The GOLF MAJORS

Records & Yearbook
1998

Compiled and Edited by
ALUN EVANS

First English Edition 1998

Brassey's Sports is an imprint of Brassey's (UK) Ltd.

UK editorial offices: Brassey's, 33 John Street, London WC1N 2AT, UK
        Email: brasseys@dial.pipex.com   Web: http://www.brasseys.com
UK and non-American orders: Marston Book Services, PO Box 267,
Abingdon, OX14 4SD, UK,

North American orders: Brassey's Inc., PO Box 960, Herndon, VA 22070, USA

Alun Evans has asserted his right under the Copyright, Designs and Patents Act, 1988, to
be identified as Author of this Work.

Library of Congress Cataloging in Publication Data
Available

British Library Cataloguing in Publication Data
A catalogue record for this book is available from the British Library

ISBN 1 85753 263 5 Flexicover

Printed in Great Britain by Page Bros (Norwich) Ltd

TO BEN HOGAN, 1912–1997

Contents

Foreword

When I take a look at tournament golf, I definitely think that the Major championships are the most significant part of the game. The yardstick used to determine a golfer's lifetime accomplishments is measured in Major championship victories.

Golf Majors are the lasting championships. Players who have won one or more Majors in their lifetimes will take their place in golf history far ahead of those who have won only a number of regular tour events.

The Majors have always held great importance – from the era of Jones and Hogan to the present. However, never before in our game's history has there been so much emphasis, media attention and fan awareness placed on a player's performance in these championships.

This book is a full and complete account of Golf Majors. It is done in a precise, to-the-point manner, so that readers and golf fans alike can easily recall, relive, or refresh their memories of the significant championships of the world.

JACK NICKLAUS
North Palm Beach, FA

November 1997

Preface

A favourite winter hobby for many golfers is to try to compare the records of contemporary players with those who have gone before. In many ways, this is meaningless, as any player taken at any particular point in time has only to beat the other players against whom he is competing. Nevertheless, to be able, by reference to one book, to examine the records of players taking part in the four majors since their inception up to the current day is a most interesting exercise and one which will keep the statisticians and golf historians occupied for many dark days and evenings.

Not only is it possible to compare the scores in the Championships, but comparisons can also be made in the value of the prize money awarded and, in this respect, it is worth noting that Harry Vardon won £30 as winner of the Open Championship at Muirfield in 1896, whereas one hundred years later, Tom Lehman's cheque was for £200,000. Equally, the winning score in the 1896 Open Championship was 316, whereas the last occasion in 1992, when the Open was also played at Muirfield, Nick Faldo's score was forty-four shots less.

The Golf Majors Records and Yearbook provides a wealth of information which will allow unlimited comparisons to be made and I congratulate Alun Evans on putting together such a comprehensive and interesting publication.

MICHAEL BONALLACK, OBE
Secretary
Royal and Ancient Golf Club of St Andrews
Scotland
November 1997

Introduction

I haven't swung a golf club for almost 10 years. Osteo-arthritis of the right ankle after a lifetime of soccer, rugby and cricket has put paid to that. Once you have played golf, however, you somehow can't get it out from under your skin.

Intrigued by the colourful commentaries of Peter Alliss, Dave Marr and others on the BBC, I became an avid TV spectator of the game. Interwoven with their descriptions of play were tales of days gone by, and of the characters central to them. A natural corollary was for me to start reading enthusiastically. I found out more about the Morrises, the Vardons, Bobby Jones and Walter Hagen. I learned for the first time about the exploits of pre-Palmer Americans and the changing influences of golf over its fascinating history. The more I read, however, the more I became aware of the apparent lack of material concentrating on the pinnacles of the golfing year – the four Major Championships – surprising, at a time when media coverage for them, and their public popularity, was at its greatest.

Why was there no combined historical record for the Masters, the US and British Opens, and the PGA, which mean so much to every golfer who competes in them? Attention has been given elsewhere to the Majors individually – some of the best reading is listed in the Bibliography – and certainly there have been many golf publications which pay lip service to them. Various golf histories, golf encyclopedias and fact books only tell the reader so much in a small section often obscured by a wealth of information relating to different aspects of the game – biographies, playing tips, golf courses and architecture, other tournaments, the Ryder Cup, and so on. But surely the Majors are now an entity and should be treated as such. So, again, why haven't the most high-profile events in the golf year been communally accorded the print space they deserve?

The answer (developed further in Part 1) lies in the ambivalent attitude taken by golf's various authorities in wanting to produce a title such as this. To understand that, it must be pointed out that the Majors grew up quite separately from each other, and at different times in history. Therefore, today we have the Royal and Ancient Club of St Andrews responsible for the running of the Open Championship: the US Golf Association (USGA), established in 1894, created the American version of the Open the following year. Then, in 1916, US professionals banded together as the Professional Golfers Association of America and introduced their own Championship (the US PGA). Finally, very much at the whim of the retired Bobby Jones, a new course was built at Augusta, Georgia, and what was initially an invitational junket for Jones' chums evolved into the Masters - run by the Augusta National Club.

The various bodies have kept records and issued publications on their own Championships, directly or indirectly, over the years, with varying degrees of enthusiasm. When asked whether they had any data on the other Majors, the R&A, through the British Golf Museum, had nothing of note on the American Majors: the USGA had nothing on the PGA and only a 1982 publication on the Masters. Augusta, traditionally very low key, particularly in commercial matters, were just updating their 1982 booklet when I approached them in 1996. The PGA, as one would expect, were at the opposite extreme and their annually-updated media guide is a browser's delight – but even they had little or no data on the other Majors.

I came to discover that each organizing body – with a quaint mixture of pride and chauvinism – regarded their event as the premier Major. And, whereas in every case I was treated with the utmost courtesy and given (mostly) as much assistance as I could expect, it was sad to detect a general lack of mutual interest. With this kind of subliminal rivalry, it became obvious to me that if this book was to be compiled, it would have to be done by someone with no affiliation to any of the organizing bodies. I would do it for my own self-gratification, if nothing else, so I sent a postage-stamp synopsis to a few British publishers in 1995. I was surprised by the encouragement I received to develop the idea, so I started to gather in the data over the course of the following months, as and when I could.

I circulated publishers last April for the second time with a revised synopsis and while I had much of the database of the book keyed into my PC, I hadn't had time to do much more. My marketing this time was ahead of my circumstances. I had planned the mailing to coincide with the 1997 Masters, but I had not budgeted for Tiger-mania. So I must thank Mr Woods (as he is not in my official list of acknowledgements) for generating interest in the Majors among commissioning editors just at the right time!

I had offers to meet with six publishers, but I chose to go with Brassey's, not just because of the charming people who put me at ease straightaway, but because they wanted an early deadline. They also had the all-important Washington DC office to secure a simultaneous launch in the States – and they had produced the impressive IOC-sanctioned Atlanta 1996 Olympic Games handbook. Furthermore, they wanted to uphold another of my sports historian's tenets – records are OK as long as they are live – by planning to make *The Golf Majors* an annual publication.

The big snag was time. I spent this past summer knocking the database into the format we now have, but hit all kinds of problems along the way. I also recorded the 1997 Majors which appear in Part 3, and, of course had to wait until the PGA had finished in the 3rd week in August before I could log the effects in Parts 4 and 5. I would like to thank everybody who has made this deadline possible.

The format of the book is one which has changed over three years of planning, but the basic outline remains. Part 1 was never going to be much more than a brief introduction as to how each Major began and developed, punctuated with stories of the winners and other characters. The heart of the book, from a statistical history point, are Parts 2 and 4.

Part 2 starts in 1860 with the first Open Championship and tells the story of events in figures but few words, of every Major since. It details the round scores and totals of the top thirty finishers and ties in every strokeplay event. This equates approximately with the top 32 qualifiers in the matchplay stage of the PGA Championship before it became medal play in 1958. The Championships are reported in strict chronological order, month-by-month, for each year, and more narrative is added where there is a greater tale to tell, or in more recent times when events are perhaps part-remembered and need memory-jogging. Part 4 strips out the characters listed in Part 2 and provides a unique Majors résumé for some 2000 players – from the gargantuan deeds of Jack Nicklaus to the once-mentioned, and long-forgotten amateur at St Andrews in the 1880s.

Sandwiched between these sections is Part 3, where the history book comes completely up-to-date. Here the 1997 Majors are fully recounted and *all* finishers are listed and some prominent players who missed the cut are named. It bridges into a short introduction on next year's Majors venues, with location maps and contact numbers. The final part – Part 5 – produces, in the author's eyes, not trivia, but the most interesting facts and figures relating to the Majors, and concludes with an attempt to project a Majors ranking for players in different generations, and for all time. All records throughout the book are current to the end of August 1997.

In the body of the book I have prefixed the four Majors by their national title, ie, either British or US. This is done for clarification, not just to upset the purists for whom (depending on which side of the Atlantic they hail) there may only be one 'Open Championship'. However, in the sections which consider The Majors specifically and individually, the familiar terms are used, eg *The* Open, *The* Masters, *The* PGA. A list of abbreviations used is explained after the Acknowledgements.

Once all the disparate data were together, I needed to improve it. This book is all about taking the raw material that is in the public domain, or has been unearthed or modified by others (who receive proper acknowledgement), and shaping it into a flowing history, a career record for players and an ongoing raft of records. Much of the original data, collected when record-taking was somewhat lax, were incomplete and sometimes inaccurate. (A glance at the only available records for the early British Opens in the first few pages of Part 2 bear this out.) Names and countries of origin have been the biggest headaches. The name situation is not finished to my satisfaction, but there are now many more complete names and identifiable players than the original records show. I intend to improve this again for next year's edition, and also obtain clearer evidence of countries of origin. Where I am in doubt I have inserted the country/countries where most of that individual's golf was played. Perhaps readers (and more Clubs and Associations) – worldwide – could shed further light?

Readers could also pick me up on the inevitable error or two. When a book includes half a million digits, there will be some mistakes. I, and others, have attempted to limit 'howlers' to an absolute minimum, but some genuine *faux pas* may have eluded us. By 'us' I mean the team of people at Brassey's who have been so helpful, led by Alan Steel and Jenny Shaw, and day-by-day, hour-by-hour, by Sue Midgley, who has waded through the proofs with me - and my family and friends, for whom this past summer hasn't been much fun. My wife, Caryl, has managed all our day-to-day affairs and at the same time given unstinting support to this (and many other of my ideas). Joanne and Katy, my daughters, have been a great help in listing, dictating, proofing and editing – and Katy and her boyfriend, Kenny Friday, did much to help deliver Part 4 on time. I am indebted to them all.

My final thanks go to Wendy Needham – for getting me started!

ALUN EVANS
Milton Keynes
England
September 1997

ACKNOWLEDGEMENTS

NANCY STULACK, USGA Museum, Far Hills – for being the biggest single reason for my carrying on with the project back in 1995, when things looked fairly hopeless. She made me appreciate that the people in golf's ivory towers were approachable.

PETER LEWIS and ELINOR CLARK, British Golf Museum, St Andrews – for consistent help and guidance, ranging from my personal visit to the unending exchange of faxes.

TERRY McSWEENEY, PGA of America, Palm Beach Gardens - for teaching me the etiquettes and protocols!

GLENN GREENSPAN, Augusta National GC – for prompt and positive responses over a long period of time.

ALAN F JACKSON – thanks to his wonderful study, *The British Professional Golfers, 1887-1930*, I was able to confirm the identity and full names of many, many early golfers.

SAL JOHNSON – his peerless *The Official US Open Almanac* did much to improve the raw detail of that Major, and in itself is an outstanding example of a complete record of a sporting event. In addition his work on PGA and Masters statistics has, sadly, been broadly unacknowledged – I am proud to put that record straight here.

My thanks also to:

MICHAEL BONALLACK
ALEX HAY
MIKE WOOD (Golf Monthly)
PGA of Argentina
BILL COLHOUN and JOHN DUNLOP (PGA of Australia)
ANNE du TOIT (PGA of South Africa)
The Clubs that sent me player names (and/or in the case of Championships sites, names, pars, yardages, course plans, brochures and pictures): Augusta National, Oak Hill, Southern Hills, Prestwick, Royal Troon, Royal Birkdale, Royal Liverpool, Royal Lytham & St Anne's, Royal St George's, Turnberry, Prince's, Royal Porthcawl, Bradford, Rhos-on-Sea, Dartford, Leven Golfing Society, Bolton Old Links, Exeter, Enfield, North Berwick, Sheringham, Hesketh, Romiley, Wilmslow, Denton, Tavistock and Wanstead.

Apologies to those I may have missed in the last-minute mayhem!

Part I

The Background to the Majors

BACKGROUND TO THE MAJORS

THIS opening section of the book is not meant to describe the history of the Majors in great detail. There are many other works which do an excellent job of this and I have mentioned a few in the bibliography. Moreover, Part 2 takes the reader Championship-by-Championship, year-by-year, as they happened – the statistics being supported by brief annotation to provide a potted version of the events. Also, every so often, these notes provide an overview of the period, a review of the record of a particular player, and so forth – thereby providing as comprehensive a history as there has ever been on the subject.

Part 1 is more concerned with the development of each of the Majors, the reasons for their coming to be, and some of the characters who have influenced or have been associated with them. It also seeks impartially to appraise the individual Championships (or Tournament in the case of the Masters), and examine why, both individually and as a group, the British and US Opens, the US PGA and Masters are held in such high regard.

This book has come together partly because golf has had no world-wide governing body to pull together, through common archives, a total history of all four Majors. With some exceptions, excellent records and anecdotal histories are to be found across a range of publications – but these only pertain to one Championship or other. These volumes, quite naturally, promote the credentials of the Championship of subject – in short, every Major Championship claims to be the best in one way or another. There has never been the perceived necessity from within the structure of the game to cross-fertilize records for the benefit of the tradition of golf as a whole, as other sports do. It has taken an outsider to knit together this history, and this section attempts to show why all four of them are worthy of being called Majors – and leaves any struggle for supremacy to the opinions of the reader.

Part 1 also considers how each Major has contributed to different phases within golf history. It looks at how, for example, the inception of a tournament may have coincided with, or influenced, a new era. In Part 5, its statistical parallel can be clearly identified in the All-Time Great lists. The first of these eras began just before 1860 . . .

THE OPEN CHAMPIONSHIP – (The British Open)

Allan Robertson was the subject of many legends. Some say he was never beaten in a singles match, and the pairing of Robertson with his assistant at St Andrews, Tom Morris (Senior, that is), over many years was probably also undefeated – and very lucrative for a time when professional sportsmen were usually only found in the ring or on the turf or cricket ground. Whatever the veracity of the stories, it is universally accepted that Robertson was the best player of his day in Scotland, which in the mid-18th Century meant the world. When he died in 1859, aged just 44, it is feasible that a golf tournament could have been arranged to discover who was to be the new king. Certainly few other valid reasons have been given for the 'Championship' which was organized for the following year. Moreover, Robertson was known in his later life to play less and less singles golf, and his objections may have been responsible for such a Championship not taking place any earlier.

During the 1850s it is known that a founder member of the Prestwick Club (1851), local squire Col. JO Fairlie, was attempting to set up a tournament for professionals, based on the less-familiar concept of medal play, but if Allan Robertson refused to compete, how much credibility would such an event have? It seems more than coincidence, therefore, despite having no support from other Clubs or Societies, that Prestwick went ahead with the competition anyway, just one year after Robertson's death.

On 16 October 1860, just eight professional golfers went out to play three rounds of Prestwick's 12 holes. Records of scoring are patchy, to say the least, and would be for many years to come, but there is no argument that Tom Morris was beaten into second place by life-long rival Willie Park. Park's reward was a belt of Moroccan leather, buckled in silver, but winner's prize money was not awarded for a few years yet. The following year, encouraged by the inaugural success, James Fairlie played himself as an amateur, thus creating the term

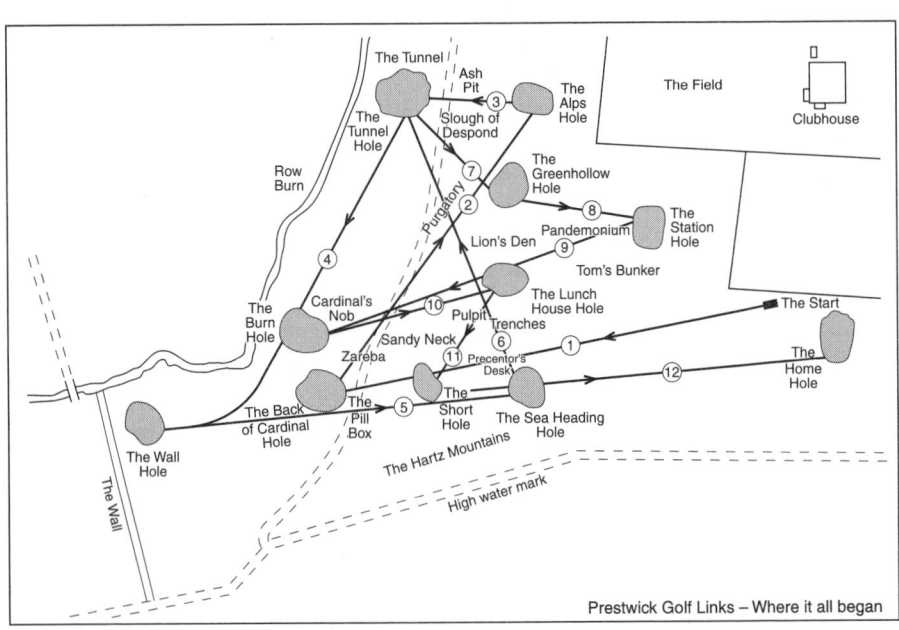

Prestwick Golf Links – Where it all began

4

'Open' Championship for the first time. This time 'Old' Tom Morris, who had become professional at Prestwick some years before, after falling out with Allan Robertson, won the Championship ahead of Park. (In 1848, the gutta-percha ball, or 'guttie' was introduced. It flew farther, had a longer life and – when you consider that the cost of the old 'feathery' ball equated to some $50 today – it was very much cheaper. Old Tom wanted to employ the new technology, but as Robertson was famed for his making of featheries, a rift ensued and Morris moved away, only returning to St Andrews in 1864 after Robertson's death.)

The older Morris and Parks dominated the Championship until 1868 when the brilliant but all too short career of Tom Morris Jr began. Just 17 when he won in 1868, this tragic figure came and went like a comet. He was to shine like a brilliant light which illuminated the golf world for the next eight years, before burning out at 25. He won the Open for three years running (1868-70) and the Belt was awarded to him for posterity. Partly because of this, and much off-course politicking, no Championship was held in 1871. When it was re-launched in 1872, Prestwick shared the organization of the event with the prestigious east coast Societies, the Royal and Ancient Club and the Honourable Company of Edinburgh Golfers, and also shared in the outlay of a new trophy – the famous silver claret jug, still presented today. The first winner was inevitably 'Young' Tom Morris, but this was also to be his last Open victory. Commonplace among Scottish professionals of the time, Morris was a heavy whisky drinker, and his health began to suffer. In 1874, he was reputedly heart-broken when his wife died in childbirth, and a combination of grief and the resultant need for succour from the bottle killed him. He was found by his father on Christmas morning.

The Open Championship consolidated its development over the following two decades by rotating Prestwick with the other Clubs' courses at St Andrews and Musselburgh. The longevity of Messrs Morris and Parks Senior was matched by very few players. The short, spectacular careers of Jamie Anderson and Bob Ferguson, both of whom won three successive Opens, ended in poverty and obscurity. By the 1890s great sea changes were occurring once more.

Golf had been exported from Scotland throughout the world during the 19th Century – and had taken root in England even earlier, following the influence of the Stuart kings who inherited the throne of England in 1603. (It is claimed that the Blackheath Club was founded in 1608, encouraged by King James I [James VI of Scotland].) The British Empire was the catalyst for the world-wide playing of many sports in the last century, but a certain contretemps with the colonials which effectively concluded in 1781, ended, or changed through evolution, many sports in the United States. Golf was played in the Carolinas, according to some records, in the mid 18th Century, but it wasn't until the 1880s that the sport was re-established.

The following decade saw a huge exodus of Scots (and some English) to work as professionals (which also included greenkeeping, club-making and the like) in the new, rapidly-forming golf hierarchies of the eastern seaboard and Great Lakes cities. The emigrations and the spreading south of the game in Britain meant that the Open took on a less-parochial feel from 1890. Indeed that year it was won by an Englishman, John Ball, for the first time. Ball was the youngest-ever competitor in any Major Championship when he competed in the 1878 Open at the tender age of 14, and he was, after the event had run for 30 years, the first amateur to win. In 1892, when Harold Hilton became the second English amateur winner, the competition was extended to four rounds over two days – and the Honourable Company left their 9-hole course at Musselburgh to host the Championship at Muirfield for the first time. The rota of courses acknowledged the importance of the English improvement in the game when the Open took in English courses at Royal St George's, Sandwich (1894) and Royal Liverpool, Hoylake (1897). And the first world stars of golf appeared.

When JH Taylor won at Sandwich in 1894 and 1895, he was to start the age of the 'Great Triumvirate'. Between then and 1914, he, Harry Vardon and James Braid won all but five Opens. Vardon and Taylor toured the US in 1900, competed in the US Open and finished first and second. At the end of their reign however, the faster development of all aspects of the game in America – administration, golf courses, ball and club technology and players – made that country the dominant force in world golf. Few Britons have won the Open since Vardon's last win, and within 25 years, total Scottish dominance of the Championship they spawned had evaporated completely. No Scotsman (emigrés Jock Hutchison and Tommy Armour apart) after Braid's last title in 1910 was to win the Open again until Sandy Lyle in 1985.

The Royal and Ancient Club (R&A) had been the prime mover in British golf developments in the 19th Century, particularly in the area of Rules, which they had based on the Honourable Company's template. By 1897, all the host clubs for the Open had adopted 'St Andrews' Rules thus giving the Club unique hegemony, like the Marylebone Club (MCC) in cricket, over the sport as a whole. Although other countries developed national bodies to monitor the game (including the USGA in America), with one or two local amendments, all looked to the R&A on the question of rules. After World War I, the British clubs were still organizing the Open Championship as a cartel, and as such differences and inconsistencies occurred.

Looking to the US where the War had not exacted such a cost and golf was suspended only for two years, the clubs saw the success the USGA had made of the US Open and the birth of the powerful PGA of America and decided that some form of rationalization was required if the British national championship was to remain competitive. In 1920, therefore, instead of setting up a national authority for golf, they vested further powers in the R&A, who took over the running of the Open Championship totally, and still does so today.

The 1920s saw the first phase of American dominance. The flashy Walter Hagen coincided with the Hollywood boom and became the world's first superstar of golf. He won four Opens in a period when only Arthur Havers was a home winner. When Hagen didn't win, it seemed that Bobby Jones must be playing. Inspired by Francis Ouimet's epoch-ending victory over Vardon and Ted Ray in the 1913 US Open, Jones (after tearing up his card in a fit of pique in 1921) won three Open titles in just three further attempts in a run which also included four US Open wins and ended with the amazing year of 1930.

The decades leading up to the next War and immediately after it were the bleakest in the history of the Open. This was caused, in part, by the inability of the R&A to match the purses on offer across the Atlantic, and the long sea crossing which took up time – an American professional could be lucratively employed in another tournament or two. There was also a difference in the size of the balls (US 1.68in. diameter v. GB 1.62in.), and most important, there was the overall strength of the American tournament players (by 1955 the US team was leading the GB team 9-2 in the Ryder Cup series). Little was remembered of the tradition which started in 1860, and even less was cared. Used to fast, manicured greens, firm, lush fairways, why should the American pro give up all that to play on links courses completely alien to him – and for comparatively little reward? Sam Snead won the 1946 Open at St Andrews, and with little grace criticized the state of the Old Course, pocketed the obviously-unsatisfactory cheque and didn't return until 1962. Ben Hogan came once, slammed Carnoustie's greens, and took the old Claret Jug. Many others didn't come at all.

Unfortunately, lessons were either not learned, or if they were understood, there was nothing the R&A could do to reverse the trend. It would be hoped that at least without US opposition there would be home victories to celebrate. This was the case in the 30s when American interest dwindled, and there were wins for Cotton, Perry, Padgham, Reg Whitcombe and Burton – but to the concerned onlooker, the Championship paled in comparison with the 20s and even the days of the 'Triumvirate'. As a world event it became second division fare.

Immediately after the War, Snead's visit apart, Fred Daly won a low-key affair at Hoylake (1947) and Cotton won his third Open (1948), but maddeningly, this, the best British player of his generation, didn't persevere with his promising early US visits and was thus not the Champion to inspire a new spate of world-beaters. Then in 1949, a rotund South African, Arthur D'Arcy Locke, better-known as Bobby, brought some colour back to the Championship. He went on to win three more times in the 1950s, when even if the Americans stayed away, the new Commonwealth was well represented. If Locke was eclipsed at all during the 50s, it was by Australia's Peter Thomson who won four times in five years to Locke's four in eight. Another South African, globe-trotting Gary Player, was to herald the new dawn with a win in 1959, while Thomson's compatriot, Kel Nagle made it 10 wins for the Commonwealth in 12 years. The only home winner during this time was Max

Faulkner, ironically the only time the Championship was not held in Great Britain – at Portrush in 1951. The only American winner from a Stars and Stripes-starved decade was Ben Hogan, who in 1953 did the unique treble of Masters, US and British Opens – but was denied the US PGA as it clashed with Carnoustie.

Meanwhile across the Atlantic the US Tour professional was, through the efforts of the PGA of America, becoming one of the world's most affluent sportsmen. Prizemoney, sponsorship and royalties were booming thanks mainly to the shrewd marketing of the game to the burgeoning TV networks. At the end of the 50s, the sport had the ideal hero for the television age – Arnold Daniel Palmer. Cigarette-smoking, with a devil-may-care approach and possessing that human touch, Palmer almost single-handedly helped to elevate the sport into a media business. The effect was not just restricted to America. Golf, through Palmer, the dashing black-clad figure of Player and the chubby young Golden Bear, Jack Nicklaus, assumed a major world-wide audience for the first time. Television relays and jet aircraft transported the stars across the globe – and the biggest beneficiary of all was the increasingly-moribund British Open Championship.

Palmer came to St Andrews in 1960 and finished second behind Kel Nagle. Two years later at Troon, he was a double Champion, posting a record 276 and beating the Australian by six shots. The R&A, witnessing the huge galleries following Palmer, had to make provision for this new-style golf fan in future Opens. The 60s saw Arnie finally superseded by Nicklaus, but not before Player had won again, Thomson added his fifth title to match Braid and Taylor, and the Open had its oldest winner in an Argentinian faithful of two decades, Roberto de Vicenzo.

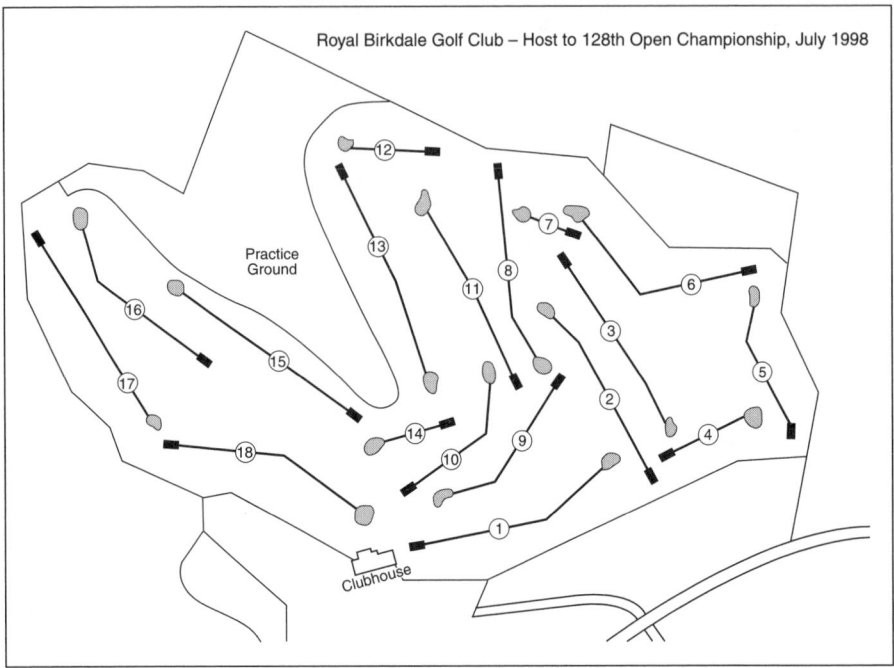

Royal Birkdale Golf Club – Host to 128th Open Championship, July 1998

If Palmer had re-ignited the spark, the man who set the Open ablaze for home supporters was Tony Jacklin. Young, good-looking, a symbol of British confidence in the 1960s, he captured the hearts of the nation at Lytham in 1969. His memorable half in the singles with a sporting Jack Nicklaus which tied the Ryder Cup at Birkdale later that year, and the win, all within 12 months, at Hazeltine in the US Open, established him as the standard-bearer for the British fightback against American rule. Whether we would have seen world-class golfers like Faldo, Lyle, Woosnam and Montgomerie if there had been no Tony Jacklin, we will never know, but his success in American eyes, closely followed in the 70s by Peter Oosterhuis, were the first signs of improving standards since the days of Dai Rees, and going further back, Henry Cotton and Abe Mitchell.

The American return to the Open, spearheaded by Arnold Palmer, carried on apace in the following decade. Lee Trevino won twice, both times at Jacklin's expense –

his chips-in at the 15th and 18th at Muirfield in 1972 are said to have unnerved the Englishman so much, his game would never be the same again. Stylish newcomers Weiskopf and Miller also won, spelling the end of the Nicklaus-Player era and ushering in the tremendous Open run of Tom Watson. Watson won the first of his five titles at Carnoustie – in fact all his first four were on different Scottish courses.

In 1979, so that competition would be more meaningful, the Ryder Cup allowed the British and Irish team to become representative of Europe. Not that this first selection was too different in composition. Apart from Antonio Garrido, there was only one non-GB & I player – another Spaniard, and current Open Champion, Severiano Ballesteros. When Ballesteros won at Lytham, the reception was like that afforded to Jacklin 10 years before. But, whereas Jacklin's applause was based on national pride, the young Spaniard's was a result of his wonderful cavalier performance. From a perspective of European golf, if Jacklin was the standard-bearer, Seve Ballesteros was his bravest captain – as he was to prove with some exciting wins in the Open and for Jacklin in the ensuing Ryder Cups.

The Open Championships since 1980 have been much more evenly-spread, with British wins for Nick Faldo (three times) and Sandy Lyle, two more for Seve, two for Australian Greg Norman and one for fellow-countryman, Ian Baker-Finch. The Zimbabwean with the English father and Welsh mother, Nick Price, won at Turnberry (the most-recent course added to the rota). The other wins have gone to America. Bill Rogers was a surprise winner at Sandwich in 1981, Tom Watson picked up titles three, four and five and Mark Calcavecchia collected his only Major at Troon. Significantly perhaps, with wins in recent years from John Daly, Tom Lehman and Justin Leonard, the balance is swinging back to the US.

The British Open is without doubt one of the most important of the Majors, if only for its venerable traditions. But as I said at the outset, it is not for the author to apply a pecking order for the Major Championships. However, the Open has the richest history as befits the home of golf, and it is unique as a Major in that it is the only one played over links courses. These semi-natural, semi-man-made amalgams of sand, gorse, marram grass and bare lies, often criss-crossed by deeply-cut burns and dykes are diametrically opposed to the lush, tree-lined parkland courses associated with the US Open, and in more-recent years the US PGA Championship. They bear no resemblance at all to the rough-free, easy fairways and lightning-fast greens of Augusta National – home of the Masters. The exposed tracts, open to the winds of the Firth of Clyde, the Irish Sea, the Channel or the North Sea in an unpredictable British summer, can result in different conditions, and a different golf course, every day. As much for the tradition then, the playing conditions make the Open Championship one of the greatest – if not the greatest – challenges in golf, and, as such, worthy to be called a Major.

The lessons of the 1930s, 40s and 50s though, must tell the R&A there is no room for complacency. Then, reliant only on its historic inertia, it was being by-passed by a more vibrant, more commercially-aware society 3000 miles away. If it wasn't for the kick-start given by the likes of Palmer and Nicklaus there would not have been famous victories for Jacklin, Seve and Faldo, and Britain and Europe may have remained a golfing backwater. The Open must never be allowed to lose its position again.

THE US OPEN

When John Reid, a Scottish immigrant to the US, asked his friend Bob Lockhart to bring back some golf equipment from a trip home to Scotland, it (indirectly and spontaneously) led to the formation of the St Andrews Club at Yonkers, NY, in 1888. We have seen that golf may have been played in America as much as a century earlier, but most golf historians agree that 1888 and St Andrews were the defining moment and location for US golf.

Six years later the St Andrews Club broke new ground by devising a tournament for professionals to go along with the events that were being organized for amateurs in some of the other infant east coast clubs. These professionals were none other than the army of Scots and more than a sprinkling of English golfers that had crossed the Atlantic to seek their golfing fortunes over the previous few years. By the turn of the century, the proliferation of golf courses in the US, which took the estimated number beyond 1000, indicated just how many Old World pros were now in the States. The 1894 'Championship' at St Andrews was contested through matchplay by Willies Dunn, Campbell and Davis, and Sam Tucker – with Dunn winning the first, but unofficial, national title. Willie Dunn had appeared in the Top 10 at the 1883 British Open, and his father (also Willie!) took part in the second British Open. Willie Campbell was runner-up to David Brown in the 1886 Open at Musselburgh, while Davis had been the pro at Carnoustie and Hoylake before coming to the Newport, Rhode Island Club in 1892. Tucker was the sole Englishman.

Dunn's win was not ratified by the other clubs. However, through the efforts of leading amateur, Charles Blair Macdonald, a meeting was called for 22 December 1894 to set up an authority recognized by all the clubs which could organize a national championship. The clubs of St Andrews, Newport, Chicago, Brookline and Shinnecock Hills met in New York City, and the United States Golf Association (USGA) was formed. In October 1895 at Newport, running concurrently with the first US Amateur Championship over the same course, the US Open Championship came into being.

The first winner, Horace Rawlins, is a bit of a mystery man. Born on the Isle of Wight, off England's south coast, in 1874, he was professional at the Mid Herts Club from 1893 to 1894, moving back to the Isle of Wight Ladies Club briefly, before arriving at Newport in January 1895. He did not compete in the British Open before emigrating, so was an unknown quantity. His 4-round, 36-hole total (it didn't become a 72-hole championship until 1898) of 173 suggested that the field was short of quality as well as quantity (only 11 competed). Rawlins would never win again.

In 1896, at Shinnecock Hills, the infant Championship nearly didn't take place. The professionals objected strongly when caddies, John Shippen and Oscar Bunn filed for entry. Shippen was (according to differing reports) either an African-American, or half African-American and half Shinnecock, and Bunn was reported to be a full native American of the same tribe. A stand-off ensued as Theodore Havermayer, the USGA President, ruled that the Open would go on even if Shippen and Bunn were the only two competitors. The professionals reluctantly fell into line.

For the first fifteen years the pattern remained broadly the same, with various Smiths', Ross's and Mac's dominating the Championship – with Willie Anderson the star of the period, collecting four wins in five years. The domination of the hired professional who had learned his golf from generations of British experience was the major feature of the early years. The American golfer was still predominantly the gentleman amateur, but slowly, as the new century wore on, a new breed of player – the home-grown caddie/professional – was starting to appear. Standards of play were undoubtedly lower than in Britain, as even the best of the emigrés – such as Alex Smith – performed only moderately when they ventured back across the Atlantic to take part in the British Open. This differential was cruelly exposed in 1900 when Harry Vardon and JH Taylor led home the US Open at Chicago by nine and seven strokes, respectively.

In 1911, however, the period of British success came to an abrupt end. Over the next decade, facilitated partly because of America's coming out of the Great War less damaged than Britain, and partly because of there being no line of succession in Britain when the time of the 'Triumvirate' came to a close, the whole emphasis in the golf world swung – permanently – to the other side of the Atlantic. The catalysts for this turnabout were to be found in the next five years of the US Open.

John J McDermott, two months short of his 20th birthday, erased the memory of his runner-up disappointment from the previous year to become the first American-born winner of the Open. The following year, proving this was no flash in the pan, he won again at the Buffalo Club. Home-grown talents, Mike Brady and Tom McNamara, were second on both occasions, suggesting that the dam was about to burst. Then, in 1913, came another twist, and a huge symbolic breakthrough. Francis Ouimet, hanging on to the coat-tails of Harry Vardon (back for the first time since his 1900 success) and Ted Ray – arguably the two best players in the world at the time – to force a three-way play-off, had the temerity to outplay

these icons and make it three US wins in a row. Now the Americans had proved they could beat the very best of British, and no-one saw this more clearly than the confident young man who tied for fourth, just behind the joint leaders – Walter Hagen.

But Ouimet was also an amateur – the first to win the US Open. The heyday of the British Amateur had flickered briefly during the 1890s when John Ball and Harold Hilton won the British Open. When Hilton won his second title in 1897, no one would know that he would be the last British amateur to win a Major Championship. In America, however, with the sport developing so rapidly across all fronts, the style of amateur was different. Unlike the British type of landowner, army officer or socialite, the socio-economic growth of America in the early decades of the 20th century meant that the successful amateur could equally spring from the ranks of the Ivy League colleges and be the heir of some industrial magnate or have learned his golf as a caddie and be holding down a regular job. Francis Ouimet was one of the latter. While Hagen was contemplating the end of British dominance, Ouimet's victory was stirring the amateur golfing ambitions of a young Atlanta schoolboy – one Robert Tyre Jones, Jr.

Hagen was fast off the mark, winning the first of his two Opens in the following year. In 1915 and 1916, while all Championship golf was suspended in Europe, two more amateurs – Jerome Travers and Chick Evans – won. This made it five American wins in a row and three amateur champions in four years. Apart from Ted Ray (1920) and various emigrés during the 20s – and following sixteen straight wins between 1895 and 1910 – the next Briton (and only the one since) to win the US Open would be Tony Jacklin in 1970.

Thereafter, along with the PGA Championship, the US Open would be viewed as an American preserve. Overseas players did enter from time to time, but they were few and far between until Gary Player's emergence in the 60s and the Europeans' re-emergence in the 80s and 90s.

Walter Hagen didn't win a US Open during his purple patch in the 1920s. Despite picking up five PGAs and four British Opens, the colourful first super-star of golf's last US Open win was in 1919. It was more than a coincidence that he never won a Major when Bobby Jones competed. This was not because Jones won every time, but the mere appearance of the man seemed to jinx Hagen. During the period 1920-30, Jones' US Open performances read 8, 5, 2, W, 2, 2, W, 11, 2, W, W. Jones, along with Hagen, and to a lesser extent, Gene Sarazen (who won the Open in 1922 and 1932), were the outstanding golfers of the decade, but, with the exception of Jones' four wins, the Open remained true to its name with an even spread of one- and two-time winners during the 20s, and, indeed, the 30s.

In 1933, Johnny Goodman became the fifth and last amateur US Open Champion. Of the 19 US Opens beginning with Ouimet's win in 1913, and ending with Goodman's triumph at North Shore, amateurs had claimed eight. The brief explosion on to the scene of Ralph Guldahl produced two wins (1937 and 1938) and ushered in the dawn of Hogan, Nelson and Snead – and World War II.

During the 30's and even more so after the War, there had been a gradual defining of the type of course required for the national championship. Partly because of historical reasons, and partly due to geography, the typical Open course was built in the early part of the century for clubs who bought up large tracts of (usually well-wooded) land close to the industrial conurbations of the east, mid-west and California. Early golf-course architects often took Scottish links characteristics like varying grades of rough and narrow fairways

and adapted them to the parkland environment. Liberal use of water and dog-legging and ubiquitous sand were employed to increase the hazards. As the century developed the US Open-style of course made it a demanding trial of any aspiring Champion's skills. In the view of architect AW Tillinghast (Baltusrol, Fresh Meadow, Inverness, Winged Foot), '...a controlled shot to a closely-guarded green is the surest test of any man's golf'.

In conjunction with this tightening of course criteria, the overwhelming prowess of the American golfer and the sad decline of the British game helped to erode the importance of the British Open – at least in American eyes – and promote the US Open as the world's premier Championship of golf. This was certainly true after the inauguration of the Masters in 1934 polarized the British Championship even further, and fewer and fewer US golfers saw the need to support what must have seemed like an outmoded and under-funded competition thousands of miles away. There was a strong argument for the US Open's hegemony over the other Majors for the next two decades.

In 1947, Lew Worsham beat Sam Snead (already 1942 PGA and 1946 British Open Champion) in a play-off. Sam was never to come as close to the Open title again – the only Major he was destined never to win, and which, in time, was to gnaw away at him. The next few years belonged to Snead's arch rival, Ben Hogan, whose courage and incredible talent were to make him probably the biggest hero in the annals of the US Open. If Bobby Jones had dominated the event in the 1920s playing a minimum of golf in between, then Hogan matched Jones now, although his limited appearances on a golf course were for other reasons.

In 1948, at the Riviera Country Club, Hogan set one of the Golf Majors' landmark low scores, when he scorched the course in an 8-

under par 276. Then, in February of the following year Hogan was badly injured in a road accident. It was feared that he might not be able to walk any more, but throughout 1949, he battled against the odds and played again in January 1950. He played in the US Open at Merion, proved that he still had enormous golfing talent, only to fade when exhaustion took over. He hung on somehow to force a play-off, and limped to a famous victory over Lloyd Mangrum and George Fazio. Thereafter, he declined to play too much golf – saving himself for the Majors. He only played one British Open, however, which he won in 1953, and eschewed the PGA completely because of the round-by-round grind of matchplay. He effectively only played in the Masters and the US Open, then – and he won them both in 1951 and again in 1953. With the British Open win as well in 1953, he still remains the only golfer to win three Grand Slam tournaments in one season.

In 1960, the new order took over when Arnold Palmer won from the still-amateur Jack Nicklaus. Nicklaus went on to equal the record of four wins between 1962 and 1980 and tie with Willie Anderson, Jones and Hogan. Americans continued to dominate during the 60s and 70s with two wins each by Billy Casper and Lee Trevino, but overseas players got a glimpse of success for the first time for many years with wins from Player, Jacklin and David Graham. In the 80s, there was no dominant force, although Curtis Strange did win back-to-back in 1988 and 1989, and there was a popular third win for 'all-time old Champion', Hale Irwin – 45 in 1990. The ominous presence of Ernie Els, winning for the second time at Congressional in 1997, could be a signpost to the future.

Since the 60s, the perceived No 1 status of the US Open may be called into question. The charisma of the Masters and the American's re-found love affair with the traditions of the British Open have tended to level out the Majors. Add to that the change in the PGA Championship from matchplay to strokeplay, its mirroring the US Open philosophy on the type of course it should be played on, and the more cosmopolitan fields since the mid-80s, the PGA has also come of age. There is no doubting the claim, however, that the US Open, year-in, year-out, is the toughest of the Majors, and as it is the only totally national championship in the US, it naturally has the support, respect and affection of the American golfer, commentator and fan alike, when it comes to choosing which Major tops the pecking order.

THE PGA CHAMPIONSHIP

The excitement created by the exploits of John McDermott, Francis Ouimet and Walter Hagen led to an enormous growth in the game of golf in America. The spread of the sport affected both recreational and professional competitive ranks. The birth of the tour professional, freed up from his greenkeeping and club-repairing duties, introduced a new stratum of golfer, and with it came the need to protect his interests.

The British PGA was founded in 1901 and as part of its role it identified sponsors who would support special golfing events. The *News of the World* Sunday newspaper was asked to sponsor the Association's own Championship and by 1916 it was a well-run, well-established 36-hole matchplay competition. On 16 January of that year, a mixture of professionals, amateurs, course architects and golf industry representatives met in New York City at the invitation of department store entrepreneur, Rodman Wanamaker. Wanamaker could see the potential the new craze for golf could have commercially, and the upshot of the meeting was the creation of the PGA of America (ratified in April, 1916) and the Wanamaker-sponsored PGA Championship.

The basis for the competition was matchplay, like its British counterpart, and was only open to professional golfers. The matchplay aspect also complemented the US Amateur Championship and provided a balance to the medal play of the British and US Opens.

Jim Barnes won the first PGA Championship, held in October 1916 at the Siwanoy Country Club, beating Scot Jock Hutchison by one hole in the final. Barnes also won the second Championship, but had to wait three years to defend it due to World War I. During the 1920s, Walter Hagen, who had attended that January 1916 meeting, won five titles, including four in a row. Before Leo Diegel beat him to go on to win the 1928 Championship, Hagen had gone 22 straight round matches without defeat. Gene Sarazen and Diegel won two PGAs in the 20s, and Sarazen went on to win a third in 1933. Sarazen's second victory – when defending his title in 1923 – featured one of the famous finals. He played a magical shot close to the pin to beat Hagen at the second extra hole. At this time, the 32 qualifiers each year had to endure 36 holes of strokeplay before the matchplay sessions. In 1935, 64 qualifiers went forward to matchplay.

Denny Shute, in 1936 and 1937, became the last player to win back-to-back Championships, and Paul Runyan also won two titles in the 30s. With wartime approaching, Byron Nelson was in devastating form, while Sam Snead won the Championship in 1942, the day before he joined the navy. Nelson won in 1940 and was runner-up to Vic Ghezzi in 1941: he was also runner-up (to Bob Hamilton) when the Championship resumed, after a break due to hostilities, in 1944. In 1945 he won the PGA for the second time at the Moraine Country Club. It was his 9th victory in a sequence of 11 straight tournament wins that season – one of those records in sport that will never ever be beaten.

The PGA Championship was deprived of one of its greatest stars during the 1950s. Having won the Championship in 1946 and 1948, Ben Hogan's terrible road accident precluded his playing in the stamina-sapping week-long event that the PGA had become. After his 1948 triumph, he stayed away until he was in semi-retirement and the Championship had switched to strokeplay. He finished as high as 9th in 1964.

The years leading up to and immediately after the dropping of matchplay were fairly nondescript in that no golfer or group of golfers dominated the Championship. In fact, between 1950 and 1970, the PGA was won by a different player each year. The end of match-play came about because of the time involved in running the Championship, the poor spectator-aspect and TV needs. A proposal by Horton Smith, who was the then President of the PGA of America, to limit matchplay to just the top seven qualifiers from the strokeplay session plus the defending champion, was superseded by one which did away with matchplay altogether. This was not a happy period for the Championship. Having to overhaul its format comprehensively in order to make it attractive to those outside golf, it was criticized from within for its selection of courses – both location and quality. That the PGA Championship, up to 1997, should have been played on 66 different courses over 25 states in its 79 years says it all. Moreover, the Masters had become a big hit with American TV audiences, and from a player's perspective, the PGA's July timing clashed with the British Open quite frequently as well as proving unpopular when the Championship was played in the steamier South.

Arnold Palmer failed to leave his mark on the PGA – surprisingly never winning. Typically, however, he couldn't be kept out of the record books. When Bobby Nichols won in 1964, Arnie became the first player to shoot sub-70 rounds throughout, without winning. He tied second with Jack Nicklaus. Nicklaus didn't have it all his own way in the 60s, winning just once, in the Dallas heat – not for the first time in a Major at the expense of Bruce Crampton. In 1968, at the age of 48, Julius Boros won, also in Texas (San Antonio), to become the oldest winner of any Major Championship.

Since the 1970s, however, when Nicklaus started to stitch together regular wins, the PGA

Championship has made up lost ground. Firstly, there has been some rationalization of the courses. The use of more courses employed by the US Open – Oakland Hills, Inverness, Pebble Beach and Winged Foot, for instance – reduced the rota and made the test as difficult as the Open. It also – finally – took its spot in August, as the finale to the Major Championship season. Over the last 25 years or so the Championship has had a base to move forward and to develop its own style. Before that, constant change and the dubious quality of both course and player, almost reduced the PGA to a non-Major.

Nicklaus went on to emulate Hagen's five wins, and for a while between 1972 and 1974, Sam Snead was having something of an Indian Summer. Then in his 60s, he collected 4th, 9th, then 3rd, positions respectively. He finally called it a day, aged 69 in 1981. He was not the oldest participant, though. Back in 1972, Gene Sarazen (who else?) appeared at the age of 70 years and 5 months, and shot two 79s to miss the cut. He thus had the distinction – and still does – of being the PGA's oldest competitor and youngest winner (20 years 5 months in 1922). Lee Trevino won twice – in 1974 and 1984 – and Tom Watson came as close as he has got to winning when he tied for first with John Mahaffey and Jerry Pate, with Mahaffey winning the sudden-death play-off. Mahaffey's win was improbable to say the least. After a First Round 75, he was never in the hunt. At the start of the Last Round he was still 7 behind Watson, but a series of brilliant putts put together a score of 66 while Tom folded to a 73.

As the PGA Championship has always been an event for the US Tour and Club professional, first and foremost, it was not until the breakthough of Gary Player in 1962 that a true overseas player won the PGA. He repeated the victory in 1972 and since 1979, when Australia's David Graham won, there has been a veritable surge of foreign winners. Whereas the Masters has been a favourite event for Europeans in the 80s and 90s, the golfers of the Southern Hemisphere have taken to the PGA. Following Player and Graham, there have been wins for Australians Wayne Grady and Steve Elkington and two for Nick Price of Zimbabwe. In between, Larry Nelson picked up two titles and when Ray Floyd won for the second time in 1982 he equalled the record of the longest span between wins of any one Major Championship (13 years – 1969). John Daly's fairytale success in 1991 heralded a new breed of super-hitter and paved the way for a certain Tiger Woods.

The PGA Championship today has every right to be a Major. Whereas the purist might pine for the days of matchplay, no-one can doubt the progress the Championship has made over the last two decades or so. Once dubbed as a second-rate parochial competition, the PGA Media Guide quoted that in 1996 at Valhalla there were 31 overseas players representing 14 countries. Not exactly the breakdown for the British Open, but a great improvement on just a few years before. The PGA Championship now proudly signs off the Majors season, attracting a better and better field every year as the Holy Grail of a Major Championship taunts the players who have never won – and those who have won, but want to win again – to effect one last try for immortality, before next year. A more important statistic from the Media Guide cited that Mark Brooks finished ahead of a field made up of 81 of the Sony World Rankings Top 100 (and 48 of the Top 50) – the classiest field of any Major in 1996.

After such an extraordinary year as 1930, Robert Tyre Jones, Jr – Bobby Jones – retired from competitive golf. He had nothing else to prove – he had done it all. Being amateur, he played his golf in the spare time he allowed himself from his law firm. Being amateur, he couldn't compete with the professional golfers in their own tournament – the PGA Championship. By 1930 then, he had achieved all that his status would allow him, but in doing so, left a series of golfing records unsurpassed by any amateur in the history of the game – records that the hugely precocious Tiger Woods, if he had remained amateur at the end of 1996, I'm sure would admit may even have been beyond him.

The 'Grand Slam' is made up of the four Majors as we know them today – the British and US Open, the PGA and the Masters. No golfer has ever achieved all four in one season, and only four – Gene Sarazen, Ben Hogan, Jack Nicklaus and Gary Player – have won every championship. Back in 1930, the Amateur Championships of America and Britain were also considered 'Majors', and the Grand Slam consisted of these plus both Opens. As an amateur, Jones won the US Amateur title five times and the British equivalent once. He took on and beat the professionals more often than not – winning the first of his four US Open titles in 1923. He also won three British Opens. His main professional rival, Walter Hagen – undoubtedly one of golf's all-time greats himself – despite winning 11 Major Championships, never won one when Jones was in the same field. These feats were achieved in just eight years.

And so to Bobby Jones' *annus mirabilis* – 1930. He appeared in the American Walker Cup side at Sandwich and stayed on to take the British Amateur. In June he went to Hoylake and beat the best of the British – and no small number of American – professionals to lift the Open Championship. The following month at Interlachen he beat an even stronger field for the US Open, before rounding off his competitive career at the Merion Cricket Club in Pennsylvania by winning his fifth US Amateur title. At the end of the year he returned to the law full-time.

During his brief but intensive career, Jones had played golf on most of the famous courses on either side of the Atlantic. No longer playing, in 1931 he switched his golfing mind to course construction, and he knew exactly what he wanted to achieve. A resident of Atlanta, Georgia, he was made aware of a 365-acre piece of land a hundred miles or so away at Augusta. It had once been a plant nursery but had gone to the wall in the Depression. Jones, with the backing of financier Clifford Roberts and Scottish golf course designer, Dr Alister Mackenzie, bought it and planned out a course that would encompass all that was best (in Jones' view) from the courses he'd known. Jones saw his course as a private member's club – open only to his closest associates, business colleagues and clients. It was, however, intended to be exclusive on a wide geographic front – hence the name it was given – Augusta National. It was also meant to provide a fitting climax to the professionals' winter tour, by invitation (from Jones) to a special tournament. The winter tour was a small offshoot of the professionals' regular summer tour, allowing them to play the Southern States 'out of season' and avoid the heat and humidity of other times. Like many clubs in the region, Augusta National closed down for the summer – and still does.

Augusta National was designed so that it wouldn't be too intimidating for Jones'

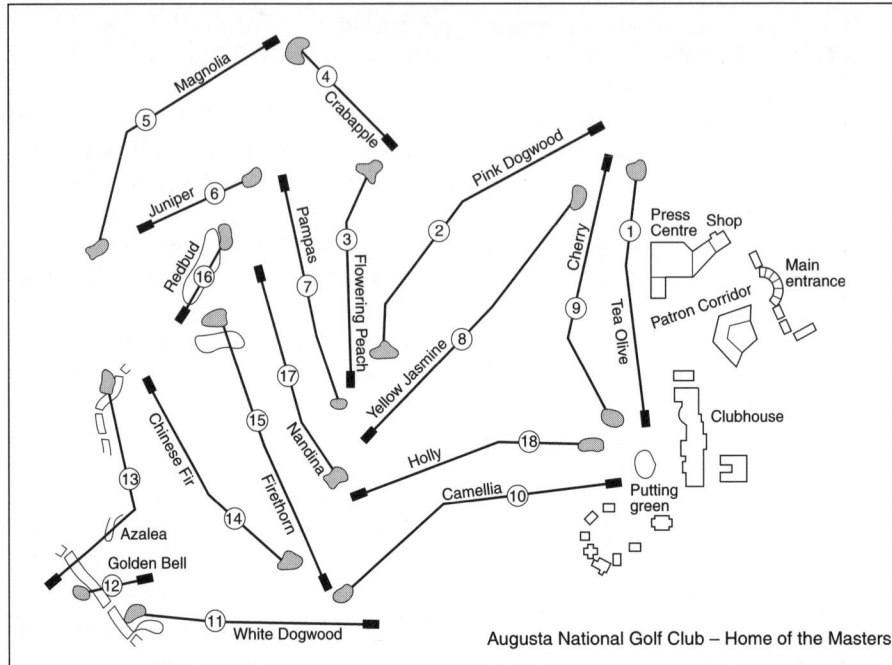

Augusta National Golf Club – Home of the Masters

members, yet it would require meticulous planning from the pros to score well. The fairways were wide and accommodating – anything a touch off-line not being penalized too severely. Bobby Jones knew how excruciating the rough could be at the Opens, but he wanted his members to continue to play the course and not be humbled by it. A hook or a slice here would probably result in nothing more punitive than the ball nestling among pine needles, and the members' sense of well-being would remain intact. Moreover, he wanted to make the playing of golf the greatest possible pleasure. No-one who has seen photographs of Augusta in spring can fail to be uplifted by the beauty of the course, fringed as it is with all manner of flowering shrubs.

In order to beat the par of 72 at Augusta, however, a strategy has to be planned hole-by-hole. Assuming that the green is reached in regulation, it depends here (more than almost anywhere else) where the ball has landed as to whether a player gets his par, better – or much,

much worse. The greens are often huge – always undulating, with several different levels. The approach shot has to be aimed at the 'right' side of the pin. Reading the contours is difficult, and the putting surfaces are lightning-fast. For example, a four foot putt from the 'wrong' side of the hole, not hit with exactly the right speed and borrow, can easily trundle past and roll on 15 feet or more.

Mackenzie and Jones completed the course for Jones' first invitation event – simply called 'The Augusta National Invitational' – in March 1934. Mackenzie unfortunately died that year, so he was unaware of the impact the tournament made. By the following year the tournament was being dubbed the Championship of Champions – the easier-off-the-tongue soubriquet 'Masters' was not long in driving that out. Horton Smith won in 1934, beating one of golf's perennial bridesmaids, Craig Wood, into second place. Bob Jones came out of retirement to tie 13th with his arch-rival, Walter Hagen. But it was not regarded yet as a Major.

To become a Major Championship, the competition has to be the best; the course has to be one of the toughest; there should at least be tradition in the organization running it. Augusta National was lacking in all three. There was no qualifying – entry was by invitation only; this was no Old Course or Olympia Fields; and the club was only formed in 1934. However, to misquote the Bard: 'Some events are born great; some events achieve greatness; and some have greatness thrust upon them'. The Opens can be thought of as the first; the PGA achieved its status through a workmanlike progress; and the Masters can thank Gene Sarazen, TV and Arnold Palmer for the third!

'Probably the best-known shot in all golf Tournament history', states Augusta National's own *Records of the Masters Tournament*. It alludes to a shot holed from all of 220 yards with fairway spoon (4 wood) by a desperate Sarazen on the 15th hole of the final round of the 1935 Tournament. Sarazen was three behind the ever-unlucky Craig Wood and his double-eagle or albatross (3 under par) on this par 5 hole enabled him to tie and force a play-off which he was to win. In doing so, Sarazen became the first player to win all four Majors as we now know them. The news story was probably blown up out of all proportion, but 'that shot' did take the infant Masters tournament on to the front page. Its real popularity, however, and therefore credibility as a Major, came in the late '50s with TV coverage and – centre-screen – the man of the people, the risk-taker, the mould-breaking Arnold Palmer. Being shown on television, the early-season combination of sunshine and Southern flowers, combined with Arnie's escapades, made for compulsive viewing. His first win, in 1958, merely set the scene. In 1960, Palmer, one behind the leader Ken Venturi with two to play, improbably birdied both holes to win. Then, in the 1962 3-way play-off, Palmer, three shots behind Gary Player at the turn, scorched the back nine in

31 to win. Comic-hero stuff, but the Masters had arrived.

Since the 1960s, coming as it does early in the season and being the smallest of all Major Championship fields, the Masters rapidly became a favourite and much-coveted tournament amongst the world's leading golfers. With his great advantage of extra length without compromising on control, Jack Nicklaus was to win an unprecedented and unsurpassed six times, the last occasion in 1986. By that time, the newly-emerging European force in golf was starting to take a fancy to Augusta in April. Seve Ballesteros had already won twice in the 80s and Benhard Langer won the first of his two titles the previous year. Sandy Lyle, Nick Faldo (three times), Ian Woosnam and Jose-Maria Olazabal would all go on to win over the next few years. American favourite Ben Crenshaw, who's 1984 win was one of the most popular of all time, delighted his supporters with a belated second Green Jacket in 1995. Greg Norman – a runner-up in 1985 and 1986 – had the field at his mercy starting out on the last round of the 1996 Tournament. His six-shot lead was turned into a five shot deficit by partner Nick Faldo, who ground out a 67 to Greg's 78 to collect a most improbable third Masters after the most incredible last round in Majors history.

Then, in 1997, a new star was born. Child prodigy and reigning US Amateur Champion, Eldrick 'Tiger' Woods, took the course and the competition apart, breaking all sorts of records along the way. A new era seemed to be dawning as Woods' power play was seen as much of a quantum leap in the sport as was Nicklaus's nearly 40 years before.

The Masters may be the fourth Major historically, but such is its charm and attraction that every golfer wants to play in it. It may, therefore, be held by many in higher regard than fourth . It certainly can argue that because it is so different to the others, it merits being a Major. At the time of the creation of the Masters, the British Open was different from the other Majors in that it was always played on seaside links and had the longest history; the US Open was arguably the sternest test of golf with narrow fairways, bunkers galore and jungle-like rough; the PGA was matchplay with tough qualifying rounds. At that time it was argued that Augusta National was too easy to be a venue for a Major Championship. Why then did so many of the game's top players fail to beat par? It was said that the Masters was a glorified putting contest – far from it. What has always mattered is where the approach shot is played .

The Masters is different in several ways – some of which we've already seen. It is also different in that it is always held at Augusta National. It has a trophy like the others, but it is not a cup. Instead the Masters trophy is a silver replica of the Clubhouse at Augusta, itself a replica of a fine *ante bellum*-style Southern homestead. It is different in that the winner is presented with the traditional Green Jacket as a member of the Augusta club – helped on for him by the previous year's champion (the first ceremony being conferred upon Sam Snead in 1949). It is different because it calls itself a tournament, not a championship. It is just different.

With holes which have names like Tea Olive, Yellow Jasmine, Magnolia, Azalea, and Redbud, the sheer style and class which reflects so much on Robert Tyre Jones Jr – the man and the gentleman golfer – the Masters can be nothing but a Major.

21

Part 2

The Championships
Year by Year

1860
17 October
BRITISH OPEN
Prestwick GC, Ayrshire, Scotland

'The holes were, for the most part, out of sight...'. So said Horace Hutchinson in a piece for Badminton Library's *Golf* in 1890. Prestwick was a 12-hole course which went '...dodging in and out among lofty sandhills', and which research has shown to have been of 3799 yards with a 'bogey' of 48.

1	**WILLIE PARK, Sr** (£nil)	55	59	60	174
2	Tom Morris, Sr	58	59	59	176
3	Andrew Strath				180
4	Robert Andrew				191
5	George Brown				192
6	Charlie Hunter				195
	Alexander Smith				
	William Steel				232?

1862
11 September
BRITISH OPEN
Prestwick GC, Ayrshire, Scotland

The last year that no monetary prize was offered - just the Championship Belt and medals. The winning margin of 13 shots is the all-time record for the Open - and any other Major.

1	**TOM MORRIS, Sr** (£nil)	52	55	56	163
2	Willie Park, Sr	59	59	58	176
3	Charlie Hunter	60	60	58	178
4	William Dow	60	58	63	181
5	James Knight (a)	62	61	63	186
6	J F Johnston (a)	64	69	75	208
	William Mitchell (a)				
	R Pollock (a)				

1861
26 September
BRITISH OPEN
Prestwick GC, Ayrshire, Scotland

Although he contrived the Championship for professionals, Col. JO Fairlie set the scene for the involvement of amateurs by taking part himself. The term 'Open' Championship may have originated from this date.

1	**TOM MORRIS, Sr** (£nil)	54	56	53	163
2	Willie Park, Sr	54	54	59	167
3	William Dow	59	58	54	171
4	David Park	58	57	57	172
5	Robert Andrew	58	61	56	175
6	Peter McEwan	56	60	62	178
7	Willie Dunn, Sr	61	59	60	180
8	James Fairlie (a)				184
9	George Brown	60	65	60	185
10	Robert Chambers, Jr (a)				187
11	Jamie Dunn	63	62	63	188
12	Charlie Hunter	67	64	59	190

1863
18 September
BRITISH OPEN
Prestwick GC, Ayrshire, Scotland

A £10 purse was shared by the professionals.

1	**WILLIE PARK, Sr** (£nil)	56	54	58	168
2	Tom Morris, Sr	56	58	56	170
3	David Park	55	63	54	172
4	Andrew Strath	61	55	58	174
5	George Brown	58	61	57	176
6	Robert Andrew	62	57	59	178
7	Charlie Hunter	61	61	62	184
8	James Knight (a)	66	65	59	190
9	James Miller (a)	63	63	66	192
10	James Paxton	65	65	66	196
11	Peter Chalmers (a)	65	67	65	197
	J F Johnston (a)	66	66	65	197
13	William Mitchell (a)	70	70	66	206
14	William Moffat (a)	75	78	80	233

16 October **1864**
BRITISH OPEN
Prestwick GC, Ayrshire, Scotland

'Old' Tom Morris continued his private battle with Willie Park. This was his last year as Prestwick's pro before returning to St Andrews.

1	**TOM MORRIS, Sr** (£6)	54	58	55	167
2	Andrew Strath	56	57	56	169
3	Robert Andrew	57	58	60	175
4	Willie Park, Sr	55	67	55	177
5	William Dow	56	58	67	181
6	William Strath	60	62	60	182

13 October **1866**
BRITISH OPEN
Prestwick GC, Ayrshire, Scotland

In these days it was impossible to know how many competitors made up the field at the start - or even completed the three rounds. As the *Ayrshire Express* reported, '...cards were not given to the secretary and cannot consequently be recorded'.

1	**WILLIE PARK, Sr** (£6)	54 56 59	169
2	David Park	58 57 56	171
3	Robert Andrew	58 59 59	176
4	Tom Morris, Sr	61 58 59	178
5	Bob Kirk	60 62 58	180
6=	William Doleman (a)	60 60 62	182
	Andrew Strath	61 61 60	182
8	John Allan	60 63 60	183
9	Tom Morris, Jr	63 60 64	187
10	Willie Dunn, Sr	64 63 62	189
11	Tom Hood (a)	61 69 61	191
12	James Hutchison	63 67 64	194

14 September **1865**
BRITISH OPEN
Prestwick GC, Ayrshire, Scotland

Official printed scorecards were introduced for the first time.

1	**ANDREW STRATH** (£8)	55	54	53	162
2	Willie Park, Sr	56	52	56	164
3	William Dow				171
4	Bob Kirk	64	54	55	173
5	Tom Morris, Sr	57	61	56	174
6	William Doleman (a)	62	57	59	178
7	Robert Andrew	61	59	59	179
8	William Strath	60	60	62	182
9	William Miller	63	60	66	189
10	Tom Hood (a)	66	66	66	198

Date unrecorded **1867**
BRITISH OPEN
Prestwick GC, Ayrshire, Scotland

Just like many successful enterprises, the early days of the venture was not too auspicious in organization or support. In 1867, the total purse was only £5-5s, having risen to all of £20 in 1865. 'Old' Tom became, at 46 years 99 days, the oldest-ever winner of the Open and of any Major until Julius Boros' USPGA title in 1968.

1	**TOM MORRIS, Sr** (£n/k)	58	54	58	170
2	Willie Park, Sr	58	56	58	172
3	Andrew Strath	61	57	56	174
4	Tom Morris, Jr	58	59	58	175
5	Bob Kirk	57	60	60	177
6	William Doleman (a)	55	66	57	178
7	Robert Andrew	56	58	65	179
8=	William Dow	62	57	65	184
	T Hunter (a)	62	60	62	184
10	Willie Dunn, Sr	64	63	62	189

1868
23 September

BRITISH OPEN
Prestwick GC, Ayrshire, Scotland

The Son of the Father. Enter 'Young' Tom Morris to dominate the Championship for several years and create new scoring records year-by-year. He recorded the Open's first hole-in-one on the 166(?)-yard 8th hole. At 17 yrs 5 mths 8 days, he is the youngest winner of the Championship – and of any of the Majors.

1	**TOM MORRIS, Jr** (£6)	50	55	52	157
2	Robert Andrew	53	54	52	159
3	Willie Park, Sr	58	50	54	162
4	Bob Kirk	56	59	56	171
5	John Allan	54	55	63	172
6	Tom Morris, Sr	56	62	58	176
7	William Dow	61	58	60	179
8	William Doleman (a)	57	63	61	181
9	Charlie Hunter	60	64	58	182
10	Willie Dunn, Sr	60	63	60	183

1869
16 September

BRITISH OPEN
Prestwick GC, Ayrshire, Scotland

Morris Jr shot the Open's first sub-50 round at Prestwick to steal the title from his Dad.

1	**TOM MORRIS, Jr** (£6)	51	54	49	154
2	Tom Morris, Sr	54	50	53	157
3	S Mure Fergusson (a)	57	54	54	165
4	Bob Kirk	53	58	57	168
5	Davie Strath	53	56	60	169
6	Jamie Anderson	60	56	57	173
7	William Doleman (a)	60	56	59	175
8	G Mitchell-Innes (a)	64	58	58	180

15 September **1870**
BRITISH OPEN
Prestwick GC, Ayrshire, Scotland

BRITISH OPEN **1871**
NO CHAMPIONSHIP

'Young' Tom became the first player to beat the course 'bogey' of 48 and the first golfer to win three Opens in succession. In recognition, he was awarded the Belt outright.

I	**TOM MORRIS, Jr** (£6)	47	51	51	149
2=	Bob Kirk	52	52	57	161
	Davie Strath	54	49	58	161
4	Tom Morris, Sr	56	52	54	162
5	William Doleman (a)	57	56	58	171
6	Willie Park, Sr	60	55	58	173
7	Jamie Anderson	59	57	58	174
8	John Allan	61	58	57	176
9=	A Doleman (a)	61	59	58	178
	Charlie Hunter	58	56	64	178
11	J Brown	66	55	59	180
12	J Millar	66	62	54	182
13	T Hunter (a)	62	63	60	185
14	F Doleman	65	64	60	189
15=	W Boyd	65	59	67	191
	J Hunter	62	65	64	191
17	William Dow	68	64	66	198

Prestwick GC, which had run the Open single-handedly since 1860, was now joined by the Royal and Ancient Club and the Honourable Company of Edinburgh Golfers in the organization of the event. It was held in abeyance for one year and it was decided that from 1872 each club should hold the Championship in rotation. A new trophy, the silver claret jug, was purchased for £30. Most importantly, it was resolved that the competition should be open to all-comers, thereby formalizing the spirit that was introduced by Col. Fairlie back in 1861.

1872

13 September

BRITISH OPEN
Prestwick GC, Ayrshire, Scotland

1873

4 October

BRITISH OPEN
Royal & Ancient GC, St Andrews, Fife, Scotland

Tom Morris Jr won his fourth Open while still only 21, and was acclaimed as the greatest golfer of his time. His is the first name on the famous claret jug.

1	**TOM MORRIS, Jr** (£8)	57	56 53	166
2	Davie Strath	56	52 61	169
3	William Doleman (a)	63	60 54	177
4=	Tom Morris, Sr	62	60 57	179
	David Park	61	57 61	179
6	Charlie Hunter	60	60 69	189
7	Hugh Brown	65	73 61	199
8	William Hunter (a)	65	63 74	202

The first Open Championship to be held at the Old Course was dominated by St Andrews golfers, of which the winner was one. Another, David Ayton, was the forerunner of various Aytons' appearances in different Majors sprinkled over the next 80 years.

1	**TOM KIDD** (£11)	91	88	179
2	Jamie Anderson	91	89	180
3=	Bob Kirk	91	92	183
	Tom Morris, Jr	94	89	183
5	Davie Strath	97	90	187
6	Walter Gourlay	92	96	188
7	Tom Morris, Sr	93	96	189
9	Henry Lamb (a)	96	96	192
10=	Willie Fernie	101	93	194
	Bob Martin	97	97	194
12=	R Armitage (a)	96	99	195
	Jas Fenton	94	101	195
	JOF Morris	96	99	195
15	S Mure Fergusson (a)	98	101	199
16	R Manzie	96	104	200
17	Jack Morris	106	100	206
18=	David Ayton	111	96	207
	R Thomson	98	109	207
20	John Chisholm	103	105	208
21	Bob Pringle	109	102	211
22	D Brand	110	103	213

10 April			**1874**

BRITISH OPEN
Honourable Co of Edinburgh Golfers,
Musselburgh, Midlothian, Scotland

Mungo Park, who shared the same name as the famous late-18th Century explorer (but it is not known whether they were related) beat 'Young' Tom, who was now reported to be suffering from ill-health. Mungo was the brother of Willie, and his son – also Mungo – became a pioneer of golf in the United States. The 75 was the record low score for any 18 holes while the Open was played over 36. It was only lowered by Harold Hilton who shot 72 on the much-criticized Muirfield Links in 1892 and by Willie Smith (71), George Duncan (71), James Braid (73&74) and others on the Old Course as late as 1910.

1	**MUNGO PARK**	75	84		159
	(£8)				
2	Tom Morris, Jr	83	78		161
3	George Paxton	80	82		162
4	Bob Martin	85	79		164
5	Jamie Anderson	82	83		165
6=	David Park	83	83		166
	William Thomson	84	82		166
8=	Bob Ferguson	83	84		167
	Tom Kidd	84	83		167
10=	J Fergusson	87	82		169
	G M'Cachnie	79	90		169
	JOF Morris	88	81		169
13	Willie Park, Sr	83	87		170
14=	Tom Hood	83	88		171
	Bob Pringle	85	86		171
16	T Hunter (a)	88	86		174
17	T Brown	87	88		175
18=	Tom Morris, Sr	90	86		176
	Davie Strath	86	90		176
20=	William Cosgrove	88	89		177
	William Doleman (a)	88	89		177
21=	R Cosgrove	92	86		178
	Willie Dunn, Sr	87	91		178
23=	J Dow	88	94		182
	Jas Fenton	90	92		182
24	William Brown	91	93		184
25	W Hutchison	90	95		185
26	Charlie Hunter	93	94		187
27	N Patrick	98	98		196
28	D Clayton	99	101		200
29	A Brown	96	106		202

10 September				**1875**

BRITISH OPEN
Prestwick GC, Ayrshire, Scotland

Willie Park picked up his 4th and last title after a few years of indifferent form. It is thought that the Morris's did not compete due the death of 'Young' Tom's wife in childbirth - a factor, coupled with the consequent heavy drinking, that led to the discovery by 'Old' Tom of his son's body on Christmas morning. The greatest golfer of his generation was dead at 24.

1	**WILLIE PARK, Sr**	56	59	51	166
	(£8)				
2	Bob Martin	56	58	54	168
3	Mungo Park	59	57	55	171
4	Bob Ferguson	58	56	58	172
5	James Rennie	61	59	57	177
6	Davie Strath	59	61	58	178
7	Bob Pringle	62	58	61	181
8=	William Doleman (a)	65	59	59	183
	Hugh Morrison	62	59	62	183
10	John Campbell	57	66	63	186
11	Neil Boon	67	60	62	189
12	James Guthrie	63	64	66	193
13	Matthew Allan	67	65	62	194
14	James Boyd	67	65	63	195

1876
30 September

BRITISH OPEN
Royal & Ancient GC, St Andrews, Fife, Scotland

1877
6 April

BRITISH OPEN
Honourable Co of Edinburgh Golfers,
Musselburgh, Midlothian, Scotland

The first-ever play-off – except it never took place. Strath protested about a claim against him for disqualification. The decision was that he and Martin should play off, but Strath refused on the basis that his protest had not been properly decided upon.

1	**BOB MARTIN***	86	90	176
	(£10)			
2	Davie Strath	86	90	176
3	Willie Park, Sr	94	89	183
4=	Tom Morris, Sr	90	95	185
	Mungo Park	95	90	185
	William Thomson	90	95	185
7	Henry Lamb (a)	94	92	186
8=	Walter Gourlay	98	89	187
	Bob Kirk	95	92	187
	George Paxton	95	92	187
11	Robert Kinsman	88	100	188
12=	Jamie Anderson	96	93	189
	David Lamb (a)	95	94	189
14=	David Anderson, Sr	93	97	190
	John Thompson	89	101	190

* See above note

Anderson's first of three wins 'back-to-back' was over four rounds of Musselburgh's nine holes.

1	**JAMIE ANDERSON**	40	42	37	41	160
	(£8)					
2	Bob Pringle	44	38	40	40	162
3=	William Cosgrove	41	39	44	40	164
	Bob Ferguson	40	40	40	44	164
5=	William Brown	39	41	45	41	166
	Davie Strath	45	40	38	43	166
7	Mungo Park					167

4 October				**1878**

BRITISH OPEN

Prestwick GC, Ayrshire, Scotland

Jamie Anderson recorded the second 'hole-in-one' in the Championship, following Morris Jr's effort in 1868. John Ball – the first amateur Champion-to-be (1890) – finished 4th in his first Open. He was aged just 14!

1	**JAMIE ANDERSON** (£8)	53	53	51	157
2	Bob Kirk	53	55	51	159
3	JOF Morris	50	56	55	161
4=	John Ball, Jr (a)	53	57	55	165
	Bob Martin	57	53	55	165
6=	William Cosgrove	55	56	55	166
	Willie Park, Sr	53	56	57	166
8	Jamie Allan	62	53	52	167
9=	John Allan	55	55	58	168
	Tom Dunn	54	60	54	168
11	Tom Morris, Sr	55	53	63	171
12	Ben Sayers	56	59	58	173
13	Edwin Paxton	58	59	58	175
14	George Strath	63	62	51	176
15	Alex Patrick	62	56	60	178
16	Jack Morris	58	57	64	179
17	Mungo Park	60	58	62	180
18	George Low	57	61	63	181
19	Neil Boon	63	54	66	183
20	William Hunter (a)	67	65	55	187
21	James Moore	62	62	65	189
22	Bob Pringle	62	65	65	192

27 September			**1879**

BRITISH OPEN

Royal & Ancient GC, St Andrews, Fife, Scotland

Anderson's 'Hat trick' had the the lowest total of all 36-hole Opens on this, his home course, until Hugh Kirkaldy's 166 in the very last one, in 1891.

1	**JAMIE ANDERSON** (£10)	84	85	169
2=	Jamie Allan	88	84	172
	Andrew Kirkaldy	86	86	172
4	George Paxton			174
5	Tom Kidd			175
6	Bob Ferguson			176
7	David Anderson, Sr			178
8=	Tom Dunn			179
	Walter Gourlay			179
	JOF Morris	92	87	179
11	AW Smith (a)			180
12=	Willie Fernie			181
	John Kirkaldy			181
	James Rennie			181
15=	Thomas Arundel			184
	David Ayton			184
	Henry Lamb (a)			184
18=	William Doleman (a)			185
	Robert Kinsman			185
	Tom Morris, Sr			185
21	Bob Martin			186
22	Ben Sayers			187
23=	D Corstorphine			189
	Robert Dow			189
	David Grant			189
	Edwin Paxton			189
	Smith (Cambridge)			189
28	Argyll Robertson (a)			190
29=	R Armitage			191
	George Strath			191

1880

9 April

BRITISH OPEN

Honourable Co of Edinburgh Golfers,
Musselburgh, Midlothian, Scotland

The early date of the Championship in 1880 caught out Jamie Anderson, who was unable to compete. This left Bob Ferguson the chance to secure the first of his three wins in a row. Anderson, although featuring strongly over the next few years, never won again, and died in a Poor House in Perth in 1912. So much for the rich pickings of the 19th Century professional golfer.

1	**BOB FERGUSON**	81	81	162
	(£8)			
2	Peter Paxton	81	86	167
3	Ned Cosgrove	82	86	168
4=	David Brown	86	83	169
	George Paxton	85	84	169
	Bob Pringle	90	79	169
7	Andrew Kirkaldy	85	85	170
8=	William Brown	87	84	171
	David Grant	87	84	171
10=	Thomas Arundel	86	93	179
	T Brown	90	89	179
	Willie Campbell	88	91	179
	J Foreman	92	87	179
14	Willie Park, Sr	89	92	181
15	Willie Park, Jr	92	90	182
16=	A Brown	91	92	183
	D Corstorphine	93	90	183
	George Strath	87	96	183
19	Ben Sayers	91	93	184
20	Mungo Park	95	92	187
21=	R Drummond	96	94	190
	William Thomson	96	94	190
23	James Beveridge	94	97	191

1881

14 October

BRITISH OPEN

Prestwick GC, Ayrshire, Scotland

A violent storm that took the lives of 180 fishermen in Scottish waters reduced the field to 22 starters, of whom only eight finished. Ferguson's winning total was the highest for Prestwick's 36 holes since 'Old' Tom's last win in 1867, and only exceeded by Willie Park's 174 in the inaugural year.

1	**BOB FERGUSON**	53	60	57	170
	(£8)				
2	Jamie Anderson	57	60	56	173
3	Ned Cosgrove	61	59	57	177
4	Bob Martin	57	62	59	178
5=	Willie Campbell	60	56	65	181
	Tom Morris, Sr	58	65	58	181
	Willie Park, Jr	66	57	58	181
8	Willie Fernie	65	62	56	183

30 September	**1882**

BRITISH OPEN
Royal & Ancient GC, St Andrews, Fife, Scotland

16 November	**1883**

BRITISH OPEN
Honourable Co of Edinburgh Golfers,
Musselburgh, Midlothian, Scotland

Ferguson held his 3-stroke 1st Round lead to pick up his third consecutive Open. Like Anderson before him, obscurity was to follow in a few years, and he resorted to greenkeeping and caddying thereafter at his home club of Musselburgh.

1	**BOB FERGUSON** (£12)	83	88	171
2	Willie Fernie	88	86	174
3=	Jamie Anderson	87	88	175
	Fitz Boothby (a)	86	89	175
	John Kirkcaldy	86	89	175
	Bob Martin	89	86	175
7=	David Ayton	90	88	178
	James Mansfield (a)	91	87	178
	Willie Park, Sr	89	89	178
	James Rennie	90	88	178
11=	Tom Kidd	87	93	180
	Henry Lamb (a)	88	92	180
13=	Andrew Alexander	93	88	181
	George Low	95	86	181
	Douglas Rolland	88	93	181
16=	W Honeyman	93	89	182
	William Thomson	95	87	182
18=	Tom Dunn	93	90	183
	Willie Park, Jr	90	93	183
	Ben Sayers	92	91	183
21=	David Anderson, Sr	91	93	184
	Peter Fernie	94	90	184
23=	Jack Burns	97	92	189
	George Forrester	94	95	189
	Bob Pringle	92	97	189
	David Simpson	98	91	189
27	Thomas Arundel	97	93	190
28	James Kirk	101	90	191
29=	James Hunter (a)	92	100	192
	Robert Kinsman	99	93	192

Willie Fernie, despite shooting the only 10 to appear on any Major winner's card in history, tied with Ferguson and denied him from making four wins in as many years - by one shot in the first contested play-off. Fernie, although St Andrews born, was then of Dumfries, thus becoming the first winner from outside the host clubs. This sums up the parochial nature of the Championship to date.

1	**WILLIE FERNIE*** (£n/k)	75	84	159
2	Bob Ferguson	78	81	159
3	William Brown	83	77	160
4	Bob Pringle	79	82	161
5=	Willie Campbell	80	83	163
	George Paxton	80	83	163
7	Ben Sayers	81	83	164
8	Willie Park, Jr	77	88	165
9	Willie Dunn, Jr	85	81	166
10=	Ben Campbell	81	86	167
	Tom Morris, Sr	86	81	167
	Peter Paxton	85	82	167
	Douglas Rolland (a)	82	85	167
14	T Grossart	82	86	168
15	F Park	84	85	169
16	William Cosgrove	79	91	170
17=	Tom Dunn	87	84	171
	Jack Simpson (a)	90	81	171
19	G Miller (a)	80	92	172
20	D Leitch (a)	88	86	174
21	Thomas Arundel	87	88	175
22	Willie Park, Sr	94	82	176
23	William Thomson	90	87	177
24=	David Brown	88	91	179
	David Grant	89	90	179
26	D Corstorphine	88	93	181
27	Mungo Park	93	89	182
28	Bob Tait	89	94	183
29	George Strath	91	93	184
30	D Baldie (a)	92	93	185

* Willie Fernie (158) beat Bob Ferguson (159) in the 36-Hole Play-off

1884
Date unrecorded
BRITISH OPEN
Prestwick GC, Ayrshire, Scotland

1885
3 October
BRITISH OPEN
Royal & Ancient GC, St Andrews, Fife, Scotland

One of several golfing brothers, Jack Simpson was the only one to win the Open. His brother Archie was runner-up in 1885 and 1890 - something that was to happen to this year's No2, Willie Fernie, on more than one occasion.

1	**JACK SIMPSON** (£n/k)	78	82	160
2=	Willie Fernie	80	84	164
	Douglas Rolland	81	83	164
4=	Willie Campbell	84	85	169
	Willie Park, Jr	86	83	169
6	Ben Sayers	83	87	170
7=	Tom Dunn			171
	George Fernie			171
9=	Peter Fernie			172
	John Kirkaldy			172
11=	Matthew Allan			173
	Willie Dunn, Jr			173
13=	JOF Morris			174
	Tom Morris, Sr			174
15	Jamie Anderson			175
16=	William Cosgrove			178
	William Doleman (a)			178
18	James Hunter (a)			179
19	David Grant			180
20	G Smith			183

Despite the piecemeal ventures of some Scottish pros to clubs south of the border, only a handful of English golfers, all amateur, had ventured north for the Championship. One of the most influential of these, Horace Hutchinson, made his debut this year. Over the ensuing few years he had much, through his playing and writing, to do with encouraging the burgeoning English talent of the 1890s to participate in the Open.

1	**BOB MARTIN** (£10)	84	87	171
2	Archie Simpson	83	89	172
3	David Ayton	89	84	173
4=	Willie Fernie	89	85	174
	Willie Park, Jr	86	88	174
	Bob Simpson	85	89	174
7	Jack Burns	88	87	175
8	Peter Paxton	85	91	176
9=	Willie Campbell	86	91	177
	JOF Morris	91	86	177
11=	Horace Hutchinson (a)	87	91	178
	John Kirkaldy	94	84	178
13=	Johnny Laidlay (a)	87	92	179
	Jack Simpson	87	92	179
15	Ben Sayers	94	86	180
16=	Leslie Balfour (a)	90	91	181
	William Greig (a)	89	92	181
18=	HSC Everard (a)	90	92	182
	George Fernie	87	95	182
	James Rennie	90	92	182
21	David Anderson, Sr	96	87	183
22	Ben Campbell	88	96	184
23	Willie Brown	91	95	186
24=	Willie Anderson, Sr	90	97	187
	S Mure Fergusson (a)	96	91	187
26	WH Goff (a)	97	91	188
27=	TS Hendry (a)	94	95	189
	Robert Kinsman	96	93	189
29=	Jamie Allan	93	97	190
	William Cosgrove	88	102	190
	Bruce Goff (a)	96	94	190
	Tom Morris, Sr	96	94	190

5 November				**1886**

BRITISH OPEN

Honourable Co of Edinburgh Golfers,
Musselburgh, Midlothian, Scotland

An unsung champion, David Brown emigrated to America where he tied with Willie Anderson for the US Open in 1903 - losing the play-off by 2 strokes.

1	**DAVID BROWN** (£8)	79	78	157
2	Willie Campbell	78	81	159
3	Ben Campbell	79	81	160
4=	Bob Ferguson	82	79	161
	Thomas Gossett	80	81	161
	Willie Park, Jr	84	77	161
	Archie Simpson	82	79	161
8=	Willie Fernie	79	83	162
	David Grant	86	76	162
	Johnny Laidlay (a)	80	82	162
11	JOF Morris	81	82	163
12=	John Lambert	78	86	164
	Thomas McWatt	81	83	164
	Jack Simpson	83	81	164
15	Bob Simpson	84	81	165
16=	Tom Dunn	83	83	166
	Horace Hutchinson (a)	81	85	166
	Bob Pringle	80	86	166
	Ben Sayers	84	82	166
20=	William Cosgrove	84	83	167
	Bob Tait	84	83	167
22	Peter Fernie	85	83	168
23	Peter Paxton	87	82	169
24=	Jacky Ferguson	83	87	170
	George Strath	86	84	170
26	David Simpson	84	88	172
27=	Willie Dunn, Jr	85	88	173
	Tom Morris, Sr	88	85	172
29=	Charlie Crawford	85	89	174
	James Keddie	84	90	174

16 September				**1887**

BRITISH OPEN

Prestwick GC, Ayrshire, Scotland

Willie Jr's win completed the second set of father-son victories. Fittingly it should be the Parks and the Morrises, the fathers having carved up the first five Championships between them. After winning again in 1889, Willie Park Jr increasingly turned his mind to club development and has been called the father of modern golf course architectutre – Sunningdale being one example.

1	**WILLIE PARK, Jr** (£8)	82	79	161
2	Bob Martin	81	81	162
3	Willie Campbell	77	87	164
4	Johnny Laidlay (a)	86	80	166
5=	Ben Sayers	83	85	168
	Archie Simpson	81	87	168
7=	Willie Fernie	86	87	173
	David Grant	89	84	173
9	David Brown	82	92	174
10=	Ben Campbell	88	87	175
	Horace Hutchinson (a)	87	88	175
12=	David Ayton	89	87	176
	James Kay	89	87	176
	John Kirkaldy	89	87	176
	Jack Simpson	85	91	176
16	Bob Simpson	90	89	179
17=	George Fernie	92	88	180
	A Monaghan	90	90	180
19	Hugh Kirkaldy	89	92	181
20=	James Boyd	95	87	182
	P Wilson (a)	90	92	182
22=	Allan Macfie (a)	94	90	184
	A Stuart (a)	96	88	184
24	Peter Fernie	95	90	185
25=	JS Carrick (a)	96	90	186
	Jack Morris	93	93	186
27	David McEwan	94	93	187

1888
6 October

BRITISH OPEN
Royal & Ancient GC, St Andrews, Fife, Scotland

1889
8 November

BRITISH OPEN
Honourable Co of Edinburgh Golfers,
Musselburgh, Midlothian, Scotland

Alex 'Sandy' Herd made the Top 10 for the first time, in his 4th year of a 54-year span in the Open Championship. His remarkable run included a win in 1902, and 2nds in 1892, 1895, 1910 and 1920. He competed in his last Open in 1939, aged 71. His brother Fred won the 1898 US Open.

1	**JACK BURNS**	86	85	171
	(£8)			

2=	David Anderson, Jr	86	86	172
	Ben Sayers	85	87	172
4	Willie Campbell	84	90	174
5	Leslie Balfour (a)	86	89	175
6=	David Grant	88	88	176
	Andrew Kirkaldy	87	89	176
8	Sandy Herd	93	84	177
9	David Ayton	87	91	178
10	Johnny Laidlay (a)	93	87	180
11=	HSC Everard (a)	93	89	182
	Hugh Kirkaldy	98	84	182
	Willie Park, Jr	90	92	182
14=	Laurie Auchterlonie	91	92	183
	Willie Fernie	91	92	183
16=	Bob Martin	86	98	184
	Archie Simpson	91	93	184
18=	Jamie Allan	95	90	185
	Willie Auchterlonie	92	93	185
	John Kirkaldy	92	93	185
	Allan MacFie (a)	94	91	185
	Bob Tait	95	90	185
23=	William Greig (a)	94	92	186
	JOF Morris	96	90	186
25	N Playfair (a)	94	93	187
26	D Leitch (a)	93	96	189
27=	Willie Anderson, Sr	98	92	190
	Tom Morris, Sr	94	96	190
	DG Rose (a)	101	89	190
30	Bob Simpson	90	101	191

The last Championship held at Musselburgh produced a course record low winning total in the tie between Willie Park Jr and Andrew Kirkaldy – the lowest at any venue since the heyday of 'Young' Tom in 1869 and 1870. The Honourable Company, in order to stay involved with the Open, forsook their 9-hole home for Muirfield. The fact that the end of the 2nd round was played in a November gloom so deep that final pairs had to be guided by street lights also triggered the move to earlier calendar dates.

1	**WILLIE PARK, Jr***	39	39	39	38	155
	(£8)					

2	Andrew Kirkaldy	39	38	39	39	155
3	Ben Sayers	39	40	41	39	159
4=	David Brown	43	39	41	39	162
	Johnny Laidlay (a)	42	39	40	41	162
6	Willie Fernie	45	39	40	40	164
7=	Willie Brown	44	43	41	37	165
	Willie Campbell	44	40	42	39	165
	David Grant	41	41	41	42	165
10=	High Kirkaldy	44	39	43	40	166
	William Thomson	43	42	40	41	166
12	Archie Simpson	44	45	37	41	167
13	AM Ross (a)	42	45	42	40	169
14	Jack Burns	47	39	42	42	170

*Willie Park Jr (158) beat Andrew Kirkaldy (163) in the 18-Hole Play-off

11 September	**1890**

BRITISH OPEN
Prestwick GC, Ayrshire, Scotland

John Ball became the first Englishman and the first amateur to win after 30 years of the Open Championship. The invasion had not yet started though - he was the only Englishman out of 31 to finish.

1	**JOHN BALL, Jr**	82	82	164
	(Amateur)			
2=	Willie Fernie	85	82	167
	Archie Simpson	85	82	167
4=	Andrew Kirkaldy	81	89	170
	Willie Park, Jr	90	80	170
6	Horace Hutchinson (a)	87	85	172
7=	David Grant	86	87	173
	Hugh Kirkaldy	82	91	173
9	William McEwan	87	87	174
10	David Brown	85	90	175
11=	James Kay	86	91	177
	Johnny Laidlay (a)	89	88	177
13	D Leitch (a)	86	93	179
14	David Anderson, Jr	90	90	180
15=	John Allan	93	88	181
	Ben Campbell	93	88	181
17=	D Anderson (a)	91	91	182
	David Ayton	97	85	182
19	Ben Sayers	90	93	183
20	A Wright	92	92	184
21	George Fernie	92	94	186
22	RB Wilson	91	96	187
23=	DD Robertson (a)	94	95	189
	Bob Mearns	96	93	189
25	Robert Adam (a)	91	99	190
26	James Mair (a)	98	96	194
27=	James Cunningham	104	95	199
	Charles Whigham (a)	93	106	199
29	James McKay	104	96	200
30	DH Gillan (a)	100	104	204

6 October	**1891**

BRITISH OPEN
Royal & Ancient GC, St Andrews, Fife, Scotland

Hugh was the only Kirkaldy brother to pick up the title although John, and particularly Andrew (who tied Willie Park Jr in 1889 but lost the play-off), featured prominently. Andrew became pro for the R&A in 1910 until his death in 1934, in direct succession to Tom Morris, Sr, and before him the legendary Allan Robertson - a dynasty of over 80 years.

1	**HUGH KIRKALDY**	83	83	166
	(£10)			
2=	Willie Fernie	84	84	168
	Andrew Kirkaldy	84	84	168
4	R Mure Fergusson (a)	86	84	170
5	WD More	84	87	171
6	Willie Park, Jr	88	85	173
7	David Brown	88	86	174
8	Willie Auchterlonie	85	90	175
9=	Ben Sayers	91	85	176
	Tom Vardon	89	87	176
11=	John Ball, Jr (a)	94	83	177
	Archie Simpson	86	91	177
13	Sandy Herd	87	91	178
14=	David Grant	84	95	179
	James Kay	93	86	179
	John Kirkaldy	90	89	179
	Bob Mearns	88	91	179
18=	Laurie Auchterlonie	87	93	180
	Charles Hutchings (a)	89	91	180
	Johnny Laidlay (a)	90	90	180
	David Simpson	91	89	180
22=	David Anderson, Jr	90	91	181
	David Ayton	94	87	181
	Ernley RH Blackwell (a)	90	91	181
	Willie Campbell	94	87	181
	Horace Hutchinson (a)	89	92	181
	George Mason	94	87	181
28=	HSC Everard (a)	89	93	182
	William Greig (a)	95	87	182
	RH Johnston (a)	95	87	182
	Freddie Tait (a)	94	88	182

1892
22-23 September

BRITISH OPEN
Honourable Company, Muirfield, Angus
Scotland

The first championship to be spread over two days and 72 holes resulted in the second win for an amateur (and an English one at that) in three years. The Honourable Company of Edinburgh Golfers were hosts at Muirfield, where the championship was held for the first time. Many critics thought that the course was not a sufficient challenge for the Championship and alterations were made for future Opens there. Entry fees, to deter mere hopefuls, were introduced.

I	**HAROLD HILTON** (Amateur)	78	81	72	74	305
2=	John Ball, Jr (a)	75	80	74	79	308
	Sandy Herd	77	78	77	76	308
	Hugh Kirkaldy	77	83	73	75	308
5=	James Kay	82	78	74	78	312
	Ben Sayers	80	76	81	75	312
7	Willie Park, Jr	78	77	80	80	315
8	Willie Fernie	79	83	76	78	316
9	Archie Simpson	81	81	76	79	317
10	Horace Hutchinson (a)	74	78	86	80	318
11	Jack White	82	78	78	81	319
12	Tom Vardon	83	75	80	82	320
13=	Edward BH Blackwell (a)	81	82	82	76	321
	Andrew Kirkaldy	84	82	80	75	321
15	S Mure Fergusson (a)	78	82	80	82	322
16=	David Anderson, Jr	76	82	79	87	324
	RT Boothby (a)	81	81	80	82	324
	Ben Campbell	86	83	79	76	324
19=	FA Fairlie (a)	83	87	79	76	325
	William McEwan	79	83	84	79	325
21=	WD More	87	75	80	84	326
	GG Smith (a)	84	82	79	81	326
	Freddie Tait (a)	81	83	84	78	326
24	David Brown	77	82	84	85	328
25=	George Douglas	81	83	86	79	329
	Douglas McEwan	84	84	82	79	329
27	Ernley RH Blackwell (a)	79	81	84	86	330
28=	Leslie Balfour (a)	83	87	80	81	331
	Jack Simpson	84	78	82	87	331
30	Charlie Crawford	79	85	85	84	333

Round Leader(s)
R1 Hutchinson; 74
R2 Hutchinson; 152
R3 Ball; 229
Lowest Scores
R2 More, Vardon; 75
R3 Hilton 72
R4 Hilton 74

31 August - 1 September 1893
BRITISH OPEN
Prestwick GC, Ayrshire, Scotland

11-12 June 1894
BRITISH OPEN
St George's GC, Sandwich, Kent, England

'Old' Tom Morris – winner of four of the first eight Opens, and playing in the Championship for the 33rd consecutive time, told *The Field* magazine that conditions on the first day were the worst ever experienced. The magazine's correspondent was more flowery: '...it rained in the most pitiless fashion from morn to eve...'. Willie Auchterlonie's brother, Laurie, made it a family double when he picked up the US Open in 1902. Willie's winning purse was £1.10.0 more than the total prizemoney 2 years earlier.

1	**W AUCHTERLONIE**	78	81	81	82	322
	(£30)					
2	Johnny Laidlay (a)	80	83	80	81	324
3	Sandy Herd	82	81	78	84	325
4=	Andrew Kirkaldy	85	82	82	77	326
	Hugh Kirkaldy	83	79	82	82	326
6=	James Kay	81	81	80	85	327
	Bob Simpson	81	81	80	85	327
8=	John Ball, Jr (a)	83	79	84	86	332
	Harold Hilton (a)	88	81	82	81	332
10=	JH Taylor	75	89	86	83	333
	Jack White	81	86	80	86	333
12	Ben Sayers	87	88	84	76	335
13	C Hutchings (a)	81	92	80	84	337
14	Archie Simpson	84	86	84	85	339
15=	S Mure Fergusson (a)	83	85	85	87	340
	John Hunter	87	85	83	85	340
17=	David Grant	86	86	85	84	341
	Joe Lloyd	85	91	84	81	341
19=	LS Anderson (a)	89	83	86	84	342
	PC Anderson (a)	93	84	83	82	342
	Willie Park, Jr	82	89	86	85	342
22	David Anderson, Jr	86	93	83	81	343
23=	John Allan	81	88	83	92	344
	T Carmichael (a)	90	87	82	85	344
	Willie Fernie	86	92	85	81	344
	Bob Mearns	86	84	86	88	344
	Harry Vardon	84	90	81	89	344
28=	FA Fairlie (a)	82	90	88	85	345
	William McEwan	88	84	90	83	345
	Tom Vardon	85	86	82	92	345

Round Leader(s)
R1   Taylor; 75
R2   Auchterlonie; 159
R3   Auchterlonie; 240
Lowest Scores
R2   Ball, H Kirkaldy; 79
R3   Herd, 78
R4   Sayers; 76

The Open left Scotland for the first time in an expanded rotation which would also take in Royal Liverpool at Hoylake in 1897. This was the first win for one of the famous 'Great Triumvirate' of JH Taylor, Harry Vardon and James Braid, who between 1894 and 1914 collected 16 Open Championships - with Vardon also raiding the US Open successfully in 1900. Joe Lloyd, in 17th place, was to achieve greater glory after emigrating, by winning the 1897 US Open.

1	**JH TAYLOR**	84	80	81	81	326
	(£30)					
2	Douglas Rolland	86	79	84	82	331
3	Andrew Kirkaldy	86	79	83	84	332
4	AH Toogood	84	85	82	82	333
5=	Willie Fernie	84	84	86	80	334
	Ben Sayers	85	81	84	84	334
	Harry Vardon	86	86	82	80	334
8	Alex Herd	83	85	82	88	338
9	Freddie Tait (a)	90	83	83	84	340
10=	AD Blyth (a)	91	84	84	82	341
	James Braid	91	84	82	84	341
12	Willie Park, Jr	88	86	82	87	343
13=	John Ball, Jr (a)	84	89	87	84	344
	David Brown	93	83	81	87	344
	Hugh Kirkaldy	90	85	80	89	344
	Archie Simpson	90	86	86	82	344
17	Joe Lloyd	95	81	86	83	345
18	S Mure Fergusson (a)	87	88	84	87	346
19	Tom Vardon	87	88	82	91	348
20=	CE Dick (a)	85	89	89	90	353
	David Grant	91	84	87	91	353
	David Herd	92	93	84	84	353
23=	Willie Auchterlonie	96	81	93	85	355
	John Rowe	90	90	84	91	355
25=	Stuart Anderson (a)	90	87	91	88	356
	CE Hambro (a)	96	90	82	88	356
	Charles Hutchings (a)	93	85	88	90	356
28	Charles Gibson	92	94	87	84	357
29	Rowland Jones	89	88	93	88	358
30	A Lumsden	90	93	87	89	359

Round Leader(s)
R1   Herd; 83
R2   Taylor; 164
R3   Taylor; 245
Lowest Scores
R2   A Kirkaldy, Rolland; 79
R3   H Kirkaldy; 80
R4   Fernie, H Vardon; 80

1895

12-13 June

BRITISH OPEN

Royal & Ancient GC, St Andrews, Fife, Scotland

1895

4 October

US OPEN

Newport GC, Newport, Rhode Island

Taylor, 3 behind Herd going into the last round, shot a 78 - 4 strokes better than anyone in the field – to overhaul the Scotsman over the last 18 holes.

I	**JH TAYLOR** (£30)	86	78	80	78	322
2	Sandy Herd	82	77	82	85	326
3	Andrew Kirkaldy	81	83	84	84	332
4	George Pulford	84	81	83	86	334
5	Archie Simpson	88	85	78	85	336
6=	David Anderson, Jr	86	83	84	84	337
	David Brown	81	89	83	84	337
	Willie Fernie	86	79	86	86	337
9=	Ben Sayers	84	87	85	82	338
	AH Toogood	85	84	83	86	338
	Harry Vardon	80	85	85	88	338
	Tom Vardon	82	83	84	89	338
13=	Laurie Auchterlonie	84	84	85	87	340
	J Robb	89	88	81	82	340
15=	Hugh Kirkaldy	87	87	83	84	341
	Freddie Tait (a)	87	86	82	86	341
17	Johnny Laidlay (a)	91	83	82	86	342
18=	John Ball, Jr (a)	85	85	88	86	344
	L Waters	86	83	85	90	344
20	David Herd	85	85	84	91	345
21	Albert Tingey, Sr	83	88	87	88	346
	Jack White	88	86	85	87	346
23	James Kinnell	84	83	88	92	347
24	Jack Ross	87	84	89	88	348
25=	James Kay	88	85	92	86	351
	David McEwan	85	90	90	86	351
27=	Willie Aveston	89	86	89	89	353
	Douglas McEwan	95	85	92	81	353
	AM Ross (a)	92	85	88	88	353
	Walter Toogood	87	91	88	87	353

Round Leader(s)
R1   H Vardon; 80
R2   S Herd; 159
R3   S Herd 241
Lowest Scores
R2   S Herd; 77
R3   Simpson; 78
R4   Taylor; 78

From one island to another - Rawlins left the Isle of Wight, England for Rhode Island, where he became pro at the Newport club. The field was made up of British professionals plus AW Smith. For the first three years the Championship was held over 36 holes, then followed the 72 example of its British counterpart.

I	**HORACE RAWLINS** ($150)	45	46	41	41	173
2	Willie Dunn, Jr	43	46	44	42	175
3=	James Foulis	46	43	44	43	176
	AW Smith (a)	47	43	44	42	176
5	Willie Davis	45	49	42	42	178
6	Willie Campbell	41	48	42	48	179
7=	John Harland	45	48	43	47	183
	John Patrick	46	48	46	43	183
9	Samuel Tucker	49	48	45	43	185
10	John Reid	49	51	55	51	206

10-11 June	**1896**
BRITISH OPEN	
Honourable Company, Muirfield, Angus, Scotland	

18 July	**1896**
US OPEN	
Shinnecock Hills GC, Southampton, New York	
4423 yards	

Harry Vardon was to eclipse his famous Triumvirate cohorts by winning six Opens (and a US Open) to Taylor's and Braid's five. This, his first, followed a play-off after a tie with Taylor at the toughened-up Muirfield course – now reputedly four strokes more difficult than in 1892. Vardon's and Taylor's total was 11 shots poorer than Hilton's four years earlier.

1	**HARRY VARDON***	83	78	78	77	316
	(£30)					
2	JH Taylor	77	78	81	80	316
3=	Willie Fernie	78	79	82	80	319
	Freddie Tait (a)	83	75	84	77	319
5	Sandy Herd	72	84	79	85	320
6	James Braid	83	81	79	80	323
7=	David Brown	80	77	81	86	324
	Ben Sayers	83	76	79	86	324
	Andrew Scott	83	84	77	80	324
10	Tom Vardon	83	82	77	83	325
11	Peter McEwan	83	81	80	84	328
12=	Willie Auchterlonie	80	86	81	82	329
	Archie Simpson	85	79	78	87	329
14=	James Kay	77	88	83	82	330
	Andrew Kirkaldy	84	85	79	82	330
	Willie Park, Jr	79	80	83	88	330
17	AH Toogood	81	85	84	84	334
18=	John Hunter	85	79	83	88	335
	Johnny Laidlay (a)	85	82	82	86	335
	David McEwan	83	89	81	82	335
	Jack Ross	83	87	84	81	335
22	Walter Toogood	87	84	80	85	336
23	Harold Hilton (a)	82	85	85	85	337
24=	David Anderson, Jr	86	89	83	81	339
	D Jackson (a)	85	84	82	88	339
	Walter Kirk	85	87	84	83	339
27	David Herd	85	87	86	82	340
28	Albert Tingey, Sr	84	84	88	86	342
29	JW Taylor	87	83	84	90	344
30	Peter Paxton	84	89	86	86	345

* Harry Vardon (157) beat JH Taylor (161) in the 36-Hole Play-off

Round Leader(s)
R1   S Herd; 72
R2   JH Taylor; 155
R3   S Herd; 235
Lowest Scores
R2   Tait; 75
R3   Scott, T Vardon; 77
R4   Tait, H Vardon; 77

The Foulis family emigrated to America *en bloc* and featured strongly in early Opens. Jim Foulis, part of the next generation, reached the QF of the PGA in 1938 and was 11th in the 1946 Masters.

1	**JAMES FOULIS**	78	74	152
	($150)			
2	Horace Rawlins	79	76	155
3	Joe Lloyd	76	81	157
4=	George Douglas	79	79	158
	AW Smith (a)	78	80	158
6=	John Shippen	78	81	159
	HJ Wigham (a)	82	77	159
8	Willie Tucker	78	82	160
9	Robert Wilson	82	80	162
10	Alfred Ricketts	80	83	163
11	WH Way	83	81	164
12	Willie Dunn, Jr	78	87	165
13	Willie Davis	83	84	167
14	Willie Campbell	85	85	170
15	WT Hoare	90	81	171
16=	JN Mackrell	89	83	172
	Alex Patrick	86	86	172
	John Reid	88	84	172
19=	Tom Gourley	82	91	173
	John Patrick	88	85	173
21	Oscar Bunn	89	85	174
22=	John I'Anson	88	92	180
	George Strath	91	89	180
24	John Harrison	92	91	183
25	WW Campbell	91	93	184
26	Willie Norton	87	98	185
27	R Anderson	92	95	187
28	T Warrender	97	93	190

1897   19-20 May
BRITISH OPEN
Royal Liverpool GC, Hoylake, Cheshire, England
6150 yards

1897   17 September
US OPEN
Chicago GC, Wheaton, Illinois
6682 yards

Hoylake's debut. Hilton's second victory made him the only amateur multiple winner of the Open until the advent of Bobby Jones in the 1920s. Joe Lloyd became the first golfer to play both British and US Opens in the same year.

Joe Lloyd was the first globe-trotting golfer, inasmuch as he was a summer pro in the US and spent his winters at the Pau club in South-West France. He collected the US title five months after finishing 20th in the British Open.

	British Open						US Open			
1	**HAROLD HILTON** (Amateur)	80	75	84	75	314	1	**JOE LLOYD** ($150)	83 79	162
2	James Braid	80	74	82	79	315	2	Willie Anderson, Jr	79 84	163
3=	George Pulford	80	79	79	79	317	3=	Willie Dunn, Jr	87 81	168
	Freddie Tait (a)	79	79	80	79	317		James Foulis	80 88	168
5	Sandy Herd	78	81	79	80	318	5	WT Hoare	82 87	169
6	Harry Vardon	84	80	80	76	320	6=	Bernard Nicholls	87 85	172
7=	David Brown	79	82	80	83	324		Alfred Ricketts	91 81	172
	Archie Simpson	83	81	81	79	324	8=	David Foulis	86 87	173
	Tom Vardon	81	81	79	83	324		Horace Rawlins	91 82	173
10=	Andrew Kirkaldy	83	83	82	82	330		HJ Wigham (a)	87 86	173
	JH Taylor	82	80	82	86	330	11=	Charles Macdonald (a)	85 89	174
12=	Ben Sayers	84	78	85	84	331		William Marshall	87 87	174
	S Mure Fergusson (a)	87	83	79	82	331		Robert Wilson	83 91	174
14=	Peter McEwan	86	79	85	82	332	14	Harry Turpie	85 90	175
	TG Renouf	86	79	83	84	332	15=	Willie Davis	88 89	177
16	Andrew Scott	83	83	84	83	333		Robert Foulis	88 89	177
17	John Ball, Jr (a)	78	81	88	87	334		Willie Tucker	90 87	177
18=	Willie Auchterlonie	84	85	85	81	335		JA Tyng (a)	86 91	177
	Jack Graham, (a)	85	80	87	83	335	19	Findlay Douglas (a)	89 91	180
20=	James Kinnell	82	83	78	93	336	20	WG Stewart (a)	91 90	181
	Joe Lloyd	86	84	82	84	336	21=	R Leslie	90 92	182
22=	Willie Fernie	81	82	93	81	337		RG McAndrews	90 92	182
	Willie Park, Jr	91	81	83	82	337		George Pearson	93 89	182
	AH Toogood	88	82	84	83	337	24	John Harrison	97 87	184
25	James Kay	86	81	86	85	338	25=	Samuel Tucker	87 98	185
26	Walter Toogood	87	89	80	83	339		WH Way	89 96	185
27	James Sherlock	85	86	84	85	340	27	R White	89 97	186
28	John Rowe	84	86	86	86	342	28	Devereux Emmet (a)	98 90	188
29	Johnny Laidlay (a)	82	86	86	89	343	29	WB Smith (a)	98 91	189
30=	John Cuthbert	89	83	87	85	344	30	AC Tolifson	91 100	191
	Charles Gibson	88	90	80	86	344				
	C Ralph Smith	88	82	94	80	344				
	JW Taylor	87	84	85	88	344				
	Albert Tingey, Sr	86	86	87	85	344				

Round Leader(s)
R1   Ball, Herd; 78
R2   Braid; 154
R3   Braid; 236
Lowest Scores
R2   Braid; 74
R3   Kinnell; 78
R4   Hilton; 75

8-9 June						**1898**
BRITISH OPEN						
Prestwick GC, Ayrshire, Scotland						
5732 yards						

17-18 June						**1898**
US OPEN						
Myopia Hunt Club, South Hamilton, Massachusetts						
6236 yards						

New restrictions on players' performances were introduced. Competitors who were 20 or more strokes behind the leader at the halfway stage were excluded from the final two rounds. The 'cut' was born. One victim was the last winner at Prestwick, Willie Auchterlonie.

The first 72-hole Championship, which meant circumnavigating Myopia's 9 holes eight times. While elder brother Sandy was to stay in Scotland and be successful in the British Open over many years, Fred Herd arrived in the US in 1898, and promptly picked up the Open Championship. However, he never came close again.

1	**HARRY VARDON**	79	75	77	76	307
	(£30)					
2	Willie Park, Jr	76	75	78	79	308
3	Harold Hilton (a)	76	81	77	75	309
4	JH Taylor	78	78	77	79	312
5	Freddie Tait (a)	81	77	75	82	315
6	David Kinnell	80	77	79	80	316
7	Willie Fernie	79	85	77	77	318
8	John Hunter	82	79	81	77	319
9	TG Renouf	77	79	81	83	320
10=	James Braid	80	82	84	75	321
	Philip Wynn	83	79	81	78	321
12	James Kay	81	81	77	83	322
13=	George Pulford	83	81	78	81	323
	Jack White	82	81	77	83	323
15=	James Kinnell	77	81	78	88	324
	Archie Simpson	83	80	82	79	324
17=	Sandy Herd	80	79	84	82	325
	Peter McEwan	83	83	77	82	325
19=	Ben Sayers	85	78	79	85	327
	Walter Toogood	82	84	83	78	327
21=	JR Gairdner (a)	84	77	82	85	328
	David Herd	79	81	83	85	328
	James Hutchinson	83	79	84	82	328
	Andrew Kirkaldy	82	84	85	77	328
	Peter Paxton	81	82	86	79	328
	Tom Williamson	86	84	77	81	328
27=	C Ralph Smith	84	78	85	82	329
	JW Taylor	83	84	80	82	329
29=	Fred Butel	81	84	86	81	332
	Andrew Scott	83	84	78	87	332
	Bob Simpson	84	81	82	85	332

Round Leader(s)
R1 Hilton, Park; 76
R2 Park; 151
R3 Park; 229
Lowest scores
R2 Park, Vardon; 75
R3 Tait; 75
R4 Braid, Hilton; 75

1	**FRED HERD**	84	85	75	84	328
	($150)					
2	Alex Smith	78	86	86	85	335
3	Willie Anderson, Jr	81	82	87	86	336
4	Joe Lloyd	87	80	86	86	339
5	Willie Smith	82	91	85	82	340
6	WV Hoare	84	84	87	87	342
7	Willie Dunn, Jr	85	87	87	84	343
8=	John Jones	83	84	90	90	347
	HC Leeds (a)	81	84	93	89	347
	RG McAndrews	85	90	86	86	347
	Bernard Nicholls	86	87	88	86	347
12	Harry Turpie	85	87	86	91	349
13	Alex Findlay	89	88	84	89	350
14=	John Lister	92	88	90	85	355
	Willie Tucker	90	89	87	89	355
16	JF Curtis (a)	87	88	88	93	356
17	John Harland	84	93	93	87	357
18	Willie Davis	91	88	95	85	359
19=	Horace Rawlins	91	90	92	88	361
	JA Tyng (a)	92	91	88	90	361
21=	QA Shaw (a)	88	85	93	98	364
	Jack Youds	92	90	92	90	364
23=	JH Mercer	85	95	93	93	366
	Gilbert Nicholls	91	92	91	92	366
25	John Dunn	91	88	91	97	367
26	Willie Campbell	93	91	97	101	382
27	HR Sweeny (a)	92	97	96	99	384
28	W Rutherford (a)	100	99	98	91	388
29	WE Stoddart	103	95	97	96	391

Round Leader(s)
R1 A Smith; 78
R2 Anderson; 163
R3 Herd; 244
Lowest Scores
R2 Lloyd; 80
R3 Herd; 75
R4 W Smith; 82
R4 W Smith; 82

1899   7–8 June
BRITISH OPEN
St George's GC, Sandwich, Kent, England
6012 yards

1899   14–15 September
US OPEN
Baltimore CC, Baltimore, Maryland

Although 101 entered, so many withdrew after the first round, only 28 finished. Vardon's 3rd win in 4 years was based on his early rounds (152 – easily the best opening 18 holes since the Open went to a 72-hole format) . This was the first occasion where the winner led from start-to-finish over four rounds. It was also Freddie Tait's last Open. He was killed the following year leading a unit of the Black Watch into battle in the Boer War.

Willie Smith was one of five brothers from Carnoustie - two of whom won the Open Championship. Alex was to win in 1906 and 1910. A third brother, Macdonald, had a few close misses in both US and British Opens and was one of the outstanding players in an era to be dominated by Walter Hagen and Bobby Jones. The winning margin is still the biggest in the Open and only falls behind Morris Sr (13 in 1862 British Open), Morris Jr (12 in 1870) and Tiger Woods (12 in 1997 Masters) in any Major. Willie went on to become pro at Mexico City where he was killed during the Revolution in 1915.

1	**HARRY VARDON** (£30)	76	76	81	77	310
2	Jack White	79	79	82	75	315
3	Andrew Kirkaldy	81	79	82	77	319
4	JH Taylor	77	76	83	84	320
5=	James Braid	78	78	85	81	322
	Willie Fernie	79	83	82	78	322
7=	James Kinnell	76	84	80	84	324
	Freddie Tait (a)	81	82	79	82	324
9=	Albert Tingey, Sr	81	81	79	85	326
	Tom Williamson	76	84	80	86	326
11	Ben Sayers	81	79	82	86	328
12=	Harold Hilton (a)	86	80	80	83	329
	TG Renouf	79	82	84	84	329
14	Willie Park, Jr	77	79	85	89	330
15	Willie Aveston	77	86	82	86	331
16=	Sandy Herd	82	81	80	89	332
	Peter Rainford	79	83	83	87	332
	Ted Ray	84	80	84	84	332
	Archie Simpson	84	84	81	83	332
20	Walter Toogood	82	86	81	84	333
21	CE Hambro (a)	78	86	88	82	334
22	T Hutchinson	82	87	82	85	336
23	AH Toogood	83	85	85	84	337
24	William McEwan	84	86	83	85	338
25=	John Ball, Jr (a)	81	82	90	86	339
	Andrew Scott	86	85	87	81	339
	JW Taylor	82	85	86	86	339
28	David Herd	80	88	83	89	340

Round Leader(s)
R1 Vardon, Williamson; 76
R2 Vardon; 152
R3 Vardon; 233
Lowest Scores
R2 Taylor, Vardon; 76
R3 Tait, Tingey; 79
R4 White; 75

1	**WILLIE SMITH** ($150)	77	82	79	77	315
2=	Val Fitzjohn	85	80	79	82	326
	George Low	82	79	89	76	326
	WH Way	80	85	80	81	326
5	Willie Anderson, Jr	77	81	85	84	327
6	Jack Park	88	80	75	85	328
7	Alex Smith	82	81	82	85	330
8	Henry Gullane	81	86	80	84	331
9=	Laurie Auchterlonie	86	87	82	78	333
	Peter Walker	84	86	79	86	333
11	AH Findlay	88	86	79	81	334
12	Alex Campbell	83	80	79	94	336
13=	HM Harriman (a)	87	88	85	79	339
	Alex Patrick	82	83	84	90	339
	Horace Rawlins	81	85	86	87	339
16	Alfred Ricketts	87	85	88	80	340
17	Bernard Nicholls	86	88	85	84	343
18=	David Foulis	83	86	91	85	345
	Harry Turpie	91	88	83	83	345
20=	James Foulis	94	84	88	80	346
	Gilbert Nicholls	90	83	86	87	346
22	Dan Leitch	87	85	85	90	347
23	Ernest Way	85	87	87	89	348
24	W Thompson	82	90	87	90	349
25=	Fred Herd	85	86	93	86	350
	John Shippen	86	88	88	88	350
27=	Robert Braid	85	90	86	90	351
	RS Patrick	85	92	88	86	351
	Willie Tucker	89	91	87	84	351
30=	William Donovan	88	89	91	96	354
	David Hunter	89	86	89	90	354

Round Leader(s)
R1 Anderson, W Smith; 77
R2 Anderson; 158
R3 W Smith; 238
Lowest Scores
R2 Low; 79
R3 Park; 75
R4 Low; 76

6–7 June					**1900**

BRITISH OPEN
Royal & Ancient GC, St Andrews, Fife, Scotland
6323 yards

4–5 October					**1900**

US OPEN
Chicago GC, Wheaton, Illinois
6032 yards

Taylor's third win was comprehensive and stopped Vardon's amazing run – at least temporarily. 'JH' led 'wire-to-wire' as did Vardon in the previous year, but Taylor also produced the lowest score in every round – a feat never repeated in any Major Championship.

The roles were reversed a few months later when Vardon, on an exhibition tour of the States, won in Chicago with Taylor second. Vardon became the first to win two different Majors. A look at the respective Top 20s this year shows the Herd and Auchterlonie Brothers represented on both sides of the Atlantic.

1	**JH TAYLOR** (£50)	79	77	78	75	309
2	Harry Vardon	79	81	80	77	317
3	James Braid	82	81	80	79	322
4	Jack White	80	81	82	80	323
5	Willie Auchterlonie	81	85	80	80	326
6	Willie Park, Jr	80	83	81	84	328
7=	Robert Maxwell (a)	81	81	86	81	329
	Archie Simpson	82	85	83	79	329
9	Ben Sayers	81	83	85	81	330
10=	Sandy Herd	81	85	81	84	331
	Andrew Kirkaldy	87	83	82	79	331
	Tom Vardon	81	85	84	81	331
13	Ted Ray	88	80	85	81	334
14=	David Anderson, Jr	81	87	85	84	337
	Tom Simpson	84	86	83	84	337
16=	William Greig (a)	93	84	80	81	338
	Harold Hilton (a)	83	87	87	81	338
18	JW Taylor	91	81	84	83	339
19=	John Kirkaldy	86	85	87	82	340
	Peter Paxton	87	87	79	87	340
21	Peter McEwan	85	80	89	87	341
22=	PJ Gaudin	85	88	81	88	342
	James Kay	84	81	87	90	342
	FM Mackenzie (a)	88	82	89	83	342
	Andrew Scott	84	84	84	90	342
26=	George Coburn	83	88	83	89	343
	WH Fowler (a)	86	85	88	84	343
	Johnny Laidlay (a)	85	87	85	86	343
29	JM Williamson	87	82	88	89	346
30=	Ted Blackwell (a)	88	86	86	89	349
	C Ralph Smith	83	87	88	91	349

1	**HARRY VARDON** ($200)	79	78	76	80	313
2	JH Taylor	76	82	79	78	315
3	David Bell	78	83	83	78	322
4=	Laurie Auchterlonie	84	82	80	81	327
	Willie Smith	82	83	79	83	327
6	George Low	84	80	85	82	331
7	Tom Hutchinson	81	87	81	84	333
8	Harry Turpie	84	87	79	84	334
9	Stewart Gardner	85	78	84	89	336
10	Val Fitzjohn	84	83	89	82	338
11=	Willie Anderson, Jr	83	88	79	89	339
	Alex Campbell	86	77	93	83	339
13	Alex Smith	90	84	82	84	340
14=	James Foulis	86	88	87	82	343
	Robert Simpson	84	84	88	87	343
16=	Fred Herd	85	89	84	86	344
	Arthur Smith	89	85	85	85	344
	WH Way	88	85	84	87	344
19=	Willie Norton	87	87	84	87	345
	Harry Rawlins	86	84	90	85	345
21	Ernest Way	89	92	81	84	346
22	JB Schlotman	85	94	83	88	350
23=	RG McAndrews	87	93	87	84	351
	Joe Mitchell	88	96	82	85	351
25=	Henry Gullane	89	89	92	82	352
	AC Tolifson	93	87	88	84	352
27=	WV Hoare	90	87	91	85	353
	John Shippen	94	87	89	83	353
29	Robert Foulis	85	89	90	90	354
30	Charles Macdonald (a)	86	90	90	89	355

Round Leader(s)
R1 Taylor, H Vardon; 79
R2 Taylor; 156
R3 Taylor; 234
Lowest Scores
R2 Taylor; 77
R3 Taylor; 78
R4 Taylor; 75

Round Leader(s)
R1 Taylor; 76
R2 Vardon; 157
R3 Vardon; 233
Lowest Scores
R2 Campbell; 77
R3 Vardon; 76
R4 Bell, Taylor; 78

1901

5–6 June

BRITISH OPEN

Honourable Company, Muirfield, Angus, Scotland
5810 yards

Braid established enough of a lead to withstand attacks from Vardon and Taylor over the last round. Braid was due the title after several good finishes in previous years, including 2nd on the same course in 1897. His great years were to come towards the end of the decade though, when he truly (in terms of Open victories) became part of the Triumvirate.

1	**JAMES BRAID** (£50)	79	76	74	80	309
2	Harry Vardon	77	78	79	78	312
3	JH Taylor	79	83	74	77	313
4	Harold Hilton (a)	89	80	75	76	320
5	Sandy Herd	87	81	81	76	325
6	Jack White	82	82	80	82	326
7=	James Kinnell	79	85	86	78	328
	Johnny Laidlay (a)	84	82	82	80	328
9=	PJ Gaudin	86	81	86	76	329
	Jack Graham (a)	82	83	81	83	329
11	Rowland Jones	85	82	81	83	331
12=	Ted Ray	87	84	74	87	332
	TG Renouf	83	86	81	82	332
	Tom Yeoman	85	83	82	82	332
15=	Fred Collins	89	80	81	84	334
	S Mure Fergusson (a)	84	86	82	82	334
	JH Oke	91	83	80	80	334
18=	Andrew Kirkaldy	82	87	86	81	336
	Alf Lewis	85	82	83	86	336
	Willie Park, Jr	78	87	81	90	336
	Andrew Scott	85	80	81	90	336
22=	Charles Neaves	84	87	81	85	337
	L Waters	86	87	86	78	337
24	C Dalziel (a)	82	84	89	83	338
25=	David Herd	90	80	82	87	339
	James Hutchison	84	83	91	81	339
	Jack Ross	84	85	86	84	339
28	Walter Toogood	87	86	85	82	340
29=	Willie Auchterlonie	86	82	88	86	342
	David McEwan	86	84	86	86	342

Round Leader(s)
R1 Vardon; 77
R2 Braid, Vardon; 155
R3 Braid; 229
Lowest Scores
R2 Braid; 76
R3 Braid, Ray, Taylor; 74
R4 Herd, Hilton, Gaudin; 76

1901

14–16 June

US OPEN

Myopia Hunt Club, South Hamilton,
Massachusetts

No such pond-hopping this year as the Opens virtually clashed, leaving anyone with the ambition to participate in both thwarted by the week-long passage. Willie Anderson from North Berwick, Scotland, won the first of his four wins in five years, after beating Alex Smith in the Open's first play-off, and his brother Willie by two.

1	**W ANDERSON, Jr*** ($200)	84	83	83	81	331
	Alex Smith	82	82	87	80	331
3	Willie Smith	84	86	82	81	333
4	Stewart Gardner	86	82	81	85	334
5=	Laurie Auchterlonie	81	85	86	83	335
	Bernard Nicholls	84	85	83	83	335
7	David Brown	86	83	83	84	336
8	Alex Campbell	84	91	82	82	339
9=	George Low	82	89	85	85	341
	Jack Park	87	84	85	85	341
11	James Foulis	88	85	85	89	347
12=	Val Fitzjohn	86	86	89	87	348
	John Jones	87	84	87	80	348
14=	Gilbert Nicholls	87	87	88	87	349
	Robert Simpson	88	87	87	87	349
16	Isaac Mackie	87	88	85	90	350
17=	AH Fenn	87	90	87	87	351
	AG Lockwood (a)	82	89	89	91	351
	Horace Rawlins	90	84	88	89	351
20	Joe Lloyd	90	87	86	89	352
21	Donald Ross	94	86	91	84	355
22=	Walter Clark	88	90	92	87	357
	Alex Taylor	94	84	92	87	357
	Harry Turpie	92	87	88	90	357
25=	David Hunter	91	92	89	87	359
	RS Patrick	90	91	87	91	359
27	Willie Davis	88	91	92	89	360
28=	John Dingwall	89	96	89	87	361
	Ed Fitzjohn	90	86	92	93	361
	John Harland	92	92	93	84	361
	Willie Hunter	88	96	91	86	361
	LC Servas	94	83	91	93	361

*Willie Anderson, Jr (85) beat Alex Smith (86) in the
18-Hole Play-off

Round Leader(s)
R1 Auchterlonie; 81
R2 A Smith; 164
R3 Gardner; 249
Lowest Scores
R2 Gardner, A Smith; 82
R3 Gardner; 81
R4 Jones, A Smith; 80

4–5 June	**1902**	10–11 October	**1902**

BRITISH OPEN
Royal Liverpool GC, Hoylake, Cheshire, England
6335 yards

US OPEN
Garden City GC, Garden City, New York
6170 yards

Herd won his only Open in a long and distinguished career. He was the first winner to use a rubber-cored ball and beat Vardon and Braid, who were still using the 'gutty', by one stroke. Braid pulled back 7 shots over the last round – not quite enough. Vardon's R1 72 equalled Herd's own record of 1896 and his halfway score of 149 was the first below 150.

Another brotherly double. Laurie emulated Willie Auchterlonie's British Open win at Prestwick in 1893, scoring sub-80 in every round for the first time in these Championships. As in the British Open the rubber-cored Haskell was used, but more widely. The result was a greater improvement in all-round scoring.

1	**SANDY HERD** (£50)	77	76	73	81	307
2=	James Braid	78	76	80	74	308
	Harry Vardon	72	77	80	79	308
4	Robert Maxwell (a)	79	77	79	74	309
5	Tom Vardon	80	76	78	79	313
6=	Harold Hilton (a)	79	76	81	78	314
	James Kinnell	78	80	79	77	314
	JH Taylor	81	76	77	80	314
9	Ted Ray	79	74	85	80	318
10=	Andrew Kirkaldy	77	78	83	82	320
	Arnaud Massy	77	81	78	84	320
12=	Willie Fernie	76	82	84	79	321
	Rowland Jones	79	78	85	79	321
14	SH Fry (a)	78	79	80	85	322
15=	John Ball, Jr (a)	79	79	84	81	323
	John Rowe	79	78	85	81	323
17	James Sherlock	79	84	80	81	324
18	Jack White	82	75	82	86	325
19	Ben Sayers	84	80	80	82	326
20=	TG Renouf	84	82	77	84	327
	Walter Toogood	83	83	80	81	327
22	George Pulford	81	81	85	81	328
23=	F Jackson	80	81	83	85	329
	Willie Park, Jr	79	82	82	86	329
25=	William McEwan	83	84	81	82	330
	Tom Yeoman	85	83	79	83	330
27	C Ralph Smith	85	79	85	82	331
28=	David Herd	82	81	84	85	332
	Peter Rainford	78	79	88	87	332
30=	Archie Simpson	88	79	85	81	333
	Tom Williamson	78	80	90	85	333

1	**L. AUCHTERLONIE** ($200)	78	78	74	77	307
2=	Stewart Gardner	82	76	77	78	313
	Walter Travis (a)	82	82	75	74	313
4	Willie Smith	82	79	80	75	316
5=	Willie Anderson, Jr	79	82	76	81	318
	John Shippen	83	81	75	79	318
7	Charles Thom	80	82	80	77	319
8	Harry Turpie	79	85	78	78	320
9	Donald Ross	80	83	78	81	322
10	Alex Ross	83	77	84	79	323
11	Willie Norton	83	82	79	81	325
12=	David Brown	80	88	82	76	326
	George Low	83	84	78	81	326
14=	Jack Campbell	77	87	79	85	328
	Jack Hobens	85	82	80	81	328
16=	AS Griffiths	79	86	82	83	330
	Horace Rawlins	89	83	79	79	330
18=	Gilbert Nicholls	88	86	73	84	331
	Alex Smith	79	86	80	86	331
20=	Alex Campbell	88	82	83	79	332
	James Foulis	81	88	82	81	332
	John Harland	82	82	83	85	332
	Willie Hunter	82	82	81	87	332
24	Fred Herd	82	79	83	89	333
25	Jack Park	79	89	85	81	334
26=	George Braid	85	81	84	85	335
	James Campbell	88	84	82	81	335
28	Bernard Nicholls	89	84	84	79	336
29	John Mackie	88	82	84	84	338
30=	Alex Findlay	85	81	87	86	339
	David Hunter	83	81	91	84	339
	RS Patrick	85	87	84	83	339

Round Leader(s)
R1 H Vardon; 72
R2 H Vardon; 149
R3 Herd; 226

Lowest Scores
R2 Ray; 74
R3 Herd; 73
R4 Braid, Maxwell; 74

Round Leader(s)
R1 Jack Campbell; 77
R2 Auchterlonie; 156
R3 Auchterlonie; 230

Lowest Scores
R2 Gardner; 76
R3 G Nicholls; 73
R4 Travis; 74

1903

9–10 June

BRITISH OPEN

Prestwick GC, Ayrshire, Scotland

5948 yards

1903

8–9 July

US OPEN

Baltusrol GC, Springfield, New Jersey

6003 yards

Vardon joined the Morrises and Willie Park Sr on 4 Open wins as he coasted home – courtesy of a 7-stroke lead after three rounds. His R3 72 was a record as were his 54- and 72-hole totals. Brother Tom finished runner-up, his highest-ever position.

1	**HARRY VARDON** (£50)	73	77	72	78	300
2	Tom Vardon	76	81	75	74	306
3	Jack White	77	78	74	79	308
4	Sandy Herd	73	83	76	77	309
5	James Braid	77	79	79	75	310
6=	Andrew Scott	77	77	83	77	314
	Robert Thomson	83	78	77	76	314
8	William Leaver	79	79	77	80	315
9=	George Cawsey	80	78	76	82	316
	JH Taylor	80	82	78	76	316
11=	Andrew Kirkaldy	82	79	78	78	317
	Tom Williamson	76	80	79	82	317
13=	Willie Hunter, Sr	81	74	79	84	318
	Robert Maxwell (a)	82	84	76	76	318
15=	Ernest Gray	77	83	79	80	319
	James Kinnell	78	86	76	79	319
	Willie Park, Jr	78	86	80	75	319
18=	David Kinnell	82	78	80	80	320
	George Pulford	79	86	79	76	320
	AH Toogood	86	77	80	77	320
21=	John Hunter	77	79	84	81	321
	Ben Sayers	79	84	80	78	321
23	Ted Ray	90	78	80	75	323
24=	Willie Fernie	78	81	76	89	324
	James Hepburn	78	82	87	77	324
	Harold Hilton (a)	81	79	83	81	324
	Rowland Jones	82	82	81	79	324
	John Milne	81	86	79	78	324
29=	George Coburn	81	82	75	87	325
	JH Oke	80	81	81	83	325
	Archie Simpson	79	85	80	81	325

Round Leader(s)
R1   Herd, H Vardon; 73
R2   H Vardon; 150
R3   H Vardon; 222
Lowest Scores
R2   W Hunter; 74
R3   H Vardon; 72
R4   T Vardon; 74

The Open's first visit to Baltusrol (pre-Tillinghast). Anderson's second win in three years and the first of three back-to-back wins may have had something to do with his settling at the Apawamis Club. Prior to 1903 he had been changing clubs annually. He was caught by 1886 British Open Champion, David Brown, in the final round, conceding a 6-stroke lead (not helped by an 8 at the 9th), before steeling himself to win the play-off by 2.

1	**W ANDERSON, Jr*** ($200)	73	76	76	82	307
2	David Brown	79	77	75	76	307
3	Stewart Gardner	77	77	82	79	315
4	Alex Smith	77	77	81	81	316
5	Donald Ross	79	79	78	82	318
6	Jack Campbell	76	83	83	77	319
7	Laurie Auchterlonie	75	79	84	83	321
8	Findlay Douglas (a)	77	79	82	84	322
9=	Jack Hobens	76	81	82	84	323
	Alex Ross	83	82	78	80	323
	Willie Smith	80	81	83	79	323
12	Horace Rawlins	82	77	78	87	324
13=	Isaac Mackie	83	80	78	84	325
	FO Reinhart (a)	81	75	89	80	325
15=	Alex Campbell	79	84	80	83	326
	Gilbert Nicholls	86	82	78	80	326
	Walter Travis (a)	83	80	81	82	326
	WH Way	84	79	82	81	326
19	Bernard Nicholls	85	78	82	83	328
20=	Willie Norton	78	81	83	87	329
	David Ogilvie	81	86	81	81	329
22	George Cummings	83	86	77	84	330
23	Harry Turpie	86	82	81	82	331
24=	Joe Lloyd	84	85	80	83	332
	John Reid	82	82	84	84	332
26=	George T Brokaw (a)	78	82	86	87	333
	James Campbell	81	84	82	86	333
	Fred McLeod	83	80	79	91	333
	Arthur Smith	80	87	83	83	333
30	AH Fenn	82	83	83	86	334

*Willie Anderson, Jr (82) beat David Brown (84) in the 18-Hole Play-off

Round Leader(s)
R1   Anderson; 73
R2   Anderson; 149
R3   Anderson; 225
Lowest Scores
R2   Reinhart, William Braid (34); 75
R3   Brown; 75
R4   Brown; 76

| 8–10 June | **1904** | 8–9 July | **1904** |

BRITISH OPEN
US OPEN
Royal St George's GC, Sandwich, Kent, England
6223 yards

Glen View GC, Golf, Illinois

A nephew of Ben Sayers from North Berwick, Jack White held off the Triumvirate by significantly lowering his numbers each round. He became the first man to break the 300 barrier, and along with Taylor and Braid was the first to record a score in the 60s at any Major. To alleviate congestion with a field of 144, play was taken into a third day for the first time.

Following the British example, the half-way cut was introduced – excluding those not within 15 strokes of the lead. Anderson's scoring, as in the previous year, set new records, with lows of 72 for any round and 303 for 72 holes. Fred MacKenzie led by 2 going into the last round but his 80 coupled with Anderson's record saw him finish third – 6 strokes off the winner.

| 1 | **JACK WHITE** (£50) | 80 | 75 | 72 | 69 | 296 |

2=	James Braid	77	80	69	71	297
	JH Taylor	77	78	74	68	297
4	Tom Vardon	77	77	75	72	301
5	Harry Vardon	76	73	79	74	302
6	James Sherlock	83	71	78	77	309
7=	Jack Graham (a)	76	76	78	80	310
	Andrew Kirkaldy	78	79	74	79	310
9	Sandy Herd	84	76	76	75	311
10=	Robert Maxwell (a)	80	80	76	77	313
	Ben Sayers	80	80	76	77	313
12=	Willie Park, Jr	84	72	81	78	315
	Ted Ray	81	81	77	76	315
	Robert Thomson	75	76	80	84	315
	AH Toogood	88	76	74	77	315
16=	George Coburn	79	82	75	80	316
	John Rowe	86	82	75	73	316
17	John Ball, Jr (a)	83	78	79	78	318
18=	George Cawsey	82	80	78	79	319
	Frederick Collins	88	77	75	79	319
	Ernest Gray	84	77	74	84	319
21	JS Worthington (a)	85	79	78	78	320
22	TG Renouf	82	79	79	81	321
23=	PJ Gaudin	79	83	80	80	322
	Alf Matthews	85	81	78	78	322
25	Alec Thompson	86	81	75	81	323
26=	Ted Blackwell (a)	88	77	81	79	325
	George Cawkwell	83	83	79	80	325
	Rowland Jones	89	77	77	82	325
29=	AE Bellworthy	82	84	83	77	326
	James Hepburn	87	80	79	80	326
	Percy Hills	85	83	80	78	326

Round Leader(s)
R1   Thomson; 75
R2   H Vardon; 149
R3   Braid; 226
Lowest Scores
R2   Sherlock; 71
R3   Braid; 69
R4   Taylor; 68

| 1 | **WILLIE ANDERSON, Jr** ($200) | 75 | 78 | 78 | 72 | 303 |

2	Gilbert Nicholls	80	76	79	73	308
3	Fred MacKenzie	76	79	74	80	309
4=	Laurie Auchterlonie	80	81	75	78	314
	Bernard Nicholls	80	77	79	78	314
6=	Percy Barrett	78	79	79	80	316
	Stewart Gardner	75	76	80	85	316
	Robert Simpson	82	82	76	76	316
9	James Foulis	83	84	78	82	317
10	Donald Ross	80	82	78	78	318
11=	Jack Hobens	77	82	80	80	319
	Charles Murray	84	81	76	78	319
13	Alex Campbell	81	87	80	82	320
14	Horace Rawlins	79	76	86	81	322
15=	George Braid	82	76	85	81	324
	Alex Ross	87	78	80	79	324
	George Thomson	78	87	81	78	324
18	Alex Smith	78	81	82	85	326
19	David Robertson	82	78	80	88	328
20=	Jack Campbell	80	88	79	82	329
	H Chandler Egan (a)	84	79	83	83	329
	Harry Turpie	81	82	86	80	329
23=	Robert Hunter (a)	83	85	79	84	331
	George Low	89	81	82	79	331
	Alex Taylor	85	83	83	80	331
26=	Kenneth Edwards (a)	84	83	80	85	332
	WH Way	88	83	79	82	332
28	George Cummings	83	83	82	85	333
29=	Tom McDeever	81	82	88	83	334
	Fred McLeod	86	88	81	79	334
	Peter Robertson	82	87	85	80	334
	James Watson	83	83	82	86	334

Round Leader(s)
R1   Anderson, Gardner; 75
R2   Gardner; 151
R3   MacKenzie; 229
Lowest Scores
R2   Foulis; 74
R3   MacKenzie; 74

1905
7–9 June
BRITISH OPEN
Royal & Ancient GC, St Andrews, Fife, Scotland
6333 yards

1905
21–22 September
US OPEN
Myopia Hunt Club, South Hamilton, Massachusetts
6300 yards

Braid's four wins over the next six years were to put him above Vardon et al. on five Open victories. His record for the decade 1901–10 was W, 2, 5, 2, W, W, 5, W, 2, W. The cut was drawn, as in the previous year's US Open, at 15 behind the leader. The Old Course took its toll on scoring, with only 10 rounds under 80 being recorded in the whole Championship.

Willie Anderson secured a place in Open history when he won his fourth title at Myopia. His feat has only been matched by Bobby Jones, Ben Hogan and Jack Nicklaus – exalted company indeed. Alex Smith became the second golfer to try his luck at both Opens in one year – finishing 16th at St Andrews and 2nd for the third time in the US Championship.

1	**JAMES BRAID** (£50)	81	78	78	81	318
2=	Rowland Jones	81	77	87	78	323
	JH Taylor	80	85	78	80	323
4	James Kinnell	82	79	82	81	324
5=	Ernest Gray	82	81	84	78	325
	Arnaud Massy	81	80	82	82	325
7	Robert Thomson	81	81	82	83	327
8	James Sherlock	81	84	80	83	328
9=	Tom Simpson	82	88	78	81	329
	Harry Vardon	80	82	84	83	329
11=	Ted Ray	85	82	81	82	330
	John Rowe	87	81	80	82	330
13=	Willie Park, Jr	84	81	85	81	331
	Tom Williamson	84	81	79	87	331
15	Sandy Herd	80	82	83	87	332
16=	TG Renouf	81	85	84	83	333
	Alex Smith	81	88	86	78	333
18=	JC Johnstone	85	86	84	80	335
	Archie Simpson	87	84	81	83	335
	Tom Watt	86	85	79	85	335
	Jack White	86	83	83	83	335
22=	Fred Collins	86	86	83	81	336
	Percy Hills	87	84	84	81	336
24=	Ernest Foord	85	86	84	83	338
	James Hepburn	84	84	87	83	338
	William Hunter	84	85	88	81	338
	Andrew Kirkaldy	83	83	83	89	338
28=	David Stephenson	84	86	83	86	339
	Walter Toogood	82	83	87	87	339
30	James Kay	85	83	85	87	340

1	**WILLIE ANDERSON, Jr** ($200)	81	80	76	77	314
2	Alex Smith	76	80	80	80	316
3=	Percy Barrett	81	80	77	79	317
	Peter Robertson	79	80	81	77	317
5	Stewart Gardner	78	78	85	77	318
6	Alex Campbell	82	76	80	81	319
7=	Jack Hobens	82	80	81	78	321
	Gilbert Nicholls	82	76	84	79	321
9	George Cummings	85	82	75	81	323
10	Arthur Smith	81	77	80	86	324
11=	AG Lockwood (a)	84	85	76	80	325
	Walter Travis (a)	81	80	80	84	325
13=	Alex Ross	79	86	78	83	326
	Willie Smith	86	81	76	83	326
15	George Low	83	82	81	81	327
16=	Joe Lloyd	75	86	83	84	328
	Fred McKenzie	81	85	80	82	328
18	Walter Clark	86	81	82	80	329
19	Fred McLeod	80	84	80	86	330
20=	Tom McNamara	81	79	82	89	331
	Bernard Nicholls	80	82	85	84	331
	George Turnbull	81	88	81	81	331
	WH Way	81	89	84	77	331
24	Laurie Auchterlonie	85	82	79	86	332
25	Donald Ross	83	83	86	81	333
26	Jack Jolly	82	83	85	85	335
	James Maiden	80	86	83	86	335
28	Robert Peebles	81	81	86	88	336
29=	Isaac Mackie	82	82	83	90	337
	Charles Murray	84	85	83	85	337

Round Leader(s)
R1   Herd, Taylor, Vardon; 80
R2   Jones; 158
R3   Braid; 237
Lowest Scores
R2   Jones; 77
R3   Braid, T Simpson, Taylor; 78
R4   Gray, Jones, Smith; 78

Round Leader(s)
R1   Lloyd; 75
R2   Gardner, A Smith; 156
R3   A Smith; 236
Lowest Scores
R2   Campbell, G Nicholls; 76
R3   Cummings; 75
R4   Anderson, Gardner, Robertson, Way; 77

13–15 June					**1906**	28–29 June						**1906**

BRITISH OPEN

Honourable Company, Muirfield, Angus, Scotland
5934 yards

US OPEN

Onwentsia Club, Lake Forest, Illinois
6107 yards

Progressively better scoring gave Braid his second win in a row. Both Taylor and Vardon were in the hunt at the end of R3, but fell away over the last 18. Muirfield, despite being 'toughened-up' was still the shortest course on the rota, and comparatively the easiest.

Alex Smith led all the way to pick up the first of two Open titles; setting a new low total of 295, bettering the 1903 total by 8 shots, and a stroke better than Jack White's British Open record. Three Smith brothers finished in the Top 18.

British Open

1	**JAMES BRAID** (£50)	77	76	74	73	300
2	JH Taylor	77	72	75	80	304
3	Harry Vardon	77	73	77	78	305
4	Jack Graham (a)	71	79	78	78	306
5	Rowland Jones	74	78	73	83	308
6	Arnaud Massy	76	80	76	78	310
7	Robert Maxwell (a)	73	78	77	83	311
8=	George Duncan	73	78	83	78	312
	Ted Ray	80	75	79	78	312
	TG Renouf	76	77	76	83	312
11	David Kinnell	78	76	80	79	313
12=	William Hunter	79	76	80	80	315
	William Leaver	80	76	78	81	315
	Tom Vardon	76	81	81	77	315
15=	George Cawsey	79	80	79	78	316
	Thomas Simpson	78	78	81	79	316
	Walter Toogood	83	79	83	71	316
	Robert Whitecross (a)	74	83	80	79	316
19=	PJ Gaudin	77	77	80	83	317
	Harry Hamill	83	78	79	77	317
	Sandy Herd	81	79	77	80	317
	David McEwan	79	79	81	78	317
	Tom Williamson	77	77	78	85	317
24=	Tom Ball	78	79	79	82	318
	Ernest Gray	77	77	78	86	318
	Donald Kenny	82	85	83	78	318
	Ernest Riseborough	81	77	80	80	318
28=	James Kinnell	81	75	82	81	319
	Alf Matthews	84	77	80	78	319
30=	Ernest Foord	78	84	78	80	320
	James Hepburn	81	78	84	77	320
	James Kay	80	79	81	80	320
	George Pulford	80	81	81	78	320
	Robert Thomson	76	78	83	83	320

Round Leader(s)
R1   Graham; 71
R2   Taylor; 149
R3   Taylor; 224
Lowest Scores
R2   Taylor; 72
R3   Jones; 73
R4   Toogood; 71

US Open

1	**ALEX SMITH** ($300)	73	74	73	75	295
2	Willie Smith	73	81	74	74	302
3=	Laurie Auchterlonie	76	78	75	76	305
	James Maiden	80	73	77	75	305
5	Willie Anderson, Jr	73	76	74	84	307
6	Alex Ross	76	79	75	80	310
7	Stewart Gardner	80	76	77	78	311
8=	H Chandler Egan (a)	79	78	76	80	313
	Gilbert Nicholls	76	81	77	79	313
10	Jack Hobens	75	84	76	79	314
11=	George Low	79	82	76	79	316
	Bernard Nicholls	79	77	79	81	316
13	Harry Turpie	80	80	76	83	319
14=	Walter Fovargue	77	84	78	81	320
	Jack Jolly	78	82	79	81	320
	Peter Robertson	79	78	80	83	320
17	Alex Baxter	83	81	81	86	321
18=	Fred Brand	78	78	85	81	322
	Alex Campbell	76	84	76	86	322
	George Cummings	79	76	84	83	322
	George Smith	79	76	82	85	322
22=	James Foulis	83	86	79	76	324
	Otto Hackbarth	82	82	82	78	324
	WR Lovekin	77	85	78	84	324
	D McIntosh	79	79	81	85	324
	William Marshall	85	77	81	81	324
27=	James Watson	76	80	81	88	325
	Ernest Way	83	81	80	81	325
29=	George O'Neill	84	82	82	78	326
	David Robertson	82	79	81	84	326

Round Leader(s)
R1   Anderson, A Smith, W Smith; 73
R2   A Smith; 147
R3   A Smith; 220
Lowest Scores
R2   Maiden; 73
R3   A Smith; 73
R4   W Smith; 74

1907

7–9 June

BRITISH OPEN
Royal Liverpool GC, Hoylake, Cheshire, England
6355 yards

1907

20–21 June

US OPEN
Philadelphia Cricket Club, Chestnut Hill, Pennsylvania
5952 yards

Arnaud Massy, from La Boulie, France, became the first overseas winner when he outplayed JH Taylor over the final holes. He is the only winner from France and the next winner from continental Europe was Severiano Ballesteros in 1979.

Yet another Scot, Alex Ross was the brother of the famous golf-course designer, Donald, who also finished in 10th place in the Championship this year.

1	**ARNAUD MASSY** (£50)	76	81	78	77	312

1	**ALEX ROSS** ($300)	76	74	76	76	302

2	JH Taylor	79	79	76	80	314
3=	George Pulford	81	78	80	78	317
	Tom Vardon	81	81	80	75	317
5=	James Braid	82	85	75	76	318
	Ted Ray	83	80	79	76	318
7=	George Duncan	83	78	81	77	319
	Harry Vardon	84	81	74	80	319
	Tom Williamson	82	77	82	78	319
10	Tom Ball	80	78	81	81	320
11	PJ Gaudin	83	84	80	76	323
12	Sandy Herd	83	81	83	77	324
13	Jack Graham (a)	83	81	80	82	326
	Walter Toogood	76	86	82	82	326
15=	John Ball, Jr (a)	88	83	79	77	327
	Frederick Collins	83	83	79	82	327
17=	Alf Matthews	82	80	84	82	328
	Charles Mayo	86	78	82	82	328
	TG Renouf	83	80	82	83	328
18	Reg Gray	83	85	81	80	329
19=	James Bradbeer	83	85	82	80	330
	G Carter	89	80	81	80	330
21	John Rowe	83	83	85	80	331
22	AH Toogood	87	83	85	77	332
23=	William Horne	91	80	81	81	333
	Harry Kidd	84	90	82	77	333
	David McEwan	89	83	80	81	333
	Charles Roberts	86	83	84	80	333
	Alex Smith	85	84	84	80	333
28=	James Kinnell	89	79	80	86	334
	JH Oke	86	85	82	81	334
30=	HH Barker (a)	89	81	82	83	335
	Harry Cawsey	85	93	77	80	335
	William McEwan	79	89	85	82	335

Round Leader(s)
R1 Massy, W Toogood; 76
R2 Massy; 157
R3 Taylor; 234
Lowest Scores
R2 Williamson; 77
R3 H Vardon; 74
R4 T Vardon; 75

2	Gilbert Nicholls	80	73	72	79	304
3	Alex Campbell	78	74	78	75	305
4	Jack Hobens	76	75	73	85	309
5=	George Low	78	76	79	77	310
	Fred McLeod	79	77	79	75	310
	Peter Robertson	81	77	78	74	310
8=	David Brown	75	80	78	78	311
	Bernard Nicholls	76	76	81	78	311
10	Donald Ross	78	80	76	78	312
11=	Laurie Auchterlonie	77	77	83	76	313
	Fred Brand	78	80	73	82	313
13	David Robertson	80	78	75	81	314
14	Tom McNamara	82	79	78	76	315
15	Willie Anderson, Jr	81	77	81	77	316
16=	Mike Brady	76	77	84	80	317
	David Hunter	77	75	85	80	317
	Martin O'Loughlin	81	81	77	78	317
19	Jack Campbell	78	79	82	80	319
20	GJ Bouse	78	78	86	78	320
21	Stewart Gardner	81	79	78	83	321
22=	James Campbell	76	85	81	80	322
	Walter Clark	78	81	79	84	322
	Isaac Mackie	82	83	79	78	322
25	Jack Jolly	78	86	81	78	323
26=	David Ogilvie	82	81	81	80	324
	Horace Rawlins	82	76	83	83	324
	WD Robinson	82	84	80	78	324
	Jerome Travers (a)	81	84	80	79	324
30=	WC Gaudin	80	86	82	77	325
	W Ogilvie	80	83	82	80	325

Round Leader(s)
R1 Brown; 75
R2 A Ross; 150
R3 Hobens; 224
Lowest Scores
R2 G Nicholls; 73
R3 G Nicholls; 72
R4 Robertson; 74

18–19 June	**1908**

BRITISH OPEN
Prestwick GC, Ayrshire, Scotland
5948 yards

27–29 August	**1908**

US OPEN
Myopia Hunt Club, South Hamilton, Massachusetts
6335 yards

Leading all the way, Braid lowered the Open (and Majors) record total even further, adding a lowest-to-date R1 score of 70; 36-hole total of 144; and 54-holes at 221. He took a 6-shot lead into the last round and stretched it to 8.

The players must have been glad to finish at Myopia - for the fourth and last time. The course has the dubious distiction of holding the three highest winning totals in the Open's history – 331 (1901), 328 (1898) and now 322. It was the wind that created the havoc in 1908, though – only Gilbert Nicholls broke 80 twice - and he was disqualified. How 5 foot 4 inch, 108 lbs Fred McLeod withstood it we'll never know. He did, tying with Willie Smith, then winning the play-off.

1	**JAMES BRAID** (£50)	70	72	77	72	291

2	Tom Ball	76	73	76	74	299
3	Ted Ray	79	71	75	76	301
4	Sandy Herd	74	74	79	75	302
5=	David Kinnell	75	73	80	78	306
	Harry Vardon	79	78	74	75	306
7=	Thomas Simpson	75	77	76	79	307
	JH Taylor	79	77	76	75	307
9=	PJ Gaudin	77	76	75	80	308
	Arnaud Massy	76	75	76	81	308
11=	James Edmundson	80	72	76	82	310
	Tom Watt	81	73	78	78	310
13=	John Ball, Jr (a)	74	78	78	81	311
	Fred Collins	78	77	77	79	311
	Ernest Gray	68	79	83	81	311
	William Leaver	79	79	75	78	311
	Tom Vardon	77	79	76	79	311
18=	George Duncan	79	77	80	76	312
	Jack Graham (a)	76	82	76	78	312
	George Pulford	81	77	74	80	312
	Fred Robson	72	79	83	78	312
	AH Toogood	82	76	77	77	312
	Walter Toogood	80	75	78	79	312
24=	George Coburn	77	79	77	81	314
	James Hepburn	80	79	79	76	314
	Rowland Jones	75	77	83	79	314
27	R Andrew (a)	83	78	77	77	315
28=	Willie Aveston	77	77	79	83	316
	TG Renouf	78	78	83	77	316
30=	Charles Mayo	83	79	80	75	317
	Ben Sayers	74	76	84	83	317
	Albert Tingey, Sr	76	82	79	80	317

1	**FRED McLEOD*** ($300)	82	82	81	77	322

2	Willie Smith	77	82	85	78	322
3	Alex Smith	80	83	83	81	327
4	Willie Anderson, Jr	85	86	80	79	330
5	John Jones	81	81	87	82	331
6=	Jack Hobens	86	81	85	81	333
	Peter Robertson	89	84	77	83	333
8=	Percy Barrett	94	80	86	78	338
	Jock Hutchison	82	84	87	85	338
10=	Richard Kimball	84	86	83	86	339
	Tom McNamara	85	82	86	86	339
12=	Donald Ball	90	81	86	83	340
	Alex Campbell	85	83	89	83	340
	George Low	92	80	84	84	340
	Robert Peebles	85	85	85	85	340
16	David Hunter	87	87	84	83	341
17=	HH Barker	84	85	88	86	343
	Mike Brady	86	87	87	83	343
	Orrin Terry	86	87	83	87	343
20	David Robertson	89	83	86	86	344
21=	Laurie Auchterlonie	85	83	83	95	346
	Harry Rawlins	85	89	88	84	346
23=	Isaac Mackie	94	88	84	81	347
	Alex Ross	89	85	91	82	347
	Walter Travis (a)	90	83	87	87	347
26	Jack Campbell	91	89	87	82	349
27=	David Brown	87	86	91	86	350
	David Ogilvie	91	89	87	83	350
29=	Arthur Smith	97	85	85	85	352
	Herbert Strong	91	89	88	84	352
	WH Way	92	88	87	85	352

Round Leaders
R1   Braid; 70
R2   Braid; 142
R3   Braid; 219
Lowest Scores
R2   Ray; 71
R3   Pulford, H Vardon; 74
R4   Braid; 72

*Fred McLeod (77) beat Willie Smith (83) in the 18-Hole Play-off

Round Leader(s)
R1   W Smith; 77
R2   W Smith; 159
R3   W Smith; 244
Lowest Scores
R2   G Nicholls (disq); 77
R3   P Robertson; 77
R4   McLeod; 77

1909
10–11 June

BRITISH OPEN

Royal Cinque Ports, Deal, Kent, England
6495 yards

In one of only two visits to Deal, The Open fell into the hands of JH Taylor for the first time since 1900. It was his 4th victory overall, and a triumph for consistently solid scoring. After a few years in America, when he featured in the US Open, Bernard Nicholls returned home to gain a Top 10 place.

1	**JH TAYLOR** (£50)	74	73	74	74	295
2=	Tom Ball	74	75	76	76	301
	James Braid	79	75	73	74	301
4	Charles Johns	72	76	79	75	302
5	TG Renouf	76	78	76	73	303
6	Ted Ray	77	76	76	75	304
7	William Horne	77	78	77	74	306
8=	James Hepburn	78	77	76	76	307
	Sandy Herd	76	75	80	76	307
10=	Bertie Lassen (a)	82	74	74	78	308
	Bernard Nicholls	78	76	77	77	308
	George Pulford	81	76	76	75	308
13	Robert Maxwell (a)	75	80	80	74	309
14=	EP Gaudin	76	77	77	80	310
	Peter Rainford	78	76	76	80	310
16	George Cawsey	79	76	78	78	311
17=	Ben Sayers	79	77	79	77	312
	Robert Thomson	81	79	75	77	312
19=	CK Hutchison (a)	75	81	78	79	313
	Tom Vardon	80	75	80	78	313
21=	Fred Collins	81	78	75	80	314
	George Duncan	77	82	80	75	314
	Ernest Foord	77	80	81	76	314
	Michael Moran	82	81	74	77	314
	Wilfred Reid	77	83	78	76	314
26=	AE Bellworthy	76	84	78	78	316
	Arthur Butchart	80	79	80	77	316
	Douglas Edgar	81	81	76	78	316
	Rowland Jones	80	79	79	78	316
	Harry Vardon	82	77	79	78	316

Round Leader(s)
R1 Johns; 72
R2 Taylor; 147
R3 Taylor; 221

Lowest Scores
R2 Taylor; 73
R3 Braid; 73
R4 Renouf; 73

1909
24–25 June

US OPEN

Englewood Golf Club, Englewood, New Jersey
6205 yards PAR 72 (288)

Sargent, after Rawlins and Lloyd, became the 3rd Englishman to win the Open in its 15-year existence. The Scottish influence on golf up to this time has to be acknowledged - only four Englishmen had won the British Open in 50 years! Sargent shot a new low total for both Majors, and McNamara – the first homegrown talent to lead the Open – set a record for both Championships for 36 and 54 holes. David Hunter, having posted a record R1 score of 68, proceeded to shoot two 84s thereafter.

1	**GEORGE SARGENT** ($300)	75	72	72	71	290
2	Tom McNamara	73	69	75	77	294
3	Alex Smith	76	73	74	72	295
4=	Willie Anderson, Jr	79	74	76	70	299
	Jack Hobens	75	78	72	74	299
	Isaac Mackie	77	75	74	73	299
7=	Tom Anderson, Jr	78	74	75	73	300
	HH Barker	75	79	73	73	300
	Andrew Campbell	71	75	77	77	300
	Tom Peebles	76	73	73	78	300
	Walter Travis (a)	72	78	77	73	300
12	Mike Brady	76	77	74	75	302
13=	Alex Campbell	75	73	81	74	303
	Fred McLeod	78	76	74	75	303
15=	Orrin Terry	78	80	73	73	304
	FR Upton, Jr (a)	72	79	78	75	304
17	Gilbert Nicholls	73	75	79	79	306
18=	Walter Fovargue	80	76	77	74	307
	David Ogilvie	76	78	79	74	307
20=	Peter Robertson	79	72	78	79	308
	Charles Rowe	74	77	76	81	308
22	Jack Campbell	74	79	75	81	309
23=	Laurie Auchterlonie	78	75	77	71	311
	Findlay Douglas (a)	82	76	78	75	311
	Jock Hutchison	79	76	77	79	311
	Tom Vardon	80	75	82	74	311
27=	John Dingwall	79	74	77	72	312
	George Low	78	75	74	85	312
	James Maiden	76	78	80	78	312
30=	Jack Burke, Sr	75	78	81	79	313
	David Hunter	68	84	84	77	313
	Charles Murray	77	75	77	84	313

Round Leader(s)
R1 Hunter; 68
R2 McNamara; 142
R3 McNamara; 217

Lowest Scores
R2 McNamara; 69
R3 Hobens, Sargent; 72
R4 Anderson; 70

17-18, 20 June	**1910**

US OPEN

Philadelphia Cricket Club, Chestnut Hill, Pennsylvania
5956 yards

The US Open preceeded the British Open for the first time this year – the last day at Philadephia Cricket Club was the day before the first at the R&A Club. Alex Smith collected his 2nd Open, in a play-off, after brother MacDonald and Champion-to-be, McDermott, finished in the first-ever 3-way tie. Brother Willie was to lead the British Open after 36 holes later that week. 4-time champion Willie Anderson, aged 30, died (probably due to a drink-related condition) several months later.

1	**ALEX SMITH***	73	73	79	73	298
	($300)					
2	John McDermott	74	74	75	75	298
3	Macdonald Smith	74	78	75	71	298
4	Fred McLeod	78	70	78	73	299
5=	Tom McNamara	73	78	73	76	300
	Gilbert Nicholls	73	75	77	75	300
7	Jack Hobens	74	77	74	76	301
8=	Tom Anderson, Jr	72	76	81	73	302
	HH Barker	75	78	77	72	302
	Jock Hutchison	77	76	75	74	302
11	Willie Anderson, Jr	74	78	76	75	303
12=	George Low	75	77	79	74	305
	Charles Thom	80	72	78	75	305
14=	Tom Bonnar	78	78	71	80	307
	George Cummings	78	73	79	77	307
16=	Alex Campbell	79	76	80	74	309
	George Sargent	77	81	74	77	309
18=	Jack Campbell	77	77	81	75	310
	James Thomson	74	80	80	76	310
20	Fred Herreshoff (a)	76	77	79	79	311
21	George Smith	76	78	79	80	313
22	Alex Ross	78	84	73	79	314
23=	Otto Hackbarth	79	82	78	76	315
	Martin O'Loughlin	77	82	80	76	315
25	AW Tillinghast (a)	80	81	79	76	316
26	WD Robinson	83	81	78	75	317
27	Jack Burke, Sr	81	77	77	84	319
28=	James Donaldson	80	78	87	75	320
	David Honeyman	83	79	79	79	320
	Irving Stringer	83	77	82	78	320

*Alex Smith (71) beat John McDermott (75) and
Macdonald Smith (77) in the 18-Hole Play-off

Round Leader(s)
R1　T Anderson; 72
R2　A Smith; 146
R3　McDermott; 223
Lowest Scores
R2　McLeod; 70
R3　Bonnar; 71
R4　M Smith; 71

21 (rain), 22–24 June	**1910**

BRITISH OPEN

Royal & Ancient GC, St Andrews, Fife, Scotland
6487 yards

Braid's magical decade was capped with his 5th Open win - then a record – beating the previous St Andrews low score by 10, and Sandy Herd by 4. Only the 60 lowest scorers (and ties) were allowed to proceed to R3. Fred MacKenzie, 3rd in the 1904 US Open, had returned (permanently) to his home course to finish 16th, while Willie Smith and Donald Ross were just visiting.

1	**JAMES BRAID**	76	73	74	76	299
	(£50)					
2	Sandy Herd	78	74	75	76	303
3	George Duncan	73	77	71	83	304
4	Laurie Ayton, Sr	78	76	75	77	306
5=	Ted Ray	76	77	74	81	308
	Fred Robson	75	80	77	76	308
	Willie Smith	77	71	80	80	308
8=	EP Gaudin	78	74	76	81	309
	James Kinnell	79	74	77	79	309
	TG Renouf	77	76	75	81	309
	Donald Ross	78	79	75	77	309
12=	Tom Ball	81	77	75	78	311
	PJ Gaudin	80	79	74	78	311
14=	Michael Moran	77	75	79	81	312
	JH Taylor	76	80	78	78	312
16=	Fred MacKenzie	78	80	75	80	313
	William Ritchie	78	74	82	79	313
	Harry Vardon	77	81	75	80	313
19=	John Ball, Jr (a)	79	75	78	82	314
	James Hepburn	78	82	76	78	314
	Tom Williamson	78	80	78	78	314
22=	Arnaud Massy	78	77	81	79	315
	John Rowe	81	74	80	80	315
24=	William Binnie	80	76	77	83	316
	CK Hutchison (a)	82	74	78	82	316
	Wilfred Reid	78	83	77	78	316
	Charles Roberts	81	73	79	83	316
28=	Willie Auchterlonie	79	76	79	83	317
	Ernest Foord	80	77	79	81	317
	Herbert Riseborough	75	81	80	81	317
	James Sherlock	77	81	80	79	317

Round Leader(s)
R1　Duncan; 73
R2　Smith; 148
R3　Duncan; 221
Lowest Scores
R2　Smith; 71
R3　Duncan; 71
R4　Braid, Herd, Robson; 76

1911

23–24 June

US OPEN

Chicago GC, Wheaton, Illinois
6605 yards

1911

26–29 June

BRITISH OPEN

Royal St George's GC, Sandwich, Kent, England
6594 yards

The much-awaited first win by a native American. Born in Philadelphia and not yet 20, McDermott tied with compatriot Mike Brady and Scot George Simpson, before winning the play-off.

James Braid's record of 5 victories was short-lived when arch-rival Vardon equalled his mark at Sandwich. Arnaud Massy, the 1907 champion, took him to the 35th extra hole, however, for the privilege.

I	**JOHN McDERMOTT*** ($300)	81	72	75	79	307
2	Mike Brady	76	77	79	75	307
3	George Simpson	76	77	79	75	307
4	Fred McLeod	77	72	76	83	308
5=	Jock Hutchison	80	77	73	79	309
	Gilbert Nicholls	76	78	74	81	309
7=	HH Barker	75	81	77	78	311
	George Sargent	76	77	84	74	311
9=	Peter Robertson	79	76	78	79	312
	Alex Ross	74	75	81	82	312
11	Albert Seckel (a)	78	80	80	75	313
12=	Alex Campbell	81	77	72	84	314
	Harry Turpie	77	76	82	79	314
14	CP Nelson	79	85	74	77	315
15=	James Donaldson	78	81	83	74	316
	George Low	80	78	82	76	316
17	RL Simpson	81	82	75	79	317
18=	John Burke	79	77	78	85	319
	DE Sawyer (a)	84	79	77	79	319
20=	Grange Alves	82	80	73	85	320
	George Cummings	82	80	79	79	320
	Mason Phelps (a)	78	78	78	86	320
23=	H Chandler Egan (a)	81	80	77	83	321
	Robert Gardner (a)	81	78	79	83	321
	JB Simpson	81	82	78	80	321
	Alex Smith	76	78	82	85	321
	RC Watson (a)	82	79	78	82	321
28	Walter Fovargue	83	81	80	78	322
29=	TJ Foulis	79	80	82	83	324
	Otto Hackbarth	78	74	83	89	324
	Robert McDonald	80	82	75	87	324
	Tom McNamara	77	87	79	81	324

*John McDermott (80) beat Mike Brady (82) and George Simpson (86) in the 18-Hole Play-off

Round Leader(s)
R1   Ross; 74
R2   McLeod, Ross; 149
R3   McLeod; 225
Lowest Scores
R2   McDermott, McLeod; 72
R3   Campbell; 72
R4   Donaldson, Sargent; 74

I	**HARRY VARDON*** (£50)	74	74	75	80	303
2	Arnaud Massy	75	78	74	76	303
3=	Sandy Herd	77	73	76	78	304
	Horace Hilton (a)	76	74	78	76	304
5=	James Braid	78	75	74	78	305
	Ted Ray	76	72	79	78	305
	JH Taylor	72	76	78	79	305
8	George Duncan	73	71	83	79	306
9	Laurie Ayton, Sr	75	77	77	78	307
10=	James Hepburn	74	77	83	75	309
	Fred Robson	78	74	79	78	309
12	Fred Collins	77	76	83	74	310
13=	J Piper	78	79	80	74	311
	TG Renouf	75	76	79	81	311
15	Tom Ball	76	77	79	80	312
16=	Rowland Jones	80	76	85	72	313
	Charles Mayo	78	78	79	78	313
	Wilfred Reid	78	79	80	76	313
	James Sherlock	73	80	76	84	313
	HE Taylor (a)	83	73	76	81	313
21=	Ernest BH Blackwell (a)	71	81	72	80	314
	Michael Moran	72	78	83	81	314
	William Watt	76	80	79	79	314
24=	Ernest Jones	77	82	81	75	315
	LB Stevens (a)	79	83	77	76	315
	Josh Taylor	79	81	80	75	315
27=	Robert Harris (a)	77	80	76	83	316
	Fred Leach	75	79	87	75	316
29=	Tom R Fernie	80	78	76	83	317
	JC Johnstone	82	79	78	78	317
	AF Kettley	79	77	81	80	317
	James Ockenden	75	78	81	83	317
	Robert Thomson	77	76	85	79	317

* Harry Vardon (143 after 35 holes) beat Arnaud Massy (148 after 34 holes) when Massy conceded at the 35th hole

Round Leader(s)
R1   Blackwell; 71
R2   Duncan; 144
R3   Vardon; 223
Lowest Scores
R2   Duncan; 71
R3   Braid, Massy; 74
R4   R Jones; 72

24–25 June   1912
BRITISH OPEN
Honourable Company, Muirfield, Angus, Scotland
6194 yards

Ted Ray was the heir apparent to the Great Triumvirate – except that they were at the top so long, he was usurped before he could properly wear the crown. Ray would surely have won more Opens (British, or US – which he collected in 1920) if Braid, Vardon and Taylor had been mere mortals – and if there wasn't an enforced sabbatical in the middle of his career, courtesy of Kaiser Wilhelm II. Leading all the way, Ray set a new 54-hole low for the Open of 220.

1	**TED RAY** (£50)	71	73	76	75	295
2	Harry Vardon	75	72	81	71	299
3	James Braid	77	71	77	78	303
4	George Duncan	72	77	78	78	305
5=	Laurie Ayton, Sr	74	80	75	80	309
	Sandy Herd	76	81	76	76	309
7=	Fred Collins	76	79	81	74	310
	Jean Gassiat	76	80	78	76	310
	Reg Wilson	82	75	75	78	310
10	Arnaud Massy	74	77	82	78	311
11=	Charles Mayo	76	77	78	81	312
	JH Taylor	75	76	77	84	312
13=	George Fotheringham	75	78	79	81	313
	Robert Thomson	73	77	80	83	313
15=	Hughie McNeill	76	78	82	78	314
	Michael Moran	76	79	80	79	314
17=	Fred Leach	75	82	81	77	315
	Tom Williamson	80	77	79	79	315
19	TG Renouf	77	80	80	79	316
20=	Douglas Edgar	77	81	80	79	317
	William Horne	73	85	82	77	317
	Wilfred Reid	80	79	79	79	317
23	PJ Gaudin	80	76	82	80	318
24=	FH Frostick	77	80	81	81	319
	Philip Taylor	76	82	81	80	319
26	Tom Ball	75	81	86	78	320
27=	Jas Batley	79	86	80	76	321
	Rowland Jones	78	82	84	77	321
	Charles Pope	83	80	77	81	321
	Charles Roberts	82	81	83	75	321

Round Leader(s)
R1 Ray; 71
R2 Ray; 144
R3 Ray; 220
Lowest Scores
R2 Braid; 71
R3 Ayton, Wilson; 75
R4 Vardon; 71

1–2 August   1912
US OPEN
Country Club of Buffalo, Buffalo, New York
6236 yards PAR 74 (296)

Proving that his 2nd in 1910 and win of the previous year were not flukes, McDermott made it back-to-back victories. He shot an impressive 294 total to lead home fellow 'home-breds' Tom McNamara and Mike Brady. Only Alex Smith of the British imports scored within 8 strokes of the winner. In 1911, the USGA officially defined the term 'par' – which meant that McDermott was 2 'under' for the Championship.

1	**JOHN McDERMOTT** ($300)	74	75	74	71	294
2	Tom McNamara	74	80	73	69	296
3=	Mike Brady	72	75	73	79	299
	Alex Smith	77	70	77	75	299
5	Alex Campbell	74	77	80	71	302
6	George Sargent	72	78	76	77	303
7=	Jack Dowling	76	79	76	74	305
	Otto Hackbarth	77	77	75	76	305
9	Charles Murray	75	78	77	76	306
10=	Tom Anderson, Jr	75	76	81	75	307
	Frank Peebles	73	76	83	75	307
	Walter Travis (a)	73	79	78	77	307
13=	Fred McLeod	79	77	75	77	308
	George Simpson	79	73	77	79	308
15	Percy Barrett	74	73	83	79	309
16=	John G Anderson (a)	80	79	78	73	310
	David Ogilvie	74	83	73	80	310
18=	Jim Barnes	77	73	79	82	311
	John Dingwall	77	77	78	79	311
	Willie MacFarlane	77	81	73	80	311
21=	Jack Croke	74	81	78	79	312
	Tom Vardon	74	83	79	76	312
23=	Jack Campbell	74	75	83	81	313
	George Cummings	78	79	77	79	313
	Jock Hutchison	78	77	82	76	313
26	AH Murray	78	79	79	78	314
27	Charles Rowe	77	78	79	81	315
28=	Dave Robertson	80	82	77	77	316
	Peter Robertson	77	82	81	76	316
30=	David Black	78	77	78	84	317
	David Honeyman	80	82	79	76	317
	David Livie	82	80	76	79	317

Round Leader(s)
R1 Brady, Sargent; 72
R2 Barrett, Brady, Smith; 147
R3 Brady; 220
Lowest Scores
R2 Smith; 70
R3 Brady, MacFarlane, McNamara, Ogilvie; 73
R4 McNamara; 69

1913

23–24 June

BRITISH OPEN

Royal Liverpool GC, Hoylake, Cheshire, England
6455 yards

Taylor joined Vardon and Braid on 5 Open wins, 19 years after his first success. His margin of 8 strokes matched his win of 1900 and Braid's of 1908 – the widest margins of victory in the Open this century. Double US Open Champion, John McDermott, became the first US-born professional to compete in the Championship, finishing tied 5th.

1	**JH TAYLOR** (£50)	73	75	77	79	304
2	Ted Ray	73	74	81	84	312
3=	Michael Moran	76	74	89	74	313
	Harry Vardon	79	75	79	80	313
5=	John McDermott	75	80	77	83	315
	TG Renouf	75	78	84	78	315
7=	James Bradbeer	78	79	81	79	317
	Arnaud Massy	77	80	81	79	317
	James Sherlock	77	86	79	75	317
	Tom Williamson	77	80	80	80	317
11=	Fred Collins	77	85	79	77	318
	Jack Graham (a)	77	79	81	81	318
	Sandy Herd	73	81	84	80	318
14=	Bertie Lassen (a)	79	78	80	82	319
	Charles Roberts	78	79	84	78	319
	Josh Taylor	80	75	85	79	319
17	Philip Taylor	78	81	83	78	320
18=	James Braid	80	79	82	80	321
	Claude Gray	80	81	79	81	321
	Ernest Jones	75	85	81	80	321
	Hughie McNeill	80	81	81	79	321
22=	Jean Gassiat	80	78	86	78	322
	Cyril Hughes	76	78	83	85	322
	Louis Tellier	77	80	85	80	322
25	TL Macnamara	80	78	85	80	323
26	Wilfred Reid	78	82	85	79	324
27=	Arthur Catlin	77	81	81	86	325
	Charles Mayo	83	82	78	82	325
	Thomas Simpson	79	83	85	78	325
30=	Laurie Ayton, Sr	78	83	86	80	327
	Tom Ball	82	83	86	76	327
	GR Buckle	81	80	87	79	327
	Jack B Ross	75	89	84	79	327

Round Leader(s)
R1 Herd, Ray, JH Taylor; 73
R2 Ray; 147
R3 JH Taylor; 225
Lowest Scores
R2 Moran, Ray; 74
R3 McDermott, JH Taylor; 77
R4 Moran; 74

1913

18–20 September

US OPEN

The Country Club, Brookline, Massachusetts
6245 yards _PAR 71 (284)_

If the Opens of 1911 and 1912 were seminal in that they witnessed the birth of the hitherto embryonic American professional, the Open Championship of 1913 showed how the golf and golfers of the New World would soon outgrow their Old World teachers. Not only did it point to the crumbling hegemony of Britain with Vardon's and Ray's defeat in a playoff – it took US golf on to the front pages and it heralded a golden era for the successful amateur. Francis Ouimet's destruction of arguably the world's two best players of the time is one of golf's biggest upsets – and turning points. Qualifying rounds were held for the first time, reducing the R1 starters to 64.

1	**FRANCIS OUIMET*** (Amateur)	77	74	74	79	304
2	Harry Vardon	75	72	78	79	304
3	Ted Ray	79	70	76	79	304
4=	Jim Barnes	74	76	78	79	307
	Walter Hagen	73	78	76	80	307
	Macdonald Smith	71	79	80	77	307
	Louis Tellier	76	76	79	76	307
8	John McDermott	74	79	77	78	308
9	Herbert Strong	75	74	82	79	310
10	Pat Doyle	78	80	73	80	311
11=	WC Fownes, Jr (a)	79	75	78	80	312
	Elmer Loving	76	80	75	81	312
13	Alex Campbell	77	80	76	80	313
14	Mike Brady	83	74	78	80	315
15	Matt Campbell	83	80	77	76	316
16=	Fred Herreshoff (a)	75	78	83	82	318
	Jock Hutchison	77	76	80	85	318
	Tom McNamara	73	86	75	84	318
	Wilfred Reid	75	72	85	86	318
	Alex Smith	82	75	82	79	318
21=	Robert Andrews (a)	83	73	83	80	319
	Jack Croke	72	83	83	81	319
	Charles Murray	80	80	80	79	319
	Peter Robertson	79	80	78	82	319
	George Sargent	75	76	79	89	319
26=	Jack Dowling	77	77	82	85	321
	Charles Thom	76	76	84	85	321
28=	Bob MacDonald	80	79	84	79	322
	Jerome Travers (a)	78	78	81	85	322
30=	Frank Bellwood	79	83	80	81	323
	James Donaldson	79	76	85	83	323
	JH Taylor	81	80	78	84	323

*Francis Ouimet (72) beat Harry Vardon (77) and Ted Ray (78) in the 18-Hole Play-off

Round Leader(s)	**Lowest Scores**
R1 Alex Ross (36), M Smith; 71	R2 Ray; 70
R2 Reid, Vardon; 147	R3 Doyle; 73
R3 Ouimet, Ray, Vardon; 225	R4 M Campbell, Tellier; 76

58

18–19 June	**1914**

BRITISH OPEN
Prestwick GC, Ayrshire, Scotland
6122 yards

20–21 August	**1914**

US OPEN
Midlothian CC, Blue Island, Illinois
6355 yards PAR 72 (288)

Vardon's last Open win – his 6th - was a record, still unsurpassed. It was the end of an era: the Great War caused a five year vacuum in the Open Championship, at the end of which the Triumvirate had reached the age of 50. Vardon was to challenge for both Opens in 1920, but that was his parting shot. American hero, Francis Ouimet, who was to add the 1914 US Amateur title to his 1913 US Open, came to Prestwick, but finished well down the field on 332.

It didn't take long for the infant US golfer to grow up. Finishing 4th behind all the excitement the previous year, Walter Hagen burst on to the scene in 1915 with a record R1 score of 68, stayed ahead of the field, and won by one stroke from fast-finishing Chick Evans, another emerging amateur. He tied George Sargent's record low total of 1909. Hagen was to go on to become the first worldwide superstar of golf – in fact, he probably invented the role with his brash but charming manner and lavish lifestyle.

1	**HARRY VARDON** (£50)	73	77	78	78	306

2	JH Taylor	74	78	74	83	309
3	Harry Simpson	77	80	78	75	310
4=	Abe Mitchell	76	78	79	79	312
	Tom Williamson	75	79	79	79	312
6	Reg Wilson	76	77	80	80	313
7	James Ockenden	75	76	83	80	314
8=	PJ Gaudin	78	83	80	74	315
	JLC Jenkins (a)	79	80	73	83	315
10=	James Braid	74	82	78	82	316
	George Duncan	77	79	80	80	316
	Arnaud Massy	77	82	75	82	316
	Ted Ray	77	82	76	81	316
14=	James Bradbeer	77	80	80	80	317
	Douglas Edgar	79	75	84	79	317
	Jean Gassiat	76	81	80	80	317
17=	William Hunter	82	77	77	83	319
	Bertie Lassen (a)	85	78	79	77	319
19=	Ernest Foord	82	81	82	76	321
	Cyril Hughes	80	81	80	80	321
21=	Jas Batley	78	83	81	80	322
	Ernest Jones	87	81	80	74	322
	Fred Leach	76	86	78	82	322
	C Ralph Smith	81	79	80	82	322
25=	Walter Hambleton	79	75	86	83	323
	Michael Moran	82	83	82	76	323
	Josh Taylor	82	79	84	78	323
	David Watt	84	80	78	81	323
29=	Sandy Herd	79	87	79	79	324
	CK Hutchison (a)	81	75	82	86	324
	JC Lonie	77	84	82	81	324
	Ernest Whitcombe	74	83	84	83	324

1	**WALTER HAGEN** ($300)	68	74	75	73	290

2	Charles Evans, Jr (a)	76	74	71	70	291
3=	Fred McLeod	78	73	75	71	297
	George Sargent	74	77	74	72	297
5=	Mike Brady	78	72	74	74	298
	James Donaldson	72	79	74	73	298
	Francis Ouimet (a)	69	76	75	78	298
8	Louis Tellier	72	75	74	78	299
9=	John McDermott	77	74	74	75	300
	Arthur Smith	79	73	76	72	300
11=	WM Rautenbusch (a)	76	75	75	75	301
	James Simpson	76	71	77	77	301
13=	Jim Barnes	73	76	80	73	302
	Charles Hoffner	77	76	77	72	302
	Tom McNamara	72	71	76	83	302
	Joe Mitchell	77	69	77	79	302
	JJ O'Brien	74	72	77	79	302
	Robert Peebles	78	75	74	75	302
	George Simpson	73	76	76	77	302
20=	Dan Kenney	76	75	76	76	303
	Tom Kerrigan	76	73	77	77	303
22=	Alex Ross	72	75	82	76	305
	Warren Wood (a)	77	73	77	78	305
24	Walter Fovargue	81	71	77	77	306
25=	Jack Munro	83	74	75	75	307
	RM Thompson	79	75	78	75	307
27	Otto Hackbarth	82	75	77	75	309
28=	Fred Brand	78	74	76	82	310
	Jack Burke, Sr	75	77	77	81	310
	CP Nelson	77	81	77	75	310

Round Leader(s)
R1 Vardon; 73
R2 Vardon; 150
R3 JH Taylor; 226
Lowest Scores
R2 Edgar, Hambleton, Hutchison; 75
R3 Jenkins; 73
R4 Gaudin, Jones; 74

Round Leader(s)
R1 Hagen; 68
R2 Hagen; 142
R3 Hagen; 217
Lowest Scores
R2 Mitchell; 69
R3 Evans; 71
R4 Evans; 70

1915–19	1915	17–18 June

BRITISH OPEN

NO CHAMPIONSHIPS

1915

US OPEN

Baltusrol GC, Springfield, New Jersey
6212 yards PAR 72 (288)

Returning to the original Baltusrol course, The Open produced its second amateur winner. Jerome Travers had won the matchplay US Amateur title four times. He gave up competitive golf shortly afterwards to concentrate on his Wall St career.

I	**JEROME TRAVERS** (Amateur)	76	72	73	76	297
2	Tom McNamara	78	71	74	75	298
3	Bob MacDonald	72	77	73	78	300
4=	Jim Barnes	71	75	76	79	301
	Louis Tellier	75	71	76	79	301
6	Mike Brady	76	71	75	80	302
7	George Low	78	74	76	75	303
8=	Jock Hutchison	74	79	76	76	305
	Fred McLeod	74	76	76	79	305
10=	Alex Campbell	76	75	74	81	306
	Emmett French	77	79	75	75	306
	Walter Hagen	78	73	76	79	306
	Tom Kerrigan	78	75	76	77	306
	Gilbert Nicholls	78	81	73	74	306
	Jack Park	77	77	75	77	306
	Wilfred Reid	77	78	75	76	306
	George Sargent	75	77	79	75	306
18	Charles Evans, Jr (a)	71	81	80	75	307
19=	James Donaldson	83	79	76	70	308
	Max Marston (a)	77	77	80	74	308
21	AJ Sanderson	77	76	77	79	309
22=	Jack Dowling	75	79	80	77	311
	Alex Smith	78	76	78	79	311
24=	HH Barker	77	78	80	77	312
	Charles Hoffner	79	79	79	75	312
26=	Joe Mitchell	76	80	74	83	313
	Herbert Strong	83	76	78	76	313
28	George Sayers	76	80	81	77	314
29=	Otto Hackbarth	80	75	79	81	315
	David Ogilvie	75	78	83	79	315
	Ben Sayers	80	79	79	77	315

Round Leader(s)
R1 Barnes, Evans; 71
R2 Barnes, Tellier; 146
R3 Travers; 221
Lowest Scores
R2 Brady, McNamara, Tellier; 71
R3 MacDonald, Nicholls, Travers; 73
R4 Donaldson; 70

US OPEN
Minikahda Club, Minneapolis, Minnesota
6130 yards PAR 72 (288)

Chick Evans became the 3rd amateur in four years to win. In doing so he shattered the record for 36 and 54 holes. There is no truth in the rumour that the recently-formed PGA of America was formed as a protectionist society, and that they wanted the upcoming PGA Championship closed to the pros to keep the amateurs out! Tom Vardon, brother of the illustrious Harry, attained his highest Open position this year after several less-successful visits, and Wilfred Reid finished 4th in his first US Open - much higher than in any British Open.

1	**CHARLES EVANS, Jr**	70	69	74	73	286
	(Amateur)					
2	Jock Hutchison	73	75	72	68	288
3	Jim Barnes	71	74	71	74	290
4=	Gilbert Nicholls	73	76	71	73	293
	Wilfred Reid	70	72	79	72	293
	George Sargent	75	71	72	75	293
7	Walter Hagen	73	76	75	71	295
8	Bob MacDonald	74	72	77	73	296
9=	Mike Brady	75	73	75	74	297
	JJ O'Brien	76	72	73	76	297
	Tom Vardon	76	72	75	74	297
12	Jack Dowling	71	76	75	76	298
13=	Walter Fovargue	76	74	74	75	299
	Louis Tellier	74	75	72	78	299
15=	Herbert Lagerblade	77	78	72	73	300
	Tom McNamara	75	79	73	73	300
	Robert Peebles	73	72	76	79	300
	JB Simpson	75	76	76	73	300
19=	Otto Hackbarth	77	80	69	75	301
	George McLean	77	76	74	74	301
21=	James Donaldson	79	75	75	73	302
	Joe Mitchell	75	75	76	76	302
	George Turnbull	83	73	72	74	302
24=	Bert Battell	76	75	75	77	303
	Arthur Fotheringham	78	78	74	73	303
	Fred McLeod	74	75	77	77	303
	George Simpson	76	76	77	74	303
28	Alex Campbell	75	75	75	79	304
29=	Alex Cunningham	79	75	75	77	306
	James Ferguson	74	75	80	77	306
	Tom Kerrigan	79	72	78	77	306

Round Leaders
R1 Evans, Reid; 70
R2 Evans; 139
R3 Evans; 213

Lowest Scores
R2 Evans; 69
R3 Hackbarth; 69
R4 Hutchison; 68

US PGA
Siwanoy CC, Bronxville, New York

MATCHPLAY
32 qualifiers after 36 holes strokeplay
All Rounds 36 holes

Jim Barnes, originally from Cornwall, England, became the first winner of the Rodman Wanamaker Trophy. The competition was based on the British PGA Championship sponsored by the News of the World newspaper – 36 hole-matchplay – which would provide an attractive alternative for the pros to the medal play of the Opens. Jock Hutchison had the dubious honour of finishing 2nd in both the year's Majors.

FINAL
JIM BARNES ($500)
beat
JOCK HUTCHISON, 1up

Round by Round Details

ROUND 1 (Last 32)
Tom Kerrigan bt Charles Adams 6&4; George McLean bt Tom NacNamara 6&5; Alex Smith bt James Ferguson 4&2; JIM BARNES bt George Fotheringham 8&7; Willie MacFarlane bt Robert McNulty 10&9; Mike Brady bt James West 7&6; Emmett French bt Eddie Towns 3&1; Jack Dowling (bye); JJ O'Brien bt Wilfred Reid 1up; George Simpson bt Walter Fovargue 6&5; Bob MacDonald bt Jimmie Donaldson 3&2; Walter Hagen bt JR Thomson 7&6; JOCK HUTCHISON bt Joe Mitchell 11&9; W Brown bt F Clarkson (default); Cyril Walker bt Louis Tellier 4&2; Jack Hobens bt Mike Sherman (default)

ROUND 2 (Last 16)
Kerrigan bt McLean 2&1
BARNES bt Smith 8&7
MacFarlane bt Brady 3&2
Dowling bt French 1up (after 37)
O'Brien bt Simpson 3&2
Hagen bt MacDonald 3&2
HUTCHISON bt Brown 11&9
Walker bt Hobens 5&4

QUARTER FINAL (QF)
BARNES bt Kerrigan 3&1
MacFarlane bt Dowling 2&1
Hagen bt O'Brien 10&9
HUTCHISON bt Walker 5&4

SEMI FINAL (SF)
BARNES bt MacFarlane 6&5
HUTCHISON bt Hagen 2up

1917–18
NO CHAMPIONSHIP

1917–18
NO CHAMPIONSHIP

1919

9–12 June

US OPEN

Brae Burn CC, West Newton, Massachusetts

PAR 71 (284)

The resurrection of the Majors after World War I saw many familiar faces returning to the golfing fray. Mike Brady, who lost in a play-off against John McDermott in 1911, suffered a similar fate at the hands of Walter Hagen this year. The 'Haig' closed a 5-shot gap over the last round to tie.

1	**WALTER HAGEN*** ($500)	78	73	75	75	301
2	Mike Brady	74	74	73	80	301
3=	Jock Hutchison	78	76	76	76	306
	Tom McNamara	80	73	79	74	306
5=	George McLean	81	75	76	76	308
	Louis Tellier	73	78	82	75	308
7	John Cowan	79	74	75	81	309
8	George Bowden	73	78	75	86	312
	Fred McLeod	78	77	79	78	312
10	Charles Evans, Jr (a)	77	76	82	78	313
11=	Jim Barnes	77	78	79	81	315
	Harry Hampton	79	81	77	78	315
13=	Clarence Hackney	83	78	81	74	316
	Charles Hoffner	72	78	77	89	316
	Isaac Mackie	82	75	78	81	316
16=	Gilbert Nicholls	81	78	82	77	318
	Alex Ross	77	78	77	86	318
18=	Pat Doyle	78	82	76	83	319
	Francis Ouimet (a)	76	79	79	85	319
	James West	79	82	80	78	319
21=	Alex Cunningham	79	81	79	81	320
	Douglas Edgar	80	78	82	80	320
	Wilfred Reid	82	78	80	80	320
24=	Jesse Guilford (a)	79	78	84	80	321
	J Sanderson	85	79	83	74	321
26=	Otto Hackbarth	77	79	82	84	322
	Tom Kerrigan	80	79	82	81	322
	Herbert Lagerblade	79	80	82	81	322
29=	George Fotheringham	81	82	79	81	323
	Bob MacDonald	81	78	80	84	323
	George Sargent	84	79	82	78	323

* Walter Hagen (77) beat Mike Brady (78)
in the 18-Hole Play-off

1919

15–20 September

US PGA

Engineers CC, Long Island, New York

MATCHPLAY
32 qualifiers after 36 holes strokeplay
All Rounds 36 holes

The hiatus caused by the War didn't stop Barnes from winning his second PGA title. He demolished 1908 US Open Champion Fred McLeod in the final. Apart from Tom Morris, Jr (1870 & 1872) he is the only champion in any Major to have won 'back-to-back' titles but not in successive years. 'Young' Tom did manage three in a row, though, before the British Open break in 1871.

FINAL
JIM BARNES ($500)
beat
FRED McLEOD, 6&5

Round by Round Details

ROUND 1 (Last 32)
JIM BARNES bt Carl Anderson 8&6; Otto Hackbarth bt Joe Sylvester 5&4; Tom Kerrigan bt Bill Mehlhorn 3&2; Emmett French bt Clarence Hackney 7&6; Bob MacDonald bt Tom Boyd 1up; George Fotheringham bt Eddie Loos 8&6; Tom MacNamara bt Louis Martucci 7&6; Jock Hutchison bt John Bredemus 6&5; Harry Hampton bt Jack Hobens 7&6; Douglas Edgar bt Joe Rosman (default); FRED McLEOD bt James Rose 9&7; George Gordon bt Dave Wilson 3&2; Wilfred Reid bt Pat Doyle 1up; Jimmy West bt Willie Kidd (default); Mike Brady bt Louis Tellier 7&6; George McLean bt Johnny Farrell 7&6

ROUND 2 (Last 16)
BARNES bt Hackbarth 3&2
French bt Kerrigan 2up
MacDonald bt Fotheringham 2&1
Hutchison bt MacNamara 8&6
Edgar bt Hampton 5&4
McLEOD bt Gordon 2up
West bt Reid 2&1
McLean bt Brady 6&5

QUARTER FINAL (QF)
BARNES bt French 3&2
MacDonald bt Hutchison 3&2
McLeod bt Edgar 8&6
McLean bt West 9&7

SEMI FINAL (SF)
BARNES bt MacDonald 5&4
McLEOD bt McLean 3&2

Jim Barnes, seen here playing in the Great Britain v America match at Wentworth, 1926. *(photo Allsport/Hulton Deutsch)*

1920

30 June – 1 July

BRITISH OPEN

Royal Cinque Ports, Deal, Kent, England
6653 yards

George Duncan's only Open win was extraordinary in its scoring. After shooting two successive 80s, he was 13 behind half-way leader Abe Mitchell, but then his final 36-holes took only 143, which had only previously been bettered by Jack White and James Braid at Sandwich in 1904. This was only the second, but also the last, visit to Deal. Many of the pros found it geographically remote (SE England, when the centre of the British golfing universe was still north of the border) and too close to Sandwich. The R&A took over the running of the Open from the host clubs and some rationalization ensued.

1	**GEORGE DUNCAN** (£75)	80	80	71	72	303
2	Sandy Herd	72	81	77	75	305
3	Ted Ray	72	83	78	73	306
4	Abe Mitchell	74	73	84	76	307
5	Len Holland	80	78	71	79	308
6	Jim Barnes	79	74	77	79	309
7=	Arthur Havers	80	78	81	74	313
	Sydney Wingate	81	74	76	82	313
9=	GR Buckle	80	80	77	78	315
	Archie Compston	79	83	75	78	315
	William Horne	80	81	73	81	315
12	JH Taylor	78	79	80	79	316
13	L Lafitte	75	85	84	73	317
14=	Eric Bannister	78	84	80	76	318
	Harry Vardon	78	81	81	78	318
16=	A Gaudin	81	82	77	79	319
	Charles Johns	82	78	81	78	319
	James Sherlock	82	81	80	76	319
	Philip Taylor	78	84	77	80	319
	Angel de la Torre	84	78	78	79	319
21=	James Braid	79	80	79	82	320
	William B Smith	81	81	77	81	320
	Dick Wheildon	82	78	83	77	320
	Reg Wilson	76	82	78	84	320
25	Cyril Hughes	83	81	80	77	321
26=	Willie Hunter Jr (a)	81	80	81	80	322
	Tom Williamson	77	86	79	80	322
28	C Ralph Smith	84	80	79	80	323
29=	Arthur Day	77	83	84	80	324
	Jean Gassiat	79	82	78	85	324
	D Grant (a)	83	76	82	83	324
	Fred Leach	83	82	78	81	324
	Arnaud Massy	81	82	80	81	324
	William Ritchie	79	86	81	78	324

Round Leader(s)
R1 Herd, Ray; 72
R2 Mitchell; 147
R3 Holland; 229

Lowest Scores
R2 Mitchell; 73
R3 Duncan, Holland; 71
R4 Duncan; 72

12–13 August	**1920**

US OPEN

Inverness Club, Toledo, Ohio
6569 yards PAR 72 (288)

Having a chastening experience in 1913 did not deter Ted Ray from trying his luck in the US Open one more time. He was 43 in 1920 and was to be the oldest winner of this championship until Ray Floyd in 1986, then Hale Irwin, 4 years later, lifted the trophy. In his two visits he tied the lead and was outright winner. His travelling companion, Harry Vardon, was aged 50, and his 3 visits, spanning 21 years, saw this sequence of results: W, 2, 2. Reigning double PGA Champion, Jim Barnes matched his 6th place in the British Open.

1	**TED RAY**	74	73	73	75	295
	($500)					
2=	Jack Burke, Sr	75	77	72	72	296
	Leo Diegel	72	74	73	77	296
	Jock Hutchison	69	76	74	77	296
	Harry Vardon	74	73	71	78	296
6=	Jim Barnes	76	70	76	76	298
	Charles Evans, Jr (a)	74	76	73	75	298
8=	Bobby Jones (a)	78	74	70	77	299
	Willie MacFarlane	76	75	74	74	299
10	Bob MacDonald	73	78	71	78	300
11	Walter Hagen	74	73	77	77	301
12	Clarence Hackney	78	74	74	76	302
13	Fred McLeod	75	77	73	79	304
14=	Mike Brady	77	76	74	78	305
	Frank McNamara	78	77	76	74	305
	Charles Rowe	76	78	77	74	305
17=	Laurie Ayton, Sr	75	78	76	77	306
	John Golden	77	80	74	75	306
	Eddie Loos	75	74	73	84	306
20=	Douglas Edgar	73	82	74	78	307
	James West	80	77	75	75	307
22	Harry Hampton	79	76	74	79	308
23=	Tom Kerrigan	77	81	74	77	309
	Gilbert Nicholls	77	82	75	75	309
	JJ O'Brien	82	77	73	77	309
	DK White	78	75	79	77	309
27=	Bill Mehlhorn	78	74	79	79	310
	Peter O'Hara	84	74	74	78	310
	Alex Ross	80	76	77	77	310
30=	George Bowden	74	80	76	81	311
	Charles Hall	77	80	76	78	311
	Willie Kidd	77	81	76	77	311
	George McLean	83	76	73	79	311
	Gene Sarazen	79	79	76	77	311

Round Leaders
R1 Hutchison; 69
R2 Hutchison; 145
R3 Vardon; 218
Lowest Scores
R2 Barnes; 70
R3 Jones; 70
R4 Burke; 72

17–21 August	**1920**

US PGA

Flossmoor CC, Chicago, Illinois

MATCHPLAY
32 qualifiers after 36 holes strokeplay
All Rounds 36 holes

Jim Barnes, despite challenging for the other Majors this year, crashed out in R2, ending a streak of 11 wins. The final was fought between St Andrews-born Jock Hutchison and JD (Douglas) Edgar of Northumberland, England. Hutchison won to make up for his defeat in the 1916 final. Although never in contention for the British Open, Edgar had taken America by storm when he emigrated in 1918. He beat a high-class field by 16 strokes to win the Canadian Open, was ahead of his time in preaching golfing techniques and induced such luminaries as Harry Vardon and Tommy Armour to rate him among the very best. He died, in mysterious circumstances, the following year in Atlanta, aged 37.

FINAL
JOCK HUTCHISON ($500)
beat
DOUGLAS EDGAR, 1up

Round by Round Details

ROUND 1 (Last 32)
Alex Cunningham bt Willie MacFarlane 2&1; Peter O'Hara bt Pat Doyle 1up; George McLean bt George Sayers 6&5; Tom Kennett bt Otto Hackbarth 3&1; DOUGLAS EDGAR bt Pat O'Hara 1up; Joe Sylvester bt Tom Boyd 4&3; Bob MacDonald bt Leo Diegel 4&3; Bill Mehlhorn bt Wallie Nelson 3&2; Harry Hampton bt Jack Gordon 6&5; George Thompson bt Isaac Mackie 3&2; Clarence Hackney bt Phil Hesler 3&2; Jim Barnes bt George Bowden 4&3; Charles Mayo bt Lloyd Gullickson 2&1; Louis Tellier bt Joe Rosman 10&9; Laurie Ayton, Sr bt Charles Hoffner 1up (after 39); JOCK HUTCHISON bt Eddie Loos 5&3

ROUND 2 (Last 16)
Peter O'Hara bt Cunningham 5&4
Mclean bt Kennett 2&1
EDGAR bt Sylvester 11&9
MacDonald bt Mehlhorn 1up
Hampton bt Thompson 5&4
Hackney bt Barnes 5&4
Tellier bt Mayo 4&2
HUTCHISON bt Ayton 5&3

QUARTER FINAL (QF)
McLean bt O'Hara 1up (after 38)
EDGAR bt MacDonald 5&4
Hampton bt Hackney 4&3
HUTCHISON bt Tellier 6&5

SEMI FINAL (SF)
EDGAR bt McLean 8&7
HUTCHISON bt Hampton 4&3

1921

23–25 June

BRITISH OPEN

Royal & Ancient GC, St Andrews, Fife, Scotland
6487 yards

Jock Hutchison won the Open on the back of the 1920 USPGA Championship. His homecoming resulted in the first win for an American golfer – albeit one who was Scottish born. Hutchison, the amateur, Wethered, and Kerrigan were all inside James Braid's 1910 St Andrews record, with Hutchison's last round 70 also a record course low in the Championship. Four Americans in the Top 10 signified that the invasion was about to begin.

1	**JOCK HUTCHISON*** (£75)	72	75	79	70	296
2	Roger Wethered (a)	78	75	72	71	296
3	Tom Kerrigan	74	80	72	72	298
4	Arthur Havers	76	74	77	72	299
5	George Duncan	74	75	78	74	301
6=	Jim Barnes	74	74	74	80	302
	Walter Hagen	74	79	72	77	302
	Sandy Herd	75	74	73	80	302
	Joe Kirkwood, Sr	76	74	73	79	302
	Fred Leach	78	75	76	73	302
	Arnaud Massy	74	75	74	79	302
	Tom Williamson	79	71	74	78	302
13=	Abe Mitchell	78	79	76	71	304
	W Pursey	74	82	74	74	304
15	JW Gaudin	78	76	75	76	305
16=	James Braid	77	75	78	76	306
	Len Holland	78	78	76	74	306
	Bill Mehlhorn	75	77	76	78	306
19=	Frank Ball	79	78	74	76	307
	P Hunter (a)	75	78	76	78	307
	Ted Ray	76	72	81	78	307
	William Watt	81	77	75	74	307
23=	Clarence Hackney	77	75	80	76	308
	Henry Kinch	73	77	81	77	308
	Harry Vardon	77	77	80	74	308
26=	Aubrey Boomer	78	80	72	79	309
	Walter Bourne	78	78	75	78	309
	Arthur Butchart	78	80	77	74	309
	Douglas Edgar	82	76	78	73	309
	Emmett French	79	76	75	79	309
	DH Kyle (a)	77	77	81	74	309
	George McLean	76	73	82	78	309
	Hugh Roberts	79	82	74	74	309
	JH Taylor	80	80	75	74	309

* Jock Hutchison (150) beat Roger Wethered (159) in the 36-Hole Play-off

Round Leader(s)
R1 Hutchison; 72
R2 Hutchison; 147
R3 Barnes, Herd; 222

Lowest Scores
R2 Williamson; 71
R3 Boomer, Hagen, Kerrigan, Wethered; 72
R4 Hutchison; 70

21–22 July	**1921**

US OPEN

Columbia CC, Chevy Chase, Maryland
6380 yards _PAR 70 (280)_

26 September – 1 October	**1921**

US PGA

Inwood CC, Far Rockaway, New York

Jim Barnes won his 3rd Major in collecting the Open Championship for the only time. He increased his lead in every round and stretched away to win by 9 shots - but still 2 short of Willie Smith's 1899 record. It is still the greatest margin of victory in the Open this century, and in any Major, it has only been matched by Jack Nicklaus at the 1965 Masters, and bettered by Tiger Woods (12 strokes) at Augusta in 1997, over the same period.

1	**JIM BARNES** ($500)	69	75	73	72	289
2=	Walter Hagen	79	73	72	74	298
	Fred McLeod	74	74	76	74	298
4	Charles Evans, Jr (a)	73	78	76	75	302
5=	Emmett French	75	77	74	77	303
	Bobby Jones (a)	78	71	77	77	303
	Alex Smith	75	75	79	74	303
8=	George Duncan	72	78	78	77	305
	Clarence Hackney	74	76	78	77	305
10	Emil Loeffler	74	77	74	81	306
11	Alfred Hackbarth	80	76	82	69	307
12	Eddie Loos	76	79	75	78	308
13	Cyril Walker	78	76	76	79	309
14=	Mike Brady	77	80	78	75	310
	Jess Sweetser (a)	78	78	77	77	310
	Louis Tellier	76	74	78	82	310
17	Gene Sarazen	83	74	77	77	311
18=	Laurie Ayton, Sr	81	74	74	83	312
	Jock Hutchison	75	83	77	77	312
	Peter O'Hara	81	82	76	73	312
21	Charles Murray	75	73	82	83	313
22=	John Golden	77	77	82	78	314
	Otto Hackbarth	79	76	80	79	314
	Harry Hampton	80	78	79	77	314
	Charles Mothersole	81	78	79	76	314
26=	Tom Boyd	81	79	79	76	315
	Bobby Cruickshank	75	77	80	83	315
	Leo Diegel	75	82	83	75	315
	Jesse Guilford (a)	79	75	78	83	315
30=	PO Hart	83	80	76	77	316
	Pat O'Hara	77	78	79	82	316

Round Leader(s)
R1 Barnes; 69
R2 Barnes; 144
R3 Barnes; 217
Lowest Scores
R2 Jones; 71
R3 Hagen; 72
R4 A Hackbarth; 69

Field selected from the Top 31 PGA available finishers in the 1921 US Open plus the defending champion (Jock Hutchison)
All Rounds 36 holes

Inwood CC was to become the first host to two different Majors when it also welcomed the US Open in 1923. Hagen's first matchplay Major win prefaced a phenomenal run in the middle of the decade. British Open Champion and defending PGA Champion, Jock Hutchison, was beaten by a 19 year-old – Gene Sarazen.

FINAL
WALTER HAGEN ($500)
beat
JIM BARNES, 3&2

Round by Round Details

ROUND 1 (Last 32)
Fred McLeod bt Fred Canausa 1up (after 37); Jack Gordon bt Bill Leach 8&7; Bobby Cruickshank bt Charlie Thom 4&3; JIM BARNES bt Clarence Hackney 3&2; George McLean bt Tom Kerrigan 2&1; Jimmy West bt Jack Pirie 1up (after 37); Charles Clarke bt Peter O'Hara 1up; Emmett French bt Joe Sylvester 8&7; Cyril Walker bt Emil Loeffler 1up (after 37); Charles Mothersole bt Johnny Farrell 1up (after 40); Gene Sarazen bt Harry Hampton 4&3; Jock Hutchison bt Pat O'Hara 1up (after 39); Tom Boyd bt Eddie Towns (default); WALTER HAGEN bt Jack Forrester 6&4; Laurie Ayton, Sr bt TJ Rajoppi 7&6; John Golden bt Robert Barnett 5&3

ROUND 2 (Last 16)
McLeod bt Gordon 4&2
BARNES bt Cruickshank 8&7
McLean bt West 8&7
French bt Clarke 8&7
Walker bt Mothersole 4&2
Sarazen bt Hutchison 8&7
HAGEN bt Boyd 6&5
Golden bt Ayton 1up

QUARTER FINAL (QF)
BARNES bt McLeod 11&9
French bt McLean 5&3
Walker bt Sarazen 5&4
HAGEN bt Golden 8&7

SEMI FINAL (SF)
BARNES bt French 5&4
HAGEN bt Walker 5&4

1922

22–23 June

BRITISH OPEN

Royal & Ancient GC, St Andrews, Fife, Scotland
6616 yards

Hagen's win meant he became the first person to take all three Majors. The Open at Sandwich was his 4th Major in a career haul of 11 – second only in the all-time lists after Jack Nicklaus - and all were achieved in the pre-Masters era.

1	**WALTER HAGEN** (£75)	76	73	79	72	300
2=	Jim Barnes	75	76	77	73	301
	George Duncan	76	75	81	69	301
4	Jock Hutchison	79	74	73	76	302
5	Charles Whitcombe	77	79	72	75	303
6	JH Taylor	73	78	76	77	304
7	Jean Gassiat	75	78	74	79	306
8=	Harry Vardon	79	79	74	75	307
	Thomas Walton	75	78	77	77	307
10	Percy Alliss	75	78	78	77	308
11	Charles Johns	78	76	80	75	309
12=	George Gadd	76	81	76	77	310
	Arthur Havers	78	80	78	74	310
	Len Holland	79	81	74	76	310
	FC Jewell	75	80	78	77	310
	Ernest R Whitcombe	77	78	77	78	310
17=	Aubrey Boomer	75	80	76	80	311
	Dick Wheildon	80	80	76	75	311
18	Abe Mitchell	79	79	78	76	312
19=	Joe Kirkwood, Sr	79	76	80	78	313
	Herbert Osborne	80	81	76	76	313
	Michael Scott (a)	77	83	79	74	313
22=	Willie Hunter Jr (a)	77	81	75	81	314
	Tom King, Sr	83	78	78	75	314
	W Pursey	77	81	80	76	314
	William B Smith	81	78	74	81	314
26	Archie Compston	81	79	75	80	315
27=	Gus Faulkner	74	81	80	81	316
	Arthur Monk	80	78	78	80	316
	William Watt	82	78	79	77	316
	Tom Williamson	83	77	75	81	316

Round Leaders
R1 Ted Ray (46), Taylor; 73
R2 Hagen; 149
R3 Hutchison; 226
Lowest Scores
R2 Hagen; 73
R3 Whitcombe; 72
R4 Duncan; 69

| 14–15 July | **1922** | 12–18 August | **1922** |

US OPEN
Skokie CC, Glencoe, Illinois
6563 yards PAR 70 (280)

US PGA
Oakmont CC, Oakmont, Pennsylvania

Gene Sarazen's long and glittering Majors career really began here at Skokie CC. His final round 68 took him from 5th place and 4 shots adrift after R3, to his first Open title. Little-known Scottish emigrant, John Black, needed two pars to tie and didn't get them. British Open Champion, Walter Hagen, threatened with a record-equalling 68 in R1 and was in the hunt until the last few holes. Admission was charged for the first time.

1	**GENE SARAZEN**	72	73	75	68	288
	($500)					
2=	John Black	71	71	75	72	289
	Bobby Jones (a)	74	72	70	73	289
4	Bill Mehlhorn	73	71	72	74	290
5	Walter Hagen	68	77	74	72	291
6	George Duncan	76	73	75	72	296
7	Leo Diegel	77	76	73	71	297
8=	Mike Brady	73	75	74	76	298
	John Golden	73	77	77	71	298
	Jock Hutchison	78	74	71	75	298
11=	Laurie Ayton, Sr	72	76	78	73	299
	Johnny Farrell	73	76	75	75	299
13=	Joe Kirkwood, Sr	77	74	75	74	300
	Bob MacDonald	73	76	75	76	300
15	Eddie Loos	75	76	73	77	301
16	Charles Evans, Jr (a)	72	76	74	80	302
17=	George Hackney	74	78	74	77	303
	Abe Mitchell	79	75	76	73	303
19=	Emmett French	76	74	77	78	305
	Jesse Guilford (a)	74	77	76	78	305
	Harry Hampton	76	75	77	77	305
	Charles Hoffner	79	76	77	73	305
	Willie Ogg	79	72	78	76	305
24=	Jim Barnes	74	75	77	80	306
	Cyril Hughes	81	74	77	74	306
	Willie Hunter Jr (a)	75	75	76	80	306
	Fred Wright Jr (a)	76	77	73	80	306
28=	Jack Burke, Sr	76	77	81	73	307
	Bobby Cruickshank	82	74	74	77	307
	Lloyd Gullickson	77	70	83	77	307

Round Leader(s)
R1 Hagen; 68
R2 Black; 142
R3 Jones, Mehlhorn; 216
Lowest Scores
R1 Gullickson; 70
R3 Jones; 70
R4 Sarazen; 68

MATCHPLAY
64 qualifiers from strokeplay
Rs 1&2,18 holes; QF, SF, F, 36 holes

Although both Jock Hutchison and Walter Hagen had been reigning PGA Champions when they respectively won the 1921 and 1922 British Opens, Gene Sarazen was the first to win two Majors in the same season. He had become US Open Champion only a month earlier. Hagen missed his opportunity due to other engagements.

FINAL
GENE SARAZEN ($500)
beat
EMMETT FRENCH, 1up

Round by Round Details

ROUND 2 (Last 32)
Francis Gallett bt Fred Brand 5&4; Bobby Cruickshank bt Al Watrous 3&2; Jack Burgess bt Peter Walsh 3&2; Charles Rowe bt Tom Boyd 3&1; Frank Sprogell bt Dan Kenny 4&3; GENE SARAZEN bt Willie Ogg 2&1; Jock Hutchison bt Dan Goss 6&4; Harry Hampton bt Charles Hoffner 3&2; Tom Kerrigan bt Charles Hilgendorf 5&4; Johnny Farrell bt Jim Barnes 1up; John Golden bt PJ Gaudin 8&7; Al Ciuci bt George Stark 4&2; Emil Loeffler bt Dave Robertson 4&3; Eddie Towns bt Matt Duffy 1up; RS Miner bt Fred Baroni 1up (after 19); EMMETT FRENCH bt Mike Brady 3&1

ROUND 3 (Last 16)
Cruickshank bt Gallett 7&6
Rowe bt Burgess 6&5
SARAZEN bt Sprogell 9&7
Hutchison bt Hampton 4&3
Kerrigan bt Farrell 4&3
Golden bt Ciuci 3&2
Loeffler bt Towns 3&1
FRENCH by Miner 8&7

QUARTER FINAL (QF)
Cruickshank bt Rowe 3&2
SARAZEN bt Hutchison 3&1
Golden bt Kerrigan 4&3
FRENCH bt Loeffler 4&2

SEMI FINAL (SF)
SARAZEN bt Cruickshank 3&2
FRENCH bt Golden 8&7

1923
14–15 June

BRITISH OPEN
Troon GC, Ayrshire, Scotland
6415 yards

For Royal Cinque Ports, read the not yet 'Royal' Troon. Troon, along with Royal Lytham in 1925 and Carnoustie in 1931 pulled the centre of gravity further north again, with Sandwich henceforward being the only Open host site in southern England. 20 year-old Arthur Havers held off a clutch of mighty Americans to be the last English winner until Henry Cotton's first win in 1934.

1	**ARTHUR HAVERS** (£75)	73	73	73	76	295
2	Walter Hagen	76	71	74	75	296
3	Macdonald Smith	80	73	69	75	297
4	Joe Kirkwood, Sr	72	79	69	78	298
5	Tom Fernie	73	78	74	75	300
6=	George Duncan	79	75	74	74	302
	Charles Whitcombe	70	76	74	82	302
8=	Herbert Jolly	79	75	75	74	303
	JH Mackenzie	76	78	74	75	303
	Abe Mitchell	77	77	72	77	303
	William Watt	76	77	72	78	303
12=	Gordon Lockhart	78	71	76	79	304
	Ted Ray	79	75	73	77	304
	Tom Williamson	79	78	73	74	304
	Sydney Wingate	80	75	74	75	304
16=	Frank Ball	76	77	77	75	305
	Tom Barber	78	80	76	71	305
	Fred Collins	76	78	72	79	305
19=	Johnny Farrell	79	73	75	79	306
	Angel de la Torre	78	80	74	74	306
	Thomas Walton	77	74	78	77	306
22=	Sid Brews	77	76	72	82	307
	Sandy Herd	82	75	74	76	307
	R Scott, Jr (a)	74	76	79	78	307
25=	Leo Diegel	80	80	73	75	308
	Len Holland	81	75	73	79	308
	FC Jewell	80	78	70	80	308
	James Ockenden	78	79	75	76	308
29=	George Gadd	78	76	79	76	309
	JW Gaudin	80	79	76	74	309
	Fred Robson	82	78	74	75	309
	Reg Wilson	78	77	75	79	309

Round Leader(s)
R1   Whitcombe; 70
R2   Havers, Whitcombe; 146
R3   Havers; 219
Lowest Scores
R2   Hagen, Lockhart; 71
R3   Kirkwood, Smith; 69
R4   Barber; 71

13–15 July	**1923**

US OPEN

Inwood CC, Inwood, New York
6532 yards _PAR 72 (288)_

Robert Tyre Jones, Jr – Bobby Jones – one of the very few immortals of golf, won the first of his seven Majors at Inwood. He had retired before the Masters era and was excluded from the PGA, so all his Majors were Opens (4 US and 3 British). At that time, the Amateur Championships were considered 'Majors' too of their type, and Jones collected 5 US and one British. All this between 1923 and 1930. Wee Bobby Cruickshank was one of the greatest players never to win a Major – so there is some irony in his losing to Jones in a play-off for the latter's first of many titles.

1	**BOBBY JONES***	71	73	76	76	296
	(Amateur)					
2	Bobby Cruickshank	73	72	78	73	296
3	Jock Hutchison	70	72	82	78	302
4	Jack Forrester	75	73	77	78	303
5=	Johnny Farrell	76	77	75	76	304
	Francis Gallett	76	72	77	79	304
	WM Reekie (a)	80	74	75	75	304
8=	Leo Diegel	77	77	76	76	306
	Bill Mehlhorn	73	79	75	79	306
	Al Watrous	74	75	76	81	306
11	Cyril Hughes	74	76	80	77	307
12=	Jim Barnes	78	81	74	75	308
	Joe Kirkwood, Sr	77	77	79	75	308
14=	Charles Evans, Jr (a)	79	80	76	74	309
	Joe Turnesa	76	81	74	78	309
16=	Charles Mothersole	77	80	71	82	310
	Gene Sarazen	79	78	73	80	310
18=	Walter Hagen	77	75	73	86	311
	Willie Ogg	74	76	80	81	311
20=	Mike Brady	74	81	76	81	312
	Macdonald Smith	77	76	81	78	312
22	Emmett French	79	78	77	79	313
23	Cyril Walker	76	78	80	80	314
24=	PO Hart	79	80	78	78	315
	Joe Sylvester	77	80	79	79	315
26=	John Black	82	76	78	80	316
	William Creavy	73	81	77	85	316
	Eddie Held (a)	80	75	79	82	316
29=	Hutt Martin	78	78	76	85	317
	Francis Ouimet (a)	82	75	78	82	317
	George Sargent	77	77	81	82	317

*Bobby Jones (76) beat Bobby Cruickshank (78) in the 18-Hole Play-off

Round Leader(s)
R1   Hutchison; 70
R2   Hutchison; 142
R3   Jones; 220

Lowest Scores
R2   Cruickshank, Gallett, Hutchison; 72
R3   Mothersole; 71
R4   Cruickshank; 73

23–29 September	**1923**

US PGA

Pelham GC, Pelham Manor, New York

MATCHPLAY
64 qualifiers from strokeplay
All Rounds 36 holes

Sarazen made it two PGAs in a row, but this time Hagen was there to compete. The two met in the final when their gargantuan battle only ended at the second extra hole. Hagen had clawed back three strokes on the final back nine to take it to sudden-death and must have thought he'd won when Sarazen's tee-shot at the 38th ended up in thick rough. Sarazen, however, hacked out to within 2 feet of the pin, while an amazed Hagen bunkered his approach.

FINAL
GENE SARAZEN ($ not available)
beat
WALTER HAGEN, 1up (after 38)

Round by Round Details

ROUND 2 (Last 32)
Bobby Cruickshank bt Herbert Obendorf 7&5; Ray Derr bt Frank Coltart 5&4; Willie MacFarlane bt Wilfred Reid 3&2; Jack Stait bt Jack Forrester 1up; Jim Barnes bt John Cowan 12&11; Cyril Walker bt Harry Cooper 2&1; Alex Campbell bt Willie Klein 4&3; GENE SARAZEN bt DK White 11&10; Clarence Hackney bt RS Miner 7&6; Fred McLeod bt James Meehan 4&3; WALTER HAGEN bt Jack Elplick 10&9; John Golden bt Robert Barnett 1up; Joe Kirkwood, Sr bt Jimmy West 2up; Johnny Farrell bt Willie Hunter, Jr 4&3; George McLean bt Jimmie Donaldson 6&4; Willie Ogg bt Carl Anderson 12&11

ROUND 3 (Last 16)
Cruickshank bt Derr 1up
MacFarlane bt Stait 5&4
Barnes bt Walker 8&7
SARAZEN bt Campbell 3&2
McLeod bt Hackney 1up
HAGEN bt Golden 4&3
Kirkwood bt Farrell 1up
McLean bt Ogg 1up (after 38)

QUARTER FINAL (QF)
Cruickshank bt MacFarlane 1up (after 39)
SARAZEN bt Barnes 1up
HAGEN bt Mcleod 5&4
McLean bt Kirkwood 5&4

SEMI FINAL (SF)
SARAZEN bt Cruickshank 6&5
HAGEN bt McLean 12&11

1924

5–6 June

US OPEN

Oakland Hills CC, Birmingham, Michigan
PAR 72 (288)

Regional qualifying (East and West) took place for the first time with the lowest 40 and ties making it to R1. Another 'first' was that steel-shafted putters were allowed. Cyril Walker was the rather surprising winner, his past form in the British Open before he emigrated not suggesting he could best a field which included the likes of Hagen, Jones, Sarazen and MacDonald Smith.

1	**CYRIL WALKER** ($500)	74	74	74	75	297
2	Bobby Jones (a)	74	73	75	78	300
3	Bill Mehlhorn	72	75	76	78	301
4=	Bobby Cruickshank	77	72	76	78	303
	Walter Hagen	75	75	76	77	303
	Macdonald Smith	78	72	77	76	303
7=	Abe Espinosa	80	71	77	77	305
	Peter O'Hara	76	79	74	76	305
9	Mike Brady	75	77	77	77	306
10=	Charles Evans, Jr (a)	77	77	76	77	307
	Eddie Loos	73	81	75	78	307
	Dave Robertson	73	76	77	81	307
13=	Tommy Armour	78	76	75	80	309
	Clarence Hackney	81	72	78	78	309
15=	Willie Ogg	75	80	76	79	310
	Joe Turnesa	76	78	78	78	310
17=	Walter Bourne	78	76	79	80	313
	Gene Sarazen	74	80	80	79	313
19=	Johnny Farrell	79	76	77	82	314
	Tom Kerrigan	77	74	89	74	314
	Jock Rogers	82	77	77	78	314
22=	Emmett French	79	79	78	79	315
	Joe Kirkwood, Sr	77	80	80	78	315
	James West	81	72	78	84	315
25=	Laurie Ayton, Sr	77	79	84	86	316
	Leo Diegel	78	78	82	78	316
	John Golden	75	83	78	80	316
25=	Jack Stait	79	77	81	79	316
29=	Wiffy Cox	82	76	81	78	317
	Jesse Guilford (a)	80	78	79	80	317

Round Leader(s)
R1 Mehlhorn; 72
R2 Jones, Mehlhorn; 147
R3 Jones, Walker; 222
Lowest Scores
R2 Espinosa; 71
R3 Jock Hutchison (31), O'Hara, Walker; 74
R4 Kerrigan; 74

26–27 June	**1924**
BRITISH OPEN	
Royal Liverpool GC, Hoylake, Cheshire, England	
6750 yards	

15–20 September	**1924**
US PGA	
French Springs, French Lick, Indiana	

Hagen's 2nd Open out of four he was to claim during the '20s was a tight affair. In a high-scoring last round he edged out Ernest Whitcombe – one of the three famous golfing brothers. Bobby Jones didn't compete – and it is worth considering, that for all Hagen's successes in the Opens, he never once won when Jones was in the field.

1	**WALTER HAGEN** (£75)	77	73	74	77	301
2	Ernest R Whitcombe	77	70	77	78	302
3=	Frank Ball	78	75	74	77	304
	Macdonald Smith	76	74	77	77	304
5	JH Taylor	75	74	79	79	307
6=	Aubrey Boomer	75	78	76	79	308
	George Duncan	74	79	74	81	308
	Len Holland	74	78	78	78	308
9=	JM Barber	78	77	79	75	309
	George Gadd	79	75	78	77	309
	James Sherlock	76	75	78	80	309
	Percy Weston	76	77	77	79	309
13=	Sandy Herd	76	79	76	79	310
	Gilbert Nicholls	75	78	79	78	310
	Tom Williamson	79	76	80	75	310
16=	JW Gaudin	79	78	80	76	313
	Charles Johns	77	77	78	81	313
18=	James Braid	80	80	78	76	314
	Albert Tingey, Jr	82	81	76	75	314
	Cyril Tolley (a)	73	82	80	79	314
21=	Archie Compston	79	81	76	79	315
	BS Weastell	76	82	78	79	315
23=	Arthur Butchart	82	75	77	82	316
	Rowland Jones	80	73	82	81	316
	Fred Leach	78	74	86	78	316
	William Robertson	84	75	77	80	316
	Fred Robson	83	80	77	76	316
	Sydney Wingate	79	79	82	76	316
29=	Arthur Havers	79	77	86	75	317
	Mark Seymour	74	81	80	82	317

Round Leader(s)
R1 Tolley; 73
R2 Whitcombe; 147
R3 Hagen, Whitcombe; 224
Lowest Scores
R2 Whitcombe; 70
R3 Ball, Duncan, Hagen; 74
R4 Barber, Havers, HJ Osborne (31), Tingey, Williamson; 75

MATCHPLAY
32 qualifiers after 36 holes strokeplay (Low - Johnny Farrell, 140)
All Rounds 36 holes

It was Hagen's turn again, in a repeat of the 1921 final. He became the first golfer to hold the British Open and one other Major in the same season, and his win record in Majors between 1919 and 1929 reads: 1919, USOP; 1921, PGA; 1922, BOP; 1924, BOP & PGA; 1925, PGA; 1926, PGA; 1927, PGA; 1928, BOP; 1929, BOP.

FINAL
WALTER HAGEN ($ not available)
beat
JIM BARNES, 2up

Round by Round Details

ROUND 1 (Last 32)
Willie MacFarlane bt George Dow 5&4; Johnny Farrell bt Neil Christian 2&1; Al Watrous bt George Aulbach 3&1; WALTER HAGEN bt Tom Harmon, Jr 6&5; Al Espinosa bt Arthur Ham 4&2; Francis Gallett bt Bill Mehlhorn 4&3; Bobby Cruickshank bt Willie Ogg 7&5; Ray Derr bt Harry Hampton 2up; Henry Ciuci bt Charles Hoffner 4&2; Dan Williams bt Fred Baroni 4&2; Gene Sarazen bt Fred McLeod 5&4; Larry Nabholtz bt Jack Forrester 1up; Mortie Dutra bt Leo Diegel 3&1; Emmett French bt Jock Robertson 6&4; Jim Barnes bt Mike Brady 1up (after 39); Eddie Towns bt Jock Hutchison 4&3

ROUND 2 (Last 16)
Farrell bt MacFarlane 2&1
HAGEN bt Watrous 4&3
Espinosa bt Gallett 4&3
Derr br Cruickshank 2&1
Ciuci bt Williams 4&3
Nabholtz bt Sarazen 2&1
French bt Dutra 3&1
BARNES bt Towns 10&9

QUARTER FINAL (QF)
HAGEN bt Farrell 3&2
Derr bt Espinosa 2&1
Nabholtz bt Ciuci 5&4
BARNES bt French 6&4

SEMI FINAL (SF)
HAGEN bt Derr 8&7
BARNES bt Nabholtz 1up

1925

3–5 June

US OPEN

Worcester CC, Worcester, Massachusetts
6430 yards _PAR 71 (284)_

The era of Scottish-born US Open Champions, and indeed Major winners in general, was just coming to an end. Willie MacFarlane, from Aberdeen, tied with Bob Jones – and tied again on 75 in the first 18-hole play-off. Jones uncharacteristically threw away a 4-stroke lead in the second play-off, to allow MacFarlane to come home in 72, and beat him by one. Earlier, in R2, MacFarlane set a new low score of 67.

I	**W MACFARLANE*** ($500)	74	67	72	78	291
2	Bobby Jones (a)	77	70	70	74	291
3=	Johnny Farrell	71	74	69	78	292
	Francis Ouimet (a)	70	73	73	76	292
5=	Walter Hagen	72	76	71	74	293
	Gene Sarazen	72	72	75	74	293
7	Mike Brady	74	72	74	74	294
8	Leo Diegel	73	68	77	78	296
9=	Laurie Ayton, Sr	75	71	73	78	297
	Al Espinosa	72	71	74	80	297
11=	Macdonald Smith	73	79	72	75	299
	Joe Turnesa	76	74	71	78	299
13=	Willie Hunter, Jr	75	77	75	73	300
	Al Watrous	78	73	74	75	300
15=	Bob MacDonald	75	77	77	72	301
	Bill Mehlhorn	78	72	75	76	301
17	Clarence Hackney	78	72	73	79	302
18=	John Golden	76	75	82	70	303
	Tom Kerrigan	75	79	74	75	303
20=	Tom Boyd	73	79	75	77	304
	Jack Forrester	71	76	76	81	304
	Emmett French	77	74	77	76	304
	Francis Gallett	73	70	84	77	304
	Harry Hampton	79	75	76	74	304
	Bob Shave	81	72	77	74	304
26	Charles Mayo	75	74	78	78	305
27=	Jock Hutchison	78	78	79	71	306
	Wilfred Reid	79	75	73	79	306
29=	Jim Barnes	75	76	71	85	307
	George Heron	75	77	77	78	307

*Willie MacFarlane (75,72) beat Bobby Jones (75, 73) after the Second 18-Hole Play-off

Round Leader(s)
R1   Ouimet; 70
R2   MacFarlane; 141
R3   MacFarlane; 213
Lowest Scores
R2   MacFarlane; 67
R3   Farrell; 69
R4   Golden; 70

| 24–26 June | **1925** | 21–26 September | **1925** |

BRITISH OPEN

Prestwick GC, Ayrshire, Scotland
6444 yards

Jim Barnes took his fourth Major title – he had already won the first 2 PGAs (1916 & 1919) and collected the US Open in 1921. He thus followed Walter Hagen's feat of winning all the contemporary Major Championships. Barnes' win – ahead of 48 year-old Ted Ray, and rising British hope, Compston – was in the last Open to be played at historic Prestwick, where of the 13 Championships held there between 1860 and 1875, the Morrisses and Willie Park had won a dozen.

1	**JIM BARNES** (£75)	70	77	79	74	300
2=	Archie Compston	76	75	75	75	301
	Ted Ray	77	76	75	73	301
3	Macdonald Smith	76	69	76	82	303
4	Abe Mitchell	77	76	75	77	305
5=	Percy Alliss	77	80	77	76	310
	Bill Davies	76	76	80	78	310
	JW Gaudin	78	81	77	74	310
	JH Taylor	74	79	80	77	310
	Sydney Wingate	74	78	80	78	310
10=	Robert Harris (a)	75	81	78	77	311
	Fred Robson	80	77	78	76	311
12	HA Gaudin	76	79	77	80	312
13=	Tom Fernie	78	74	77	85	314
	Sandy Herd	76	79	82	77	314
	Joe Kirkwood, Sr	83	79	76	76	314
16=	JI Cruickshank (a)	80	78	82	75	315
	Jack Smith	75	78	82	80	315
	Harry Vardon	79	80	77	79	315
19=	Arthur Havers	77	80	80	79	316
	Duncan McCulloch	76	77	84	79	316
	James Ockenden	80	78	80	78	316
	Reg Whitcombe	81	80	79	76	316
23=	Frank Ball	76	78	81	82	317
	Dick May	82	77	78	80	317
25=	Aubrey Boomer	79	82	76	81	318
	Ernest R Whitcombe	81	83	77	77	318
27=	James Adwick	81	77	82	80	320
	George Duncan	79	77	83	81	320
	Cedric Sayner	83	80	78	79	320
	Cyril Tolley (a)	82	81	78	79	320

Round Leader(s)
R1   Barnes; 70
R2   M Smith; 145
R3   M Smith; 221
Lowest Scores
R2   M Smith; 69
R3   Compston, Mitchell, Ray; 75
R4   Ray; 73

US PGA

Olympia Fields CC, Olympia Fields, Illinois

MATCHPLAY
32 qualifiers after 36 holes strokeplay (Low - Al Watrous, 140)
All Rounds 36 holes

Although convincingly beating 'Wild Bill' Mehlhorn in the final, Walter Hagen's 3rd PGA win in 1925 was not without a fright or two along the way, when he was taken into extra holes by Al Watrous and Leo Diegel. Having seen Jim Barnes match a record of his when Barnes won the British Open in June, Hagen now equalled Barnes' (and Sarazen's) feat of back-to-back PGA titles.

FINAL
WALTER HAGEN ($ not available)
beat
BILL MEHLHORN, 6&5

Round by Round Details

ROUND 1 (Last 32)
WALTER HAGEN bt Al Watrous 1 up (after 39); Mike Brady bt JS Collins 10&9; Leo Diegel bt Laurie Ayton, Sr 2&1; Bobby Cruickshank bt Bill Leach 4&3; Harry Cooper bt Jack Blakeslee 7&6; Jack Burke, Sr bt Gene Sarazen 8&7; Johnny Farrell bt William Creavy 6&4; Ray Derr bt Abe Espinosa 4&3; BILL MEHLHORN bt Emmett French 5&4; Al Espinosa bt George Howard 5&3; Tom Kerrigan bt George Smith 5&3; Dan Williams bt Charles Hoffner 4&3; Motrie Dutra bt Willie Ogg 2&1; Ed Dudley bt Mike Patton 3&2; Tommy Armour bt George Griffin 3&1; John Golden bt Dave Robertson 9&8

ROUND 2 (Last 16)
HAGEN bt Brady 7&6
Diegel bt Cruickshank 2&1
Cooper bt Burke 2&1
Farrell bt Derr 1 up (after 37)
MEHLHORN bt Al Espinosa 1 up
Kerrigan bt Williams 2 up
Dutra bt Dudley 6&5
Armour bt Golden 6&5

QUARTER FINAL (QF)
HAGEN bt Diegel 1 up (after 40)
Cooper bt Farrell 2&1
MEHLHORN bt Kerrigan 7&6
Dutra bt Armour 2 up

SEMI FINAL (SF)
HAGEN bt Cooper 3&1
MEHLHORN bt Dutra 8&6

1926
BRITISH OPEN
22–24 June

Royal Lytham and St Anne's GC, Lancashire, England
6456 yards

With sectional qualifying and expanding the competition over 3 days, the Opens were beginning to think in unison – except on the question of the calendar. This year, the British Open preceded its US counterpart once more. The Lancashire links of Royal Lytham were hosting the Championship for the first time – and Bobby Jones won for the first time. He was the first amateur to win since Harold Hilton in 1897.

1	**BOBBY JONES** (Amateur)	72	72	73	74	291
2	Al Watrous	71	75	69	78	293
3=	Walter Hagen	68	77	74	76	295
	George Von Elm (a)	75	72	76	72	295
5=	Tom Barber	77	73	78	71	299
	Abe Mitchell	78	78	72	71	299
7	Fred McLeod	71	75	76	79	301
8=	Emmett French	76	75	74	78	303
	Jose Jurado	77	76	74	76	303
	Bill Mehlhorn	70	74	79	80	303
10=	HA Gaudin	78	78	71	77	304
	JH Taylor	75	78	71	80	304
12	Tommy Armour	74	76	75	80	305
13=	WL Hartley (a)	74	77	79	76	306
	Harry Walker	74	77	78	77	306
	Reg Whitcombe	73	82	76	75	306
	Tom Williamson	78	76	76	76	306
17=	Jim Barnes	77	80	72	78	307
	Fred Robson	79	76	77	75	307
	Cyril Walker	79	71	80	77	307
20=	George Duncan	75	79	80	74	308
	Sandy Herd	81	76	75	76	308
21	Herbert Jolly	79	76	79	75	309
22=	Edward Douglas	79	78	75	78	310
	George Gadd	80	71	78	81	310
	Joe Kirkwood, Sr	81	76	78	75	310
	Charles Whitcombe	79	78	75	78	310
26=	James Braid	82	75	75	79	311
	Arthur Havers	75	76	82	78	311
28=	Fred Boobyer	79	79	80	74	312
	Charles Corlett	77	80	76	79	312
	Jean Gassiat	78	78	79	77	312
	J MacDowell	75	82	75	80	312
	Ted Ray	78	80	74	80	312

Round Leader(s)
R1   Hagen; 68
R2   Jones, Mehlhorn; 144
R3   Watrous; 215
Lowest Scores
R2   Gadd, Walker; 71
R3   Watrous; 69
R4   Barber, Mitchell; 71

8–10 July					**1926**

US OPEN

Scioto CC, Columbus, Ohio
PAR 72 (288)

Returning to the States, Jones picked up his 2nd Major in succession, and became the first player to win both Opens in the same year. Joe Turnesa's 2nd place was to start a runner's-up jinx over many years – on him and his brothers, Mike and Jim, until Jim broke it by picking up the 1952 PGA.

1	**BOBBY JONES** (Amateur)	70	79	71	73	293
2	Joe Turnesa	71	74	72	77	294
3=	Leo Diegel	72	76	75	74	297
	Johnny Farrell	76	79	69	73	297
	Bill Mehlhorn	68	75	76	78	297
	Gene Sarazen	78	77	72	70	297
7	Walter Hagen	73	77	74	74	298
8	Willie Hunter, Jr	75	77	69	79	300
9=	Tommy Armour	76	76	74	75	301
	Willie Klein	76	74	75	76	301
	Macdonald Smith	82	76	68	75	301
	Dan Williams	72	74	80	75	301
13=	Al Espinosa	71	79	78	74	302
	Charles Evans, Jr (a)	75	75	73	79	302
	Jack Forrester	76	73	77	76	302
16=	Laurie Ayton, Sr	76	78	76	76	306
	Mike Brady	77	82	76	71	306
	George McLean	74	74	79	79	306
	Jimmy Thomson	77	82	73	74	306
20=	Willie MacFarlane	72	79	75	81	307
	Jock Rogers	80	79	75	73	307
22	Clarence Hackney	77	77	74	80	308
23=	Arthur De Mane	76	80	78	75	309
	PO Hart	76	81	76	76	309
	Harrison Johnston (a)	79	76	77	77	309
	Tom Stevens	79	78	76	76	309
27=	Emmett French	74	79	76	81	310
	Harry Hampton	81	75	78	76	310
	Tom Harmon, Jr	73	81	76	80	310
	Bob MacDonald	77	79	77	77	310
	Eddie Murphy	74	77	80	79	310

Round Leader(s)
R1   Mehlhorn; 68
R2   Mehlhorn; 143
R3   Ternesa; 217
Lowest Scores
R2   Forrester; 73
R3   Smith; 68
R4   Sarazen; 70

20–25 September	**1926**

US PGA

Salisbury GL, Westbury, Long Island, New York

MATCHPLAY
32 qualifiers after 36 holes strokeplay (Low - Walter Hagen, 140)
All Rounds 36 holes

Bobby Jones may have been having all his own way in the Opens, but in matchplay, Walter Hagen was peerless during the mid-'20s. If Jones was elegible to compete in the PGA, it would have been a very mouth-watering prospect to contemplate he and Hagen head-to-head. As it was, in 1926, the 'Haig' demolished the opposition round-by-round to take his 4th PGA – and the 3rd in succession.

FINAL
WALTER HAGEN ($ not available)
beat
LEO DIEGEL, 5&3

Round by Round Details

ROUND 1 (Last 32)
Marshall Crichton bt Francis Gallett 1up; Pat Doyle bt Willie Maguire 2&1; Dick Grout bt Jock Hendry 4&3; WALTER HAGEN bt Joe Turnesa 3&2; Dick Linnars bt Fred McLeod 5&4; Johnny Farrell bt Al Watrous 6&5; Harry Hampton bt Larry Nabholtz 6&5; Tom Harmon, Jr bt Al Espinosa 6&4; Abe Espinosa bt Gunnar Nelson 7&6; Mike Brady bt George Aulbach 1up (after 37); LEO DIEGEL bt Mike Patton 8&7; Neal McIntyre bt Bobby Cruickshank 4&2; John Golden bt Harry Cooper 5&3; Gene Sarazen bt Jim Barnes 5&4; Bill Leach bt Laurie Ayton, Sr 3&2; George Christ bt Leo Shea 3&2

ROUND 2 (Last 16)
Doyle by Crichton 3&2
HAGEN bt Grout 7&6
Farrell bt Linnars 6&5
Hampton bt Harmon 6&5
Abe Espinosa bt Brady 1up
DIEGEL bt McIntyre 6&5
Golden bt Sarazen 4&3
Christ bt Leach 1up (after 38)

QUARTER FINAL (QF)
HAGEN bt Doyle 6&5
Farrell bt Hampton 3&1
DIEGEL bt Abe Espinosa 3&2
Golden bt Christ 7&6

SEMI FINAL (SF)
HAGEN bt Farrell 6&5
DIEGEL bt Golden 1up

1927

14–17 June

US OPEN

Oakmont CC, Oakmont, Pennsylvania
6965 yards PAR 72 (288)

Tommy Armour won the first of his 3 Majors over the classic Oakmont parkland course. He tied 'Light Horse' Harry Cooper – another for whom a Major Championship was just beyond the grasp – and comfortably won the play-off. Armour was the last Scots-born player to win the US Open. Ted Ray, the Champion of 1920, said farewell to America at the age of 50.

1	**TOMMY ARMOUR*** ($500)	78	71	76	76	301
2	Harry Cooper	74	76	74	77	301
3	Gene Sarazen	74	74	80	74	302
4	Emmett French	75	79	77	73	304
5	Bill Mehlhorn	75	77	80	73	305
6	Walter Hagen	77	73	76	81	307
7=	Archie Compston	79	74	76	79	308
	Johnny Farrell	81	73	78	76	308
	John Golden	83	77	75	73	308
	Harry Hampton	73	78	80	77	308
11=	Bobby Cruickshank	77	78	76	78	309
	Leo Diegel	78	74	80	77	309
	Bobby Jones (a)	76	77	79	77	309
	Eddie Loos	78	75	79	77	309
15=	Fred Baroni	80	72	79	79	310
	Perry Del Vecchio	79	79	76	76	310
	Arthur Havers	79	77	74	80	310
18=	Al Espinosa	83	80	79	69	311
	Harrison Johnston (a)	73	74	87	77	311
	Willie MacFarlane	82	76	80	73	311
	Macdonald Smith	78	76	81	76	311
	Al Watrous	82	74	78	77	311
23	Jock Hutchison	80	77	77	78	312
24=	Jim Barnes	78	75	81	79	313
	PO Hart	77	77	86	73	313
	Larry Nabholtz	75	81	78	79	313
27=	Ted Ray	76	83	77	78	314
	Joe Turnesa	81	79	78	76	314
29=	Tom Harmon, Jr	79	77	80	79	315
	Bob MacDonald	77	83	78	77	315

*Tommy Armour (76) beat Harry Cooper (79) in the 18-Hole Play-off

Round Leader(s)
R1 Hampton, Johnston; 73
R2 Johnston; 147
R3 Cooper; 224
Lowest Scores
R2 Armour; 71
R3 Cooper, Havers; 74
R4 Espinosa; 69

13–15 July	**1927**	31 October–5 November	**1927**
BRITISH OPEN		**US PGA**	
Royal & Ancient GC, St Andrews, Fife, Scotland		Cedar Crest CC, Dallas, Texas	
6572 yards			

Bobby Jones continued to re-write the record books - record low score for either Open, first back-to-back British Open win for an amateur, 3rd win in row in eligible Championships (he won both Opens in 1926), and so on. St Andrews introduced a larger scoreboard for spectators – the precursor of the modern leaderboard.

1	**BOBBY JONES** (Amateur)	68	72	73	72	285
2=	Aubrey Boomer	76	70	73	72	291
	Fred Robson	76	72	69	74	291
4=	Joe Kirkwood, Sr	72	72	75	74	293
	Ernest R Whitcombe	74	73	73	73	293
6	Charles Whitcombe	74	76	71	75	296
7=	Arthur Havers	80	74	73	70	297
	Bert Hodson	72	70	81	74	297
8	Henry Cotton	73	72	77	76	298
9=	Percy Alliss	73	74	73	80	300
	Sandy Herd	76	75	78	71	300
	Phil Perkins (a)	76	78	70	76	300
	Phillip H Rodgers	76	73	74	77	300
	WB Torrance	72	80	74	74	300
	RD Vickers	75	75	77	73	300
	Tom Williamson	75	76	78	71	300
16=	Jim Barnes	76	76	72	77	301
	GR Buckle	77	69	77	78	301
	O Johns	74	78	73	76	301
19=	Donald Curtis	73	76	79	74	302
	Jean Gassiat	76	77	73	76	302
	Tom Stevens	76	73	74	79	302
22=	Archie Compston	74	78	79	72	303
	Len Holland	75	75	71	82	303
	Henry Kinch	80	73	73	77	303
	Jack Smith	81	73	73	76	303
26	Duncan McCulloch	74	77	78	75	304
27=	Chas Gadd	74	74	78	79	305
	Tom King, Jr	73	74	74	84	305
29=	James Braid	75	77	76	78	306
	W Kennett	78	75	75	78	306
	D Murray	72	78	77	79	306
	Ted Ray	78	73	77	78	306
	W Tweddell (a)	78	74	78	76	306
	William Twine	75	78	78	75	306

Round Leader(s)

R1 Jones; 68
R2 Jones; 140
R3 Jones; 213

Lowest Scores

R2 Buckle; 69
R3 Robson; 69
R4 Havers; 70

MATCHPLAY

32 qualifiers after 36 holes strokeplay (Low - Walter Hagen, 141)
All Rounds 36 holes

Hagen set his remarkable record of 4 consecutive wins in the PGA. He joined Tom Morris, Jr as the only player in history to win the same Major Championship 4 times in succession – and the only one to do it 4 years in a row ('Young' Tom won 4 British Opens between 1868 and 1872, but there was no Championship in 1871).

FINAL

WALTER HAGEN ($ not available)
beat
JOE TURNESA, 1up

Round by Round Details

ROUND 1 (Last 32)
Tommy Armour bt Johnny Farrell 4&3; Tom Harmon, Jr bt Johnny Perelli 4&3; Tony Manero bt Bobby Cruickshank 4&3; WALTER HAGEN bt Jack Farrell 3&2; Mortie Dutra bt Albert Alcroft 12&11; Charles Guest bt Roland Hancock 3&2; Al Espinosa bt Mel Smith 5&4; Harry Cooper bt Eddie Murphy 7&6; Ed Dudley bt James Gullane 8&7; Gene Sarazen by Jack Curley 1up (after 37); Willie Klein bt Bill Mehlhorn 1up; JOE TURNESA bt Charles McKenna 5&3; John Golden bt Charles Koontz 2&1; Harold Long bt Willie Kidd 4&3; Francis Gallett bt Bob Shave 4&3; Ralph Beach bt Fred Baroni 1up

ROUND 2 (Last 16)
Armour bt Harmon, Jr 7&6
HAGEN bt Manero 11&10
Dutra bt Guest 2up
Espinosa bt Cooper 5&4
Sarazen bt Dudley 4&3
TURNESA bt Klein 1up
Golden bt Long 1up (after 37)
Gallett bt Beach 2up

QUARTER FINAL (QF)
HAGEN bt Armour 4&3
Espinosa bt Dutra 1up
TURNESA bt Sarazen 3&2
Golden bt Gallett 4&2

SEMI FINAL (SF)
HAGEN bt Espinosa 1up (after 37)
TURNESA bt Golden 7&6

1928
9–11 June
BRITISH OPEN
Royal St George's, Sandwich, Kent, England
6751 yards

Walter Hagen edged away from his arch-rival pro, Gene Sarazen, over the second 36 holes to win his 2nd Open at Sandwich. He lowered his own 1922 record there by 8 strokes. In the last appearance of members of the Triumvirate among the finishers, James Braid shot a 316 to finish tied-41st and Harry Vardon tied-47th (317).

1	**WALTER HAGEN** (£75)	75	73	72	72	292
2	Gene Sarazen	72	76	73	73	294
3	Archie Compston	75	74	73	73	295
4=	Percy Alliss	75	76	75	72	298
	Fred Robson	79	73	73	73	298
6=	Jim Barnes	81	73	76	71	301
	Aubrey Boomer	79	73	77	72	301
	Jose Jurado	74	71	76	80	301
9	Bill Mehlhorn	71	78	76	77	302
10	Bill Davies	78	74	79	73	304
11=	Fred Taggart	76	74	77	78	305
	Albert Whiting	78	76	76	75	305
13	Jack Smith	79	77	76	74	306
14=	Phil Perkins (a)	80	79	76	72	307
	William Twine	75	79	77	76	307
16	Stewart Burns	76	74	75	83	308
17	CO Hezlet (a)	79	76	78	76	309
18=	Henry Cotton	77	75	83	75	310
	Duncan McCulloch	78	78	78	76	310
	George Duncan	75	77	78	80	310
21=	Abe Mitchell	78	75	82	76	311
	Tom Williamson	77	73	77	84	311
23=	Bob Bradbeer	83	76	78	75	312
	George Gadd	83	73	78	78	312
	Jean Gassiat	76	77	81	78	312
	WL Hope (a)	84	75	75	78	312
	James Ockenden	80	78	79	75	312
	Reg Whitcombe	79	77	81	75	312
	Reg Wilson	82	73	77	80	312
	Sydney Wingate	75	82	79	76	312

Round Leader(s)
R1   Mehlhorn; 71
R2   Jurado; 145
R3   Hagen; 220
Lowest Scores
R2   Jurado; 71
R3   Hagen; 72
R4   Barnes; 71

21–23 June	**1928**	1–6 October	**1928**

US OPEN
Olympia Fields CC, Matteson, Illinois
PAR 71 (284)

US PGA
Five Farms CC, Baltimore, Maryland

The number of entries had been steadily rising in all Majors, but in 1928, the 1000 mark was passed, here, at Olympia Fields near Chicago, for the first time. The Championship went to a tie once more, and although he was to win the 4th of his 5 US Amateur titles in the coming September, did Jones, as in 1925, give a glimpse of a slight weakness in matchplay golf? Willie MacFarlane beat him then: this year it was Johnny Farrell.

1	**JOHNNY FARRELL*** ($500)	77	74	71	72	294
2	Bobby Jones (a)	73	71	73	77	294
3	Roland Hancock	74	77	72	72	295
4=	Walter Hagen	75	72	73	76	296
	George Von Elm (a)	74	72	76	74	296
6=	Henry Ciuci	70	77	72	80	299
	Waldo Crowder	74	74	76	75	299
	Ed Dudley	77	79	68	75	299
	Bill Leach	72	74	73	80	299
	Gene Sarazen	78	76	73	72	299
	Denny Shute	75	73	79	72	299
	Macdonald Smith	75	77	75	72	299
	Joe Turnesa	74	77	74	74	299
14=	Al Espinosa	74	74	77	75	300
	Willie MacFarlane	73	74	73	80	300
16	Tommy Armour	76	75	77	73	301
17	Jack Forrester	77	76	75	74	302
18=	Billy Burke	74	79	73	77	303
	Neil Christian	80	78	74	71	303
	Leo Diegel	72	79	75	77	303
	Charles Hilgendorf	76	77	79	71	303
22=	Frank Ball	70	81	78	75	304
	Archie Compston	76	81	75	72	304
	Harrison Johnston (a)	77	75	79	73	304
25=	Harry Hampton	77	76	72	80	305
	Leonard Schmutte	71	81	75	78	305
27	Frank Walsh	74	74	80	78	306
28=	Willie Hunter, Jr	73	83	73	78	307
	Felix Serafin	75	76	77	79	307
	Horton Smith	72	79	76	80	307

*Johnny Farrell (143) beat Bobby Jones (144) in the 36-Hole Play-off

Round Leader(s)
R1 Ball, Ciuci; 70
R2 Jones; 144
R3 Jones; 217
Lowest Scores
R2 Craig Wood (46); 70
R3 Dudley; 68
R4 Bill Mehlhorn (49); 70

MATCHPLAY
32 qualifiers after 36 holes strokeplay (Low - Al Espinosa, 142)
All Rounds 36 holes

Leo Diegel broke Walter Hagen's 4-year run and 22 consecutive match wins when he won at the 35th hole in the quarter final. Only Gene Sarazen before that had beaten Hagen in PGA Championship matches going back to 1921. Diegel then demolished Sarazen before easily beating Al Espinosa in the final.

FINAL
LEO DIEGEL ($ not available)
beat
AL ESPINOSA, 6&5

Round by Round Details

ROUND 1 (Last 32)
Willie McFarlane beat Jim Foulis 9&7; Horton Smith bt Billy Burke 2&1; Glen Spencer bt Fred McDermott 8&6; Perry Del Vecchio bt Jack Burke, Sr 1up (after 37); AL ESPINOSA bt John Golden 8&7; Bob MacDonald bt Willie Kidd 2up; Jock Hutchison bt Willie Klein 3&2; Pat Doyle bt Mortie Dutra 6&4; Jim Barnes bt Tommy Armour 3&2; Gene Sarazen bt Bill Mehlhorn 3&2; Al Watrous bt Olin Dutra 2&1; Ed Dudley bt Wiffy Cox 3&2; George Christ bt Albert Alcroft 1up (after 38); LEO DIEGEL bt Tony Manero 10&8; Walter Hagen bt Willie Ogg 4&3; Julian Blanton bt Ed McElligott 9&8

ROUND 2 (Last 16)
Smith bt MacFarlane 1up
Del Vecchio bt Spencer 1up (after 37)
ESPINOSA by MacDonald 1up (after 37)
Hutchison bt Doyle 1up
Sarazen bt Barnes 3&2
Dudley bt Watrous 3&2
DIEGEL bt Christ 6&4
Hagen bt Blanton 2up

QUARTER FINAL (QF)
Smith bt Del Vecchio 2up
ESPINOSA bt Hutchison 5&4
Sarazen bt Dudley 7&6
DIEGEL bt Hagen 2&1

SEMI FINAL (SF)
ESPINOSA bt Smith 6&5
DIEGEL bt Sarazen 9&8

1929
8–10 May
BRITISH OPEN
Honourable Company, Muirfield, Angus, Scotland
6738 yards

Hagen repeated his 1928 victory when the first three on the leaderboard were the three reigning Majors champions from 1928. A startling record-equalling 67 in R2 and a bad R3 from Diegel made the difference, with Hagen only having to play solid golf over the last 18 to win his 4th – and last – Open. He stands, with a group of players, one behind Taylor, Braid, Peter Thomson and Tom Watson and two behind Vardon – in the list of most wins.

1	**WALTER HAGEN** (£75)	75	67	75	75	292
2	Johnny Farrell	72	75	76	75	298
3	Leo Diegel	71	69	82	77	299
4=	Percy Alliss	69	76	76	79	300
	Abe Mitchell	72	72	78	78	300
6	Bobby Cruickshank	73	74	78	76	301
7	Jim Barnes	71	80	78	74	303
8=	Gene Sarazen	73	74	81	76	304
	Al Watrous	73	79	75	77	304
10	Tommy Armour	75	73	79	78	305
11	Arthur Havers	80	74	76	76	306
12	Archie Compston	76	73	77	81	307
13=	Johnny Golden	74	73	86	75	308
	Jimmy Thomson	78	78	75	77	308
15=	Aubrey Boomer	74	74	80	81	309
	Herbert Jolly	72	80	78	79	309
	Macdonald Smith	73	78	78	80	309
18=	Sid Brews	76	77	78	79	310
	Bill Davies	79	76	81	74	310
	Ed Dudley	72	80	80	78	310
	Mark Seymour	75	74	78	83	310
22	George Duncan	78	76	81	76	311
23=	William Nolan	80	76	79	77	312
	Phil Perkins (a)	79	73	80	80	312
25=	Jose Jurado	77	73	81	82	313
	W Willis Mackenzie (a)	80	71	80	82	313
	Cedric Sayner	80	75	78	80	313
	Horton Smith	76	76	84	77	313
	Cyril Tolley (a)	74	76	87	76	313
	Joe Turnesa	78	74	81	80	313
	Tom Williamson	73	78	80	82	313

Round Leader(s)
R1 Alliss; 69
R2 Diegel; 140
R3 Hagen; 217
Lowest Scores
R2 Hagen; 67
R3 Hagen, Thomson, Watrous; 75
R4 Barnes, Davies; 74

27–30 June					**1929**

US OPEN

Winged Foot GC, Mamaroneck, New York
6786 yards *PAR 72 (288)*

2–7 December	**1929**

US PGA

Hillcrest CC, Los Angeles, California

Al Espinosa may have wished he hadn't bothered to tie with Bobby Jones. Jones had two 7s in his last round 79 and only made the play-off courtesy of a 12-foot putt on the last green. In his 4th Open play-off though, Jones played golf as majestic as Espinosa's was abject, winning by 23 shots, and landed his 3rd US Open.

1	**BOBBY JONES*** (Amateur)	69	75	71	79	294
2	Al Espinosa	70	72	77	75	294
3=	Gene Sarazen	71	71	76	78	296
	Denny Shute	73	71	76	76	296
5=	Tommy Armour	74	71	76	76	297
	George Von Elm (a)	79	70	74	74	297
7	Henry Ciuci	78	74	72	75	299
8=	Leo Diegel	74	74	76	77	301
	Peter O'Hara	74	76	73	78	301
10	Horton Smith	76	77	74	75	302
11=	Wiffy Cox	74	76	80	75	305
	Jock Rogers	78	76	77	74	305
13=	PO Hart	76	78	75	77	306
	Charles Hilgendorf	72	79	75	80	306
15	Billy Burke	75	80	78	74	307
16=	Louis Chiapetta	78	79	72	79	308
	George Smith	77	77	77	77	308
	Craig Wood	79	71	80	78	308
19=	Walter Hagen	76	81	74	78	309
	Joe Kirkwood, Sr	75	82	76	76	309
21=	Jim Barnes	78	78	81	73	310
	Massie Miller	75	82	75	78	310
23=	Jack Forrester	77	76	75	83	311
	Ted Longworth	74	82	73	82	311
	Macdonald Smith	77	78	80	76	311
26=	Jack Burke, Sr	77	80	74	81	312
	Willie Hunter, Jr	76	77	76	83	312
	Willie MacFarlane	79	78	76	79	312
	Leonard Schmutte	73	75	89	75	312
30=	Tom Boyd	79	80	74	80	313
	Emerick Kocsis	79	76	77	81	313

* Bobby Jones (141) beat Al Espinosa (164) in the 36-Hole Play-off

Round Leader(s)
R1   Jones; 69
R2   Espinosa, Sarazen; 142
R3   Jones; 215
Lowest Scores
R2   Von Elm; 70
R3   Jones; 71
R4   Barnes; 73

MATCHPLAY
32 qualifiers after 36 holes strokeplay (Low - Fred Morrison, 136)
All Rounds 36 holes

Leo Diegel not only repeated his 1928 win, he had to negotiate prevous multiple Champions – Sarazen in the QF, then Hagen in the semis - in doing it. In his 4th meeting with Hagen in 5 years, Diegel squared the series. He went on to beat 1928 US Open winner, Johnny Farrell.

FINAL
LEO DIEGEL ($ not available)
beat
JOHNNY FARRELL, 6&4

Round by Round Details

ROUND 1 (Last 32)
Larry Nabholtz bt Albert Alcroft 1 up; Al Watrous bt Neal McIntyre 4&3; Al Espinosa bt Dave Hackney 5&4; Bill Mehlhorn bt Guy Paulsen 7&6; Neil Christian bt Frank Walsh 7&6; Craig Wood bt Horton Smith 1 up (after 37); Henry Ciuci bt Clarence Clark 3&2; JOHNNY FARRELL bt John Golden 1 up; Tony Manero by Denny Shute 6&5; Eddie Schultz bt Wiffy Cox 5&4; Walter Hagen bt Bob Shave 9&8; Charles Guest bt Mortie Dutra 1 up; LEO DIEGEL bt PO Hart 10&9; Herman Barron bt Clarence Doser 5&4; Gene Sarazen bt Jock Hendry 3&2; Fred Morrison bt Joe Kirkwood, Sr 5&4

ROUND 2 (Last 16)
Watrous bt Nabholtz 9&7
Espinosa bt Mehlhorn 1 up (after 40)
Wood bt Christian 3&2
FARRELL by Ciuci 3&1
Manero bt Schultz 6&5
Hagen Bt Guest 5&4
DIEGEL bt Barron 10&9
Sarazen bt Morrison 3&2

QUARTER FINAL (QF)
Watrous bt Espinosa 2up
FARRELL bt Wood 1 up (after 37)
Hagen bt Manero 6&5
DIEGEL bt Sarazen 3&2

SEMI FINAL (SF)
FARRELL bt Watrous 6&5
DIEGEL bt Hagen 3&2

1930   18–20 June
BRITISH OPEN
Royal Liverpool GC, Hoylake, Cheshire, England
6750 yards

This was Bobby Jones' year. As if his performances as an amateur over the previous 8 years – against amateurs and pros – were not enough, his feats in 1930 will never be repeated. Jones played steady golf to win by 2 from a clutch of outstanding Americans, and the best of British – who, Compston and Cotton apart, were not of the best vintage.

1	**BOBBY JONES** (Amateur)	70	72	74	75	291
2=	Leo Diegel	74	73	71	75	293
	Macdonald Smith	70	77	75	71	293
4=	Fred Robson	71	72	78	75	296
	Horton Smith	72	73	78	73	296
6=	Jim Barnes	71	77	72	77	297
	Archie Compston	74	73	68	82	297
8	Henry Cotton	70	79	77	73	299
9=	Tom Barber	75	76	72	77	300
	Auguste Boyer	73	77	70	80	300
	Charles Whitcombe	74	75	72	79	300
12	Bert Hodson	74	77	76	74	301
13=	Abe Mitchell	75	78	77	72	302
	Reg Whitcombe	78	72	73	79	302
15=	Donald Moe (a)	74	73	76	80	303
	Phillip H Rodgers	74	73	76	80	303
17=	Percy Alliss	75	74	77	79	305
	William Large	78	74	77	76	305
	Ernest R Whitcombe	80	72	76	77	305
	Arthur Young	75	78	78	74	305
21=	H Crapper	78	73	80	75	306
	Pierre Hirigoyen	75	79	76	76	306
	Harry Large	79	74	78	75	306
24=	Stewart Burns	77	75	80	75	307
	Bill Davies	78	77	73	79	307
	Arthur Lacey	78	79	74	76	307
	Ted Ray	78	75	76	78	307
	Norman Sutton	72	80	76	79	307
29	Tom Green	73	79	78	78	308
30=	Duncan McCulloch	78	78	79	74	309
	Alf Perry	78	74	75	82	309

Round Leader(s)
R1 Cotton, Jones, M Smith; 70
R2 Jones; 142
R3 Compston; 215
Lowest Scores
R2 Cyril Tolley (52); 71
R3 Compston; 68
R4 M Smith; 71

| 10–12 July | **1930** | 8–13 September | **1930** |

US OPEN

Interlachen CC, Minneapolis, Minnesota
6609 yards _PAR 72 (288)_

US PGA

Fresh Meadows CC, Flushing, New York

The Jones Bandwagon rolled on. Already possessing the British Amateur and Open titles, he won the US Open at Interlachen by 2 from British Open runner-up Macdonald Smith. In doing so he was the only player under par for the 4 rounds; he notched up his 4th US Open; and the 3rd leg of the never-to-be-repeated Grand Slam. By winning the US Amateur the following September his challenge was complete, and he retired to practise law full-time at the age of 28.

| 1 | **BOBBY JONES** | 71 | 73 | 68 | 75 | 287 |
| | (Amateur) | | | | | |

2	Macdonald Smith	70	75	74	70	289
3	Horton Smith	72	70	76	74	292
4	Harry Cooper	72	72	73	76	293
5	Johnny Golden	74	73	71	76	294
6	Tommy Armour	70	76	75	76	297
7	Charles Lacey	74	70	77	77	298
8	Johnny Farrell	74	72	73	80	299
9=	Bill Mehlhorn	76	74	75	75	300
	Craig Wood	73	75	72	80	300
11=	Leo Diegel	75	75	76	75	301
	Johnny Goodman (a)	74	80	72	75	301
	Al Heron (a)	76	78	74	73	301
	Peter O'Hara	75	77	73	76	301
	George Smith	72	81	74	74	301
	George Von Elm (a)	80	74	73	74	301
17=	Ed Dudley	74	75	78	76	303
	Mortie Dutra	76	80	69	78	303
	Charles Guest	76	73	77	77	303
	Walter Hagen	72	75	76	80	303
	Willie Hunter, Jr	76	76	78	73	303
	Bob Shave	76	72	78	77	303
	Joe Turnesa	73	78	78	74	303
	Al Watrous	79	73	73	78	303
25=	Olin Dutra	73	79	78	75	305
	Francis Gallett	76	75	74	80	305
	Denny Shute	76	78	77	74	305
28=	Herman Barron	77	78	74	77	306
	Billy Burke	76	72	82	76	306
	Jack Forrester	73	75	80	78	306
	Charles Hilgendorf	74	81	76	75	306
	Walter Kozak	74	76	78	78	306
	Gene Sarazen	76	78	77	75	306
	Frank Walsh	75	78	77	76	306

Round Leader(s)
R1 M Smith; 70
R2 H Smith; 142
R3 Jones; 212
Lowest Scores
R2 Lacey, H Smith; 70
R3 Jones; 68
R4 M Smith; 70

MATCHPLAY
32 qualifiers after 36 holes strokeplay (Low - Johnny Farrell, Horton Smith, 145).
All Rounds 36 holes

The 'Silver Scot', Tommy Armour, became the last British-born golfer to win the PGA and it was not until Jim Ferrier in 1947 that the American stranglehold on the Championship was next broken. Ex-champions Hagen and Barnes didn't make it to the matchplay stage, but, another, finalist Gene Sarazen, had his best PGA since winning in 1923.

FINAL
TOMMY ARMOUR ($ not available)
beat
GENE SARAZEN, 1up

Round by Round Details

ROUND 1 (Last 32)
Al Watrous bt Eric Seavall 3&1; Charles Lacey bt Charles Guest 3&2; Harold Sampson bt Clarence Ehresman 4&3; Leo Diegel bt Henry Ciuci 8&7; TOMMY ARMOUR bt Clarence Hackney 11&10; Bob Shave bt Joseph Kenny 1up; Denny Shute bt Joe Frank 8&6; Johnny Farrell bt Norman Smith 7&5; GENE SARAZEN bt Charles Schneider 1up; Bob Crowley bt Wiffy Cox 4&3; Harry Cooper bt Bill Mehlhorn 2&1; Al Espinosa bt Mark Fry 2&1; Joe Kirkwood, Sr bt Gunnar Johnson 8&7; JS Collins bt John Golden 5&4; Horton Smith bt Billy Burke 2&1; Laurie Ayton, Sr bt Earl Fry 4&3

ROUND 2 (Last 16)
Lacey bt Watrous 5&4
Sampson bt Diegel 1up (after 38)
ARMOUR bt Shave 7&5
Farrell bt Shute 1up
SARAZEN bt Crowley 7&6
Espinosa bt Cooper 4&3
Kirkwood bt Collins 1up (after 37)
Horton Smith bt Ayton 5&4

QUARTER FINAL (QF)
Lacey bt Sampson 4&3
ARMOUR bt Farrell 2&1
SARAZEN bt Espinosa 2&1
Kirkwood bt Horton Smith 1up

SEMI FINAL (SF)
ARMOUR bt Lacey 1up
SARAZEN bt Kirkwood 5&4

1931
3–5 June

BRITISH OPEN
Carnoustie GC, Angus, Scotland

Reigning US PGA Champion, Tommy Armour, won his 3rd different Major on the Open's 1st visit to Muirfield. This is the most-northerly site of any Major Championship course, and, curiously, Argentina (with apologies to Chile!) – the southernmost stronghold of world golf – was well represented, with 3 players in the first 11 places. In fact, Jurado was leading, 7 better than the winner going into the last round. Armour was the last Scot to win the Open before Sandy Lyle 54 years later – and the last in Scotland.

1	**TOMMY ARMOUR** (£100)	73	75	77	71	296
2	Jose Jurado	76	71	73	77	297
3=	Percy Alliss	74	78	73	73	298
	Gene Sarazen	74	76	75	73	298
5=	Johnny Farrell	72	77	75	75	299
	Macdonald Smith	75	77	71	76	299
7=	Marcos Churio	76	75	78	71	300
	Bill Davies	76	78	71	75	300
8	Arthur Lacey	74	80	74	73	301
9=	Henry Cotton	72	75	79	76	302
	Arthur Havers	75	76	72	79	302
11=	Gus Faulkner	77	76	76	74	303
	Tomas Genta	75	78	75	75	303
	Abe Mitchell	77	74	77	75	303
	Horton Smith	77	79	75	72	303
	Tom Williamson	77	76	73	77	303
16=	Marcel Dallemagne	74	77	78	75	304
	Willie Hunter Jr	76	75	74	79	304
	William Oke	74	80	75	75	304
	Reg Whitcombe	75	78	71	80	304
20=	Aubrey Boomer	76	77	80	73	306
	Fred Robson	80	76	76	74	306
22=	Len Holland	80	74	78	75	307
	Mark Seymour	80	79	75	73	307
	Ernest R Whitcombe	79	76	76	76	307
25=	Bert Hodson	77	76	78	77	308
	Joe Kirkwood, Sr	75	75	77	81	308
	William Twine	72	78	79	79	308
28=	Archie Compston	77	76	75	81	309
	Ernest WH Kenyon	75	78	78	78	309
	Duncan McCulloch	76	78	77	78	309
	William McMinn	78	78	79	74	309
	Phillip H Rodgers	77	74	78	80	309
	Charles Whitcombe	80	76	75	78	309

Round Leader(s)

R1   Cotton, Farrell, Twine; 72
R2   Cotton, Jurado; 147
R3   Jurado; 220

Lowest Scores

R2   Jurado; 71
R3   Davies, M Smith, R Whitcombe; 71
R4   Armour, Churio; 71

| 2–6 July | **1931** | 7–14 September | **1931** |
| US OPEN | | US PGA | |

Inverness GC, Toledo, Ohio

6529 yards PAR 71 (284)

Wannamoisett CC, Rumford, Rhode Island

It took the 6th play-off in 9 years to decide who was to fill the vaccum left by Bobby Jones. The play-off had the effect of doubling the amount of golf the protagonists had to play as the result was only known at the 36th extra hole. Perhaps surprisingly, Billy Burke and recently-turned pro, Von Elm, tied for the lead ahead of a more-fancied Top 10, with Burke winning by 1 shot.

| 1 | **BILLY BURKE*** | 73 | 72 | 74 | 73 | 292 |
| | ($1000) | | | | | |

2	George Von Elm	75	69	73	75	292
3	Leo Diegel	75	73	74	72	294
4=	Wiffy Cox	75	74	74	72	295
	Bill Mehlhorn	77	73	75	71	296
	Gene Sarazen	74	78	74	80	296
7=	Mortie Dutra	71	77	73	76	297
	Walter Hagen	74	74	73	76	297
	Phil Perkins (a)	78	76	73	70	297
10=	Al Espinosa	72	78	75	74	299
	Johnny Farrell	78	70	79	72	299
	Macdonald Smith	73	73	75	78	299
13=	Guy Paulsen	74	72	74	80	300
	Frank Walsh	73	77	75	75	300
15=	Herman Barron	71	75	78	77	301
	Harry Cooper	76	75	75	75	301
	Ed Dudley	75	76	76	74	301
	Al Watrous	74	78	76	73	301
19=	Charles Guest	71	75	76	80	302
	Tony Manero	74	75	80	73	302
21=	Olin Dutra	76	76	76	75	303
	John Kinder	79	72	75	77	303
23=	Laurie Ayton, Sr	76	79	74	75	304
	Willie Klein	75	80	70	79	304
25=	Denny Shute	79	73	77	76	305
	Eddie Williams	71	74	81	79	305
27=	Johnny Golden	79	75	78	74	306
	Horton Smith	77	78	75	76	306
29=	Auguste Boyer	75	80	72	80	307
	Henry Ciuci	73	79	81	74	307
	Bill Davies	73	83	74	77	307

* Billy Burke beat George Von Elm after two
36-Hole Play-offs:
5 July – Burke (149) tied with Von Elm (149)
6 July – Burke (148) beat Von Elm (149)

Round Leader(s)

R1	Barron, M Dutra, Guest,	**Lowest Scores**	
	Williams; 71	R2	Von Elm; 69
R2	Von Elm; 144	R3	Klein; 70
R3	Von Elm; 217	R4	Perkins, Sarazen; 70

MATCHPLAY
31 qualifiers, plus the defending champion (Tommy Armour), after 36 holes strokeplay (Low - Gene Sarazen, 145) All Rounds 36 holes

Tom Creavy beat former US Open Champions, Cyril Walker and Gene Sarazen on his way to a Major at the age of 20. After featuring quite well for the next year or two in the PGA and appearing in the US Open Top 10 of 1934, he was struck down by a debilitating illness and faded into obscurity.

FINAL
TOM CREAVY ($1000)
beat
DENNY SHUTE, 2&1

Round by Round Details

ROUND 1 (Last 32)
Paul Runyan bt Arthur Gusa 3&2; Gene Sarazen bt Al Espinosa 9&8; Willie MacFarlane bt Henry Ciuci 3&2; Horton Smith bt Walter Bemish 7&6; Cyril Walker bt Ed Dudley 3&2; John Golden bt Alfred Sargent 3&2; Peter O'Hara bt Walter Hagen 4&3; TOM CREAVY bt Jack Collins 5&4; Bob Crowley bt Pat Circelli 1up; Billy Burke bt Dave Hackney 5&3; Abe Espinosa by Vincent Eldred 4&3; Bill Mehlhorn bt Leo Diegel 3&2; DENNY SHUTE bt Tony Butler 1up (after 38); Jim Foulis bt Johnny Farrell 2up; Tommy Armour bt Joe Kirkwood, Sr 2&1; Walter Murray bt Eddie Schultz 6&5

ROUND 2 (Last 16)
Sarazen bt Runyan 7&6
Smith bt McaFarlane 6&5
Walker bt Golden 5&4
CREAVY bt O'Hara 2up
Burke bt Crowley 5&4
Abe Espinosa bt Mehlhorn 2&1
SHUTE bt Foulis 2&1
Armour bt Murray 5&3

QUARTER FINAL (QF)
Sarazen bt Smith 5&4
CREAVY bt Walker 3&1
Burke bt Abe Espinosa 5&3
SHUTE bt Armour 3&1

SEMI FINAL (SF)
CREAVY bt Sarazen 5&3
SHUTE bt Burke 1up

1932

8–10 June

BRITISH OPEN

Prince's GC, Sandwich, Kent, England
6983 yards *PAR 71 (284)*

Sarazen joined Hagen, Barnes and Armour in a select band who had won all 3 Majors. A record 36- and 54- hole total for either Open set the scene for a comfortable victory. The Prince's Club, adjacent to Royal St George's, was host to the Open for the one and only time.

1	**GENE SARAZEN**	70	69	70	74	283
	(£100)					
2	Macdonald Smith	71	76	71	70	288
3	Arthur Havers	74	71	68	76	289
4=	Percy Alliss	71	71	78	72	292
	Alf Padgham	76	72	74	70	292
	Charles Whitcombe	71	73	73	75	292
7=	Bill Davies	71	73	74	75	293
	Arthur Lacey	73	73	71	76	293
9	Fred Robson	74	71	78	71	294
10=	Archie Compston	74	70	75	76	295
	Henry Cotton	74	72	77	72	295
	Abe Mitchell	77	71	75	72	295
13=	Syd Easterbrook	74	75	72	77	298
	H Prowse	75	75	75	73	298
15=	CS Denny	73	81	72	73	299
	WL Hope (a)	74	79	75	71	299
17=	Tommy Armour	75	70	74	81	300
	Bert Hodson	77	73	77	73	300
	Alf Perry	73	76	77	74	300
	Charlie Ward	73	77	77	73	300
	Reg Whitcombe	75	74	75	76	300
22=	Ernest WH Kenyon	74	73	76	78	301
	Mark Seymour	74	75	81	71	301
	TA Torrance (a)	75	73	76	77	301
25=	Alf Beck	78	71	74	79	302
	Lister Hartley (a)	76	73	80	73	302
	Phillip H Rodgers	74	79	75	74	302
	William Twine	80	74	71	77	302
29=	Pierre Hirigoyen	79	73	75	76	303
	LO Munn (a)	74	75	78	76	303
	W Purse	76	75	73	79	303
	Cedric Sayner	74	74	79	76	303
	Percy Weston	75	79	76	73	303

Round Leader (s)
R1   Sarazen; 70
R2   Sarazen; 139
R3   Sarazen; 209
Lowest Scores
R2   Sarazen; 69
R3   Havers; 68
R4   Padgham, Smith; 70

| 23–25 June | **1932** | 31 August–4 September | **1932** |

US OPEN

Fresh Meadow CC, Flushing, New York
PAR 70 (280)

After setting records at the British Open earlier in the month, Gene Sarazen became the 2nd man after Bobby Jones to lift both Opens in the same season. If the earlier rounds were his strength at Sandwich, it was his 2nd 36-hole low of 136 (including a record for both Opens with his last round of 66) which provided the victory at Fresh Meadow. English amateur Phil Perkins (runner-up to Bob Jones in the 1928 US Amateur) turned professional and led after 54 holes, eventually tying 2nd. His game was somewhat hampered in future after picking up a gun-shot wound to the thigh later that year.

1	**GENE SARAZEN** ($1000)	74	76	70	66	286
2=	Bobby Cruickshank	78	74	69	68	289
	Phil Perkins	76	69	74	70	289
4	Leo Diegel	73	74	73	74	294
5	Wiffy Cox	80	73	70	72	295
6	Jose Jurado	74	71	75	76	296
7=	Billy Burke	75	77	74	71	297
	Harry Cooper	77	73	73	74	297
	Olin Dutra	69	77	75	76	297
10	Walter Hagen	75	73	79	71	298
11	Clarence Clark	79	72	74	75	300
12=	Vincent Eldred	78	73	77	73	301
	Paul Runyan	79	77	69	76	301
14=	Henry Ciuci	77	74	77	74	302
	Ed Dudley	80	74	71	77	302
	Johnny Goodman (a)	79	78	77	68	302
	Fred Morrison	77	80	69	76	302
	Denny Shute	78	76	76	72	302
	Macdonald Smith	80	76	74	72	302
	Craig Wood	79	71	79	73	302
21=	Tommy Armour	82	73	77	71	303
	George Smith	81	76	72	74	303
23=	Mortie Dutra	77	77	75	75	304
	Joe Kirkwood, Sr	76	77	75	76	304
	Charles Lacey	77	76	78	73	304
	Jack Patroni	79	77	77	71	304
27=	John Fischer (a)	81	78	74	73	306
	Bob MacDonald	82	77	74	73	306
	George Von Elm	79	73	77	77	306
	Al Zimmerman	79	77	73	77	306

Round Score(s)
R1 O Dutra; 69
R2 Jurado, Perkins; 145
R3 Perkins; 219
Lowest Scores
R2 Perkins; 69
R3 Cruickshank, Morrison, Runyan; 69
R4 Sarazen; 66

| 31 August–4 September | **1932** |

US PGA

Keller GC, St Paul, Minnesota

MATCHPLAY
31 qualifiers, plus the defending champion (Tom Creavy), after 36 holes strokeplay (Low - Olin Dutra, 140)
All Rounds 36 holes

Olin Dutra proved that his qualifying score was no fluke. However, he was helped by notables such as Armour, Cooper and Billy Burke not making the matchplay 32, and the early round exits of Horton Smith and Walter Hagen. In R1, a generous act by Al Watrous backfired. 9up with just 12 to play, he conceded a testing 2-footer to Cruickshank. The match result speaks for itself.

FINAL
OLIN DUTRA ($1000)
beat
FRANK WALSH, 4&3

Round by Round Details

ROUND 1 (Last 32)
OLIN DUTRA bt George Smith 9&8; Reggie Myles bt Horton Smith 1up (after 37); Herman Barron bt Neal McIntyre 8&7; Abe Espinosa bt Eddie Schultz 4&3; Henry Picard bt Charles Lacey 6&4; Ed Dudley bt Joe Turnesa 8&7; Al Collins bt Gunnar Nelson 5&4; John Golden bt Walter Hagen (after 43); Vincent Eldred bt Paul Runyan 1up (after 38); Bobby Cruickshank bt Al Watrous 1up (after 41 holes); Gene Kunes bt Craig Wood 3&2; FRANK WALSH bt Ted Longworth 7&6; Ralph Stonehouse bt Vic Ghezzi 6&5; John Kinder bt Joe Kirkwood, Sr 1up; Johnny Perelli bt Denny Shute 3&2; Tom Creavy bt Jimmy Hines 7&6

ROUND 2 (Last 16)
DUTRA by Myles 5&3
Barron bt Espinosa 1up (after 38)
Dudley bt Picard 10&9
Collins bt Golden 1up
Cruickshank bt Eldred 3&1
WALSH bt Kunes 9&8
Stonehouse bt Kinder 3&2
Creavy bt Perelli 1up

QUARTER FINAL (QF)
DUTRA bt Barron 5&4
Dudley bt Collins 1up (after 38)
WALSH bt Cruickshank 8&7
Creavy bt Stonehouse 3&2

SEMI FINAL (SF)
DUTRA bt Dudley 3&2
WALSH bt Creavy 1up (after 38)

1933
5–7 July
BRITISH OPEN
Royal & Ancient GC, St Andrews, Fife, Scotland

Always listed in British records and newspapers as 'Densmore', Denny Shute won his 1st Major, and only British Open, at the home of golf. In a tight finish only 3 shots covered the 1st 11 home. Craig Wood tied him on 292, but, inevitably, it seems, lost the play-off.

1	**DENNY SHUTE*** (£100)	73	73	73	73	292
2	Craig Wood	77	72	68	75	292
3=	Leo Diegel	75	70	71	77	293
	Syd Easterbrook	73	72	71	77	293
	Gene Sarazen	72	73	73	75	293
6	Olin Dutra	76	76	70	72	294
7=	Henry Cotton	73	71	72	79	295
	Ed Dudley	70	71	76	78	295
	Abe Mitchell	74	68	74	79	295
	Alf Padgham	74	73	74	74	295
	Reg Whitcombe	76	75	72	72	295
12=	Archie Compston	72	74	77	73	296
	Ernest R Whitcombe	73	73	75	75	296
14=	Auguste Boyer	76	72	70	79	297
	Arthur Havers	80	72	71	74	297
	Joe Kirkwood, Sr	72	73	71	81	297
	Horton Smith	73	73	75	76	297
18=	Aubrey Boomer	74	70	76	78	298
	Jack M'Lean (a)	75	74	75	74	298
	Cyril Tolley (a)	70	73	76	79	298
21	Laurie Ayton, Sr	78	72	76	74	300
22=	Bert Gadd	75	73	73	80	301
	Walter Hagen	68	72	79	82	302
	DC Jones	75	72	78	76	301
	Fred Robertson	71	71	77	82	301
26	Alf Perry	79	73	74	76	302
27	Allan Dailey	74	74	77	78	303
28=	Ross Somerville (a)	72	78	75	79	304
	W Spark	73	72	79	80	304
	Charlie Ward	76	73	76	79	304

* Denny Shute (149) beat Craig Wood (154) in the 36 - Hole Play-off

Round Leader(s)
R1   Dudley; 70
R2   Dudley; 141
R3   Easterbrook, Diegel; 146
Lowest Scores
R2   Mitchell; 68
R3   Wood; 68
R4   Dutra, R Whitcombe; 72

1–2 August	**1933**	8–13 August	**1933**

US OPEN
North Shore CC, Glenview, Illinois
6927 yards _PAR 72 (288)_

US PGA
Blue Mound CC, Milwaukee, Wisconsin

Johnny Goodman was the last amateur to win any Major. He equalled Sarazen's Open low of 66 in R2 and was never headed after that. Like Ouimet, Evans and Jones previously, he won the Open before taking the Amateur Championship (in 1937). Hagen, aged 41, also shot a 66 – in R4 – his best strokeplay score in the Majors. After this year (apart from peculiar changes around, and just after, wartime with the PGA Championship) the present order of Majors in the golfing calendar was to prevail.

1	**JOHNNY GOODMAN** (Amateur)	75	66	70	76	287
2	Ralph Guldahl	76	71	70	71	288
3	Craig Wood	73	74	71	72	290
4=	Tommy Armour	68	75	76	73	292
	Walter Hagen	73	76	77	66	292
6	Mortie Dutra	75	73	72	74	294
7=	Olin Dutra	75	71	75	74	295
	Gus Moreland (a)	76	76	71	72	295
9=	Clarence Clark	80	72	72	72	296
	Johnny Farrell	75	77	72	72	296
	Willie Goggin	79	73	73	71	296
	Joe Kirkwood, Sr	74	70	79	73	296
13=	Herman Barron	77	77	74	69	297
	Al Watrous	74	76	77	70	297
15=	Henry Ciuci	73	79	74	72	298
	Johnny Revolta	73	76	75	74	298
17=	George Dawson (a)	78	74	71	76	299
	Leo Diegel	78	71	75	75	299
19=	Lester Bolstad (a)	76	74	73	77	300
	Macdonald Smith	77	72	77	74	300
21=	Johnny Golden	79	76	74	72	301
	Archie Hambrick	81	71	75	74	301
	Denny Shute	76	77	72	76	301
24=	Abe Espinosa	76	73	78	75	302
	Horton Smith	75	76	76	75	302
26=	Bob Crowley	75	75	81	72	303
	Ky Laffoon	74	78	79	72	303
	Gene Sarazen	74	77	77	75	303
29=	Harry Cooper	78	76	75	75	304
	Tony Manero	79	73	77	75	304
	Bill Schwartz	75	81	72	76	304
	Frank Walsh	79	73	72	80	304

Round Leader(s)
R1 Armour; 68
R2 Goodman; 141
R3 Goodman; 211
Lowest scores
R2 Goodman; 66
R3 Goodman, Guldahl; 70
R4 Hagen; 66

MATCHPLAY
31 qualifiers, plus the defending champion (Olin Dutra), after 36 holes strokeplay (Low - Mortie Dutra, Jimmy Hines, 138)
All Rounds 36 holes

'Pretty good for a washed up golfer', commented Gene Sarazen, when he collected his 3rd PGA title – countering a jibe from Tommy Armour that the little man was past his best. Hagen, along with the pair who tied for the British Open a month earlier – Shute and Wood – declined to enter the Championship. I don't think Sarazen minded too much as Major No 6 went into the record books.

FINAL
GENE SARAZEN ($1000)
beat
WILLIE GOGGIN, 5&4

Round by Round Details

ROUND 1 (Last 32)
Jimmy Hines bt Mortie Dutra 3&2; Henry Picard bt Willie Klein 2&1; Frank Walsh bt Jack Curley 3&2; Tom Creavy bt Dick Metz 3&2; Al Espinosa bt Charles Schneider 3&2; WILLIE GOGGIN bt Leo Diegel 4&3; Paul Runyan bt Al Houghton 6&5; Johnny Revolta bt Alex Gerlak 12&11; Clarence Clark bt Horton Smith 6&5; Ed Dudley bt Ben Pautke 2&1; GENE SARAZEN bt Vincent Eldred 8&7; Harry Cooper bt Dave Hackney 6&5; John Golden bt Gunnar Johnson 4&3; Bobby Cruickshank bt Bunny Torpey 3&2; Johnny Farrell bt Vic Ghezzi 1up; Olin Dutra bt Reggie Myles 4&3

ROUND 2 (Last 16)
Hines bt Picard 5&3
Creavy bt Walsh 2&1
GOGGIN bt Espinosa 9&7
Runyan bt Revolta 1&1
Dudley bt Clark 3&1
SARAZEN bt Cooper 4&3
Golden bt Cruickshank 2&1
Farrell bt Olin Dutra 1up

QUARTER FINAL (QF)
Hines bt Creavy 4&3
GOGGIN bt Runyan 6&5
SARAZEN bt Dudley 6&5
Farrell bt Golden 5&4

SEMI FINAL (SF)
GOGGIN bt Hines 1up
SARAZEN bt Farrell 5&4

1934

22–25 March

THE MASTERS
Augusta National GC, Augusta, Georgia
6925 yards PAR 72 (288)

At the inaugural 'Masters' – properly called the Augusta National Invitational – Horton Smith's 20-foot putt for a birdie at 17 sealed the fate of Craig Wood once again. Bobby Jones came out of retirement to play in this – the tournament he devised, on a course he helped design – and finished in a tie for 13th with his erstwhile adversary, Walter Hagen.

1	**HORTON SMITH** ($1500)	70	72	70	72	284
2	Craig Wood	71	74	69	71	285
3=	Billy Burke	72	71	70	73	286
	Paul Runyan	74	71	70	71	286
5	Ed Dudley	74	69	71	74	288
6	Willie MacFarlane	74	73	70	74	291
7=	Al Espinosa	75	70	75	72	292
	Jimmy Hines	70	74	74	74	292
	Harold McSpaden	77	74	72	69	292
	MacDonald Smith	74	70	74	74	292
11=	Mortie Dutra	74	75	71	73	293
	Al Watrous	74	74	71	74	293
13=	Walter Hagen	71	76	70	77	294
	Bobby Jones (a)	76	74	72	72	294
	Denny Shute	73	73	76	72	294
16=	Leo Diegel	73	72	74	76	295
	Ralph Stonehouse	74	70	75	76	295
18=	Ky Laffoon	72	79	72	73	296
	Johnny Revolta	75	72	75	74	296
	WJ Schwartz	75	72	71	78	296
21=	Johnny Golden	71	75	74	77	297
	Charlie Yates (a)	76	72	77	72	297
23=	John Dawson (a)	74	73	76	75	298
	Henry Picard	71	76	75	76	298
25=	Henry Ciuci	74	73	74	78	299
	Tom Creavy	74	73	80	72	299
	Vic Ghezzi	77	74	74	74	299
28=	Bobby Cruickshank	74	74	80	72	300
	Jim Foulis	78	74	76	72	300
	Mike Turnesa	75	74	77	74	300

Round Leader(s)
R1   Emmett French (w/d), Hines, H Smith; 70
R2   H Smith; 142
R3   H Smith; 212
Lowest Scores
R2   Dudley; 69
R3   Wood; 69
R4   McSpaden; 69

1934

7–9 June

US OPEN
Merion Cricket Club, Ardmore, Pennsylvania
6694 yards PAR 70 (280)

Olin Dutra made up 8 strokes on the 36-hole leader, Bobby Cruickshank to add a 2nd Major to his 1932 PGA triumph. Despite not having played golf for 10 days due to crippling dysentery, he picked up 2 birdies on the last 9 holes to overhaul Cruickshank, Cox and Sarazen – the last shooting a 3 over par 7 at the 11th hole.

1	**OLIN DUTRA** ($1000)	76	74	71	72	293
2	Gene Sarazen	73	72	73	76	294
3=	Harry Cooper	76	74	74	71	295
	WiffyCox	71	75	74	75	295
	Bobby Cruickshank	71	71	77	76	295
6=	Billy Burke	76	71	77	72	296
	Macdonald Smith	75	73	78	70	296
8=	Tom Creavy	79	76	78	76	299
	Ralph Guldahl	78	73	70	78	299
	Jimmy Hines	80	70	77	72	299
	Johnny Revolta	76	73	77	73	299
12=	Joe Kirkwood, Sr	75	73	78	74	300
	Ted Luther	78	71	78	73	300
14=	Willie Hunter, Jr	75	74	80	72	301
	Alvin Krueger	76	75	75	75	301
16	Mark Fry	79	75	74	74	302
17=	Henry Ciuci	74	74	79	76	303
	Leo Diegel	76	71	78	78	303
	Johnny Golden	75	76	74	78	303
	Horton Smith	74	73	79	77	303
21=	Al Espinosa	76	74	76	78	304
	Phil Perkins	78	74	79	73	304
23=	Herman Barron	79	72	76	78	305
	Ky Laffoon	76	73	80	76	305
25=	Lawson Little (a)	83	72	76	75	306
	Eddie Loos	76	75	78	77	306
	Orville White	76	79	76	75	306
28=	Rodney Bliss, Jr (a)	74	73	82	78	307
	Mortie Dutra	74	77	79	77	307
	Zell Eaton (a)	76	73	78	80	307
	Paul Runyan	74	78	79	76	307
	George Schneiter	76	76	79	76	307
	Bill Schwartz	81	74	73	79	307
	George Von Elm	74	76	80	77	307

Round Leader(s)
R1   Cox, Cruickshank; 71
R2   Cruickshank; 142
R3   Sarazen; 218
Lowest Scores
R2   Hines; 70
R3   Guldahl; 70
R4   Creavy; 66

27–29 June	**1934**	24–29 July	**1934**

BRITISH OPEN
Royal St George's GC, Sandwich, Kent, England
6776 yards

US PGA
Park Club of Buffalo, Williamsville, New York

After ten years of American dominance, there was a British winner at Sandwich. Henry Cotton's second round score of 65 was not beaten in the Open until 1977. His 36- and 54-hole totals smashed all existing Majors records. Macdonald Smith was the leading American – 9 behind Cotton – but it is fair to say that the trans-Atlantic presence was not as great as in previous years.

1	**HENRY COTTON** (£100)	67	65	72	79	283
2	Sid Brews	76	71	70	71	288
3	Alf Padgham	71	70	75	74	290
4=	Marcel Dallemagne	71	73	71	77	292
	Joe Kirkwood, Sr	74	69	71	78	292
	Macdonald Smith	77	71	72	72	292
7=	Bert Hodson	71	74	74	76	295
	Charles Whitcombe	71	72	74	78	295
9=	Percy Alliss	73	75	71	77	296
	Ernest R Whitcombe	72	77	73	74	296
11	William Twine	72	76	75	74	297
12	John Burton	80	72	72	74	298
13=	Bill Davies	76	68	73	82	299
	Edward Jarman	74	76	74	75	299
	Charlie Ward	76	71	72	70	299
16=	Allan Dailey	74	73	78	75	300
	James McDowall	73	74	76	77	300
	Jack M'Lean (a)	77	76	69	78	300
	Reg Whitcombe	75	76	74	75	300
20	Denny Shute	71	72	80	78	301
21=	Alf Beck	78	72	78	74	302
	Bert Gadd	76	74	74	78	302
	William Nolan	73	71	75	83	302
	Gene Sarazen	75	73	74	80	302
	Percy Weston	72	76	77	77	302
26=	Jimmy Adams	73	78	73	79	303
	Tom Green	75	73	74	81	303
	Alf Perry	76	76	74	77	303
29=	Auguste Boyer	78	75	77	74	304
	LT Cotton	76	73	79	76	304

Round Leader(s)
R1   Cotton; 67
R2   Cotton; 132
R3   Cotton; 204
Lowest Scores
R2   Cotton; 65
R3   M'Lean; 69
R4   Brews; 71

MATCHPLAY
31 qualifiers, plus the defending champion (Gene Sarazen), after 36 holes strokeplay (Low Bob Crowley, 138)
All Rounds 36 holes

In a match of incredibly-low scoring, Craig Wood wreaked revenge on Denny Shute for his 1933 British Open play-off defeat. Victory was still not to be for Wood, though, as he missed out again after extra holes to leading money-winner, Paul Runyan.

FINAL
PAUL RUNYAN ($1000)
beat
CRAIG WOOD, 1up (after 38)

Round by Round Details

ROUND 1 (Last 32)
Gene Sarazen bt Herman Barron 3&2; Al Watrous bt Errie Ball 8&7; Harry Cooper bt Bill Mehlhorn 4&2; CRAIG WOOD bt Leo Fraser 6&5; Ky Laffoon bt George Smith 12&10; Denny Shute bt Walter Hagen 4&3; Al Houghton bt George Christ 7&6; Fay Coleman bt Leo Diegel 4&2; Dick Metz bt Joe Paletti 6&5; Tommy Armour bt Byron Nelson 4&3; Vic Ghezzi bt Eddie Burke 2&1; PAUL RUNYAN bt Johnny Farrell 8&6; Johnny Revolta bt Jim Foulis 7&6; Gene Kunes bt Orville White 3&2; Ted Turner bt Willie Goggin 1up (after 37); Bob Crowley bt Eddie Loos 3&2

ROUND 2 (Last 16)
Watrous bt Sarazen 4&3
WOOD bt Cooper 4&3
Shute bt Laffoon 3&2
Houghton bt Coleman 4&3
Metz bt Armour 3&2
RUNYAN bt Ghezzi 2&1
Kunes bt Revolta 2&1
Crowley bt Turner 1up

QUARTER FINAL (QF)
WOOD bt Watrous 2&1
Shute bt Houghton 6&5
RUNYAN bt Metz 1up
Kunes bt Crowley 4&3

SEMI FINAL (SF)
WOOD bt Shute 2&1
RUNYAN bt Kunes 4&2

1935
THE MASTERS
4–8 April

Augusta National GC, Augusta, Georgia
6925 yards _PAR 72 (288)_

The Masters reputation was forever set with just one golf shot. Gene Sarazen's double-eagle on the par 15th, hit with a fairway wood from 220 yards, did for – yes – poor Craig Wood again. The ensuing newspaper hype brought national attention to this Southern off-season tournament – and the rest is history. Sarazen also made history of another kind. He became the first of only 4 players (Hogan, Nicklaus and Player, the others) to win all 4 Majors – the first modern Grand Slam. This was his last Majors win.

1	**GENE SARAZEN***	68	71	73	70	282
	($1500)					
2	Craig Wood	69	72	68	73	282
3	Olin Dutra	70	70	70	74	284
4	Henry Picard	67	68	76	75	286
5	Denny Shute	73	71	70	73	287
6	Lawson Little (a)	74	72	70	72	288
7	Paul Runyan	70	72	75	72	289
8	Vic Ghezzi	73	71	73	73	290
9=	Bobby Cruickshank	76	70	73	72	291
	Jimmy Hines	70	70	77	74	291
	Byron Nelson	71	74	72	74	291
	Joe Turnesa	73	71	74	73	291
13=	Ray Mangrum	68	71	76	77	292
	Johnny Revolta	70	74	73	75	292
15=	Walter Hagen	73	69	72	79	293
	Sam Parks Jr	74	70	74	75	293
17=	John Dawson (a)	75	72	72	75	294
	Al Espinosa	76	72	73	73	294
19=	Clarence Clark	77	75	73	71	296
	Leo Diegel	72	73	74	77	296
	Ed Dudley	73	73	74	76	296
	Harold McSpaden	75	72	75	74	296
	Horton Smith	74	75	74	73	296
	Charlie Yates (a)	75	70	76	75	296
25=	Harry Cooper	73	76	74	74	297
	Bobby Jones (a)	74	72	73	78	297
	Mike Turnesa	72	74	75	76	297
28=	Gene Kunes	76	72	77	73	298
	Ky Laffoon	76	73	72	77	298
	Phil Perkins	77	71	75	75	298

* Gene Sarazen (144) beat Craig Wood (149) in the 36-Hole Play-off

Round Leader(s)
R1 Picard; 67
R2 Picard; 135
R3 Wood; 209
Lowest Scores
R2 Picard; 68
R3 Wood; 68
R4 Sarazen; 70

1935
US OPEN
6–8 June

Oakmont CC, Oakmont, Pennsylvania
6981 yards _PAR 72 (288)_

The 11-over par winning total was a testimony to the Oakmont trial. A look at the final round scores says more than any words can. Sam Parks Jr, fresh out of college, was a surprise winner. He was pro at the nearby South Hills CC, though, and was certainly helped by his local knowledge of Oakmont.

1	**SAM PARKS, Jr**	77	73	73	76	299
	($1000)					
2	Jimmy Thomson	73	73	77	78	301
3	Walter Hagen	77	76	73	76	302
4=	Ray Mangrum	76	76	72	79	303
	Denny Shute	78	73	76	76	303
6=	Alvin Krueger	71	77	78	80	306
	Henry Picard	79	78	70	79	306
	Gene Sarazen	75	74	78	79	306
	Horton Smith	73	79	79	75	306
10=	Dick Metz	77	76	76	78	307
	Paul Runyan	76	77	79	75	307
12=	Olin Dutra	77	76	78	77	308
	Vincent Eldred	75	77	77	79	308
14=	Herman Barron	73	79	78	79	309
	Bobby Cruickshank	78	76	77	78	309
	Mortie Dutra	75	77	80	77	309
	Macdonald Smith	74	82	76	77	309
	Ted Turner	80	71	81	77	309
	Al Watrous	75	80	79	75	309
20	Vic Ghezzi	75	78	81	77	311
21=	Sid Brews	76	81	78	77	312
	Ed Dudley	74	83	75	80	312
	Bill Kaiser	78	82	78	74	312
	Gene Kunes	76	79	77	80	312
	Craig Wood	76	80	79	77	312
26=	Ted Luther	80	76	84	73	313
	Frank Walsh	76	82	82	73	313
28=	Harry Cooper	77	81	79	77	314
	Al Espinosa	75	76	78	85	314
	Willie Hunter, Jr	78	80	80	76	314
	Ky Laffoon	75	83	81	75	314

Round Leader(s)
R1 Krueger; 71
R2 Thomson; 146
R3 Parks, Thomson; 223
Lowest Scores
R2 Turner; 71
R3 Picard; 70
R4 Luther, Walsh; 73

26–28 June	**1935**

BRITISH OPEN

Honourable Company, Muirfield, Angus, Scotland
6806 yards

Once again a light assault from the Americans facilitated another home victory. Alf Perry's only win owed much to an excellent start and a record-equalling R3. With Fred (no relation) winning at Wimbledon it was a good year for the Perrys! Double-double Amateur Champion in the making (US & British, 1934-35), Lawson Little, was the best-placed overseas player.

1	**ALF PERRY** (£100)	69	75	67	72	285
2	Alf Padgham	70	72	74	71	287
3	Charles Whitcombe	71	68	73	76	288
4=	Bert Gadd	72	75	71	71	289
	Lawson Little (a)	75	71	74	69	289
6	Henry Picard	72	73	72	75	292
7=	Henry Cotton	68	74	76	75	293
	Syd Easterbrook	75	73	74	71	293
8	William Branch	71	73	76	74	294
9	Laurie Ayton, Sr	74	73	77	71	295
10	Auguste Boyer	74	75	76	71	296
11=	Aubrey Boomer	76	69	75	77	297
	Jack Busson	75	76	70	76	297
	Bill Cox	76	69	77	75	297
	Ernest WH Kenyon	70	74	74	79	297
15=	Percy Alliss	72	76	75	75	298
	JA Jacobs	78	74	75	71	298
17=	W Laidlaw	74	71	75	79	299
	Philip H Rodgers	74	76	74	75	299
	Mark Seymour	75	76	75	73	299
	Macdonald Smith	69	77	75	78	299
	Ernest R Whitcombe	75	72	74	78	299
22=	Reg Cox	75	73	76	76	300
	Sam King	76	74	75	75	300
	Arthur Lacey	71	75	74	80	300
	Laddie Lucas (a)	74	73	72	81	300
26=	Frank Ball	76	75	73	77	301
	Alf Beck	74	76	77	74	301
	Len Holland	72	74	78	77	301
	PWL Risdon (a)	78	74	75	74	301
30=	Sid Brews	79	74	75	74	302
	Dai Rees	75	73	77	77	302
	Cyril Thomson	74	76	75	77	302

Round Leader(s)
R1   Cotton; 68
R2   C Whitcombe; 139
R3   Perry; 211
Lowest Scores
R2   C Whitcombe; 68
R3   Perry; 67
R4   Little; 69

18–23 October	**1935**

US PGA

Twin Hills CC, Oklahoma City, Oklahoma

MATCHPLAY
63 qualifiers, plus the defending champion (Paul Runyan), after 36 holes strokeplay (Low - Walter Hagen, 139)
Rs1&2, 18 holes: R3,QF,SF&F, 36 holes

The Championship format was changed from this year to allow more players into the matchplay stage. It was to remain in this format for most of the remaining years until it gave way to medal play totally in 1958. Johnny Revolta stopped Tommy Armour claiming his 2nd PGA with a comfortable win in a final which was played in quite wintry conditions.

FINAL
JOHNNY REVOLTA ($1000)
beat
TOMMY ARMOUR, 5&4

Round by Round Details

ROUND 2 (Last 32)
Paul Runyan bt Mortie Dutra 3&2; Tony Manero bt Clarence Doser 1up; Levi Lynch bt Art Bell 4&2; Al Zimmerman bt Vic Ghezzi 2&1; Pat Cicelli bt Orville White 3&2; JOHNNY REVOLTA bt Jimmy Hines 1up; Alvin Krueger bt Gene Sarazen 2&1; Eddie Schultz bt G Slingerland 2&1; Al Watrous bt Harold Sampson 2&1; Sam Parks, Jr bt Francis Scheider 1up; Horton Smith bt Ray Mangrum 1up; Denny Shute bt Henry Bontempo 4&3; Jimmy Thomson bt JG Collins 6&4; Ed Dudley bt Dick Metz 3&1; Ky Laffoon bt Eddie Loos 1up (after 21); TOMMY ARMOUR bt Charles Schneider 3&2

ROUND 3 (Last 16)
Runyan bt Manero 9&8
Zimmerman bt Lynch 7&6
REVOLTA bt Circelli 4&2
Schultz bt Krueger 1up (after 37)
Watrous bt Parks, Jr 4&3
Smith bt Shute 2&1
Dudley bt Thomson 6&4
ARMOUR bt Laffoon 3&2

QUARTER FINAL (QF)
Zimmerman bt Runyan 3&2
REVOLTA bt Schultz 4&2
Watrous bt Smith 1up
ARMOUR bt Dudley 1up (after 39)

SEMI FINAL (SF)
REVOLTA bt Zimmerman 4&3
ARMOUR bt Watrous 2&1

1936
THE MASTERS
2–5 April

Augusta National GC, Augusta, Georgia
6925 yards PAR 72 (288)

Horton Smith won his 2nd and last Masters and 2nd and last Major. He overcame Harry Cooper – another with the regular propensity to lose Majors when in contention – to turn a 3-shot deficit into a 1-stroke victory. Smith chipped in from 50 feet at the 14th and came home under par from there.

1	**HORTON SMITH** ($1500)	74	71	68	72	285
2	Harry Cooper	70	69	71	76	286
3	Gene Sarazen	78	67	72	70	287
4=	Bobby Cruickshank	75	69	74	72	290
	Paul Runyan	76	69	70	75	290
6=	Ed Dudley	75	75	70	73	293
	Ky Laffoon	75	70	75	73	293
	Ray Mangrum	76	73	68	76	293
9=	John Dawson (a)	77	70	70	77	294
	Henry Picard	75	72	74	73	294
11=	Walter Hagen	77	74	73	72	296
	Denny Shute	76	68	75	77	296
13=	Wiffy Cox	82	69	75	72	298
	Byron Nelson	76	71	77	74	298
15=	Al Espinosa	72	73	75	79	299
	Vic Ghezzi	77	70	77	75	299
	Harold McSpaden	77	75	71	76	299
	Jimmy Thomson	76	78	71	74	299
	Orville White	78	73	77	71	299
20=	Tommy Armour	79	74	72	75	300
	Chick Chin	76	74	71	79	300
	Lawson Little	75	75	73	77	300
	Sam Parks, Jr	76	75	72	77	300
	Craig Wood	88	67	69	76	300
25	Johnny Revolta	77	72	76	76	301
26	Albert Campbell (a)	82	73	68	79	302
27	Dick Metz	79	78	76	70	303
28	Billy Burke	74	77	74	79	304
29=	Johnny Farrell	78	75	74	78	305
	Joe Kirkwood, Sr	81	76	73	75	305
	Torchy Toda	81	84	75	75	305
	Al Watrous	78	76	73	78	305

Round Leader(s)
R1 Cooper; 70
R2 Cooper; 139
R3 Cooper; 210
Lowest Scores
R2 Sarazen, Wood; 67
R3 Campbell, Mangrum, Smith; 68
R4 Metz, Sarazen; 70

1936
US OPEN
4–6 June

Baltusrol GC, Springfield, New Jersey
6866 yards PAR 72 (288)

Just to prove he could do it again – only 2 months after the Masters – Cooper, 5 strokes clear over the field, saw Tony Manero charge past with a brilliant 67 to win by 2. Chick Evans' 20-year low score of 286 for the US Open had been finally beaten, as had the 283 set (successively) by Sarazen, Cotton and Perry in the British Open. Manero was relatively unknown, and although would be around for a few years, he never won another Major.

1	**TONY MANERO** ($1000)	73	69	73	67	282
2	Harry Cooper	71	70	70	73	284
3	Clarence Clark	69	75	71	72	287
4	Macdonald Smith	73	73	72	70	288
5=	Wiffy Cox	74	74	69	72	289
	Ky Laffoon	71	74	70	74	289
	Henry Picard	70	71	74	74	289
8=	Ralph Guldahl	73	70	73	74	290
	Paul Runyan	69	75	73	73	290
10	Denny Shute	72	69	73	77	291
11=	Herman Barron	73	74	69	76	292
	Tom Kerrigan	70	75	72	75	292
	Ray Mangrum	69	71	76	76	292
14=	Charles Kocsis (a)	72	71	73	77	293
	Frank Moore	70	74	75	74	293
	Johnny Revolta	70	71	77	75	293
	Jimmy Thomson	74	73	71	75	293
18=	Billy Burke	72	76	72	74	294
	Vic Ghezzi	70	70	73	81	294
	Willie Goggin	73	73	72	76	294
	Harold McSpaden	75	71	78	70	294
22=	Tommy Armour	74	76	74	71	295
	Johnny Farrell	75	75	70	75	295
	Jerry Gianferante	74	73	71	77	295
	Johnny Goodman (a)	75	73	73	74	295
	Felix Serafin	72	73	74	76	295
	Horton Smith	75	75	72	73	295
28=	Al Brosch	73	75	72	76	296
	Zell Eaton	72	75	72	77	296
	Dick Metz	74	73	73	76	296
	Jack Munger (a)	74	70	76	76	296
	Gene Sarazen	75	72	75	74	296

Round Leader(s)
R1 Clark, Mangrum, Runyon; 69
R2 Ghezzi, Mangrum; 140
R3 Cooper; 211
Lowest Scores
R2 Manero, Shute; 69
R3 Barron, Cox; 69
R4 Manero; 67

24–26 June					**1936**
BRITISH OPEN					

Royal Liverpool GC, Hoylake, Cheshire, England
7078 yards

Consistent solid golf gave Alf Padgham his only Open win. Gene Sarazen was there, but precious few other US stars. Although no official par figures are available for the Open Championship courses via the R&A at this time, where figures do appear they are courtesy of the clubs or contemporary newspaper reports. Hoylake's Scratch score was 76 in 1936.

I	**ALF PADGHAM**	73	72	71	71	287
	(£100)					
2	Jimmy Adams	71	73	71	73	288
3=	Henry Cotton	73	72	70	74	289
	Marcel Dallemagne	73	72	75	69	289
5=	Percy Alliss	74	72	74	71	291
	Tom Green	74	72	70	75	291
	Gene Sarazen	73	75	70	73	291
8=	Arthur Lacey	76	74	72	72	294
	Bobby Locke (a)	75	73	72	74	294
	Reg Whitcombe	72	77	71	74	294
II	Dai Rees	77	71	72	75	295
12=	Dick Burton	74	71	75	76	296
	Bill Cox	70	74	79	73	296
14	Bill Davies	72	76	73	77	298
15=	Aubrey Boomer	74	75	75	75	299
	Wally Smithers	75	73	77	74	299
	Hector Thomson (a)	76	76	73	74	299
	Ted Turner	75	74	76	74	299
19=	Gordon Good	75	73	79	73	300
	Charles Whitcombe	73	76	79	72	300
21=	Max Faulkner	74	75	77	75	301
	Bert Gadd	74	72	77	78	301
23=	Errie Ball	74	77	72	79	302
	Johnny Fallon	78	73	78	73	302
	Francis Francis (a)	73	72	79	78	302
	Willie Goggin	74	78	73	77	302
	Norman Sutton	75	72	78	77	302
28=	Sam King	79	74	75	76	304
	HR Manton	76	78	77	73	304
	Jean Saubaber	74	78	75	77	304

Round Leader(s)
R1   Cox; 70
R2   Adams, Cox; 144
R3   Adams, Cotton; 215
Lowest Scores
R2   Burton, Rees; 71
R3   Cotton, Green, Sarazen; 70
R4   Dallemagne; 69

17–22 November	**1936**
US PGA	

Pinehurst CC, Pinehurst, North Carolina

MATCHPLAY
63 qualifiers, plus the defending champion (Johnny Revolta), after 36 holes strokeplay (Low - Fay Coleman, 143)
Rs 1&2, 18 holes: R3,QF,SF,&F, 36 holes

FINAL
DENNY SHUTE ($1000)
beat
JIMMY THOMSON, 3&2

Shute beat Jimmy Thomson to add a PGA title to his 1933 British Open. It was a bad event for former Champions. Hagen and Diegel didn't qualify and Sarazen, Armour and Runyan were eliminated in R1. Defending Champion, Revolta, also went out early.

Round by Round Details

ROUND 2 (Last 32)
    Harold McSpaden bt Johnny Revolta 1up (after 19); Leo Walper bt Clarence Hackney 2&1; JIMMY THOMSON bt Willie Klein 3&2; Henry Picard bt Alvin Krueger 5&4; Harry Cooper bt Clarence Doser 3&2; Craig Wood bt Frank Walsh 1up; Bobby Cruickshank bt Errie Ball 2&1; Tony Manero bt Mortie Dutra 6&5; Horton Smith bt Jack Patroni 6&5; Willie Goggin bt Les Madison 5&4; DENNY SHUTE bt Al Zimmerman 3&2; Billy Burke bt Ky Laffoon 4&3; Bill Mehlhorn bt Dick Metz 1up (after 23); Ed Dudley bt Tom LoPresti 2&1; Jimmy Hines bt Ray Mangrum 2&1; Vic Ghezzi bt Fay Coleman 1up

ROUND 3 (Last 16)
    McSpaden bt Walper 4&3
    THOMSON bt Picard 4&2
    Wood bt Cooper 2&1
    Manero bt Cruickshank 4&2
    Smith bt Goggin 2&1;
    SHUTE bt Burke 2&1
    Mehlhorn bt Dudley 6&4;
    Hines bt Ghezzi 4&3

QUARTER FINAL (QF)
    THOMSON bt McSpaden 1up
    Wood bt Manero 5&4
    SHUTE bt Smith 3&2
    Mehlhorn bt Hines 4&2

SEMI FINAL (SF)
    THOMSON bt Wood 5&4
    SHUTE bt Mehlhorn 1up

1937
THE MASTERS
1–4 April

Augusta National GC, Augusta, Georgia
6925 yards PAR 72 (288)

Byron Nelson burst on to the scene. After a faltering start to his career, the 1937 Masters was his big breakthrough. He set a new low of 66 for the Tournament and led at half-way. Then a bad R3 let in Ralph Guldahl for a 4-stroke lead going into the last round. A combination of the latter's bad figures thereafter, and Nelson's 2 under par last round, turned it all round.

1	**BYRON NELSON** ($1500)	66	72	75	70	283
2	Ralph Guldahl	69	72	68	76	285
3	Ed Dudley	70	71	71	74	286
4	Harry Cooper	73	69	71	74	287
5	Ky Laffoon	73	70	74	73	290
6	Jimmy Thomson	71	73	74	73	291
7	Al Watrous	74	72	71	75	292
8=	Tommy Armour	73	75	73	72	293
	Vic Ghezzi	72	72	72	77	293
10=	Leonard Dodson	71	75	71	77	294
	Jimmy Hines	77	72	68	77	294
12	Wiffy Cox	70	72	77	76	295
13=	Clarence Clark	77	75	70	74	296
	Tony Manero	71	72	78	75	296
	Johnny Revolta	71	72	72	81	296
	Denny Shute	74	75	71	76	296
17	Bobby Cruickshank	79	69	71	78	297
18	Sam Snead	76	72	71	79	298
19=	Lawson Little	70	79	74	76	299
	Willie MacFarlane	73	76	73	77	299
	Paul Runyan	74	77	72	76	299
	Felix Serafin	75	76	71	77	299
	Horton Smith	75	72	77	75	299
24=	Ray Mangrum	71	80	72	77	300
	Gene Sarazen	74	80	73	73	300
26=	Craig Wood	79	77	74	71	301
	Charlie Yates (a)	76	73	74	78	301
28	Francis Francis (a)	77	74	75	76	302
29=	Billy Burke	77	71	75	80	303
	Al Espinosa	72	76	79	76	303
	Bobby Jones (a)	79	74	73	77	303

Round Leader(s)
R1   Nelson; 66
R2   Nelson; 138
R3   Guldahl; 209
Lowest Scores
R2   Cooper, Cruickshank; 69
R3   Guldahl, Hines; 68
R4   Nelson; 70

1937
US PGA
26–30 May

Pittsburgh Field Club, Aspinwall, Pennsylvania

MATCHPLAY
63 qualifiers, plus the defending champion (Denny Shute), after 36 holes strokeplay (Low – Byron Nelson, 139)
Rs1&2, 18 holes: R3,QF,SF&F, 36 holes

Denny Shute's back-to-back PGA titles took his Majors wins to 3, and he became the 5th multiple winner of the Championship. He beat Harold 'Jug' McSpaden over extra holes – something that McSpaden had experienced against Bunny Torpey and Henry Picard in earlier rounds.

FINAL
DENNY SHUTE ($1000)
beat
HAROLD McSPADEN, 1UP (after 37)

Round by Round Details

ROUND 2 (Last 32)
DENNY SHUTE bt Olin Dutra 3&2; Ed Dudley bt Pat Wilcox 4&3; Paul Runyan bt Willie Goggin 2&1; Jimmy Hines bt Al Espinosa 1up; Harry Cooper bt Johnny Revolta 1up; Jim Foulis bt Gene Sarazen 1up; Vic Ghezzi bt Sam Parks, Jr 1up; Tony Manero bt Willie MacFarlane 4&3; Byron Nelson bt Craig Wood 4&2; Johnny Farrell bt Charles Schneider 1up; Ky Laffoon bt Billy Burke 2&1; Jimmy Thomson bt Ralph Guldahl 2&1; HAROLD McSPADEN bt Bunny Torpey 1up (after 20); Sam Snead bt Alvin Krueger 2up; Henry Picard bt Sam Bernardi 1up; Horton Smith bt Al Watrous 1up (after 19)
ROUND 3 (Last 16)
SHUTE bt Dudley   3&2
Hines bt Runyan 2&1
Cooper bt Foulis 5&4
Manero by Ghezzi 3&1
Nelson bt Farrell 5&4
Laffoon bt Thomson 4&3
McSPADEN bt Snead 3&2
Picard bt Smith 4&3

QUARTER FINAL (QF)
SHUTE bt Hines 4&3
Manero bt Cooper 1up
Laffoon bt Nelson 2up
McSPADEN bt Picard 1up (after 39)

SEMI FINAL (SF)
SHUTE bt Manero 1up
McSPADEN bt Laffoon 2&1

10–12 June

US OPEN 1937
Oakland Hills CC, Birmingham, Michigan
7037 yards _PAR 72 (288)_

Guldahl made up for his Masters disappointment with a stunning win, lowering Manero's US Open record of the previous year. The win was the dawn of Guldahl's great but brief reign at the top of world golf. A new era was coming in, with Nelson's Masters win and the entry of Sam Snead into the record books as runner-up in the 1937 US Open. This started a 38-year span of Majors Top 10s for Snead – he finished tied for 3rd in the PGA as late as 1974.

1	**RALPH GULDAHL** ($1000)	71	69	72	69	281
2	Sam Snead	69	73	70	71	283
3	Bobby Cruickshank	73	73	67	72	285
4	Harry Cooper	72	70	73	71	286
5	Ed Dudley	70	70	71	76	287
6	Al Brosch	74	73	68	73	288
7	Clarence Clark	72	75	73	69	289
8	Johnny Goodman (a)	70	73	72	75	290
9	Frank Strafaci (a)	70	72	77	72	291
10=	Charles Kocsis (a)	72	73	76	71	292
	Henry Picard	71	75	72	74	292
	Gene Sarazen	78	69	71	74	292
	Denny Shute	69	76	75	72	292
14=	Ray Mangrum	75	75	71	72	293
	Paul Runyan	76	72	73	72	293
16=	Billy Burke	75	73	71	75	294
	Jimmy Demaret	72	74	76	72	294
	Sam Parks, Jr	74	74	72	74	294
	Pat Sawyer	72	70	75	77	294
20=	Vic Ghezzi	72	71	78	74	295
	Jimmy Hines	75	72	76	72	295
	Ky Laffoon	74	74	74	73	295
	Harold McSpaden	74	75	73	73	295
	Fred Morrison	71	76	74	74	295
	Byron Nelson	73	78	71	73	295
	Bob Stupple	73	73	73	76	295
	Frank Walsh	70	70	78	77	295
28=	Leo Mallory	73	74	76	73	296
	Toney Penna	76	74	75	71	296
	Johnny Revolta	75	73	75	73	296
	Jimmy Thomson	74	66	78	78	296

Round Leader(s)
R1 Shute, Snead; 69
R2 Dudley, Guldahl, Thomson, Walsh; 140
R3 Dudley; 211
Lowest Scores
R2 Thomson; 66
R3 Cruickshank; 67
R4 Clark, Guldahl; 69

7–9 July

BRITISH OPEN 1937
Carnoustie GC, Angus, Scotland
7135 yards

Nelson's good form continued on his only serious visit to the Open Championship – but he still finished 6 behind Henry Cotton. Many Americans now saw the British Open as less relevant than their domestic Majors. There were several reasons for this in the '30s. Post-Depression USA was commercially more lucrative for a professional golfer – and the time taken by sea would mean 2 extra tournaments sacrificed. Also, the US golfers saw themselves post-Vardon, et al, as in the ascendancy (the Ryder Cup wins – started in 1927 – were going their way). Perhaps Cotton might have been the British champion to throw down the gauntlet in the USA – but it wasn't to be.

1	**HENRY COTTON** (£100)	74	73	72	71	290
2	Reg Whitcombe	72	70	74	76	292
3	Charles Lacey	76	75	70	72	293
4	Charles Whitcombe	73	71	74	76	294
5	Byron Nelson	75	76	71	74	296
6	Ed Dudley	70	74	78	75	297
7=	Arthur Lacey	75	73	75	75	298
	W Laidlaw	77	72	73	76	298
	Alf Padgham	72	74	76	76	298
10	Horton Smith	77	71	79	72	299
11=	Ralph Guldahl	77	72	74	77	300
	Sam Snead	75	74	75	76	300
13	Bill Branch	72	75	73	81	301
14	Denny Shute	73	73	76	80	302
15=	Percy Alliss	75	76	75	77	303
	Henry Picard	76	77	70	80	303
17=	Jimmy Adams	74	78	76	76	304
	Arthur Havers	77	75	76	76	304
	Bobby Locke (a)	74	74	77	79	304
	Fred Robertson	73	75	78	78	304
21=	Bill Cox	74	77	81	73	305
	Dai Rees	75	73	78	79	305
23	Jack Busson	74	77	79	76	306
24	Tom Collinge	75	75	83	74	307
25	Douglas Cairncross	73	76	77	82	308
26=	Marcel Dallemagne	78	75	79	77	309
	Walter Hagen	76	72	80	81	309
	Jack M'Lean	78	74	81	76	309
29=	John Burton	76	75	82	77	310
	Sam King	79	74	75	82	310
	Ernest E Whitcombe	76	76	81	77	310

Round Leader(s)
R1 Dudley; 70
R2 R Whitcombe; 142
R3 R Whitcombe; 216
Lowest Scores
R2 R Whitcombe; 70
R3 C Lacey; 70
R4 Cotton; 71

99

1938

1–4 April

THE MASTERS
Augusta National GC, Augusta, Georgia
6925 yards _PAR 72 (288)_

Harry Cooper again came in 2nd (tied this time), failing to capitalize on a good start. Henry Picard's 1st Major was compensation for his 1935 diasppointment in the Masters. Leading by 4 after 36 holes, he fell away badly then, but this time a solid 2nd half saw him home.

1	**HENRY PICARD** ($1500)	71	72	72	70	285
2=	Harry Cooper	68	77	71	71	287
	Ralph Guldahl	73	70	73	71	287
4	Paul Runyan	71	73	74	70	288
5	Byron Nelson	73	74	70	73	290
6=	Ed Dudley	70	69	77	75	291
	Felix Serafin	72	71	78	70	291
8=	Dick Metz	70	77	74	71	292
	Jimmy Thomson	74	70	76	72	292
10=	Vic Ghezzi	75	74	70	74	293
	Jimmy Hines	75	71	75	72	293
	Lawson Little	72	75	74	72	293
13=	Billy Burke	73	73	76	73	295
	Gene Sarazen	78	70	68	79	295
15	Stanley Horne	74	74	77	71	296
16=	Bobby Jones (a)	76	74	72	75	297
	Harold McSpaden	72	75	77	73	297
18=	Bobby Cruickshank	72	75	77	74	298
	Johnny Revolta	73	72	76	77	298
	Tommy Taller	74	69	75	80	298
22=	Chuck Kocsis (a)	76	73	77	73	299
	Horton Smith	75	75	78	71	299
24	Sam Parks, Jr	75	75	76	74	300
25=	Wiffy Cox	74	78	74	75	301
	Ben Hogan	75	76	78	72	301
27=	Ky Laffoon	78	76	74	74	302
	Tony Manero	72	78	82	70	302
	Frank Walsh	74	75	77	76	302
	Al Watrous	73	77	76	76	302

Round Leader(s)
R1   Cooper; 68
R2   Dudley; 139
R3   Picard; 215
Lowest Scores
R2   Dudley, Tailer; 69
R3   Sarazen; 68
R4   Manero, Picard, Runyan, Serafin; 70

1938

9–11 June

US OPEN
Cherry Hills CC, Denver, Colorado
6888 yards _PAR 71 (284)_

Guldahl's easy back-to-back win was only the 4th time it had happened in the Open. Willie Anderson, John McDermott and Bobby Jones were the other successful defending champions. Ray Ainsley set a record which he would never crow about. He took 19 at the par 4 16th in R2. He missed the cut.

1	**RALPH GULDAHL** (£1000)	74	70	71	69	284
2	Dick Metz	73	68	70	79	290
3=	Harry Cooper	76	69	76	71	292
	Toney Penna	78	72	74	68	292
5=	Byron Nelson	77	71	74	72	294
	Emery Zimmerman	72	71	73	78	294
7=	Frank Moore	79	73	72	71	295
	Henry Picard	70	70	77	78	295
	Paul Runyan	78	72	71	74	295
10	Gene Sarazen	74	74	75	73	296
11=	Vic Ghezzi	79	71	75	72	297
	Jimmy Hines	70	75	69	83	297
	Denny Shute	77	71	72	77	297
	George Von Elm	78	72	71	76	297
15	Willie Hunter, Jr	73	72	78	75	298
16=	Olin Dutra	74	71	77	77	299
	Harold McSpaden	76	67	74	82	299
	Johnny Revolta	74	72	77	76	299
19=	Jim Foulis	74	74	75	77	300
	Horton Smith	80	73	73	74	300
	Al Zimmerman	76	77	75	72	300
22	Charles Lacey	77	75	75	75	302
23	Tommy Armour	78	70	75	80	303
24=	Al Huske	76	79	76	73	304
	Johnny Rogers	71	76	73	84	304
26	Charles Sheppard	79	73	74	79	305
27=	Joe Belfore	75	73	80	78	306
	Stanley Kertes	77	72	82	75	306
	Alvin Krueger	79	69	79	79	306
	Ray Mangrum	77	77	73	79	306

Round Leader(s)
R1   Hines, Picard; 70
R2   Picard; 140
R3   Metz; 211
Lowest Scores
R2   McSpaden; 67
R3   Hines; 69
R4   Penna; 68

1938
BRITISH OPEN
Royal St George's GC, Sandwich, Kent, England
6728 yards

1938
US PGA
Shawnee CC, Shawnee-on-Delaware,
Pennsylvania

Reg Whitcombe, the youngest of the family after Ernest (R) and Charles, improved on his previous-year's runner-up position to take the Open at Sandwich. The winds on the last day were the strongest since Muirfield in 1929, and the Exhibition Tent collapsed. Padgham drove the green on the 384-yard 11th for an eagle-2, while the opposite happened to Cyril Tolley who, on the 14th saw his 1 iron clear water only for it to blow back. He'd already hit a driver off the tee.

1	**REG WHITCOMBE** (£100)	71	71	75	78	295
2	Jimmy Adams	70	71	78	78	297
3	Henry Cotton	74	73	77	74	298
4=	Dick Burton	71	69	78	85	303
	Jack Busson	71	69	83	80	303
	Allan Dailey	73	72	80	78	303
	Alf Padgham	74	72	75	82	303
8=	Fred Bullock	73	74	77	80	304
	Bill Cox	70	70	84	80	304
10=	Bert Gadd	71	70	84	80	305
	Bobby Locke	73	72	81	79	305
	Charles Whitcombe	71	75	79	80	305
13=	Sid Brews	76	70	84	77	307
	Dai Rees	73	72	79	83	307
15=	JH Ballingall	76	72	83	77	308
	Alf Perry	71	74	77	86	308
17	Arthur Lacey	74	72	82	81	309
18	Bill Shankland	74	74	84	81	311
19	Ernest R Whitcombe	70	77	83	82	312
20=	Jimmy Black	72	72	83	86	313
	PJ Mahon	73	74	83	83	313
22	Jack M'Lean	72	74	83	85	314
23=	Marcel Dallemagne	70	74	86	85	315
	Willie Hastings	74	74	83	84	315
	Sam King	74	73	83	85	315
26=	Johnny Fallon	70	75	82	89	316
	Eustace Storey (a)	77	71	84	84	316
28=	Ernest WH Kenyon	77	71	86	83	317
	Bob Pemberton	74	72	91	80	317
	Cyril Tolley (a)	77	68	86	86	317

Round Leader(s)
R1 Adams, Cox, E Whitcombe, Dallemagne, Fallon; 70
R2 Burton, Busson, Cox; 140
R3 R Whitcombe; 217
Lowest Scores
R2 Tolley; 68
R3 Padgham, R Whitcombe; 75
R4 Cotton; 74

MATCHPLAY
63 qualifiers, plus the defending champion (Denny Shute), after 36 holes strokeplay (Low – Frank Moore, 136)
Rs1&2, 18 holes: R3,QF,SF&F, 36 holes

Paul Runyan immediately followed Denny Shute into the record books as a two-time winner of the PGA. He joined Shute, Jim Barnes, Walter Hagen, Gene Sarazen and Leo Diegel as the only golfers to have won the Championship more than once. Despite being taken to an extra hole by Horton Smith, Runyan had a reasonably trouble-free ride to the final where he demoralized the young Sam Snead.

FINAL
PAUL RUNYAN ($1100)
beat
SAM SNEAD, 8&7

Round by Round Details

ROUND 2 (Last 32)
Denny Shute bt John Thoren 7&6; Jimmy Hines bt Frank Walsh 2&1; Byron Nelson bt Alvin Krueger 1 up (after 20); Harry Bassler bt Ed Dudley 4&3; Marvin Stahl bt George Whitehead 6&5; Jim Foulis bt Jimmy Thomson 1 up; SAM SNEAD bt Terl Johnson 4&3; Felix Serafin bt Ky Laffoon 3&2; Billy Burke bt Frank Moore 1 up (after 19); Horton Smith bt Leo Diegel 2&1; Ray Mangrum bt Harold McSpaden 1 up (after 20); PAUL RUNYAN bt Tony Manero 3&2; Gene Sarazen bt Harry Nettlebladt 6&5; Jimmy Demaret bt Johnny Revolta 2up; Henry Picard bt Bob Shave 3&2; Dick Metz bt Ralph Guldahl 1 up

ROUND 3 (Last 16)
Hines bt Shute 2&1
Nelson bt Bassler 11&10
Foulis bt Stahl 6&5
SNEAD bt Serafin 4&3
Smith bt Burke 3&2
RUNYAN bt Mangrum 1 up (after 37)
Sarazen bt Demaret 1 up (after 38)
Picard bt Metz 4&3

QUARTER FINAL (QF)
Hines by Nelson 2&1
SNEAD bt Foulis 8&7
RUNYAN bt Smith 4&3
Picard bt Sarazen 3&2

SEMI FINAL (SF)
SNEAD bt Hines 1 up
RUNYAN bt Picard 4&3

1939   30 March–2 April
THE MASTERS
Augusta National GC, Augusta, Georgia
6925 yards PAR 72 (288)

Sam Snead set a new low for all Majors and looked a certainty to win the Masters, until Guldahl came home in 33 to set the first-ever sub-280 total. This also established a record of 8 under par for Major Championships.

1	**RALPH GULDAHL** ($1500)	72	68	70	69	279
2	Sam Snead	70	70	72	68	280
3=	Billy Burke	69	72	71	70	282
	Lawson Little	72	72	68	70	282
5	Gene Sarazen	73	66	72	72	283
6	Craig Wood	72	73	71	68	284
7	Byron Nelson	71	69	72	75	287
8	Henry Picard	71	71	76	71	289
9	Ben Hogan	75	71	72	72	290
10=	Ed Dudley	75	75	69	72	291
	Toney Penna	72	75	72	72	291
12=	Tommy Armour	71	74	76	72	293
	Vic Ghezzi	73	76	72	72	293
	Harold McSpaden	75	72	74	72	293
15	Denny Shute	78	71	73	72	294
16=	Paul Runyan	73	71	75	76	295
	Felix Serafin	74	76	73	72	295
18=	Chick Harbert	74	73	75	74	296
	Jimmy Thomson	75	71	73	77	296
	Charlie Yates (a)	74	73	74	75	296
21	Tommy Taller	78	75	73	71	297
22	Jimmy Hines	76	73	74	75	298
	Ky Laffoon	72	75	73	78	298
	Frank Moore	75	74	75	74	298
25	Al Watrous	75	75	74	75	299
26=	Tony Manero	76	73	77	74	300
	Horton Smith	75	79	74	72	300
	Willie Turnesa (a)	78	70	79	73	300
29=	Jess Sweetser (a)	75	75	75	77	302
	Frank Walsh	76	76	72	78	302

Round Leader(s)
R1   Burke; 69
R2   Sarazen; 139
R3   Guldahl; 210

Lowest Scores
R2   Sarazen; 66
R3   Little; 68
R4   Snead, Wood; 68

1939   8–12 June
US OPEN
Philadelphia CC, Philadelphia, Pennsylvania

Byron Nelson's 2nd Major, after a triple-tie, should have belonged to Sam Snead. Building on a good start, Snead led, or had a share of the lead, throughout. Arriving at the 18th tee he needed a par-5 to win, shot 8, and didn't even make the play-off . Craig Wood has the dubious honour of being the first man to finish 2nd in every Major. He holds the equally-undesirable record of having been beaten in a play-off (extra holes in the PGA) in every Major.

1	**BYRON NELSON*** ($1000)	72	73	71	68	284
2	Craig Wood	70	71	71	72	284
3	Denny Shute	70	72	70	72	284
4	Bud Ward (a)	69	73	71	72	285
5	Sam Snead	68	71	73	74	286
6	Johnny Bulla	72	71	68	76	287
7=	Ralph Guldahl	71	73	72	72	288
	Dick Metz	76	72	71	69	288
9=	Ky Laffoon	76	70	73	70	289
	Harold McSapden	70	73	71	75	289
	Paul Runyan	76	70	71	72	289
12=	Harry Cooper	71	72	75	72	290
	Ed Dudley	76	72	73	69	290
	Henry Picard	72	72	72	74	290
15	Horton Smith	72	68	75	76	291
16=	Sam Byrd	75	71	72	74	292
	Olin Dutra	70	74	70	78	292
	Clayton Heafner	73	73	66	80	292
	Wilford Wehrle (a)	71	77	69	75	292
20=	Jimmy Hines	73	74	77	69	293
	Johnny Rogers	75	70	69	79	293
22=	Tommy Armour	70	75	69	80	294
	Jimmy Demaret	72	76	72	74	294
	Johnny Revolta	73	76	71	74	294
25=	Bobby Cruickshank	73	74	73	75	295
	Jim Foulis	73	75	77	70	295
	Dutch Harrison	75	72	74	74	295
	Matt Kowal	69	76	75	75	295
29=	Vic Ghezzi	73	71	76	76	296
	Ed Oliver	75	77	72	72	296
	Felix Serafin	80	72	71	73	296

* Byron Nelson beat Craig Wood and Denny Shute after two 18-Hole Play-offs:
11 July – Nelson (68) tied with Wood (68) - Shute (76) eliminated;
12 July – Nelson (70) beat Wood (73)

Round Leader(s)	**Lowest Scores**
R1 Snead; 68	R2 Smith; 68
R2 Snead; 139	R3 Heafner; 66
R3 Bulla; 211	R4 Nelson; 68

| 5–7 July | **1939** | 9–15 July | **1939** |

BRITISH OPEN
Royal & Ancient GC, St Andrews, Fife, Scotland
6842 yards

US PGA
Pomonock CC, Flushing, New York

The last Open Championship before the second great war in Europe was to intervene, was won for the only time by Dick Burton. He does hold the record though for holding the Claret Jug for the longest time! It was the end of an era in more ways than one. The 1902 Champion, Sandy Herd, ended his 54-year relationship with The Open at the age of 71. In his 1st Open, in 1885, he was in a field that included Old Tom Morris; and his younger brother Fred won the US Open as long ago as 1898. He is undoubtedly *the* stepping stone linking the origins of Major Championships in 1860 to modern times.

1	**DICK BURTON**	70	72	77	71	290
	(£100)					
2	Johnny Bulla	77	71	71	73	292
3=	Johnny Fallon	71	73	71	79	294
	Sam King	74	72	75	73	294
	Alf Perry	71	74	73	76	294
	Bill Shankland	72	73	72	77	294
	Reg Whitcombe	71	75	74	74	294
8	Martin Pose	71	72	76	76	295
9=	Percy Alliss	75	73	74	74	296
	Ernest WH Kenyon	73	75	74	74	296
	Bobby Locke	70	75	76	75	296
12	Dai Rees	71	74	75	77	297
13=	Jimmy Adams	73	74	75	76	298
	Enrique Bertolino	73	75	75	75	298
	Jimmy Bruen (a)	72	75	75	76	298
	Henry Cotton	74	72	76	76	298
17=	Bill Anderson	73	74	77	75	299
	Enrique Serra	77	72	73	77	299
19	WH Green	75	75	72	78	300
20=	Bill Davies	71	79	74	77	301
	Syd Easterbrook	74	71	80	76	301
	Alex Kyle (a)	74	76	75	76	301
23=	LG Crawley (a)	72	76	80	74	302
	Max Faulkner	70	76	76	80	302
25	Harry Busson	70	75	81	77	303
26=	Laurie Ayton, Jr	72	77	78	77	304
	WS Collins	75	74	79	76	304
	Fred Taggart	73	77	76	78	304
29	Aurelio Castanon	77	73	80	75	305
30=	Laurie Ayton, Sr	76	72	82	76	306
	Charlie Ward	71	74	78	83	306

Round Leader(s)
R1   Burton, Busson, Faulkner, Locke; 70
R2   Burton; 142
R3   Fallon; 215
Lowest Scores
R2   Bulla, Easterbrook; 71
R3   Bulla, Fallon; 71
R4   Burton;

MATCHPLAY
64 qualifiers after 36 holes strokeplay (Low – Dutch Harrison, Ben Hogan, Ky Laffoon, Emerick Kocsis, 138)
Rs1&2, 18 holes: R3,QF,SF&F, 36 holes

Byron Nelson was denied consecutive Majors victories when Henry Picard birdied the 36th to take the final into overtime - and repeated the dose on the 37th. This was Picard's 2nd Major (he collected the Masters in the previous year) but he was not destined to add to them. Poor health was shortly to curtail his career - but his driver lived for many years and did great things. He gave it to Sam Snead.

FINAL
HENRY PICARD ($1100)
beat
BYRON NELSON, 1up (after 37)

Round by Round Details

ROUND 2 (Last 32)
Paul Runyan bt Frank Champ 3&2; Ben Hogan bt Abe Espinosa 5&4; Billy Burke bt Herman Barron 2&1; Dick Metz bt Al Brosch 1up; Tom O'Connor bt Ky Laffoon 2up; Rod Munday bt Jack Ryan 2up; HENRY PICARD v Joe Zarhardt 2up; Al Watrous bt Ken Tucker 5&3; Dutch Harrison bt Johnny Farrell 3&2; Bruce Coltart bt Mike Turnesa 1up (after 21); Clarence Doser bt Ralph Guldahl 2up; Horton Smith bt Ray Mangrum 3&2; Emerick Kocsis bt Vic Ghezzi 3&1; Denny Shute bt Leo Diegel 3&1; Johnny Revolta bt Tony Manero 3&2; BYRON NELSON bt William Francis 3&1

ROUND 3 (Last 16)
Runyan bt Hogan 3&2
Metz bt Burke 6&4
Munday bt O'Connor 2up
PICARD bt Watrous 8&7
Harrison bt Coltart 10&9
Smith bt Doser 4&2
Kocsis bt Shute 3&1
NELSON bt Revolta 6&4

QUARTER FINAL (QF)
Metz bt Runyan 2&1
PICARD bt Munday 2&1
Harrison bt Smith 4&3
NELSON bt Kocsis 10&9

SEMI FINAL (SF)
PICARD bt Metz 1up
NELSON bt Harrison 9&8

1940
4–7 April
THE MASTERS
Augusta National GC, Augusta, Georgia
6925 yards _PAR 72 (288)_

1940
6–9 June
US OPEN
Canterbury GC, Cleveland, Ohio
6894 yards _PAR 72 (288)_

Records fell to Jimmy Demaret who posted 30 on the back 9 – and Lloyd Mangrum whose low of 64 beat the previous record for any Major. Demaret gradually clawed his way back into the Tournament and eventually won by a then Masters record margin of 4. Demaret was to become a feature in a few Masters to come and went on to regain the title in 1947 and 1950. He was less lucky in the other Majors, though.

Former multiple Amateur Champion, Lawson Little, beat Gene Sarazen after a play-off. Sarazen had pulled back 3 shots over the final holes to tie. Ed Oliver scored 287, but was disqualified for starting his last round earlier than scheduled due to the threat of a storm. Lawson became the 6th player to have won both US Amateur and Open Championships, but the first of them to win the Open as a professional.

I	**JIMMY DEMARET** ($1500)	67	72	70	71	280
2	Lloyd Mangrum	64	75	71	74	284
3	Byron Nelson	69	72	74	70	285
4=	Harry Cooper	69	75	73	70	287
	Ed Dudley	73	72	71	71	287
	Willie Goggin	71	72	73	71	287
7=	Henry Picard	71	71	71	75	288
	Sam Snead	71	72	69	76	288
	Craig Wood	70	75	67	76	288
10=	Ben Hogan	73	74	69	74	290
	Toney Penna	73	73	72	72	290
12=	Paul Runyan	72	73	72	74	291
	Frank Walsh	73	75	69	74	291
14=	Sam Byrd	73	74	72	73	292
	Johnny Farrell	76	72	70	74	292
	Ralph Guldahl	74	73	71	74	292
17=	Harold McSpaden	73	71	74	75	293
	Charlie Yates (a)	72	75	71	75	293
19=	Lawson Little	70	77	75	72	294
	Ed Oliver	73	75	74	72	294
21=	Johnny Bulla	73	73	74	75	295
	Dick Metz	71	74	75	75	295
	Gene Sarazen	74	71	77	73	295
	Bud Ward (a)	74	68	75	78	295
	Al Watrous	75	70	73	77	295
26	Jim Ferrier	73	74	75	74	296
27=	Jimmy Hines	75	76	74	72	297
	Johnny Revolta	74	74	74	75	297
29=	Jim Foulis	74	75	73	76	298
	Tony Manero	75	75	73	75	298

Round Leader(s)
R1 Mangrum; 64
R2 Demaret, Mangrum; 139
R3 Demaret; 209
Lowest Scores
R2 Ward; 68
R3 Wood; 67
R4 Cooper, Nelson; 70

I	**LAWSON LITTLE*** ($1000)	72	69	73	73	287
2	Gene Sarazen	71	74	70	72	287
3	Horton Smith	69	72	78	69	288
4	Craig Wood	72	73	72	72	289
5=	Ralph Guldahl	73	71	76	70	290
	Ben Hogan	70	73	74	73	290
	Lloyd Mangrum	75	70	71	74	290
	Byron Nelson	72	74	70	74	290
9	Dick Metz	75	72	72	72	291
10=	Ed Dudley	73	75	71	73	292
	Frank Walsh	73	69	71	79	292
12=	Tommy Armour	73	74	75	71	293
	Harold McSpaden	74	72	70	77	293
	Henry Picard	73	73	71	76	293
15	Vic Ghezzi	70	74	75	75	294
16=	Jim Foulis	73	73	77	72	295
	Gene Kunes	76	72	73	74	295
	Johnny Revolta	73	74	72	76	295
	Sam Snead	67	74	73	81	295
20=	Andrew Gibson	71	75	77	73	296
	Jimmy Hines	73	74	77	72	296
	Felix Serafin	77	74	71	74	296
23=	Jock Hutchison, Jr	73	72	75	77	297
	Eddie Kirk	73	77	74	73	297
	Wilford Wehrle (a)	78	73	72	74	297
	Leland Wilcox	75	73	74	75	297
27	Ray Mangrum	73	78	75	72	298
28	Johnny Farrell	75	77	76	71	299
29=	Bruce Coltart	80	72	74	74	300
	Jim Ferrier (a)	73	74	78	75	300
	Al Huske	70	80	76	74	300
	Sam Parks, Jr	69	74	79	78	300
	Henry Ransom	75	77	74	74	300
	Jack Ryan	75	75	77	73	300
	Andrew Szwedko (a)	76	77	76	71	300

* Lawson Little (70) beat Gene Sarazen (73) in the 18-Hole Play-off

Round Leader(s)
R1 Snead; 67
R2 Little, Smith, Snead; 141
R3 Walsh; 213

Lowest Scores
R2 Little, Walsh; 69
R3 McSpaden, Nelson, Sarazen; 70
R4 Smith; 69

1940–45
BRITISH OPEN
NO CHAMPIONSHIPS

26 August–2 September

US PGA
Hershey CC, Hershey, Pennsylvania

1940

MATCHPLAY
64 qualifiers after 36 holes strokeplay (Low - Dick Metz, 140)
Rs1,2&3, 18 holes: QF,SF&F, 36 holes

Byron Nelson matched Hagen, Sarazen, Barnes and Armour by winning his 3rd different Major. Sam Snead was still searching for his first title when he went down to Nelson at the 36th hole. Hagen's victory was his 40th and last match win in the PGA, while rival Sarazen, in beating Ray Mangrum, notched up win No 43 - and still had some years to go.

FINAL
BYRON NELSON
($1100) beat
SAM SNEAD, 1up

Round by Round Details

ROUND 2 (Last 32)
Henry Picard bt Alex Gerlak 4&3; Gene Sarazen bt Ray Mangrum 2&1; Jimmy Hines bt Ray Hill 2&1; SAM SNEAD bt Charles Sheppard 3&2; Ed Dudley bt John Gibson 2&1; Paul Runyan bt Al Watrous 3&2; Walter Hagen bt Vic Ghezzi 2&1; Harold McSpaden bt Herman Keiser 2&1; Dick Metz bt Ky Laffoon 3&2; BYRON NELSON bt Frank Walsh 1up (after 20); Arthur Clark bt Billy Burke 1up; Eddie Kirk bt Jimmy Demaret 2&1; Al Brosch bt Red Francis 5&4; Ben Hogan bt Harry Nettlebladt 5&4; Ralph Guldahl bt John Kinder 6&5; Jim Foulis bt Craig Wood 1up (after 19)

ROUND 3 (Last 16)
Sarazen bt Picard 1up
SNEAD bt Hines 2&1
Runyan bt Dudley 4&3
McSpaden bt Hagen 1up
NELSON bt Metz 2&1
Kirk bt Clark 5&4
Hogan bt Brosch 5&4
Guldahl bt Foulis 5&3

QUARTER FINAL (QF)
SNEAD by Sarazen 1up
McSpaden bt Runyan 8&6
NELSON bt Kirk 6&5
Guldahl bt Hogan 3&2

SEMI FINAL (SF)
SNEAD bt McSpaden 5&4
NELSON bt Guldahl 3&2

1941

3–6 April

THE MASTERS

Augusta National GC, Augusta, Georgia
6925 yards _PAR 72 (288)_

Craig Wood's luck had changed. After a decade and more of disappointment he won his 1st Major. The US entered the War before the end of the year, so Wood's success seemed to arrive just in time. His win equalled the record under par score – 8 – and set a new 1st 36-hole low for the Masters.

1	**CRAIG WOOD** ($1500)	66	71	71	72	280
2	Byron Nelson	71	69	73	70	283
3	Sam Byrd	73	70	68	74	285
4	Ben Hogan	71	72	75	68	286
5	Ed Dudley	73	72	75	68	288
6=	Vic Ghezzi	77	71	71	70	289
	Sam Snead	73	75	72	69	289
8	Lawson Little	71	70	74	75	290
9=	Willie Goggin	71	72	72	76	291
	Harold McSpaden	75	74	72	70	291
	Lloyd Mangrum	71	72	72	76	291
12=	Jimmy Demaret	77	69	71	75	292
	Clayton Heafner	73	70	76	73	292
14=	Harry Cooper	72	73	75	73	293
	Ralph Guldahl	76	71	75	71	293
17	Jack Ryan	73	74	74	74	295
18	Denny Shute	77	75	74	70	296
19=	Dick Chapman (a)	76	73	70	78	297
	Jimmy Hines	76	74	75	72	297
	Gene Kunes	76	74	76	71	297
	Dick Metz	74	72	75	76	297
	Sam Parks, Jr	75	76	75	71	297
	Toney Penna	73	74	80	70	297
	Gene Sarazen	76	72	74	75	297
	Felix Serafin	72	79	74	72	297
	Horton Smith	74	72	77	74	297
28	Ray Mangrum	76	70	78	74	298
29=	Jim Ferrier	75	76	73	75	299
	Jim Foulis	76	75	71	77	299
	Martin Pose	77	74	76	72	299

Round Leader(s)
R1   Wood; 66
R2   Wood; 137
R3   Wood; 208
Lowest Scores
R2   Demaret, Nelson; 69
R3   Byrd; 68
R4   Dudley, Hogan; 68

1941

5–7 June

US OPEN

Colonial CC, Fort Worth, Texas
7005 yards _PAR 70 (280)_

As if to make up for all his previous failures, Craig Wood made it two in a row when he won the Open at Colonial in June. Just as sweet as the win was to be able to turn the tables on Denny Shute – something of a _bête noir_ to Woods over the years. Par golf over the 2nd 36 holes kept him ahead of the field.

1	**CRAIG WOOD** ($1000)	73	71	70	70	284
2	Denny Shute	69	75	72	71	287
3=	Johnny Bulla	75	71	72	71	289
	Ben Hogan	74	77	68	70	289
5=	Herman Barron	75	71	74	71	291
	Paul Runyan	73	72	71	75	291
7=	Dutch Harrison	70	82	71	71	294
	Harold McSpaden	71	75	74	74	294
	Gene Sarazen	74	73	72	75	294
10=	Ed Dudley	74	74	74	73	295
	Lloyd Mangrum	73	74	72	76	295
	Dick Metz	71	74	76	74	295
13=	Henry Ransom	72	74	75	75	296
	Horton Smith	73	75	73	75	296
	Sam Snead	76	70	77	73	296
	Harry Todd (a)	72	77	76	71	296
17=	Lawson Little	71	73	79	74	297
	Byron Nelson	73	73	74	77	297
19	Vic Ghezzi	70	79	77	72	298
20	Gene Kunes	71	79	74	75	299
21=	Ralph Guldahl	79	76	72	73	300
	Clayton Heafner	72	72	78	78	300
	Johnny Palmer	74	76	76	74	300
24	Jimmy Hines	74	75	76	76	301
25	Joe Zarhardt	74	76	77	75	302
26=	Sam Byrd	76	78	75	74	303
	Herman Keiser	74	77	76	76	303
	Johnny Morris	72	73	81	77	303
	Henry Picard	77	79	72	75	303
30=	Jim Ferrier	77	71	81	75	304
	Jerry Gianferante	76	77	74	77	304
	Bud Ward (a)	76	77	75	76	304

Round Leader(s)
R1   Shute; 69
R2   Heafner, Little, Shute, Wood; 144
R3   Wood; 214
Lowest Scores
R2   Snead; 70
R3   Hogan; 68
R4   Hogan, Wood; 70

1940–45	7–13 July	**1941**
BRITISH OPEN	**US PGA**	
NO CHAMPIONSHIPS	Cherry Hills CC, Denver, Colorado	

MATCHPLAY

63 qualifiers, plus the defending champion (Byron Nelson), after 36 holes strokeplay (Low - Sam Snead, 138)
Rs1&2, 18 holes: R3,QF,SF&F, 36 holes

Wood's bid to win all 3 US Majors in one season failed at the 2nd fence in the PGA, when he was hammered 6&5 by little-known Mark Fry. Vic Ghezzi had been competing in the PGA for some years without proceeding to the later stages. Now wins over Lloyd Mangrum in the SF and an overtime win in the final over Byron Nelson made him a worthy Champion.

FINAL
VIC GHEZZI ($1100)
beat
BYRON NELSON, 1up (after 38)

Round by Round Details

ROUND 2 (Last 32)
BYRON NELSON bt William Heinlein 1up; Ralph Guldahl bt Gene Kunes 2&1; Ben Hogan bt Bud Oakley 2up; Horton Smith bt Ralph Stonehouse 3&2; Denny Shute bt Jim Foulis 1up; Leonard Ott bt Jack Ryan (default); Bruce Coltart bt George Fazio 1up (after 19); Gene Sarazen bt Toney Penna 1up (after 19); Sam Snead bt Phil Greenwaldt 7&6; Mike Turnesa bt Harry Bassler 4&2; Mark Fry bt Craig Wood 6&5; Lloyd Mangrum bt Charles Sheppard 3&1; Jack Grout bt Fay Coleman 1up; VIC GHEZZI bt Augie Nordone 1up; Harold McSpaden bt George Schneiter 3&2; Jimmy Hines bt Ed Dudley 3&2

ROUND 3 (Last 16)
NELSON bt Guldahl 4&3
Hogan bt Smith 2&1
Shute bt Ott 5&3
Sarazen bt Coltart 9&7
Snead bt Turnesa 1up
Mangrum bt Fry 1up
GHEZZI bt Grout 1up
Hines bt McSpaden 6&4

QUARTER FINAL (QF)
NELSON bt Hogan 2&1
Sarazen bt Shute 7&6
Mangrum bt Snead 6&4
GHEZZI bt Hines 6&4

SEMI FINAL (SF)
NELSON bt Sarazen 2up
GHEZZI bt Mangrum 1up

1942

9–13 April

THE MASTERS

Augusta National GC, Augusta, Georgia
6925 yards _PAR 72 (288)_

1942–45

US OPEN

NO CHAMPIONSHIPS

The Clash of the Titans. The two biggest names in the game at that time went to an historic play-off. Hogan had reduced Nelson's 36-hole lead of 8 to tie on a record-equalling 280 after the latter's 135 – another Masters low. In the play-off, Hogan raced away to lead by 3, but starting at the 6th, Nelson started to reel him in and pass him to win by one.

1	**BYRON NELSON***	68	67	72	73	280
	($1500)					
2	Ben Hogan	73	70	67	70	280
3	Paul Runyan	67	73	72	71	283
4	Sam Byrd	68	68	75	74	285
5	Horton Smith	67	73	74	73	287
6	Jimmy Demaret	70	70	75	75	290
7=	Dutch Harrison	74	70	71	77	292
	Lawson Little	71	74	72	75	292
	Sam Snead	78	69	72	73	292
10=	Chick Harbert	73	73	72	75	293
	Gene Kunes	74	74	74	71	293
12	Jimmy Thomson	73	70	74	77	294
13	Chandler Harper	75	75	76	69	295
14	Willie Goggin	74	70	78	74	296
15=	Bobby Cruickshank	72	79	71	75	297
	Jim Ferrier	71	76	80	70	297
	Henry Picard	75	72	75	75	297
18=	Harry Cooper	74	77	76	72	299
	Harold McSpaden	74	72	79	74	299
	Felix Serafin	75	74	77	73	299
21	Ralph Guldahl	74	74	76	76	300
22	Toney Penna	74	79	73	75	301
23=	Billy Burke	71	79	80	72	302
	Herman Keiser	74	74	78	76	302
	Craig Wood	72	75	72	73	302
26=	Jim Foulis	75	71	79	78	303
	Johnny Palmer	78	75	75	75	303
28=	Tommy Armour	74	79	76	75	304
	Bobby Jones (a)	72	75	79	78	304
	Gene Sarazen	80	74	75	75	304
	Bud Ward (a)	76	73	80	75	304
	Charlie Yates (a)	78	76	74	76	304

* Byron Nelson (69) beat Ben Hogan (70) in the 18-Hole Play-off

Round Leader(s)	**Lowest Scores**
R1 Runyan, Smith; 67	R2 Nelson; 67
R2 Nelson; 135	R3 Hogan; 67
R3 Nelson; 207	R4 Harper; 69

1943–45
NO CHAMPIONSHIPS

1940–45	23–31 May	**1942**
BRITISH OPEN	**US PGA**	
NO CHAMPIONSHIPS	Seaview CC, Atlantic City, New Jersey	

MATCHPLAY
31 qualifiers, plus the defending champion (Vic Ghezzi), after 36 holes strokeplay (Low - Harry Cooper, 138)
All Rounds 36 holes

Unlike the other Majors, World War II did not disrupt the PGA in the same way. There was no Championship in 1943, but otherwise it was business as usual. Some pros had volunteered, others were conscripted, but in 1942 the PGA could still attract a strong field. There was a military feel to the final, all the same, when Army Cpl (shortly to become Sgt) Jim Turnesa lost out to Sam Snead, due to join the US Navy the following day, in a closer match than most people predicted. Snead made his Majors breakthrough, and went to war.

FINAL
SAM SNEAD ($1000)
beat
JIM TURNESA, 2&1

Round by Round Details

ROUND 1 (Last 32)
Jimmy Demaret bt Vic Ghezzi 4&3; Tom Harmon, Jr bt Bruce Coltart 3&2; Craig Wood bt Rod Munday 5&4; Leland Gibson bt Jimmy Gauntt 10&9; SAM SNEAD bt Sam Byrd 7&6; Willie Goggin bt Eddie Burke 2&1; Ed Dudley bt Denny Shute 3&2; Toney Penna bt Jimmy Hines 3&2; Harry Cooper bt Mike Turnesa 3&1; Lloyd Mangrum bt Dick Metz 6&5; Byron Nelson bt Harry Nettlebladt 5&3; Joe Kirkwood, Sr bt Jimmy Thomson 4&2; JIM TURNESA bt Dutch Harrison 6&5; Harold McSpaden bt Sam Parks, Jr 7&5; Ben Hogan bt Ben Loving 7&6; Ky Laffoon bt Vic Bass 12&11

ROUND 2 (Last 16)
Demaret bt Harmon 3&2
Wood bt Gibson 7&6
SNEAD bt Goggin 9&8
Dudley bt Penna 4&2
Cooper bt Mangrum 1 up
Nelson bt Kirkwood 2&1
JIM TURNESA bt McSpaden 1 up
Hogan bt Laffoon 9&8

QUARTER FINAL (QF)
Demaret bt Wood 7&6
SNEAD bt Dudley 1 up
Nelson bt Cooper 1 up (after 39)
JIM TURNESA bt Hogan 2&1

SEMI FINAL (SF)
SNEAD bt Demaret 3&2
JIM TURNESA bt Nelson 1 up (after 37)

1943–45
NO CHAMPIONSHIPS

1944
14–20 August
US PGA
Manito G&CC, Spokane, Washington

1945
9–15 July
US PGA
Moraine CC, Dayton, Ohio

MATCHPLAY
32 qualifiers after 36 holes strokeplay (Low - Byron Nelson)
All Rounds 36 holes

There was a less-familiar look to the competitors when the Championship resumed in 1944. It looked to be a foregone conclusion for Byron Nelson as he coasted through an under-strength field to meet little-known Bob Hamilton. Hamilton was 10-1 to beat Nelson, but in one of golf's biggest upsets, he did just that. Hamilton did less well in future – hampered as he was with burns from an aircraft accident, although he reappeared to contest the 1946 Masters.

FINAL
BOB HAMILTON ($3500)
beat
BYRON NELSON, 1up

Round by Round Details

ROUND 1 (Last 32)
BYRON NELSON bt Mike DeMassey 5&4; Mark Fry bt Neil Christian 2&1; Willie Goggin bt Purvis Ferree 8&7; Tony Manero bt Clayton Aleridge 1up (after 38); Sam Byrd bt WA Stackhouse 4&3; Chuck Congdon bt Henry Williams, Jr 7&6; Ed Dudley bt Steve Savel 7&6; Jimmy Hines bt Thurman Edwards 7&6; Harold McSpaden bt Bruce Coltart 7&5; Fred Annon bt Harry Nettlebladt 5&4; BOB HAMILTON bt Gene Kunes 6&5; Harry Bassler bt Joe Mozel 6&5; Art Bell bt Joe Zarhardt 1up (after 37); Craig Wood bt Jimmy D'Angelo 5&4; Toney Penna bt Morrie Gravatt 3&2; George Schneiter bt Ted Longworth 7&6

ROUND 2 (Last 16)
NELSON bt Fry 7&6
Goggin bt Manero 4&3
Congdon bt Byrd 2&1
Dudley bt Hines 1up (after 37)
McSpaden bt Annon 8&7
HAMILTON bt Bassler 6&5
Bell bt Wood 3&2
Schneiter bt Penna 4&3

QUARTER FINAL (QF)
NELSON bt Goggin 4&3
Congdon bt Dudley 6&5
HAMILTON bt McSpaden 2&1
Schneiter bt Bell 2&1

SEMI FINAL (SF)
NELSON bt Congdon 8&7
HAMILTON bt Schneiter 1up

MATCHPLAY
31 qualifiers, plus the defending champion (Bob Hamilton), after 36 holes strokeplay (Low - Byron Nelson, Johnny Revolta, 138)
All Rounds 36 holes

If 1930 was the year of Bobby Jones, then surely 1945 was Byron Nelson's year. Although no other Major was played, the PGA Championship was part of the Players' Tour which restarted the previous year. Chastened perhaps by his 1994 PGA defeat, Nelson was not going to allow a repetition to occur – in any event he played. From March to August 1945, he won every tournament he entered, to put together a consecutive sequence of wins, which just like Jones' achievement in 1930, will never be beaten. He won 11 altogether, including the PGA in July - which, with the winner's purse at $3750, was easily the richest of the Majors for several years to come.

FINAL
BYRON NELSON ($3750)
beat
SAM BYRD, 4&3

Round by Round Details

ROUND 1 (Last 32)
Jack Grout bt Bob Hamilton 5&4; Ky Laffoon bt Felix Serafin 4&3; Clarence Doser bt Harold McSpaden 5&4; Toney Penna bt Wayne Timberman 2up; Johnny Revolta bt Frank Kringle 10&9; SAM BYRD bt Augie Nordone 4&3; Herman Barron bt Harry Nettlebladt 5&3; Vic Ghezzi bt Ed Dudley 7&6; BYRON NELSON bt Gene Sarazen 4&3; Mike Turnesa bt John Gibson 5&4; Denny Shute bt Barney Clark 4&3; Bob Kepler bt George Schneiter 2&1; Terl Johnson bt Dutch Harrison 1up; Ralph Hutchison bt Ted Huge 6&5; Jim Turnesa bt Byron Harcke 6&5; Claude Harmon bt Verl Stinchcomb 2&1

ROUND 2 (Last 16)
Laffoon bt Grout 5&4
Doser bt Penna 1up
BYRD bt Revolta 2&1
Ghezzi bt Barron 2up
NELSON bt Mike Turnesa 1up
Shute bt Kepler 5&4
Hutchison bt Johnson 6&5
Harmon bt Jim Turnesa 8&7

QUARTER FINAL (QF)
Doser bt Laffoon 2&1
BYRD bt Ghezzi 7&6
NELSON bt Shute 3&2
Harmon bt Hutchison 4&3

SEMI FINAL (SF)
BYRD bt Doser 7&6
NELSON bt Harmon 5&4

BYRON NELSON (1912–) Won the PGA in 1945 – within a run of 11 consecutive tour victories between March and August
(Photo Hulton Getty)

1946
4–7 April
THE MASTERS
Augusta National GC, Augusta, Georgia
6925 yards _PAR 72 (288)_

Normal service was resumed in 1946 with all the Majors taking place. Herman Keiser surprisingly won the first post-war Masters, leaving Ben Hogan then with the longest reign of any golfer as runner-up in a Major – at least for a few months. Keiser's excellent start meant that Hogan had to charge the last round. This he duly did and had the chance to tie on the 18th when Keiser 3-putted. That Hogan did precisely the same was somewhat of an anticlimax.

1	**HERMAN KEISER** ($2500)	69	68	71	74	282
2	Ben Hogan	74	70	69	70	283
3	Bob Hamilton	75	69	71	72	287
4=	Jimmy Demaret	75	70	71	73	289
	Jim Ferrier	74	72	68	75	289
	Ky Laffoon	74	73	70	72	289
7=	Chick Harbert	69	75	76	70	290
	Clayton Heafner	74	69	71	76	290
	Byron Nelson	72	73	71	74	290
	Sam Snead	74	75	70	71	290
11	Jim Foulis	75	70	72	74	291
12	Cary Middlecoff (a)	72	76	70	74	292
13=	Vic Ghezzi	71	79	67	76	293
	George Schneiter	73	73	72	75	293
15	Fred Haas	71	75	68	80	294
16=	Johnny Bulla	72	76	73	74	295
	Lloyd Mangrum	76	75	72	72	295
18	Claude Harmon	76	75	74	71	296
19	Chandler Harper	74	76	73	74	297
20	Frank Stranahan (a)	76	74	73	75	298
21=	Lawson Little	74	74	78	73	299
	Toney Penna	71	73	80	75	299
	Felix Serafin	76	75	79	69	299
	Horton Smith	78	77	75	69	299
25=	Herman Barron	74	73	74	79	300
	Henry Picard	79	73	72	77	300
	Denny Shute	79	77	71	73	300
	Jimmy Thomson	72	70	79	79	300
29=	Gene Kunes	76	72	77	76	301
	Harold McSpaden	75	74	75	77	301
	Al Zimmerman	76	76	74	75	301

Round Leader(s)
R1 Harbert, Keiser; 69
R2 Keiser; 137
R3 Keiser; 208
Lowest Scores
R2 Keiser; 68
R3 Ghezzi; 67
R4 Serafin, Smith; 69

1946
13–16 June
US OPEN
Canterbury GC, Cleveland, Ohio
6926 yards _PAR 72 (288)_

Vic Ghezzi was denied his 2nd Major and Nelson his 6th, when Lloyd Mangrum won the three-way play-off at Cleveland. The 1st play-off was indecisive and in the repeat, with Mangrum 3 down on Ghezzi and 2 on Hogan with 6 to play, all look lost. 3 successive birdies changed all that and Mangrum's 2nd 72 was too good for the others.

1	**LLOYD MANGRUM*** ($1500)	74	70	68	72	284
2=	Vic Ghezzi	71	69	72	72	284
	Byron Nelson	71	71	69	73	284
4=	Herman Barron	72	72	72	69	285
	Ben Hogan	72	68	73	72	285
6=	Jimmy Demaret	71	74	73	68	286
	Ed Oliver	71	71	74	70	286
8=	Chick Harbert	72	78	67	70	287
	Dick Metz	76	70	72	69	287
10=	Dutch Harrison	75	71	72	70	288
	Lawson Little	72	69	76	71	288
12=	Ed Furgol	77	69	74	69	289
	Clayton Heafner	75	72	71	71	289
	Henry Picard	71	73	71	74	289
15=	Claude Harmon	72	77	70	72	291
	Chandler Harper	76	74	67	74	291
	Steve Kovach	71	72	73	75	291
	Toney Penna	69	77	74	71	291
19=	Gene Kunes	74	73	73	72	292
	Sam Snead	69	75	74	74	292
21	Paul Runyan	75	72	76	70	293
22=	Johnny Bulla	72	74	73	75	294
	Henry Ransom	71	73	73	77	294
	Harry Todd	75	73	70	76	294
	Lew Worsham	73	74	76	71	294
26=	Leland Gibson	74	71	78	72	295
	Smiley Quick (a)	75	76	72	72	295
	Mike Turnesa	70	76	74	75	295
	Ellsworth Vines	73	72	75	75	295
	Bud Ward (a)	74	77	72	72	295

* Lloyd Mangrum beat Vic Ghezzi and Byron Nelson after two 18-Hole Play-offs:
(am) Mangrum (72) tied with Ghezzi (72) and Nelson (72)
(pm) Mangrum (72) beat Ghezzi (73) and Nelson (73)

Round Leader(s)
R1 Penna, Snead; 69
R2 Ghezzi, Hogan; 140
R3 Nelson; 211
Lowest Scores
R2 Hogan; 68
R3 Harbert, Harper; 67
R4 Demaret; 68

3–5 July	**1946**

BRITISH OPEN

Royal & Ancient GC, St Andrews, Fife, Scotland
6923 yards

19–25 August	**1946**

US PGA

Portland GC, Portland, Oregon

It was fitting that the first post-war Open Championship, just like the last pre-war one, should be held over the Old Course at St Andrews. Unfortunately, Sam Snead did not consider his 1st Major all that important – and the Americans stayed away in their droves for another decade or more. All but one that is. Johnny Bulla remained faithful to the British Open for several years to come – and it was he that relieved Ben Hogan of his longevity crown for runner-up, set the previous April at Augusta.

1	**SAM SNEAD** (£150)	71	70	74	75	290
2=	Johnny Bulla	71	72	72	79	294
	Bobby Locke	69	74	75	76	294
4=	Henry Cotton	70	70	76	79	295
	Norman von Nida	70	76	74	75	295
	Dai Rees	75	67	73	80	295
	Charlie Ward	73	73	73	76	295
8=	Fred Daly	77	71	76	74	298
	Joe Kirkwood, Sr	71	75	78	74	298
10	Lawson Little	78	75	72	74	299
11	Harry Bradshaw	76	75	76	73	300
12	Dick Burton	74	76	76	76	302
13	Bill Shankland	76	76	77	75	304
14=	Bill Anderson	76	76	78	75	305
	Reg Whitcombe	71	76	82	76	305
16	Laurie Ayton, Jr	77	74	80	75	306
17	Percy Alliss	74	72	82	79	307
18=	Archie Compston	77	74	77	80	308
	Frank Jowle	78	74	76	80	308
	Arthur Lees	77	71	78	82	308
21=	G Knight	77	75	82	76	310
	Ernest E Whitcombe	75	79	77	79	310
23=	RK Bell (a)	81	73	81	77	312
	JA Jacobs	76	77	80	79	312
25=	Alf Perry	78	77	78	80	313
	JC Wilson (a)	78	76	81	78	313
27=	Flory van Donck	76	78	83	78	315
	A Dowie (a)	81	71	80	83	315
	AM Robertson	79	75	80	81	315
30=	Tom Haliburton	78	76	81	81	316
	Alf Padgham	79	74	76	87	316
	Ronnie White (a)	76	79	84	77	316

Round Leader(s)
R1   Locke; 69
R2   Cotton; 140
R3   Bulla, Rees, Snead; 215
Lowest Scores
R2   Rees; 67
R3   Bulla, Little; 72
R4   Bradshaw; 73

MATCHPLAY
63 qualifiers, plus the defending champion (Byron Nelson), after 36 holes strokeplay (Low - Jim Ferrier, 134)
Rs1&2, 18 holes: R3,QF,SF&F, 36 holes

After a compacted matchplay format during the War years, the PGA reverted to the 1941 set-up once more. Australian Jim Ferrier shot a round of 63 in his record qualifying score, and although the field was back to strength no-one could stop Ben Hogan ripping it apart. Big defeats of Art Bell and Frank Moore preceded the SF demolition of ex-Masters Champion, Jimmy Demaret. Hogan then blasted away Ed Oliver in the final. Byron Nelson, after his amazing year previously, and with a haul of 5 Majors, dramatically and prematurely retired from tournament golf. He did, however, play in a smattering of Major Championships for another 20 years.

FINAL
BEN HOGAN ($3500)
beat
ED OLIVER, 6&4

Round by Round Details

ROUND 2 (Last 32)
Byron Nelson bt Larry Lamberger 3&2; Herman Barron bt Fay Coleman 3&2; ED OLIVER bt Dick Metz 3&1; Chandler Harper bt Jimmy Thomson 2&1; Dutch Harrison bt Toney Penna 1up; Harold McSpaden bt Bob Hamilton 4&3; Chuck Congdon bt Newton Bassler 1up (after 19); George Schneiter bt Sam Snead 6&5; Jim Ferrier bt Lawson Little 3&2; Jimmy Demaret bt Dave Tinsley 3&2; Jim Turnesa bt Henry Ransom 1up; Dick Shoemaker bt Vic Ghezzi 1up; BEN HOGAN bt William Heinlein 4&3; Art Bell bt Al Nelson 4&3; Frank Moore bt George Fazio 2&1; Harry Bassler bt Lew Worsham 1up

ROUND 3 (Last 16)
Nelson bt Barron 3&2
OLIVER bt Harper 5&4
McSpaden bt Harrison 4&3
Congdon bt Schneiter 2&1
Demaret bt Ferrier 3&2
Turnesa bt Shoemaker 5&4
HOGAN bt Bell 5&4
Moore bt Harry Bassler 4&3

QUARTER FINAL (QF)
OLIVER bt Nelson 1up
McSpaden bt Congdon 5&3
Demaret bt Turnesa 6&5
HOGAN bt Moore 5&4

SEMI FINAL (SF)
OLIVER bt McSpaden 6&5
HOGAN bt Demaret 10&9

1947
THE MASTERS
3–6 April

Augusta National GC, Augusta, Georgia
6925 yards PAR 72 (288)

1947
US OPEN
12–15 June

St Louis CC, St Louis, Missouri
6532 yards PAR 71 (284)

Jimmy Demaret, badly beaten finalist in the PGA of 1946, was on much more familiar territory in the 1st Major of 1947 at Augusta National. Charged with a R1 69, he led from start to finish to win his 2nd Masters. The outstanding amateur of the next decade, Frank Stranahan, finished 3rd.

1	**JIMMY DEMARET** ($2500)	69	71	70	71	281
2=	Byron Nelson	69	72	72	70	283
	Frank Stranahan (a)	73	72	70	68	283
4=	Ben Hogan	75	68	71	70	284
	Harold McSpaden	74	69	70	71	284
6=	Jim Ferrier	70	71	73	72	286
	Henry Picard	73	70	72	71	286
8=	Chandler Harper	77	72	68	70	287
	Lloyd Mangrum	76	73	68	70	287
	Dick Metz	72	72	72	71	287
	Ed Oliver	70	72	74	71	287
	Toney Penna	71	70	75	71	287
13	Johnny Bulla	70	75	74	69	288
14=	Dick Chapman (a)	72	71	74	72	289
	Lawson Little	71	71	76	71	289
	Bobby Locke	74	74	71	70	289
17=	Herman Barron	71	71	74	74	290
	Fred Haas	70	74	73	73	290
	Johnny Palmer	70	73	74	73	290
20	Denny Shute	73	75	72	71	291
21	Vic Ghezzi	73	77	71	71	292
22=	Horton Smith	72	70	76	75	293
	Sam Snead	72	71	75	75	293
24=	Herman Keiser	74	75	73	72	294
	Ellsworth Vines	75	71	75	73	294
26=	Claude Harmon	73	69	76	77	295
	Gene Sarazen	75	76	74	70	295
	George Schneiter	70	75	78	72	295
29=	Dutch Harrison	74	71	74	77	296
	Clayton Heafner	75	73	75	73	296
	Cary Middlecoff	71	69	76	80	296
	Harry Todd	74	74	71	77	296

Round Leader(s)
R1 Demaret, Nelson; 69
R2 Demaret, Middlecoff; 140
R3 Demaret; 210

Lowest Scores
R2 Hogan; 68
R3 Harper, Mangrum; 68
R4 Stranahan; 68

Sam Snead never won the US Open – the only jewel missing from the crown. In the previous September the original trophy was destroyed by fire. Old trophy or new, Snead was never to get as close as 1947, when he and Lew Worsham tied. Worsham won the play-off on the last green in controversial circumstances. Worsham asked for a measure after Snead had addressed his 2½ foot putt. The measure still meant that Snead was first to putt. He missed, and Worsham made his to win.

1	**LEW WORSHAM*** ($2000)	70	70	71	71	282
2	Sam Snead	72	70	70	70	282
3=	Bobby Locke	68	74	70	73	285
	Ed Oliver	73	70	71	71	285
5	Bud Ward (a)	69	72	73	73	287
6=	Jim Ferrier	71	70	74	74	289
	Vic Ghezzi	74	73	73	69	289
	Leland Gibson	69	76	73	71	289
	Ben Hogan	70	75	70	74	289
	Johnny Palmer	72	70	75	72	289
	Paul Runyan	71	74	72	72	289
12	Chick Harbert	67	72	81	70	290
13=	Ed Furgol	70	75	72	74	291
	Dutch Harrison	76	72	70	73	291
	Dick Metz	69	70	78	74	291
	Bill Nary	77	71	70	73	291
	Frank Stranahan (a)	73	74	72	72	291
	Harry Todd	67	75	77	72	291
19=	Claude Harmon	74	72	74	72	292
	Gene Kunes	71	77	72	72	292
	George Payton	71	75	75	71	292
	Alfred Smith	70	73	76	73	292
23=	Sam Byrd	72	74	70	77	293
	Joe Kirkwood, Sr	72	73	70	78	293
	Lloyd Mangrum	77	72	69	75	293
	James McHale, Jr (a)	79	72	65	77	293
27=	Herman Barron	74	71	75	74	294
	Billy Burke	74	75	71	74	294
29=	Bob Hamilton	75	71	75	74	295
	Henry Ransom	67	74	79	75	295

* Lew Worsham (69) beat Sam Snead (70) in the 18-Hole Play-off

Round Leader(s)
R1 Harbert, Ransom, Todd; 67
R2 Harbert, Metz; 139
R3 Worsham; 211

Lowest Scores
R2 Demaret (39); 69
R3 McHale Jr; 65
R4 Ghezzi; 69

18–24 June		1947

US PGA

Plum Hollow CC, Detroit, Michigan

2–4 July		1947

BRITISH OPEN

Royal Liverpool GC, Hoylake, Cheshire, England

MATCHPLAY

63 qualifiers, plus the defending champion (Ben Hogan), after 36 holes strokeplay (Low - Jimmy Demaret, 137)
Rs1&2, 18holes: R3,QF,SF&F, 36 holes

Jim Ferrier became the first non-American born winner of the PGA since Tommy Armour in 1930. It was also the first final since 1937 without Hogan, Nelson or Snead. Good putting (just 52 over the 35 holes played) was Ferrier's secret. It was just as well as his driving off the tee and approach play were erratic. It is reported that he struck 7 spectators during the course of the final.

FINAL
JIM FERRIER ($3500)
beat
CHICK HARBERT, 5&4

Round by Round Details

ROUND 2 (Last 32)
Ky Laffoon bt Toney Penna 1up; Gene Sarazen bt Sam Snead 2&1; Dick Metz bt Henry Ransom 1up; Art Bell bt Johnny Bulla 4&3; Claude Harmon bt Jim Milward 5&3; JIM FERRIER bt Herman Barron 3&2; Mike Turnesa bt Chandler Harper 1up (after 22); Lloyd Mangrum bt Ed Dudley 4&3; Vic Ghezzi bt Earl Martin 6&5; Jim Turnesa bt Walter Ambo 4&3; Lew Worsham bt Clarence Doser 5&4; Reggie Myles bt George Schneiter 1up; CHICK HARBERT bt Clayton Heafner 1up (after 20); Ed Oliver bt Harry Bassler 4&3; Eddie Joseph bt Lloyd Wadkins 1up; Leland Gibson bt Jack Smith 3&2

ROUND 3 (Last 16)
Laffoon bt Sarazen 4&3
Bell bt Metz 1up (after 37)
FERRIER bt Harmon 1up (after 37)
Mangrum bt Mike Turnesa 1up
Ghezzi bt Jim Turnesa 4&3
Worsham bt Myles 7&6
HARBERT bt Oliver 3&2
Gibson bt Joseph 1up (after 37)

QUARTER FINAL (QF)
Bell bt Laffoon 2up
FERRIER bt Mangrum 4&3
Ghezzi bt Worsham 3&2
HARBERT bt Gibson 2up

SEMI FINAL (SF)
FERRIER bt Bell 10&9
HARBERT bt Ghezzi 6&5

Ulsterman Fred Daly became the only Irish player to win a Major. As Liverpool is often considered as a cultural extension of the Emerald Isle, I suppose the win at Hoylake was apposite. Laurie Ayton is the 3rd generation of that family to feature strongly in Major Championships.

1	**FRED DALY**	73	70	78	72	293
	(£150)					
2=	Reg Horne	77	74	72	71	294
	Frank Stranahan (a)	71	79	72	72	294
4	Bill Shankland	76	74	75	70	295
5	Dick Burton	77	71	77	71	296
6=	Johnny Bulla	80	72	74	71	297
	Henry Cotton	69	78	74	76	297
	Sam King	75	72	77	73	297
	Arthur Lees	75	74	72	76	297
	Norman von Nida	74	76	71	76	297
	Charlie Ward	76	73	76	72	297
12	Jimmy Adams	73	80	71	75	299
13=	Alf Padgham	75	75	74	76	300
	Reg Whitcombe	75	77	71	77	300
15=	Laurie Ayton, Jr	69	80	74	79	302
	Fred Bullock	74	78	78	72	302
17	Norman Sutton	77	76	73	77	303
18=	Vic Ghezzi	75	78	72	79	304
	Alf Perry	76	77	70	81	304
	Ernest E Whitcombe	77	76	74	77	304
21=	Dai Rees	77	74	73	81	305
	Flory van Donck	73	76	81	75	305
23	Alan Waters	75	78	76	77	306
24	John Burton	73	79	76	71	309
25=	Harry Busson	80	76	71	83	310
	JA Jacobs	75	80	76	79	310
27=	Ken Bousfield	78	76	79	78	311
	Arthur Havers	80	76	79	76	311
	N Quigley	79	77	76	79	311
	B Shepard	78	78	77	78	311

Round Leader(s)
R1   Ayton, Cotton; 69
R2   Daly, 143
R3   Daly, Lees, Von Nida; 221
Lowest Scores
R2   Daly; 70
R3   Perry; 70
R4   Shankland; 70

1948
THE MASTERS
8–11 April

Augusta National GC, Augusta, Georgia
6925 yards PAR 72 (288)

1948
US PGA
19–25 May

Norwood Hills CC, St Louis, Missouri

Claude Harmon was the first non-tournament playing professional to win the Masters. No-one would have noticed – he equalled Ralph Guldahl's low score set in 1939 and won by the biggest margin to date.

1	**CLAUDE HARMON** ($2500)	70	70	69	70	279
2	Cary Middlecoff	74	71	69	70	284
3	Chick Harbert	71	70	70	76	287
4=	Jim Ferrier	71	71	75	71	288
	Lloyd Mangrum	69	73	75	71	288
6=	Ed Furgol	70	72	73	74	289
	Ben Hogan	70	71	77	71	289
8=	Byron Nelson	71	73	72	74	290
	Harry Todd	72	67	80	71	290
10=	Herman Keiser	70	72	76	73	291
	Bobby Locke	71	71	74	75	291
	Dick Metz	71	72	75	73	291
13=	Johnny Bulla	74	72	76	71	293
	Dutch Harrison	73	77	73	70	293
	Skee Riegel (a)	71	74	73	75	293
16=	Al Smith	73	73	74	74	294
	Sam Snead	74	75	72	73	294
18=	Jimmy Demaret	73	72	78	72	295
	Ed Dudley	73	76	75	71	295
	Vic Ghezzi	75	73	73	74	295
	Fred Haas	75	75	76	69	295
	Bob Hamilton	72	72	76	75	295
23=	Art Bell	71	74	74	77	296
	Gene Sarazen	77	74	73	72	296
25=	Herman Barron	73	77	71	76	297
	Henry Cotton	72	73	75	77	297
	Henry Picard	73	73	74	77	297
28=	Johnny Palmer	75	73	76	74	298
	Elsworth Vines	76	71	77	74	298
30=	Bud Ward (a)	74	74	77	74	299
	Lew Worsham	74	78	71	76	299

Round Leader(s)
R1 Mangrum; 69
R2 Todd; 139
R3 Harmon; 209
Lowest Scores
R2 Todd; 67
R3 Harman, Middlecoff; 69
R4 Haas; 69

MATCHPLAY
63 qualifiers, plus the defending champion (Jim Ferrier), after 36 holes strokeplay (Low - Skip Alexander, 134)
Rs1&2, 18 holes: R3,QF,SF&F, 36 holes

Having the choice of dates for many of the War years, the PGA still hadn't decided on a fixed time of the year for their Championship. While the Masters and both Open Championship dates remained quite static, the PGA in 1947 was the 3rd Major of the season; 1948 and 1949 it was 2nd on the calendar; 1950 through to 1953, back to 3rd; and 4th from then on. Even then it didn't settle into its August slot until 1969 and, still experimenting, it took place in 1971, rather eccentrically, in February! The Hogan era was well and truly here as he added a 2nd PGA to his 1946 title, with a 3rd Turnesa brother experiencing the anguish of runner-up in a Major. An accident involving a Greyhound bus on 2 February 1949 cut short Hogan's PGA career. He was to return to it again only in 1960.

FINAL
BEN HOGAN ($3500)
beat
MIKE TURNESA, 7&6

Round by Round Details

ROUND 2 (Last 32)
Claude Harmon bt Jim Ferrier 1up; Henry Ransom bt Lloyd Mangrum 3&2; Sam Snead bt Frank Moore 4&3; Leland Gibson bt Pete Cooper 1up; Johnny Bulla bt Armand Farina 4&3; Ky Laffoon bt Chandler Harper 3&2; MIKE TURNESA bt Zell Eaton 1up (after 21); Al Smith bt Jimmy Hines 4&3; Skip Alexander bt Al Brosch 2up; Chick Harbert bt Eddie Burke 1up (after 26); BEN HOGAN bt Johnny Palmer 1up; Gene Sarazen bt Jackson Bradley 2&1; Jimmy Demaret bt George Getchell 3&1; Lew Worsham bt Errie Ball 7&6; Ed Oliver bt Sherman Elworthy 3&2; George Fazio bt Henry Williams Jr 7&6

ROUND 3 (Last 16)
Harmon bt Ransom 2&1
Snead bt Gibson 5&3
Bulla bt Laffoon 6&5
TURNESA bt Smith 3&2
Harbert bt Alexander 11&10
HOGAN bt Sarazen 1up
Demaret bt Worsham 3&2
Fazio bt Oliver 1up

QUARTER FINAL (QF)
Harmon bt Snead 1up (after 42)
TURNESA bt Bulla 6&5
HOGAN bt Harbert 2&1
Demaret bt Fazio 5&4

SEMI FINAL (SF)
TURNESA bt Harmon 1up (after 37)
HOGAN bt Demaret 2&1

10–12 June	**1948**

US OPEN

Riviera CC, Pacific Palisades, California
7020 yards _PAR 71 (284)_

30 June–2 July	**1948**

BRITISH OPEN

Honourable Company, Muirfield, Angus, Scotland
6806 yards

Ben Hogan's first US Open win was his 2nd Major in successive events, and 3rd in total. His 276 was a landmark record in the US Open. It was not lowered until Jack Nicklaus' 275 at Baltusrol in 1967. In fact, up until 1964 only one total bettered this in any Major – 274 in the 1954 Masters by – yes – Ben Hogan.

1	**BEN HOGAN**	67	72	68	69	276
	($2000)					
2	Jimmy Demaret	71	70	68	69	278
3	Jim Turnesa	71	69	70	70	280
4	Bobby Locke	70	69	73	70	282
5	Sam Snead	69	69	73	72	283
6	Lew Worsham	67	74	71	73	285
7	Herman Barron	73	70	71	72	286
8=	Johnny Bulla	73	72	75	67	287
	Toney Penna	70	72	73	72	287
	Smiley Quick	73	71	69	74	287
11	Skip Alexander	71	73	71	73	288
12=	Charles Congdon	71	70	71	77	289
	Harold McSpaden	74	69	69	77	289
14=	Vic Ghezzi	72	74	74	70	290
	Leland Gibson	71	76	69	74	290
	Otto Greiner	74	73	71	72	290
	Herman Keiser	71	71	73	75	290
	George Schneiter	73	68	75	74	290
	Herschel Spears	72	71	76	71	290
	Ellsworth Vines	75	72	69	74	290
21=	Joe Kirkwood, Jr	72	70	72	77	291
	Lloyd Mangrum	71	72	74	74	291
	Cary Middlecoff	74	71	73	73	291
	Alfred Smith	73	72	77	69	291
25=	Art Bell	72	75	71	74	292
	Pete Cooper	76	72	72	72	292
	George Fazio	72	72	76	72	292
28=	Marty Furgol	72	74	73	74	293
	Chick Harbert	72	72	77	72	293
	Joe Kirkwood, Sr	73	75	73	72	293
	Frank Moore	73	75	73	72	293

Round Leader(s)
R1 Hogan, Worsham; 67
R2 Snead; 138
R3 Hogan; 207
Lowest Scores
R2 Schnieter; 68
R3 Demaret, Hogan; 68
R4 Bulla; 67

Cotton won his 3rd Open at the age of 41, courtesy of a 2nd round of 66 – a score only beaten by his own 65 at Sandwich 14 years before. This gave him enough of a cushion to hold off defending champion Daly. US veteran, Bobby Cruickshank, 54, finished down the field on 302.

1	**HENRY COTTON**	71	66	75	72	284
	(£150)					
2	Fred Daly	72	71	73	73	289
3=	Roberto de Vicenzo	70	73	72	75	290
	Jack Hargreaves	76	68	73	73	290
	Norman von Nida	71	72	76	71	290
	Charlie Ward	69	72	75	74	290
7=	Johnny Bulla	74	72	73	72	291
	Sam King	69	72	74	76	291
	Alf Padgham	73	70	71	77	291
	Flory van Donck	69	73	73	76	291
11=	Mario Gonzales	76	72	70	75	293
	EC Kingsley (a)	77	69	77	70	293
	Arthur Lees	73	79	73	78	293
	Alan Waters	75	71	70	77	293
15=	Max Faulkner	75	71	74	74	294
	Dai Rees	73	71	76	74	294
	Ernest E Whitcombe	74	73	73	74	294
18=	Dick Burton	74	70	74	77	295
	Frank Jowle	70	78	74	73	295
	Reg Whitcombe	77	67	77	74	295
21=	Ken Bousfield	76	71	73	76	296
	Johnny Fallon	73	74	74	75	296
23=	Tom Haliburton	73	74	76	74	297
	Alf Perry	77	71	76	73	297
	Frank Stranahan (a)	77	71	75	74	297
	Norman Sutton	72	73	77	75	297
27	Claude Harmon	75	73	78	72	298
28=	Otway Hayes	74	73	75	78	300
	Reg Horne	71	77	73	79	300
30=	Arthur Clark	74	71	75	81	301
	Harold Gould	75	73	78	75	301

Round Leader(s)
R1 King, Van Donck, Ward; 69
R2 Cotton; 137
R3 Cotton; 212
Lowest Scores
R2 Cotton; 66
R3 Gonzales, Waters; 70
R4 Kingsley; 70

1949

7–10 April

THE MASTERS

Augusta National GC, Augusta, Georgia

6925 yards _PAR 72 (288)_

1949

25–31 May

US PGA

Hermitage CC, Richmond, Virginia

Snead's first Masters was down to a superb 2nd 36 holes. The R4 67 included 8 birdies. This was his 2nd Major, but another was just around the corner. Bulla, after two experiences in the British Open, became a runner-up for the 3rd time. He was also 3rd in the 1941 US Open, but was never to come so close again.

1	**SAM SNEAD** ($2750)	73	75	67	67	282
2=	Johnny Bulla	74	73	69	69	285
	Lloyd Mangrum	69	74	72	70	285
4=	Johnny Palmer	73	71	70	72	286
	Jim Turnesa	73	72	71	70	286
6	Lew Worsham	76	75	70	68	289
7	Joe Kirkwood, Jr	73	72	70	75	290
8=	Jimmy Demaret	76	72	73	71	292
	Clayton Heafner	71	74	72	75	292
	Byron Nelson	75	70	74	73	292
11=	Claude Harmon	73	75	73	72	293
	Herman Keiser	75	68	78	72	293
13=	Herman Barron	73	75	71	75	294
	Leland Gibson	71	77	74	72	294
	Bobby Locke	74	74	74	72	294
16=	Charles R Coe (a)	77	72	72	74	295
	John Dawson (a)	78	72	72	73	295
	Jim Ferrier	77	72	67	79	295
19=	Tony Holguin	81	70	71	74	296
	Frank Stranahan (a)	70	77	75	74	296
21=	Pete Cooper	76	75	72	74	297
	Henry Picard	74	77	73	73	297
23=	Bob Hamilton	77	79	69	73	298
	Dutch Harrison	73	78	75	72	298
	Lawson Little	72	77	73	76	298
	Cary Middlecoff	76	77	72	73	298
	Toney Penna	74	76	76	72	298
	Horton Smith	75	72	78	73	298
29	Fred Haas	75	70	75	79	299
30=	Skip Alexander	74	77	75	74	300
	George Fazio	78	76	71	75	300
	Dick Metz	71	76	76	77	300
	Skee Riegel (a)	75	74	74	77	300

Round Leader(s)

R1   Mangrum; 69
R2   Keiser, Mangrum; 143
R3   Palmer; 214

Lowest Scores

R2   Keiser; 68
R3   Ferrier, Snead; 67
R4   Snead; 67

MATCHPLAY

64 qualifiers (the defending champion Ben Hogan was unable to compete) after 36 holes strokeplay (Low - Ray Hill, 136) Rs1&2, 18 holes: R3,QF,SF&F, 36 holes

It is very difficult to win a Masters and a PGA in the same season. They are usually at the opposite ends of the calendar, which requires the sustaining of form in a notoriously fickle sport over several months, or the ability to 'peak' twice in the same year. Sam Snead's feat was no doubt facilitated by another springtime PGA – and the absence of Ben Hogan due to his horrendous road accident.

FINAL
SAM SNEAD
($3500) beat
JOHNNY PALMER, 3&2

Round by Round Details

ROUND 2 (Last 32)
Ray Hill bt Jack Isaacs 3&2; Walter Romans bt Frank Moore 4&2; Herman Barron bt Jimmy Thomson 2&1; LLoyd Mangrum bt Bob Hamilton 3&2; JOHNNY PALMER bt Clay Gaddie 8&6; Lew Worsham by George Schneiter 5&4; Henry Williams Jr bt Jack Harden 1up; Al Brosch bt Horton Smith 5&4; SAM SNEAD bt Henry Ransom 3&1; Dave Douglas bt Mike DeMassey 3&2; Jimmy Demaret by George Fazio 3&1; Jim Turnesa bt Johnny Bulla 1up; Clyton Heafner bt Claude Harmon 2&1; Jack Patroni bt Jimmy Johnson 1up; Jim Ferrier bt Skip Alexander 1up; Marty Furgol bt Eddie Burke 2&1

ROUND 3 (Last 16)
Hill bt Romans 5&4
Mangrum bt Barron 4&3
PALMER bt Worsham 2&1
Williams Jr bt Brosch 7&6
SNEAD bt Douglas 1up
Demaret bt Turnesa 5&3
Heafner bt Patroni 5&4
Ferrier bt Furgol 8&6

QUARTER FINAL (QF)
Mangrum bt Hill 7&6
PALMER bt Williams Jr 7&6
SNEAD bt Demaret 4&3
Ferrier bt Heafner 3&2

SEMI FINAL (SF)
PALMER bt Mangrum 6&5
SNEAD bt Ferrier 3&2

9–11 June	**1949**

US OPEN
Medinah CC, Medinah, Illinois
6936 yards PAR 71 (284)

Hogan was crippled for 12 months and played no part in any of the 1949 Majors. Cary Middlecoff won the first of his 2 Opens, winning at Medinah by just holding off late challenges by Heafner, and especially Snead.

1	**CARY MIDDLECOFF** ($2000)	75	67	69	75	286
2=	Clayton Heafner	72	71	71	73	287
	Sam Snead	73	73	71	70	287
4=	Bobby Locke	74	71	73	71	289
	Jim Turnesa	78	69	70	72	289
6=	Dave Douglas	74	73	70	73	290
	Buck White	74	68	70	78	290
8=	Pete Cooper	71	73	74	73	291
	Claude Harmon	71	72	74	74	291
	Johnny Palmer	71	75	72	73	291
11=	Eric Monti	75	72	70	75	292
	Herschel Spears	76	71	71	74	292
13	Al Brosch	70	71	73	79	293
14=	Johnny Bulla	73	75	72	74	294
	Lloyd Mangrum	74	74	70	76	294
	Skee Riegel (a)	72	75	73	74	294
	Harry Todd	76	72	73	73	294
	Ellsworth Vines	73	72	71	78	294
19=	Fred Haas	74	73	73	75	295
	Les Kennedy	69	74	79	73	295
	Gene Webb	73	77	70	75	295
22	Ralph Guldahl	71	75	73	77	296
23=	Jim Ferrier	74	75	74	74	297
	Chick Harbert	70	78	75	74	297
	Jack Isaacs	73	73	74	77	297
	Horton Smith	72	75	74	76	297
27=	Skip Alexander	76	72	77	73	298
	Herman Barron	70	78	76	74	298
	Sam Bernardi	80	69	76	73	298
	Jack Burke, Jr	74	74	75	75	298
	Charles Farlow	70	77	76	75	298
	James McHale, Jr (a)	72	76	74	76	298
	Craig Wood	76	73	76	73	298
	Lew Worsham	71	76	71	80	298

Round Leader(s)
R1 Kennedy; 69
R2 Brosch; 141
R3 Middlecoff; 211
Lowest Scores
R2 Middlecoff; 67
R3 Middlecoff; 69
R4 Snead; 70

6–8 July	**1949**

BRITISH OPEN
Royal St George's, Sandwich, Kent, England
6728 yards

In 1949, Bobby Locke of South Africa was undoubtedly the best non-American golfer in the world. He had already won several times on the US tour and featured well in the US Open and was about to embark on an orgy of British Open Championships. He had to endure a 2nd 36-hole dogfight with Harry Bradshaw first – then an easier head-to-head in the play-off. Bradshaw's R2 77 was not helped by his having to play one shot out of a broken beer bottle. It meant having to address the bottle and hope that the follow-through would pick up the ball as well. It did!

1	**BOBBY LOCKE*** (£300)	69	76	68	70	283
2	Harry Bradshaw	68	77	68	70	283
3	Roberto de Vicenzo	68	75	73	69	285
4=	Sam King	71	69	74	72	286
	Charlie Ward	73	71	70	72	286
6=	Max Faulkner	71	71	71	74	287
	Arthur Lees	74	70	72	71	287
8=	Jimmy Adams	67	77	72	72	288
	Johnny Fallon	69	75	72	72	288
	Wally Smithers	72	75	70	71	288
11=	Ken Bousfield	69	77	76	67	289
	Bill Shankland	69	73	74	73	289
13	Frank Stranahan (a)	71	73	74	72	290
14=	Bill Branch	71	75	74	71	291
	Dick Burton	73	70	74	74	291
	J Knipe	76	71	72	72	291
17	Walter Lees	74	72	69	78	293
18	Alan Waters	70	76	75	73	294
19	Norman Sutton	69	78	75	73	295
20=	Reg Horne	73	74	75	74	296
	Arthur Lacey	72	73	73	78	296
	Gregor McIntosh	70	77	76	73	296
	William McMinn	70	75	78	73	296
	EA Southerden	69	76	74	77	296
25	Jim Wade	71	74	77	75	297
26	Herbert Osborne	73	74	75	76	298
27	Johnny Bulla	71	73	76	79	299
28	Ugo Grappasoni	70	76	77	77	300
29	Ernest WH Kenyon	72	75	77	77	301
30	Bill White	74	71	80	78	303

* Bobby Locke (135) beat Harry Bradshaw (147) in the 36-Hole Play-off

Round Leader(s)
R1 Adams; 67
R2 King; 140
R3 Bradshaw, Faulkner, Locke; 68
Lowest Scores
R2 King, 69
R3 Bradshaw, Locke; 68
R4 Bousfield; 67

1950
THE MASTERS
6–9 April

Augusta National GC, Augusta, Georgia
6925 yards _PAR 72 (288)_

Jim Ferrier conceded 7 strokes over the final 6 holes to lose to Jimmy Demaret. Although Demaret kept up the pressure by playing these holes in 2 under par – Ferrier's game collapsed as he dropped 5 shots. Demaret's win was his 3rd – the first to achieve this number in the Masters. After 12 months, when to walk again was considered optimistic, Ben Hogan finished in par to tie for 4th place.

1	**JIMMY DEMARET** ($2400)	70	72	72	69	283
2	Jim Ferrier	70	67	73	75	285
3	Sam Snead	71	74	70	72	287
4=	Ben Hogan	73	68	71	67	288
	Byron Nelson	75	70	69	74	288
6	Lloyd Mangrum	76	74	73	68	291
7=	Clayton Heafner	74	77	69	72	292
	Cary Middlecoff	75	76	68	73	292
9	Lawson Little	70	73	75	75	293
10=	Fred Haas	74	76	73	71	294
	Gene Sarazen	80	70	72	72	294
12=	Roberto de Vicenzo	76	76	73	71	296
	Horton Smith	70	79	75	72	296
14=	Skip Alexander	78	74	73	72	297
	Vic Ghezzi	78	75	70	74	297
	Leland Gibson	78	73	72	74	297
	Herman Keiser	75	72	75	75	297
	Joe Kirkwood, Jr	75	74	77	71	297
	Henry Picard	74	71	77	75	297
	Frank Stranahan (a)	74	79	73	71	297
21=	George Fazio	73	74	78	73	298
	Toney Penna	71	75	77	75	298
	Skee Riegel	69	75	78	76	298
24=	Chick Harbert	76	75	73	75	299
	Johnny Palmer	72	76	76	75	299
26	Eric Monti	74	79	74	73	300
27=	Herschel Spears	70	74	79	78	301
	Norman Von Nida	77	74	74	76	301
29=	Billy Burke	80	75	76	71	302
	Pete Cooper	74	77	77	74	302

Round Leader(s)
R1   Riegel; 69
R2   Ferrier; 137
R3   Ferrier; 210
Lowest Scores
R2   Ferrier; 67
R3   Middlecoff; 68
R4   Mangrum; 68

1950
US OPEN
8–11 June

Merion GC, Ardmore, Pennsylvania
6694 yards _PAR 70 (280)_

Lee Mackey's R1 score of 64 equalled the lowest for any Major to date. Hogan's comeback was complete when he repeated his 1948 Open win at the Riviera CC, here at Merion. He was to achieve it the hard way, however, with the 3-way tie taking him to the physical limit. The 36-holes on the final day proved almost too much for him, but, refreshed for the Sunday play-off, he shot a 69 to win comfortably. This lesson was to dissuade Hogan from playing too much golf – and thereafter the demanding matchplay schedule of the PGA Championship was eschewed in favour of the Opens and the Masters.

1	**BEN HOGAN*** ($4000)	72	69	72	74	287
2	Lloyd Mangrum	72	70	69	76	287
3	George Fazio	73	72	72	70	287
4	Dutch Harrison	72	67	73	76	288
5=	Jim Ferrier	71	69	74	75	289
	Joe Kirkwood, Jr	71	74	74	70	289
	Henry Ransom	72	71	73	73	289
8	Bill Nary	73	70	74	73	290
9	Julius Boros	68	72	77	74	291
10=	Cary Middlecoff	71	71	71	79	292
	Johnny Palmer	73	70	70	79	292
12=	Al Besselink	71	72	76	75	294
	Johnny Bulla	74	66	78	76	294
	Dick Mayer	73	76	73	72	294
	Henry Picard	71	71	79	73	294
	Skee Riegel	73	69	79	73	294
	Sam Snead	73	75	72	74	294
18=	Skip Alexander	68	74	77	76	295
	Fred Haas	73	74	76	72	295
20=	Jimmy Demaret	72	77	71	76	296
	Marty Furgol	75	71	72	78	296
	Dick Metz	76	71	71	78	296
	Bob Toski	73	69	80	74	296
	Harold Williams	69	75	75	77	296
25=	Bobby Cruickshank	72	77	76	72	297
	Ted Kroll	75	72	78	72	297
	Lee Mackey, Jr	64	81	75	77	297
	Paul Runyan	76	73	73	75	297
29=	Pete Cooper	75	72	76	75	298
	Henry Williams, Jr	69	76	76	77	298

* Ben Hogan (69) beat Lloyd Mangrum (73) and George Fazio (75) in the 18-Hole Play-off

Round Leader(s)
R1   Mackey Jr; 64
R2   Harrison; 139
R3   Mangrum; 211
Lowest Scores
R2   Bulla; 66
R3   Mangrum; 69
R4   Fazio, Kirkwood Jr; 70

21–27 June	**1950**

US PGA
Scioto CC, Columbus, Ohio

5–7 July	**1950**

BRITISH OPEN
Troon GC, Ayrshire, Scotland
6583 yards

MATCHPLAY

63 qualifiers, plus the defending champion (Sam Snead), after 36 holes strokeplay (Low - Sam Snead, 140)

Rs1&2, 18 holes: R3,QF,SF&F, 36 holes

Hogan's absence, and the defeat of Sam Snead in R2, made for a very open PGA Championship at Scioto. Experienced campaigners like Jimmy Demaret and Lloyd Mangrum were then favourites, but it was 36-year old Chandler Harper who defeated Demaret in the SF to go on and gain his only Major. The final was played between two men who's best PGA record previously was Harper's R3 in 1946

FINAL

CHANDLER HARPER ($3500)

beat

HENRY WILLIAMS Jr, 4&3

Round by Round Details

ROUND 2 (Last 32)
Eddie Burke bt Sam Snead 1up; Ray Gafford by Leonard Schmutte 1up; Denny Shute bt Elsworth Vines 4&3; Jimmy Demaret bt Rod Munday 5&3; Lloyd Mangrum bt Skip Alexander 1up; Chick Harbert bt Harold Williams 5&3; Bob Toski bt George Fazio 1up; CHANDLER HARPER bt Dick Metz 1up; Claude Harmon bt Al Brosch 2&1; HENRY WILLIAMS Jr by Emery Thomas 6&5; Elmer Reed bt Jim Ferrier 5&4; Dave Douglas bt Jimmy Hines 5&4; Jackson Bradley by George Shafer 4&3; Henry Picard bt Clarence Doser 4&2; Johnny Palmer bt Lew Worsham 4&2; Ted Kroll bt Al Watrous 2&1

ROUND 3 (Last 16)
Gafford bt Burke 4&3
Demaret bt Shute 4&3
Mangrum bt Harbert 6&5
HARPER bt Toski 2&1
WILLIAMS Jr bt Harmon 1up (after 38)
Douglas bt Reed 3&2
Picard bt Bradley 1up
Palmer bt Kroll 1up

QUARTER FINAL (QF)
Demaret bt Gafford 5&4
HARPER bt Mangrum 1up
WILLIAMS Jr bt Douglas 1up
Picard bt Palmer 10&8

SEMI FINAL (SF)
HARPER bt Demaret 2&1
WILLIAMS Jr bt Picard 1up (after 38)

From this year onwards – after 15 wins on the US Tour, apart for the odd US Open, Bobby Locke concentrated his time more in Europe and his native S Africa . He collected the 1st back-to-back Open Championship win since Hagen's in 1929. In doing so he set a new low of 279. Johnny Bulla apart, American professional interest waned even further, as the PGA only finished 8 days before the Open started - and there was some disparity in the respective purses.

1	**BOBBY LOCKE** (£300)	69	72	70	68	279
2	Roberto de Vicenzo	72	71	68	70	281
3=	Fred Daly	75	72	69	66	282
	Dai Rees	71	68	72	71	282
5=	Max Faulkner	72	70	70	71	283
	Eric Moore	74	68	73	68	283
7=	Fred Bullock	71	71	71	71	284
	Arthur Lees	68	76	68	72	284
9=	Sam King	70	75	68	73	286
	Frank Stranahan (a)	77	70	73	66	286
	Flory van Donck	73	71	72	70	286
12=	Jimmy Adams	73	75	69	70	287
	Wally Smithers	74	70	73	70	287
14=	Johnny Bulla	73	70	71	74	288
	Hector Thomson	71	72	73	72	288
16	Harry Bradshaw	73	71	75	70	289
17=	Reg Horne	73	75	71	71	290
	James McHale (a)	73	73	74	70	290
	Ernest E Whitcombe	69	76	72	73	290
20=	Alf Padgham	77	71	74	69	291
	John Panton	76	69	70	76	291
	Norman von Nida	74	72	76	69	291
23	Eric Brown	73	73	73	73	292
24=	Trevor Allen	77	70	75	71	293
	Bill Branch	71	69	78	75	293
	Stewart Field	73	71	73	76	293
	Norman Sutton	71	75	74	73	293
	Bill White	74	74	73	72	293
29	Fred Allott	72	71	77	74	294
30=	David Blair (a)	72	72	77	74	295
	H Hassanein	73	72	77	73	295

Round Leader(s)

R1 Lees; 68
R2 Rees; 139
R3 De Vicenzo, Locke, Rees; 211

Lowest Scores

R2 Moore, Rees; 68
R3 De Vicenzo, King, Lees; 68
R4 Daly, Stranahan; 66

1951
THE MASTERS
5–8 April

Augusta National GC, Augusta, Georgia
6925 yards *PAR 72 (288)*

1951
US OPEN
14–16 June

Oakland Hills CC, Birmingham, Michigan
6927 yards *PAR 70 (280)*

Ben Hogan won his 1st Masters to keep his incredible comeback going. It was his 7th Major title, and 2nd since his accident. Recently-turned professional, 1947 US Amateur Champion, Skee Riegel, finished at 6 under par for the Tournament, but the power and experience of Hogan overcame him in R4.

Hogan made it two US Opens in a row – and 3 consecutive Major Championships wins in which he had entered. Still playing a modicum of golf to conserve his strength, but enough to stay sharp, Hogan made it a last round special performance once again, burning up Oakland Hills in 67 – 32 on the back 9. He considered this his best-ever round of golf.

1	**BEN HOGAN** ($3000)	70	72	70	68	280
2	Skee Riegel	73	68	70	71	282
3=	Lloyd Mangrum	69	74	70	73	286
	Lew Worsham	71	71	72	72	286
5	Dave Douglas	74	69	72	73	288
6	Lawson Little	72	73	72	72	289
7	Jim Ferrier	74	70	74	72	290
8=	Johnny Bulla	71	72	73	75	291
	Byron Nelson	71	73	73	74	291
	Sam Snead	69	74	68	80	291
11	Jack Burke, Jr	73	72	74	73	292
12=	Charles R Coe (a)	76	71	73	73	293
	Cary Middlecoff	73	73	69	78	293
	Gene Sarazen	75	74	73	71	293
15=	Ed Furgol	80	71	72	71	294
	Dutch Harrison	76	71	76	71	294
17	Julius Boros	76	72	74	73	295
18=	George Fazio	68	74	74	80	296
	Bob Toski	75	73	73	75	296
20=	Al Besselink	76	73	71	77	297
	Dick Chapman (a)	72	76	72	77	297
	Clayton Heafner	74	72	73	78	297
	Joe Kirkwood, Jr	73	71	78	75	297
	Roberto de Vicenzo	75	74	74	74	297
25=	Ted Kroll	76	75	71	76	298
	Dick Mayer	71	75	79	73	298
	Bill Nary	76	73	73	76	298
	Henry Ransom	74	74	74	76	298
	Sam Urzetta	73	72	78	75	298
30=	Jimmy Demaret	76	74	78	71	299
	Johnny Palmer	73	74	77	75	299

Round Leader(s)
R1 Fazio; 68
R2 Riegel; 141
R3 Riegel, Snead; 211
Lowest Scores
R2 Riegel; 68
R3 Snead; 68
R4 Hogan; 68

1	**BEN HOGAN** ($4000)	76	73	71	67	287
2	Clayton Heafner	72	75	73	69	289
3	Bobby Locke	73	71	74	73	291
4=	Julius Boros	74	74	71	74	293
	Lloyd Mangrum	75	74	74	70	293
6=	Al Besselink	72	77	72	73	294
	Dave Douglas	75	70	75	74	294
	Fred Hawkins	76	72	75	71	294
	Paul Runyan	73	74	72	75	294
10=	Al Brosch	73	74	76	72	295
	Smiley Quick	73	76	74	72	295
	Skee Riegel	75	76	71	73	295
	Sam Snead	71	78	72	74	295
14=	Jimmy Demaret	74	74	70	78	296
	Lew Worsham	76	71	76	73	296
16=	Charles Kocsis (a)	75	74	76	72	297
	Henry Ransom	74	74	76	73	297
	Buck White	76	75	74	72	297
19=	Raymond Gafford	76	74	74	74	298
	Johnny Revolta	78	72	72	76	298
21=	Charles Bassler	79	71	74	75	299
	Joe Kirkwood, Jr	74	78	73	74	299
23	Marty Furgol	78	72	74	76	300
24=	Cary Middlecoff	76	73	79	73	301
	Ed Oliver	81	71	77	72	301
	Johnny Palmer	73	78	76	74	301
	Henry Picard	78	73	78	72	301
	Earl Stewart	74	74	78	75	301
29=	Tommy Bolt	77	72	75	78	302
	Roberto de Vicenzo	75	76	74	77	302
	Fred Haas	77	75	77	73	302
	George Kinsman	75	73	75	79	302
	Sam Urzetta (a)	78	71	78	75	302
	Bo Wininger (a)	75	71	77	79	302

Round Leader(s)
R1 Snead; 71
R2 Locke; 144
R3 Demaret, Locke; 218
Lowest Scores
R2 Johnny Bulla (52), Douglas; 70
R3 Demaret; 70
R4 Hogan; 67

27 June–3 July	**1951**

US PGA

Oakmont CC, Oakmont, Pennsylvania

4–6 July	**1951**

BRITISH OPEN

Royal Portrush GC, Co Antrim, Northern Ireland
6802 yards

MATCHPLAY
63 qualifiers, plus the defending champion (Chandler Harper), after 36 holes strokeplay (Low - Pete Cooper, Claude Harmon, Lloyd Mangrum, 142)
Rs1&2, 18 holes: R3,QF,SF&F, 36 holes

After squeaking past Fred Haas in R1, and needing 3 extra holes before disposing of Marty Furgol, Sam Snead really came to life in the SF. From there he annihilated Charles Bassler and Walter Burkemo to become the last multiple PGA Champion until Nicklaus repeated his 1st win in 1971 - making it 19 different winners in succession.

FINAL
SAM SNEAD ($3500)
beat
WALTER BURKEMO, 7&6

Round by Round Details

ROUND 2 (Last 32)
    Charles Bassler bt Jim Turnesa 5&4; George Bolesta bt Ed Oliver 2&1; Al Brosch bt Lew Worsham 5&4; Jack Harden bt Toney Penna 5&3; Lloyd Mangrum bt Buck White 2&1; SAM SNEAD bt Marty Furgol 1up (after 21); Jack Burke, Jr bt Gene Sarazen 5&3; Gene Kunes bt Ray Gafford 2&1; Dick Shoemaker bt Lawson Little 2&1; WALTER BURKEMO bt Chick Harbert 1up (after 19); Vic Ghezzi bt Rod Munday 4&3; Reggie Myles by Mike Pavella 1up (after 20); Jackson Bradley bt Denny Shute 2&1; Elsworth Vines bt Henry Picard 1up; Jim Ferrier bt Milon Marusic 3&2; Johnny Bulla bt Bob Hamilton 5&3

ROUND 3 (Last 16)
    Bassler bt Bolesta 1up (after 37)
    Brosch bt Harden 6&5
    SNEAD bt Mangrum 3&2
    Burke Jr bt Kunes 4&3
    BURKEMO by Shoemaker 2&1
    Myles bt Ghezzi 1up
    Vines bt Bradley 2&1
    Bulla bt Ferrier 9&8

QUARTER FINAL (QF)
    Bassler bt Brosch 1up
    SNEAD bt Burke Jr 2&1
    BURKEMO bt Myles 1up
    Vines bt Bulla 1up

SEMI FINAL (SF)
    SNEAD bt Bassler 9&8
    BURKEMO bt Vines 1up (after 37)

The Open left the shores of Great Britain for the one and only time and visited picturesque Royal Portrush. Max Faulkner interrupted Bobby Locke's recent stranglehold, building up enough of any early lead to hold off fast-finishing Argentinian, Antonio Cerda. This year, the US PGA and the British Open effectively overlapped, with the finals of the latter held on the day before R1 in Ulster.

1	**MAX FAULKNER** (£300)	71	70	70	74	285
2	Antonio Cerda	74	72	71	70	287
3	Charlie Ward	75	73	74	68	290
4=	Jimmy Adams	68	77	75	72	292
	Fred Daly	74	70	75	73	292
6=	Bobby Locke	71	74	74	74	293
	Bill Shankland	73	76	72	72	293
	Norman Sutton	73	70	74	76	293
	Peter Thomson	70	75	73	75	293
	Harry Weetman	73	71	75	74	293
11	John Panton	73	72	74	75	294
12=	Dick Burton	74	77	71	73	295
	Dai Rees	70	77	76	72	295
	Frank Stranahan (a)	75	75	72	73	295
15	Harry Bradshaw	80	71	74	71	296
16	Eric Cremin	73	75	75	74	297
17=	Kep Enderby (a)	76	74	75	73	298
	Alan Waters	74	75	78	71	298
19=	Ugo Grappasoni	73	73	77	76	299
	Jack Hargreaves	73	78	79	69	299
	Willie John Henderson	77	73	76	73	299
	Kel Nagle	76	76	72	75	299
	Christy O'Connor, Sr	79	74	72	74	299
24=	Joe Carr (a)	75	76	73	76	300
	P Traviani	74	79	73	74	300
	Flory van Donck	72	76	76	76	300
	Ernest E Whitcombe	74	74	76	76	300
28=	J McKenna	74	76	76	76	302
	Alan Poulton	77	77	73	75	302
	Wally Smithers	75	73	76	78	302

Round Leader(s)
R1   Adams; 68
R2   Faulkner; 141
R3   Faulkner; 211
Lowest Scores
R2   Daly, Faulkner, Sutton; 70
R3   Faulkner; 70
R4   Ward; 68

1952

THE MASTERS

3–6 April

Augusta National GC, Augusta, Georgia
6925 yards _PAR 72 (288)_

1952

US OPEN

12–14 June

Northwood GC, Dallas, Texas
6782 yards _PAR 70 (280)_

Sam Snead overcame high winds which affected scoring generally over the last 2 rounds to post 286 – the only score better than par in the Tournament. It was his 2nd Masters and 6th Major title. Ray Gafford tied for the lead after R1 with a 69 – but followed it with an 80.

Julius Boros didn't turn professional until 1950, when he was already 30 years old. This was his 1st of 3 Majors – the other 2 occurred in the next decade, when he was to set records for his age. The odds were in favour of Hogan winning again when he equalled the Open 36-hole low score. The heat and 36 holes on the last day did for him this time though.

1	**SAM SNEAD**	70	67	77	72	286
	($4000)					

2	Jack Burke, Jr	76	67	78	69	290
3=	Al Besselink	70	76	71	74	291
	Tommy Bolt	71	71	75	74	291
	Jim Ferrier	72	70	77	72	291
6	Lloyd Mangrum	71	74	75	72	292
7=	Julius Boros	73	73	76	71	293
	Fred Hawkins	71	73	78	71	293
	Ben Hogan	70	70	74	79	293
	Lew Worsham	71	75	73	74	293
11	Cary Middlecoff	72	72	72	78	294
12	Johnny Palmer	69	74	75	77	295
13	Johnny Revolta	71	71	77	77	296
14=	George Fazio	72	71	78	76	297
	Claude Harmon	73	74	77	73	297
	Chuck Kocsis (a)	75	78	71	73	297
	Ted Kroll	74	74	76	73	297
	Skee Riegel	75	71	78	73	297
19=	Joe Kirkwood, Jr	71	77	74	76	298
	Frank Stranahan (a)	72	74	76	76	298
21=	Doug Ford	71	74	79	75	299
	Bobby Locke	74	71	79	75	299
	E Harvie Ward, Jr (a)	72	71	78	78	299
24=	Arnold Blum (a)	74	77	77	74	302
	Clayton Heafner	76	74	74	78	302
	Byron Nelson	72	75	78	77	302
27=	Skip Alexander	71	73	77	82	303
	Smiley Quick	73	76	79	75	303
	Norman Von Nida	77	77	73	76	303
30=	Dave Douglas	76	69	81	78	304
	Vic Ghezzi	77	77	76	74	304
	Ed Oliver	72	72	77	83	304
	Horton Smith	74	73	77	80	304

1	**JULIUS BOROS**	71	71	68	71	281
	($4000)					

2	Ed Oliver	71	72	70	72	285
3	Ben Hogan	69	69	74	74	286
4	Johnny Bulla	73	68	73	73	287
5	George Fazio	71	69	75	75	290
6	Dick Metz	70	74	76	71	291
7=	Tommy Bolt	72	76	71	73	292
	Ted Kroll	71	75	76	70	292
	Lew Worsham	72	71	74	75	292
10=	Lloyd Mangrum	75	74	72	72	293
	Sam Snead	70	75	76	72	293
	Earl Stewart	76	75	70	72	293
13=	Clarence Doser	71	73	73	77	294
	Harry Todd	71	76	74	73	294
15=	Al Brosch	68	79	77	71	295
	Jimmy Demaret	74	77	73	71	295
	Milon Marusic	73	76	74	72	295
	Horton Smith	70	73	76	76	295
19=	Doug Ford	74	74	74	74	296
	James Jackson (a)	74	76	75	71	296
	Bill Trombley	72	73	81	70	296
22=	Leland Gibson	73	76	72	76	297
	Paul Runyan	73	78	73	73	297
24=	Chick Harbert	75	75	73	75	298
	Cary Middlecoff	75	74	75	74	298
	Felice Torza	74	76	70	78	298
	Bo Wininger	78	72	69	79	298
28=	Zell Eaton	71	79	73	76	299
	Raymond Gafford	77	74	75	73	299
	Dick Mayer	74	77	69	79	299
	Stan Mosel (a)	71	77	75	76	299
	P Patrick	74	76	73	76	299

Round Leader(s)
R1 Ray Gafford (49), Palmer; 69
R2 Snead; 137
R3 Hogan, Snead; 214
Lowest Scores
R2 Burke, Snead; 67
R3 Besselink, Kocsis ; 71
R4 Burke; 69

Round Leader(s)
R1 Brosch; 68
R2 Hogan; 138
R3 Boros; 210
Lowest Scores
R2 Bulla; 68
R3 Boros; 68
R4 Kroll, Trombley; 70

18–25 June	**1952**

US PGA

Big Spring CC, Louisville, Kentucky

9–11 July	**1952**

BRITISH OPEN

Royal Lytham and St Anne's GC, Lancashire, England
6657 yards

MATCHPLAY

63 qualifiers plus the defending champion (Sam Snead) after 36 holes strokeplay (Low - Dutch Harrison, 136)
Rs1&2, 18 holes: R3,QF,SF&F, 36 holes

At the age of 40 and after 26 years and four Major Championship 2nd places for him and his brothers (Joe and Mike), Jim Turnesa finally buried the family jinx at Big Spring. The youngest of the seven Turnesa brothers to make a mark was Willie – winner of the US Amateur title in 1938 and 1948 – but he never turned pro. Sam Snead, the defending champion, went out in R1 to Lew Worsham.

FINAL

JIM TURNESA ($3500)
beat
CHICK HARBERT, 1 UP

Round by Round Details

ROUND 2 (Last 32)
Ray Honsberger bt Jim Ferrier 1up; Ted Kroll bt Lloyd Mangrum 2up; Cary Middlecoff bt Gharles Harter 3&2; Al Smith bt Labron Harris 1up (after 19); JIM TURNESA bt Chandler Harper 3&1; Roberto de Vicenzo bt Jack Burke Jr 1up; Clarence Doser bt Bob Gajda 3&2; Jack Isaacs bt Marty Furgol 3&2; Fred Haas bt Lew Worsham 1up; Milon Marusic bt Zell Eaton (default); Henry Williams Jr bt Jack Jones 1up; CHICK HARBERT bt Leonard Schmutte 3&2; Frank Champ bt John Trish 2&1; Walter Burkemo bt Dave Douglas 1up; Vic Ghezzi bt Mel Carpenter 5&3; Bob Hamilton bt Sam Bernardi 3&1

ROUND 3 (Last 16)
Kroll bt Honsberger 1up (after 38)
Middlecoff bt Smith 4&2
TURNESA bt de Vicenzo 5&4
Doser bt Isaacs 1up
Haas bt Marusic 1up (after 38)
HARBERT bt Williams Jr 6&5
Champ bt Burkemo 3&1
Hamilton bt Ghezzi 9&8

QUARTER FINAL (QF)
Kroll bt Middlecoff 1up (after 38)
TURNESA bt Doser 2&1
HARBERT bt Haas 2&1
Hamilton bt Champ 2&1

SEMI FINAL (SF)
TURNESA bt Kroll 4&2;
HARBERT bt Hamilton 2&1

Emulating Harry Vardon and James Braid, Locke won his 3rd Open in 4 years. He held firm in the last round under the challenge of young Australian, Peter Thomson. Gene Sarazen, at the age of 50, made a creditable 17th place, 18 years after his success at Prince's, Sandwich. Otherwise the field was almost bereft of an American challenge.

1	**BOBBY LOCKE** (£300)	69	71	74	73	287
2	Peter Thomson	68	73	77	70	288
3	Fred Daly	67	69	77	76	289
4	Henry Cotton	75	74	74	71	294
5=	Antonio Cerda	73	73	76	73	295
	Sam King	71	74	74	76	295
7	Flory van Donck	74	75	71	76	296
8	Fred Bullock	76	72	72	77	297
9=	Harry Bradshaw	70	74	75	79	298
	Eric Brown	71	72	78	77	298
	Willie Goggin	71	74	75	78	298
	Arthur Lees	76	72	76	74	298
	Syd Scott	75	69	76	78	298
	Norman von Nida	77	70	74	77	298
15=	John Panton	72	72	78	77	299
	Harry Weetman	74	77	71	77	299
17=	Max Faulkner	72	76	79	73	300
	Gene Sarazen	74	73	77	76	300
	Wally Smithers	73	74	76	77	300
20	Norman Sutton	72	74	79	76	301
21=	Fred Allott	77	71	76	78	302
	Ken Bousfield	72	73	79	78	302
	Jimmy Hines	73	78	74	77	302
	Eddie Noke	72	78	76	76	302
25=	JA Jacobs	74	72	81	76	303
	Alan Poulton	71	74	76	82	303
27=	Jack Hargreaves	75	75	79	75	304
	John Jacobs	72	76	79	77	304
	JW Jones (a)	73	70	78	83	304
	Dai Rees	76	74	77	77	304

Round Leader(s)
R1 Daly; 67
R2 Daly; 136
R3 Daly; 213

Lowest Scores
R2 Daly, Scott; 69
R3 Van Donck, Weetman; 71
R4 Thomson; 70

1953
THE MASTERS
9–12 April

Augusta National GC, Augusta, Georgia
6925 yards _PAR 72 (288)_

1953
US OPEN
11–13 June

Oakmont CC, Oakmont, Pennsylvania
6916 yards _PAR 72 (288)_

Ben Hogan, in winning his 2nd Masters title, lowered the Masters' and all Majors' low score to 274 – trimming the Augusta National Tournament's record, and beating the field, by 5 shots. Conditions were benign, but Hogan played what was reported as 'the best 72-hole stretch of golf played by anyone anywhere'. The Masters' record low was to stand until taken by Nicklaus in 1965, and equalled by Ray Floyd 11 years later. It was then reduced to 270 by Tiger Woods in 1997.

Returning to Oakmont for the 1st time since 1935 (although the course was host site to the PGA 2 years earlier), the Open saw Hogan rewriting the record books once again. In beating top rival Snead by 6 strokes, Hogan drew level with Willie Anderson's and Bobby Jones' 4 US Opens and it was the first wire-to-wire win since Jim Barnes in 1921. He also repeated his 1951 feat of lifting the Masters and US Open in the same year.

1	**BEN HOGAN** ($4000)	70	69	66	69	274
2	Ed Oliver	69	73	67	70	279
3	Lloyd Mangrum	74	68	71	69	282
4	Bob Hamilton	71	69	70	73	283
5=	Tommy Bolt	71	75	68	71	285
	Chick Harbert	68	73	70	74	285
7	Ted Kroll	71	70	73	72	286
8	Jack Burke, Jr	78	69	69	71	287
9	Al Besselink	69	75	70	74	288
10=	Julius Boros	73	71	75	70	289
	Chandler Harper	74	72	69	74	289
	Fred Hawkins	75	70	74	70	289
13	Johnny Palmer	74	73	72	71	290
14=	Frank Stranahan (a)	72	75	69	75	291
	E Harvie Ward, Jr (a)	73	74	69	75	291
16=	Charles R Coe (a)	75	74	72	71	292
	Jim Ferrier	74	71	76	71	292
	Dick Mayer	73	72	71	76	292
	Sam Snead	71	75	71	75	292
	Earl Stewart, Jr	75	72	70	75	292
21=	Jerry Barber	73	76	72	72	293
	Doug Ford	73	73	72	75	293
23=	Leland Gibson	73	71	72	78	294
	Al Mengert	77	70	75	72	294
	Dick Metz	73	72	71	78	294
26	Fred Haas	74	73	71	77	295
27=	Cary Middlecoff	75	76	68	77	296
	Jim Turnesa	73	74	73	76	296
29=	Skip Alexander	72	78	74	73	297
	Byron Nelson	73	73	78	73	297
	Skee Riegel	74	72	76	75	297
	Felice Torza	78	73	72	74	297
	Bo Wininger	80	70	72	75	297

1	**BEN HOGAN** ($5000)	67	72	73	71	283
2	Sam Snead	72	69	72	76	289
3	Lloyd Mangrum	73	70	74	75	292
4=	Pete Cooper	78	75	71	70	294
	Jimmy Demaret	71	76	71	76	294
	George Fazio	70	71	77	76	294
7=	Ted Kroll	76	71	74	74	295
	Dick Metz	75	70	74	76	295
9=	Marty Furgol	73	74	76	73	296
	Jay Hebert	72	72	74	78	296
	Frank Souchak (a)	70	76	76	74	296
12=	Fred Haas	74	73	72	78	297
	Bill Ogden	71	78	75	73	297
14=	Jack Burke, Jr	76	73	72	77	298
	Dutch Harrison	77	75	70	76	298
	Bobby Locke	78	70	74	76	298
17=	Julius Boros	75	72	76	76	299
	Clarence Doser	74	76	78	71	299
	Bill Nary	76	74	73	76	299
	Jim Turnesa	75	78	72	74	299
21=	Gardner Dickinson	77	73	76	74	300
	Doug Ford	74	77	74	75	300
	Al Mengert	75	71	78	76	300
	Bob Rosburg	76	72	78	74	300
	Frank Stranahan (a)	75	75	75	75	300
26=	Clayton Heafner	75	75	76	75	301
	James McHale, Jr (a)	79	74	75	73	301
	Peter Thomson	80	73	73	75	301
	Art Wall	80	72	77	72	301
30=	Louis Barbaro	72	79	74	77	302
	Jerry Barber	72	75	76	79	302
	Toby Lyons	73	78	74	77	302

Round Leader(s)
R1 Harbert; 68
R2 Hogan; 139
R3 Hogan; 205
Lowest Scores
R2 Mangrum; 68
R3 Hogan; 66
R4 Hogan, Mangrum; 69

Round Leader(s)
R1 Hogan; 67
R2 Hogan; 139
R3 Hogan; 212
Lowest Scores
R2 Snead; 69
R3 Harrison; 70
R4 Cooper; 70

1–7 July	**1953**	8–10 July	**1953**

US PGA

Birmingham CC, Birmingham, Michigan

BRITISH OPEN

Carnoustie GC, Angus, Scotland
7103 yards

MATCHPLAY
63 qualifiers plus the defending champion (Jim Turnesa) after 36 holes strokeplay (Low - Johnny Palmer, 134)
Rs1&2, 18 holes: R3,QF,SF&F, 36 holes

Once more the PGA clashed with the British Open, so even if Ben Hogan did contemplate a Grand Slam in 1953, he would have been denied it. He was persuaded to try the British Open instead. Walter Burkemo was a local boy and his match wins were cheered on by a partisan crowd. His one and only Major win, and his 2nd place in the PGA in 1951, picked him out as a match-player and he was selected for the 1953 Ryder Cup. He lost his only match.

FINAL
WALTER BURKEMO ($5000)
beat
FELICE TORZA, 2&1

Round by Round Details

ROUND 2 (Last 32)
FELICE TORZA bt Jim Turnesa 4&3; Wally Ulrich bt Buck White 2&1; Jimmy Clark bt Cary Middlecoff 5&4; Henry Williams Jr bt Charles Bassler 3&1; Jack Isaacs bt Fred Haas 1up; Labron Harris bt Marty Furgol 1up; Al Smith bt Iverson Martin 3&2; Henry Ransom bt Bob Toski 3&2; Jackson Bradley bt Tommy Bolt 1up (after 19); WALTER BURKEMO bt Mike Turnesa 3&1; Pete Cooper bt Leonard Dodson 6&5; Bill Nary bt Dutch Harrison 1up; Jim Browning bt Broyles Plemmons 3&1; Ed Furgol bt Jim Ferrier 3&1; Claude Harmon bt Jack Grout 4&2

ROUND 3 (Last 16)
TORZA bt Ulrich 1up (after 38)
Clark bt Williams Jr 4&3
Isaacs bt Harris 5&4
Ransom bt Smith 1up
Douglas bt Bradley 1up (after 37)
BURKEMO bt Cooper 3&2
Nary bt Browning 6&5
Harmon bt Furgol 5&3

QUARTER FINAL (QF)
TORZA bt Clark 1up
Isaacs bt Ransom 1up
BURKEMO bt Douglas 2up
Harmon bt Nary 6&5

SEMI FINAL (SF)
TORZA bt Isaacs 1up (after 39)
BURKEMO bt Harmon 1up

Ben Hogan paid his only visit to the Open Championship, adapted very quickly to conditions and the size of the ball – the British still used the 1.62 inch small ball, whereas the American big ball (1.68 inch) had been in operation since 1932 – and won the title. His reducing round-by-round score of 282 meant he was the first – and only – golfer to win 3 modern Majors in one season. In doing so he joined Sarazen as the 2nd man to achieve the Grand Slam. This was his last Major title (his 9th, 2 behind Walter Hagen). He had played in few other tournaments apart from Majors since the accident in 1949, but his sequence in Majors played between 1950 and 1953 was: 5, W, W, W, 7, 3, W, W, W.

1	**BEN HOGAN** (£500)	73	71	70	68	282
2=	Antonio Cerda	75	71	69	71	286
	Dai Rees	72	70	73	71	286
	Frank Stranahan (a)	70	74	73	69	286
	Peter Thomson	72	72	71	71	286
6	Roberto de Vicenzo	72	71	71	73	287
7	Sam King	74	73	72	71	290
8	Bobby Locke	72	73	74	72	291
9=	Peter Alliss	75	72	74	71	292
	Eric Brown	71	71	75	75	292
11	Fred Daly	73	75	71	75	294
12	Max Faulkner	74	71	73	77	295
13	Arthur Lees	76	76	72	72	296
14=	THT Fairbairn	74	71	73	79	297
	John Jacobs	79	74	71	73	297
	Harry Weetman	80	73	72	72	297
17=	H Hassanein	78	71	73	76	298
	Eric Lester	83	70	72	73	298
	Charlie Ward	78	71	76	73	298
20=	Reg Horne	76	74	75	74	299
	Flory van Donck	77	71	78	73	299
22=	Syd Scott	74	74	78	74	300
	Hector Thomson	76	74	74	76	300
24=	Reg Knight	74	79	74	74	301
	Lloyd Mangrum	75	76	74	76	301
	Christy O'Connor, Sr	77	77	72	75	301
27=	Ugo Grappasoni	77	75	72	78	302
	John Panton	79	74	76	73	302
29=	R Ferguson	77	75	74	77	303
	Tom Haliburton	75	76	76	76	303
	Alan Poulton	75	77	75	76	303
	Norman Sutton	76	72	76	79	303

Round Leader(s)
R1 Stranahan; 70
R2 Brown, Rees; 142
R3 De Vicenzo, Hogan; 214

Lowest Scores
R2 Lester, Rees; 70
R3 Cerda; 69
R4 Hogan; 68

1954
THE MASTERS
8–12 April

Augusta National GC, Augusta, Georgia
6925 yards PAR 72 (288)

1954
US OPEN
17–19 June

Baltusrol GC, Springfield, New Jersey
7027 yards PAR 70 (280)

Hogan could have made that famous sequence four in a row had not Sam Snead chipped away at the great man's lead in R4. Hogan slipped to 3 over for the round, allowing Snead to force a tie through his solid par play. Snead then won the head-to-head between the world's two greatest players of the time, to become 3-time Masters Champion.

National TV covered the 1954 Open to witness Ed Furgol just hold off 1953 US Amateur Champion – now professional – Gene Littler, to win his only Major. The human interest story here was that Furgol had a withered left arm after a childhood accident. Amateur, Billy Joe Patton, after leading and almost tying the Masters, took the lead again here, after 18 holes.

1	**SAM SNEAD***	74	73	70	72	289
	($5000)					
2	Ben Hogan	72	73	69	75	289
3	Billy Joe Patton (a)	70	74	75	71	290
4=	Dutch Harrison	70	79	74	68	291
	Lloyd Mangrum	71	75	76	69	291
6=	Jerry Barber	74	76	71	71	292
	Jack Burke, Jr	71	77	73	71	292
	Bob Rosburg	73	73	76	70	292
9=	Al Besselink	74	74	74	72	294
	Cary Middlecoff	73	76	70	75	294
11	Dick Chapman (a)	75	75	75	70	294
12=	Tommy Bolt	73	74	72	77	296
	Chick Harbert	73	75	75	73	296
	Byron Nelson	73	76	74	73	296
	Lew Worsham	74	74	74	74	296
16=	Julius Boros	76	79	68	74	297
	Jay Hebert	79	74	74	70	297
	Peter Thomson	76	72	76	73	297
	Ken Venturi (a)	76	74	73	74	297
20=	Charles R Coe (a)	76	75	73	74	298
	E Harvie Ward, Jr (a)	78	75	74	71	298
22=	Walter Burkemo	74	77	75	73	299
	Pete Cooper	73	76	75	75	299
	Marty Furgol	76	79	75	69	299
	Gene Littler	79	75	73	72	299
	Ed Oliver	75	75	75	74	299
	Earl Stewart, Jr	78	75	75	71	299
	Bob Toski	80	74	71	74	299
29=	Jimmy Demaret	80	75	72	73	300
	Vic Ghezzi	73	79	73	75	300
	Dick Mayer	76	75	72	77	300

* Sam Snead (70) beat Ben Hogan (71) in the 18-hole Play-off

Round Leader(s)
R1   Harrison, Patton; 70
R2   Patton; 144
R3   Hogan; 214
Lowest Scores
R2   Thomson; 72
R3   Boros; 68
R4   Harrison; 68

1	**ED FURGOL**	71	70	71	72	284
	($6000)					
2	Gene Littler	70	69	76	70	285
3=	Lloyd Mangrum	72	71	72	71	286
	Dick Mayer	72	71	70	73	286
5	Bobby Locke	74	70	74	70	288
6=	Tommy Bolt	72	72	73	72	289
	Fred Haas	73	73	71	72	289
	Ben Hogan	71	70	76	72	289
	Shelley Mayfield	73	75	72	69	289
	Billy Joe Patton (a)	69	76	71	73	289
11=	Cary Middlecoff	72	71	72	75	290
	Sam Snead	72	73	72	73	290
13=	Rudy Horvath	75	72	71	73	291
	Al Mengert	71	72	73	75	291
15=	Jack Burke, Jr	73	73	72	75	293
	Claude Harmon	75	72	72	74	293
17	Jay Hebert	77	70	70	77	294
18=	Marty Furgol	73	74	73	75	295
	Leland Gibson	72	77	69	77	295
	Bob Toski	70	74	78	73	295
21=	Dick Chapman (a)	77	67	77	75	296
	Johnny Weitzel	74	76	69	77	296
23=	Julius Boros	78	71	78	70	297
	William Campbell (a)	75	73	73	76	297
	Max Evans	76	74	73	74	297
	Lew Worsham	72	77	77	71	297
27=	George Fazio	74	77	74	73	298
	Ted Kroll	70	79	73	76	298
29=	Jimmy Demaret	79	71	76	73	299
	Dick Metz	75	75	72	77	299
	Johnny Revolta	72	75	73	79	299
	Bob Rosburg	74	77	74	74	299

Round Leader(s)
R1   Patton; 69
R2   Littler; 139
R3   Furgol; 212
Lowest Scores
R2   Chapman; 67
R3   Gibson, Weitzel; 69
R4   Mayfield; 69

7–9 July	**1954**

BRITISH OPEN

Birkdale GC, Southport, Lancashire, England
6867 yards

21–27 July	**1954**

US PGA

Keller GC, St Paul, Minnesota

Following Ben Hogan's famous interruption the previous year, Bobby Locke must have wondered what had happened to his Open hegemony when Peter Thomson converted his 2 previous runner-up spots into his first Open win, to put the South African into joint-2nd place. Sarazen again belied his age and there were Top 10 performances from other US veterans, Jim Turnesa and Jimmy Demaret. To put British golf of this era in perspective, the US won 6 of the 7 Ryder Cups in the period 1949-61. Over the same period, apart from Faulkner in 1951, the Opens were monopolized by 2 Americans, 2 South Africans and 2 Australians. The British had to wait until Tony Jacklin in 1969 for their next home success.

1	**PETER THOMSON** (£750)	72	71	69	71	283
2=	Bobby Locke	74	71	69	70	284
	Dai Rees	72	71	69	72	284
	Syd Scott	76	67	69	72	284
5=	Jimmy Adams	73	75	69	69	286
	Antonio Cerda	71	71	73	71	286
	Jim Turnesa	72	72	71	71	286
8=	Peter Alliss	72	74	71	70	287
	Sam King	69	74	74	70	287
10=	Jimmy Demaret	73	71	74	71	289
	Flory van Donck	77	71	70	71	289
12=	Alfonso Angelini	76	70	73	71	290
	Harry Bradshaw	72	72	73	73	290
	JW Spence	69	72	74	75	290
15=	Bobby Halsall	72	73	73	73	291
	Peter Toogood (a)	72	75	73	71	291
17=	Ugo Grappasoni	72	75	74	71	292
	C Kane	74	72	74	72	292
	Gene Sarazen	75	74	73	70	292
20=	Norman Drew	76	71	74	72	293
	Max Faulkner	73	78	69	73	293
	Jack Hargreaves	77	72	77	67	293
	John Jacobs	71	73	80	69	293
	Eric Lester	72	75	73	73	293
	Christy O'Connor, Sr	74	72	72	75	293
	Lambert Topping	75	76	69	73	293
27=	Norman Sutton	70	80	72	72	294
	EB Williamson	76	73	75	70	294
29=	Jimmy Hitchcock	73	72	76	74	295
	Ben Shelton	74	77	71	73	295
	Frank Stranahan (a)	73	75	71	76	295

Round Leader(s)

R1   Alliss, Spence; 69
R2   Spence, 141
R3   Rees, Scott,
       Thomson; 212

Lowest Scores

R2   Scott; 67
R3   Adams, Faulkner, Locke,
       Rees, Scott, Thomson,
       Topping; 69
R4   Hargreaves; 67

MATCHPLAY

63 qualifiers plus the defending champion (Walter Burkemo) after 36 holes strokeplay (Low - Ed Oliver, 136)
Rs1&2, 18 holes: R3,QF,SF&F, 36 holes

Settling finally (give or take a year) for its position in the Majors calendar, the 1954 PGA Championship was won by 1952 runner-up Chick Harbert. Burkemo again confirmed his reputation in matchplay, but was no match in this instance for Harbert, who took control of the final early into the 2nd 18 holes.

FINAL
CHICK HARBERT ($5000)
beat
WALTER BURKEMO, 4&3

Round by Round Details

ROUND 2 (Last 32)
Tommy Bolt bt Arthur Doering 2&1; Jim Browning bt Ed Furgol 1up; Sam Snead bt Jin Milward 4&3; Dutch Harrison bt Johnny Palmer 4&3; Charles Bassler bt Bill Trombley 5&4; Jerry Barber bt Fred Haas 1up (after 19); CHICK HARBERT bt John O'Donnell 3&1; Ed Oliver bt Bill Nary (1up); WALTER BURKEMO bt Claude Harmon 2&1; Johnny Revolta bt Toby Lyons 5&4; Roberto de Vicenzo bt Henry Ransom; 4&3; Elroy Marti bt Henry Williams Jr 2up; Cary Middlecoff bt Bob Toski 2&1; Ted Kroll bt Max Evans 1up (after 24); Shelley Mayfield bt Wally Ulrich 5&4; Horton Smith bt Jack Isaacs 3&2

ROUND 3 (Last 16)
Bolt bt Browning 2&1
Snead bt Harrison 4&3
Barber bt Bassler 1up (after 38)
HARBERT bt Oliver 3&1
BURKEMO bt Revolta 4&3
de Vicenzo bt Marti 8&6
Middlecoff bt Kroll 5&4
Mayfield bt Smith 3&2

QUARTER FINAL (QF)
Bolt bt Snead 1up (after 39)
HARBERT bt Barber 1up
BURKEMO bt de Vicenzo 5&4
Middlecoff bt Mayfield 3&1

SEMI FINAL (SF)
HARBERT bt Bolt 1up
BURKEMO bt Middlecoff 1up (after 37)

1955

THE MASTERS

7–10 April

Augusta National GC, Augusta, Georgia
6925 yards _PAR 72 (288)_

Thanks to a blistering 65 in R2, Cary Middlecoff finished a remarkable 7 shots clear of Hogan, and 8 of Snead. This was the 2nd Major win for dentist Middlecoff, having beaten Snead into 2nd place earlier in the 1949 US Open at Medinah. 1954 US Amateur Champion, 26 year-old Arnold Daniel Palmer, finished 10th.

1	**CARY MIDDLECOFF**	72	65	72	70	279
	($5000)					
2	Ben Hogan	73	68	72	73	286
3	Sam Snead	72	71	74	70	287
4=	Julius Boros	71	75	72	71	289
	Bob Rosburg	72	72	72	73	289
	Mike Souchak	71	74	72	72	289
7	Lloyd Mangrum	74	73	72	72	291
8=	E Harvie Ward, Jr (a)	77	69	75	71	292
	Stan Leonard	77	73	68	74	292
10=	Dick Mayer	78	72	72	71	293
	Byron Nelson	72	75	74	72	293
	Arnold Palmer	76	76	72	69	293
13=	Jack Burke, Jr	67	76	71	80	294
	Skee Riegel	73	73	73	75	294
15=	Walter Burkemo	73	73	72	77	295
	Jay Hebert	75	74	74	72	295
	Frank Stranahan	77	76	71	71	295
18=	Joe Conrad (a)	77	71	74	75	297
	Billy Maxwell (a)	77	72	77	71	297
	Johnny Palmer	77	73	72	75	297
	Peter Thomson	74	73	74	76	297
22=	Tommy Bolt	76	70	77	75	298
	Gene Littler	75	72	76	75	298
24=	Pete Cooper	73	73	78	75	299
	Ed Furgol	74	72	78	75	299
	Hillman Robbins, Jr (a)	77	76	74	72	299
27	Max Evans	76	75	75	76	302
28=	William L Goodloe, Jr (a)	74	73	81	75	303
	Claude Harmon	77	75	78	73	303
30=	Don Cherry	79	75	78	82	304
	Bud Ward	77	73	77	77	304

Round Leader(s)
R1   Burke; 67
R2   Middlecoff; 137
R3   Middlecoff; 209
Lowest Scores
R2   Middlecoff; 65
R3   Leonard; 68
R4   Palmer; 69

1955

US OPEN

16–19 June

Olympic CC, San Francisco, California
6700 yards _PAR 70 (280)_

Jack Fleck, in his 1st full year on the Tour, held his nerve to beat 43 year-old Ben Hogan in a play-off. He had arrived there after birdying 2 of the last 4 holes to tie. With a par of 70, the difficult Olympic CC course took its toll, with only 7 rounds beating par throughout the Championship – including the play-off. Fittingly, Fleck achieved 3 of them. After his momentous year in 1953, Hogan's Majors sequence read: 2, 8, 2, 2. He was never to get any higher again.

1	**JACK FLECK***	76	69	75	67	287
	($6000)					
2	Ben Hogan	72	73	72	70	287
3=	Tommy Bolt	67	77	75	73	292
	Sam Snead	79	69	70	74	292
5=	Julius Boros	76	69	73	77	295
	Bob Rosburg	78	74	67	76	295
7=	Doug Ford	74	77	74	71	296
	Bud Holscher	77	75	71	73	296
	E Harvie Ward, Jr (a)	74	70	76	76	296
10=	Jack Burke, Jr	71	77	72	77	297
	Mike Souchak	73	79	72	73	297
12=	Shelley Mayfield	75	76	75	72	298
	Frank Stranahan	80	71	76	71	298
14	Walker Inman, Jr	70	75	76	78	299
15	Gene Littler	76	73	73	78	300
16=	Al Mengert	76	76	72	77	301
	Smiley Quick	76	74	74	77	301
	Art Wall	77	78	72	74	301
19=	Fred Hawkins	73	78	75	76	302
	George Schneiter	78	74	77	73	302
21=	Bob Harris	77	71	78	77	303
	Cary Middlecoff	76	78	74	75	303
	Arnold Palmer	77	76	74	76	303
	Ernie Vossler	77	76	76	74	303
25=	Marty Furgol	76	77	78	73	304
	Leland Gibson	76	78	76	74	304
27	Billy Maxwell	77	74	75	79	305
28=	Art Bell	74	76	81	75	306
	Max Evans	77	73	76	80	306
	Dow Finsterwald	84	71	74	77	306
	Eric Monti	76	76	78	76	306
	Byron Nelson	77	74	80	75	306
	Charles Rotar	76	75	80	75	306

* Jack Fleck (69) beat Ben Hogan (72) in the 18-Hole Play-off

Round Leader(s)
R1   Bolt; 67
R2   Bolt, Ward; 144
R3   Hogan; 217

Lowest Scores
R2   Boros, Fleck, Snead; 69
R3   Rosburg; 67
R4   Fleck; 67

6–8 July	**1955**
BRITISH OPEN	
Royal and Ancient GC, St Andrews, Fife, Scotland	
6526 yards	

20–26 July	**1955**
US PGA	
Meadowbrook CC, Northville, Michigan	

Despite never winning a tournament, Johnny Fallon came close to the Open Championship twice – both times at St Andrews. In 1939 he finished 3rd and achieved one better in 1955. Peter Thomson won his 2nd Open in a row, but the aficionados gathered around the Old Course more to see the legend that was Byron Nelson. Effectively retired for almost a decade, he deided to take a golfing 'holiday' in Europe. Aged 43, he won the French Open, but his last British Open placing was 33rd, after shooting 296.

1	**PETER THOMSON**	71	68	70	72	281
	(£1000)					
2	Johnny Fallon	73	67	73	70	283
3	Frank Jowle	70	71	69	74	284
4	Bobby Locke	74	69	70	72	285
5=	Ken Bousfield	71	75	70	70	286
	Antonio Cerda	73	71	71	71	286
	Bernard Hunt	70	71	74	71	286
	Flory van Donck	71	72	71	72	286
	Harry Weetman	71	71	70	74	286
10=	Romualdo Barbieri	71	71	73	72	287
	Christy O'Connor, Sr	71	75	70	71	287
12=	Eric Brown	69	70	73	76	288
	Fred Daly	75	72	70	71	288
	John Jacobs	71	70	71	76	288
15=	Iain Anderson	71	72	77	69	289
	Willie John Henderson	74	71	72	72	289
17=	DF Smalldon	70	69	78	73	290
	Arturo Soto	72	73	72	73	290
20=	Ed Furgol	71	76	72	73	292
	Kel Nagle	72	72	74	74	292
	Syd Scott	69	77	73	73	292
23=	Harry Bradshaw	72	70	73	78	293
	Bill Branch	75	72	73	73	293
	Joe Conrad (a)	72	76	74	71	293
	Bobby Halsall	71	74	76	72	293
	Reg Horne	72	75	75	71	293
28=	H Hassanein	73	72	76	73	294
	Dai Rees	69	79	73	73	294
	Norman Sutton	71	74	75	74	294

Round Leader(s)
R1 Brown, Rees, Scott; 69
R2 Brown, Smalldon, Thomson; 139
R3 Thomson; 209
Lowest Scores
R2 Fallon; 67
R3 Jowle; 69
R4 Anderson; 69

MATCHPLAY
64 qualifiers after 36 holes strokeplay (Low - Doug Ford, 136)
Rs1&2, 18 holes: R3,QF,SF&F, 36 holes

Doug Ford became only the 4th player, after Walter Hagen, in 1926 and 1927,Olin Dutra in 1932 and – inevitably, in 1945 – Byron Nelson, to shoot the lowest qualifying score and then go on to win the matchplay series. He overcame reigning Masters Champion, Cary Middlecoff, in a final that could have gone either way until he picked up birdies at 29, 30 and 32, for a three shot lead he was not going to give away.

FINAL
DOUG FORD ($5000)
beat
CARY MIDDLECOFF, 4&3

Round by Round Details

ROUND 2 (Last 32)
Brien Charter bt Lionel Hebert 1up; Don Fairfield bt Vic Ghezzi 1up (after 23); Shelley Mayfield by Gene Sarazen 4&3; Claude Harmon bt Eldon Briggs 2&1; Ed Furgol bt Gus Salerno 1up (after 20); Fred Hawkins bt Fred Haas 2up; Wally Ulrich bt Leonard Wagner 2up; DOUG FORD bt Ted Kroll 2&1; Johnny Palmer bt Chick Harbert 1up; Lew Worsham bt Ray Hill 2&1; Tommy Bolt bt Sam Snead 3&2; Jack Fleck bt Jay Hebert 2&1; CARY MIDDLECOFF bt Bill Nary 3&2; Mike Pavella bt Jim Browning 4&3; Marty Furgol bt Tony Holguin 1up; Jack Burke Jr bt Dave Douglas 8&6

ROUND 3 (Last 16)
Fairfield bt Charter 2&1
Mayfield bt Harmon 1up
Hawkins bt E Furgol 6&5
FORD bt Ulrich 12&10
Worsham bt Palmer 6&5
Bolt bt Fleck 3&1
MIDDLECOFF bt Pavella 8&6
Burke Jr bt M Furgol 2&1

QUARTER FINAL(QF)
Mayfield bt Fairfield 3&2
FORD bt Hawkins 5&4
Bolt bt Worsham 8&7
MIDDLECOFF bt Burke Jr 1up (after 40)

SEMI FINAL(SF)
FORD bt Mayfield 4&3
MIDDLECOFF bt Bolt 4&3

1956
THE MASTERS
5–8 April

Augusta National GC, Augusta, Georgia
6925 yards PAR 72 (288)

1956
US OPEN
14–16 June

Oak Hill CC, Rochester, New York
6902 yards PAR 70 (280)

Jack Burke achieved what his father never could when he won a Major Championship in the most dramatic fashion at Augusta. Amateur Ken Venturi led Cary Middlecoff by 4 going into the last round, with Burke back in the pack, 8 off the leader. The young Venturi crumbled in a generally high-scoring round, allowing Burke to come through on the rails to win by one.

Middlecoff's 2nd US Open and 3rd Major came after a nail-biting few minutes watching his pursuers. To tie, first Hogan (for a par) missed a 2½ foot putt on the 17th; then Boros (for birdie) rattled the cup on the final hole. Peter Thomson, in the middle of his unassailable period in the British Open, finished in his highest position in a US Major.

1	**JACK BURKE, Jr** ($6000)	72	71	75	71	289
2	Ken Venturi (a)	66	69	75	80	290
3	Cary Middlecoff	67	72	75	77	291
4=	Lloyd Mangrum	72	74	72	74	292
	Sam Snead	73	76	72	71	292
6=	Jerry Barber	71	72	76	75	294
	Doug Ford	70	72	75	77	294
8=	Tommy Bolt	68	74	78	76	296
	Ben Hogan	69	78	74	75	296
	Shelley Mayfield	68	74	80	74	296
11	Johnny Palmer	76	74	74	73	297
12=	Pete Cooper	72	70	77	79	298
	Gene Littler	73	77	74	74	298
	Billy Joe Patton (a)	70	76	79	73	298
	Sam Urzetta	73	75	76	74	298
16	Bob Rosberg	70	74	81	74	299
17=	Walter Burkemo	72	74	78	76	300
	Roberto de Vicenzo	75	72	78	75	300
	Hillman Robbins, Jr (a)	73	73	78	76	300
	Mike Souchak	73	73	74	80	300
21	Arnold Palmer	73	75	74	79	301
22=	Frank Stranahan	72	75	79	76	302
	Jim Turnesa	74	74	74	80	302
24=	Julius Boros	73	78	72	80	303
	Dow Finsterwald	74	73	79	77	303
	Ed Furgol	74	75	78	76	303
	Stan Leonard	75	75	79	74	303
	Al Mengert	74	72	79	78	303
29=	Al Balding	75	78	77	74	304
	Vic Ghezzi	74	77	77	76	304
	Fred Haas	78	72	75	79	304
	Fred Hawkins	71	73	76	84	304
	Walker Inman, Jr	73	75	74	82	304

1	**CARY MIDDLECOFF** ($6000)	71	70	70	70	281
2=	Julius Boros	71	71	71	69	282
	Ben Hogan	72	68	72	70	282
4=	Ed Furgol	71	70	73	71	285
	Ted Kroll	72	70	70	73	285
	Peter Thomson	70	69	75	71	285
7	Arnold Palmer	72	70	72	73	287
8	Ken Venturi (a)	77	71	68	73	289
9=	Jerry Barber	72	69	74	75	290
	Wes Ellis, Jr	71	70	71	78	290
	Doug Ford	71	75	70	74	290
12	Billy Maxwell	72	71	76	72	291
13	Billy Joe Patton (a)	75	73	70	74	292
14=	Billy Casper	75	71	71	76	293
	Pete Cooper	73	74	76	70	293
	Fred Haas	72	71	72	78	293
17=	Henry Cotton	74	72	73	75	294
	Dutch Harrison	72	76	72	74	294
	Jay Hebert	71	76	73	74	294
	Bill Ogden	76	73	76	69	294
	Bob Toski	76	71	74	73	294
22=	Errie Ball	71	75	73	76	295
	Tommy Bolt	74	71	73	77	295
24=	Johnny Bulla	77	72	73	74	296
	Robert Kay	75	74	76	71	296
	Sam Snead	75	71	77	73	296
27=	Roberto de Vicenzo	76	69	77	75	297
	Doug Higgins	74	75	72	76	297
29=	Walter Burkemo	73	74	76	75	298
	Mike Dietz	73	74	70	81	298
	Shelley Mayfield	75	71	75	77	298
	Mike Souchak	78	71	72	77	298
	Frank Taylor, Jr (a)	72	71	80	75	298

Round Leader(s)
R1 Venturi; 66
R2 Venturi; 135
R3 Venturi; 210
Lowest Scores
R2 Venturi; 69
R3 Boros, Mangrum, Snead; 72
R4 Burke, Snead; 71

Round Leader(s)
R1 Bob Rosburg (45); 68
R2 Thomson; 139
R3 Middlecoff; 211
Lowest Scores
R2 Hogan; 68
R3 Venturi; 68
R4 Boros, Ogden; 69

4–6 July	**1956**

BRITISH OPEN
Royal Liverpool GC, Hoylake, Cheshire, England
6960 yards

20–24 July	**1956**

US PGA
Blue Hill G&CC, Canton, Massachusetts

Peter Thomson achieved something that had not happened since Bob Ferguson did it in 1882 – he won the Open Championship 3 times in succession. Only Jamie Anderson and Tom Morris Jr, moving progressively backwards from Ferguson, had achieved the same: only Willie Anderson (US Open) and Walter Hagen (PGA) – in the history of the Major Championships - had achieved it. No-one has achieved it since.

1	**PETER THOMSON** (£1000)	70	70	72	74	286
2	Flory van Donck	71	74	70	74	289
3	Roberto de Vicenzo	71	70	79	70	290
4	Gary Player	71	76	73	71	291
5	John Panton	74	76	72	70	292
6=	Enrique Bertolino	69	72	76	76	293
	Henry Cotton	72	76	71	74	293
8=	Antonio Cerda	72	81	68	73	294
	Mike Souchak	74	74	74	72	294
10=	Christy O'Connor, Sr	73	78	74	70	295
	Harry Weetman	72	76	75	72	295
12	Frank Stranahan	72	76	72	76	296
13=	Bruce Crampton	76	77	72	72	297
	Angel Miguel	71	74	75	77	297
	Dai Rees	75	74	75	73	297
16	John Jacobs	73	77	76	72	298
17=	Al Balding	70	81	76	73	300
	Jack Hargreaves	72	80	75	73	300
	Ricardo Rossi	75	77	72	76	300
	Dave Thomas	70	78	77	75	300
	Charlie Ward	73	75	78	74	300
22=	Ken Bousfield	73	77	76	75	301
	Gerard de Wit	76	73	74	78	301
	Eric Lester	70	76	77	78	301
25=	Jimmy Adams	75	76	76	75	302
	Laurie Ayton, Jr	74	78	78	72	302
	Eric Moore	75	75	78	74	302
28=	KWC Adwick	77	76	74	76	303
	Syd Scott	78	74	74	77	303
	DF Smalldon	68	79	78	78	303

Round Leader(s)
R1 Smalldon; 68
R2 Thomson; 140
R3 Thomson; 212
Lowest Scores
R2 De Vicenzo, Thomson; 70
R3 Cerda; 68
R4 De Vicenzo, O'Connor, Panton; 70

MATCHPLAY
128 players
Rs1,2,3&4, 18 holes: QF,SF&F, 36 holes

In the penultimate year of matchplay, the format was changed to allow matchplay for 128 competitors. Jack Burke became the 11th player to win 2 or more Majors in the same season - by doing the difficult Masters-PGA double. He beat Ted Kroll, who had finished well up in the US Open, in the final. Kroll strolled to the final after a SF which saw Bill Johnston commit golfing suicide with a morning 81.

FINAL
JACK BURKE Jr ($5000)
beat
TED KROLL, 3&2

Round by Round Details

ROUND 3 (Last 32)
Walter Burkemo bt Doug Ford 5&3; Bill Johnston bt Tony Fortino 4&3; Henry Ransom bt Claude Harmon 1up (after 23); Lew Worsham bt Shelley Mayfield 5&4; Sam Snead bt Bob Toski 4&3; Gene Sarazen bt Mike Krak 3&2; Jim Turnesa bt Jack Fleck 1up; Charles Harper Jr bt Babe Lichardus 1up; JACK BURKE Jr bt Fred Haas 1up (after 20); Fred Hawkins bt Art Wall 1up (after 19); Lionel Hebert bt Skee Riegel 3&1; Toby Lyons bt Charles Lepre 3&2; Terl Johnson bt Charles DuPree 4&2; Robert Kay bt Mike Fetchick 1up; Ed Furgol bt Jerry Barber 2&1

ROUND 4 (Last 16)
Johnston bt Burkemo 1up
Ransom bt Worsham 2up
Snead bt Sarazen 5&4
KROLL bt Turnesa 1up
BURKE Jr bt Harper Jr 3&2
Hawkins bt Hebert 4&3
Johnson bt Lyons 1up (after 19)
Furgol bt Kay 4&3

QUARTER FINAL (QF)
Johnston bt Ransom 3&2
KROLL bt Snead 2&1
BURKE Jr bt Hawkins 4&2
Furgol bt Johnson 1up

SEMI FINAL (SF)
KROLL bt Johnston 10&8
BURKE Jr bt Furgol 1up (after 37)

1957

4–7 April

THE MASTERS
Augusta National GC, Augusta, Georgia
6925 yards _PAR 72 (288)_

1957

13–15 June

US OPEN
Inverness GC, Toledo, Ohio
6919 yards _PAR 70 (280)_

A 36-hole cut was applied for the first time in the '57 Masters. Doug Ford added to his 1955 PGA title as a 6-shot swing occurred over the last 18 holes. R3 leader Sam Snead shot par, but Ford's record last round 66 took him from 3 behind to 3 in front. Snead, at 45 was 2nd, and Masters expert Jimmy Demaret who finished 3rd, was 47. Henry Cotton, making a rare visit to the US was 13th at the age of 50; Byron Nelson 16th at 45.

1	**DOUG FORD**	72	73	72	66	283
	($8750)					
2	Sam Snead	72	68	74	72	286
3	Jimmy Demaret	72	70	75	70	287
4	E Harvie Ward, Jr (a)	73	71	71	73	288
5	Peter Thomson	72	73	73	71	289
6	Ed Furgol	73	71	72	74	290
7=	Jack Burke, Jr	71	72	74	74	291
	Dow Finsterwald	74	74	73	70	291
	Arnold Palmer	73	73	69	76	291
10	Jay Hebert	74	72	76	70	292
11=	Marty Furgol	73	74	73	73	293
	Stan Leonard	75	72	68	78	293
13=	Henry Cotton	73	73	72	76	294
	Frank M Taylor, Jr (a)	74	74	77	69	294
	Ken Venturi	74	76	74	70	294
16=	Al Balding	73	73	73	76	295
	Billy Casper	75	75	75	70	295
	Mike Fetchick	74	73	72	76	295
	Fred Hawkins	75	74	72	74	295
	Byron Nelson	74	72	73	76	295
21=	Bruce Crampton	72	75	78	71	296
	Al Mengert	75	75	71	75	296
	Henry Ransom	75	73	72	76	296
24=	Johnny Palmer	77	73	73	74	297
	Gary Player	77	72	75	73	297
26=	Jerry Barber	73	77	78	70	298
	Jack Fleck	76	74	75	73	298
28=	Bill Johnston	77	70	78	74	299
	Lawson Little	76	72	77	74	299
	Lloyd Mangrum	77	71	74	77	299

Round Leader(s)
R1   Burke; 71
R2   Snead; 140
R3   Snead; 214
Lowest Scores
R2   Snead; 68
R3   Leonard; 68
R4   Ford; 66

Dick Mayer won his only Major and stopped a Middlecoff double when he outplayed him in the play-off. A tie had resulted after 72 holes when Mayer's 138 over the first 36 holes (shared with Billy Joe Patton) was compensated by Middlecoff's 136 over the last 36 (this equalled a 25 year-old record set by Gene Sarazen at Fresh Meadow). Demaret was again in the hunt and was leading going into R4.

1	**DICK MAYER***	70	68	74	70	282
	($7200)					
2	Cary Middlecoff	71	75	68	68	282
3	Jimmy Demaret	68	73	70	72	283
4=	Julius Boros	69	75	70	70	284
	Walter Burkemo	74	73	72	65	284
6=	Fred Hawkins	72	72	71	71	286
	Ken Venturi	69	71	75	71	286
8=	Roberto de Vicenzo	72	70	72	76	290
	Chick Harbert	68	79	71	72	290
	Billy Maxwell	70	76	72	72	290
	Billy Joe Patton (a)	70	68	76	76	290
	Sam Snead	74	74	69	73	290
13=	Mike Fetchick	74	71	71	75	291
	Dow Finsterwald	74	72	72	73	291
	William Hyndman III (a)	77	73	72	69	291
	Frank Stranahan	72	76	69	74	291
17=	Don Fairfield	78	72	73	69	292
	Jim Ferree	74	74	73	71	292
	Doug Ford	69	71	80	72	292
	Bud Ward	70	74	70	78	292
21	Bo Wininger	70	71	76	76	293
22=	George Bayer	73	77	69	75	294
	Joe Campbell (a)	74	72	73	75	294
	Ed Oliver	74	73	73	74	294
	Peter Thomson	71	72	74	77	294
26=	Jack Fleck	72	76	73	74	295
	Gerald Kesselring	74	71	75	75	295
	Sam Penecale	71	73	73	78	295
	E Harvie Ward, Jr (a)	72	75	74	74	295
30=	Leo Biagetti	73	75	72	76	296
	Johnny Revolta	76	74	74	72	296

* Dick Mayer (72) beat Cary Middlecoff (79) in the 18-Hole Play-off

Round Leader(s)
R1   Demaret, Harbert; 68
R2   Mayer, Patton; 138
R3   Demaret; 211
Lowest Scores
R2   Mayer, Patton; 68
R3   Middlecoff; 68
R4   Burkemo; 65

3–5 July	**1957**

BRITISH OPEN

Royal & Ancient GC, St Andrews, Fife, Scotland
6936 yards

17–21 July	**1957**

US PGA

Miami Valley GC, Dayton, Ohio

TV cameras caught the finish 'live' for the for 1st time, as Bobby Locke regained the crown after 4 years from Peter Thomson. This was Locke's 4th and last Open (and Major) win, to put him level with Willie Park Sr and Tom Morris (Sr and Jr) - but one behind Taylor and Braid, 2 behind Vardon (who also, of course, was US Open Champion in 1900). Token American interest came in the form of current US Open runner-up, Cary Middlecoff, and the now professional Frank Stranahan.

1	**BOBBY LOCKE**	69	72	68	70	279
	(£1000)					
2	Peter Thomson	73	69	70	70	282
3	Eric Brown	67	72	73	71	283
4	Angel Miguel	72	72	69	72	285
5=	Tom Haliburton	72	73	68	73	286
	Dick Smith (a)	71	72	72	71	286
	Dave Thomas	72	74	70	70	286
	Flory van Donck	72	68	74	72	286
9=	Antonio Cerda	71	71	72	73	287
	Henry Cotton	74	72	69	72	287
	Max Faulkner	74	70	71	72	287
12=	Peter Alliss	72	74	74	68	288
	Harry Weetman	75	71	71	71	288
14	Cary Middlecoff	72	71	74	72	289
15=	Norman Drew	70	75	71	74	290
	Eric Lester	71	76	70	73	290
	Sebastian Miguel	71	75	76	68	290
	John Panton	71	72	74	73	290
19=	Harry Bradshaw	73	74	69	75	291
	Johnny Fallon	75	67	73	76	291
	Christy O'Connor, Sr	77	69	72	73	291
	Frank Stranahan	74	71	74	72	291
23	Jimmy Hitchcock	69	74	73	76	292
24=	Reg Horne	76	72	72	73	293
	Bernard Hunt	72	72	74	75	293
	Sam King	76	72	70	75	293
	Gary Player	71	74	75	73	293
	Trevor Wilkes	75	73	71	74	293
29	Harold Henning	75	73	71	75	294
30=	Laurie Ayton, Jr	67	76	75	77	295
	Peter Butler	77	71	74	73	295
	Reg Knight	71	73	75	76	295
	Dai Rees	73	72	79	71	295
	Norman Sutton	69	76	73	77	295

Round Leader(s)

R1	Ayton, Brown; 67
R2	Brown; 139
R3	Locke; 209

Lowest Scores

R2	Fallon; 67
R3	Haliburton, Locke; 68
R4	Alliss, Miguel; 68

MATCHPLAY
128 players
Rs1,2,3&4, 18 holes: QF,SF&F, 36 holes

Due to commercial demands brought on by the burgeoning TV era, and not altogether approved of by the professionals, matchplay in the PGA was brought to a close in 1957. To be fair, the Championship still took 5 days as against 3 or 4 for the other Majors – so it was perhaps a little unwieldy. Strokeplay ensued thereafter. Lionel Hebert beat Dow Finsterwald in the last matchplay final.

FINAL
LIONEL HEBERT ($8000)
beat
DOW FINSTERWALD, 3&1

Round by Round Details

ROUND 3 (Last 32)
Milon Marusic bt Mike Krak 2&1; Donald Whitt bt Ellsworth Vines 4&3; Ted Kroll bt Ewing Pomeroy 4&3; Dick Mayer bt Al Smith 5&3; Warren Smith bt Skee Riegel 3&2; Charles Sheppard bt Buck White 1up; Sam Snead bt John Thoren 3&2; DOW FINSTERWALD bt Joe Kirkwood Jr 2&1; Nike Souchak bt Brien Charter 4&3; LIONEL HEBERT bt Charles Farlow 3&1; Claude Harmon bt Charles Bassler 4&3; Tommy Bolt bt Eldon Briggs 7&6; Henry Ransom bt Herman Keiser 5&3; Walter Burkemo bt Tony Holguin 1up; Jay Hebert bt Charles Harper Jr 1up; Doug Ford bt Bob Gajda 3&2

ROUND 4 (Last 16)
Whitt bt Marusic 2&1
Mayer bt Kroll 1up
Sheppard bt Smith 4&3
FINSTERWALD bt Snead 2&1
L HEBERT bt Souchak 2&1
Harmon bt Bolt 1up
Burkemo bt Ransom 5&4
J Hebert bt Ford 3&2

QUARTER FINAL (QF)
Whitt bt Mayer 2&1
FINSTERWALD bt Sheppard 2up
L HEBERT bt Harmon 2&1
Burkemo bt J Hebert 3&2

SEMI FINAL (SF)
FINSTERWALD bt Whitt 2up
L HEBERT bt Burkemo 3&1

1958
THE MASTERS
3–6 April

Augusta National GC, Augusta, Georgia
6925 yards _PAR 72 (288)_

1958
US OPEN
12–14 June

Southern Hills CC, Tulsa, Oklahoma
6907 yards _PAR 70 (280)_

It was somehow appropriate that the 1st 5-figure winner's purse should go to Arnold Palmer. Over the next 2 decades he, more than anyone else, is associated with the commercial revolution that took place in golf. Arnie's 1st win made him, at 28, the youngest winner of the Masters since Byron Nelson in 1938. He was almost caught by Ford and Hawkins over the last holes, but they both missed holeable birdie putts on the 18th.

The number of entries topped 2000 for the 1st time and Sam Snead, after 18 consecutive years of making the final day, missed the cut. Irascible Tommy Bolt's humour was tempered by his leading all the way to collect his solitary Major Championship victory. A 2nd Top 5 placing in two years for Walter Burkemo belied the myth he was just a matchplay golfer. Despite a wrist injury, Ben Hogan still finished 10th.

1	**ARNOLD PALMER**	70	73	68	73	284
	($11250)					
2=	Doug Ford	74	71	70	70	285
	Fred Hawkins	71	75	68	71	285
4=	Stan Leonard	72	70	73	71	286
	Ken Venturi	68	72	74	72	286
6=	Cary Middlecoff	70	73	69	75	287
	Art Wall	71	72	70	74	287
8	Billy Joe Patton (a)	72	69	73	74	288
9=	Claude Harmon	71	76	72	70	289
	Jay Hebert	72	73	73	71	289
	Billy Maxwell (a)	71	70	72	76	289
	Al Mengert	73	71	69	76	289
13	Sam Snead	72	71	68	79	290
14=	Jimmy Demaret	69	79	70	73	291
	Ben Hogan	72	77	69	73	291
	Mike Souchak	72	75	73	71	291
17=	Dow Finsterwald	72	71	74	75	292
	Chick Harbert	69	74	73	76	292
	Bo Winninger	69	73	71	79	292
20=	Billy Casper	76	71	72	74	293
	Byron Nelson	71	77	74	71	293
22	Phil Rodgers	77	72	73	72	294
23=	Charles R Coe (a)	73	76	69	77	295
	Ted Kroll	73	75	75	72	295
	Peter Thomson	72	74	73	76	295
26=	Al Balding	75	72	71	78	296
	Bruce Crampton	73	76	72	75	296
	William Hyndman III (a)	71	76	70	79	296
29=	George Bayer	74	75	72	76	297
	Arnold Blum (a)	72	74	75	76	297
	Joe E Campbell (a)	73	75	74	75	297

1	**TOMMY BOLT**	71	71	69	72	283
	($8000)					
2	Gary Player	75	68	73	71	287
3	Julius Boros	71	75	72	71	289
4	Gene Littler	74	73	67	76	290
5=	Walter Burkemo	75	74	70	72	291
	Bob Rosburg	75	74	72	70	291
7=	Jay Hebert	77	76	71	69	293
	Don January	79	73	68	73	293
	Dick Metz	71	78	73	71	293
10=	Ben Hogan	75	73	75	71	294
	Tommy Jacobs	76	75	71	72	294
	Frank Stranahan	72	72	75	75	294
13=	Billy Casper	79	70	75	71	295
	Charles R Coe (a)	75	71	75	74	295
	Marty Furgol	75	74	74	72	295
16	Bob Goetz	75	75	77	69	296
17=	Tom Nieporte	75	73	74	75	297
	Jerry Pittman	75	77	71	74	297
19=	Jerry Barber	79	73	73	73	298
	Bruce Crampton	73	75	74	76	298
	Jim Ferree	76	74	73	75	298
	Jerry Magee	76	77	75	70	298
23=	Dutch Harrison	76	76	73	74	299
	Dick Mayer	76	74	71	78	299
	Arnold Palmer	75	75	77	72	299
	Earl Stewart	75	74	77	73	299
27=	Stan Dudas	76	73	76	75	300
	Don Fairfield	78	75	72	75	300
	Mike Fetchick	78	76	73	73	300
	Labron Harris	74	72	77	77	300
	Billy Maxwell	78	76	76	70	300
	Cary Middlecoff	75	79	75	71	300
	Bo Wininger	78	74	74	74	300

Round Leader(s)
R1   Venturi; 68
R2   Venturi; 140
R3   Palmer, Snead; 211

Lowest Scores
R2   Patton; 69
R3   Hawkins, Palmer, Snead; 68
R4   Ford, Harmon; 70

Round Leader(s)
R1   Bolt, Boros, Metz; 71
R2   Bolt; 142
R3   Bolt; 211

Lowest Scores
R2   Player; 68
R3   Littler; 67
R4   Hebert, Goetz; 69

2–4 July	**1958**

BRITISH OPEN
Royal Lytham and St Anne's GC, Lancashire, England
6635 yards

The game of musical chairs between Locke and Thomson continued at Lytham. Between them they had claimed the Open 8 times since 1949. Only Max Faulkner (1951) and Ben Hogan (1953) disturbed their party game. Thomson's 4th win placed him alongside Locke in the all-time lists, and only James Braid had more wins in the century. Thomson's sequence in the event since 1952: 2, 2, W, W, W, 2, W. In 1958, he was taken to the wire – and beyond – though, by Dave Thomas.

1	**PETER THOMSON*** (£1000)	66	72	67	73	278
2	Dave Thomas	70	68	69	71	278
3=	Eric Brown	73	70	65	71	279
	Christy O'Connor, Sr	67	68	73	71	279
5=	Leopoldo Ruiz	71	65	72	73	281
	Flory van Donck	70	70	67	74	281
7	Gary Player	68	74	70	71	283
8=	Henry Cotton	68	75	69	72	284
	Eric Lester	73	66	71	74	284
	Harry Weetman	73	67	73	71	284
11=	Peter Alliss	72	70	70	73	285
	Don Swaelens	74	67	74	70	285
13	Harold Henning	70	71	72	73	286
14=	Jean Garaialde	69	74	72	72	287
	Dai Rees	77	69	71	70	287
16=	Max Faulkner	68	71	71	78	288
	Bobby Locke	76	70	72	70	288
	Eric Moore	72	72	70	74	288
	Gene Sarazen	73	73	70	72	288
20=	AB Coop	69	71	75	75	290
	Fred Daly	71	74	72	73	290
	Norman Drew	69	72	75	74	290
	Christy Greene	75	71	72	72	290
24=	Harry Bradshaw	70	73	72	76	291
	Gerard de Wit	71	75	72	73	291
26=	Antonio Cerda	72	71	74	75	292
	Sebastian Miguel	74	71	73	74	292
	Trevor Wilkes	76	70	69	77	292
29	Angel Miguel	71	70	75	77	293
30=	Bernard Hunt	70	70	76	79	295
	Sam King	71	73	76	75	295
	David Snell	72	72	72	79	295

* Peter Thomson (139) beat Dave Thomas (143) in the 36-Hole Play-off

Round Leader(s)
R1   Thomson; 66
R2   O'Connor; 135
R3   Thomson; 205

Lowest Scores
R2   Ruiz; 65
R3   Thomson, Van Donck; 67
R4   Locke, Rees, Swaelens; 70

17–20 July	**1958**

US PGA
Llanerch CC, Havertown, Pennsylvania
6710 yards PAR 70 (280)

Dow Finsterwald became the 1st strokeplay winner of the PGA – atoning for his defeat in the last matchplay final the previous year, by Lionel Hebert. It was Lionel's brother, Jay, who was the early threat this time. For Sam Snead, the scenario was not too dissimilar from the Masters of the previous year. Again he led into the final round, but was once more overhauled by a superb round. This time, for Doug Ford's 66 read Finsterwald's 67.

1	**DOW FINSTERWALD** ($5500)	67	72	70	67	276
2	Billy Casper	73	67	68	70	278
3	Sam Snead	73	67	67	73	280
4	Jack Burke, Jr	70	72	69	70	281
5=	Tommy Bolt	72	70	73	70	285
	Julius Boros	72	68	73	72	285
	Jay Hebert	68	71	73	73	285
8=	Buster Cupit	71	74	69	73	287
	Ed Oliver	74	73	71	69	287
	Mike Souchak	75	69	69	74	287
11=	Doug Ford	72	70	70	76	288
	Bob Rosburg	71	73	76	68	288
	Art Wall	71	78	67	72	288
14=	Fred Hawkins	72	75	70	73	290
	Dick Mayer	69	76	69	76	290
16=	John Barnum	75	69	74	73	291
	Walter Burkemo	76	73	66	76	291
	Lionel Hebert	69	73	74	75	291
	Bo Wininger	76	73	69	73	291
20=	Ted Kroll	69	74	75	74	292
	Cary Middlecoff	71	73	76	72	292
	Eric Monti	73	71	73	75	292
	Bob Toski	79	70	71	72	292
	Ken Venturi	72	73	74	73	292
25=	Pete Cooper	74	77	73	69	293
	George Fazio	72	74	73	74	293
	Bob Gajda	75	70	75	73	293
	Billy Maxwell	75	69	74	75	293
29=	Dick Shoemaker	79	72	73	70	294
	Don Whitt	71	72	73	78	294

Round Leader(s)
R1   Finsterwald; 67
R2   Finsterwald, Hebert; 139
R3   Snead; 207

Lowest Scores
R2   Casper, Snead; 67
R3   Burkemo; 66
R4   Finsterwald; 67

1959
THE MASTERS
2–5 April

Augusta National GC, Augusta, Georgia
6925 yards _PAR 72 (288)_

Art Wall was to be the leading money winner on the Tour in 1959 – set up by the biggest-ever 1st prize in a Major to date. His 66 in R4 to squeeze out Middlecoff was remarkable in its 5 under par sequence over the last 4 holes. Wall was a remarkable golfer in many ways. He won a Tour tournament aged 51 as late as 1975; he also claims the world record for holes-in-one – an astonishing 42! This was to be his only Major win, though.

1	**ART WALL**	73	74	71	66	284
	($15000)					
2	Cary Middlecoff	74	71	68	72	285
3	Arnold Palmer	71	70	71	74	286
4=	Stan Leonard	69	74	69	75	287
	Dick Mayer	73	75	71	68	287
6	Charles R Coe (a)	74	74	67	73	288
7	Fred Hawkins	77	71	68	73	289
8=	Julius Boros	75	69	74	72	290
	Jay Hebert	72	73	72	73	290
	Gene Littler	72	75	72	71	290
	Billy Maxwell (a)	73	71	72	74	290
	Billy Joe Patton (a)	75	70	71	74	290
	Gary Player	73	75	71	71	290
14=	Chick Harbert	74	72	74	71	291
	Chandler Harper	71	74	74	72	291
	Ted Kroll	76	71	73	71	291
	Ed Oliver	75	69	73	74	291
18=	Dow Finsterwald	79	68	73	72	292
	Jack Fleck	74	71	71	76	292
	William Hyndman III (a)	73	72	76	71	292
	Bo Wininger	75	70	72	75	292
22=	Walter Burkemo	75	70	71	77	293
	Chuck Kocsis (a)	73	75	70	75	293
	Sam Snead	74	73	72	74	293
25=	Don Cherry	77	71	75	71	294
	Doug Ford	76	73	73	72	294
	Paul Harney	75	69	77	73	294
	Angel Miguel	72	72	76	74	294
	Mike Souchak	73	71	74	76	294
30=	Tommy Bolt	72	75	72	76	295
	Ben Hogan	73	74	76	72	295
	Bob Rosburg	75	74	73	73	295
	Dave Thomas	73	71	77	74	295

Round Leader(s)
R1   Leonard; 69
R2   Palmer; 141
R3   Leonard, Palmer; 212
Lowest Scores
R2   Finsterwald; 68
R3   Coe; 67
R4   Wall; 66

1959
US OPEN
11–13 June

Winged Foot GC, Mamaroneck, New York
6873 yards _PAR 70 (280)_

The increasing number of entrants forced the introduction of local and final qualifying sessions. Billy Casper hung on to his halfway lead to head up an unfancied Top 4. Disappointing last rounds for Palmer, Hogan and Snead reduced the pressure on him in a Championship where his putting had kept his scores together. He putted just 122 times throughout.

1	**BILLY CASPER**	71	68	69	74	282
	($12000)					
2	Bob Rosburg	75	70	67	71	283
3=	Claude Harmon	72	71	70	71	284
	Mike Souchak	71	70	72	71	284
5=	Doug Ford	72	69	72	73	286
	Arnold Palmer	71	69	72	74	286
	Ernie Vossler	72	70	72	72	286
8=	Ben Hogan	69	71	71	76	287
	Sam Snead	73	72	67	75	287
10	Dick Knight	69	75	73	73	290
11=	Dow Finsterwald	69	73	75	74	291
	Fred Hawkins	76	72	69	74	291
	Ted Kroll	71	73	73	74	291
	Gene Littler	69	74	75	73	291
15=	Dave Marr	75	73	69	75	292
	Gary Player	71	69	76	76	292
17=	Gardner Dickinson	77	70	71	75	293
	Jay Hebert	73	70	78	72	293
19=	Jack Fleck	74	74	69	77	294
	Mac Hunter	75	74	73	72	294
	Don January	71	73	73	77	294
	Cary Middlecoff	71	73	73	77	294
	Johnny Pott	77	72	70	75	294
	Bo Wininger	71	73	72	78	294
25	Joe Campbell	73	71	75	76	295
26=	Chick Harbert	78	68	76	74	296
	Billy Maxwell	75	75	70	76	296
28=	Julius Boros	76	74	72	75	297
	Lionel Hebert	71	74	70	82	297
	Henry Ransom	72	77	71	77	297
	Fred Wampler	74	73	75	75	297

Round Leader(s)
R1   Finsterwald, Hogan, Knight, Littler; 69
R2   Casper; 139
R3   Casper; 208
Lowest Scores
R2   Cooper, Harbert; 68
R3   Rosburg, Snead; 67
R4   Harman, Rosburg, Souchak; 71

1–3 July	**1959**

BRITISH OPEN

Honourable Company, Muirfield, Angus, Scotland
6806 yards

Gary Player had announced his arrival when he finished 4th in the British Open in 1956 and 2nd in the US Open in 1958. The South African's 1st Major Championship win of an illustrious career coincided with the nadir of the Open's gradual decline in comparative importance with the US Open. The influx of top-class American challengers had dwindled to a trickle since the mid '30s until, by 1959, there were none. It was soon to change...

1	**GARY PLAYER**	75	71	70	68	284
	(£1000)					
2=	Fred Bullock	68	70	74	74	286
	Flory van Donck	70	70	73	73	286
4	Syd Scott	73	70	73	71	287
5=	Reid Jack (a)	71	75	68	74	288
	Sam King	70	74	68	76	288
	Christy O'Connor, Sr	73	74	72	69	288
	John Panton	72	72	71	73	288
9=	Dai Rees	73	73	69	74	289
	Leopoldo Ruiz	72	74	69	74	289
11=	Michael Bonallack (a)	70	72	72	76	290
	Ken Bousfield	73	73	71	73	290
	Jimmy Hitchcock	75	68	70	77	290
	Bernard Hunt	73	75	71	71	290
	Arnold Stickley	68	74	77	71	290
16=	Peter Alliss	76	72	76	67	291
	Harry Bradshaw	71	76	72	72	291
	Antonio Cerda	69	74	73	75	291
	Harry Weetman	72	73	76	70	291
	Guy Wolstenholme (a)	78	70	73	70	291
21=	Neil Coles	72	74	71	75	292
	Jean Garaialde	75	70	74	73	292
23=	Harold Henning	73	73	72	76	294
	Geoff Hunt	72	73	74	75	294
	Reg Knight	71	71	74	78	294
	Peter Mills	75	71	72	76	294
	JR Moses	72	73	73	76	294
	Peter Thomson	74	74	72	74	294
29=	Jimmy Adams	71	74	75	75	295
	Tom Haliburton	74	69	74	78	295
	Bobby Locke	73	73	76	73	295
	PJ Shanks	76	70	75	74	295
	Ernest E Whitcombe	71	77	74	73	295

Round Leader(s)
R1 Bullock, Stickley; 68
R2 Bullock; 138
R3 Bullock, King; 212
Lowest Scores
R2 Haliburton; 69
R3 Jack, King; 68
R4 Alliss; 67

30 July–2 August	**1959**

US PGA

Minneapolis GC, St Louis Park, Minnesota
6850 yards PAR 70 (280)

Bob Rosburg made up for his 2nd place disappointment in the US Open by taking his one and only Major at Minneapolis. Nine people (3 of whom would miss the cut) tied at the end of R1 – the largest leadership grouping for any Major. Rosburg, 9 behind Barber at halfway, and 6 after 54 holes, blasted a R4 66 to win by one.

1	**BOB ROSBURG**	71	72	68	66	277
	($8250)					
2=	Jerry Barber	69	65	71	73	278
	Doug Sanders	72	66	68	72	278
4	Dow Finsterwald	71	68	71	70	280
5=	Bob Goalby	72	69	72	68	281
	Mike Souchak	69	67	71	74	281
	Ken Venturi	70	72	70	69	281
8=	Cary Middlecoff	72	68	70	72	282
	Sam Snead	71	73	68	70	282
10	Gene Littler	69	70	72	73	284
11=	Doug Ford	71	73	71	70	285
	Billy Maxwell	70	76	70	69	285
	Ed Oliver	75	70	69	71	285
14=	Paul Harney	74	71	71	70	286
	Tommy Jacobs	73	71	68	74	286
	Arnold Palmer	72	72	71	71	286
17=	Tommy Bolt	76	69	68	74	287
	Jack Burke, Jr	70	73	72	72	287
	Walter Burkemo	69	72	73	73	287
	Billy Casper	69	71	73	74	287
	Pete Cooper	78	70	68	71	287
	Buster Cupit	70	72	72	73	287
	Babe Lichardus	71	73	72	71	287
	Ernie Vossler	75	71	72	69	287
25=	Jay Hebert	72	70	69	77	288
	Ted Kroll	72	74	71	71	288
	Art Wall	70	72	73	73	288
28=	Clare Emery	74	74	72	69	289
	Chick Harbert	73	71	71	74	289
	Fred Hawkins	72	69	72	76	289

Round Leader(s)
R1 Barber, Jackson Bradley (31), Burkemo, Casper, Dick Hart (Cut), Chuck Klein (Cut), Mike Krak (Cut), Littler, Souchak; 69
R2 Barber; 134
R3 Barber; 205
Lowest Scores
R2 Barber; 65
R3 Bolt, Cooper, Jacobs, Rosburg, Sanders, Snead; 68
R4 Rosburg; 66

1960
7–10 April
THE MASTERS
Augusta National GC, Augusta, Georgia
6925 yards PAR 72 (288)

Palmer's 2nd Masters triumph swept in the new decade like the breath of fresh air the '60s' was to become on many fronts. Post-War colourless austerity, and cloying formalities and conventions gave way to new freedoms of expression - and none freer than in golf, personified by the phenomenon of Arnold Palmer. The people's man, he took the playing of golf into a new dimension through his vision and daring. He almost single-handedly, through the media of press and, particularly, TV, popularized the sport for spectators and created a surge in new players like no time before. At Augusta in 1960, in front of a TV audience sitting on the edge of their seats, he dramatically birdied 17 and 18 to beat the disbelieving Ken Venturi by one.

1	**ARNOLD PALMER** ($17500)	67	73	72	70	282
2	Ken Venturi	73	69	71	70	283
3	Dow Finsterwald	71	70	72	71	284
4	Billy Casper	71	71	71	74	287
5	Julius Boros	72	71	70	75	288
6=	Walter Burkemo	72	69	75	73	289
	Ben Hogan	73	68	72	76	289
	Gary Player	72	71	72	74	289
9=	Lionel Hebert	74	70	73	73	290
	Stan Leonard	72	72	72	74	290
11=	Jack Burke, Jr	72	72	74	74	292
	Sam Snead	73	74	72	73	292
13=	Ted Kroll	72	76	71	74	293
	Jack Nicklaus (a)	75	71	72	75	293
	Billy Joe Patton	75	72	74	72	293
16=	Bruce Crampton	74	73	75	72	294
	Claude Harmon	69	72	75	78	294
	Fred Hawkins	69	78	72	75	294
	Mike Souchak	72	75	72	75	294
20=	Tommy Bolt	73	74	75	73	295
	Don January	70	72	74	79	295
	Ed Oliver	74	75	73	73	295
	Bob Rosburg	74	74	71	76	295
	Frank M Taylor, Jr (a)	70	74	73	78	295
25=	Tommy Aaron	74	75	75	73	297
	Doug Ford	74	72	80	81	297
	Billy Maxwell (a)	72	71	79	75	297
	Dave Ragan	74	73	75	75	297
29=	George Bayer	73	73	80	72	298
	Deane Beman (a)	71	72	77	78	298
	Richard Crawford	74	72	75	77	298
	Doug Sanders	73	71	81	73	298

Round Leader(s)
R1   Palmer; 67
R2   Palmer; 140
R3   Palmer; 212

Lowest Scores
R2   Hogan; 68
R3   Boros; 70
R4   Palmer, Venturi; 70

1960
16–18 June
US OPEN
Cherry Hills CC, Denver, Colorado
7004 yards PAR 71 (284)

Two months later Palmer was still rolling on. Once more, he saved his heroics until R4, when trailing leader Mike Souchak he went out in a record-equalling 30 to make 65 and leapfrog the leading pack. Jack Nicklaus entered the scene when he took the highest place claimed by an amateur since Goodman's win in 1933. Along with Palmer and British Open Champion, Player, the emergence of the 'Golden Bear' heralded the modern version of the Great Triumvirate. From Arnie's 1958 Master's win to Jack's last Major in 1986, they were to scoop 34 Major titles between them.

1	**ARNOLD PALMER** ($14400)	72	71	72	65	280
2	Jack Nicklaus (a)	71	71	69	71	282
3=	Julius Boros	73	69	68	73	283
	Dow Finsterwald	71	69	70	73	283
	Jack Fleck	70	70	72	71	283
	Dutch Harrison	74	70	70	69	283
	Ted Kroll	72	69	75	67	283
	Mike Souchak	68	67	73	75	283
9=	Jerry Barber	69	71	70	74	284
	Don Cherry (a)	70	71	71	72	284
	Ben Hogan	75	67	69	73	284
12=	George Bayer	72	72	73	69	286
	Billy Casper	71	70	73	72	286
	Paul Harney	73	70	72	71	286
15=	Bob Harris	73	71	71	72	287
	Johnny Pott	75	68	69	75	287
17=	Dave Marr	72	73	70	73	288
	Donald Whitt	75	69	72	72	288
19=	Jackson Bradley	73	73	69	74	289
	Bob Goalby	73	70	72	74	289
	Gary Player	70	72	71	76	289
	Sam Snead	72	69	73	75	289
23=	Al Feminelli	75	71	71	73	290
	Lloyd Mangrum	72	73	71	74	290
	Bob Rosburg	72	75	71	72	290
	Ken Venturi	71	73	74	72	290
27=	Claude Harmon	73	73	75	70	291
	Lionel Hebert	73	72	71	75	291
	Bob Shave, Jr	72	71	71	77	291
	Richard Stranahan	70	73	73	75	291

Round Leader(s)
R1   Souchak; 68
R2   Souchak; 135
R3   Souchak; 208

Lowest Scores
R2   Rex Baxter (33), Hogan, Souchak; 67
R3   Boros; 68
R4   Palmer; 65

6–8 July **1960**
BRITISH OPEN
Royal & Ancient GC, St Andrews, Fife, Scotland
6936 yards

21–24 July **1960**
US PGA
Firestone CC, Akron, Ohio
7165 yards PAR 70 (280)

Another R4 Palmer charge just failed to net him the Centenary Open Championship on his 1st visit, and thus emulate the great Ben Hogan's triple in 1953. The Commonwealth succession continued in the person of Australian Kel Nagle. Palmer's presence, however, and the introduction of a new style of play – and player – had a 2-pronged effect. It blew new life into an increasingly-parochial Championship: it also re-introduced the British Open to a new generation of US golfers.

Jay Hebert followed younger brother Lionel as PGA Champion – the only brothers to achieve this (albeit one matchplay, one strokeplay) – as he pipped 1947 winner, Jim Ferrier, for the 1960 title. The Parks, Sr – Willie & Mungo (BOP); the Auchterlonies – Willie (BOP) and Laurie (USOP); the Herds – Fred (USOP) and Sandy (BOP); and the Smiths – Willie and Alex (USOP), are the only other sets of brothers to win Majors. Palmer's outstanding year continued when he led after R1, but 2 poor rounds dropped him to 7th.

1	**KEL NAGLE** (£1250)	69	67	71	71	278
2	Arnold Palmer	70	71	70	68	279
3=	Roberto de Vicenzo	67	67	75	73	282
	Harold Henning	72	72	69	69	282
	Bernard Hunt	72	73	71	66	282
6	Guy Wolstenholme (a)	74	70	71	68	283
7	Gary Player	72	71	72	69	284
8	Joe Carr (a)	72	73	67	73	285
9=	David Blair (a)	70	73	71	72	286
	Eric Brown	75	68	72	71	286
	Dai Rees	73	71	73	69	286
	Syd Scott	73	71	67	75	286
	Peter Thomson	72	69	75	70	286
	Harry Weetman	74	70	71	71	286
15	Ramon Sota	74	72	71	70	287
16=	Fidel de Luca	69	73	75	71	288
	Reid Jack (a)	74	71	70	73	288
	Angel Miguel	72	73	72	71	288
	Ian Smith	74	70	73	71	288
20	Peter Mills	71	74	70	74	289
21=	Ken Bousfield	70	75	71	74	290
	Alec Deboys (a)	76	70	73	71	290
	George Low	72	74	71	73	290
	John MacDonald	76	71	69	74	290
	Ralph Moffitt	72	71	76	71	290
26=	Bill Johnston	75	74	71	71	291
	Sebastian Miguel	73	68	74	76	291
28=	Laurie Ayton, Jr	73	69	75	75	292
	Fred Boobyer	74	74	73	71	292
	Geoff Hunt	76	69	72	75	292
	Jimmy Martin	72	72	72	76	292

Round Leader(s)
R1 De Vicenzo; 67
R2 De Vicenzo; 134
R3 Nagle; 207
Lowest Scores
R2 De Vicenzo, Nagle; 67
R3 Carr, Scott; 67
R4 Hunt; 66

1	**JAY HEBERT** ($11000)	72	67	72	70	281
2	Jim Ferrier	71	74	66	71	282
3=	Doug Sanders	70	71	69	73	283
	Sam Snead	68	73	70	72	283
5	Don January	70	70	72	72	284
6	Wes Ellis, Jr	72	72	72	69	285
7=	Doug Ford	75	70	69	72	286
	Arnold Palmer	67	74	75	70	286
9	Ken Venturi	70	72	73	72	287
10=	Fred Hawkins	73	69	72	74	288
	Dave Marr	75	71	69	73	288
12=	Bill Collins	71	75	71	73	290
	Ted Kroll	73	71	72	74	290
	Mike Souchak	73	73	70	74	290
15=	Pete Cooper	73	74	70	74	291
	Dow Finsterwald	73	73	69	76	291
	Johnny Pott	75	72	72	72	291
18=	Paul Harney	69	78	73	72	292
	Lionel Hebert	75	72	70	75	292
	Gene Littler	74	70	75	73	292
	Tom Nieporte	72	74	74	72	292
22=	Dave Ragan	75	75	68	75	293
	Mason Rudolph	72	71	76	74	293
24=	Julius Boros	76	73	72	73	294
	Walter Burkemo	72	77	73	72	294
	Billy Casper	73	75	75	71	294
	Billy Maxwell	74	77	72	71	294
	Ernie Vossler	71	77	74	72	294
29=	Jack Burke, Jr	73	72	78	72	295
	Cary Middlecoff	73	74	73	75	295
	Bo Wininger	73	77	71	74	295

Round Leader(s)
R1 Palmer; 67
R2 Hebert; 139
R3 Sanders; 210
Lowest Scores
R2 Hebert; 67
R3 Ferrier; 66
R4 Ellis, Jr; 69

1961 — 6–10 April (Sunday play washed out)
THE MASTERS
Augusta National GC, Augusta, Georgia
6925 yards PAR 72 (288)

Gary Player's 1st Masters and 2nd Major came after an extra day was required due to the weather. He collected golf's 1st $20000 winning purse and was the 1st non-American to win the Masters (and the 1st since Jim Ferrier in the 1947 PGA to win any US Major). His victory was built on a 54 hole-total of 206, allowing him a cushion of 4 strokes over Palmer and 6 over Coe going into R4. He was to need every one.

1	**GARY PLAYER** ($20000)	69	68	69	74	280
2=	Charles R Coe, Jr (a)	72	71	69	69	281
	Arnold Palmer	68	69	73	71	281
4=	Tommy Bolt	72	71	74	68	285
	Don January	74	68	72	71	285
6	Paul Harney	71	73	68	74	286
7=	Jack Burke, Jr	76	70	68	73	287
	Billy Casper	72	77	69	69	287
	Bill Collins	74	72	67	74	287
	Jack Nicklaus (a)	70	75	70	72	287
11=	Walter Burkemo	74	69	73	72	288
	Robert Gardner (a)	74	71	72	71	288
	Doug Sanders	76	71	68	73	288
	Ken Venturi	72	71	72	73	288
15=	Stan Leonard	72	74	72	74	289
	Gene Littler	72	73	72	72	289
	Bob Rosburg	68	73	73	75	289
	Sam Snead	74	73	69	73	289
19=	Dick Mayer	76	72	70	73	291
	Johnny Pott	71	75	72	73	291
	Peter Thomson	73	76	68	74	291
22=	Roberto de Vicenzo	73	74	71	74	292
	Lew Worsham	74	71	73	74	292
24=	Antonio Cerda	73	73	72	75	293
	Fred Hawkins	74	75	72	72	293
	Ted Kroll	73	70	72	78	293
27	Al Balding	74	74	70	76	294
28=	Mason Rudolph	77	69	72	77	295
	Mike Souchak	75	72	75	73	295
30=	Jay Hebert	72	75	69	80	296
	Lionel Hebert	74	69	74	79	296

Round Leader(s)
R1   Palmer, Rosburg; 68
R2   Palmer, Player; 137
R3   Player; 206
Lowest Scores
R2   January, Player; 68
R3   Collins; 67
R4   Bolt; 68

1961 — 15–17 June
US OPEN
Oakland Hills CC, Birmingham, Michigan
6907 yards PAR 70 (280)

Gene Littler's Open win, after a fine closing round took him past Sanders, Goalby and Souchak, came relatively early in a long career. After winning the US Amateur in 1953 (thereby becoming the 8th player to pick up the Amateur-Open double), much was expected – but perhaps he just missed that dedicated edge which is required to be the very top in any field. Ben Hogan missed a Top 10 finish for the 1st time in any Open he competed in since 1940.

1	**GENE LITTLER** ($14000)	73	68	72	68	281
2=	Bob Goalby	70	72	69	71	282
	Doug Sanders	72	67	71	72	282
4=	Jack Nicklaus (a)	75	69	70	70	284
	Mike Souchak	73	70	68	73	284
6=	Dow Finsterwald	72	71	71	72	286
	Doug Ford	72	69	71	74	286
	Eric Monti	74	67	72	73	286
9=	Jacky Cupit	72	72	67	76	287
	Gardner Dickinson	72	69	71	75	287
	Gary Player	75	72	69	71	287
12=	Deane Beman (a)	74	72	72	70	288
	Al Geiberger	71	70	73	74	288
14=	Dave Douglas	72	72	75	70	289
	Ben Hogan	71	72	73	73	289
	Arnold Palmer	74	75	70	70	289
17=	Billy Casper	74	71	73	72	290
	Dutch Harrison	74	71	76	69	290
	Kel Nagle	71	71	74	74	290
	Sam Snead	73	70	74	73	290
21	Bob Rosburg	72	67	74	78	291
22=	Tommy Bolt	70	73	73	76	292
	Bob Brue	69	72	73	78	292
	Bruce Crampton	71	71	74	76	292
	Jim Ferrier	74	72	71	75	292
	Billy Maxwell	73	74	72	73	292
27=	Jack Fleck	73	71	79	70	293
	Ted Kroll	78	69	73	73	293
29=	Edward Brantly (a)	75	70	72	77	294
	Chick Harbert	75	71	69	79	294
	Robert Harrison	79	70	71	74	294
	Milon Marusic	75	74	71	74	294
	Jerry Steelsmith	74	74	72	74	294

Round Leader(s)
R1   Brue; 69
R2   Rosburg, Sanders; 139
R3   Sanders; 210
Lowest Scores
R2   Bob Harris (34), Monti, Rosburg, Sanders; 67
R3   Cupit; 67
R4   Littler; 68

| 12–14 July | **1961** | 27–31 July | **1961** |

BRITISH OPEN

Birkdale GC, Southport, Lancashire, England
6844 yards

US PGA

Olympia Fields CC, Olympia Fields, Illinois
6722 yards PAR 70 (280)

Dai Rees, according to Peter Alliss, was probably the best British player never to win his native Championship. He was undoubtedly the best golfer to come out of Wales until Ian Woosnam appeared on the scene – and was captain of the victorious British Ryder Cup team of 1957, when he beat Ed Furgol in the Singles, 7&6. His 3rd 2nd place in the Open after a tooth-and-nail struggle with the best player in the world, was to be his last serious challenge. Palmer's 1st win in the Open seemed inevitable after his runner's-up place the previous year.

1	**ARNOLD PALMER**	70	73	69	72	284
	(£1400)					
2	Dai Rees	68	74	71	72	285
3=	Neil Coles	70	77	69	72	288
	Christy O'Connor, Sr	71	77	67	73	288
5=	Eric Brown	73	76	70	70	289
	Kel Nagle	68	75	75	71	289
7	Peter Thomson	75	72	70	73	290
8=	Peter Alliss	73	75	72	71	291
	Ken Bousfield	71	77	75	68	291
10=	Harold Henning	68	74	75	76	293
	Syd Scott	76	75	71	71	293
12	Ramon Sota	71	76	72	76	295
13	AB Coop	71	79	73	74	297
14=	Norman Johnson	69	80	70	79	298
	Reg Knight	71	80	73	74	298
	Angel Miguel	73	79	74	72	298
	Sebastian Miguel	71	80	70	77	298
18=	Dennis Hutchinson	72	80	74	73	299
	Paul Runyan	75	77	75	72	299
20=	Harry Bradshaw	73	75	78	74	300
	Peter Butler	72	76	78	74	300
	John Jacobs	71	79	76	74	300
	Lionel Platts	70	80	71	79	300
26=	Jean Garaialde	69	81	76	75	301
	Brian Huggett	72	77	75	77	301
	Eric Lester	71	77	75	78	301
	Ralph Moffitt	73	80	73	75	301
30=	David Miller	69	79	80	74	302
	George Will	74	75	75	78	302

Round Leader(s)
R1   Henning, Nagle, Rees; 68
R2   Henning, Rees; 142
R3   Palmer; 212

Lowest Scores
R2   Thomson; 72
R3   O'Connor, Sr; 67
R4   Bousfield; 68

With 3 holes to play, Don January led Jerry Barber by 4 strokes. Thanks to 2 dropped shots and 3 big putts by Barber (2 for birdie), the latter drew level – and after a few traumas, went on to win the play-off. At 45, Barber was the oldest man to win the PGA and he overtook Ted Ray's 1920 record to become the oldest player this century to win a Major - at least for a few years.

1=	**JERRY BARBER***	69	67	71	70	277
	($11000)					
2	Don January	72	66	67	72	277
3	Doug Sanders	70	68	74	68	280
4	Ted Kroll	72	68	70	71	281
5=	Wes Ellis, Jr	71	71	68	72	282
	Doug Ford	69	73	74	66	282
	Gene Littler	71	70	72	69	282
	Arnold Palmer	73	72	69	68	282
	Johnny Pott	71	73	67	71	282
	Art Wall	67	72	73	70	282
11=	Paul Harney	70	73	69	71	283
	Cary Middlecoff	74	69	71	69	283
13	Jay Hebert	68	72	72	72	284
14	Walter Buekemo	71	71	73	70	285
15=	Billy Casper	74	72	69	71	286
	Bob Goalby	73	72	68	73	286
	Ernie Vossler	68	72	71	75	286
	Don Whitt	76	72	70	68	286
19=	Gardner Jackson	71	71	71	74	287
	Jack Fleck	70	74	73	70	287
	Bob Rosburg	70	71	73	73	287
22=	George Bayer	73	71	72	72	288
	Don Fairfield	70	71	74	73	288
	Fred Hawkins	75	73	71	69	288
	Dave Marr	72	74	73	69	288
	Shelley Mayfield	70	74	72	72	288
27=	Billy Maxwell	71	72	73	73	289
	Sam Snead	72	71	71	75	289
29=	Charles Bassler	73	73	72	72	290
	Bob Keller	72	73	72	73	290
	Al Mengert	72	74	72	72	290
	Gary Player	72	74	71	73	290

* Jerry Barber (67) beat Don January (68) in the 18-Hole Play-off

Round Leader(s)
R1   Wall; 67
R2   Barber; 136
R3   January; 205

Lowest Scores
R2   January; 66
R3   January, Pott; 67
R4   Ford; 66

1962
THE MASTERS
5–9 April

Augusta National GC, Augusta, Georgia
6925 yards _PAR 72 (288)_

1962
US OPEN
14–17 June

Oakmont CC, Oakmont, Pennsylvania
6894 yards _PAR 72 (288)_

All the 1961 Major Champions featured in the Top 5 in the 1st Major of the year – two of them, along with Dow Finsterwald, in the 3-way play-off. Palmer's supremacy was maintained, however, when he reeled in Gary Player – the pretender to his crown – pulling back 3 shots to win with a home 9 score of 31.

Two months later Palmer was not so lucky in the play-off. He succumbed to 22 year-old Jack Nicklaus, who was in his 1st year as a professional. Nicklaus was the 1st player since Bobby Jones to hold the US Amateur and US Open titles at the same time. The balance of power was changing again. Although Palmer would remain at the very top for some years yet, this was definitely the start of the Jack Nicklaus era. Between 1962 and 1986 – a record span – a blend of power and precision never before witnessed on a golf course was to reap him a harvest of 18 Majors, 7 more than the next man, Walter Hagen.

1	**ARNOLD PALMER*** ($20000)	70	66	69	75	280
2	Gary Player	67	71	71	71	280
3	Dow Finsterwald	74	68	65	73	280
4	Gene Littler	71	68	71	72	282
5=	Jerry Barber	72	72	69	74	287
	Jimmy Demaret	73	73	71	70	287
	Billy Maxwell (a)	71	73	72	71	287
	Mike Souchak	70	72	74	71	287
9=	Charles R Coe (a)	72	74	71	71	288
	Ken Venturi	75	70	71	72	288
11=	Julius Boros	69	73	72	76	290
	Gay Brewer	74	71	70	75	290
	Jack Fleck	72	75	74	69	290
	Harold Henning	75	73	72	70	290
15=	Billy Casper	73	73	73	72	291
	Gardner Dickinson	70	71	72	78	291
	Paul Harney	74	71	74	72	291
	Jack Nicklaus	74	75	70	72	291
	Sam Snead	72	75	70	74	291
20=	Jacky Cupit	73	73	72	74	292
	Lionel Hebert	72	73	71	76	292
	Don January	71	73	74	74	292
	Johnny Pott	77	71	75	69	292
24	Al Balding	75	68	78	72	293
25=	Bob Charles	75	72	73	74	294
	Bob Goalby	74	74	73	73	294
	Ted Kroll	72	74	72	76	294
	Dave Ragan	70	73	76	75	294
29=	Bill Collins	75	70	75	75	295
	Bruce Crampton	72	75	74	74	295
	Cary Middlecoff	75	74	73	73	295
	Lew Worsham	75	70	78	72	295

*Arnold Palmer (68) beat Gary Player (71) and Dow Finsterwald (77) in the 18-hole Play-off

Round Leader(s)
R1   Player; 67
R2   Palmer; 136
R3   Palmer; 205

Lowest Scores
R2   Palmer; 66
R3   Finsterwald; 65
R4   Fleck, Pott; 69

1	**JACK NICKLAUS*** ($17500)	72	70	72	69	283
2	Arnold Palmer	71	68	73	71	283
3=	Bobby Nichols	70	72	70	73	285
	Phil Rodgers	74	70	69	72	285
5	Gay Brewer	73	72	73	69	287
6=	Tommy Jacobs	74	71	73	70	288
	Gary Player	71	71	72	74	288
8=	Doug Ford	74	75	71	70	290
	Gene Littler	69	74	72	75	290
	Billy Maxwell	71	70	75	74	290
11=	Doug Sanders	74	74	74	69	291
	Art Wall	73	72	72	74	291
13	Bob Rosburg	70	69	74	79	292
14=	Deane Beman (a)	74	72	80	67	293
	Bob Goalby	73	74	73	73	293
	Mike Souchak	75	73	72	73	293
17=	Jacky Cupit	73	72	72	77	294
	Jay Hebert	75	72	73	74	294
	Earl Stewart	75	73	75	71	294
	Donald Whitt	73	71	75	75	294
	Bo Wininger	73	74	69	78	294
22	Miller Barber	73	70	77	75	295
23=	Gardner Dickinson	76	74	75	71	296
	Lionel Hebert	75	72	75	74	296
25=	Stan Leonard	72	73	78	74	297
	Edward Meister, Jr (a)	78	72	76	71	297
27	Frank Boynton	71	75	74	78	298
28=	Joe Campbell	78	71	72	78	299
	Dave Douglas	74	70	72	83	299
	Paul Harney	73	73	71	72	299
	Dean Refram	75	73	77	74	299
	Mason Rudolph	74	74	73	78	299

* Jack Nicklaus (71) beat Arnold Palmer (74) in the 18-Hole Play-off

Round Leader(s)
R1   Littler; 69
R2   Palmer, Rosburg; 139
R3   Palmer, Nichols; 212

Lowest Scores
R2   Palmer; 68
R3   Rodgers, Wininger; 69
R4   Beman; 67

<table>
<tr><td>11–13 July</td><td>1962</td></tr>
</table>

BRITISH OPEN
Troon GC, Ayrshire, Scotland
7045 yards

Nicklaus was not to get all his own way yet. He won't forget his 1st visit to Troon, where rounds of 80 and 79 contributed to a humbling score of 305, and a tie for 34th place. Palmer, on the other hand, found the links much to his liking, setting a new record low for the Championship and tying Hogan's famous score in the 1948 US Open. His lead from the end of R2 increased from 2, to 4, to 6, over Kel Nagle.

1	**ARNOLD PALMER** (£1400)	71	69	67	69	276
2	Kel Nagle	71	71	70	70	282
3=	Brian Huggett	75	71	74	69	289
	Phil Rodgers	75	70	72	72	289
5	Bob Charles	75	70	70	75	290
6=	Sam Snead	76	73	72	71	292
	Peter Thomson	70	77	75	70	292
8=	Peter Alliss	77	69	74	73	293
	Dave Thomas	77	70	71	75	293
10	Syd Scott	77	74	75	68	294
11	Ralph Moffitt	75	70	74	76	295
12=	Jean Garaialde	76	73	76	71	296
	Sebastian Miguel	72	79	73	72	296
	Harry Weetman	75	73	73	75	296
	Ross Whitehead	74	75	72	75	296
16=	Roger Foreman	77	73	72	75	297
	Bernard Hunt	74	75	75	73	297
	Dennis Hutchinson	78	73	76	70	297
	Jimmy Martin	73	72	76	76	297
	Christy O'Connor, Sr	74	78	73	72	297
	John Panton	74	73	79	71	297
22	AB Coop	76	75	75	72	298
23	Don Swaelens	72	79	74	74	299
24=	Brian Bamford	77	73	74	76	300
	Lionel Platts	78	74	76	72	300
	Guy Wolstenholme	78	74	76	72	300
27=	Hugh Boyle	73	78	74	76	301
	Keith MacDonald	69	77	76	79	301
29	George Low	77	75	77	73	302
30=	Harry Bradshaw	72	75	81	75	303
	Harold Henning	74	73	79	77	303
	Jimmy Hitchcock	78	74	72	79	303

Round Leader(s)
R1 MacDonald; 69
R2 Palmer; 140
R3 Palmer; 207

Lowest Scores
R2 Alliss, Palmer; 69
R3 Palmer; 67
R4 Scott; 68

<table>
<tr><td>19–22 July</td><td>1962</td></tr>
</table>

US PGA
Aronimink GC, Newtown Square, Pennsylvania
7045 yards <u>PAR 70 (280)</u>

Gary Player – in just 4 years – won his 3rd different Major. He was the 10th player to achieve it, and the 1st non-American since Tommy Armour in 1931. Two others, Snead and Palmer, were also in the Top 20. Scoring was tough on this 7000+ yard, Par 70 course.

1	**GARY PLAYER** ($13000)	72	67	69	70	278
2	Bob Goalby	69	72	71	67	279
3=	George Bayer	69	70	71	71	281
	Jack Nicklaus	71	75	69	67	281
5	Doug Ford	69	69	73	71	282
6	Bobby Nichols	72	70	71	70	283
7=	Jack Fleck	74	69	70	71	284
	Paul Harney	70	73	72	69	284
	Dave Ragan	72	74	70	68	284
10	Jay Hebert	73	72	70	70	285
11=	Julius Boros	73	69	74	70	286
	Dow Finsterwald	73	70	70	73	286
	Chick Harbert	68	76	69	73	286
	Bob McCallister	74	66	70	76	286
15=	Cary Middlecoff	73	66	74	74	287
	Doug Sanders	76	69	73	69	287
17=	Jack Burke, Jr	73	69	71	75	288
	Bruce Crampton	76	73	67	72	288
	Billy Farrell	73	71	73	71	288
	Arnold Palmer	71	72	73	72	288
	Sam Snead	75	70	71	72	288
	Frank Stranahan	69	73	72	74	288
23=	Fred Haas	75	71	74	69	289
	Tommy Jacobs	73	73	73	70	289
	Gene Littler	73	75	72	69	289
	Art Wall	72	75	71	71	289
27=	Joe Campbell	70	74	74	73	291
	Don January	70	74	72	75	291
	Johnny Pott	71	77	71	72	291
30=	Tommy Bolt	72	74	72	74	292
	Pete Cooper	73	71	74	74	292
	Buster Cupit	76	70	76	70	292
	Wes Ellis, Jr	75	72	73	72	292
	Dick Hart	70	73	76	73	292
	Ted Kroll	73	70	76	73	292
	Shelley Mayfield	74	70	74	74	292
	Tom Nieporte	75	75	69	73	292
	Don Whitt	74	73	70	75	292

Round Leader(s)
R1 John Barnum (57); 66
R2 Ford; 138
R3 Player; 208

Lowest Scores
R2 McCallister, Middlecoff; 66
R3 Crampton; 67
R4 Nicklaus, Goalby; 67

1963
THE MASTERS
4–7 April

Augusta National GC, Augusta, Georgia
6925 yards _PAR 72 (288)_

1963
US OPEN
20–23 June

The Country Club, Brookline, Massachusetts
6870 yards _PAR 71 (284)_

Nicklaus' 2nd Major was gained when confronting Augusta National at its most difficult. Weather conditions accounted for the relatively high scoring, but Nicklaus made the best of it when it relented during R2. At 23, he was the youngest winner of the Masters to date.

From the youngest winner of the Masters we come to the oldest – American – winner of the Open. Julius Boros, in adding to his 1952 Open title, was just 26 days younger than Ted Ray when he won at Inverness in 1920. A 3-way play-off resulted when Boros caught Palmer, who missed a 2-footer at the 17th, and Jackie Cupit, who dropped 3 shots over 17 and 18. Paul Harney also bogeyed the last to miss the play-off.

1	**JACK NICKLAUS** ($20000)	74	66	74	72	286
2	Tony Lema	74	69	74	70	287
3=	Julius Boros	76	69	71	72	288
	Sam Snead	70	73	74	71	288
5=	Dow Finsterwald	74	73	73	69	289
	Ed Furgol	70	71	74	74	289
	Gary Player	71	74	74	70	289
8	Bo Wininger	69	72	77	72	290
9=	Don January	73	75	72	71	291
	Arnold Palmer	74	73	73	71	291
11=	Billy Casper	79	72	71	70	292
	Bruce Crampton	74	74	72	72	292
	Doug Ford	75	73	75	69	292
	Mike Souchak	69	70	79	74	292
15=	Bob Charles	74	72	76	71	293
	Chen Ching-po	76	71	71	75	293
	Billy Maxwell (a)	72	75	76	70	293
	Dick Mayer	73	70	80	70	293
	Mason Rudolph	75	72	72	74	293
	Dan Sikes	74	76	72	71	293
21=	Stan Leonard	74	72	73	75	294
	Johnny Pott	75	76	74	69	294
	Art Wall	75	74	73	72	294
24=	Wes Ellis, Jr	74	72	79	70	295
	Gene Littler	77	72	78	68	295
	Bobby Nichols	76	74	73	72	295
27	Jay Hebert	70	70	81	75	296
28=	George Bayer	71	75	84	67	297
	Tommy Jacobs (a)	78	74	73	72	297
	Doug Sanders	73	74	77	73	297
	Alvie Thompson	79	72	75	71	297

Round Leader(s)
R1 Souchak, Wininger; 69
R2 Souchak; 139
R3 Nicklaus; 214
Lowest Scores
R2 Nicklaus; 66
R3 Boros, Casper, Ching-po; 71
R4 Bayer; 67

1	**JULIUS BOROS*** ($17500)	71	74	76	72	293
2	Jacky Cupit	70	72	76	75	293
3	Arnold Palmer	73	69	77	74	293
4	Paul Harney	78	70	73	73	294
5=	Bruce Crampton	74	72	75	74	295
	Tony Lema	71	74	74	76	295
	Billy Maxwell	73	73	75	74	295
8=	Walter Burkemo	72	71	76	77	296
	Gary Player	74	75	75	72	296
10	Dan Sikes	77	73	73	74	297
11	Don January	72	74	78	75	299
12=	Dow Finsterwald	73	69	79	79	300
	Dave Ragan	78	74	74	74	300
14=	Mike Fetchick	74	76	75	77	302
	Lionel Hebert	71	79	76	76	302
	Davis Love, Jr	71	74	78	79	302
	Bobby Nichols	74	75	75	78	302
	Dean Refram	72	71	80	79	302
19=	Bob Charles	74	76	76	77	303
	Ken Still	76	75	78	74	303
21=	Jack Burke, Jr	75	76	78	75	304
	Gardner Dickinson	76	71	78	79	304
	Gene Littler	75	77	80	72	304
	Dave Marr	75	74	77	78	304
	Bob McCallister	75	77	76	76	304
	Doug Sanders	77	74	75	78	304
27=	Otto Greiner	74	75	76	80	305
	Ted Makalena	75	77	76	77	305
	Mason Rudolph	76	75	78	76	305
30=	Bob Goetz	79	72	80	75	306
	Bill Ogden	73	76	78	79	306

* Julius Boros (70) beat Jacky Cupit (73) and Arnold Palmer (76) in the 18-Hole Play-off

Round Leader(s)
R1 Bob Gadja (46); 69
R2 Cupit, Finsterwald, Palmer; 142
R3 Cupit; 218
Lowest Scores
R2 Finsterwald, Palmer; 69
R3 Harney, Sikes; 73
R4 Boros, Littler, Player; 72

10–12 July						**1963**
BRITISH OPEN						
Royal Lytham and St Anne's GC, Lancashire, England						
6836 yards						

The first New Zealander to win a Major, Bob Charles tied with Phil Rodgers before comfortably winning the play-off. They both, along with 3rd-placed Nicklaus, beat the Lytham links scratch score of 70 (280), playing off Championship tees accumulatively adding 79 yards to the members' course.

1	**BOB CHARLES***	68	72	66	71	277
	(£1500)					
2	Phil Rodgers	67	68	73	69	277
3	Jack Nicklaus	71	67	70	70	278
4	Kel Nagle	69	70	73	71	283
5	Peter Thomson	67	69	71	78	285
6	Christy O'Connor, Sr	74	68	76	68	286
7=	Gary Player	75	70	72	70	287
	Ramon Sota	69	73	73	72	287
9=	Jean Garaialde	72	69	72	75	288
	Sebastian Miguel	73	69	73	73	288
11=	Bernard Hunt	72	71	73	73	289
	Alex King	71	73	73	72	289
13	Sewsunker Sewgolum	71	74	73	72	290
14=	Brian Allen	75	71	71	74	291
	Brian Huggett	73	74	70	74	291
	Hugh Lewis	71	77	69	74	291
	Ian MacDonald	71	71	74	75	291
18=	Peter Alliss	74	71	77	80	292
	Frank Phillips	70	73	75	74	292
20=	Neil Coles	73	75	72	73	293
	Max Faulkner	77	71	71	74	293
	Harold Henning	76	68	71	78	293
	Malcolm Leeder	76	73	74	70	293
	John MacDonald	73	75	75	70	293
	Brian Wilkes	70	77	74	72	293
26=	Jimmy Hitchcock	75	73	70	76	294
	Arnold Palmer	76	71	71	76	294
	Doug Sewell	75	72	73	74	294
	Dave Thomas	74	74	75	71	294
30=	Ken Bousfield	73	75	71	76	295
	Tom Haliburton	68	73	77	77	295
	Tony Jacklin	73	72	76	74	295

* Bob Charles (140) beat Phil Rodgers (148) in the 36-Hole Play-off

Round Leader(s)
R1 Rodgers, Thomson; 67
R2 Rodgers; 135
R3 Charles; 206
Lowest Scores
R2 Nicklaus; 67
R3 Charles; 66
R4 O'Connor, Sr; 68

18–21 July						**1963**
US PGA						
Dallas Athletic Club, Dallas, Texas						
7046 yards PAR 71 (284)						

Nicklaus emulated Gary Player's feat of the previous year - except Jack's 3rd different Major was achieved in just a 2-year span. He also became only the 4th player, after Sarazen, Nelson and Hogan to lift all the US Majors; the 4th player after Snead, Hogan and Jack Burke Jr to do the Masters-PGA double in the same year; and the 8th to have won 2 Majors in one season. And this was only his 2nd full year as a pro!

1	**JACK NICKLAUS**	69	73	69	68	279
	($13000)					
2	Dave Ragan	75	70	67	69	281
3=	Bruce Crampton	70	73	65	74	282
	Dow Finsterwald	72	72	66	72	282
5=	Al Geiberger	72	73	69	70	284
	Billy Maxwell	73	71	69	71	284
7	Jim Ferrier	73	73	70	69	285
8=	Gardner Dickinson	72	74	74	66	286
	Tommy Jacobs	74	72	70	70	286
	Bill Johnson	71	72	72	71	286
	Gary Player	74	75	67	70	286
	Art Wall	73	76	66	71	286
13=	Julius Boros	69	72	73	73	287
	Bob Charles	69	76	72	70	287
	Tony Lema	70	71	77	69	287
	Jack Sellman	75	70	74	68	287
17=	Manuel de la Torre	71	71	74	72	288
	Wes Ellis, Jr	71	74	71	72	288
	Bob Goalby	74	70	74	70	288
	Dick Hart	66	72	76	74	288
	Dave Hill	73	72	69	74	288
	Doug Sanders	74	69	70	75	288
23=	Paul Harney	72	74	71	72	289
	Bobby Nichols	74	73	71	71	289
	Mason Rudolph	69	75	71	74	289
	Mike Souchak	72	72	73	72	289
27=	Doug Ford	70	72	71	77	290
	JC Goosie	74	74	74	68	290
	Fred Haas	80	70	70	70	290
	Sam Snead	71	73	70	76	290
	Earl Stewart	70	77	70	73	290
	Bert Weaver	76	73	71	70	290
	Bo Wininger	75	71	71	73	290

Round Leader(s)
R1 Hart; 66
R2 Hart; 138
R3 Crampton; 208
Lowest Scores
R2 Sanders; 69
R3 Crampton; 65
R4 Dickinson; 66

1964
THE MASTERS
9–12 April

Augusta National GC, Augusta, Georgia
6925 yards PAR 72 (288)

1964
US OPEN
18–20 June

Congressional CC, Bethesda, Maryland
7053 yards PAR 70 (280)

Arnold Palmer led all the way to win an unprecedented 4th Masters – putting him above Sam Snead and Jimmy Demaret. His victory by 6 from Dave Marr was his 7th and last Major, and he joined a stellar band of golfers on this mark – Vardon, Jones, Sarazen and Snead. 49 year-old former PGA Champion, Jim Ferrier, was a surprising Top 10 finisher.

After 2 momentous failures in the Masters, Ken Venturi put his past behind him to take a Major Championship. In 1956, as an amateur, he blew up and shot a last-round 80 to concede 9 strokes to Jack Burke, and the Tournament. Then in 1960, the nightmare returned – this time in the guise of Arnold Palmer's birdie-birdie finish, to pip him at the last. On this occasion Venturi came from behind in R4 to overtake the collapsing Tommy Jacobs, who in R2 had equalled Lee Mackey's 14 year-old low.

1	**ARNOLD PALMER** ($20000)	69	68	69	70	276
2=	Dave Marr	70	73	69	70	282
	Jack Nicklaus	71	73	71	67	282
4	Bruce Devlin	72	72	67	73	284
5=	Billy Casper	76	72	69	69	286
	Jim Ferrier	71	73	69	73	286
	Paul Harney	73	72	71	70	286
	Gary Player	69	72	72	73	286
9=	Dow Finsterwald	71	72	75	69	287
	Ben Hogan	73	75	67	72	287
	Tony Lema	75	68	74	70	287
	Mike Souchak	73	74	70	70	287
13=	Peter Butler	72	72	69	75	288
	Al Geiberger	75	73	70	70	288
	Gene Littler	70	72	78	68	288
	Johnny Pott	74	70	71	73	288
	Dan Sikes	76	68	71	73	288
18=	Don January	70	72	75	72	289
	Billy Maxwell (a)	73	73	69	74	289
	Mason Rudolph	75	72	69	73	289
21=	Bruce Crampton	74	72	73	71	290
	Kel Nagle	69	77	71	73	290
	Chi Chi Rodriguez	71	73	73	73	290
	Bo Wininger	74	71	69	76	290
25=	Deane Beman (a)	74	71	70	76	291
	Gay Brewer	75	72	73	71	291
	Gary Cowan (a)	71	77	72	71	291
	Bobby Nichols	75	71	75	70	291
	Phil Rodgers	75	72	72	72	291
30=	Jay Hebert	74	74	69	75	292
	Dean Refram	74	72	73	73	292

Round Leader(s)
R1 Bob Goalby (37), Davis Love, Jr (34); Nagle, Palmer, Player; 69
R2 Palmer, 137
R3 Palmer; 206
Lowest Scores
R2 Lema, Palmer, Sikes; 68
R3 Devlin, Hogan; 67
R4 Nicklaus; 67

1	**KEN VENTURI** ($17500)	72	70	66	70	278
2	Tommy Jacobs	72	64	70	76	282
3	Bob Charles	72	72	71	68	283
4	Billy Casper	71	74	69	71	285
5=	Gay Brewer	76	69	73	68	286
	Arnold Palmer	68	69	75	74	286
7	Bill Collins	70	71	74	72	287
8	Dow Finsterwald	73	72	71	72	288
9=	Johnny Pott	71	73	73	72	289
	Bob Rosburg	73	73	70	73	289
11=	George Bayer	75	73	72	71	291
	Don January	75	73	74	69	291
	Gene Littler	73	71	74	73	291
14=	Bruce Crampton	72	71	75	74	292
	Terry Dill	73	73	75	71	292
	Ray Floyd	73	70	72	77	292
	Ed Furgol	72	74	72	74	292
	Al Geiberger	74	70	75	73	292
	Bobby Nichols	72	72	76	72	292
20	Tony Lema	71	72	75	75	293
21=	Lionel Hebert	73	74	72	75	294
	Bill Ogden	73	73	73	75	294
23=	Ted Makalena	73	74	75	73	295
	Jack Nicklaus	72	73	77	73	295
	Gary Player	75	74	72	74	295
	Dudley Wysong	74	73	75	73	295
27	Charles Sifford	72	70	77	77	296
28=	Jacky Cupit	75	71	75	76	297
	Don Fairfield	75	72	74	76	297
	John Farquhar (a)	74	73	77	73	297
	Labron Harris, Jr	72	76	74	75	297

Round Leader(s)
R1 Palmer; 68
R2 Jacobs; 136
R3 Jacobs; 206
Lowest Scores
R2 Jacobs; 64
R3 Venturi; 66
R4 Brewer, Charles; 68

8–10 July	**1964**

BRITISH OPEN

Royal & Ancient GC, St Andrews, Fife, Scotland
6926 yards _PAR 72 (288)_

'Champagne' Tony Lema won the Open Championship at his 1st attempt. His 9 under par performance over the Old Course was stunning, finishing 5 clear of Nicklaus, who had hauled himself into contention early in R4, and Lema's star seemed to be in the ascendant. He was to finish prominently in a few more Majors, but before his true worth could be assessed, he was tragically killed in a private plane crash in 1966.

1	**TONY LEMA** (£1500)	73	68	68	70		279
2	Jack Nicklaus	76	74	66	68		284
3	Roberto de Vicenzo	76	72	70	67		285
4	Bernard Hunt	73	74	70	70	.	287
5	Bruce Devlin	72	72	73	73		290
6=	Christy O'Connor, Sr	71	73	74	73		291
	Harry Weetman	72	71	75	73		291
8=	Harold Henning	78	73	71	70		292
	Angel Miguel	73	76	72	71		292
	Gary Player	78	71	73	70		292
11	Doug Sanders	78	73	74	68		293
12	Frank Phillips	77	75	72	70		294
13=	Jean Garaialde	71	74	79	72		296
	Christy Greene	74	76	73	73		296
	Ralph Moffitt	76	72	74	74		296
	Dave Thomas	75	74	75	72		296
17=	Alex Caygill	77	74	71	75		297
	Bob Charles	79	71	69	78		297
19=	Malcolm Gregson	78	70	74	76		298
	John MacDonald	78	74	74	72		298
	A Murray	77	73	76	72		298
	Phil Rodgers	74	79	74	71		298
	Syd Scott	75	74	73	76		298
24=	AB Coop	75	72	76	76		299
	Doug Ford	75	76	76	72		299
	Liang-Huan Lu	76	71	78	74		299
	Jimmy Martin	74	72	79	74		299
	Peter Thomson	79	73	72	75		299
29	George Will	74	79	71	76		300
30=	Peter Butler	78	75	74	74		301
	Geoff Hunt	77	75	74	75		301
	Ramon Sota	77	74	74	76		301

Round Leader(s)
R1 Garaialde, O'Connor, Sr; 71
R2 Lema; 141
R3 Lema; 209
Lowest Scores
R2 Lema; 68
R3 Nicklaus; 66
R4 De Vicenzo; 67

16–19 July	**1964**

US PGA

Columbus CC, Columbus, Ohio
6851 yards _PAR 70 (280)_

In a Championship of records, 28 year-old Bobby Nichols, partially paralysed only a few years earlier, won over Nicklaus and Palmer by 3 strokes. Record-equalling 64s came from Nichols and Nicklaus; and the new low total of 271 for the PGA, was also – by 3 strokes – the record for any Major Championship. A consistent player for the next decade or so, Nichols never won another Major, and his form left him after he was struck, along with Lee Trevino and Jerry Heard, by lightning during the Western Open in 1975.

1	**BOBBY NICHOLS** ($18000)	64	71	69	67	271
2=	Jack Nicklaus	67	73	70	64	274
	Arnold Palmer	68	68	69	69	274
4	Mason Rudolph	73	66	68	69	276
5=	Tom Nieporte	68	71	68	72	279
	Ken Venturi	72	65	73	69	279
7	Bo Wininger	69	68	73	70	280
8	Gay Brewer	72	71	71	67	281
9=	Billy Casper	68	72	70	72	282
	Jon Gustin	69	76	71	66	282
	Ben Hogan	70	72	68	72	282
	Tony Lema	71	68	72	71	282
13=	Ed Furgol	71	69	72	71	283
	Billy Maxwell	72	71	70	70	283
	Gary Player	70	71	71	71	283
	Mike Souchak	67	73	71	72	283
17=	Walter Burkemo	70	71	72	71	284
	Jacky Cupit	72	71	72	69	284
19=	Bob Charles	68	71	73	73	285
	Al Geiberger	73	72	72	68	285
21=	Tommy Aaron	72	74	70	70	286
	Julius Boros	70	73	71	72	286
23=	Gardner Dickinson	74	74	68	71	287
	Mike Fetchick	74	73	74	66	287
	Ed Kroll	75	72	72	68	287
	Ted Kroll	72	73	72	70	287
	Dick Rhyan	71	72	71	73	287
28=	Bill Bisdorf	73	72	73	70	288
	Jim Ferree	70	72	75	71	288
	Dick Hart	73	73	72	70	288
	George Knudson	76	69	72	71	288
	Doug Sanders	71	73	76	68	288

Round Leader(s)
R1 Nichols; 64
R2 Nichols; 135
R3 Nichols; 204
Lowest Scores
R2 Venturi; 65
R3 Dickinson, Chick Harbert (44), Hogan, Nieporte, Rudolph; 68
R4 Nicklaus; 64

1965

8–11 April

THE MASTERS

Augusta National GC, Augusta, Georgia
6925 yards _PAR 72 (288)_

Jack Nicklaus dismantled Ben Hogan's Masters low and equalled Lloyd Mangrum's 1940 course record 64 when he shot 271, 17 under par, to win. The under par figures and the margin of victory – 9 strokes – were also records, and the low total matched Bobby Nicholls' outstanding effort in the previous year's PGA, to become the best-equal for any Major.

1	**JACK NICKLAUS**	67	71	64	69	271
	($20000)					
2=	Arnold Palmer	70	68	72	70	280
	Gary Player	69	72	72	73	280
4	Mason Rudolph	70	75	66	72	283
5	Dan Sikes	67	72	71	75	285
6=	Gene Littler	71	74	67	74	286
	Ramon Sota	71	73	70	72	286
8=	Frank Beard	68	77	72	70	287
	Tommy Bolt	69	78	69	71	287
10	George Knudson	72	73	69	74	288
11=	Tommy Aaron	67	74	71	77	289
	Bruce Crampton	72	72	74	71	289
	Paul Harney	74	74	71	70	289
	Doug Sanders	69	72	74	74	289
15=	George Bayer	69	74	75	72	290
	Bruce Devlin	71	76	73	70	290
	Wes Ellis, Jr	69	76	72	73	290
	Tommy Jacobs	71	74	72	73	290
	Kel Nagle	75	70	74	71	290
	Byron Nelson	70	74	72	74	290
21=	Dow Finsterwald	72	75	72	72	291
	Ben Hogan	71	75	71	74	291
	Tony Lema	67	73	77	74	291
24=	Terry Dill	72	73	75	72	292
	Al Geiberger	75	72	74	71	292
26=	Bernard Hunt	71	74	74	74	293
	Tomoo Ishii	74	74	70	75	293
	Billy Maxwell (a)	74	72	76	71	293
	Tom Nieporte	71	73	75	74	293
	Bo Wininger	70	72	75	76	293

Round Leader(s)
R1 Player; 65
R2 Nicklaus, Palmer, Player; 138
R3 Nicklaus; 202
Lowest Scores
R2 Palmer; 68
R3 Nicklaus; 64
R4 Nicklaus; 69

1965

17–21 June

US OPEN

Bellerive CC, St Louis, Missouri

South Africa's Gary Player became the 1st overseas winner of the Open since Ted Ray in 1920, beating 1960 British Open Champion, Kel Nagle, after a play-off. In doing so he joined Gene Sarazen and Ben Hogan as only one of three golfers to win all four Majors – the Grand Slam. Player achieved this feat in 6 years, compared with 7 for Hogan (who, of course only entered the British Open once – at the end of his winning span in 1953) and 13 for Sarazen.

1	**GARY PLAYER***	70	70	71	71	282
	($26000)					
2	Kel Nagle	68	73	72	69	282
3	Frank Beard	74	69	70	71	284
4=	Julius Boros	72	75	70	70	287
	Al Geiberger	70	76	70	71	287
6=	Bruce Devlin	72	73	72	71	288
	Ray Floyd	72	72	76	68	288
8=	Tony Lema	72	74	73	70	289
	Gene Littler	73	71	73	72	289
	Dudley Wysong	72	75	70	72	289
11=	Deane Beman (a)	69	73	76	72	290
	Mason Rudolph	69	72	73	76	290
	Doug Sanders	77	73	69	71	290
14	Billy Maxwell	76	73	71	71	291
15	Steve Oppermann	72	77	73	70	292
16	Gay Brewer	72	74	71	76	293
17=	Billy Casper	73	73	76	72	294
	Charles Huckaby	73	74	73	74	294
	George Knudson	80	69	73	72	294
	Bob Verwey	73	74	75	72	294
21=	Gardner Dickinson	77	73	71	74	295
	Eric Monti	76	71	75	73	295
23	Lou Graham	70	77	76	73	296
24=	Wes Ellis, Jr	73	76	77	71	297
	Labron Harris, Jr	74	76	74	73	297
	Ted Kroll	76	74	72	75	297
	Sam Snead	75	71	77	74	297
28=	Dutch Harrison	78	72	72	76	298
	Tommy Jacobs	76	71	74	77	298
	Dean Refram	71	79	72	76	298
	Terry Wilcox	74	73	73	78	298

* Gary Player (71) beat Kel Nagle (74) in the 18-Hole Play-off

Round Leader(s)
R1 Nagle; 68
R2 Player; 140
R3 Player; 211
Lowest Scores
R2 Beard, Knudson; 69
R3 Sanders; 69
R4 Floyd; 68

7–9 July	**1965**
BRITISH OPEN	
Royal Birkdale GC, Southport, Lancashire, England	
7037 yards PAR 73 (292)	

12–15 August	**1965**
US PGA	
Laurel Valley GC, Ligonier, Pennsylvania	
7090 yards PAR 71 (284)	

Returning to the scene of his 1st Open victory in 1954, Peter Thomson picked up his 5th win, and thereby joined Braid and Taylor on this mark - just one behind Harry Vardon's all-time record of 6. It will always be argued that Thomson's 4 wins during the '50s were somewhat devalued because the competition was not of the very best – this is strengthened by Thomson's modest success in US Majors. However, no-one can argue against his 5th, and final, win, with a strong American contingent trailing in his wake.

Dave Marr won his only Major when he cast off Tommy Aaron's challenge, whose 40 going out in R4 put him out of contention, then held firm to weather assaults from Nicklaus and Casper. 53 year-old ex-Champions, Sam Snead and Ben Hogan, came home 6th and 15th, respectively, while contemporary giants of the game, Palmer and Player, could only tie 33rd.

1	**PETER THOMSON**	74	68	72	71	285
	(£1750)					
2=	Brian Huggett	73	68	76	70	287
	Christy O'Connor, Sr	69	73	74	71	287
4	Roberto de Vicenzo	74	69	73	72	288
5=	Bernard Hunt	74	74	70	71	289
	Tony Lema	68	72	75	74	289
	Kel Nagle	74	70	73	72	289
8=	Bruce Devlin	71	69	75	75	290
	Sebastian Miguel	72	73	72	73	290
10=	Max Faulkner	74	72	74	73	293
	John Panton	74	74	75	70	293
12=	Hugh Boyle	73	69	76	76	294
	Neil Coles	73	74	77	70	294
	Jack Nicklaus	73	71	77	73	294
	Lionel Platts	72	72	73	77	294
16	Arnold Palmer	70	71	75	79	295
17=	Eric Brown	72	70	77	77	296
	Tommy Horton	75	73	76	72	296
	Cobie Legrange	76	73	75	72	296
	Guy Wolstenholme	72	75	77	72	296
21=	Brian Bamford	72	76	74	75	297
	Christy Greene	72	77	74	74	297
	Dennis Hutchinson	74	72	76	75	297
	George Will	75	69	74	79	297
25=	Fred Boobyer	74	73	73	78	298
	Tony Jacklin	75	73	73	77	298
	Doug Sewell	72	75	74	77	298
	Ramon Sota	75	70	78	75	298
29=	Michael Burgess (a)	74	73	78	74	299
	Harry Weetman	76	69	80	74	299

1	**DAVE MARR**	70	69	70	71	280
	($25000)					
2=	Billy Casper	70	70	71	71	282
	Jack Nicklaus	69	70	72	71	282
4	Bo Wininger	73	72	72	66	283
5	Gardner Dickinson	67	74	69	74	284
6=	Bruce Devlin	68	75	72	70	285
	Sam Snead	68	75	70	72	285
8=	Tommy Aaron	66	71	72	78	287
	Jack Burke, Jr	75	71	72	69	287
	Jacky Cupit	72	76	70	69	287
	Rod Funseth	75	72	69	71	287
	Bob McCallister	76	68	70	73	287
13=	Wes Ellis, Jr	73	76	70	69	288
	RH Sykes	71	71	71	75	288
15=	Ben Hogan	72	75	72	70	289
	Mike Souchak	70	72	77	70	289
17=	Julius Boros	75	72	73	70	290
	Ray Floyd	68	73	72	77	290
19	Al Geiberger	74	71	71	75	291
20=	Bruce Crampton	77	74	70	71	292
	Jack Fleck	76	71	72	73	292
	Doug Ford	73	70	77	72	292
	Gordon Jones	72	76	71	73	292
	George Knudson	75	69	73	75	292
	Kel Nagle	74	75	71	72	292
	Mason Rudolph	67	76	75	74	292
	Doug Sanders	71	73	74	74	292
28=	Gay Brewer	75	70	73	75	293
	Paul Kelly	76	71	75	71	293
	Gene Littler	78	70	70	75	293
	Johnny Pott	76	70	74	73	293

Round Leader(s)
R1   Lema; 68
R2   Devlin, Lema; 140
R3   Thomson; 214
Lowest Scores
R2   Huggett, Thomson; 68
R3   Hunt; 70
R4   Coles, Huggett, Panton; 70

Round Leader(s)
R1   Aaron; 66
R2   Aaron; 137
R3   Aaron, Marr; 209
Lowest Scores
R2   McCallister; 68
R3   Funseth, Dickinson; 69
R4   Wininger; 66

TOM MORRIS, Snr (1821–1908) – 'Old' Tom Morris in 1880. He played in every Open Championship from 1860-1893. *Allsport/Hulton Deutsch*

TOM MORRIS, Jnr (1851–1875) – Tragic Tommy in happier times – proudly wearing the Championship Belt which he won outright after his third straight Open win in 1870. *Allsport/Hulton Deutsch*

JH TAYLOR (1871–1963) – The first of the Great Triumvirate (Vardon and Braid were the others) to win the Open – at Sandwich in 1894. *Allsport/Hulton Deutsch*

HARRY VARDON (1870–1937) – Holds the record of Open wins – 6 – and also won the US Open in 1900.
Allsport/Hulton Deutsch

JAMES BRAID (1870–1950) – Made the decade 1901–1910 his own, winning the Open 5 times.
Allsport/Hulton Deutsch

WALTER HAGEN (1892–1969) – The flamboyant multi-Majors winner from upstate New York was golf's first superstar. *Allsport/Hulton Deutsch*

GENE SARAZEN (1895–) – The 'Squire' – the youngest winner of the PGA Championship (and the oldest competitor)! *Allsport*

BOBBY JONES (1902–1971) – As close as anyone in golf to immortality. *Allsport/Hulton Deutsch*

BEN HOGAN (1912-1997) – Probably the most venerated of golf's greats – coming back from a horrendous accident to dominate the Majors of the early 1950s. *Allsport/Hulton Deutsch*

SAM SNEAD (1912–) – Finished tied-3rd in the PGA at the age of 62 – but never won the US Open. *Allsport*

ARNOLD PALMER (1929–) & JACK NICKLAUS (1940–) – Two of the 'Big Three' with Gary Player – they did more to popularize the game in the modern era than any other players. *Allsport*

GARY PLAYER (1935–) – Inspired by Bobby Locke, the South African became the first globetrotting golfer. *Allsport*

SEVERIANO BALLESTEROS (1957–) – The irrepressible Spaniard who single-handedly gave European golf its current credibility. *Allsport*

TOM WATSON (1949–) – Winner of 5 British Opens – and 8 Majors in all (but not the PGA). *Allsport*

NICK FALDO (1957–) – The last in the line of Major title gatherers with 3 British Opens and 3 Masters to date. *Allsport*

155

1966
THE MASTERS
7–11 March

Augusta National GC, Augusta, Georgia
6925 yards PAR 72 (288)

1966
US OPEN
16–20 June

Olympic GC, San Francisco, California
6719 yards PAR 70 (280)

Nicklaus' 3rd Masters win was the 1st ever back-to-back. His 5th Major title took him equal with Braid and Taylor, Byron Nelson and Peter Thomson, but it was not his easiest. In a Tournament where the lead changed hands 17 times, a play-off seemed inevitable. Nicklaus had more trouble seeing off Tommy Jacobs, than Gay Brewer, who struggled to a 78.

Arnold Palmer's attempt to collect his 2nd Open and 8th Major folded on the back 9 of R4. Although he eventually succumbed to Billy Casper in a play-off, in R4 Palmer dropped 7 shots to the eventual winner after completing the 1st half in 32. This was Casper's 2nd title, following his win at Winged Foot in 1959. Unknown Rives McBee equalled the low score of 64 in R2.

1	JACK NICKLAUS*	68	76	72	72	288
	($20000)					
2	Tommy Jacobs	75	71	70	72	288
3	Gay Brewer	74	72	72	70	288
4=	Arnold Palmer	74	70	74	72	290
	Doug Sanders	74	70	75	71	290
6=	Don January	71	73	73	75	292
	George Knudson	73	76	72	71	292
8=	Ray Floyd	72	73	74	74	293
	Paul Harney	75	68	76	74	293
10=	Billy Casper	71	75	76	72	294
	Jay Hebert	72	74	73	75	294
	Bob Rosburg	73	71	76	74	294
13=	Tommy Aaron	74	73	77	71	295
	Peter Butler	72	71	79	73	295
	Ben Hogan	74	71	73	77	295
16	Ken Venturi	75	74	73	74	296
17=	Tommy Bolt	75	72	78	72	297
	Bruce Crampton	74	75	71	77	297
	Terry Dill	75	72	74	76	297
	Doug Ford	75	73	73	76	297
	Phil Rodgers	76	73	75	73	297
22=	Frank Beard	77	71	77	73	298
	Chen Ching-po	75	77	76	70	298
	Roberto de Vicenzo	74	76	74	74	298
	Harold Henning	77	74	70	77	298
	Tony Lema	74	74	74	76	298
	Bobby Nichols	77	73	74	74	298
28=	Julius Boros	77	73	73	76	299
	Bruce Devlin	75	77	72	77	299
	Gardner Dickinson	76	75	76	72	299
	James A Grant (a)	74	74	78	73	299
	Gary Player	74	77	76	72	299

1	BILLY CASPER*	69	68	73	68	278
	($26500)					
2	Arnold Palmer	71	66	70	71	278
3	Jack Nicklaus	71	71	69	74	285
4=	Tony Lema	71	74	70	71	286
	Dave Marr	71	74	68	73	286
6	Phil Rodgers	70	70	73	74	287
7	Bobby Nichols	74	72	71	72	289
8=	Wes Ellis, Jr	71	75	74	70	290
	Johnny Miller (a)	70	72	74	74	290
	Mason Rudolph	74	72	71	73	290
	Doug Sanders	70	75	74	71	290
12	Ben Hogan	72	73	76	70	291
13=	Rod Funseth	75	75	69	73	292
	Rives McBee	76	64	74	78	292
15=	Bob Murphy (a)	73	72	75	73	293
	Gary Player	78	72	74	69	293
17=	George Archer	74	72	76	72	294
	Frank Beard	76	74	69	75	294
	Julius Boros	74	69	77	74	294
	Don January	73	73	75	73	294
	Ken Venturi	73	77	71	73	294
22=	Walter Burkemo	76	72	70	77	295
	Bob Goalby	71	73	71	80	295
	Dave Hill	72	71	79	73	295
	Bob Verwey	72	73	75	75	295
26=	Miller Barber	74	76	77	69	296
	Bruce Devlin	74	75	71	76	296
	Al Mengert	67	77	71	81	296
	Bob Shave	76	71	74	75	296
30=	Tommy Aaron	73	75	71	78	297
	Deane Beman (a)	75	76	70	76	297
	Al Geiberger	75	75	74	73	297
	Vince Sullivan	77	73	73	74	297

*Jack Nicklaus (70) beat Tommy Jacobs (72) and Gay Brewer (78) in the 18-hole Play-off

* Billy Casper (69) beat Arnold Palmer (73) in the 18-Hole Play-off

Round Leader(s)   **Lowest Scores**
R1   Nicklaus; 68   R2   Harney; 68
R2   Butler, Harney; 143   R3   Henning, Jacobs; 70
R3   Jacobs, Nicklaus; 216   R4   Brewer, Ching-po; 70

Round Leader(s)   **Lowest Scores**
R1   Mengert; 67   R2   McBee; 64
R2   Casper, Palmer; 137   R3   Marr; 68
R3   Palmer; 207   R4   Casper; 68

6–9 July		**1966**	21–24 July					**1966**

BRITISH OPEN
Honourable Company, Muirfield, Angus, Scotland
6887 yards

US PGA
Firestone CC, Akron, Ohio
7180 yards PAR 70 (280)

Jack Nicklaus became the 4th (and last, to date) golfer to win a clean sweep of all the Major Championships. If you consider the Bobby Jones Grand Slam, then Nicklaus' record is neither that, nor exactly equivalent to the professional feats of Sarazen, Hogan and Player, in that Jack won the US Amateur (twice), but not the British Amateur. It is, indeed an unique achievement. His professional Grand Slam was accumulated over just 4 years. The R&A decided to follow the example of the US Open and spread the Championship over 4 days. The Masters had been a 4 day event since inception – the PGA since opting for medal play.

Al Geiberger was the only player to achieve par as the course defeated the likes of Casper and Player (2 over), Boros, Palmer and Snead (3 over) and Nicklaus (8 over). It was the only Major Championship for Geiberger, who will be better remembered for his 59 in the 1977 Memphis Classic - the 1st sub-60 score in a US Tour event. He went out in 30, back in 29, and shot 11 birdies, 1 eagle and no bogeys.

1	**JACK NICKLAUS**	70	67	75	70	282
	(£2100)					
2=	Doug Sanders	71	70	72	70	283
	Dave Thomas	72	73	69	69	283
4=	Bruce Devlin	73	69	74	70	286
	Kel Nagle	72	68	76	70	286
	Gary Player	72	74	71	69	286
	Phil Rodgers	74	66	70	76	286
8=	Dave Marr	73	76	69	70	288
	Sebastian Miguel	74	72	70	72	288
	Arnold Palmer	73	72	69	74	288
	Peter Thomson	73	75	69	71	288
12	RH Sikes	73	72	73	72	290
13=	Harold Henning	71	69	75	76	291
	Christy O'Connor, Sr	73	72	74	72	291
15	Julius Boros	73	71	76	72	292
16=	Peter Butler	73	65	80	75	293
	Alex Caygill	72	71	73	77	293
	Jimmy Hitchcock	70	77	74	72	293
	Ronnie Shade (a)	71	70	75	77	293
20=	Peter Alliss	74	72	75	73	294
	Roberto de Vicenzo	74	72	71	77	294
	Doug Sewell	76	69	74	75	294
23=	Eric Brown	78	72	71	74	295
	Peter Townsend (a)	73	75	72	75	295
	George Will	74	75	73	73	295
26	Keith MacDonald	75	74	70	77	296
27=	Michael Bonallack (a)	73	76	75	73	297
	Denis Hutchinson	74	73	73	77	297
	Bob Stanton	73	72	73	79	297
30=	Fred Boobyer	72	76	77	73	298
	Bobby Cole (a)	73	75	73	77	298
	Christy Greene	72	76	76	74	298
	Alan Henning	73	73	74	78	298
	Tony Jacklin	74	76	72	76	298
	Tony Lema	71	76	76	75	298

1	**AL GEIBERGER**	68	72	68	72	280
	($25000)					
2	Dudley Wysong	74	72	66	72	284
3=	Billy Casper	73	73	70	70	286
	Gene Littler	75	71	71	69	286
	Gary Player	73	70	70	73	286
6=	Julius Boros	69	72	75	71	287
	Jacky Cupit	70	73	73	71	287
	Arnold Palmer	75	73	71	68	287
	Doug Sanders	69	74	73	71	287
	Sam Snead	68	71	75	73	287
11	Frank Beard	73	72	69	74	288
12=	Dow Finsterwald	74	70	73	72	289
	Jay Hebert	75	73	70	71	289
	Don January	69	71	73	76	289
15=	Paul Harney	74	73	71	72	290
	Bill Martindale	73	75	70	72	290
	Ken Venturi	74	75	69	72	290
18=	Gardner Dickinson	74	72	73	72	291
	Ray Floyd	74	75	74	68	291
	Dave Marr	75	75	68	73	291
	Ernie Vossler	77	70	75	69	291
22=	Tommy Aaron	71	72	75	74	292
	Frank Boynton	73	74	73	72	292
	Billy Farrell	73	70	71	78	292
	Jack Nicklaus	75	71	75	71	292
	Mason Rudolph	74	73	76	69	292
27	Gay Brewer	73	73	76	71	293
28=	Butch Baird	73	74	73	74	294
	Bruce Devlin	76	71	71	76	294
	Ron Howell	76	71	75	72	294
	Don Massengale	74	72	75	73	294
	Dan Sikes	72	76	74	72	294
	RH Sikes	75	72	73	74	294

Round Leader(s)
R1 Geiberger, Snead; 68
R2 Snead; 139
R3 Geiberger; 208

Lowest Scores
R2 Farrell, Finsterwald, Player, Riggins (75), Vossler; 70
R3 Wysong; 66
R4 Floyd, Palmer; 68

Round Leader(s)
R1 Hitchcock, Nicklaus; 70
R2 Nicklaus; 137
R3 Rodgers; 210

Lowest Scores
R2 Rodgers; 66
R3 Marr, Palmer, Thomas, Thomson; 69
R4 Player, Thomas; 69

1967

6–9 April

THE MASTERS

Augusta National GC, Augusta, Georgia
6925 yards _PAR 72 (288)_

After disappointing in the 3-way play-off the previous year, Gay Brewer won his only Major, one stroke clear of 1964 PGA Champion, Bobby Nichols, at Augusta National. With Bert Yancey fading, Brewer and Nichols fought tooth and nail over the last round, the winner getting in front for the first time at the 13th.

I	**GAY BREWER**	73	68	72	67	280
	($20000)					
2	Bobby Nichols	72	69	70	70	281
3	Bert Yancey	67	73	71	73	284
4	Arnold Palmer	73	73	70	69	285
5	Julius Boros	71	70	70	75	286
6=	Paul Harney	73	71	74	69	287
	Gary Player	75	69	72	71	287
8=	Tommy Aaron	75	68	74	71	288
	Lionel Hebert	77	71	67	73	288
10=	Roberto de Vicenzo	73	72	74	71	290
	Bruce Devlin	74	70	75	71	290
	Ben Hogan	74	73	66	77	290
	Mason Rudolph	72	76	72	70	290
	Sam Snead	72	76	71	71	290
15	Jacky Cupit	73	76	67	75	291
16=	George Archer	75	67	72	78	292
	Wes Ellis, Jr	79	71	74	68	292
	Tony Jacklin	71	70	74	77	292
	Dave Marr	73	74	70	75	292
	Doug Sanders	74	72	73	73	292
21=	Jay Hebert	72	77	68	76	293
	Bob Rosburg	73	72	76	72	293
	Ken Venturi	76	73	71	73	293
24=	Peter Butler	72	73	77	72	294
	Billy Casper	70	74	75	75	294
26=	Frank Beard	74	75	75	71	295
	Tommy Bolt	72	77	72	74	295
	Don January	74	74	76	71	295
28=	Gene Littler	72	74	74	75	295
	Juan Rodriguez	73	73	73	76	295

Round Leader(s)
R1   Yancey; 67
R2   Yancey; 140
R3   Boros, Nichols, Yancey; 211
Lowest Scores
R2   Archer; 67
R3   Hogan; 66
R4   Brewer; 67

1967

15–18 June

US OPEN

Baltusrol GC, Springfield, New Jersey
7015 yards _PAR 70 (280)_

Arnold Palmer may have been the 1st person in US Open history to shoot below 280 on more than one occasion, but he could not stop Nicklaus' 2nd Open win, nor his lowering of the record total – a record which had stood since 1948 when Hogan took the Riviera CC apart. At 27 Nicklaus was now well into his purple patch, collecting his 7th Major, to tie with Vardon, Jones, Sarazen, Snead and Palmer.

I	**JACK NICKLAUS**	71	67	72	65	275
	($30000)					
2	Arnold Palmer	69	68	73	69	279
3	Don January	69	72	70	70	281
4	Billy Casper	69	70	71	72	282
5	Lee Trevino	72	70	72	70	284
6=	Deane Beman	69	71	71	73	284
	Gardner Dickinson	70	73	68	73	284
	Bob Goalby	72	71	70	71	284
9=	Dave Marr	70	74	70	71	285
	Kel Nagle	70	72	72	71	285
	Art Wall	69	73	72	71	285
12=	Al Balding	75	72	71	68	286
	Wes Ellis, Jr	74	69	70	73	286
	Gary Player	69	73	73	71	286
15	Tom Weiskopf	72	71	74	70	287
16=	Dutch Harrison	70	76	72	70	288
	Jerry Pittman	72	72	75	69	288
18=	Miller Barber	71	71	69	78	289
	Marty Fleckman (a)	67	73	69	80	289
	Paul Harney	71	75	72	71	289
	Dave Hill	76	69	69	75	289
	Bob Verwey	75	71	69	74	289
23=	Bruce Devlin	72	68	77	73	290
	Billy Farrell	76	71	73	70	290
	Howie Johnson	74	73	71	72	290
	Bob Murphy (a)	73	73	75	69	290
	Bobby Nichols	74	71	73	72	290
28=	Charles Coody	77	71	75	68	291
	Mike Fetchick	73	71	76	71	291
	Al Geiberger	71	73	73	74	291
	Lou Graham	71	75	76	69	291
	Labron Harris, Jr	75	71	72	73	291
	Ken Venturi	74	74	72	71	291

Round Leader(s)
R1   Fleckman; 67
R2   Palmer; 137
R3   Fleckman; 209
Lowest Scores
R2   Dick Lotz (60), Nicklaus; 67
R3   Dickinson; 68
R4   Nicklaus; 65

12–15 July	**1967**

BRITISH OPEN

Royal Liverpool GC, Hoylake, Cheshire, England
6995 yards PAR 70 (280)

Already 44, Argentinian Roberto de Vicenzo became Britain's Champion Golfer, after being runner-up as long ago as 1950. The best player to come out of South America, de Vicenzo was to collect 12 different national titles in all, over a professional career spanning 40 years. He then progressed to the Seniors tour, winning the US title twice, and the World's senior title in 1974. Royal Liverpool GC at Hoylake played host to the Open for the 10th and last time.

1	**ROBERTO de VICENZO**	70	71	67	70	278
	(£2100)					
2	Jack Nicklaus	71	69	71	69	280
3=	Clive Clark	70	73	69	72	284
	Gary Player	72	71	67	74	284
5	Tony Jacklin	73	69	73	70	285
6=	Harold Henning	74	70	71	71	286
	Sebastian Miguel	72	74	68	72	286
8=	Al Balding	74	71	69	73	287
	Hugh Boyle	74	74	71	68	287
	Bruce Devlin	70	70	72	75	287
	Tommy Horton	74	74	69	70	287
	Peter Thomson	71	74	70	72	287
13=	Deane Beman	72	76	68	73	289
	M Hoyle	74	75	69	71	289
	Stanley Peach	71	75	73	70	289
	Lionel Platts	68	73	72	76	289
	Guy Wolstenholme	74	71	73	71	289
18=	Barry Coxon	73	76	71	70	290
	Hedley Muscroft	72	73	72	73	290
	Doug Sanders	71	73	73	73	290
21	Christy O'Connor, Sr	70	74	71	76	291
22=	Denis Hutchinson	73	72	71	76	292
	Peter Mills	72	75	73	72	292
	Kel Nagle	70	74	69	79	292
25=	Brian Barnes	71	75	74	73	293
	Robin Davenport	76	69	75	73	293
	Barry Franklin	70	74	73	76	293
	Brian Huggett	73	75	72	73	293
29=	Fred Boobyer	70	71	74	79	294
	Jimmy Hume	69	72	73	80	294

Round Leader(s)
R1 Platts; 68
R2 Nicklaus; 140
R3 de Vicenzo; 208

Lowest Scores
R2 Jacklin, Nicklaus; 69
R3 de Vicenzo, Player; 67
R4 Boyle; 68

20–24 July	**1967**

US PGA

Columbine CC, Denver, Colorado
7436 yards PAR 72 (288)

Columbine hosted a Major for the one and only time and holds the record as being the longest course for any Major. For Don January, who had perished in the 1961 play-off, the extra holes this time were not to hold any gremlins. His 69 was too good for Don Massengale's 1 under par effort.

1=	**DON JANUARY***	71	72	70	68	281
	($25000)					
2	Don Massingale	70	75	70	66	281
3=	Jack Nicklaus	67	75	69	71	282
	Dan Sikes	69	70	70	73	282
5=	Julius Boros	69	76	70	68	283
	Al Geiberger	73	71	69	70	283
7=	Frank Beard	71	74	70	70	285
	Don Bies	69	70	76	70	285
	Bob Goalby	70	74	68	73	285
	Gene Littler	73	72	71	69	285
11=	Billy Farrell	75	72	69	70	286
	Dave Hill	66	73	74	73	286
	Ken Venturi	73	74	71	68	286
14=	Sam Carmichael	75	71	69	72	287
	Lionel Hebert	75	71	70	71	287
	Bobby Nichols	75	75	67	70	287
	Arnold Palmer	70	71	72	74	287
	RH Sikes	72	71	71	73	287
19	Billy Casper	75	70	75	68	288
20=	Tommy Aaron	70	65	76	78	289
	Bill Bisdorf	72	71	77	69	289
	Dick Crawford	76	73	73	67	289
	Ray Floyd	74	69	74	72	289
	Mike Souchak	70	73	70	76	289
25	Wes Ellis Jr	76	71	72	71	290
26=	Bruce Crampton	71	77	74	69	291
	Earl Stewart	77	70	72	72	291
28=	Gay Brewer	75	74	71	72	292
	Gardner Dickinson	75	72	69	76	292
	Phil Rodgers	71	76	72	73	292
	Mason Rudolph	72	73	73	74	292
	Doug Sanders	72	71	76	73	292

* Don January (69) beat Don Massingale (71) in the 18-Hole Play-off

Round Leader(s)
R1 Hill; 66
R2 Aaron; 135
R3 Sikes; 209

Lowest Scores
R2 Aaron; 65
R3 Nichols; 67
R4 Massengale; 66

1968 THE MASTERS

11–14 April

Augusta National GC, Augusta, Georgia
6925 yards _PAR 72 (288)_

Following his late-career win in the British Open in 1967, Roberto de Vicenzo tied with Bob Goalby – after birdying 17 and dropping a shot at the last. The Argentinian was annoyed about that bogey at 18, but completely distraught when he was penalized one stroke for signing an incorrect card. The 3 at 17 was entered as a 4 – a mistake that was to haunt de Vicenzo, and Tommy Aaron, who was marking his playing partner's card – for some time to come. Goalby, in rather unsatisfactory circumstances, was outright winner.

1	**BOB GOALBY**	70	70	71	66	277
	($20000)					
2	Roberto de Vicenzo	69	73	70	66	278
3	Bert Yancey	71	71	72	65	279
4	Bruce Devlin	69	73	69	69	280
5=	Frank Beard	75	65	71	70	281
	Jack Nicklaus	69	71	74	67	281
7=	Tommy Aaron	68	72	72	69	282
	Ray Floyd	71	71	69	71	282
	Lionel Hebert	72	71	71	68	282
	Jerry Pittman	70	73	70	69	282
	Gary Player	72	67	71	72	282
12=	Miller Barber	75	69	68	71	283
	Doug Sanders	76	69	70	68	283
14=	Don January	71	68	72	73	284
	Mason Rudolph	73	73	72	66	284
16=	Julius Boros	73	71	70	71	285
	Billy Casper	68	75	73	69	285
	Tom Weiskopf	74	71	69	71	285
19	Bob Charles	75	71	70	70	286
20=	Dave Marr	74	71	71	71	287
	Kermit Zarley	70	73	74	70	287
22=	George Archer	75	71	72	70	288
	Gardner Dickinson	74	71	72	71	288
	Marvin Giles III (a)	71	72	72	73	288
	Harold Henning	72	71	71	74	288
	Tony Jacklin	69	73	74	72	288
	Art Wall	74	74	73	67	288
28=	Jay Hebert	74	71	71	73	289
	George Knudson	75	71	72	71	289
30=	Charles Coody	76	72	72	70	290
	Al Geiberger	76	70	72	72	290
	Kel Nagle	76	71	72	71	290
	Bobby Nichols	74	73	73	70	290
	Bob Rosburg	74	73	71	72	290

Round Leader(s)
R1   Casper; 68
R2   January, Player; 139
R3   Player; 210
Lowest Scores
R2   Beard; 65
R3   Barber; 68
R4   Yancey; 65

1968 US OPEN

13–16 June

Oak Hill CC, Rochester, New York
6962 yards _PAR 70 (280)_

Equalling Jack Nicklaus' previous year low total, Lee Trevino became the 1st man in history to win any Major with all 4 rounds under par and sub-70. When he wasn't winning, Nicklaus was notching up a high percentage of 2nd places. Bert Yancey set a new Open 54-hole low of 205; and Sam Snead, now 56, still made the Top 10. Entries for the Open passed 3000 for the 1st time.

1	**LEE TREVINO**	69	68	69	69	275
	($30000)					
2	Jack Nicklaus	72	70	70	67	279
3	Bert Yancey	67	68	70	76	281
4	Bobby Nichols	74	71	68	69	282
5=	Don Bies	70	70	75	69	284
	Steve Spray	73	75	71	65	284
7=	Bob Charles	73	69	72	71	285
	Jerry Pittman	73	67	74	71	285
9=	Gay Brewer	71	71	75	69	286
	Billy Casper	75	68	71	72	286
	Bruce Devlin	71	69	75	71	286
	Al Geiberger	72	74	68	72	286
	Sam Snead	73	71	74	68	286
	Dave Stockton	72	73	69	72	286
15	Dan Sikes	71	71	73	72	287
16=	George Archer	74	72	73	69	288
	Julius Boros	71	71	71	75	288
	Charles Coody	69	71	72	76	288
	Rod Funseth	74	72	69	73	288
	Dave Hill	74	68	74	72	288
	Gary Player	76	69	70	73	288
22=	Mac McLendon	72	76	70	71	289
	Hugh Royer, Jr	75	72	73	69	289
24=	Miller Barber	74	68	78	70	290
	Roberto de Vicenzo	72	76	72	70	290
	Bob Erickson	75	68	72	75	290
	Don January	71	75	71	73	290
	Bob Lunn	74	73	73	70	290
	Pat Schwab	76	70	75	69	290
	Tom Weiskopf	75	72	70	73	290
	Larry Ziegler	71	71	74	74	290

Round Leader(s)
R1   Yancey; 67
R2   Yancey; 135
R3   Yancey; 205
Lowest Scores
R2   Pittman; 67
R3   Geiberger, Nichols; 68
R4   Spray; 65

10–13 July					**1968**

BRITISH OPEN

Carnoustie GC, Angus, Scotland
7252 yards _PAR 72 (288)_

Gary Player won his 5th Major when he won the Open at Carnoustie – over the longest course set for the Championship. He beat a strong field which boasted 6 other Majors winners in the Top 10 and ties. A 54-hole cut was introduced for the 1st time, reducing the number to 45 who went out on the last day.

1	**GARY PLAYER**	74	71	71	73	289
	(£3000)					
2=	Bob Charles	72	72	71	76	291
	Jack Nicklaus	76	69	73	73	291
4	Billy Casper	72	68	74	78	292
5	Maurice Bembridge	71	75	73	74	293
6=	Brian Barnes	70	74	80	71	295
	Gay Brewer	74	73	72	76	295
	Neil Coles	75	76	71	73	295
9	Al Balding	74	76	74	72	296
10=	Roberto de Vicenzo	77	72	74	74	297
	Bruce Devlin	77	73	72	75	297
	Arnold Palmer	77	71	72	77	297
13=	Peter Alliss	73	78	72	75	298
	Bobby Cole	75	76	72	75	298
	Tommy Horton	77	74	73	74	298
	Brian Huggett	76	71	75	76	298
	Kel Nagle	74	75	75	74	298
18=	Eric Brown	76	76	74	73	299
	Tony Jacklin	72	72	75	80	299
	Paddy Skerritt	72	73	77	77	299
21=	Michael Bonallack (a)	70	77	74	79	300
	Sebastian Miguel	73	75	76	76	300
	DL Webster	77	71	78	74	300
24=	Alex Caygill	79	76	71	75	301
	Keith MacDonald	80	71	73	77	301
	Peter Thomson	77	71	78	75	301
27=	Malcolm Gregson	77	75	76	74	302
	Bob Shaw	75	76	73	78	302
	Dave Thomas	75	71	78	78	302
	Sandy Wilson	73	81	74	74	302

Round Leader(s)
R1 Barnes, Bonallack; 70
R2 Barnes, Charles, Jacklin; 144
R3 Casper; 214
Lowest Scores
R2 Casper; 68
R3 Caygill, Charles, Coles, Player; 71
R4 Barnes; 71

18–21 July					**1968**

US PGA

Pecan Valley CC, San Antonio, Texas
7096 yards _PAR 70 (280)_

If Julius Boros failed by a few days to set the record for the oldest winner of the US Open in 1963, he certainly set one which is going to be difficult to beat when he won the PGA at Pecan Valley at the age of 48. Before that, the oldest winner of any Major was 46 year-old Tom Morris, Sr – and the oldest this century, Jerry Barber in 1961, also in the PGA, was positively juvenile at 45!

1	**JULIUS BOROS**	71	71	70	69	281
	($25000)					
2=	Bob Charles	72	70	70	70	282
	Arnold Palmer	71	69	72	20	282
4=	George Archer	71	69	74	69	283
	Marty Fleckman	66	72	72	73	283
6=	Frank Beard	68	70	72	74	284
	Billy Casper	74	70	70	70	284
8=	Miller Barber	70	70	72	73	285
	Frank Boynton	70	73	72	70	285
	Charles Coody	70	77	70	68	285
	Al Geiberger	70	73	71	71	285
	Bob Goalby	73	72	70	70	285
	Lou Graham	73	70	70	72	285
	Doug Sanders	72	67	73	73	285
	Dan Sikes	70	72	73	70	285
	Kermit Zarley	72	75	68	70	285
17=	Dave Hill	72	74	69	71	286
	Mason Rudolph	69	75	70	72	286
	Dave Stockton	75	71	68	72	286
20=	Gay Brewer	71	72	72	72	287
	Al Mengert	71	73	70	73	287
	Dick Rhyan	72	72	68	75	287
23=	Bruce Crampton	71	75	70	72	288
	Lee Trevino	69	71	72	76	288
	Bert Yancey	75	71	70	72	288
26=	Tommy Aaron	73	73	73	70	289
	Don Bies	69	73	74	73	289
	Dick Crawford	71	75	73	70	289
	Steve Reid	73	73	71	72	289
30=	Gardner Dickinson	74	69	76	71	290
	Lionel Hebert	75	71	70	74	290
	Gene Littler	73	74	74	69	290
	Bob Lunn	72	75	72	71	290

Round Leader(s)
R1 Fleckman; 66
R2 Beard, Fleckman; 138
R3 Beard, Fleckman; 210
Lowest Scores
R2 Sanders; 67
R3 Rhyan, Stockton, Zarley; 68
R4 Coody; 68

1969
THE MASTERS
10–13 April

Augusta National GC, Augusta, Georgia
6925 yards _PAR 72 (288)_

George Archer only came to prominence in Major Championships in the PGA of 1968, when he finished 4th – 2 behind Julius Boros. Billy Casper, who had made all the running, wilted, leaving Archer the Masters Champion when Tom Wieskopf and Canadian George Knudson couldn't mount a sufficient challenge over the final holes.

1	**GEORGE ARCHER** ($20000)	67	73	69	72	281
2=	Billy Casper	66	71	71	74	282
	George Knudson	70	73	69	70	282
	Tom Weiskopf	71	71	69	71	282
5=	Charles Coody	74	68	69	72	283
	Don January	74	73	70	66	283
7	Miller Barber	71	71	68	74	284
8=	Tommy Aaron	71	71	73	70	285
	Lionel Hebert	69	73	70	73	285
	Gene Littler	69	75	70	71	285
11	Mason Rudolph	69	73	74	70	286
12	Dan Sikes	69	71	73	74	287
13=	Bruce Crampton	69	73	74	72	288
	Al Geiberger	71	71	74	72	288
	Harold Henning	73	72	71	72	288
	Takaaki Kono	71	75	68	74	288
	Bert Yancey	69	75	71	73	288
18	Dave Stockton	71	71	75	72	289
19=	Frank Beard	72	74	70	74	290
	Deane Beman	74	73	74	69	290
	Bruce Devlin	67	70	76	77	290
	Dale Douglass	73	72	71	74	290
	Lee Trevino	72	74	75	69	290
24=	Jack Burke, Jr	73	72	70	76	291
	Dave Hill	75	73	72	71	291
	Jack Nicklaus	68	75	72	76	291
27	Arnold Palmer	73	75	70	74	292
28	Johnny Pott	72	72	71	78	293
29=	Roberto Bernardini	76	71	72	75	294
	Bob Charles	70	76	72	76	294
	Gardner Dickinson	73	74	71	76	294
	Bobby Nichols	78	69	74	73	294

Round Leader(s)
R1   Casper; 66
R2   Casper, Devlin; 137
R3   Casper; 208
Lowest Scores
R2   Coody; 68
R3   Barber, Kono; 68
R4   January; 66

1969
US OPEN
12–15 June

Champions GC, Houston, Texas
6967 yards _PAR 70 (280)_

Failing to make the cut in his 1st attempt the previous year, former career soldier Orville Moody won his only Major in only his 2nd year on the Tour. Miller Barber held a 3-stroke lead over Moody after 54 holes, but blew up, allowing Moody to close out Beman, Geiberger and 1959 PGA Champion Bob Rosburg over the final 18.

1	**ORVILLE MOODY** ($30000)	71	70	68	72	281
2=	Deane Beman	68	69	73	72	282
	Al Geiberger	68	72	72	70	282
	Bob Rosburg	70	69	72	71	282
5	Bob Murphy	66	74	72	71	283
6=	Miller Barber	67	71	68	78	284
	Bruce Crampton	73	72	68	71	284
	Arnold Palmer	70	73	69	72	284
9	Bunky Henry	70	72	68	75	285
10=	George Archer	69	74	73	70	286
	Bruce Devlin	73	74	70	69	286
	Dave Marr	75	69	71	71	286
13=	Julius Boros	71	73	70	73	287
	Charles Coody	72	68	72	75	287
	Dale Douglass	76	69	70	72	287
	Ray Floyd	79	68	68	72	287
	Dave Hill	73	74	70	70	287
	Howie Johnson	72	73	72	70	287
	Dean Refram	69	74	70	74	287
	Phil Rodgers	76	70	69	72	287
	Kermit Zarley	74	72	70	71	287
22=	Bob Stanton	74	70	71	73	288
	Tom Weiskopf	69	75	71	73	288
	Bert Yancey	71	71	74	72	288
25=	Joe Campbell	73	74	73	69	289
	Richard Crawford	70	75	73	71	289
	Tony Jacklin	71	70	73	75	289
	Bobby Mitchell	72	74	66	77	289
	Jack Nicklaus	74	67	75	73	289
	Dave Stockton	75	69	72	73	289

Round Leader(s)
R1   Murphy; 66
R2   Beman; 137
R3   Barber; 206
Lowest Scores
R2   Nicklaus, Bob E Smith (31); 67
R3   Mitchell; 66
R4   Campbell, Devlin; 69

9–12 July						14–17 August					

BRITISH OPEN **1969**

Royal Lytham and St Anne's GC, Lancashire, England
6848 yards _PAR 71 (284)_

US PGA **1969**

NCR CC, Dayton, Ohio
6915 yards _PAR 71(284)_

After a wait of 18 years, the old Claret Jug was lifted by a home player again. Englishman Tony Jacklin became a national hero when he finished 4 under par and ahead of 3 former Champions to win at Lytham. It may be simplistic to say that Jacklin's emergence at the top of world golf, albeit for a short time, was a pivotal point in the game's history, in that the emphasis of total American dominance was to change – but his exploits did act as a catalyst to Britain in that the interest in golf surged, and within the next 15 years, 2 multiple Majors winners, Faldo and Lyle, had emerged – as well as parity or better in the Ryder Cup.

Raymond Floyd won the 1st of his 2 PGA titles, and 4 Majors, in holding out Gary Player over the last round. Player was the subject of anti-apartheid demonstrations during the Championship, but displaying his famous iron will he pushed Floyd all the way, pulling back 4 shots in R4, but just failing to tie. As in the PGA of 1959, it was claustrophobic at the top of the R1 leaderboard, with 9 tying for the lead.

1	**TONY JACKLIN**	68	70	70	72	280
	(£4250)					
2	Bob Charles	66	69	75	72	282
3=	Roberto de Vicenzo	72	73	66	72	283
	Peter Thomson	71	70	70	72	283
5	Christy O'Connor, Sr	71	65	74	74	284
6=	Davis Love, Jr	70	73	71	71	285
	Jack Nicklaus	75	70	68	72	285
8	Peter Alliss	73	74	73	66	286
9	Kel Nagle	74	71	72	70	287
10	Miller Barber	69	75	75	69	288
11=	Neil Coles	75	76	70	68	289
	Tommy Horton	71	76	70	72	289
	Cobie Legrange	79	70	71	69	289
	Guy Wolstenholme	70	71	76	72	289
15	Gay Brewer	76	71	68	75	290
16=	Eric Brown	73	76	69	73	291
	Bruce Devlin	71	73	75	72	291
	Harold Henning	72	71	75	73	291
	Brian Huggett	72	72	69	78	291
	Orville Moody	71	70	74	76	291
	Peter Townsend	73	70	76	72	291
	Bert Yancey	72	71	71	77	291
23=	Bernard Hunt	73	71	75	73	292
	Gary Player	74	68	76	74	292
25=	Fred Boobyer	74	70	76	73	293
	Billy Casper	70	70	75	78	293
	Alex Caygill	71	67	79	76	293
28=	Hedley Muscroft	68	77	73	76	294
	Peter Tupling (a)	73	71	78	72	294
30=	Max Faulkner	71	74	76	74	295
	Jean Garaialde	69	77	76	73	295
	Mike Ingham	73	73	74	75	295
	Don Swaelens	72	73	76	74	295

1	**RAY FLOYD**	69	66	67	74	276
	($35000)					
2	Gary Player	71	65	71	70	277
3	Bert Greene	71	68	68	71	278
4	Jimmy Wright	71	68	69	71	279
5=	Miller Barber	73	75	64	68	280
	Larry Ziegler	69	71	70	70	280
7=	Charles Coody	69	71	72	69	281
	Orville Moody	70	68	71	72	281
	Terry Wilcox	72	71	72	66	281
10	Frank Beard	70	75	68	69	282
11=	Don Bies	74	64	71	74	283
	Bunky Henry	69	68	70	76	283
	Larry Mowry	69	71	69	74	283
	Jack Nicklaus	70	68	74	71	283
15=	Bruce Crampton	70	70	72	72	284
	Dave Hill	74	75	67	68	284
	Don January	75	70	70	69	284
	Chi Chi Rodriguez	72	72	71	69	284
19=	Howie Johnson	73	68	72	72	285
	Johnny Pott	69	75	71	70	285
21=	Ron Cerrudo	74	66	70	76	286
	Bobby Cole	72	74	71	69	286
	Bob Lunn	69	74	73	70	286
	Tom Shaw	69	75	73	70	286
25=	Julius Boros	72	74	70	71	287
	Gay Brewer	74	71	76	66	287
	Bob Dickson	74	72	70	71	287
	Tony Jacklin	73	70	73	71	287
	George Knudson	70	75	67	75	287
	Fred Marti	73	70	71	73	287
	Dan Sikes	71	74	69	73	287

Round Leader(s)
R1 Coody, Floyd, Al Geiberger (35), Henry, Lunn, Mowry, Pott, Shaw, Ziegler; 69
R2 Floyd; 135
R3 Floyd; 202

Lowest Scores
R2 Bies; 64
R3 Barber; 64
R4 Brewer, Wilcox; 66

Round Leader(s)
R1 Charles; 66
R2 Charles; 135
R3 Jacklin; 208

Lowest Scores
R2 O'Connor; 65
R3 De Vicenzo; 66
R4 Alliss; 66

1970
9–13 April
THE MASTERS
Augusta National GC, Augusta, Georgia
6925 yards PAR 72 (288)

1970
18–21 June
US OPEN
Hazeltine National GC, Minneapolis, Minnesota
7151 yards PAR 72 (288)

Billy Casper compensated for his defeat the previous year when he took the Masters in a play-off from 1961 Open Champion Gene Littler. R4 was very tight with 5 players jockeying for the lead, before Casper and Littler prevailed. This was Casper's 3rd Major, following 2 successes in the US Open.

Reigning British Open Champion Jacklin achieved a rare double with a remarkable win at Hazeltine. His victory by 7 shots was the biggest since Jim Barnes in 1921; he led wire-to-wire, increasing his lead round-by-round; he was the only player under par. 2nd-placed Dave Hill was so critical of Robert Trent Jones' alterations to the course, he was fined $150 by the USGA for his remarks.

1	**BILLY CASPER***	72	68	68	71	279
	($25000)					

1	**TONY JACKLIN**	71	70	70	70	281
	($30000)					

2	Gene Littler	69	70	70	70	279
3	Gary Player	74	68	68	70	280
4	Bert Yancey	69	70	72	70	281
5=	Tommy Aaron	68	74	69	72	283
	Dave Hill	73	70	70	70	283
	Dave Stockton	72	72	69	70	283
8	Jack Nicklaus	71	75	69	69	284
9	Frank Beard	71	76	68	70	285
10=	Bob Lunn	70	70	75	72	287
	Chi Chi Rodriguez	70	76	73	68	287
12=	Charles Coody	70	74	67	77	288
	Bert Greene	75	71	70	72	288
	Tony Jacklin	73	74	70	71	288
	Don January	76	73	69	70	288
	Takaaki Kono	75	68	71	74	288
17	Bob Charles	75	71	71	72	289
18=	Howie Johnson	75	71	73	71	290
	Dick Lotz	74	72	72	72	290
	Orville Moody	73	72	71	74	290
21=	Miller Barber	76	73	77	65	291
	Terry Wilcox	79	70	70	72	291
23=	Deane Beman	74	72	72	74	292
	Julius Boros	75	71	74	72	292
	Charles R Coe (a)	74	71	72	75	292
	Bob Murphy	78	70	73	71	292
	Sam Snead	76	73	71	72	292
	Tom Weiskopf	73	73	72	74	292
29=	Yung-Yo Hsieh	75	75	69	74	293
	Jimmy Wright	75	72	71	75	293

*Billy Casper (69) beat Gene Littler (74) in the 18-hole Play-off

Round Leader(s)
R1   Aaron; 68
R2   Littler, Yancey; 139
R3   Casper; 208
Lowest Scores
R2   Casper, Kono, Player; 68
R3   Coody; 67
R4   Barber; 65

2	Dave Hill	75	69	71	73	288
3=	Bob Charles	76	71	75	67	289
	Bob Lunn	77	72	70	70	289
5	Ken Still	78	71	71	71	291
6	Miller Barber	75	75	72	70	292
7	Gay Brewer	75	71	71	76	293
8=	Billy Casper	75	75	71	73	294
	Bruce Devlin	75	75	71	73	294
	Lee Trevino	77	73	74	70	294
	Larry Ziegler	75	73	73	73	294
12=	Julius Boros	73	75	70	77	295
	Bobby Cole	78	75	71	71	295
	Joel Goldstrand	76	76	71	72	295
	Howie Johnson	75	72	75	73	295
	Gene Littler	77	72	71	75	295
	Bobby Mitchell	74	78	74	69	295
18=	Al Balding	75	74	75	72	296
	Paul Harney	78	73	75	70	296
	Johnny Miller	79	73	73	71	296
	Randy Wolff	78	67	76	75	296
22=	Frank Beard	75	73	79	70	297
	Richard Crawford	74	71	76	76	297
	Ray Floyd	78	73	70	76	297
	Ted Hayes, Jr	79	73	73	72	297
	Bert Yancey	81	72	73	71	297
27=	Chi Chi Rodriguez	73	77	75	73	298
	Mason Rudolph	73	75	73	77	298
	Dan Sikes	81	69	72	76	298
30=	George Archer	76	73	77	73	299
	Bruce Crampton	79	71	74	75	299
	Bunky Henry	80	68	77	74	299
	Dave Marr	82	69	74	74	299
	Kel Nagle	78	75	73	73	299
	Tom Weiskopf	76	73	78	72	299

Round Leader(s)
R1   Jacklin; 71
R2   Jacklin; 141
R3   Jacklin; 211
Lowest Scores
R2   Wolff; 67
R3   Boros, Floyd, Jacklin, Lunn; 70
R4   Charles; 67

8–11 July	**1970**

BRITISH OPEN

Royal & Ancient GC, St Andrews, Fife, Scotland
6951 yards PAR 72 (288)

Doug Sanders never won a Major but will always be remembered for his glorious failure at St Andrews. Once Trevino fell away, Sanders always seemed to have the edge over Nicklaus. However, needing a par 4 at the relatively-easy 18th, he missed a 4 foot putt for outright victory. In the play-off, Sanders, one behind going to the last, birdied the same hole – only for Nicklaus to do likewise and pick up his 2nd Open and 1st Major for 3 years.

1	**JACK NICKLAUS***	68	69	73	73	283
	(£5250)					
2	Doug Sanders	68	71	71	73	283
3=	Harold Henning	67	72	73	73	285
	Lee Trevino	68	68	72	77	285
5	Tony Jacklin	67	70	73	76	286
6=	Neil Coles	65	74	72	76	287
	Peter Oosterhuis	73	69	69	76	287
8	Hugh Jackson	69	72	73	74	288
9=	Tommy Horton	66	73	75	75	289
	John Panton	72	73	73	71	289
	Peter Thomson	68	74	73	74	289
12	Arnold Palmer	68	72	76	74	290
13=	Maurice Bembridge	67	74	75	76	292
	Bob Charles	72	73	73	74	292
	JC Richardson	67	72	76	77	292
	Bert Yancey	71	71	73	77	292
17=	Roberto Bernadini	75	69	74	75	293
	Billy Casper	71	74	73	75	293
	Clive Clark	69	70	77	77	293
	Roberto de Vicenzo	71	76	71	75	293
	Christy O'Connor, Sr	72	68	74	79	293
22=	Walter Godfrey	71	75	74	74	294
	Tom Weiskopf	70	74	72	78	294
	Guy Wolstenholme	68	77	72	77	294
25=	Bruce Devlin	72	76	72	75	295
	Graham Marsh	75	72	74	74	295
	Ronnie Shade	72	75	69	79	295
28=	Stuart Brown	73	73	71	79	296
	Bobby Cole	71	76	71	78	296
	Brian Huggett	68	78	73	77	296
	Tom Shaw	73	71	73	79	296

* Jack Nicklaus (72) beat Doug Sanders (73) in the 18-hole play-off

Round Leader(s)
R1 Coles; 65
R2 Trevino; 136
R3 Trevino; 208
Lowest Scores
R2 O'Connor, Trevino; 68
R3 Oosterhuis, Shade; 69
R4 Panton; 71

13–16 August	**1970**

US PGA

Southern Hills CC, Tulsa, Oklahoma
6962 yards PAR 70 (280)

Arnold Palmer's 3rd 2nd place in the PGA was to be his last serious attempt to be the 5th player to win all 4 Majors. The PGA was to elude him. Dave Stockton's R3 66 took him clear of the field and although Arnie was gradually clawing his way back he couldn't make enough of an impact on the leader to exert pressure.

1	**DAVE STOCKTON**	70	70	66	73	279
	($40000)					
2=	Bob Murphy	71	73	71	66	281
	Arnold Palmer	70	72	69	70	281
4=	Larry Hinson	69	71	74	68	282
	Gene Littler	72	71	69	70	282
6=	Bruce Crampton	73	75	68	67	283
	Jack Nicklaus	68	76	73	66	283
8=	Ray Floyd	71	73	65	75	284
	Dick Lotz	72	70	75	67	284
10=	Billy Maxwell	72	71	73	69	285
	Mason Rudolph	71	70	73	71	285
12=	Don January	73	71	73	69	286
	Johnny Miller	68	77	70	71	286
	Gary Player	74	68	74	70	286
	Sam Snead	70	75	68	73	286
16=	Al Geiberger	72	74	71	71	288
	Mike Hill	70	71	74	73	288
18=	Billy Casper	72	70	74	73	289
	Bruce Devlin	75	70	71	73	289
	Al Mengert	76	72	70	71	289
	Dan Sikes	74	70	75	70	289
22=	Lou Graham	75	68	74	73	290
	Bob Stanton	71	74	72	73	290
	Bert Yancey	74	69	75	72	290
	Kermit Zarley	73	74	73	70	290
26=	Julius Boros	72	71	72	76	291
	Bob Charles	74	73	72	72	291
	Terry Dill	72	71	75	73	291
	Bobby Nichols	72	76	72	72	291
	Lee Trevino	72	77	77	65	291

Round Leader(s)
R1 Miller, Nicklaus; 68
R2 Hinson, Stockton; 140
R3 Stockton; 206
Lowest Scores
R2 Graham, Player; 68
R3 Floyd; 65
R4 Trevino; 65

1971
25–28 February
US PGA
PGA National GC, Palm Beach Gardens, Florida
7096 yards PAR 72 (288)

1971
8–11 April
THE MASTERS
Augusta National GC, Augusta, Georgia
6925 yards PAR 72 (288)

Going completely against the grain of previous years, the 1971 PGA Championship was held in February, making it the 1st not the last Major of the season. The time of year made no difference to Jack Nicklaus though. He won, coasting home with shots to spare. In winning, he performed a unique double Grand Slam. Nicklaus became – and still is – the only golfer to win all the Major Championships at least twice.

In 1969, dropped shots over the last 3 holes cost Charles Coody the Masters Tournament. This year, despite Johnny Miller's 6 under par charge to hole 16 in R4, Coody held his game together to see off both Miller, who eventually ran out of steam, and Jack Nicklaus.

1	**JACK NICKLAUS**($40000)	66	69	70	73	281
2	Billy Casper	71	73	71	68	283
3	Tommy Bolt	72	74	69	69	284
4=	Miller Barber	72	68	75	70	285
	Gary Player	71	73	68	73	285
6=	Gibby Gilbert	74	67	72	73	286
	Dave Hill	74	71	71	70	286
	Jim Jamieson	72	72	72	70	286
9=	Jerry Heard	73	71	72	71	287
	Bob Lunn	72	70	73	72	287
	Fred Marti	72	71	74	70	287
	Bob Rosburg	74	72	70	71	287
13=	Frank Beard	74	71	73	70	288
	Bob Charles	70	75	70	73	288
	Bruce Devlin	71	71	74	72	288
	Larry Hinson	71	73	73	71	288
	Lee Trevino	71	73	75	69	288
18=	Herb Hooper	74	71	73	71	289
	Arnold Palmer	75	71	70	73	289
20=	Johnny Miller	71	76	72	71	290
	Bob E Smith	73	70	75	72	290
22=	Brad Anderson	71	75	75	70	291
	Chuck Courtney	74	71	74	72	291
	Hale Irwin	73	72	72	74	291
	Jerry McGee	73	74	71	73	291
	John Schroeder	72	74	74	71	291
	Tom Weiskopf	72	70	77	72	291
	Larry Wood	74	71	72	74	291
	Bert Yancey	71	74	70	76	291
30=	Terry Dill	75	68	75	74	292
	Gene Borek	72	70	73	77	292
	Rod Funseth	72	47	75	71	292
	Al Geiberger	74	69	77	72	292

Round Leader(s)
R1   Nicklaus; 69
R2   Nicklaus; 138
R3   Nicklaus; 208
Lowest Scores
R2   Gilbert; 67
R3   Player; 68
R4   Casper; 68

1	**CHARLES COODY**($25000)	66	73	70	70	279
2=	Johnny Miller	72	73	68	68	281
	Jack Nicklaus	70	71	68	72	281
4=	Don January	69	69	73	72	283
	Gene Littler	72	69	73	69	283
6=	Gary Player	72	72	71	69	284
	Ken Still	72	71	72	69	284
	Tom Weiskopf	71	69	72	72	284
9=	Frank Beard	74	73	69	70	286
	Roberto de Vicenzo	76	69	72	69	286
	Dave Stockton	72	73	69	72	286
12	Bert Greene	73	73	71	70	287
13=	Billy Casper	72	73	71	72	288
	Bruce Devlin	72	70	72	74	288
	Ray Floyd	69	75	73	71	288
	Hale Irwin	69	72	71	76	288
	Bob Murphy	69	70	76	73	288
18=	Bruce Crampton	73	72	74	70	289
	Arnold Palmer	73	72	71	73	289
20=	Dave Eichelberger	76	71	70	73	290
	Orville Moody	79	69	70	72	290
22=	Tommy Aaron	76	72	74	69	291
	Bobby Mitchell	72	70	74	75	291
24=	Al Geiberger	73	75	72	72	292
	Dick Lotz	77	72	73	70	292
	Steve Melnyk	73	70	75	74	292
27=	Dale Douglass	70	71	76	76	293
	Dave Hill	74	73	70	76	293
	Art Wall	71	76	72	74	293
30=	Larry Hinson	75	71	76	72	294
	Yung-Yo Hsieh	75	69	77	73	294
	Juan Rodriguez	73	75	71	75	294
	Larry Ziegler	73	70	77	74	294

Round Leader(s)
R1   Coody; 66
R2   January; 138
R3   Coody, Nicklaus; 209
Lowest Scores
R2   Hsieh, January, Littler, Moody, de Vicenzo, Weiskopf; 69
R3   Miller, Nicklaus; 68
R4   Miller; 68

1971

17–21 June

US OPEN

Merion GC, Ardmore, Pennsylvania
6544 yards PAR 70 (280)

Lee Trevino's 2nd Open came after a superb 68 saw off Jack Nicklaus in a play-off. Amateur Jim Simons held a 2-stroke lead at the end of R3, thanks to a 65. Nicklaus collected his 2nd runner-up prize of the season, while 1971 winner, Tony Jacklin, missed the cut, as had 5 other defending champions from the previous 8 years. Entries passed 4000 for the 1st time.

1	**LEE TREVINO***	70	72	69	69	280
	($30000)					
2	Jack Nicklaus	69	72	68	71	280
3=	Jim Colbert	69	69	73	71	282
	Bob Rosburg	71	72	70	69	282
5=	George Archer	71	70	70	72	283
	Johnny Miller	70	73	70	70	283
	Jim Simons (a)	71	71	65	76	283
8	Ray Floyd	71	75	67	71	284
9=	Gay Brewer	70	70	73	72	285
	Larry Hinson	71	71	70	73	285
	Bobby Nichols	69	72	69	75	285
	Bert Yancey	75	69	69	72	285
13=	Bob Charles	72	75	69	70	286
	Bobby Cole	72	71	72	71	286
	Jerry Heard	73	71	73	69	286
	Jerry McGee	72	67	77	70	286
	Chi Chi Rodriguez	70	71	73	72	286
	Lanny Wadkins (a)	68	75	75	68	286
19=	Homero Blancas	71	71	75	70	287
	Dave Eichelberger	72	72	70	73	287
	Bob Goalby	68	76	74	69	287
	Hale Irwin	72	73	72	70	287
	Ken Still	71	72	69	75	287
24=	Dick Lotz	72	72	73	71	288
	Arnold Palmer	73	68	73	74	288
	Bob E Smith	71	74	71	72	288
27=	Ben Crenshaw (a)	74	74	68	73	289
	Bruce Devlin	72	69	71	77	289
	Don January	75	73	71	70	289
	Ralph Johnston	70	75	73	71	289
	Bob Lunn	71	73	71	74	289
	Bobby Mitchell	72	74	72	71	289
	Orville Moody	71	71	76	71	289
	Gary Player	76	71	72	70	289
	John Schroeder	72	73	69	75	289
	Kermit Zarley	74	70	72	73	289

* Lee Trevino (68) beat Jack Nicklaus (71) in the 18-Hole Play-off

Round Leader(s)
R1 Labron Harris (46); 67
R2 Colbert, Bob Erickson (37);
138
R3 Simons; 207

Lowest Scores
R2 Erickson, McGee; 67
R3 Simons; 65
R4 Wadkins; 68

1971

7–9 July

BRITISH OPEN

Royal Birkdale GC, Southport, Lancashire, England
7080 yards PAR 73 (292)

The year of 'Mr Lu' and the constantly-doffed pork-pie hat: the 1st of Lee Trevino's British Opens. Liang-Huan Lu, from Taiwan, charmed the Birkdale crowds – and TV audiences – as he so nearly became the 1st Asian golfer to win a Major. Trevino's R1 69 was to make all the difference as the pair matched each other's scores from there in. His 2nd consecutive Major of the year meant he joined Jones (twice), Sarazen and Hogan as the only players to lift both Opens in the same year.

1	**LEE TREVINO**	69	70	69	70	278
	(£5500)					
2	Liang-Huan Lu	70	70	69	70	279
3	Tony Jacklin	69	70	70	71	280
4	Craig DeFoy	72	72	68	69	281
5=	Charles Coody	74	71	70	68	283
	Jack Nicklaus	71	71	72	69	283
7=	Billy Casper	70	72	75	67	284
	Gary Player	71	70	71	72	284
9=	Doug Sanders	73	71	74	67	285
	Peter Thomson	70	73	73	69	285
11=	Harry Bannerman	73	71	72	71	287
	Roberto de Vicenzo	71	70	72	74	287
	Kel Nagle	70	75	73	69	287
	Ramon Sota	72	72	70	73	287
	Dave Stockton	74	74	68	71	287
	Bert Yancey	75	70	71	71	287
17	Dale Hayes	71	72	70	75	288
18=	Bob Charles	77	71	71	70	289
	Peter Oosterhuis	76	71	66	76	289
20=	Bernard Hunt	74	73	73	70	290
	Howie Johnson	69	76	72	73	290
22=	Michael Bonallack (a)	71	72	75	73	291
	Neil Coles	76	72	72	71	291
	Hugh Jackson	71	73	72	75	291
25=	Peter Butler	73	73	73	73	292
	Vicente Fernandez	69	79	73	71	292
	Malcolm Gregson	71	71	73	77	292
	Brian Huggett	73	73	74	72	292
	Bill Large	73	75	73	71	292
	John Lister	74	71	74	73	292
	Doug Sewell	73	74	74	71	292
	Randall Vines	75	71	73	73	292

Round Leader(s)
R1 Fernandez, Jacklin, Johnson, Trevino; 69
R2 Jacklin, Trevino; 139
R3 Trevino; 208

Lowest Scores
R2 de Vicenzo, Jacklin, Lu, Player, Trevino, Yancey; 70
R3 Oosterhuis; 66
R4 Casper, Sanders; 67

1972
THE MASTERS
6–9 April

Augusta National GC, Augusta, Georgia
6925 yards _PAR 72 (288)_

After a period of three seasons when he won nothing, Jack Nicklaus was winning Majors again – and continuing to break records. He won his 4th Masters, tying the record of Arnold Palmer, and 10th Major overall, one ahead of Ben Hogan, one behind Walter Hagen. Australian Bruce Crampton was to follow Jack home in this and his next 2 Major Championship wins.

1	**JACK NICKLAUS**	68	71	73	74	286
	($25000)					

2=	Bruce Crampton	72	75	69	73	289
	Bobby Mitchell	73	72	71	73	289
	Tom Weiskopf	74	71	70	74	289
5=	Homero Blancas	76	71	69	74	290
	Bruce Devlin	74	75	70	71	290
	Jerry Heard	73	71	72	74	290
	Jim Jamieson	72	70	71	77	290
	Jerry McGee	73	74	71	72	290
10=	Gary Player	73	75	72	71	291
	Dave Stockton	76	70	74	71	291
12=	George Archer	73	75	72	72	292
	Charles Coody	73	70	74	75	292
	Al Geiberger	76	70	74	72	292
	Steve Melnyk	72	72	74	74	292
	Bert Yancey	72	69	76	75	292
17=	Billy Casper	75	71	74	74	294
	Bob Goalby	73	76	72	73	294
19=	Ben Crenshaw (a)	73	74	74	74	295
	Takaaki Kono	76	72	73	74	295
	Lanny Wadkins	72	72	77	74	295
22=	Bob Charles	72	76	74	74	296
	Roberto de Vicenzo	75	69	76	76	296
	Gardner Dickinson	77	72	73	74	296
	Hubert Green	75	74	74	73	296
	Paul Harney	71	69	75	81	296
27=	Tony Jacklin	72	76	75	74	297
	Tom Kite	74	74	76	73	297
	Sam Snead	69	75	76	77	297
30	JC Snead	74	77	72	75	298

Round Leader(s)
R1 Nicklaus; 68
R2 Nicklaus; 139
R3 Nicklaus; 212
Lowest Scores
R2 Harney, de Vicenzo, Yancey; 69
R3 Blancas, Crampton; 69
R4 Devlin, Player, Stockton; 71

1972
US OPEN
15–18 June

Pebble Beach GL, Pebble Beach, California
6812 yards _PAR 72 (288)_

Spectacular Pebble Beach played host to a Major Championship for the 1st time – and it proved a tough test. Nicklaus' 2nd consecutive Major win was the 5th time the Masters-US Open double in the same year was recorded. Craig Wood, Ben Hogan (twice) and Arnold Palmer had previously accomplished it. It was Jack's 3rd US Open title and it also put him level with Walter Hagen in the all-time lists with 11 – MAS (4), USOP (3), BOP (2), PGA (2) – more than any other player. Mason Rudolph shot the low score for Rs1 & 4, but scored 80 and 86 in between to finish in 40th place.

1	**JACK NICKLAUS**	71	73	72	74	290
	($30000)					

2	Bruce Crampton	74	70	73	76	293
3	Arnold Palmer	77	68	73	76	294
4=	Homero Blancas	74	70	76	75	295
	Lee Trevino	74	72	71	78	295
6	Kermit Zarley	71	73	73	79	296
7	Johnny Miller	74	73	71	79	297
8	Tom Weiskopf	73	74	73	78	298
9=	Chi Chi Rodriguez	71	75	78	75	299
	Cesar Sanudo	72	72	78	77	299
11=	Billy Casper	74	73	79	74	300
	Don January	76	71	74	79	300
	Bobby Nichols	77	74	72	77	300
	Bert Yancey	75	79	70	76	300
15=	Don Massengale	72	81	70	78	301
	Orville Moody	71	77	79	74	301
	Gary Player	72	74	75	78	299
	Jim Simons (a)	75	75	79	72	301
19=	Lou Graham	75	73	75	79	302
	Tom Kite (a)	75	73	79	75	302
21=	Al Geiberger	80	74	76	73	303
	Paul Harney	79	72	75	77	303
	Bobby Mitchell	74	80	73	76	303
	Charles Sifford	79	74	72	78	303
25=	Gay Brewer	77	77	72	78	304
	Rod Funseth	73	73	84	74	304
	Lanny Wadkins	76	68	79	81	304
	Jim Wiechers	74	79	69	82	304
29=	Miller Barber	76	76	73	80	305
	Julius Boros	77	77	74	77	305
	Dave Eichelberger	76	71	80	78	305
	Lee Elder	75	71	79	80	305
	Jerry Heard	73	74	77	81	305
	Dave Hill	74	78	74	79	305
	Tom Watson	74	79	76	76	305

Round Leader(s)
R1 Moody, Nicklaus, Rodriguez, Mason Rudolph (40), Tom Shaw (40), Zarley; 71
R2 Blancas, Crampton, Nicklaus, Sanudo, Wadkins, Zarley; 144
R3 Nicklaus; 216

Lowest Scores
R2 Palmer, Wadkins; 68
R3 Wiechers; 69
R4 Mason Rudolph (40); 70

12–15 July **1972**
BRITISH OPEN
Honourable Company, Muirfield, Angus, Scotland
6892 yards _PAR 71 (284)_

3–6 August **1972**
US PGA
Oakland Hills CC, Birmingham, Michigan
6815 yards _PAR 70 (280)_

Lee Trevino's back-to-back Open win was destined to be. In R3, he scrambled 5 consecutive birdies over the final 5 holes with an array of chips-in and outlandish putting unlikely to be seen again . . . or so Tony Jacklin hoped. It was bad enough seeing his immaculate 67 being overhauled by Trevino's antics in R3, but when, tied going into the last, he was 15 feet away from the hole in 3 and saw Trevino, through the back of the green in 4, run it in, it destroyed Jacklin - some say as a golfing force forever. Jacklin 3-putted and allowed a Nicklaus charge to deprive him of even 2nd place, Jack just failing to emulate Hogan's 1953 3 Majors in-a-row record.

I	**LEE TREVINO**	71	70	66	71	278
	(£5500)					
2	Jack Nicklaus	70	72	71	66	279
3	Tony Jacklin	69	72	67	72	280
4	Doug Sanders	71	71	69	70	281
5	Brian Barnes	71	72	69	71	283
6	Gary Player	71	71	76	67	285
7=	Guy Hunt	75	72	67	72	286
	Arnold Palmer	73	73	69	71	286
	David Vaughan	74	73	70	69	286
	Tom Weiskopf	73	74	70	69	286
11=	Clive Clark	72	71	73	71	287
	Dave Marr	70	74	71	72	287
13=	Roberto Bernadini	73	71	76	68	288
	Peter Townsend	70	72	76	70	288
15=	Peter Butler	72	75	73	69	289
	Bob Charles	75	70	74	70	289
	Jan Dorrestein	74	71	72	72	289
	Johnny Miller	76	66	72	75	289
19=	Harry Bannerman	77	73	73	67	290
	Frank Beard	70	76	74	70	290
	Maurice Bembridge	73	71	75	71	290
	Bert Yancey	73	72	72	73	290
23=	Craig DeFoy	70	75	71	75	291
	Doug McClelland	73	74	72	72	291
	Christy O'Connor, Sr	73	74	73	71	291
26=	Bruce Devlin	75	70	77	70	292
	Brian Huggett	73	72	79	68	292
28=	John Garner	71	71	76	75	293
	Jerry Heard	75	75	71	72	293
	Peter Oosterhuis	75	75	73	70	293

Round Leader(s)
R1 Jacklin; 69
R2 Jacklin, Trevino; 141
R3 Trevino; 207
Lowest Scores
R2 Miller; 66
R3 Trevino; 66
R4 Nicklaus; 66

Just when it was rumoured that Gary Player was losing his form, and like Arnold Palmer – another of the modern triumvirate now known as the 'Big Three' – he would never win another Major, he picked up his 2nd PGA title and 6th Major. He was now ranked above Taylor, Braid, Nelson and Thomson in the all-time lists, but still one behind the next group of Vardon, Jones, Sarazen, Snead and the aforementioned Palmer.

I	**GARY PLAYER**	71	71	67	72	281
	(£45000)					
2=	Tommy Aaron	71	71	70	71	283
	Jim Jamieson	69	72	72	70	283
4=	Billy Casper	73	70	67	74	284
	Ray Floyd	69	71	74	70	284
	Sam Snead	70	74	71	69	284
7=	Gay Brewer	71	70	70	74	285
	Jerry Heard	69	70	72	74	285
	Phil Rodgers	71	72	68	74	285
	Doug Sanders	72	72	68	73	285
11=	Hale Irwin	71	69	75	71	286
	Lee Trevino	73	71	71	71	286
13=	Jack Nicklaus	72	75	68	72	287
	Dan Sikes	70	72	73	73	287
15	Charles Coody	71	73	70	74	288
16=	Miller Barber	73	74	72	70	289
	Hubert Green	75	71	73	70	289
	Arnold Palmer	69	75	72	73	289
	Lanny Wadkins	74	68	72	75	289
20=	Johnny Miller	70	76	70	74	290
	Bob Shaw	72	72	74	72	290
	JC Snead	72	72	71	75	290
	Larry Wise	74	71	67	78	290
24=	Bruce Crampton	73	74	68	76	291
	Lee Elder	73	71	71	76	291
	Chi Chi Rodriguez	71	74	73	73	291
	Bob E Smith	72	69	76	74	291
	Art Wall	72	71	75	73	291
29=	Jerry McGee	73	74	72	73	292
	Mike Souchak	73	73	71	75	292
	Jim Wiechers	70	73	69	80	292
	Bert Yancey	72	74	71	75	292

Round Leader(s)
R1 Buddy Allin (53), Stan Thirsk (72); 68
R2 Heard; 139
R3 Player; 209
Lowest Scores
R2 Wadkins; 68
R3 Casper, Player, Wise; 67
R4 Snead; 69

1973 THE MASTERS
5–9 April – (Saturday washed out)

Augusta National GC, Augusta, Georgia
6925 yards _PAR 72 (288)_

Local boy Tommy Aaron won his 1st and last Major over JC Snead – Sam's nephew. Englishman Peter Oosterhuis held a 3-shot lead going into R4, but couldn't hold it together, as Aaron, Snead and Jamieson challenged. A string of 8 consecutive birdies helped Jack Nicklaus race up the leaderboard to tie with the Briton and Jamieson.

1	**TOMMY AARON** ($30000)	68	73	74	68	283
2	JC Snead	70	71	73	70	284
3=	Jim Jamieson	73	71	70	71	285
	Jack Nicklaus	69	77	73	66	285
	Peter Oosterhuis	73	70	68	74	285
6=	Bob Goalby	73	70	71	74	288
	Johnny Miller	75	69	71	73	288
8=	Bruce Devlin	73	72	72	72	289
	Jumbo Ozaki	69	74	73	73	289
10=	Gay Brewer	75	66	74	76	291
	Gardner Dickinson	74	70	72	75	291
	Don January	75	71	75	70	291
	Chi Chi Rodriguez	72	70	73	76	291
14=	Hubert Green	72	74	75	71	292
	Mason Rudolph	72	72	77	71	292
	Dave Stockton	72	74	71	75	292
17=	Billy Casper	75	73	72	73	293
	Bob Dickson	70	71	76	76	293
	Lou Graham	77	73	72	71	293
	Babe Hiskey	74	73	72	74	293
	Gene Littler	77	72	71	73	293
	Kermit Zarley	74	71	77	71	293
23	Phil Rodgers	71	75	75	73	294
24=	Frank Beard	73	75	71	76	295
	Ben Crenshaw (a)	73	72	74	76	295
	Paul Harney	77	71	74	73	295
	Bobby Nichols	79	72	76	68	295
	Arnold Palmer	77	72	76	70	295
29=	Bob Charles	74	70	74	78	296
	Charles Coody	74	73	79	70	296
	David Graham	72	74	77	73	296
	Sam Snead	74	76	73	73	296
	Lanny Wadkins	75	74	71	76	296

Round Leader(s)
R1 Aaron; 68
R2 Aaron, Brewer, Dickson, Snead; 141
R3 Oosterhuis; 211
Lowest Scores
R2 Brewer; 66
R3 Oosterhuis; 68
R4 Nicklaus; 66

1973 US OPEN
14–17 June

Oakmont CC, Oakmont, Pennsylvania
6921 yards _PAR 71 (284)_

Johnny Miller followed up his 6th place at Augusta with his 1st Majors win – the Open at Oakmont. In doing so he beat the Open low round score of 64 jointly held by Lee Mackey, Tommy Jacobs and Rives McBee – his 63 being the lowest score in any Major to date.

1	**JOHNNY MILLER** ($35000)	71	69	76	63	279
2	John Schlee	73	70	67	70	280
3	Tom Weiskopf	73	69	69	70	281
4=	Jack Nicklaus	71	69	74	68	282
	Arnold Palmer	71	71	68	72	282
	Lee Trevino	70	72	70	70	282
7=	Julius Boros	73	69	68	73	283
	Jerry Heard	74	70	66	73	283
	Lanny Wadkins	74	69	75	65	283
10	Jim Colbert	70	68	74	72	284
11	Bob Charles	71	69	72	74	286
12	Gary Player	67	70	77	73	287
13=	Al Geiberger	73	72	71	72	288
	Ralph Johnston	71	73	76	68	288
	Larry Ziegler	73	74	69	72	288
16	Ray Floyd	70	73	75	71	289
17	Marvin Giles (a)	74	69	74	73	290
18=	Gene Littler	71	74	70	76	291
	Rocky Thompson	73	71	71	76	291
20=	Rod Funseth	75	74	70	74	293
	Hale Irwin	73	74	75	71	293
	Denny Lyons	72	74	75	72	293
	Bob Murphy	77	70	75	71	293
	Bobby Nichols	75	71	74	73	293
25=	Miller Barber	74	71	71	78	294
	Frank Beard	74	75	68	77	294
	Tom Shaw	73	71	74	76	294
	Bert Yancey	73	70	75	76	294
29=	Don Bies	77	73	73	72	295
	Charles Coody	74	74	73	74	295
	John Mahaffey	74	72	74	75	295
	Chi Chi Rodriguez	75	71	75	74	295
	Sam Snead	75	74	73	73	295

Round Leader(s)
R1 Player; 67
R2 Player; 137
R3 Boros, Heard, Palmer, Schlee; 210
Lowest Scores
R2 Gene Borek (38); 65
R3 Heard, 66
R4 Miller; 63

BRITISH OPEN 1973

Troon GC, Ayrshire, Scotland
7064 yards PAR 72 (288)

Tom Weiskopf's good finish in the US Open was in a run of superb form on the US Tour. Running up to Pebble Beach, his results sequence read: W, W, 2, W. He played one event between the Opens, and must have been disappointed to finish 5th. His win at Troon, therefore, was as expected as it was popular – for if the game of golf awarded marks for artistic impression, then Weiskopf would have won more than one Major.

1	**TOM WEISKOPF**	68	67	71	70	276
	(£5500)					
2=	Neil Coles	71	72	70	66	279
	Johnny Miller	70	68	69	72	279
4	Jack Nicklaus	69	70	76	65	280
5	Bert Yancey	69	69	73	70	281
6	Peter Butler	71	72	74	69	286
7=	Bob Charles	73	71	73	71	288
	Christy O'Connor, Sr	73	68	74	73	288
	Lanny Wadkins	71	73	70	74	288
10=	Brian Barnes	76	67	70	76	289
	Gay Brewer	76	71	72	70	289
	Harold Henning	73	73	73	70	289
	Lee Trevino	75	73	73	68	289
14=	Tony Jacklin	75	73	72	70	290
	Doug McClelland	76	71	69	74	290
	Arnold Palmer	72	76	70	72	290
	Gary Player	76	69	76	69	290
18=	Hugh Baiocchi	75	74	69	74	292
	Hugh Boyle	75	75	69	73	292
	Bruce Crampton	71	76	73	72	292
	Bruce Devlin	72	78	71	71	292
	Bernard Gallacher	73	69	75	75	292
	DJ Good	75	74	73	70	292
	Dave Hill	75	74	74	69	292
	Peter Oosterhuis	80	71	69	72	292
	Eddie Polland	74	73	73	72	292
	Peter Wilcock	71	76	72	73	292
28=	Roberto de Vicenzo	72	75	74	72	293
	Chi Chi Rodriguez	72	73	73	75	293
	Doug Sanders	79	72	72	70	293

Round Leader(s)
R1   Weiskopf; 68
R2   Weiskopf; 135
R3   Weiskopf; 206
Lowest Scores
R2   Barnes, Weiskopf; 67
R3   Baiocchi, Boyle, McClelland, Miller, Oosterhuis; 69
R4   Nicklaus; 65

US PGA 1973

Canterbury GC, Cleveland, Ohio
6852 yards PAR 71 (284)

Jack Nicklaus made history when he won his 12th Major and became the greatest player of Major Championships the game had ever seen. In passing Walter Hagen's total, he also – to the statistician's delight – eclipsed the old version of Grand Slam titles, which include the US and British Amateur Championships, held by Bobby Jones for 43 years. Nicklaus' 2 US Amateur wins took his total past Jones' tally of 13 titles.

1	**JACK NICKLAUS**	72	68	68	69	277
	($45000)					
2	Bruce Crampton	71	73	67	70	281
3=	Mason Rudolph	69	70	70	73	282
	JC Snead	71	74	68	69	282
	Lanny Wadkins	73	69	71	69	282
6=	Don Iverson	67	72	70	74	283
	Dan Sikes	72	68	72	71	283
	Tom Weiskopf	70	71	71	71	283
9=	Hale Irwin	76	72	68	68	284
	Sam Snead	71	71	71	71	284
	Kermit Zarley	76	71	68	69	284
12=	Bobby Brue	70	72	73	70	285
	Jim Colbert	72	70	69	74	285
	Larry Hinson	73	70	71	71	285
	Denny Lyons	73	70	67	75	285
	Dave Stockton	72	69	75	69	285
	Tom Watson	75	70	71	69	285
18=	Al Geiberger	67	76	74	69	286
	Gibby Gilbert	70	70	73	73	286
	Bob Goalby	75	70	71	70	286
	Jim Jamieson	71	73	71	71	286
	Johnny Miller	72	71	74	69	286
	Lee Trevino	76	70	73	67	286
24=	Miller Barber	73	73	70	71	287
	Bruce Devlin	73	70	74	70	287
	Lee Elder	71	76	70	70	287
	Mike Hill	69	73	75	70	287
	Chi Chi Rodriguez	72	71	74	70	287
	Bert Yancey	74	72	69	72	287
30=	Don Bies	70	72	71	75	288
	Lou Graham	74	71	73	70	288
	John Mahaffey	75	71	72	70	288
	Orville Moody	73	74	70	71	288

Round Leader(s)
R1   Geiberger, Iverson; 67
R2   Iverson, Rudolph; 139
R3   Nicklaus; 208
Lowest Scores
R2   Charles Coody (35), Nicklaus, Sikes; 68
R3   Buddy Allin (34), Crampton, Lyons; 67
R4   Trevino; 67

1974
THE MASTERS
11–14 April

Augusta National GC, Augusta, Georgia
6925 yards _PAR 72 (288)_

Gary Player's 7th Major, but only his 2nd Masters after a 13 year span. 1970 PGA Champion Dave Stockton had led for much of the Tournament, but was caught and passed by Player in an exciting back 9. A 9-iron to within inches of the pin at 17 set up the birdie that was to clinch it for the South African. Englishman Maurice Bembridge equalled the low score with a 64 to finish tied for 9th.

1	**GARY PLAYER**	71	71	66	70	278
	($35000)					
2=	Dave Stockton	71	66	70	73	280
	Tom Weiskopf	71	69	70	70	280
4=	Jim Colbert	67	72	69	73	281
	Hale Irwin	68	70	72	71	281
	Jack Nicklaus	69	71	72	69	281
7=	Bobby Nichols	73	68	68	73	282
	Phil Rodgers	72	69	68	73	282
9=	Maurice Bembridge	73	74	72	64	283
	Hubert Green	68	70	74	71	283
11=	Bruce Crampton	73	72	69	70	284
	Jerry Heard	70	70	73	71	284
	Dave Hill	71	72	70	71	284
	Arnold Palmer	76	71	70	67	284
15=	Bud Allin	73	73	70	69	285
	Miller Barber	75	67	72	71	285
	Ralph Johnston	72	71	70	72	285
	Johnny Miller	72	74	69	70	285
	Dan Sikes	69	71	74	71	285
20=	Chi Chi Rodriguez	70	74	71	71	286
	Sam Snead	72	72	71	71	286
22=	Frank Beard	69	70	72	76	287
	Ben Crenshaw	75	70	70	72	287
	Ray Floyd	69	72	76	70	287
	Bob Goalby	76	71	72	68	287
26=	Julius Boros	75	70	69	74	288
	John Schlee	75	71	71	71	288
	JC Snead	73	68	74	73	288
29=	Charles Coody	74	72	76	67	289
	Don Iverson	68	74	73	74	289

Round Leader(s)
R1   Colbert; 67
R2   Stockton; 137
R3   Stockton; 207
Lowest Scores
R2   Stockton; 66
R3   Player; 66
R4   Bembridge; 64

1974
US OPEN
13–16 June

Winged Foot GC, Mamaroneck, New York
6961 yards _PAR 70 (280)_

Hale Irwin won his 1st Major by playing solid golf over the tough West Course at Winged Foot. That he was 7 over par is testament to the demands of the golf course. 23 year-old Tom Watson held the lead after 54 holes, but collapsed – coming home in 41 – as the pack overwhelmed him.

1	**HALE IRWIN**	73	70	71	73	287
	($35000)					
2	Forrest Fezler	75	70	74	70	289
3=	Lou Graham	71	75	74	70	290
	Bert Yancey	76	69	73	72	290
5=	Jim Colbert	72	77	69	74	292
	Arnold Palmer	73	70	73	76	292
	Tom Watson	73	71	69	79	292
8=	Tom Kite	74	70	77	72	293
	Gary Player	70	73	77	73	293
10=	Brian Allin	76	71	74	73	294
	Jack Nicklaus	75	74	76	69	294
12=	Frank Beard	77	69	72	77	295
	John Mahaffey	74	73	75	73	295
	Larry Ziegler	78	68	78	71	295
15=	Ray Floyd	72	71	78	75	296
	Mike Reasor	71	76	76	73	296
	Tom Weiskopf	76	73	72	75	296
18=	Dale Douglass	77	72	72	76	297
	Al Geiberger	75	76	78	68	297
	David Graham	73	75	76	73	297
21=	JC Snead	76	71	76	75	298
	Leonard Thompson	75	75	76	72	298
23=	Bruce Crampton	72	77	76	74	299
	Larry Hinson	75	76	75	73	299
	Bobby Mitchell	77	73	73	76	299
26=	Hubert Green	81	67	76	76	300
	Jim Jamieson	77	73	75	75	300
	Chi Chi Rodriguez	75	75	77	73	300
	Lanny Wadkins	75	73	76	76	300
30=	Ron Cerrudo	78	75	75	73	301
	Rod Funseth	73	75	78	75	301
	David Glenz	76	74	75	76	301
	Rik Massengale	79	72	74	76	301
	Jerry McGee	77	72	78	74	301

Round Leader(s)
R1   Player; 70
R2   Floyd, Irwin, Palmer, Player; 143
R3   Watson; 213
Lowest Scores
R2   Green; 67
R3   Colbert, Watson; 69
R4   Geiberger; 68

10–13 July
BRITISH OPEN **1974**
Royal Lytham and St Anne's GC, Lancashire, England
6822 yards PAR 71 (284)

8–11 August **1974**
US PGA
Tanglewood GC, Clemmons, North Carolina
7050 yards PAR 70 (280)

Gary Player won his 3rd Open and 8th Major in all when he was the only one to beat par at Royal Lytham. He climbed to 4th place outright in the all-time list, behind Nicklaus, Hagen and Hogan. The British Open, thanks to its support from Player (Champion 1st in 1959) and the Americans led by Palmer and Nicklaus, was unrecognizable from a decade or so before. Only one Englishman finished in the cosmopolitan Top 10, which also featured 2 South Africans, 5 Americans, a Taiwanese and a Belgian.

Wet conditions throughout the Championship favoured the maverick shotmaking genius that was Lee Trevino. He won his 1st PGA, and 5th Major, after shooting a R1 73 which left him tied-43rd, 5 shots off the lead. Thereafter he played brilliant golf in the conditions to card 203 for the last 54 holes. Jack Nicklaus continued to collect as many runner-up prizes as wins. Sam Snead, at the age of 62, was having a remarkable Indian summer in the PGA, finishing 4th, 9th and 3rd over the last 3 years. It was 32 years after his 1st of 7 Major titles.

1	**GARY PLAYER**	69	68	75	70	282
	(£5500)					
2	Peter Oosterhuis	71	71	73	71	286
3	Jack Nicklaus	74	72	70	71	287
4	Hubert Green	71	74	72	71	288
5=	Danny Edwards	70	73	76	73	292
	Liang-Huan Lu	72	72	75	73	292
7=	Bobby Cole	70	72	76	75	293
	Don Swaelens	77	73	74	69	293
	Tom Weiskopf	72	72	74	75	293
10	Johnny Miller	72	75	73	74	294
11=	John Garner	75	78	73	69	295
	David Graham	76	74	76	69	295
13=	Neil Coles	72	75	75	74	296
	Al Geiberger	76	70	76	74	296
	John Morgan	69	75	76	76	296
	Alan Tapie	73	77	73	73	296
	Peter Townsend	79	76	72	69	296
18=	Peter Dawson	74	74	73	76	297
	Tony Jacklin	74	77	71	75	297
	Gene Littler	77	76	70	74	297
	Dewitt Weaver	73	80	70	74	297
22=	Ronnie Shade	78	75	73	72	298
	Lanny Wadkins	78	71	75	74	298
24=	Bernard Gallacher	76	72	76	75	299
	Angel Gallardo	74	77	75	73	299
	Hale Irwin	76	73	79	71	299
	Christy O'Connor, Jr	78	76	72	73	299
28=	Ben Crenshaw	74	80	76	70	300
	David Jagger	80	71	76	73	300
	Doug McClelland	75	79	73	73	300

1	**LEE TREVINO**	73	66	68	69	276
	($45000)					
2	Jack Nicklaus	69	69	70	69	277
3=	Bobby Cole	69	68	71	71	279
	Hubert Green	68	68	73	70	279
	Dave Hill	74	69	67	69	279
	Sam Snead	69	71	71	68	279
7	Gary Player	73	64	73	70	280
8	Al Geiberger	70	70	75	66	281
9=	Don Bies	73	71	68	70	282
	John Mahaffey	72	72	71	67	282
11=	Tommy Aycock	73	68	73	70	284
	Frank Beard	73	67	69	75	284
	Lee Elder	74	69	72	69	284
	Ray Floyd	68	73	74	70	284
	Mike Hill	76	72	68	68	284
	Tom Watson	69	72	73	70	284
17=	Gay Brewer	72	72	72	69	285
	Tom Jenkins	70	73	71	71	285
	John Schlee	68	67	75	75	285
	Dan Sikes	71	75	71	68	285
	Leonard Thompson	69	71	70	75	285
22=	Stan Brion	71	71	74	70	286
	Bruce Devlin	70	74	70	72	286
24=	Don Massengale	74	71	70	72	287
	JC Snead	72	72	75	68	287
26=	Larry Hinson	74	73	69	72	288
	Dave Stockton	71	73	70	74	288
28=	Jim Colbert	70	76	70	73	289
	Gene Littler	76	72	70	71	289
	Arnold Palmer	72	75	70	72	289
	Victor Regalado	70	72	77	70	289

Round Leader(s)
R1   Morgan, Player; 69
R2   Player; 137
R3   Player; 212
Lowest Scores
R2   Player; 68
R3   Littler, Nicklaus, Weaver; 70
R4   Garner, Graham, Swaelens, Townsend; 69

Round Leader(s)
R1   Green, Floyd, Schlee; 68
R2   Schlee; 135
R3   Trevino; 207
Lowest Scores
R2   Player; 64
R3   Hill; 67
R4   Geiberger; 66

1975
10–13 April
THE MASTERS
Augusta National GC, Augusta, Georgia
6925 yards PAR 72 (288)

1975
19–23 June
US OPEN
Medinah CC, Medinah, Illinois
7032 yards PAR 71 (284)

Nicklaus' 5th win was a record for the Masters, while Tom Weiskopf equalled Ben Hogan's 4 2nd places. The 2 fought out a real dogfight over the last 9 holes, but when Weiskopf missed his birdie putt on 18, Jack was home and dry for Major No13. Attempting to make up 11 shots on Nicklaus over the last 36 holes, Johnny Miller fired 131, but just failed to tie for the lead when he too missed a birdieable putt at the last.

With 3 strokes covering the 1st 11 players home, a play-off was perhaps inevitable. Frank Beard led by 3 going into the final round from Tom Watson and Pat Fitzsimons, but all played R4 poorly allowing John Mahaffey through to tie with Lou Graham, who took a 1-over 5 at the last. Graham steadied himself for the play-off to win his only Major. Unusually, Jack Nicklaus dropped a shot at each of the last 3 holes, and fell back into the pack.

1	**JACK NICKLAUS** ($40000)	68	67	73	68	276
2=	Johnny Miller	75	71	65	66	277
	Tom Weiskopf	69	72	66	70	277
4=	Hale Irwin	73	74	71	64	282
	Bobby Nichols	67	74	72	69	282
6	Billy Casper	70	70	73	70	283
7	Dave Hill	75	71	70	68	284
8=	Hubert Green	74	71	70	70	285
	Tom Watson	70	70	72	73	285
10=	Tom Kite	72	74	71	69	286
	JC Snead	69	72	75	70	286
	Lee Trevino	71	70	74	71	286
13=	Arnold Palmer	69	71	75	72	287
	Larry Ziegler	71	73	74	69	287
15=	Bobby Cole	73	71	73	71	288
	Rod Curl	72	70	76	70	288
	Bruce Devlin	72	70	76	70	288
	Allen Miller	68	75	72	73	288
	Art Wall	72	74	72	70	288
20=	Bud Allin	73	69	73	74	289
	Ralph Johnston	74	73	69	73	289
22=	Hugh Baiocchi	76	72	72	70	290
	Pat Fitzsimons	73	68	79	70	290
	Gene Littler	72	72	72	74	290
	Graham Marsh	75	70	74	71	290
26=	Miller Barber	74	72	72	73	291
	Maurice Bembridge	75	72	75	69	291
	Jerry Heard	71	75	72	73	291
	Dave Stockton	72	72	73	74	291
30=	George Burns	72	72	76	72	292
	Ben Crenshaw	72	71	75	74	292
	Forrest Fezler	76	71	71	74	292
	Ray Floyd	72	73	79	68	292
	Gary Player	72	74	73	73	292
	Victor Regalado	76	72	72	72	292
	Bert Yancey	74	71	74	73	292

1	**LOU GRAHAM*** ($40000)	74	72	68	73	287
2	John Mahaffey	73	71	72	71	287
3=	Frank Beard	74	69	67	78	288
	Ben Crenshaw	70	68	76	74	288
	Hale Irwin	74	71	73	70	288
	Bob Murphy	74	73	72	69	288
7=	Jack Nicklaus	72	70	75	72	289
	Peter Oosterhuis	69	73	72	75	289
9=	Pat Fitzsimons	67	73	73	77	290
	Arnold Palmer	69	75	73	73	290
	Tom Watson	67	68	78	77	290
12=	Ray Floyd	76	71	72	72	291
	Andy North	75	72	72	72	291
14=	Joe Inman	72	72	71	77	292
	Rik Massengale	71	74	71	76	292
	Eddie Pearce	75	71	70	76	292
	Jim Wiechers	68	73	76	75	292
18=	Terry Dill	72	69	77	75	293
	Hubert Green	74	73	68	78	293
	Gary Groh	73	74	73	73	293
	Jay Haas (a)	74	69	72	78	293
	Grier Jones	69	73	79	72	293
	Jerry Pate (a)	79	70	72	72	293
24=	Brian Allin	76	70	73	75	294
	Miller Barber	74	71	71	78	294
	Dale Douglass	71	77	72	74	294
	Forrest Fezler	73	75	71	75	294
	Kermit Zarley	73	71	75	75	294
29=	Tommy Aaron	73	71	82	69	295
	David Graham	71	76	74	74	295
	Jerry Heard	77	67	78	73	295
	Don January	75	71	74	75	295
	Steve Melnyk	75	73	74	73	295
	Ed Sneed	75	74	73	73	295
	Nate Starks	75	72	76	72	295
	Lee Trevino	72	75	73	75	295
	Tom Weiskopf	75	71	74	75	295

Round Leader(s)

R1	Nichols; 67
R2	Nicklaus; 135
R3	Weiskopf; 207

Lowest Scores

R2	Nicklaus; 67
R3	Miller; 65
R4	Irwin; 64

* Lou Graham (71) beat John Mahaffey (73) in the 18-Hole Play-off

Round Leader(s)

R1	Fitzsimons, Watson; 67
R2	Watson; 135
R3	Beard; 210

Lowest Scores

R2	Heard; 67
R3	Beard; 67
R4	Aaron, Murphy; 69

9–12 July	**1975**
BRITISH OPEN	

Carnoustie GC, Angus, Scotland
7065 yards PAR 72 (288)

7–10 August	**1975**
US PGA	

Firestone CC, Akron, Ohio
7180 yards PAR 70 (280)

After succumbing to final round pressures in the US Open the previous month, and blowing up at Winged Foot in 1974, there was something of a question mark over Tom Watson's credentials when it came to converting winning positions into wins in Major Championships. There was always going to be something different about seaside golf for Watson, however – especially in Scotland – as he became only the 3rd American after Ben Hogan and Tony Lema to play the British Open (and its particular linksland game) 'blind', and win at the 1st attempt.

1	**TOM WATSON***	71	67	69	72	279
	(£7500)					
2	Jack Newton	69	71	75	74	279
3=	Bobby Cole	72	66	66	76	280
	Johnny Miller	71	69	66	74	280
	Jack Nicklaus	69	71	68	72	280
6	Graham Marsh	72	67	71	71	281
7=	Neil Coles	72	69	67	74	282
	Peter Oosterhuis	68	70	71	73	282
9	Hale Irwin	69	70	69	75	283
10=	George Burns	71	73	69	71	284
	John Mahaffey	71	68	69	76	284
12=	Bob Charles	74	73	70	69	286
	P Leonard	70	69	73	74	286
	Andries Oosthuizen	69	69	70	78	286
15	Tom Weiskopf	73	72	70	72	287
16=	Maurice Bembridge	75	73	67	73	288
	Arnold Palmer	74	72	69	73	288
	Alan Tapie	70	72	67	79	288
19=	Bernard Gallacher	72	67	72	78	289
	Lon Hinckle	76	72	69	72	289
	Tommy Horton	72	71	71	75	289
	Sam Torrance	72	74	71	72	289
23=	Brian Barnes	71	74	72	73	290
	Hugh Baiocchi	72	72	73	73	290
	Danny Edwards	70	74	71	75	290
	Ray Floyd	71	72	76	71	290
	Martin Foster	72	74	73	71	290
28=	Roberto de Vicenzo	71	74	72	74	291
	David Graham	74	70	72	75	291
	Simon Hobday	70	70	76	75	291
	Guy Hunt	73	68	76	74	291

* Tom Watson (71) beat Jack Newton (72) in the 18-Hole Play-off

Round Leader(s)
R1 Oosterhuis; 68
R2 Cole, Oosterhuis, Oosthuizen, Watson; 138
R3 Cole; 204
Lowest Scores
R2 Cole; 66
R3 Newton; 65
R4 Charles; 69

Jack Nicklaus became the 1st person to do the Masters-PGA double in the same year - twice. Sam Snead and Jack Burke Jr, had achieved the feat once. Playing steady golf based on an overnight 4-shot lead, Nicklaus coasted to his 14th Major, ahead of Bruce Crampton – 2nd to Jack for the 4th time in a Major Championship. Crampton had the consolation of setting a new low of 63, however - the best in the PGA, and matching Johnny Miller in the 1973 US Open to tie for the all-time low in a Major.

1	**JACK NICKLAUS**	70	68	67	71	276
	($45000)					
2	Bruce Crampton	71	63	75	69	278
3	Tom Weiskopf	70	71	70	68	279
4	Andy North	72	74	70	65	281
5=	Billy Casper	69	72	72	70	283
	Hale Irwin	72	65	73	73	283
7=	Dave Hill	71	71	74	68	284
	Gene Littler	76	71	66	71	284
9	Tom Watson	70	71	71	73	285
10=	Buddy Allin	73	72	70	71	286
	Ben Crenshaw	73	72	71	70	286
	Ray Floyd	70	73	72	71	286
	David Graham	72	70	70	74	286
	Don January	72	70	71	73	286
	John Schlee	71	68	75	72	286
	Leonard Thompson	74	69	72	71	286
17=	Dale Douglass	74	72	74	67	287
	Gibby Gilbert	73	70	77	67	287
	Mike Hill	72	71	70	74	287
	Steve Melnyk	71	72	74	70	287
	Gil Morgan	73	71	71	72	287
22=	Ed Dougherty	69	70	72	77	288
	Mark Hayes	67	71	75	75	288
	Chi Chi Rodriguez	73	72	74	69	288
25=	Jerry Heard	75	70	70	74	289
	Mac McLendon	73	71	70	75	289
	Bob Murphy	75	68	69	77	289
28=	Larry Hinson	68	73	72	77	290
	John Mahaffey	71	70	75	74	290
	JC Snead	73	67	75	75	290
	Bob Wynn	69	69	80	72	290

Round Leader(s)
R1 Hayes; 67
R2 Crampton; 134
R3 Nicklaus; 205
Lowest Scores
R2 Crampton; 63
R3 Littler; 66
R4 North; 65

1976
8–11 April
THE MASTERS
Augusta National GC, Augusta, Georgia
6925 yards _PAR 72 (288)_

1976
17–20 June
US OPEN
Atlanta Athletic Club, Atlanta, Georgia
7015 yards _PAR 70 (280)_

Ray Floyd's 2nd Major came as a result of spectacular scoring at Augusta. In tying Jack Nicklaus' all-time low for the Masters (and any Major Championship) he set new 36-and 54-hole record scores, to win by 8 – only 1 shot less than Jack's 1965 margin. At the end of R3 Floyd led Nicklaus by 8, but as the latter faded, and Ben Crenshaw charged, he held firm to maintain the same gap.

Spectators numbered more than 100000 for the 4 days for the 1st time, to see Jerry Pate play golf of a consistently-high standard to win from 1966 PGA Champion, Al Geiberger and the British Open Champion of 1973, Tom Weiskopf. After Nicklaus in 1962, Pate, at 22, was the youngest Open winner since Bobby Jones in 1923.

1	**RAY FLOYD** ($40000)	65	66	70	70	271
2	Ben Crenshaw	70	70	72	67	279
3=	Jack Nicklaus	67	69	73	73	282
	Larry Ziegler	67	71	72	72	282
5=	Charles Coody	72	69	70	74	285
	Hale Irwin	71	77	67	70	285
	Tom Kite	73	67	72	73	285
8	Billy Casper	71	76	71	69	287
9=	Roger Maltbie	72	75	70	71	288
	Graham Marsh	73	68	75	72	288
	Tom Weiskopf	73	71	70	74	288
12=	Jim Colbert	71	72	74	72	289
	Lou Graham	68	73	72	76	289
	Gene Littler	71	72	74	72	289
15=	Al Geiberger	75	70	73	73	291
	Dave Hill	69	73	76	73	291
	Jerry McGee	71	73	72	75	291
	Curtis Strange (a)	71	76	73	71	291
19=	Bud Allin	69	76	72	75	292
	Bruce Devlin	77	69	72	74	292
	Hubert Green	71	66	78	77	292
	Dale Hayes	75	74	73	70	292
23=	Gay Brewer	75	74	71	73	293
	Rik Massengale	70	72	78	73	293
	Johnny Miller	71	73	74	75	293
	Peter Oosterhuis	76	74	75	68	293
27	Bruce Crampton	74	76	71	73	294
28=	Bob Murphy	72	74	76	73	295
	Eddie Pearce	71	71	79	74	295
	Gary Player	73	73	70	79	295
	Lee Trevino	75	75	69	76	295
	Art Wall	74	71	75	75	295

1	**JERRY PATE** ($42000)	71	69	69	68	277
2=	Al Geiberger	70	69	71	69	279
	Tom Weiskopf	73	70	68	68	279
4=	Butch Baird	71	71	71	67	280
	John Mahaffey	70	68	69	73	280
6	Hubert Green	72	70	71	69	282
7	Tom Watson	74	72	68	70	284
8=	Ben Crenshaw	72	68	72	73	285
	Lyn Lott	71	71	70	73	285
10	Johnny Miller	74	72	69	71	286
11=	Rod Funseth	70	70	72	75	287
	Jack Nicklaus	74	70	75	68	287
13	Ray Floyd	70	75	71	72	288
14=	Mark Hayes	74	74	70	71	289
	Don January	71	74	69	75	289
	Mike Morley	71	71	70	77	289
	Andy North	74	72	69	74	289
	JC Snead	73	69	71	76	289
19=	Danny Edwards	73	75	70	72	290
	Randy Glover	72	74	76	68	290
21=	Dave Eichelberger	73	70	74	74	291
	Larry Nelson	75	74	70	72	291
23=	Joe Inman	75	73	74	70	292
	Calvin Peete	76	69	74	73	292
	Gary Player	72	77	73	70	292
26=	Hale Irwin	75	72	75	71	293
	Tom Jenkins	72	74	75	72	293
28=	Lou Graham	75	74	72	73	294
	Barry Jaeckel	74	77	69	74	294
	Grier Jones	76	69	71	78	294
	Wayne Levi	74	73	74	73	294
	Bob E Smith	72	75	74	73	294

Round Leader(s)
R1 Floyd; 65
R2 Floyd; 131
R3 Floyd; 201
Lowest Scores
R2 Floyd, Green; 66
R3 Irwin; 67
R4 Crenshaw; 67

Round Leader(s)
R1 Mike Reid (a, 50); 67
R2 Mahaffey; 138
R3 Mahaffey; 207
Lowest Scores
R2 Mahaffey, Crenshaw; 68
R3 Weiskopf, Watson; 68
R4 Baird; 67

7–10 July	**1976**

BRITISH OPEN

Royal Birkdale GC, Southport, Lancashire, England
7001 yards _PAR 72 (288)_

12–16 August – rain affected	**1976**

US PGA

Congressional CC, Bethesda, Maryland
7054 yards _PAR 70 (280)_

Johnny Miller became the 13th winner of both Opens, 1st achieved by Harry Vardon in 1900. In doing so he pulled away from the exciting, erratic Spaniard – the 19 year-old Severiano Ballesteros – with a blistering last round 66. Over the final 36 holes Miller used his 1 iron no fewer than 21 times. His achievement almost took a back seat to Ballesteros' antics. Flirting with the Birkdale dunes, his scrambling brilliance was shown to the world for the 1st time. This was no ordinary golfer.

Dave Stockton won the PGA for the 2nd time. He repeated his 1970 success by holing an awkward 10 foot putt for par at the last, to avoid a play-off with the 1967 and 1969 Champions. Congressional was at its meanest – denying par to any competitor over the 72 holes.

1	**JOHNNY MILLER**	72	68	73	66	279
	(£7500)					
2=	Seve Ballesteros	69	69	73	74	285
	Jack Nicklaus	74	70	72	69	285
4	Ray Floyd	76	67	73	70	286
5=	Hubert Green	72	70	78	68	288
	Tommy Horton	74	69	72	73	288
	Mark James	76	72	74	66	288
	Tom Kite	70	74	73	71	288
	Christy O'Connor, Jr	69	73	75	71	288
10=	George Burns	75	69	75	70	289
	Peter Butler	74	72	73	70	289
	Vicente Fernandez	79	71	69	70	289
	Norio Suzuki	69	75	75	70	289
14	Brian Barnes	70	73	75	72	290
15=	Eamonn Darcy	78	71	71	71	291
	John Fourie	71	74	75	71	291
17=	Graham Marsh	71	73	72	76	292
	Jack Newton	70	74	76	72	292
	Tom Weiskopf	73	72	76	71	292
	Guy Wolstenholme	76	72	71	73	292
21=	Stewart Ginn	78	72	72	71	293
	David Graham	77	70	75	71	293
	Simon Hobday	79	71	75	68	293
	Chi-San Hsu	81	69	71	72	293
	David Huish	73	74	72	74	293
	Bob Shearer	76	73	75	69	293
	Alan Tapie	74	72	75	72	293
28=	Neil Coles	74	77	70	73	294
	Nick Faldo	78	71	76	69	294
	Gary Player	72	72	79	71	294
	Doug Sanders	77	73	73	71	294

Round Leader(s)
R1 Ballesteros, O'Connor, Suzuki; 69
R2 Ballesteros; 138
R3 Ballesteros; 211
Lowest Scores
R2 Floyd; 67
R3 Fernandez; 69
R4 James, Miller; 66

1	**DAVE STOCKTON**	70	72	69	70	281
	($45000)					
2=	Ray Floyd	72	68	71	71	282
	Don January	70	69	71	72	282
4=	David Graham	70	71	70	72	283
	Jack Nicklaus	71	69	69	74	283
	Jerry Pate	69	73	72	69	283
	John Schlee	72	71	70	70	283
8=	Charles Coody	68	72	67	77	284
	Ben Crenshaw	71	69	74	70	284
	Jerry McGee	68	72	72	72	284
	Gil Morgan	66	68	75	75	284
	Tom Weiskopf	65	74	73	72	284
13=	Tom Kite	66	72	73	75	286
	Gary Player	70	69	72	75	286
15=	Lee Elder	68	74	70	75	287
	Mark Hayes	69	72	73	73	287
	Mike Hill	72	70	73	72	287
	Mike Morley	69	72	72	74	287
	Arnold Palmer	71	76	68	72	287
	JC Snead	74	71	70	72	287
	Tom Watson	70	74	70	73	287
22=	Lou Graham	74	70	70	74	288
	Jerry Heard	72	74	69	73	288
	Dave Hill	76	66	75	71	288
	Joe Inman Jr	72	69	74	73	288
	Gene Littler	71	69	73	75	288
	Don Massengale	71	74	73	70	288
	Leonard Thompson	73	69	72	74	288
29	Joe Porter	72	71	70	76	289
30=	Hubert Green	73	70	73	74	290
	Grier Jones	71	70	75	74	290
	Rik Massengale	71	72	73	74	290
	Bob Zender	69	71	73	77	290

Round Leader(s)
R1 Weiskopf; 65
R2 Morgan; 134
R3 Coody; 207
Lowest Scores
R2 Hill; 66
R3 Coody; 67
R4 Pate; 69

1977
THE MASTERS
7–10 April

Augusta National GC, Augusta, Georgia
6925 yards _PAR 72 (288)_

1977
US OPEN
16–19 June

Southern Hills CC, Tulsa, Oklahoma
6873 yards _PAR 70 (280)_

Reigning British Open Champion, Tom Watson, won his 2nd Major in under a year, when he beat Jack Nicklaus. Nicklaus' sequence of scores in the Majors before this event and following his success in the 1973 PGA, were as follows: 4, 10, 3, 2, W, 7, 3, W, 11, 2, 4 – recording an amazing consistency, and posing a threat at every Championship. Watson's 20 foot birdie putt at 17 sealed his victory.

Hubert Green hung on to a lead he'd had since the 1st day to squeeze out 1975 Champion, Lou Graham, whose record-equalling last 36 holes took him to within one of a tie. Birdie-par-bogey over the last 3 holes, Green just about handled the pressure to stay ahead of Graham, already in the Clubhouse.

1	**TOM WATSON** ($40000)	70	69	70	67	276
2	Jack Nicklaus	72	70	70	66	278
3=	Tom Kite	70	73	70	67	280
	Rik Massengale	70	73	67	70	280
5	Hale Irwin	70	74	70	68	282
6=	David Graham	75	67	73	69	284
	Lou Graham	75	71	69	69	284
8=	Ben Crenshaw	71	69	69	76	285
	Ray Floyd	71	72	71	71	285
	Hubert Green	67	74	72	72	285
	Don January	69	76	69	71	285
	Gene Littler	71	72	73	69	285
	John Schlee	75	73	69	68	285
14=	Billy Casper	72	72	73	69	286
	Jim Colbert	72	71	69	74	286
	Rod Funseth	72	67	74	73	286
	Jerry Pate	70	72	74	70	286
	Tom Weiskopf	73	71	71	71	286
19=	George Archer	74	74	69	70	287
	Andy Bean	74	70	71	72	287
	Danny Edwards	72	74	68	73	287
	Lee Elder	76	68	72	71	287
	Gary Player	71	70	72	74	287
24=	Billy Kratzert	69	71	78	70	288
	Andy North	74	74	71	69	288
	Arnold Palmer	76	71	71	70	288
	Bob Wynn	75	73	70	70	288
28=	Isao Aoki	73	76	70	70	289
	Bruce Lietzke	73	71	72	73	289
	Jerry McGee	73	73	72	71	289

Round Leader(s)
R1   Green; 67
R2   Funseth, Watson; 139
R3   Crenshaw, Watson; 209

Lowest Scores
R2   Funseth, Graham, Bob Shearer (37); 67
R3   Massengale; 67
R4   Nicklaus; 66

1	**HUBERT GREEN** ($45000)	69	67	72	70	278
2	Lou Graham	72	71	68	68	279
3	Tom Weiskopf	71	71	68	71	281
4	Tom Purtzer	69	69	72	72	282
5=	Jay Haas	72	68	71	72	283
	Gary Jacobsen	73	70	67	73	283
7=	Terry Diehl	69	68	73	74	284
	Lyn Lott	73	72	71	67	284
	Tom Watson	74	72	71	67	284
10=	Rod Funseth	69	70	72	74	285
	Al Geiberger	70	71	75	69	285
	Mike McCullough	73	73	69	70	285
	Jack Nicklaus	74	68	71	72	285
	Peter Oosterhuis	71	70	74	70	285
	Gary Player	72	67	71	75	285
16=	Wally Armstrong	71	70	70	75	286
	Joe Inman	70	70	72	74	286
	Steve Melnyk	70	73	70	73	286
19=	Bill Kratzert	73	69	75	70	287
	Bruce Lietzke	74	68	71	74	287
	Jerry McGee	76	69	76	66	287
	Arnold Palmer	70	72	73	72	287
23=	Sam Adams	70	69	76	73	288
	Andy Bean	71	70	68	79	288
	Ron Streck	73	73	71	71	288
26	Gay Brewer	73	72	70	74	289
27=	George Archer	73	72	74	71	290
	Tom Kite	71	73	70	76	290
	John Lister	72	73	68	77	290
	Johnny Miller	71	73	70	76	290
	Mike Morley	70	73	74	73	290
	Don Padgett	70	74	66	80	290
	JC Snead	72	75	68	75	290
	Lee Trevino	74	70	73	73	290

Round Leader(s)
R1   Diehl, Funseth, Green, Grier Jones (35),
      Florentino Molina (39), Larry Nelson (54),
      Purtzer; 69
R2   Green; 136
R3   Green; 208

Lowest Scores
R2   Green, Player, Jim Simons (35); 67
R3   Padgett; 66
R4   McGee; 66

6–9 July

BRITISH OPEN 1977

Turnberry GC, Ayrshire, Scotland
6875 yards PAR 70 (280)

11–14 August

US PGA 1977

Pebble Beach Golf Links, Pebble Beach, California
6804 yards PAR 72 (288)

The Open came to Turnberry, a few miles south of Prestwick and Troon, for the 1st time, and the Ailsa course with its dramatic sea views also saw its fair share of drama on the links. Tom Watson defended his title and became the 5th player to do the Masters-British Open double in the same year – following no lesser lights than Hogan, Palmer, Nicklaus (twice) and Player. His 268 in a wonderfully-stirring two-horse race with (who else but) Nicklaus, beat the Championship record by 8 shots and lowered Jack's, Bobby Nichols' and Ray Floyd's record score for any Major. Watson also set a new low of 130 for 36-holes. Nicklaus was 10 shots clear of US Open Champion, Hubert Green, at the end. Mark Hayes' 63 was a new Championship low and tied with Johnny Miller's and Bruce Crampton's record for any Major.

1	**TOM WATSON**	68	70	65	65	268
	(£10000)					
2	Jack Nicklaus	68	70	65	66	269
3	Hubert Green	72	66	74	67	279
4	Lee Trevino	68	70	72	70	280
5=	George Burns	70	70	72	69	281
	Ben Crenshaw	71	69	66	75	281
7	Arnold Palmer	73	73	67	69	282
8	Ray Floyd	70	73	68	72	283
9=	Mark Hayes	76	63	72	73	284
	Tommy Horton	70	74	65	75	284
	Johnny Miller	69	74	67	74	284
	John Schroeder	66	74	73	71	284
13=	Howard Clark	72	68	72	74	286
	Peter Thomson	74	72	67	73	286
15=	Seve Ballesteros	69	71	73	74	287
	Peter Butler	71	68	75	73	287
	Bobby Cole	72	71	71	73	287
	Guy Hunt	73	71	71	72	287
	Graham Marsh	73	69	71	74	287
	Jerry Pate	74	70	70	73	287
	Bob Shearer	72	69	72	74	287
22=	Peter Dawson	74	68	73	73	288
	John Fourie	74	69	70	75	288
	Gary Player	71	74	74	69	288
	Tom Weiskopf	74	71	71	72	288
26=	Gaylord Burrows	69	72	68	80	289
	Martin Foster	67	74	75	73	289
	Angel Gallardo	78	65	72	74	289
	David Ingram	73	74	70	72	289
	Roger Maltbie	71	66	72	80	289
	Rik Massengale	73	71	74	71	289
	John O'Leary	74	73	68	74	289
	Norio Suzuki	74	71	69	75	289

Round Leader(s)   **Lowest Scores**
R1 Schroeder; 66   R2 Hayes; 63
R2 Maltbie; 137   R3 Horton; 65
R3 Nicklaus, Watson; 203   R4 Watson; 65

In the 1st-ever sudden-death playoff employed in any Major, Lanny Wadkins won his only Major when he beat 1961 US Open Champion, Gene Littler. The tie was somewhat presented to Wadkins, who, 5 shots adrift at the turn, saw Littler bogey 5 of the next 6 holes, and Jack Nicklaus, who was then tying with Littler, drop a shot at the 17th. Wadkins then drew level with Littler by shooting the only birdie of his round at the last.

1	**LANNY WADKINS***	69	71	72	70	282
	($45000)					
2	Gene Littler	67	69	70	76	282
3	Jack Nicklaus	69	71	70	73	283
4	Charles Coody	70	71	70	73	284
5	Jerry Pate	73	70	69	73	285
6=	Al Geiberger	71	70	73	72	286
	Lou Graham	71	73	71	71	286
	Don January	75	69	70	72	286
	Jerry McGee	68	70	77	71	286
	Tom Watson	68	73	71	74	286
11=	Joe Inman Jr	72	69	73	73	287
	Johnny Miller	70	74	73	70	287
13=	Tom Kite	73	73	70	72	288
	Lee Trevino	71	73	71	73	288
15=	George Cadle	69	73	70	77	289
	Bruce Lietzke	74	70	74	71	289
	Gil Morgan	74	68	70	77	289
	Leonard Thompson	72	73	69	75	289
19=	George Archer	70	73	76	72	291
	George Burns	71	76	70	74	291
	Mark Hayes	68	75	74	74	291
	Arnold Palmer	72	73	73	73	291
	John Schroeder	73	76	68	74	291
	JC Snead	76	71	72	72	291
25=	Miller Barber	77	68	69	78	292
	Grier Jones	72	74	72	74	292
	Bill Kratzert	71	76	75	70	292
	Lyn Lott	76	75	67	74	292
	Bob Murphy	72	72	72	76	292
	Jim Simons	74	74	69	75	292

* Lanny Wadkins beat Gene Littler at 3rd extra hole in Sudden Death Play-off

Round Leader(s)
R1 Littler; 67
R2 Littler; 136
R3 Littler; 206
Lowest Scores
R2 Morgan, Barber; 68
R3 Danny Edwards (36), Lott; 67
R4 Kratzert, Miller, Wadkins; 70

1978
THE MASTERS
6–9 April

Augusta National GC, Augusta, Georgia
6925 yards _PAR 72 (288)_

1978
US OPEN
15–18 June

Cherry Hills CC, Denver, Colorado
7083 yards _PAR 71 (284)_

Gary Player, aged 42, won his 9th and last Major Championship at the Masters, thus drawing level with Ben Hogan to tie 3rd on the all-time list. His 1st Major was back in 1959 when he lifted the British Open title at Muirfield, and his span of wins matched that of JH Taylor (1894–1913). 7 birdies over the last 10 holes set up his 3rd Masters win – an improbable result when Hubert Green was defending a 7 shot lead after R3 and went round the last 18 holes in par. Tommy Nakajima of Japan shot 13 at the 13th – unlucky, perhaps, but he missed the cut.

No-one beat par at Cherry Hills. Andy North went to 4 under par after 7 holes on the last day – a lead of 5 – with the benefit of 2 birdies, but the next few holes saw some eccentric scoring from him: bogey, bogey, bogey, birdie, birdie, bogey, double-bogey! Then at the 15th North's lead was cut to one when Dave Stockton birdied, but his bogey at the 18th meant North only needed the same to win. He duly did.

1	**GARY PLAYER**	72	72	69	64	277
	($45000)					
2=	Rod Funseth	73	66	70	69	278
	Hubert Green	72	69	65	72	278
	Tom Watson	73	68	68	69	278
5=	Wally Armstrong	72	70	70	68	280
	Billy Kratzert	70	74	67	69	280
7	Jack Nicklaus	72	73	69	67	281
8	Hale Irwin	73	67	71	71	282
9=	David Graham	75	69	67	72	283
	Joe Inman, Jr	69	73	72	69	283
11=	Don January	72	70	72	70	284
	Jerry McGee	71	73	71	69	284
	Tom Weiskopf	72	71	70	71	284
14=	Peter Oosterhuis	74	70	70	71	285
	Lee Trevino	70	69	72	74	285
16=	Ray Floyd	76	71	71	68	286
	Lindy Miller (a)	74	71	70	71	286
18=	Seve Ballesteros	74	71	68	74	287
	Tom Kite	71	74	71	71	287
	Gil Morgan	73	73	70	71	287
	Jerry Pate	72	71	72	72	287
	Ed Sneed	74	70	70	73	287
	Lanny Wadkins	74	70	73	70	287
24=	Miller Barber	75	67	73	73	288
	Andy Bean	76	68	73	71	288
	Gene Littler	72	68	70	78	288
	Leonard Thompson	72	69	75	72	288
28	Bobby Cole	77	70	70	72	289
29=	Gay Brewer	73	71	69	77	290
	Mac McLendon	72	72	72	74	290
	Bill Rogers	76	70	68	76	290

1	**ANDY NORTH**	70	70	71	74	285
	(£45000)					
2=	JC Snead	70	72	72	72	286
	Dave Stockton	71	73	70	72	286
4=	Hale Irwin	69	74	75	70	288
	Tom Weiskopf	77	73	70	68	288
6=	Andy Bean	72	72	71	74	289
	Bill Kratzert	72	74	70	73	289
	Johnny Miller	78	69	68	74	289
	Jack Nicklaus	73	69	74	73	289
	Gary Player	71	71	70	77	289
	Tom Watson	74	75	70	70	289
12=	Ray Floyd	75	70	76	70	291
	Joe Inman	72	72	74	73	291
	Mike McCullough	75	75	73	68	291
	Lee Trevino	72	71	75	73	291
16=	Seve Ballesteros	75	69	71	77	292
	Artie McNickle	74	75	70	73	292
	Jerry Pate	73	72	74	73	292
	Bob Shearer	78	72	71	71	292
20=	Wally Armstrong	73	73	74	73	293
	Phil Hancock	71	73	75	74	293
	Tom Kite	73	73	70	77	293
	Bruce Lietzke	72	73	72	76	293
24=	Dale Douglass	74	75	74	72	295
	Tom Purtzer	75	72	72	76	295
	Victor Regalado	74	72	73	76	295
27=	Jerry McGee	74	76	71	75	296
	Pat McGowan	74	73	72	77	296
	Peter Oosterhuis	72	72	78	74	296
30=	Billy Casper	71	76	73	77	297
	Bobby Clampett (a)	70	73	80	84	297
	Charles Coody	74	76	76	71	297
	Rod Curl	78	72	74	73	297
	Lee Elder	76	73	73	75	297

Round Leader(s)
R1   John Schlee (44); 68
R2   Funseth, Trevino; 139
R3   Green; 206
Lowest Scores
R2   Funseth; 66
R3   Green; 65
R4   Player; 64

Round Leader(s)
R1   Irwin; 69
R2   North; 140
R3   North; 211
Lowest Scores
R2   Ballesteros, Nicklaus, Miller, Bill Rogers (44); 69
R3   Miller, 68
R4   McCullough, Weiskopf; 68

12–15 July	**1978**
BRITISH OPEN	
Royal & Ancient GC, St Andrews, Fife, Scotland	
6933 yards <u>*PAR 72 (288)*</u>	

In a Championship of 'might-have-beens' it was totally fitting that Jack Nicklaus should win what was to be his last Open Championship at the home of golf. It was his 15th Major and his 1st for 3 years – and it gave him a record that may never be beaten. He now became the only player to win each of the Grand Slam titles 3 times or more. New Zealander Simon Owen, building on his R3 67, took the lead when he chipped in at the 15th. At this point he was playing the best golf of the round, and an upset seemed likely. However, he dropped 2 shots over the last 3 holes to tie 2nd. After his disaster in the Masters, Nakajima effectively put himself out of contention when he took 9 at the 17th (Road Hole) in R3.

I	**JACK NICKLAUS**	71	72	69	69	281
	(£12500)					
2=	Ben Crenshaw	70	69	73	71	283
	Ray Floyd	69	75	71	68	283
	Tom Kite	72	69	72	70	283
	Simon Owen	70	75	67	71	283
6	Peter Oosterhuis	72	70	69	73	284
7=	Isao Aoki	68	71	73	73	285
	Nick Faldo	71	72	70	72	285
	John Schroeder	74	69	70	72	285
	Bob Shearer	71	69	74	71	285
11=	Michael Cahill	71	72	75	68	286
	Dale Hayes	74	70	71	71	286
	Orville Moody	73	69	74	70	286
14=	Mark Hayes	70	75	75	67	287
	Jumbo Ozaki	72	69	75	71	287
	Tom Watson	73	68	70	76	287
17=	Seve Ballesteros	69	70	76	73	288
	Bob Byman	72	69	74	73	288
	Guy Hunt	71	73	71	73	288
	Tommy Nakajima	70	71	76	71	288
	Tom Weiskopf	69	72	72	75	288
22=	Bernard Gallacher	72	71	76	70	289
	Nick Job	73	75	68	73	289
24=	Antonio Garrido	73	71	76	70	290
	Hale Irwin	75	71	76	78	290
	Carl Mason	70	74	72	74	290
	Jack Newton	69	76	71	74	290
	Peter Thomson	72	70	72	76	290
29=	Tienie Britz	73	74	72	72	291
	Hubert Green	78	70	67	76	291
	John Morgan	74	68	77	72	291
	Greg Norman	72	73	74	72	291
	Lee Trevino	75	72	73	71	291

Round Leader(s)   **Lowest Scores**

R1   Aoki; 68   R2   Morgan, Watson; 68
R2   Aoki, Crenshaw; 139   R3   Owen; 67
R3   Aoki, Crenshaw, Nicklaus,   R4   Hayes; 67
     Oosterhuis; 212

3–6 August	**1978**
US PGA	
Oakmont CC, Oakmont, Pennsylvania	
6989 yards <u>*PAR 72 (284)*</u>	

Trailing Tom Watson by 7 going into the last round, John Mahaffey shot a 66 to tie him and Jerry Pate. He then birdied the 2nd extra hole to win the 1st 3-way sudden-death play-off and his only Majors title. This was the 1st strokeplay PGA hosted by Oakmont CC, but 2 Championships were held there in matchplay days – and 5 US Opens to that date. This made Oakmont the most-used venue for Majors in the US after Augusta National.

I	**JOHN MAHAFFEY***	75	67	68	66	276
	($50000)					
2=	Jerry Pate	72	70	66	68	276
	Tom Watson	67	69	67	73	276
4=	Gil Morgan	76	71	66	67	280
	Tom Weiskopf	73	67	69	71	280
6	Craig Stadler	70	74	67	71	282
7=	Andy Bean	72	72	70	70	284
	Graham Marsh	72	74	68	70	284
	Lee Trevino	69	73	70	74	284
10	Fuzzy Zoeller	75	69	73	68	285
11	Joe Inman Jr	72	68	69	77	286
12=	Hale Irwin	73	71	73	70	287
	Bill Kratzert	70	77	73	67	287
	Larry Nelson	76	71	70	70	287
	John Schroeder	76	69	70	72	287
16=	Ben Crenshaw	69	71	75	73	288
	Phil Hancock	70	73	70	75	288
	Grier Jones	70	73	71	74	288
19=	Wally Armstrong	71	73	75	70	289
	George Burns	79	68	70	72	289
	Bob Gilder	74	71	70	74	289
	Don January	73	72	75	69	289
	Bobby Nichols	75	67	73	74	289
	Dave Stockton	68	75	74	72	289
	Kermit Zarley	75	71	67	76	289
26=	George Cadle	74	74	74	68	290
	Rod Curl	76	72	73	70	290
	Hubert Green	71	71	74	74	290
	Peter Oosterhuis	73	72	72	73	290
	Gary Player	76	72	71	71	290
	Greg Powers	75	70	75	70	290
	Bob Shearer	73	73	71	73	290
	Bob Zender	73	69	74	74	290

* John Mahaffey beat Jerry Pate and Tom Watson at the
2nd extra hole in the Sudden Death Play-off

Round Leader(s)   **Lowest Scores**

R1   Watson; 67   R2   George Archer (61), Mahaffey,
R2   Watson; 136   Nichols, Weiskopf; 67
R3   Watson; 203   R3   Morgan, Pate; 66
                  R4   Mahaffey; 66

1979
THE MASTERS
12–15 April

Augusta National GC, Augusta, Georgia
6925 yards _PAR 72 (288)_

Frank Urban (Fuzzy) Zoeller wrote himself into the record books with his 1st Major, by winning the 1st-ever sudden-death play-off in the Masters. He also collected the 1st $50000 winner's prize. Ed Sneed saw fame and glory dissipate after squandering a 5 stroke lead at the start of the day. After the 15th he was still 3 clear, but 3 bogeys necessitated a play-off. For Tom Watson, after the 1978 PGA, it was his 2nd successive 3-way sudden-death play-off - but he was no luckier at Augusta. Zoeller's birdie at the 2nd extra hole saw to that.

1	**FUZZY ZOELLER***	70	71	69	70	280
	($50000)					
2=	Ed Sneed	68	67	69	76	280
	Tom Watson	68	71	70	71	280
4	Jack Nicklaus	69	71	72	69	281
5	Tom Kite	71	72	68	72	283
6	Bruce Lietzke	67	75	68	74	284
7=	Craig Stadler	69	66	74	76	285
	Leonard Thompson	68	70	73	74	285
	Lanny Wadkins	73	69	70	73	285
10=	Hubert Green	74	69	72	71	286
	Gene Littler	74	71	69	72	286
12=	Seve Ballesteros	72	68	73	74	287
	Miller Barber	75	64	72	76	287
	Jack Newton	70	72	69	76	287
	Andy North	72	72	74	69	287
	Lee Trevino	73	71	70	73	287
17=	Lee Elder	73	70	74	71	288
	Ray Floyd	70	68	73	77	288
	Billy Kratzert	73	68	71	76	288
	Artie McNickle	71	72	74	71	288
	Gary Player	71	72	74	71	288
22	JC Snead	73	71	72	73	289
23=	Bobby Clampett	73	71	73	73	290
	Lou Graham	69	71	76	74	290
	Joe Inman, Jr	68	71	76	75	290
	Hale Irwin	72	70	74	74	290
	Jim Simons	72	70	75	73	290
28=	Tommy Aaron	72	73	76	70	291
	Andy Bean	69	74	74	74	291
	Graham Marsh	71	72	73	75	291

*Fuzzy Zoeller beat Ed Sneed and Tom Watson at the 2nd extra hole of the Sudden-death Play-off

Round Leader(s)
R1   Lietzke; 67
R2   Sneed, Stadler; 135
R3   Sneed; 204
Lowest Scores
R2   Barber; 64
R3   Kite, Lietzke; 68
R4   Nicklaus, North; 69

1979
US OPEN
14–17 June

Inverness GC, Toledo, Ohio
6982 yards _PAR 71 (284)_

Par over the tough 72 holes at Inverness was only achieved by Hale Irwin, giving him another Open title to add to that of 1974. Leading Tom Weiskopf by 3 overnight, he had extended his advantage to 5 by the 16th. Then the wheels almost came off. At the 17th, bunkered and 2-putting, he carded a double-bogey 6, then found sand again at the last to limp home just 2 ahead.

1	**HALE IRWIN**	74	68	67	75	284
	($50000)					
2=	Jerry Pate	71	74	69	72	286
	Gary Player	73	73	72	68	286
4=	Larry Nelson	71	68	76	73	288
	Bill Rogers	71	72	73	72	288
	Tom Weiskopf	71	74	67	76	288
7	David Graham	73	73	70	73	289
8	Tom Purtzer	70	69	75	76	290
9=	Keith Fergus	70	77	72	72	291
	Jack Nicklaus	74	77	72	68	291
11=	Ben Crenshaw	75	71	72	75	293
	Lee Elder	74	72	69	78	293
	Andy North	77	74	68	74	293
	Calvin Peete	72	75	71	75	293
	Ed Sneed	72	73	75	73	293
16=	Bob Gilder	77	70	69	78	294
	Graham Marsh	77	71	72	74	294
	Jim Simons	74	74	78	68	294
19=	Al Geiberger	74	74	69	78	295
	Lee Trevino	77	73	73	72	295
	Lanny Wadkins	73	74	71	77	295
	Bobby Walzel	74	72	71	78	295
	DA Weibring	74	76	71	74	295
24	Hubert Green	74	77	73	72	296
25=	Andy Bean	70	76	71	80	297
	Lou Graham	70	75	77	75	297
	Wayne Levi	77	73	75	72	297
	Bob Murphy	72	79	69	77	297
	Bobby Nichols	76	75	71	75	297
	Mike Reid	74	75	74	74	297
	Bob E Smith	77	71	69	80	297

Round Leader(s)
R1   Bean, Fergus, Graham, Purtzer; 70
R2   Nelson, Purtzer; 139
R3   Irwin; 209
Lowest Scores
R2   Irwin, Nelson; 68
R3   Irwin, Weiskopf; 67
R4   Nicklaus, Player, Simons; 68

18–21 July
BRITISH OPEN 1979
Royal Lytham and St Anne's GC, Lancashire, England
6822 yards _PAR 71 (284)_

2–5 August
US PGA 1979
Oakland Hills CC, Birmingham, Michigan
7014 yards _PAR 70 (280)_

Ballesteros' victory at Lytham will not be remembered for the 1st Open Championship to be won by a continental European since Arnaud Massy in 1907, but for the manner in which it was won. A new star in the ascendant, the flamboyant Spaniard was aggressive and headstrong, foolish and cavalier in his approach to the game – and he announced himself to the world displaying all those characteristics in just 18 holes on Saturday 21 July 1979. Bashing his way from rough to sand to car park to green with scant regard for the fairway - only replacing brute strength with sublime touch when he neared his destination – Seve broke the hearts of Crenshaw and Nicklaus. As much as icons like Ouimet, Jones, Hogan, Palmer or Nicklaus, he was changing the face of golf once again. European golf was stirring.

David Graham became the 2nd Australian, after Jim Ferrier in 1947, to take the PGA Championship. With play-offs coming thick and fast in recent Majors, this PGA was no exception, but while Ben Crenshaw played beautifully for his R4 67, Graham's 65 should have been a 63 (he double-bogeyed the last) and no play-off would have been necessary. Graham then sank 2 very-missable putts before birdying the 3rd extra hole for victory.

1	**SEVE BALLESTEROS**	73	65	75	70	283
	(£15000)					
2=	Ben Crenshaw	72	71	72	71	286
	Jack Nicklaus	72	69	73	72	286
4	Mark James	76	69	69	73	287
5	Rodger Davis	75	70	70	73	288
6	Hale Irwin	68	68	75	78	289
7=	Isao Aoki	70	74	72	75	291
	Bob Byman	73	70	72	76	291
	Graham Marsh	74	68	75	74	291
10=	Bob Charles	78	72	70	72	292
	Greg Norman	73	71	72	76	292
	Jumbo Ozaki	75	69	75	73	292
13=	Wally Armstrong	74	74	73	72	293
	Terry Gale	71	74	75	73	293
	John O'Leary	73	73	74	73	293
	Simon Owen	75	76	74	68	293
17=	Peter McEvoy (a)	71	74	72	77	294
	Lee Trevino	71	73	74	76	294
19=	Ken Brown	72	71	75	77	295
	Nick Faldo	74	74	78	69	295
	Sandy Lyle	74	76	75	70	295
	Orville Moody	71	74	76	74	295
	Gary Player	77	74	69	75	295
24=	Tony Jacklin	73	74	76	73	296
	Tohru Nakamura	77	75	67	77	296
26=	Jerry Pate	69	74	76	78	297
	Ed Sneed	76	75	70	76	297
	Peter Thomson	76	75	72	74	297
	Tom Watson	72	68	76	81	297
30=	Mark Hayes	75	75	77	71	298
	Simon Hobday	75	77	71	75	298
	Tom Kite	73	74	77	74	298
	Bill Longmuir	65	74	77	82	298
	Armando Saavedra	76	76	73	73	298
	Bobby Verwey	75	77	74	72	298

Round Leader(s)

			Lowest Scores	
R1	Longmuir; 65		R2	Ballesteros; 65
R2	Irwin; 136		R3	Nakamura; 67
R3	Irwin; 211		R4	Owen; 68

1	**DAVID GRAHAM***	69	68	70	65	272
	($60000)					
2	Ben Crenshaw	69	67	69	67	272
3	Rex Caldwell	67	70	66	71	274
4	Ron Streck	68	71	69	68	276
5=	Gibby Gilbert	69	72	68	69	278
	Jerry Pate	69	69	69	71	278
7=	Jay Haas	68	69	73	69	279
	Don January	69	70	71	69	279
	Howard Twitty	70	73	69	67	279
10=	Lou Graham	69	74	68	69	280
	Gary Koch	71	71	71	67	280
12=	Andy Bean	76	69	68	68	281
	Jerry McGee	73	69	71	68	281
	Jack Renner	71	74	66	70	281
	Tom Watson	66	72	69	74	281
16=	Bob Gilder	73	71	68	70	282
	Hubert Green	69	70	72	71	282
	Bruce Lietzke	69	69	71	73	282
	Gene Littler	71	71	67	73	282
	Graham Marsh	69	70	71	72	282
21=	Bob Byman	73	72	69	69	283
	John Schroeder	72	72	70	69	283
23=	Frank Conner	70	73	69	72	284
	Rod Funseth	70	69	76	69	284
	Peter Jacobsen	70	74	67	73	284
	Gary Player	73	70	70	71	284
	Alan Tapie	73	65	76	70	284
28=	Miller Barber	73	72	69	71	285
	George Burns	71	74	67	73	285
	Mark McCumber	75	68	70	72	285
	Artie McNickle	69	70	72	74	285
	Gil Morgan	72	73	70	70	285
	Larry Nelson	70	75	70	70	285
	Ed Sneed	77	67	70	71	285

*David Graham beat Ben Crenshaw at the 3rd extra hole in the Sudden Death Play-off

Round Leader(s)

			Lowest Scores	
R1	Watson; 66		R2	Tapie; 65
R2	Crenshaw; 136		R3	Caldwell, Renner; 66
R3	Caldwell; 203		R4	D Graham; 65

1980
THE MASTERS
10–13 April

Augusta National GC, Augusta, Georgia
6925 yards _PAR 72 (288)_

1980
US OPEN
12–15 June

Baltusrol GC, Springfield, New Jersey
7076 yards _PAR 70 (280)_

Seve Ballesteros led the Masters by 10 strokes going into the back 9 on the last day. Typically, the flawed genius made some unspeakable errors coming home, so that in the end his lead was cut to 4. If he had parred in from there, the Masters low total was his for the taking. But that was not the Ballesteros way. As it was, Seve's 2nd Major was his 1st in the US and, after leading wire-to-wire, he became, at 23, the youngest winner of the Masters.

1980 was to be Jack Nicklaus' last big year. Tom Watson's year-round play on the US Tour had been superior to Jack's for the last 3 years, but now turning 40, he honed himself pre-season for one last assault on the Majors. After disappointing in the Masters, he won the Open for the 4th time and joined the ranks of Willie Anderson, Bobby Jones and Ben Hogan, setting a new low total in the process. This included a 63, which tied Johnny Miller (1973) and Tom Weiskopf (in R1) on the Open record round score.

1	**SEVE BALLESTEROS**	66	69	68	72	275
2=	Gibby Gilbert	70	74	68	67	279
	Jack Newton	68	74	69	68	279
4	Hubert Green	68	74	71	67	280
5	David Graham	66	73	72	70	281
6=	Ben Crenshaw	76	70	68	69	283
	Ed Fiori	71	70	69	73	283
	Tom Kite	69	71	74	69	283
	Larry Nelson	69	72	73	69	283
	Jerry Pate	72	68	76	67	283
	Gary Player	71	71	71	70	283
12=	Andy Bean	74	72	68	70	284
	Tom Watson	73	69	71	71	284
14=	Jim Colbert	72	70	70	73	285
	Jack Renner	72	70	72	71	285
	JC Snead	73	69	69	74	285
17=	Ray Floyd	75	70	74	67	286
	Jay Haas	72	74	70	70	286
19=	Billy Kratzert	73	69	72	73	287
	Gil Morgan	74	71	75	67	287
	Calvin Peete	73	71	76	67	287
	Jim Simons	70	70	72	75	287
	Fuzzy Zoeller	72	70	70	75	287
24=	Andy North	70	72	69	77	288
	Arnold Palmer	73	73	73	69	288
26=	Keith Fergus	72	71	72	74	289
	Lou Graham	71	74	71	73	289
	Jay Sigel (a)	71	71	73	74	289
	Craig Stadler	74	70	72	73	289
	Dave Stockton	74	70	76	69	289
	Lee Trevino	74	71	70	74	289

Round Leader(s)
R1 Ballesteros, Graham, Jeff Mitchell (41); 66
R2 Ballesteros; 135
R3 Ballesteros; 203
Lowest Scores
R2 Rex Caldwell (38); 66
R3 Ballesteros, Bean, Crenshaw, Gilbert; 68
R4 Floyd, Gilbert, Green, Morgan, Pate, Peete; 67

1	**JACK NICKLAUS**	63	71	70	68	272
	($55000)					
2	Isao Aoki	68	68	68	70	274
3=	Keith Fergus	66	70	70	70	276
	Lon Hinkle	66	70	69	71	276
	Tom Watson	71	68	67	70	276
6=	Mark Hayes	66	71	69	74	280
	Mike Reid	69	67	75	69	280
8=	Hale Irwin	70	70	73	69	282
	Mike Morley	73	68	69	72	282
	Andy North	68	75	72	67	282
	Ed Sneed	72	70	70	70	282
12=	Bruce Devlin	71	70	70	72	283
	Joe Hager	72	70	71	70	283
	Lee Trevino	68	72	69	74	283
	Bobby Wadkins	72	71	68	72	283
16=	Joe Inman	74	69	69	72	284
	Pat McGowan	69	69	73	73	284
	Gil Morgan	73	70	70	71	284
	Bill Rogers	69	72	70	73	284
	Craig Stadler	73	67	69	75	284
	Curtis Strange	69	74	71	70	284
22=	Gary Hallberg (a)	74	68	70	73	285
	Peter Jacobsen	70	69	72	74	285
	Jim Simons	70	72	71	72	285
	JC Snead	69	71	73	72	285
26=	Jay Haas	67	74	70	75	286
	Mark Lye	68	72	77	69	286
28=	George Burns	75	69	73	70	287
	David Edwards	73	68	72	74	287
	John Mahaffey	72	73	69	73	287
	Calvin Peete	67	76	74	70	287

Round Leader(s)
R1 Nicklaus; 63
R2 Nicklaus; 134
R3 Aoki, Nicklaus; 204
Lowest Scores
R2 Reid, Stadler; 67
R3 Hubert Green (32); 65
R4 North; 67

17–20 July	**1980**	7–10 August					**1980**

BRITISH OPEN

Honourable Company, Muirfield, Angus, Scotland
6806 yards _PAR 71 (284)_

US PGA

Oak Hill CC, Rochester, New York
6964 yards _PAR 70 (280)_

Tom Watson collected his 3rd Open on Scottish links (all different) ahead of a resurgent Lee Trevino, and the man at that time who was 'probably the best player never to win a Major', Ben Crenshaw. 8 Americans, an Englishman, a Scotsman and an Australian made up the Top 10 and tie. Watson's 4th Major rubber-stamped the contention that he was the best player in the world in 1980.

Gene Sarazen in 1922 was the only man in history to win both American National Championships – the US Open and the US PGA – in the same season. 58 years later the feat was eventually emulated by Jack Nicklaus – adding another record, or share of a record, to his name. He stretched his lead in the all-time list with this 1980 double to 17 Majors, and tied Walter Hagen's redoubtable PGA record of 5 wins.

1	**TOM WATSON**	68	70	64	69	271
	(£25000)					

2	Lee Trevino	68	67	71	69	275
3	Ben Crenshaw	70	70	68	69	277
4=	Carl Mason	72	69	70	69	280
	Jack Nicklaus	73	67	71	69	280
6=	Andy Bean	71	69	70	72	282
	Ken Brown	70	68	68	76	282
	Hubert Green	77	69	64	72	282
	Craig Stadler	72	70	69	71	282
10=	Gil Morgan	70	70	71	72	283
	Jack Newton	69	71	73	70	283
12=	Isao Aoki	74	74	63	73	284
	Nick Faldo	69	74	71	70	284
	Sandy Lyle	70	71	70	73	284
	Larry Nelson	72	70	71	71	284
16=	John Bland	73	70	70	73	285
	Jerry Pate	71	67	74	73	285
	Tom Weiskopf	72	72	71	70	285
19=	Seve Ballesteros	72	68	72	74	286
	Bruce Lietzke	74	69	73	70	286
	Bill Rogers	76	73	68	69	286
	Norio Suzuki	74	68	72	72	286
23=	Gary Cullen	72	72	69	74	287
	Bill McColl	75	73	68	71	287
	Mark McNulty	71	73	72	71	287
	Peter Oosterhuis	72	71	75	69	287
27=	Tom Kite	72	72	74	70	288
	Nick Price	72	71	71	74	288
29=	Hugh Baiocchi	76	67	69	77	289
	Neil Coles	75	69	69	76	289
	David Graham	73	71	68	77	289

Round Leader(s)
R1 Trevino, Watson; 68
R2 Trevino; 135
R3 Watson; 202
Lowest Scores
R2 Horacio Carbonetti (Cut); 64
R3 Aoki; 63
R4 Crenshaw, Mason, Nicklaus, Oosterhuis,
Rogers, Trevino, Watson; 69

1	**JACK NICKLAUS**	70	69	66	69	274
	($60000)					

2	Andy Bean	72	71	68	70	281
3=	Lon Hinckle	70	69	69	75	283
	Gil Morgan	68	70	73	72	283
5=	Curtis Strange	68	72	72	72	284
	Howard Twitty	68	74	71	71	284
7	Lee Trevino	74	71	69	69	285
8=	Bill Rogers	71	71	72	72	286
	Bobby Walzel	68	76	71	71	286
10=	Terry Diehl	72	72	68	76	288
	Peter Jacobsen	71	73	74	70	288
	Jerry Pate	72	73	70	73	288
	Tom Watson	75	74	72	67	288
	Tom Weiskopf	71	73	72	72	288
15=	John Mahaffey	71	77	69	72	289
	Andy North	72	70	73	74	289
17=	George Archer	70	73	75	72	290
	Ray Floyd	70	76	71	73	290
	Joe Inman Jr	72	71	75	72	290
20=	Rex Caldwell	73	70	73	75	291
	Rod Curl	74	71	75	71	291
	Tom Kite	73	70	76	72	291
	Bob Murphy	68	80	72	71	291
	Jack Newton	72	73	73	73	291
	Alan Tapie	74	75	69	73	291
26=	Lee Elder	70	75	74	73	292
	David Graham	69	75	73	75	292
	Gary Player	72	74	71	75	292
	Leonard Thompson	71	75	73	73	292
30=	Jim Colbert	73	75	77	68	293
	Bruce Devlin	76	73	71	73	293
	Bob Eastwood	72	73	73	75	293
	David Edwards	73	76	73	71	293
	Hale Irwin	69	76	74	74	293
	Bruce Lietzke	71	75	74	73	293
	Artie McNickle	71	71	76	75	293
	Scott Simpson	74	74	74	71	293
	Mike Sullivan	71	74	76	72	293
	Doug Tewell	73	71	75	74	293
	Lanny Wadkins	76	72	72	73	293

Round Leader(s)
R1 Craig Stadler (55); 67
R2 Morgan; 138
R3 Nicklaus; 205

Lowest Scores
R2 Ed Sneed (55); 66
R3 Nicklaus; 66
R4 Watson; 67

1981
9–12 April
THE MASTERS
Augusta National GC, Augusta, Georgia
6925 yards PAR 72 (288)

1981
18–21 June
US OPEN
Merion GC, Ardmore, Pennsylvania
6544 yards PAR 70 (280)

Tom Watson's contemporary superiority over Jack Nicklaus continued into 1981, when he won the 1st Major of the year at Augusta. A R3 75 undid Jack, who held a 4-shot lead after 36 holes, and he was joined in 2nd place by Johnny Miller. This win was Watson's 2nd Green Jacket and 5th Major overall.

David Graham added the US Open to the PGA Championship he picked up in 1979. He became the 1st Australian to win the Open and the 1st overseas player since Tony Jacklin in 1970. He turned a 3-stroke deficit going into R4 into a victory by the same margin, thanks to a superb 67, and turned the tables on George Burns who had led from R2.

1	**TOM WATSON** ($60000)	71	68	70	71	280
2=	Johnny Miller	69	72	73	68	282
	Jack Nicklaus	70	65	75	72	282
4	Greg Norman	69	70	72	72	283
5=	Tom Kite	74	72	70	68	284
	Jerry Pate	71	72	71	70	284
7	David Graham	70	70	74	71	285
8=	Ben Crenshaw	71	72	70	73	286
	Ray Floyd	75	71	71	69	286
	John Mahaffey	72	71	69	74	286
11=	George Archer	74	70	72	71	287
	Hubert Green	70	70	74	73	287
	Peter Jacobsen	71	70	72	74	287
	Bruce Lietzke	72	67	73	75	287
15=	Gay Brewer	75	68	71	74	288
	Bob Gilder	72	75	69	72	288
	Gary Player	73	73	71	71	288
	Jim Simons	70	75	71	72	288
19=	Don Pooley	71	75	72	71	289
	Curtis Strange	69	79	70	71	289
21=	John Cook	70	71	72	77	290
	Gil Morgan	74	73	70	73	290
	Calvin Peete	75	70	71	74	290
	Lanny Wadkins	72	71	71	76	290
25=	Jim Colbert	73	68	74	76	291
	Hale Irwin	73	74	70	74	291
	Wayne Levi	72	71	73	75	291
28=	Gibby Gilbert	71	71	76	74	292
	Lon Hinkle	69	70	74	79	292
	Sandy Lyle	73	70	76	73	292

Round Leader(s)
R1 Hinckle, Miller, Norman, Strange; 69
R2 Nicklaus; 135
R3 Watson; 209
Lowest Scores
R2 Nicklaus; 65
R3 Gilder, Mahaffey; 69
R4 Kite, Miller; 68

1	**DAVID GRAHAM** ($55000)	68	68	70	67	273
2=	George Burns	69	66	68	73	276
	Bill Rogers	70	68	69	69	276
4=	John Cook	68	70	71	70	279
	John Schroeder	71	68	69	71	279
6=	Frank Conner	71	72	69	68	280
	Lon Hinkle	69	71	70	70	280
	Jack Nicklaus	69	68	71	72	280
	Sammy Rachels	70	71	69	70	280
	Chi Chi Rodriguez	68	73	67	72	280
11=	Isao Aoki	72	71	71	67	281
	Ben Crenshaw	70	75	64	72	281
	Jim Thorpe	66	73	70	72	281
14=	Mark Hayes	71	70	72	69	282
	Calvin Peete	73	72	67	70	282
	Lanny Wadkins	71	68	72	71	282
17=	Bruce Lietzke	70	71	71	71	283
	Jack Renner	68	71	72	72	283
	Curtis Strange	71	69	72	71	283
20=	Tom Kite	73	74	67	70	284
	Larry Nelson	70	73	69	72	284
	Mike Reid	71	72	69	72	284
23=	Johnny Miller	69	71	73	72	285
	Scott Simpson	72	67	71	75	285
	Tom Watson	70	69	73	73	285
26=	Jim Colbert	71	69	77	69	286
	Bruce Devlin	73	71	70	72	286
	Rik Massengale	70	75	70	71	286
	Jerry Pate	70	69	72	75	286
	Gary Player	72	72	71	71	286
	Craig Stadler	71	76	68	71	286
	Tom Valentine	69	68	72	77	286

Round Leader(s)
R1 Thorpe; 66
R2 Burns; 135
R3 Burns; 203
Lowest Scores
R2 Burns; 66
R3 Crenshaw; 64
R4 Aoki, Graham; 67

16–19 July

BRITISH OPEN 1981

Royal St George's, Sandwich, Kent, England
6857 yards _PAR 70 (280)_

6–9 August

US PGA 1981

Atlanta Athletic Club, Duluth, Georgia
7070 yards _PAR 70 (280)_

The Open returned to Sandwich after a break of 32 years. Bill Rogers, who had finished strongly to tie for 2nd in the US Open the previous month, played the best golf of his life to win on a links course at his 1st attempt – as had Hogan, Lema and Watson before him. His strength lay in the middle rounds, enabling him to take a 5-shot lead into R4, and comfortably hold off 2 young European hopefuls, Langer and James, and double-Majors winner Floyd – who was never to get closer than this in the Open.

Vietnam veteran Larry Nelson won his 1st Major at the Atlanta Athletic Club – just a few minutes from his front door. He hung on to Bob Murphy's coat-tails as Murphy blazed away with a 66, 69 start, then pulled away from the field with a 66 of his own to take a lead of 4 over Fuzzy Zoeller. He maintained the differential over the final round to cruise home.

1	**BILL ROGERS**	72	66	67	71	276
	(£25000)					
2	Bernhard Langer	73	67	70	70	280
3=	Ray Floyd	74	70	69	70	283
	Mark James	72	70	68	73	283
5=	Sam Torrance	72	69	73	70	284
	Bruce Lietzke	76	69	71	69	285
	Manuel Pinero	73	74	68	70	285
8=	Howard Clark	72	76	70	68	286
	Ben Crenshaw	72	67	76	71	286
	Brian Jones	73	76	66	71	286
11=	Isao Aoki	71	73	69	74	287
	Nick Faldo	77	68	69	73	287
	Lee Trevino	77	67	70	73	287
14=	Brian Barnes	76	70	70	72	288
	Eamonn Darcy	79	69	70	70	288
	David Graham	71	71	74	72	288
	Nick Job	70	69	75	74	288
	Sandy Lyle	73	73	71	71	288
19=	Gordon J Brand	78	65	74	72	289
	Graham Marsh	75	71	72	71	289
	Jerry Pate	73	73	69	74	289
	Peter Townsend	73	70	73	73	289
23=	Hubert Green	75	72	74	69	290
	Tony Jacklin	71	71	73	75	290
	Mark McNulty	74	74	74	68	290
	Jack Nicklaus	83	66	71	70	290
	Simon Owen	71	74	70	75	290
	Arnold Palmer	72	74	73	71	290
	Nick Price	77	68	76	69	290
	Tom Watson	73	69	75	73	290

1	**LARRY NELSON**	70	66	66	71	273
	($60000)					
2	Fuzzy Zoeller	70	68	68	71	277
3	Dan Pohl	69	67	73	69	278
4=	Isao Aoki	75	68	66	70	279
	Keith Fergus	71	71	69	68	279
	Bob Gilder	74	69	70	76	279
	Tom Kite	71	67	69	72	279
	Bruce Lietzke	70	70	71	68	279
	Jack Nicklaus	71	68	71	69	279
	Greg Norman	73	67	68	71	279
11=	Vance Heafner	68	70	70	72	280
	Andy North	68	69	70	73	280
	Jerry Pate	71	68	70	71	280
	Tommy Valentine	73	70	71	66	280
15	JC Snead	70	71	70	70	281
16=	David Edwards	71	69	70	72	282
	Hale Irwin	71	74	68	69	282
18	Bob Murphy	66	69	73	75	283
19=	John Cook	72	69	70	73	284
	Ray Floyd	71	70	71	72	284
	Jay Haas	73	68	74	69	284
	Joe Inman Jr	73	71	67	73	284
	Don January	70	72	70	72	284
	Gil Morgan	70	69	74	71	284
	Don Pooley	74	70	69	71	284
	Tom Purtzer	70	70	73	71	284
27=	Bobby Clampett	75	71	70	69	285
	Hubert Green	71	74	71	69	285
	Peter Jacobsen	74	71	71	69	285
	Bill Rogers	72	75	66	72	285
	Curtis Strange	73	72	74	66	285
	Tom Weiskopf	71	72	72	70	285

Round Leader(s)
R1 Job; 70
R2 Rogers; 138
R3 Rogers; 205
Lowest Scores
R2 Nicklaus, Rogers; 66
R3 Jones; 66
R4 Clark, McNulty; 68

Round Leader(s)
R1 Murphy; 66
R2 Murphy; 135
R3 Nelson; 202
Lowest Scores
R2 Nelson; 66
R3 Aoki, Nelson, Rogers; 66
R4 Gilder, Strange, Valentine; 66

1982
THE MASTERS
8–11 April

Augusta National GC, Augusta, Georgia
6925 yards *PAR 72 (288)*

1982
US OPEN
17–20 June

Pebble Beach GL, Pebble Beach, California
6815 yards *PAR 72 (288)*

Craig Stadler answered the $64000 question when he defeated Dan Pohl in the sudden-death play-off. He was being asked it all through the 2nd half of the Tournament as Pohl, who shot an anonymous 150 for the 1st 36, then tore up the course with 2 67s. He made up 6 shots on the 'Walrus', but Stadler clung on for a tie, steadied himself, and prevailed in overtime.

Watson's penchant for seaside golf, and delight in keeping Jack Nicklaus at bay, was doubly manifested at Pebble Beach. His 1st – and so far, only US Open – was won after another titanic struggle between the two great golfers was only settled at the 17th, when Tom memorably pitched in for a birdie. Another record was set for entries filed, taking the figure over 5000 for the 1st time.

1	**CRAIG STADLER*** ($64000)	75	69	67	73	284
2	Dan Pohl	75	75	67	67	284
3=	Seve Ballesteros	73	73	68	71	285
	Jerry Pate	74	73	67	71	285
5=	Tom Kite	76	69	73	69	287
	Tom Watson	77	69	70	71	287
7=	Ray Floyd	74	72	69	74	289
	Larry Nelson	79	71	70	69	289
	Curtis Strange	74	70	73	72	289
10=	Andy Bean	75	72	73	70	290
	Mark Hayes	74	73	73	70	290
	Tom Weiskopf	75	72	68	75	290
	Fuzzy Zoeller	72	76	70	72	290
14	Bob Gilder	79	71	66	75	291
15=	Yakata Hagawa	75	74	71	72	292
	Jack Nicklaus	69	77	71	75	292
	Gary Player	74	73	71	74	292
	Jim Simons	77	74	69	72	292
19	David Graham	73	77	70	73	293
20=	Peter Jacobsen	78	75	70	71	294
	Bruce Lietzke	76	75	69	74	294
	Jodie Mudd (a)	77	74	67	76	294
	Jack Renner	72	75	76	71	294
24=	Ben Crenshaw	74	80	70	71	295
	Danny Edwards	75	74	74	72	295
	Morris Hatalsky	73	77	75	70	295
	Wayne Levi	77	76	72	70	295
	Peter Oosterhuis	73	74	75	73	295
	John Schroeder	77	71	70	77	295
30=	George Archer	79	74	72	71	296
	Calvin Peete	77	72	73	74	296

*Craig Stadler beat Dan Pohl in the Sudden-death Play-off

Round Leader(s)
R1 Nicklaus; 69
R2 Stadler, Strange; 144
R3 Stadler; 211
Lowest Scores
R2 Kite, Stadler, Watson; 69
R3 Gilder; 66
R4 Pohl; 67

1	**TOM WATSON** ($60000)	72	72	68	70	282
2	Jack Nicklaus	74	70	71	69	284
3=	Bobby Clampett	71	73	72	70	286
	Dan Pohl	72	74	70	70	286
	Bill Rogers	70	73	69	74	286
6=	David Graham	73	72	69	73	287
	Jay Haas	75	74	70	68	287
	Gary Koch	78	73	69	67	287
	Lanny Wadkins	73	76	67	71	287
10=	Bruce Devlin	70	69	75	74	288
	Calvin Peete	71	72	72	73	288
12=	Chip Beck	76	75	69	69	289
	Danny Edwards	71	75	73	70	289
	Lyn Lott	72	71	75	71	289
15=	Larry Rinker	74	67	75	74	290
	Scott Simpson	73	69	72	76	290
	JC Snead	73	75	71	71	290
	Fuzzy Zoeller	72	76	71	71	290
19=	Ben Crenshaw	76	74	68	73	291
	Larry Nelson	74	72	74	71	291
	Hal Sutton	73	76	72	70	291
22=	Mike Brannan	75	74	71	72	292
	Joe Hager	78	72	72	70	292
	Gene Littler	74	75	72	71	292
	John Mahaffey	77	72	70	73	292
	Gil Morgan	75	75	68	74	292
	Andy North	72	71	77	72	292
	Craig Stadler	76	70	70	76	292
29	Tom Kite	73	71	75	74	293
30=	Isao Aoki	77	74	72	71	294
	Don Bies	73	74	74	73	294
	George Burns	72	72	70	80	294
	Peter Oosterhuis	73	78	67	76	294
	Greg Powers	77	71	74	72	294
	Jack Renner	74	71	77	72	294
	Jim Thorpe	72	73	72	77	294

Round Leader(s)
R1 Devlin, Rogers; 70
R2 Devlin; 139
R3 Rogers, Watson; 212

Lowest Scores
R2 Rinker; 67
R3 Oosterhuis, Wadkins; 67
R4 Koch; 67

15–18 July					
BRITISH OPEN					**1982**
Royal Troon GC, Ayrshire, Scotland					
7067 yards PAR 72 (288)					

5–8 August					
US PGA					**1982**
Southern Hills CC, Tulsa, Oklahoma					
6862 yards PAR 70 (280)					

Troon GC received its Royal Charter in the Queen's Silver Jubilee year of 1977. That year Tom Watson won his 2nd British Open 20 miles down the coast at Turnberry, and in 1982 collected his 4th - all at different Scottish courses. He joined the Morrises, Willie Park Sr, Walter Hagen and Bobby Locke on 4 wins; he also joined Bobby Jones (twice), Gene Sarazen, Ben Hogan and Lee Trevino as the only winners of both Opens in the same year. He was chased hard by Peter Oosterhuis, and Nick Price, and especially Bobby Clampett, were left to contemplate what might have been.

Raymond Floyd's 3rd Major was also his 2nd PGA - after a gap of 13 years – the joint-longest wait for a second win in any single Major. The records were not to stop there: 63 equalled the all-time low in the PGA and any Major; 200 was the low for any 54 holes in any Major; Floyd was the only winner of the PGA wire-to-wire on more than one occasion. 52 year-old Gene Littler, the 1961 US Open Champion, shot the low score of R3.

1	**TOM WATSON**	69	71	74	70	284
	(£32000)					
2=	Peter Oosterhuis	74	67	74	70	285
	Nick Price	69	69	74	73	285
4=	Nick Faldo	73	73	71	69	286
	Masahiro Kuramoto	71	73	71	71	286
	Tom Purtzer	76	66	75	69	286
	Des Smyth	70	69	74	73	286
8=	Sandy Lyle	74	66	73	74	287
	Fuzzy Zoeller	73	71	73	70	287
10=	Bobby Clampett	67	66	78	77	288
	Jack Nicklaus	77	70	72	69	288
12	Sam Torrance	73	72	73	71	289
13=	Seve Ballesteros	71	75	73	71	290
	Bernhard Langer	70	69	78	73	290
15=	Ben Crenshaw	74	75	72	70	291
	Ray Floyd	74	73	77	67	291
	Curtis Strange	72	73	76	70	291
	Denis Watson	75	69	73	74	291
19	Ken Brown	70	71	79	72	292
20=	Isao Aoki	75	69	75	74	293
	Tohru Nakamura	77	68	77	71	293
22=	Jose-Maria Canizares	71	72	79	72	294
	Johnny Miller	71	76	75	72	294
	Bill Rogers	73	70	76	75	294
25=	Bernard Gallacher	75	71	74	75	295
	Graham Marsh	76	76	72	71	295
27=	David Graham	73	70	76	77	296
	Jay Haas	78	72	75	71	296
	Greg Norman	73	75	76	72	296
	Arnold Palmer	71	73	78	74	296
	Lee Trevino	78	72	71	75	296

Round Leader(s)
R1 Clampett; 67
R2 Clampett; 133
R3 Clampett; 211
Lowest Scores
R2 Clampett, Lyle, Purtzer; 66
R3 Faldo, Kuramoto, Trevino; 71
R4 Floyd; 67

1	**RAY FLOYD**	63	69	68	72	272
	($65000)					
2	Lanny Wadkins	71	68	69	67	275
3=	Fred Couples	67	71	72	66	276
	Calvin Peete	69	70	68	69	276
5=	Jay Haas	71	66	68	72	277
	Greg Norman	66	69	70	72	277
	Jim Simons	68	67	73	69	277
8	Bob Gilder	66	68	72	72	278
9=	Lon Hinkle	70	68	71	71	280
	Tom Kite	73	70	70	67	280
	Jerry Pate	72	69	70	69	280
	Tom Watson	72	69	71	68	280
13	Seve Ballesteros	71	68	69	73	281
14=	Nick Faldo	67	70	73	72	282
	Curtis Strange	72	70	71	69	282
16=	Jim Colbert	70	72	72	69	283
	Dan Halldorsan	69	71	72	71	283
	Bruce Lietzke	73	71	70	69	283
	Jack Nicklaus	74	70	72	67	283
	Tom Purtzer	73	69	73	68	283
	Craig Stadler	71	70	70	72	283
22=	Danny Edwards	71	71	68	74	284
	Gil Morgan	76	66	68	74	284
	Peter Oosterhuis	72	72	74	66	284
	Mark Pfeil	68	73	76	67	284
	Ron Streck	71	72	71	70	284
	Doug Tewell	72	70	72	70	284
	Leonard Thompson	72	72	71	69	284
29=	Mike Holland	71	73	70	71	285
	Bill Rogers	73	71	70	71	285
	Hal Sutton	72	68	70	75	285

Round Leader(s)
R1 Floyd; 63
R2 Floyd; 132
R3 Floyd; 200
Lowest Scores
R2 Haas, Morgan; 66
R3 Gene Littler (49); 67
R4 Couples, Oosterhuis; 66

1983
7–11 April (Friday washed out)
THE MASTERS
Augusta National GC, Augusta, Georgia
6925 yards PAR 72 (288)

1983
16–20 June
US OPEN
Oakmont CC, Oakmont, Pennsylvania
6972 yards PAR 71 (284)

Ballesteros' 2nd Masters and 3rd Major win was a typical mixture of brilliance and bravura. He shot a last round 69 to overhaul the crumbling 1982 Champion Craig Stadler and the reigning PGA Champion, Ray Floyd. Eligible 'bridesmaids' Crenshaw and Kite were still awaiting the bouquet to be thrown in their direction. Both shot sub-70 but had too much ground to make up on the Spaniard.

Larry Nelson's 2nd Major followed his 1981 PGA triumph – but victory was far from his mind after the 1st 36 holes, when he was standing on 148, 7 shots back, and tying for 25th place. He then broke the Open record for 36 holes with a 10 under par 132 – 4 strokes better than the previous low. Arnold Palmer equalled Gene Sarazen's record of 31 consecutive Open appearances, and finished tied for 60th.

1	**SEVE BALLESTEROS**	68	70	73	69	280
	($90000)					

2=	Ben Crenshaw	76	70	70	68	284
	Tom Kite	70	72	73	69	284
4=	Ray Floyd	67	72	71	75	285
	Tom Watson	70	71	71	73	285
6=	Hale Irwin	72	73	72	69	286
	Craig Stadler	69	72	69	76	286
8=	Gil Morgan	67	70	76	74	287
	Dan Pohl	74	72	70	71	287
	Lanny Wadkins	73	70	73	71	287
11	Scott Simpson	70	73	72	73	288
12=	George Archer	71	73	71	74	289
	Wayne Levi	72	70	74	73	289
	Johnny Miller	72	72	71	74	289
	J C Snead	68	74	74	73	289
16=	Keith Fergus	70	69	74	77	290
	Tommy Nakajima	72	70	72	76	290
	Jack Renner	67	75	78	70	290
19	Isao Aoki	70	76	74	71	291
20=	Nick Faldo	70	70	76	76	292
	Mark Hayes	71	73	76	72	292
	Peter Jacobsen	73	71	76	72	292
	Peter Oosterhuis	73	69	78	72	292
	Lee Trevino	71	72	72	77	292
	Tom Weiskopf	75	72	71	74	292
	Fuzzy Zoeller	70	74	76	72	292
27=	Jay Haas	73	69	73	78	293
	Scott Hoch	74	69	74	76	293
	Hal Sutton	73	73	70	77	293
30=	Greg Norman	71	74	70	79	294
	Andy North	72	75	72	75	294

Round Leader(s)
R1   Floyd, Morgan, Renner; 67
R2   Morgan; 137
R3   Floyd, Stadler; 210
Lowest Scores
R2   Fred Couples (32), Jodie Mudd (42); 68
R3   Stadler; 69
R4   Crenshaw; 68

1	**LARRY NELSON**	75	73	65	67	280
	($72000)					

2	Tom Watson	72	70	70	69	281
3	Gil Morgan	73	72	70	68	283
4=	Seve Ballesteros	69	74	69	74	286
	Calvin Peete	75	68	70	73	286
6	Hal Sutton	73	70	73	71	287
7	Lanny Wadkins	72	73	74	69	288
8=	David Graham	74	75	73	69	291
	Ralph Landrum	75	73	69	74	291
10=	Chip Beck	73	74	74	71	292
	Andy North	73	71	72	76	292
	Craig Stadler	76	74	73	69	292
13=	Lennie Clements	74	71	75	73	293
	Ray Floyd	72	70	72	79	293
	Pat McGowan	75	71	75	72	293
	Mike Nicolette	76	69	73	75	293
	David Ogrin	75	69	75	74	293
	Scott Simpson	73	71	73	76	293
	Jim Thorpe	75	70	75	73	293
20=	Tom Kite	75	76	70	73	294
	Griff Moody	76	72	73	73	294
	Gary Player	73	74	76	71	294
	DA Weibring	71	74	80	79	294
24=	Gary Koch	78	71	72	74	295
	Tom Weiskopf	75	73	74	73	295
26=	Bob Ford	76	73	75	72	296
	Ken Green	77	73	71	75	296
	Mark Hayes	75	72	74	75	296
	Tommy Nakajima	75	74	74	73	296
	Joey Rassett	72	69	78	77	296
	Curtis Strange	74	72	78	72	296

Round Leader(s)
R1   Ballesteros, John Mahaffey (34),
     Bob Murphy (50); 69
R2   Mahaffey, Rassett; 141
R3   Ballesteros, Watson; 212
Lowest Scores
R2   Peete; 68
R3   Nelson; 65
R4   Nelson; 67

14–17 July

BRITISH OPEN 1983

Royal Birkdale GC, Southport, Lancashire, England
6968 yards PAR 71 (284)

4–7 August

US PGA 1983

Riviera CC, Pacific Palisades, California
6946 yards PAR 71 (284)

Playing steady golf as only he could, Tom Watson capitalized on a good start and mistakes by Craig Stadler to take a lead after 54 holes. He was headed by Nick Faldo briefly in R4, but kept his game together better than the 26 year-old Englishman, who was urged on by an excited home crowd. Last round charges by Andy Bean and twice US Open Champion, Hale Irwin, were not quite enough to undermine Watson – nor was a new R4 low for the Championship by Australian Graham Marsh. Watson, proving he could win south of the border, joined the rarified level of 5 Open wins – joint 2nd all-time with Taylor, Braid and Thomson, and one behind Vardon. This was his 8th and last (so far) Major title.

1	**TOM WATSON**	67	68	70	70	275
	(£40000)					
2=	Andy Bean	70	69	70	67	276
	Hale Irwin	69	68	72	67	276
4	Graham Marsh	69	70	74	64	277
5	Lee Trevino	69	66	73	70	278
6=	Seve Ballesteros	71	71	69	68	279
	Harold Henning	71	69	70	69	279
8=	Denis Durnian	73	66	74	67	280
	Nick Faldo	68	68	71	73	280
	Christy O'Connor, Jr	72	69	71	68	280
	Bill Rogers	67	71	73	69	280
12=	Peter Jacobsen	72	69	70	70	281
	Craig Stadler	64	70	72	75	281
14=	Ray Floyd	72	66	69	75	282
	David Graham	71	69	67	75	282
	Gary Koch	75	71	66	70	282
	Mike Sullivan	72	68	74	68	282
	Fuzzy Zoeller	71	71	67	73	282
19=	Tienie Britz	71	74	69	69	283
	Bernard Gallacher	72	71	70	70	283
	Hubert Green	69	74	72	68	283
	Jay Haas	73	72	68	70	283
	Simon Hobday	70	73	70	70	283
	Greg Norman	75	71	70	67	283
	Brian Waites	70	70	73	70	283
26=	Howard Clark	71	72	69	72	284
	Eamonn Darcy	69	72	74	69	284
	Rodger Davis	70	71	70	73	284
29=	Terry Gale	72	66	72	75	285
	Mark James	70	70	74	71	285
	Tom Kite	71	72	72	70	285
	CS Lu	71	72	74	68	285
	Mike McCullough	74	69	72	70	285
	Tohru Nakamura	73	69	72	71	285
	Jack Nicklaus	71	72	72	70	285
	Curtis Strange	74	68	70	73	285
	Hal Sutton	68	71	75	71	285
	Lanny Wadkins	72	73	72	68	285

Round Leader(s)   **Lowest Scores**
R1 Stadler; 64   R2 Durnian, Floyd, Gale, Trevino; 66
R2 Stadler; 134   R3 Koch; 66
R3 Watson; 205   R4 Marsh; 64

The Riviera CC, scene of Hogan's and Demaret's dismantling of the US Open and all-Majors low total in 1948, was host to a Major Championship for the 1st time since. Although the 1948 figure was lowered, the impact on the golfing world this time around was not so great – unless of course your name was Hal Sutton. Nothing could have seemed better for Sutton, winning his 1st Major in the season following his 'Rookie of the Year' award – but he had to withstand heavy pressure from Nicklaus and Peter Jacobsen to win through.

1	**HAL SUTTON**	65	66	72	71	274
	($100000)					
2	Jack Nicklaus	73	65	71	66	275
3	Peter Jacobsen	73	70	68	65	276
4	Pat McGowan	68	67	73	69	277
5	John Fought	67	69	71	71	278
6=	Bruce Lietzke	67	71	70	71	279
	Fuzzy Zoeller	72	71	67	69	279
8	Dan Pohl	72	70	69	69	280
9=	Ben Crenshaw	68	66	71	77	282
	Jay Haas	68	72	69	73	282
	Mike Reid	69	71	72	70	282
	Scott Simpson	66	73	70	73	282
	Doug Tewell	74	72	69	67	282
14=	Keith Fergus	68	70	72	73	283
	David Graham	79	69	74	70	283
	Hale Irwin	72	70	73	68	283
	Roger Maltbie	71	71	71	70	283
	Jim Thorpe	68	72	74	69	283
	Lee Trevino	70	68	74	71	283
20=	John Cook	74	71	68	71	284
	Danny Edwards	67	76	71	70	284
	Ray Floyd	69	75	71	69	284
23=	Chip Beck	72	71	70	72	285
	Fred Couples	71	70	73	71	285
	Jerry Pate	69	72	70	74	285
	Don Pooley	72	68	74	71	285
27=	Seve Ballesteros	71	76	72	67	286
	Bobby Wadkins	73	72	74	67	286
	Buddy Whitten	66	70	73	77	286
30=	Andy Bean	71	73	71	72	287
	Bob Boyd	70	77	72	68	287
	Johnny Miller	72	75	73	67	287
	Mark Pfeil	73	71	70	73	287
	Jim Simons	69	75	72	71	287
	Tom Weiskopf	76	70	69	72	287

Round Leader(s)   **Lowest Scores**
R1 Sutton; 65   R2 Nicklaus; 65
R2 Sutton; 131   R3 Barry Jaeckel (42), Zoeller; 67
R3 Sutton; 203   R4 Jacobsen; 65

1984

12–15 April

THE MASTERS

Augusta National GC, Augusta, Georgia
6925 yards _PAR 72 (288)_

1984

14–18 June

US OPEN

Winged Foot GC, Mamaroneck, New York
6930 yards _PAR 70 (280)_

After 10 Top 10 finishes, incuding 3 runners-up places (one a 1st-tied for the 1979 PGA, when David Graham won the play-off), Ben Crenshaw cast off the mantle of 'nearly man' and won his 1st Major. In doing so he collected the 1st 6-figure 1st prize in a Major Championship and left Tom Kite the media's 'best player never to have won a Major' tag. Kite held the lead at the end of R3, but disintegrated to finish 5 shots behind Crenshaw.

Greg Norman's 1st of several near misses over the next few years gave Fuzzy Zoeller his 2nd Major Championship. Zoeller led by 3 at the turn, but Norman scrambled on to level terms, courtesy of a birdie at 17, then a 15-yard putt to save par at the last. His relief and ambition were only temporary however, and when Fuzzy sank a putt of almost 25 yards at the 2nd play-off hole and Greg made a double-bogey – that was the beginning of the end for the 'Shark'.

1	**BEN CRENSHAW**	67	72	70	68	277
	($108000)					
2	Tom Watson	74	67	69	69	279
3=	David Edwards	71	70	72	67	280
	Gil Morgan	73	71	69	67	280
5	Larry Nelson	76	69	66	70	281
6=	Ronnie Black	71	74	69	68	282
	David Graham	69	70	70	73	282
	Tom Kite	70	68	69	75	282
	Mark Lye	69	66	73	74	282
10	Fred Couples	71	73	67	72	283
11=	Rex Caldwell	71	71	69	73	284
	Wayne Levi	71	72	69	72	284
	Larry Mize	71	70	71	72	284
	Jack Renner	71	73	71	69	284
15=	Nick Faldo	70	69	70	76	285
	Ray Floyd	70	73	70	72	285
	Calvin Peete	79	66	70	70	285
18=	Andy Bean	71	70	72	73	286
	Danny Edwards	72	71	70	73	286
	Jack Nicklaus	73	73	70	70	286
21=	Jay Haas	74	71	70	72	287
	Hale Irwin	70	71	74	72	287
	Gary Player	71	72	73	71	287
	Payne Stewart	76	69	68	74	287
25=	Isao Aoki	69	72	73	74	288
	George Archer	70	74	71	73	288
	Rick Fehr (a)	72	71	70	75	288
	Peter Jacobsen	72	70	75	71	288
	Greg Norman	75	71	73	69	288
	Tom Purtzer	69	74	76	69	288

Round Leader(s)
R1 Crenshaw; 67
R2 Lye; 135
R3 Kite; 207

Lowest Scores
R2 Lye, Peete; 66
R3 Nelson; 66
R4 Edwards, Morgan; 67

1	**FUZZY ZOELLER***	71	66	69	70	276
	($94000)					
2	Greg Norman	70	68	69	69	276
3	Curtis Strange	69	70	74	68	281
4=	Johnny Miller	74	68	70	70	282
	Jim Thorpe	68	71	70	73	282
6	Hale Irwin	68	68	69	79	284
7=	Peter Jacobsen	72	73	73	67	285
	Mark O'Meara	71	74	71	69	285
9=	Fred Couples	69	71	74	72	286
	Lee Trevino	71	72	69	74	286
11=	Andy Bean	70	71	75	71	287
	Jay Haas	73	73	70	71	287
	Tim Simpson	72	71	68	76	287
	Lanny Wadkins	72	71	72	72	287
	Tom Watson	72	72	74	69	287
16=	Isao Aoki	72	70	72	74	288
	Lennie Clements	69	76	72	71	288
	Mark McCumber	71	73	71	73	288
	Tom Purtzer	73	72	72	71	288
	Hal Sutton	72	72	74	70	288
21=	Chip Beck	72	74	71	72	289
	David Graham	71	72	70	76	289
	Gil Morgan	70	74	72	73	289
	Jack Nicklaus	71	71	70	77	289
25=	Bill Glasson	72	75	71	72	290
	Joe Hager	74	73	71	72	290
	Peter Oosterhuis	73	71	71	75	290
	Scott Simpson	72	75	74	69	290
	Mike Sullivan	70	73	70	77	290
30=	Jim Albus	77	69	74	71	291
	Seve Ballesteros	69	73	74	75	291
	Hubert Green	68	75	72	76	291
	John Mahaffey	72	74	77	68	291

* Fuzzy Zoeller (67) beat Greg Norman (75) in the 18-Hole Play-off

Round Leader(s)
R1 Mike Donald (34), Green, Irwin, Thorpe; 68
R2 Irwin; 136
R3 Irwin; 205

Lowest Scores
R2 Zoeller; 66
R3 Simpson; 68
R4 Jacobsen; 67

19–22 July	**1984**	16–19 August	**1984**

BRITISH OPEN

Royal & Ancient GC, St Andrews, Fife, Scotland
6933 yards PAR 72 (288)

US PGA

Shoal Creek CC, Birmingham, Alabama
7145 yards PAR 72 (288)

Seve Ballesteros won his 2nd Open to double his haul of Major wins, thereby denying Tom Watson immortality and a share in Harry Vardon's record of 6 Open wins. Neck-and-neck coming to the 17th, Ballesteros (via the rough, of course) found the green in regulation for the 1st time that week, and the usually rock-steady Watson sent his approach over the green to within 2 feet of the wall abutting the road by which the 17th hole at St Andrews is named. A dropped shot here coincided with Seve's birdie at 18, and there was no way back for Tom.

Lee Trevino, at 44, won his 2nd PGA, 10 years after his win at Tanglewood. In doing so he frustrated Gary Player, now 48, from achieving his 10th Major win, even though the South African shot a PGA low of 63 in R2. Lanny Wadkins, Champion in 1977, fought hard against the veteran maestros, but first he, then Player buckled under the power of Trevino's impressive play on the greens. The affable Texan walked away with the record prize for any Major – his 6th title (2MAS, 2BOP and 2PGA) put him 11th overall on the all-time list.

1	**SEVE BALLESTEROS**	69	68	70	69	276
	(£50000)					

1	**LEE TREVINO**	69	68	67	69	273
	($125000)					

2=	Bernard Langer	71	68	68	71	278
	Tom Watson	71	68	66	73	278
4=	Fred Couples	70	69	74	68	281
	Lanny Wadkins	70	69	73	69	281
6=	Nick Faldo	69	68	76	69	282
	Greg Norman	67	74	74	67	282
8	Mark McCumber	74	67	72	70	283
9=	Hugh Baiocchi	72	70	70	72	284
	Ian Baker-Finch	68	66	71	79	284
	Graham Marsh	70	74	73	67	284
	Ronan Rafferty	74	72	67	71	284
	Sam Torrance	74	74	66	70	284
14=	Andy Bean	72	69	75	69	285
	Bill Bergin	75	73	66	71	285
	Ken Brown	74	71	72	68	285
	Hale Irwin	75	68	70	72	285
	Sandy Lyle	75	71	72	67	285
	Peter Senior	74	70	70	71	285
	Lee Trevino	70	67	75	73	285
	Fuzzy Zoeller	71	72	71	71	285
22=	Ben Crenshaw	72	75	70	69	286
	Peter Jacobsen	67	73	73	73	286
	Tom Kite	69	71	74	72	286
	Gil Morgan	71	71	71	73	286
	Corey Pavin	71	74	72	69	286
	Paul Way	73	72	69	72	286
28=	Terry Gale	71	74	72	70	287
	Jaime Gonzalez	69	71	76	71	287
	Craig Stadler	75	70	70	72	287

2=	Gary Player	74	63	69	71	277
	Lanny Wadkins	68	69	68	72	277
4	Calvin Peete	71	70	69	68	278
5	Seve Ballesteros	70	69	70	70	279
6=	Gary Hallberg	69	71	68	72	280
	Larry Mize	71	69	67	73	280
	Scott Simpson	69	69	72	70	280
	Hal Sutton	74	73	64	69	280
10=	Russ Cochran	73	68	73	67	281
	Tommy Nakajima	72	68	67	74	281
	Victor Regalado	69	69	73	70	281
13	Ray Floyd	68	71	69	74	282
14=	Hubert Green	70	74	66	73	283
	Mike Reid	68	72	72	71	283
16=	Andy Bean	69	75	70	70	284
	Donnie Hammond	70	69	71	74	284
18=	Peter Jacobsen	70	72	72	71	285
	Craig Stadler	71	73	73	68	285
20=	Fred Couples	72	72	75	67	286
	Nick Faldo	69	73	74	70	286
	Keith Fergus	72	72	72	70	286
	John Mahaffey	72	72	72	70	286
	Corey Pavin	73	72	74	67	286
25=	Chip Beck	69	77	70	71	287
	Rex Caldwell	71	71	74	71	287
	Jim Colbert	71	72	74	70	287
	Hale Irwin	71	70	74	72	287
	Jack Nicklaus	77	70	71	69	287
	Mark O'Meara	75	69	71	72	287
	Tim Simpson	73	70	72	72	287
	Doug Tewell	72	71	71	73	287

Round Leader(s)
R1 Jacobsen, Norman; 67
R2 Baker-Finch; 134
R3 Baker-Finch, Watson; 205
Lowest Scores
R2 Baker-Finch; 66
R3 Bergin, Torrance, Watson; 66
R4 Lyle, Marsh, Norman; 67

Round Leader(s)
R1 Floyd, Reid, Wadkins; 68
R2 Trevino, Wadkins; 137
R3 Trevino; 204
Lowest Scores
R2 Player; 63
R3 Sutton; 64
R4 Cochran, Couples, Pavin; 67

1985

11–14 April

THE MASTERS
Augusta National GC, Augusta, Georgia
6925 yards _PAR 72 (288)_

After tying 2nd with Tom Watson at St Andrews the previous year, Bernhard Langer became the 1st German, and only the 3rd continental European (after Arnaud Massy and Ballesteros) to win a Major Championship. Seve jointly led the chasing group, but despite catching the overnight leaders Floyd and Strange, he had no answer to the German's R4 68.

1	**BERNHARD LANGER**	72	74	68	68	282
	($126000)					
2=	Seve Ballesteros	72	71	71	70	284
	Ray Floyd	70	73	69	72	284
	Curtis Strange	80	65	68	71	284
5	Jay Haas	73	73	72	67	285
6=	Gary Hallberg	68	73	75	70	286
	Bruce Lietzke	72	71	73	70	286
	Jack Nicklaus	71	74	72	69	286
	Craig Stadler	73	67	76	70	286
10=	Fred Couples	75	73	69	70	287
	David Graham	74	71	71	71	287
	Lee Trevino	70	73	72	72	287
	Tom Watson	69	71	75	72	287
14=	Bill Kratzert	73	77	69	69	288
	John Mahaffey	72	75	70	71	288
16=	Isao Aoki	72	74	71	72	289
	Gary Koch	72	70	73	74	289
18=	Wayne Levi	75	72	70	73	290
	Mark McCumber	73	73	79	65	290
	Sam Randolph (a)	70	75	72	73	290
	Tim Simpson	73	72	75	70	290
	Jim Thorpe	73	71	72	74	290
	Lanny Wadkins	72	73	72	73	290
24	Mark O'Meara	73	76	72	70	291
25=	Andy Bean	72	74	73	73	292
	Nick Faldo	73	73	75	71	292
	Sandy Lyle	78	65	76	73	292
	Johnny Miller	77	68	76	71	292
	Corey Pavin	72	75	75	70	292
	Payne Stewart	69	71	76	76	292

Round Leader(s)
R1   Hallberg; 68
R2   Stadler, Stewart, Watson; 140
R3   Floyd; 212
Lowest Scores
R2   Lyle, Strange; 65
R3   Langer, Strange; 68
R4   McCumber; 65

1985

13–16 June

US OPEN
Oakland Hills CC, Birmingham, Michigan
6966 yards _PAR 70 (280)_

Andy North repeated his 1978 win at Cherry Hills by just holding off Dave Barr of Canada, and Taiwan's T-C Chen. Chen was 4 strokes to the good when he lost all his advantage with a disastrous 8 at the 5th. North went ahead, but after bogeying 9, 10 and 11, slipped behind Barr. Nerves got to everybody in the run-in and all but North dropped shots up to 17. North then bogeyed the final hole - but had a 2-stroke buffer at the tee, to edge home.

1	**ANDY NORTH**	70	65	70	74	279
	($103000)					
2=	Dave Barr	70	68	70	72	280
	Tze-Chung Chen	65	69	69	77	280
	Dennis Watson	72	65	73	70	280
5=	Seve Ballesteros	71	70	69	71	281*
	Payne Stewart	70	70	71	70	281
	Lanny Wadkins	70	72	69	70	281
8	Johnny Miller	74	71	68	69	282
9=	Rick Fehr	69	67	73	74	283
	Corey Pavin	72	68	73	70	283
	Jack Renner	72	69	72	70	283
	Fuzzy Zoeller	71	69	72	71	283
13	Tom Kite	69	70	71	74	284
14	Hale Irwin	73	72	70	70	285
15=	Andy Bean	69	72	73	72	286
	Jay Haas	69	66	77	74	286
	Greg Norman	72	71	71	72	286
	Mark O'Meara	72	67	75	72	286
	Don Pooley	73	69	73	71	286
	Tony Sills	75	70	71	70	286
	Scott Simpson	73	73	68	72	286
	Joey Sindelar	72	72	69	73	286
23=	Ray Floyd	72	67	73	75	287
	David Frost	74	68	74	71	287
	Fred Funk	75	70	72	70	287
	David Graham	73	72	74	68	287
	Gil Morgan	71	72	72	72	287
	Mike Reid	69	75	70	73	287
	Tom Sieckmann	73	73	70	71	287
	Hal Sutton	74	71	74	68	287

Round Leader(s)
R1   Chen; 65
R2   Chen; 134
R3   Chen; 203
Lowest Scores
R2   North; Watson; 65
R3   Miller, Simpson; 68
R4   Graham, Sutton; 68

18–21 July

BRITISH OPEN 1985

Royal St George's, Sandwich, Kent, England
6857 yards PAR 70 (280)

8–11 August

US PGA 1985

Cherry Hills CC, Englewood, Colorado
7145 yards PAR 72 (288)

Jock Hutchison and Tommy Armour excepted (who, in 1921 and 1931, were domiciled in the USA), James Braid was the last Scotsman to win the Open Championship – in 1910. This was a desperate return for a nation which had given the world the ancient game. Then, as a consequence of the sport's resurgence in Britain and Europe - with Jacklin perhaps the catalyst, and Ballesteros very much its swash-buckling lead role – Sandy Lyle won his 1st Major amid patriotic scenes at St George's. With this result, Langer's win at the Masters, the development of Faldo and the emergence of Woosnam, the Ryder Cup – now the British Isles and Europe against the Americans (since 1979) – was won for the 1st time since 1957.

Lee Trevino, leading at the halfway point, could not consolidate to win back-to-back PGAs. His 75 in R3 let in 1977 US Open Champion, Hubert Green, for his 2nd Major. After 8 years of anonymous performances, Green, despite his early pedigree, was not expected to win another Major title – but obviously 'they' failed to tell Hubert that!

1	**HUBERT GREEN** ($125000)	67	69	70	72	278

2	Lee Trevino	66	68	75	71	280
3=	Andy Bean	71	70	72	68	281
	Tze-Ming Chen	69	76	71	65	281
5	Nick Price	73	73	65	71	282
6=	Fred Couples	70	65	76	72	283
	Buddy Gardner	73	73	70	67	283
	Corey Pavin	66	75	73	69	283
	Tom Watson	67	70	74	72	283
10=	Peter Jacobsen	66	71	75	72	284
	Lanny Wadkins	70	69	73	72	284
12=	Scott Hoch	70	73	73	69	285
	Tom Kite	69	75	71	70	285
	Dan Pohl	72	74	69	70	285
	Scott Simpson	72	68	72	73	285
	Payne Stewart	72	72	73	68	285
	Doug Tewell	64	72	77	72	285
18=	Bob Gilder	73	70	74	69	286
	Wayne Levi	72	69	74	71	286
	Bruce Lietzke	70	74	72	70	286
	Calvin Peete	69	72	75	70	286
	Craig Stadler	72	73	74	67	286
23=	TC Chen	73	74	74	66	287
	John Mahaffey	74	73	71	69	287
	Larry Mize	71	70	73	73	287
	Larry Nelson	70	74	71	72	287
	Willie Wood	71	73	74	69	287
28=	Roger Maltbie	69	73	72	74	288
	Gil Morgan	69	77	72	70	288
	Mark O'Meara	71	76	71	70	288
	Joey Sindelar	71	75	71	71	288

Round Leader(s)
R1 Tewell; 64
R2 Trevino; 134
R3 Green; 206
Lowest Scores
R2 Couples; 65
R3 Price; 65
R4 Chen; 65

1	**SANDY LYLE** (£65000)	68	71	73	70	282
2	Payne Stewart	70	75	70	68	283
3=	David Graham	68	71	70	75	284
	Bernhard Langer	72	69	68	75	284
	Christy O'Connor, Jr	64	76	72	72	284
	Mark O'Meara	70	72	70	72	284
	Jose Rivero	74	72	70	68	284
8=	Anders Forsbrand	70	76	69	70	285
	Tom Kite	73	73	67	72	285
	DA Weibring	69	71	74	71	285
11=	Jose-Maria Canizares	72	75	70	69	286
	Eamonn Darcy	76	68	74	68	286
	Peter Jacobsen	71	74	68	73	286
	Gary Koch	75	72	70	69	286
	Fuzzy Zoeller	69	76	70	71	286
16=	Simon Bishop	71	75	72	69	287
	Greg Norman	71	72	71	73	287
	Sam Torrance	74	74	69	70	287
	Ian Woosnam	70	71	71	75	287
20=	Ian Baker-Finch	71	73	74	70	288
	Jaime Gonzalez	72	72	73	71	288
	Mark James	71	78	66	73	288
	Graham Marsh	71	75	69	73	288
	Lee Trevino	73	76	68	71	288
25=	Gordon J Brand	73	72	72	72	289
	Michael Cahill	72	74	71	72	289
	David Frost	70	74	73	72	289
	Robert Lee	68	73	74	74	289
	Kristen Moe	70	76	73	70	289
	Jose-Maria Olazabal (a)	72	76	71	70	289
	Philip Parkin	68	76	77	68	289
	Manuel Pinero	71	73	72	73	289

Round Leader(s)
R1 O'Connor; 64
R2 Graham, Lyle; 139
R3 Graham, Langer; 209

Lowest Scores
R2 Darcy; 68
R3 James; 66
R4 Darcy, Parkin, Rivero, Stewart; 68

1986
10–13 April
THE MASTERS
Augusta National GC, Augusta, Georgia
6925 yards _PAR 72 (288)_

1986
12–15 June
US OPEN
Shinnecock Hills GC, Southampton, New York
6912 yards _PAR 70 (280)_

I doubt if there was ever a more popular win in the Majors than the one achieved at Augusta by Jack Nicklaus in 1986. Now aged 46, and not having won a Major for 6 years, the odds on the Golden Bear picking up another title to add to the seemingly insurmountable tally of 17 were very long indeed. Nearly-men old and new, Kite and Norman (who agonizingly bogeyed the last) were shattered by a vintage Nicklaus charge which took him to a final round 65 - and title No 18 (6 MAS - a record, 4 USOP – a tied record, 3 BOP and 5 PGA - another tied record).

90 years after hosting the 2nd-ever Championship, the Open returned to a very different Shinnecock Hills. Ray Floyd, 43, picked up his 4th Major title, but in this, his 1st Open win, he beat Ted Ray's 66 year-old record for the being the oldest winner, by some 5 months. He also joined a group of only 12 players to have won 3 different Majors – Tom Watson being the last to do so in 1982. High quality last rounds by Chip Beck and Lanny Wadkins weren't quite enough and shooting a 66 of his own, Floyd came home 2 ahead.

1	**JACK NICKLAUS**	74	71	69	65	279
	($144000)					
2=	Tom Kite	70	74	68	68	280
	Greg Norman	70	72	68	70	280
4	Seve Ballesteros	71	68	72	70	281
5	Nick Price	79	69	63	71	282
6=	Jay Haas	76	69	71	67	283
	Tom Watson	70	74	68	71	283
8=	Tommy Nakajima	70	71	71	72	284
	Payne Stewart	75	71	69	69	284
	Bob Tway	70	73	71	70	284
11=	Donnie Hammond	73	71	67	74	285
	Sandy Lyle	76	70	68	71	285
	Mark McCumber	76	67	71	71	285
	Corey Pavin	71	72	71	71	285
	Calvin Peete	75	71	69	70	285
16=	Dave Barr	70	77	71	68	286
	Ben Crenshaw	71	71	74	70	286
	Gary Koch	69	74	71	72	286
	Bernhard Langer	74	68	69	75	286
	Larry Mize	75	74	72	65	286
21=	Curtis Strange	73	74	68	72	287
	Fuzzy Zoeller	73	73	69	72	287
23=	Tze Chung Chen	69	73	75	71	288
	Roger Maltbie	71	75	69	73	288
25=	Bill Glasson	72	74	72	71	289
	Peter Jacobsen	75	73	68	73	289
	Scott Simpson	76	72	67	74	289
28=	Danny Edwards	71	71	72	76	290
	David Graham	76	72	74	68	290
	Johnny Miller	74	70	77	69	290

Round Leader(s)
R1   Ken Green (44), Bill Kratzert (42); 68
R2   Ballesteros; 139
R3   Norman; 210
Lowest Scores
R2   McCumber; 67
R3   Price; 63
R4   Mize, Nicklaus; 65

1	**RAY FLOYD**	75	68	70	66	279
	($115000)					
2=	Chip Beck	75	73	68	65	281
	Lanny Wadkins	74	70	72	65	281
4=	Hal Sutton	75	70	66	71	282
	Lee Trevino	74	68	69	71	282
6=	Ben Crenshaw	76	69	69	69	283
	Payne Stewart	76	68	69	70	283
8=	Bernhard Langer	74	70	70	70	284
	Mark McCumber	74	71	68	71	284
	Jack Nicklaus	77	72	67	68	284
	Bob Tway	70	73	69	72	284
12=	Greg Norman	71	68	71	75	285
	Dennis Watson	72	70	71	72	285
14	Mark Calcavecchia	75	75	72	65	287
15=	David Frost	72	72	77	67	288
	David Graham	76	71	69	72	288
	Gary Koch	73	73	71	71	288
	Jodie Mudd	73	75	69	71	288
	Joey Sindelar	81	66	70	71	288
	Craig Stadler	74	71	74	69	288
	Scott Verplank	75	72	67	74	288
	Bobby Wadkins	75	69	72	72	288
	Fuzzy Zoeller	75	74	71	68	288
24=	Seve Ballesteros	75	73	68	73	289
	Andy Bean	76	72	73	68	289
	Lennie Clements	75	72	67	75	289
	Dave Eichelberger	80	70	72	67	289
	Larry Mize	75	71	73	70	289
	Calvin Peete	77	73	70	69	289
	Don Pooley	75	71	74	69	289
	Mike Reid	74	73	76	66	289
	Larry Rinker	77	71	70	71	289
	Tom Watson	72	71	71	75	289

Round Leader(s)
R1   Tway; 70
R2   Norman; 139
R3   Norman; 210
Lowest Scores
R2   Sindelar; 66
R3   Reid, Sutton; 66
R4   Beck, Calcavecchia, Wadkins; 65

17–20 July					**1986**

BRITISH OPEN

Turnberry GC, Ayrshire, Scotland
6957 yards PAR 70 (280)

7–10 August					**1986**

US PGA

Inverness Club, Toledo, Ohio
6982 yards PAR 71 (284)

Greg Norman put away former miseries – including the recent US Open R4 failure – and silenced his critics to boot, with a wonderful win over a Turnberry links whipped up by heavy winds. His belated 1st Major was a performance of power tempered by worldy-wise experience. Now 31, his five years on the European Tour - as much as his previous close calls – helped him tame the conditions and silence the field. He seemed to have broken his jinx and was destined to win more Major Honours – but, as we are about to see, old habits were to return. Only 2 Americans from a strong contingent made the Top 10.

In only his 2nd year on the US Tour, Bob Tway was to burst Greg Norman's bubble and allow all the old doubts about his losing Majors from winning positions to return. Norman, leading all the way, and by 4 going into R4, was caught by Tway as he squandered shots down the back 9. Then – in the cruellest way of all, when brittle confidence is starting to crumble – Tway won the Championship by chipping in from a bunker for a birdie at 18. Uniquely, Norman held the 54-hole lead in every Major of 1986.

1	**GREG NORMAN**	74	63	74	69	280
	(£70000)					
2	Gordon J Brand	71	68	75	71	285
3=	Bernhard Langer	72	70	76	68	286
	Ian Woosnam	70	74	70	72	286
5	Nick Faldo	71	70	76	70	287
6=	Seve Ballesteros	76	75	73	64	288
	Gary Koch	73	72	72	71	288
8=	Brian Marchbank	78	70	72	69	289
	Tommy Nakajima	74	67	71	77	289
	Fuzzy Zoeller	75	73	72	69	289
11=	Jose-Maria Canizares	76	68	73	73	290
	David Graham	75	73	70	72	290
	Christy O'Connor, Jr	75	71	75	69	290
14=	Andy Bean	74	73	73	71	291
	Curtis Strange	79	69	74	69	291
16=	Ray Floyd	78	67	73	74	292
	Anders Forsbrand	71	73	77	71	292
	Jose-Maria Olazabal	78	69	72	73	292
19=	Bob Charles	76	72	73	72	293
	Manuel Pinero	78	71	70	74	293
21=	Derrick Cooper	72	79	72	71	294
	Ben Crenshaw	77	69	75	73	294
	Danny Edwards	77	73	70	74	294
	Vicente Fernandez	78	70	71	75	294
	Robert Lee	71	75	75	73	294
	Philip Parkin	78	70	72	74	294
	Ronan Rafferty	75	74	75	70	294
	Vaughan Somers	73	77	72	72	294
	Sam Torrance	78	69	71	76	294
30=	Masahiro Kuramoto	77	73	73	72	295
	Sandy Lyle	78	73	70	74	295
	John Mahaffey	75	73	75	72	295
	Ian Stanley	72	74	78	71	295
	DA Weibring	75	70	76	74	295

1	**BOB TWAY**	72	70	64	70	276
	($140000)					
2	Greg Norman	65	68	69	76	278
3	Peter Jacobsen	68	70	70	71	279
4	DA Weibring	71	72	68	69	280
5=	Bruce Lietzke	69	71	70	71	281
	Payne Stewart	70	67	72	72	281
7=	David Graham	75	69	71	67	282
	Mike Hulbert	69	68	74	71	282
	Jim Thorpe	71	67	73	71	282
10	Doug Tewell	73	71	68	71	283
11=	Ben Crenshaw	72	73	72	67	284
	Donnie Hammond	70	71	68	75	284
	Lonnie Nielsen	73	69	72	70	284
	Lee Trevino	71	74	69	70	284
	Lanny Wadkins	71	75	70	68	284
16=	Chip Beck	71	73	71	70	285
	Jack Nicklaus	70	68	72	75	285
	Don Pooley	71	74	69	71	285
	Tony Sills	71	72	69	73	285
	Tom Watson	72	69	72	72	285
21=	Ronnie Black	68	71	74	73	286
	David Frost	70	73	68	75	286
	Wayne Grady	68	76	71	71	286
	Corey Pavin	71	72	70	73	286
	Hal Sutton	73	71	70	72	286
26=	Ken Green	71	72	71	73	287
	Hale Irwin	76	70	73	68	287
	Tom Kite	72	73	71	71	287
	Dan Pohl	71	71	74	71	287
30=	Wayne Levi	68	73	71	76	288
	Calvin Peete	72	73	69	74	288
	Gene Sauers	69	73	70	76	288
	Jeff Sluman	70	71	76	71	288
	Craig Stadler	67	74	73	74	288
	Ian Woosnam	72	70	75	71	288

Round Leader(s)

R1	Woosnam; 70
R2	Norman; 137
R3	Norman; 211

Lowest Scores

R2	Norman; 63
R3	Edwards, Graham, Lyle, Pinero, Woosnam; 70
R4	Ballesteros; 64

Round Leader(s)

R1	Norman; 65
R2	Norman; 133
R3	Norman; 202

Lowest Scores

R2	Stewart, Thorpe, Mark Wiebe (47); 67
R3	Tway; 64
R4	Crenshaw, Graham; 67

1987 THE MASTERS
9–12 April

Augusta National GC, Augusta, Georgia
6925 yards PAR 72 (288)

Greg Norman would have hoped that the memory of last August's PGA nightmare might have faded during the winter, and have disappeared altogether with the optimistic airs of spring. He certainly came to Augusta full of expectation, and a R3 66 took him to the wire to tie with twice-Champion Ballesteros, and hitherto modest performer, Larry Mize. Seve blew out on the 1st extra hole, and with Norman on the green and Mize, to the right of it, some 30 yards from the flag, Greg was in prime position. The nightmare recurred when Mize, in an action which, in a less-gentlemanly sport would surely have been classed as sadistic, chipped in, leaving Norman crushed once more.

1	**LARRY MIZE*** ($162000)	70	72 72	71	285
2=	Seve Ballesteros	73	71 70	71	285
	Greg Norman	73	74 66	72	285
4=	Ben Crenshaw	75	70 67	74	286
	Roger Maltbie	76	66 70	74	286
	Jodie Mudd	74	72 71	69	286
7=	Jay Haas	72	72 72	73	289
	Bernhard Langer	71	72 70	76	289
	Jack Nicklaus	74	72 73	70	289
	Tom Watson	71	72 74	72	289
	DA Weibring	72	75 71	71	289
12=	Chip Beck	75	72 70	73	290
	Tze-Chung Chen	74	69 71	76	290
	Mark McCumber	75	71 69	75	290
	Curtis Strange	71	70 73	76	290
	Lanny Wadkins	73	72 70	75	290
17=	Paul Azinger	77	73 69	72	291
	Mark Calcavecchia	73	72 78	68	291
	Sandy Lyle	77	74 68	72	291
	Craig Stadler	74	74 72	71	291
21	Bobby Wadkins	76	69 73	74	292
22=	Gary Koch	76	75 72	70	293
	Nick Price	73	73 71	76	293
24=	John Cook	69	73 74	78	294
	Tom Kite	73	74 74	73	294
	Mark O'Meara	75	74 71	74	294
27=	David Graham	73	77 72	73	295
	Donnie Hammond	73	75 74	73	295
	Corey Pavin	71	71 81	72	295
	Scott Simpson	72	75 72	76	295
	Denis Watson	76	74 73	72	295
	Fuzzy Zoeller	76	71 76	72	295

*Larry Mize beat Seve Ballesteros and Greg Norman in the Sudden-death Play-off

Round Leader(s)
R1 Cook; 69
R2 Strange; 141
R3 Crenshaw, Maltbie; 212

Lowest Scores
R2 Maltbie; 66
R3 Norman; 66
R4 Calcavecchia; 68

1987 US OPEN
16–19 June

Olympic GC, San Francisco, California
6709 yards PAR 70 (280)

Overnight leader Tom Watson was denied a 2nd Open when Scott Simpson birdied 14,15, and 16 in R4 to overtake him and win his 1st Major title. Watson was undergoing a long slump in form, but still managed to raise his game for the events that mattered, and just failed to tie Simpson when his 45-foot putt for birdie at the 18th ended up just inches from the hole.

1	**SCOTT SIMPSON** ($150000)	71	68 70	68	277
2	Tom Watson	72	65 71	70	278
3	Seve Ballesteros	68	75 68	71	282
4=	Ben Crenshaw	67	72 72	72	283
	Bernhard Langer	69	69 73	72	283
	Larry Mize	71	68 72	72	283
	Curtis Strange	71	72 69	71	283
	Bobby Wadkins	71	71 70	71	283
9=	Lennie Clements	70	70 70	74	284
	Tommy Nakajima	68	70 74	72	284
	Mac O'Grady	71	69 72	72	284
	Dan Pohl	75	71 69	69	284
	Jim Thorpe	70	68 73	73	284
14=	Isao Aoki	71	73 70	71	285
	Bob Eastwood	73	66 75	71	285
	Tim Simpson	76	66 70	73	285
17=	Mark Calcavecchia	73	68 73	72	286
	David Frost	70	72 71	73	286
	Kenny Knox	72	71 69	74	286
	Jodie Mudd	72	75 71	68	286
	Jumbo Ozaki	71	69 72	74	286
	Nick Price	69	74 69	74	286
	Jim Woodward	71	74 72	69	286
24=	Jay Don Blake	70	75 71	71	287
	Danny Edwards	72	70 72	73	287
	Peter Jacobsen	72	71 71	73	287
	John Mahaffey	72	72 67	76	287
	Steve Pate	71	72 72	72	287
	Don Pooley	74	72 72	69	287
	Craig Stadler	72	68 74	73	287

Round Leader(s)
R1 Crenshaw; 67
R2 Watson, Mark Wiebe (58); 137
R3 Watson; 208

Lowest Scores
R2 Watson; 65
R3 Keith Clearwater (31); 64
R4 Ken Green (31), Mudd, Simpson; 68

16–19 July | **1987**

BRITISH OPEN

Honourable Company, Muirfield, Angus, Scotland
6963 yards _PAR 71 (284)_

6–9 August | **1987**

US PGA

PGA National GC, Palm Beach Gardens, Florida
7002 yards _PAR 72 (288)_

Nick Faldo, for many years the heir-apparent to Tony Jacklin, eventually came out of the shadow of the double Open winner, and nearly 3 years of technical rehabilitation with guru David Leadbeater, to win his 1st Major. He had been playing the Open since 1976 when he was a teenager, and although consistently winning on the European Tour, he was not by his own demanding standards making the breakthrough in the Majors. Leadbeater effectively rebuilt Faldo's swing. He won in the Muirfield haar (sea mist), grinding down Paul Azinger with 18 straight pars in R4, eventually nudging ahead at the last when the American missed his 30-foot par putt.

Larry Nelson may not have been the most consistent performer in the Majors, but he is only one of 15 players to have won the PGA Championship more than once. When the Championship returned to the Florida home of the PGA, he tied with 1977 Champion, Lanny Wadkins, then added to his 1981 success when Wadkins bogeyed the 1st hole in sudden death.

1	**LARRY NELSON***	70	72	73	72	287
	($150000)					
2	Lanny Wadkins	70	70	74	73	287
3=	Scott Hoch	74	74	71	69	288
	DA Weibring	73	72	67	76	288
5=	Mark McCumber	74	69	69	77	289
	Don Pooley	73	71	73	72	289
7=	Ben Crenshaw	72	70	74	74	290
	Bobby Wadkins	68	74	71	77	290
9	Curtis Strange	70	76	71	74	291
10=	Seve Ballesteros	72	70	72	78	292
	David Frost	75	70	71	76	292
	Tom Kite	72	77	71	72	292
	Nick Price	76	71	70	75	292
14=	Curt Byrum	74	75	68	76	293
	David Edwards	69	75	77	72	293
	Ray Floyd	70	70	73	80	293
	Dan Pohl	71	78	75	69	293
	Jeff Sluman	72	69	78	74	293
	Tom Watson	70	79	73	71	293
20	Peter Jacobsen	73	75	73	73	294
21=	Jim Hallett	73	78	73	71	295
	Bernhard Langer	70	78	77	70	295
	Gil Morgan	75	74	70	76	295
24=	Ken Brown	73	74	73	76	296
	Jack Nicklaus	76	73	74	73	296
	Gene Sauers	76	74	68	78	296
	Payne Stewart	72	75	75	74	296
28=	Ronnie Black	76	70	76	75	297
	Bobby Clampett	71	72	77	77	297
	Russ Cochran	73	76	69	79	297
	John Cook	76	70	72	79	297
	Brad Fabel	73	73	77	74	297
	Nick Faldo	73	73	77	74	297
	Jay Haas	74	70	76	77	297
	Bruce Lietzke	75	76	74	72	297
	Roger Maltbie	74	72	75	76	297
	Chris Perry	75	75	74	73	297
	Craig Stadler	75	72	75	75	297
	Hal Sutton	73	74	74	76	297

1	**NICK FALDO**	68	69	71	71	279
	(£75000)					
2=	Paul Azinger	68	68	71	73	280
	Rodger Davis	64	73	74	69	280
4=	Ben Crenshaw	73	68	72	68	281
	Payne Stewart	71	66	72	72	281
6	David Frost	70	68	70	74	282
7	Tom Watson	69	69	71	74	283
8=	Nick Price	68	71	72	73	284
	Craig Stadler	69	69	71	75	284
	Ian Woosnam	71	69	72	72	284
11=	Mark Calcavecchia	69	70	72	74	285
	Graham Marsh	69	70	72	74	285
	Mark McNulty	71	69	75	70	285
	Jose-Maria Olazabal	70	73	70	72	285
	Jumbo Ozaki	69	72	71	73	285
	Hal Sutton	71	70	73	71	285
17=	Ken Brown	69	73	70	74	286
	Eamonn Darcy	74	69	72	71	286
	Ray Floyd	72	68	70	76	286
	Wayne Grady	70	71	76	69	286
	Bernhard Langer	69	69	76	72	286
	Sandy Lyle	76	69	71	70	286
	Mark Roe	74	68	72	72	286
	Lee Trevino	67	74	73	72	286
25	Gerard Taylor	69	68	75	75	287
26=	Gordon Brand, Jr	73	70	75	70	288
	David Feherty	74	70	77	67	288
	Larry Mize	68	71	76	73	288
29=	Danny Edwards	71	73	72	73	289
	Anders Forsbrand	73	69	73	74	289
	Ken Green	67	76	74	72	289
	Lanny Wadkins	72	71	75	71	289
	Fuzzy Zoeller	71	70	76	72	289

*Larry Nelson beat Lanny Wadkins at 1st extra hole in Sudden Death Play-off

Round Leader(s)

R1	Davis; 64	
R2	Azinger; 136	
R3	Azinger; 207	

Lowest Scores

R2	Stewart; 66
R3	Brown, Floyd, Frost, Olazabal; 70
R4	Feherty; 67

Round Leader(s)

R1	Wadkins; 68
R2	Floyd, Wadkins; 140
R3	McCumber, Weibring; 212

Lowest Scores

R2	McCumber, Sluman; 69
R3	Weibring; 67
R4	Hoch, Pohl; 69

1988
THE MASTERS
7–10 April

Augusta National GC, Augusta, Georgia
6925 yards _PAR 72 (288)_

1988
US OPEN
16–20 June

The Country Club, Brookline, Massachusetts
7010 yards _PAR 71 (284)_

Sandy Lyle became the 1st Briton to win the Masters, and the 3rd European in the decade so far. His R2 67 gave him the platform and he led again after 54 holes. However, Mark Calcavecchia caught Lyle and they were level when Lyle teed off at the last. Going for birdie, the Scot caught a fairway trap some 140 yards from the flag. Then, in one of the most dramatic approaches seen at Augusta's 18th, Lyle's 7 iron shot sailed out of the bunker, over the pin and span back to within 10 feet of the hole. He birdied against Calcavecchia's par to take the Green Jacket.

Sandy Lyle projected his Masters form into the Open to shoot 68 and share the lead, but dropped out of contention after that. Another Briton, Nick Faldo, was trying to emulate Tony Jacklin by winning the US Open while still Britain's Champion Golfer, and tied with Curtis Strange when Strange bogeyed the 17th. The play-off – the 3rd in 3 visits to Brookline (including the momentous 1913 affair between Ouimet, Vardon and Ray) – saw Curtis play much the better golf, and he held the lead from the 7th, Faldo bogeying 3 of the last 4 holes.

1	**SANDY LYLE**	71	67	72	71	281
	($183800)					
2	Mark Calcavecchia	71	69	72	70	282
3	Craig Stadler	76	69	70	68	283
4	Ben Crenshaw	72	73	67	72	284
5=	Fred Couples	75	68	71	71	285
	Greg Norman	77	73	71	64	285
	Don Pooley	71	72	72	70	285
8	David Frost	73	74	71	68	286
9=	Bernhard Langer	71	72	71	73	287
	Tom Watson	72	71	73	71	287
11=	Seve Ballesteros	73	72	70	73	288
	Ray Floyd	80	69	68	71	288
	Lanny Wadkins	74	75	69	70	288
14=	Nick Price	75	76	72	66	289
	Doug Tewell	75	73	68	73	289
16=	Mark McNulty	74	71	73	72	290
	Dan Pohl	78	70	69	73	290
	Fuzzy Zoeller	76	66	72	76	290
19=	Tze-Chung Chen	76	73	72	70	291
	Hubert Green	74	70	75	72	291
21=	Chip Beck	73	70	76	73	292
	Jack Nicklaus	75	73	72	72	292
	Curtis Strange	76	70	72	74	292
24	Mark McCumber	79	71	72	71	293
25=	Isao Aoki	74	74	73	73	294
	Gary Koch	72	73	74	75	294
	Payne Stewart	75	76	71	72	294
	Robert Wrenn	69	75	76	74	294
29	Rodger Davis	77	72	71	75	295
30=	Nick Faldo	75	74	75	72	296
	Steve Jones	74	74	75	73	296
	Mac O'Grady	74	73	76	73	296

1	**CURTIS STRANGE***	70	67	69	72	278
	($180000)					
2	Nick Faldo	72	67	68	71	278
3=	Mark O'Meara	71	72	66	71	280
	Steve Pate	72	69	72	67	280
	DA Weibring	71	69	68	72	280
6=	Paul Azinger	69	70	76	66	281
	Scott Simpson	69	66	72	74	281
8=	Bob Gilder	68	69	70	75	282
	Fuzzy Zoeller	73	72	71	66	282
10=	Fred Couples	72	67	71	73	283
	Payne Stewart	73	73	70	67	283
12=	Andy Bean	71	71	72	70	284
	Ben Crenshaw	71	72	74	67	284
	Larry Mize	69	67	72	76	284
	Dan Pohl	74	72	69	69	284
	Lanny Wadkins	70	71	70	73	284
17=	Ray Floyd	73	72	73	67	285
	Hale Irwin	71	71	72	71	285
	Mark McNulty	73	72	72	68	285
	Joey Sindelar	76	68	70	71	285
21=	Chip Beck	73	72	71	70	286
	Bob Eastwood	74	72	69	71	286
	Scott Hoch	71	72	71	72	286
	Peter Jacobsen	76	70	76	64	286
25=	Dave Barr	73	72	72	20	287
	Jay Haas	73	67	74	73	287
	Sandy Lyle	68	71	75	73	287
	Billy Mayfair (a)	71	72	71	73	287
	Craig Stadler	70	73	71	73	287
	Bob Tway	77	68	73	69	287
	Mark Wiebe	75	70	73	69	287

* Curtis Strange (71) beat Nick Faldo (75) in the 18-Hole Play-off

Round Leader(s)
R1 Larry Nelson (33), Wrenn; 69
R2 Lyle; 138
R3 Lyle; 210
Lowest Scores
R2 Zoeller; 66
R3 Crenshaw; 67
R4 Norman; 64

Round Leader(s)
R1 Gilder, Lyle, Mike Nicolette (40); 68
R2 Simpson; 135
R3 Strange; 206
Lowest Scores
R2 Simpson; 66
R3 O'Meara; 66
R4 Jacobsen; 64

1988 BRITISH OPEN

14–18 July (Rain washed out 3rd day)

Royal Lytham and St Anne's GC, Lancashire, England
6857 yards *PAR 71 (284)*

1988 US PGA

11–14 August

Oak Tree GC, Edmond, Oklahoma
7015 yards *PAR 71 (284)*

Seve Ballesteros' 3rd Open and 5th Major title came where it all started for the Spaniard in 1979. At his lucky Lytham links, Ballesteros' stunning 65 broke the heart of defending Champion, Faldo, and only Zimbabwean Nick Price could mount a challenge. In the end he had to capitulate to Seve's masterful performance. Rain washed away Day 3, disappointing the 36000 crowd, and after 117 Opens over 128 years, there was play on a Monday for the first time.

1	**SEVE BALLESTEROS**	67	71	70	65	273
	(£80000)					
2	Nick Price	70	67	69	69	275
3	Nick Faldo	71	69	68	71	279
4=	Fred Couples	73	69	71	68	281
	Gary Koch	71	72	70	68	281
6	Peter Senior	70	73	70	69	282
7=	Isao Aoki	72	71	73	67	283
	David Frost	71	75	69	68	283
	Sandy Lyle	73	69	67	74	283
	Payne Stewart	73	75	68	67	283
11=	Brad Faxon	69	74	70	71	284
	David J Russell	71	74	69	70	284
13=	Larry Nelson	73	71	68	73	285
	Eduardo Romero	72	71	69	73	285
	Curtis Strange	79	69	69	68	285
16=	Andy Bean	71	70	71	74	286
	Ben Crenshaw	73	73	68	72	286
	Don Pooley	70	73	69	74	286
	Jose Rivero	75	69	70	72	286
20=	Gordon Brand, Jr	72	76	68	71	287
	Bob Charles	71	74	69	73	287
	Rodger Davis	76	71	72	68	287
	Tom Kite	75	71	73	68	287
	Bob Tway	71	71	72	73	287
25=	Jack Nicklaus	75	70	75	68	288
	Ian Woosnam	76	71	72	69	288
27	Mark O'Meara	75	69	75	70	289
28=	Tommy Armour III	73	72	72	73	290
	Chip Beck	72	71	74	73	290
	Jim Benepe	75	72	70	73	290
	Howard Clark	71	72	75	72	290
	Mark McNulty	73	73	72	72	290
	Tom Watson	74	72	72	72	290

Round Leader(s)
R1 Ballesteros; 67
R2 Price; 137
R3 Faldo, Price; 208
Lowest Scores
R2 Price; 67
R3 Lyle; 67
R4 Ballesteros; 65

Just as Ballesteros had done at Royal Lytham the previous month, a charging 65 from Jeff Sluman gave him his 1st Major Championship win. For Paul Azinger, it was sense of Muirfield déjà vu, except instead of being ground down by Nick Faldo, he was blasted away by Sluman. All-round scoring was lower than expected on a notoriously difficult course.

1	**JEFF SLUMAN**	69	70	68	65	272
	($160000)					
2	Paul Azinger	67	66	71	71	275
3	Tommy Nakajima	69	68	74	67	278
4=	Tom Kite	72	69	71	67	279
	Nick Faldo	67	71	70	71	279
6=	Bob Gilder	66	75	71	68	280
	Dave Rummells	73	64	68	75	280
8	Dan Pohl	69	71	70	71	281
9=	Ray Floyd	68	68	74	72	282
	Steve Jones	69	68	72	73	282
	Kenny Knox	72	69	68	73	282
	Greg Norman	68	71	72	71	282
	Mark O'Meara	70	71	70	71	282
	Payne Stewart	70	69	70	73	282
15=	John Mahaffey	71	71	70	71	283
	Craig Stadler	68	73	75	67	283
17=	Mark Calcavecchia	73	69	70	72	284
	Ben Crenshaw	70	71	69	74	284
	David Graham	70	67	73	74	284
	Mark McNulty	73	70	67	74	284
	Jay Overton	68	66	76	74	284
	Corey Pavin	71	70	75	68	284
	Nick Price	74	70	67	73	284
	Richard Zokol	70	70	74	70	284
25=	Ronnie Black	71	71	70	73	285
	Jay Don Blake	71	73	72	69	285
	David Edwards	71	69	77	68	285
	Scott Hoch	74	69	68	74	285
	Blaine McCallister	73	67	75	70	285
	Lanny Wadkins	74	69	70	72	285

Round Leader(s)
R1 Gilder; 66
R2 Azinger; 133
R3 Azinger; 204
Lowest Scores
R2 Rummells; 64
R3 McNulty, Price; 67
R4 Sluman; 65

1989
THE MASTERS
6–9 April

Augusta National GC, Augusta, Georgia
6925 yards _PAR 72 (288)_

With Nick Faldo winning his 2nd Major in successive years, he also perpetuated the mini-stranglehold that Europeans had on the Masters. After Ballesteros (twice), Langer and Lyle, Faldo's win meant that half the decade's Masters titles went overseas – a somewhat different picture to the previous 46 years of the Tournament. Faldo had to put together something special over the last round after an incongruous 77 in R3, and his best-of-the-event 65 tied him with Scott Hoch, and set him up for the play-off win and the 1st prize of $200000 – a record for any Major.

1	**NICK FALDO***	68	73	77	65	283
	($200000)					
2	Scott Hoch	69	74	71	69	283
3=	Ben Crenshaw	71	72	70	71	284
	Greg Norman	74	75	68	67	284
5	Seve Ballesteros	71	72	73	69	285
6	Mike Reid	72	71	71	72	286
7	Jodie Mudd	73	76	72	76	287
8=	Chip Beck	74	76	70	68	288
	Jose-Maria Olazabal	77	73	70	68	288
	Jeff Sluman	74	72	74	68	288
11=	Fred Couples	72	76	74	67	289
	Ken Green	74	69	73	73	289
	Mark O'Meara	74	71	72	72	289
14=	Paul Azinger	75	75	69	71	290
	Don Pooley	70	77	76	67	290
	Tom Watson	72	73	74	71	290
	Ian Woosnam	74	76	71	69	290
18=	David Frost	76	72	73	70	291
	Tom Kite	72	72	72	75	291
	Jack Nicklaus	73	74	73	71	291
	Jumbo Ozaki	71	75	73	72	291
	Curtis Strange	74	71	74	72	291
	Lee Trevino	67	74	81	69	291
24=	Tom Purtzer	71	76	73	72	292
	Payne Stewart	73	75	74	70	292
26=	Bernhard Langer	74	75	71	73	293
	Larry Mize	72	77	69	75	293
	Steve Pate	76	75	74	68	293
	Lanny Wadkins	76	71	73	73	293
	Fuzzy Zoeller	76	74	69	74	293

*Nick Faldo (5,3) beat Scott Hoch (5,4) in the Sudden-death Play-off

Round Leader(s)
R1 Trevino; 67
R2 Faldo, Trevino; 141
R3 Crenshaw; 213
Lowest Scores
R2 Green; 69
R3 Norman; 68
R4 Faldo; 65

1989
US OPEN
15–18 June

Oak Hill CC, Rochester, New York
6902 yards _PAR 70 (280)_

Curtis Strange became the 1st player since Ben Hogan in 1951 to win back-to-back Opens, and the 6th in all. Along with Hogan, he joined Willie Anderson, John McDermott, Bobby Jones and Ralph Guldahl. His win over Chip Beck, Mark McCumber and Welshman Ian Woosnam was a little more comfortable than his play-off win over Faldo the previous year. He could afford to 3-putt the 18th and still win. With odds against it happening of 332000 to 1, 4 players – Doug Weaver, Mark Wiebe, Jerry Pate and Nick Price – all achieved a hole-in-one on the 167-yard 6th, and all within a few hours during R2.

1	**CURTIS STRANGE**	71	64	73	70	278
	($200000)					
2=	Chip Beck	71	69	71	68	279
	Mark McCumber	70	68	72	69	279
	Ian Woosnam	70	68	73	68	279
5=	Brian Claar	71	72	68	69	280
6=	Jumbo Ozaki	70	71	68	72	281
	Scott Simpson	67	70	69	75	281
8	Peter Jacobsen	71	70	71	70	282
9=	Paul Azinger	71	72	70	70	283
	Hubert Green	69	72	74	68	283
	Tom Kite	67	69	69	78	283
	Jose-Maria Olazabal	69	72	70	72	283
13=	Scott Hoch	70	72	70	72	284
	Mark Lye	71	69	72	72	284
	Larry Nelson	68	73	68	75	284
	Tom Pernice	67	75	68	74	284
	Payne Stewart	66	75	72	71	284
18=	Jay Don Blake	66	71	72	76	285
	Nick Faldo	68	72	73	72	285
	David Frost	73	72	70	70	285
21=	Fred Couples	74	71	67	74	286
	Steve Elkington	70	70	78	68	286
	Bill Glasson	73	70	70	73	286
	Nolan Henke	75	69	72	70	286
	DA Weibring	70	74	73	69	286
26=	Ray Floyd	68	74	74	71	287
	Don Pooley	74	69	71	73	287
	Robert Wrenn	74	71	73	69	287
29=	Emlyn Aubrey	69	73	73	73	288
	Dan Pohl	71	71	73	73	288
	Hal Sutton	69	75	72	72	288
	Scott Taylor	69	71	76	72	288

Round Leader(s)
R1 Blake, Bernhard Langer (59), Stewart; 66
R2 Strange; 135
R3 Kite; 205

Lowest Scores
R2 Strange; 64
R3 Couples; 67
R4 Beck, Elkington, Green, Woosnam; 68

20–23 July
BRITISH OPEN 1989
Royal Troon GC, Ayrshire, Scotland
7067 yards _PAR 71 (284)_

10–13 August
US PGA 1989
Kemper Lakes GC, Hawthorn Woods, Illinois
7217 yards _PAR 72 (288)_

Another play-off was needed to settle a Major when the 1988 Masters runner-up, Mark Calcavecchia, tied with Australians Wayne Grady and Greg Norman at Troon. Norman had fought his way into contention with a record-equalling R4 score, only to miss out again when it really mattered. Grady lost touch early in the play-off, and after controlling events early on, Norman's game collapsed over holes 3 and 4, to let Calcavecchia back in.

1	**M CALCAVECCHIA*** (£80000)	71	68	68	68	275
2=	Wayne Grady	68	67	69	71	275
	Greg Norman	69	70	72	64	275
4	Tom Watson	69	68	68	72	277
5	Jodie Mudd	73	67	68	70	278
6=	Fred Couples	68	71	68	72	279
	David Feherty	71	67	69	72	279
8=	Paul Azinger	68	73	67	72	280
	Eduardo Romero	68	70	75	67	280
	Payne Stewart	72	65	69	74	280
11=	Nick Faldo	71	71	70	69	281
	Mark McNulty	75	70	70	66	281
13=	Roger Chapman	76	68	67	71	282
	Howard Clark	72	68	72	70	282
	Mark James	69	70	71	72	282
	Steve Pate	69	70	70	73	282
	Craig Stadler	73	69	69	71	282
	Philip Walton	69	74	69	70	282
19=	Derrick Cooper	69	70	76	68	283
	Tom Kite	70	74	67	72	283
	Larry Mize	71	74	66	72	283
	Don Pooley	73	70	69	71	283
23=	Davis Love III	72	70	73	69	284
	Jose-Maria Olazabal	68	72	69	75	284
	Vijay Singh	71	73	69	71	284
26=	Chip Beck	75	69	68	73	285
	Stephen Bennett	75	69	68	73	285
	Scott Simpson	73	66	72	74	285
	Lanny Wadkins	72	70	69	74	285
30=	Ian Baker-Finch	72	69	70	75	286
	Mark Davis	77	68	67	74	286
	Jeff Hawkes	75	67	69	75	286
	Peter Jacobsen	71	74	71	70	286
	Gary Koch	72	71	74	69	286
	Brian Marchbank	69	74	73	70	286
	Miguel Martin	68	73	73	72	286
	Jack Nicklaus	74	71	71	70	286
	Jumbo Ozaki	71	73	70	72	286

* Mark Calcavecchia (4-3-3-3) beat Wayne Grady (4-4-4-4) and Greg Norman (3-3-4-x) in the 4-Hole Play-off

Round Leader(s)
R1 Azinger, Couples, Grady, Martin, Olazabal, Romero; 68
R2 Grady; 135
R3 Grady; 204

Lowest Scores
R2 Stewart; 65
R3 Mize; 66
R4 Norman; 64

For the 1st time in the same year, the 3 American Majors paid out the same amount to the winner. Payne Stewart, along with Australia's Rodger Davis, the only 2 top golfers of the day who regularly wore traditional plus-fours or knickers, collected his 1st Major, after strong performances in recent years. At the 13th hole in R4, a win looked most unlikely, but a 7-shot swing between Stewart (4 birdies) and Mike Reid (bogey at 16, double-bogey at 17) allowed Payne to squeeze by and also pip Andy Bean – already home with a 66.

1	**PAYNE STEWART** ($200000)	74	66	69	67	276
2=	Andy Bean	70	67	74	66	277
	Mike Reid	66	67	70	74	277
	Curtis Strange	70	68	70	69	277
5	Dave Rummells	68	69	69	72	278
6	Ian Woosnam	68	70	70	71	279
7=	Scott Hoch	69	69	69	73	280
	Craig Stadler	71	64	72	73	280
9=	Nick Faldo	70	73	69	69	281
	Ed Fiori	70	67	75	69	281
	Tom Watson	67	69	74	71	281
12=	Seve Ballesteros	72	70	66	74	282
	Jim Gallagher Jr	73	69	68	72	282
	Greg Norman	74	71	67	70	282
	Mike Sullivan	76	66	67	73	282
	Mark Wiebe	71	70	69	72	282
17=	Isao Aoki	72	71	65	75	283
	Ben Crenshaw	68	72	72	71	283
	Buddy Gardner	72	71	70	70	283
	Davis Love III	73	69	72	69	283
	Blaine McCallister	71	72	70	70	283
	Larry Mize	73	71	68	71	283
	Chris Perry	67	70	70	76	283
24=	Tommy Armour	70	69	73	72	284
	Dan Pohl	71	69	74	70	284
	Jeff Sluman	75	70	69	70	284
27=	David Frost	70	74	69	72	285
	Mike Hulbert	70	71	72	72	285
	Peter Jacobsen	70	70	73	72	285
	Jack Nicklaus	68	72	73	72	285
	Tim Simpson	69	70	73	73	285
	Brian Tennyson	71	69	72	73	285
	Howard Twitty	72	71	68	74	285

Round Leader(s)
R1 Reid, Leonard Thompson (34); 66
R2 Reid; 133
R3 Reid; 203

Lowest Scores
R2 Stadler; 64
R3 Aoki; 65
R4 Bean; 66

1990

THE MASTERS

5–8 April

Augusta National GC, Augusta, Georgia
6925 yards PAR 72 (288)

1990

US OPEN

14–18 June

Medinah CC, Medinah, Illinois
7195 yards PAR 72 (288)

Nick Faldo joined Jack Nicklaus (1965–66) to be the only players to have won consecutive Masters Tournaments. This time Faldo needed to play-off against 48 year-old Raymond Floyd, and became the only man in Majors history to have to play off to win back-to-back titles. It was his 3rd Major title. Mike Donald's 64 led by 2 after the 1st day: he then shot an 82 to make the cut by one. He played the final 54 holes in 19-over par – a Masters record since the halfway cut was introduced in 1957 – to come in 47th out of 49 finishers.

No concessions are given for age, as 45 year-old Hale Irwin will testify. He was taken into a sudden-death extension to the play-off – effectively made to play 91 holes – for the privilege of becoming the oldest winner of the Open. It was his 3rd win – only Anderson, Jones, Hogan and Nicklaus had achieved more. Irwin beat Mike Donald, who led him by 4 shots going into the last regulation 18 holes. Donald, whose adventures in the Masters had not fazed him, had won his private duel with Billy Ray Brown, only to find Irwin in the Clubhouse on 280 as well. There was a new record for entries filed – 6198.

1	**NICK FALDO***	71	72	66	69	278
	($225000)					
2	Ray Floyd	70	68	68	72	278
3=	John Huston	66	74	68	75	283
	Lanny Wadkins	72	73	70	68	283
5	Fred Couples	74	69	72	69	284
6	Jack Nicklaus	72	70	69	74	285
7=	Seve Ballesteros	74	73	68	71	286
	Bill Britton	68	74	71	73	286
	Bernhard Langer	70	73	69	74	286
	Scott Simpson	74	71	68	73	286
	Curtis Strange	70	73	71	72	286
	Tom Watson	77	71	67	71	286
13	Jose-Maria Olazabal	72	73	68	74	287
14=	Ben Crenshaw	72	74	73	69	288
	Scott Hoch	71	68	73	76	288
	Tom Kite	75	73	66	74	288
	Larry Mize	70	76	71	71	288
	Ronan Rafferty	72	74	69	73	288
	Craig Stadler	72	70	74	72	288
20=	Mark Calcavecchia	74	73	73	69	289
	Steve Jones	77	69	72	71	289
	Fuzzy Zoeller	72	74	73	70	289
23	Jumbo Ozaki	70	71	77	72	290
24=	Donnie Hammond	71	74	75	71	291
	Gary Player	73	74	68	76	291
	Lee Trevino	78	69	72	72	291
27=	Wayne Grady	72	75	72	73	292
	Andy North	71	73	77	71	292
	Jeff Sluman	78	68	75	71	292
30=	Peter Jacobsen	67	75	76	75	293
	Jodie Mudd	74	70	73	76	293
	Ian Woosnam	72	75	70	76	293

1	**HALE IRWIN***	69	70	74	67	280
	($220000)					
2	Mike Donald	67	70	72	71	280
3=	Billy Ray Brown	69	71	69	72	281
	Nick Faldo	72	72	68	69	281
5=	Mark Brooks	68	70	72	73	283
	Greg Norman	72	73	69	69	283
	Tim Simpson	66	69	75	73	283
8=	Scott Hoch	70	73	69	72	284
	Steve Jones	67	76	74	67	284
	Jose-Maria Olazabal	73	69	69	73	284
	Tom Sieckmann	70	74	68	72	284
	Craig Stadler	71	70	72	71	284
	Fuzzy Zoeller	73	70	68	73	284
14=	Jim Benepe	72	70	73	70	285
	John Huston	68	72	73	72	285
	John Inman	72	71	70	72	285
	Larry Mize	72	70	69	74	285
	Larry Nelson	74	67	69	75	285
	Scott Simpson	66	73	73	73	285
	Jeff Sluman	66	70	74	75	285
21=	Steve Elkington	73	71	73	69	286
	Curtis Strange	73	70	68	75	286
	Ian Woosnam	70	70	74	72	286
24=	Paul Azinger	72	72	69	74	287
	Webb Heintzelman	70	75	74	68	287
	Jumbo Ozaki	73	72	74	68	287
	Corey Pavin	74	70	73	70	287
	Billy Tuten	74	70	72	71	287
29=	Chip Beck	71	71	73	73	288
	Brian Claar	70	71	71	76	288
	Mike Hulbert	76	66	71	75	288
	Phil Mickelson (a)	74	71	71	72	288

*Nick Faldo (4,4) beat Ray Floyd (4,5) in the Sudden-death Play-off

* Hale Irwin (74) beat Mike Donald (74) at the 1st extra hole after the 18-Hole Play-off was tied

Round Leader(s)	Lowest Scores
R1 Mike Donald (47); 64	R2 Floyd, Hoch, Sluman; 68
R2 Floyd; 138	R3 Faldo, Kite; 66
R3 Floyd; 206	R4 Wadkins; 68

Round Leader(s)	Lowest Scores
R1 S Simpson, T Simpson,	R2 Hulbert; 66
Sluman; 66	R3 Faldo, Jack Nicklaus (33),
R2 T Simpson; 135	Craig Parry (46), Mike Reid (33),
R3 Brown, Donald; 209	Sieckmann, Strange, Zoeller; 68
	R4 Irwin, Jones; 67

19–22 July	**1990**
BRITISH OPEN	

Royal & Ancient GC, St Andrews, Fife, Scotland
6933 yards PAR 72 (288)

9–12 August	**1990**
US PGA	

Shoal Creek CC, Birmingham, Alabama
7145 yards PAR 72 (288)

Nick Faldo shot the lowest total for any Major since Tom Watson's all-time low of 268 (and Nicklaus' 269) at Turnberry in 1977. In some ways, Faldo's performance could be considered superior, in that his total was 18 under par, compared to Watson's 12 under; he finished 5 ahead of reigning PGA Champion Payne Stewart and Zimbabwean, Mark McNulty, themselves leading home a classy–looking Top 10. It was Faldo's 2nd Open Championship, and 4th Major, in under 4 years. In that time, since the influence of David Leadbeater on his technique, his Majors sequence read: W, 28, 30, 2, 3, 4, W, 18, 11, 9, W, 3, W – a consistency over a period of time only put together by the very best in golfing history.

1	**NICK FALDO**	67	65	67	71	270
	(£85000)					
2=	Mark McNulty	74	68	68	65	275
	Payne Stewart	68	68	68	71	275
4=	Jodie Mudd	72	66	72	66	276
	Ian Woosnam	68	69	70	69	276
6=	Ian Baker-Finch	68	72	64	73	277
	Greg Norman	66	66	76	69	277
8=	David Graham	72	71	70	66	279
	Donnie Hammond	70	71	68	70	279
	Steve Pate	70	68	72	69	279
	Corey Pavin	71	69	68	71	279
12=	Paul Broadhurst	74	69	63	74	280
	Robert Gamez	70	72	67	71	280
	Tim Simpson	70	69	69	72	280
	Vijay Singh	70	69	72	69	280
16=	Peter Jacobsen	68	70	70	73	281
	Steve Jones	72	67	72	70	281
	Sandy Lyle	72	70	67	72	281
	Frank Nobilo	72	67	68	74	281
	Jose-Maria Olazabal	71	67	71	72	281
	Mark Roe	71	70	72	68	281
22=	Eamonn Darcy	71	71	72	68	282
	Craig Parry	68	68	69	77	282
	Jamie Spence	72	65	73	72	282
25=	Fred Couples	71	70	70	72	283
	Christy O'Connor, Jr	68	72	71	72	283
	Nick Price	70	67	71	75	283
	Jose Rivero	70	70	70	73	283
	Jeff Sluman	72	70	70	71	283
	Lee Trevino	69	70	73	71	283

Round Leader(s)
R1 Norman; 66
R2 Faldo, Norman; 132
R3 Faldo; 199
Lowest Scores
R2 Faldo, Spence; 65
R3 Broadhurst; 63
R4 McNulty; 65

After tying for the British Open in 1989, Wayne Grady no doubt benefitted from that experience as he played par golf coming home behind Fred Couples, who, feeling the pressure, lost out through bogeys at 13, 14, 15 and 16. Grady was the 3rd Australian, after Jim Ferrier and David Graham, to hold the PGA title, which, along with the US Open, is the most American-dominated Major Championship.

1	**WAYNE GRADY**	72	67	72	71	282
	($225000)					
2	Fred Couples	69	71	73	72	285
3	Gil Morgan	77	72	65	72	286
4	Bill Britton	72	74	72	71	289
5=	Chip Beck	70	71	78	71	290
	Billy Mayfair	70	71	75	74	290
	Loren Roberts	73	71	70	76	290
8=	Mark McNulty	74	72	75	71	292
	Don Pooley	75	74	71	72	292
	Tim Simpson	71	73	75	73	292
	Payne Stewart	71	72	70	79	292
12=	Hale Irwin	77	72	70	74	293
	Larry Mize	72	68	76	77	293
14=	Billy Andrade	75	72	73	74	294
	Morris Hatalsky	73	78	71	72	294
	Jose Maria Olazabal	73	77	72	72	294
	Corey Pavin	73	75	72	74	294
	Fuzzy Zoeller	72	71	76	75	294
19=	Bob Boyd	74	74	71	76	295
	Nick Faldo	71	75	80	69	295
	Blaine McCallister	75	73	74	73	295
	Greg Norman	77	69	76	73	295
	Mark O'Meara	69	76	79	71	295
	Tom Watson	74	71	77	73	295
	Mark Wiebe	74	73	75	73	295
26=	Mark Brooks	78	69	76	73	296
	Peter Jacobsen	74	75	71	76	296
	Chris Perry	75	74	72	75	296
	Ray Stewart	73	73	75	75	296
	Brian Tennyson	71	77	71	77	296

Round Leader(s)
R1 Bobby Wadkins (66); 68
R2 Grady; 139
R3 Grady; 211
Lowest Scores
R2 Grady; 67
R3 Morgan; 65
R4 Faldo; 69

205

1991
THE MASTERS
11–14 April

Augusta National GC, Augusta, Georgia
6925 yards PAR 72 (288)

Ask any self-respecting Welshman what he associates with 1991, he conveniently overlooks the debacle of the Rugby World Cup and proudly states that Welshmen won both Best Acting Oscar and the US Masters. Ian Woosnam may be no Hannibal Lecter, as much as Anthony Hopkins may be no great shakes as a golfer, but Woosie's 'bite' lay in his ability to make approach irons pitch and stop as well as anyone in the world at that time. Not that such control was in evidence at Augusta, coming into 18. Woosnam, tied with the young Spaniard Olazabal and the old maestro Watson, missed the green with his approach but scrambled up and down for a par while the others dropped shots.

1	**IAN WOOSNAM** ($243000)	72	66	67	72	277
2	Jose-Maria Olazabal	68	71	69	70	278
3=	Ben Crenshaw	70	73	68	68	279
	Steve Pate	72	73	69	65	279
	Lanny Wadkins	67	71	70	71	279
	Tom Watson	68	68	70	73	279
7=	Ian Baker-Finch	71	70	69	70	280
	Andrew Magee	70	72	68	70	280
	Jodie Mudd	70	70	71	69	280
10=	Hale Irwin	70	70	75	66	281
	Tommy Nakajima	74	71	67	69	281
12=	Mark Calcavecchia	70	68	77	67	282
	Nick Faldo	72	73	67	70	282
	Billy Mayfair	72	72	72	66	282
	Craig Stadler	70	72	71	69	282
	Fuzzy Zoeller	70	70	75	67	282
17=	Ray Floyd	71	68	71	73	283
	Jim Gallagher, Jr	67	74	71	71	283
	Peter Jacobsen	73	70	68	72	283
	Mark McCumber	67	71	73	72	283
	Larry Mize	72	71	66	74	283
22=	Seve Ballesteros	75	70	69	70	284
	Steve Elkington	72	69	74	69	284
	Rocco Mediate	72	69	71	72	284
	Corey Pavin	73	70	69	72	284
	Scott Simpson	69	73	69	73	284
27=	Jay Don Blake	74	72	68	71	285
	Mark O'Meara	74	68	72	71	285
29=	Morris Hatalsky	71	72	70	73	286
	John Huston	73	72	71	70	286
	Jeff Sluman	71	71	72	72	286

Round Leader(s)
R1 Gallagher, McCumber, Wadkins; 67
R2 Watson; 136
R3 Woosnam; 205
Lowest Scores
R2 Billy Ray Brown (42); 65
R3 Mize; 66
R4 Pate; 65

1991
US OPEN
13–17 June

Hazeltine National GC, Minneapolis, Minnesota
7149 yards PAR 72 (288)

Payne Stewart had been injured for much of the early season, and didn't compete in the Masters. However, fit again, he led home an all-American Top 10 to collect his 2nd Major Championship – adding to the PGA title he won in 1989. Leading almost throughout, he surrendered the lead to 1987 Champion, Scott Simpson between holes 10 and 15 in R4, when Simpson held a 2-shot advantage. Simpson then bogeyed 16 and 18 to go into the 3rd play-off in 4 years. Both played nondescript golf, but Stewart was just the steadier to win. A freak lightning storm on the 1st day unfortunately killed a spectator – unhappily to occur again this year at Crooked Stick, during the PGA.

1	**PAYNE STEWART*** ($235000)	67	70	73	72	282
2	Scott Simpson	70	68	72	72	282
3=	Fred Couples	70	70	75	70	285
	Larry Nelson	73	72	72	68	285
5	Fuzzy Zoeller	72	73	74	67	286
6	Scott Hoch	69	71	74	73	287
7	Nolan Henke	67	71	77	73	288
8=	Ray Floyd	73	72	76	68	289
	Jose-Maria Olazabal	73	71	75	70	289
	Corey Pavin	71	67	79	72	289
11=	Jim Gallagher, Jr	70	72	75	73	290
	Hale Irwin	71	75	70	74	290
	Davis Love III	70	76	73	71	290
	Craig Parry	70	73	73	74	290
	DA Weibring	76	71	75	68	290
16=	Nick Faldo	72	74	73	72	291
	Sandy Lyle	72	70	74	75	291
	Tom Watson	73	71	77	70	291
19=	Mark Brooks	73	73	73	73	292
	Billy Ray Brown	73	71	77	71	292
	John Cook	76	70	72	74	292
	Peter Persons	70	75	75	72	292
	Nick Price	74	69	71	78	292
	Tom Sieckmann	74	70	74	74	292
	Craig Stadler	71	69	77	75	292
26=	Rick Fehr	74	69	73	77	293
	Jodie Mudd	71	70	77	75	293
	Mike Reid	74	72	74	73	293
	Bob Tway	75	69	75	74	293

* Payne Stewart (75) beat Scott Simpson (77) in the 18-Hole Play-off

Round Leader(s)
R1 Henke, Stewart; 67
R2 Stewart; 137
R3 Simpson, Stewart; 210
Lowest Scores
R2 Pavin; 67
R3 Irwin; 70
R4 Zoeller; 67

206

18–21 July	**1991**

BRITISH OPEN

Royal Birkdale GC, Southport, Lancashire, England
6940 yards PAR 70 (280)

8–11 August	**1991**

US PGA

Crooked Stick GC, Carmel, Indiana
7295 yards PAR 72 (288)

In 1984, then aged 23, Australian Ian Baker-Finch shot a R4 79 over the Old Course at St Andrews to bow out of Open Championship contention. That, after 54 holes of 68, 66, 71 (205) and a share of the lead, gave birth to the unkind tabloid nickname of Ian Baker-*Flinch*. Baker-Finch was not the 1st person to blow up in the last round of a Major, and won't be the last, but the combination of surnames made him a headline writer's delight. It was with some satisfaction, then, when the most famous hyphen in golf became the 1st double-barrelled surname to win any Major. This time, the Australian saved all his sparkling golf to the end - shooting a record-equalling R3 score, and birdying 5 of the 1st 7 holes on the last day. Although chased hard by compatriot, Mike Harwood, this burst of scoring secured him the title. Englishman, Richard Boxhall, trailing the lead in R3 by just 3, freakishly broke his leg while driving off the 3rd tee.

Every sport has its share of fairy stories – golf more than most. There have not been many more remarkable than when John Daly won the PGA in 1991. Virtually unknown, he didn't qualify high enough to merit an automatic entry for the Championship. In fact, he was only 9th on the reserve list – 9th alternate – and his chance only came when Nick Price scratched to be at the birth of his child, and several higher on the list declined the invitation to play. Daly hit the ball consistently longer, and usually straighter, than any player before in the history of the Majors. Without a practice round he shot a 69 and, from R2 onwards – his ferocious hitting combined with some magical pressure putting – he was not headed, finally victorious by 3 strokes.

1	**IAN BAKER-FINCH**	71	71	64	66	272
	(£90000)					

2	Mike Harwood	68	70	69	67	274
3=	Fred Couples	72	69	70	64	275
	Mark O'Meara	71	68	67	69	275
5=	Eamonn Darcy	73	68	66	70	277
	Jodie Mudd	72	70	72	63	277
	Bob Tway	75	66	70	66	277
8	Craig Parry	71	70	69	68	278
9=	Seve Ballesteros	66	73	69	71	279
	Bernhard Langer	71	71	70	67	279
	Greg Norman	74	68	71	66	279
12=	Roger Chapman	74	66	71	69	280
	Rodger Davis	70	71	73	66	280
	Vijay Singh	71	69	69	71	280
	Magnus Sunesson	72	73	68	67	280
	David Williams	74	71	68	67	280
17=	Chip Beck	67	78	70	66	281
	Paul Broadhurst	71	73	68	69	281
	Nick Faldo	68	75	70	68	281
	Barry Lane	68	72	71	70	281
	Mark Mouland	68	74	68	71	281
	Peter Senior	74	67	71	69	281
	Andrew Sherborne	73	70	68	70	281
	Lee Trevino	71	72	71	67	281
	Ian Woosnam	70	72	69	70	281
26=	Wayne Grady	69	70	73	70	282
	Mark James	72	68	70	72	282
	Colin Montgomerie	71	69	71	71	282
	Mike Reid	68	71	70	73	282
	Eduardo Romero	70	73	68	71	282
	Tom Watson	69	72	72	69	282

Round Leader(s)

		Lowest Scores	
R1	Ballesteros; 66	R2	Chapman, Tway; 66
R2	Harwood; 138	R3	Baker-Finch; 64
R3	Baker-Finch, O'Meara; 206	R4	Mudd; 63

1	**JOHN DALY**	69	67	69	71	276
	($230000)					

2	Bruce Lietzke	68	69	72	70	279
3	Jim Gallagher, Jr	70	72	72	67	281
4	Kenny Knox	67	71	70	74	282
5=	Bob Gilder	73	70	67	73	283
	Steven Richardson	70	72	72	69	283
7=	David Feherty	71	74	71	68	284
	Ray Floyd	69	74	72	69	284
	John Huston	70	72	70	72	284
	Steve Pate	70	75	70	69	284
	Craig Stadler	68	71	69	76	284
	Hal Sutton	74	67	72	71	284
13=	Jay Don Blake	75	70	72	68	285
	Andrew Magee	69	73	68	75	285
	Payne Stewart	74	70	71	70	285
16=	Nick Faldo	70	69	71	76	286
	Ken Green	68	73	71	74	286
	Wayne Levi	73	71	72	70	286
	Sandy Lyle	68	75	71	72	286
	Rocco Mediate	71	71	73	71	286
	Gil Morgan	70	71	74	71	286
	Howard Twitty	70	71	75	70	286
23=	Seve Ballesteros	71	72	71	73	287
	Chip Beck	73	73	70	71	287
	Mike Hulbert	72	72	73	70	287
	Jack Nicklaus	71	72	73	71	287
27=	Fred Couples	74	67	76	71	288
	Rick Fehr	70	73	71	74	288
	Jim Hallett	69	74	73	72	288
	Mark McNulty	75	71	69	73	288
	Loren Roberts	72	74	72	70	288

Round Leader(s)

R1	Knox, Ian Woosnam (48); 67
R2	Daly; 136
R3	Daly; 205

Lowest Scores

R2	Daly, Couples, Sutton; 67
R3	Gilder; 67
R4	Gallagher; 67

1992

9–12 April

THE MASTERS

Augusta National GC, Augusta, Georgia
6925 yards _PAR 72 (288)_

1992

18–21 June

US OPEN

Pebble Beach GL, Pebble Beach, California
6809 yards _PAR 72 (288)_

Ian Woosnam, tying with Craig Parry at halfway, looked to be on course to a successful defence of his title, but disappointingly fell away to finish 8 shots adrift of Freddie Couples at the end. Parry still led after 54 holes, but the Australian of Woosnamesque stature also capitulated, shooting a R4 78. Couples' 1st Major was extremely popular, and he played a consistent, and at times brilliant, set of 4 rounds to head Ray Floyd – 6 months short of his 50th birthday – by 2.

1	**FRED COUPLES** ($270000)	69	67	69	70	275
2	Ray Floyd	69	68	69	71	277
3	Corey Pavin	72	71	68	67	278
4=	Mark O'Meara	74	67	69	70	280
	Jeff Sluman	65	74	70	71	280
6=	Ian Baker-Finch	70	69	68	74	281
	Nolan Henke	70	71	70	70	281
	Larry Mize	73	69	71	68	281
	Greg Norman	70	70	73	68	281
	Steve Pate	73	71	70	67	281
	Nick Price	70	71	67	73	281
	Ted Schultz	68	69	72	72	281
13=	Nick Faldo	71	72	68	71	282
	Wayne Grady	68	75	71	68	282
	Bruce Lietzke	69	72	68	73	282
	Craig Parry	69	66	69	78	282
	Dillard Pruitt	75	68	70	69	282
	Scott Simpson	70	71	71	70	282
19=	Billy Ray Brown	70	74	70	69	283
	John Daly	71	71	73	68	283
	Mike Hulbert	68	74	71	70	283
	Andrew Magee	73	70	70	70	283
	Ian Woosnam	69	66	73	75	283
	Fuzzy Zoeller	71	70	73	69	283
25=	Bruce Fleisher	73	70	72	69	284
	Jim Gallagher, Jr	74	68	71	71	284
	John Huston	69	73	73	69	284
	Davis Love III	68	72	72	72	284
	Craig Stadler	70	71	70	73	284
	DA Weibring	71	68	72	73	284

Round Leader(s)
R1   Sluman, Lanny Wadkins (48); 65
R2   Parry, Woosnam; 135
R3   Parry; 204
Lowest Scores
R2   Parry, Woosnam; 66
R3   Price; 67
R4   Mark Calcavecchia (31); 65

Tom Kite probably held the tag of 'best player never..', etc, longer than most. That he had appeared in the Open as far back as 1970 and had 3 runner-up slots in Major Championships, suggested that, at the age of 42, his career (in which he became the biggest money-earner in golf history) was going to end without that elusive claim to immortality – a Major. It took a wild and windy Pebble Beach to elevate his status into Majors folklore – an Open that also confirmed Jeff Sluman's credentials as a worthy Major Champion (he won the 1988 PGA title) and the promise of Scotsman, Colin Montgomerie, while being 46 year-old Gil Morgan's last serious attempt to win.

1	**TOM KITE** ($275000)	71	72	70	72	285
2	Jeff Sluman	73	74	69	71	287
3	Colin Montgomerie	70	71	77	70	288
4=	Nick Faldo	70	76	68	77	291
	Nick Price	71	72	77	71	291
6=	Billy Andrade	72	74	72	74	292
	Jay Don Blake	70	74	75	73	292
	Bob Gilder	73	70	75	74	292
	Mike Hulbert	74	73	70	75	292
	Tom Lehman	69	74	72	77	292
	Joey Sindelar	74	72	68	78	292
	Ian Woosnam	72	72	69	79	292
13=	Ian Baker-Finch	74	71	72	76	293
	John Cook	72	72	74	75	293
	Mark McCumber	70	76	73	74	293
	Gil Morgan	66	69	77	81	293
17=	Fred Couples	72	70	78	74	294
	Andy Dillard	68	70	79	77	294
	Wayne Grady	74	76	81	73	294
	Andrew Magee	77	69	72	76	294
	Tray Tyner	74	72	78	70	294
	Willie Wood	70	75	75	74	294
23=	Seve Ballesteros	71	76	69	79	295
	Brad Bryant	71	76	75	73	295
	Jay Haas	70	77	74	74	295
	Donnie Hammond	73	73	73	76	295
	Dudley Hart	76	71	71	77	295
	Jim Kane	73	71	76	75	295
	Bernhard Langer	73	72	75	75	295
	Billy Mayfair	74	73	75	73	295
	Jumbo Ozaki	77	70	72	76	295
	Curtis Strange	67	78	76	74	295

Round Leader(s)
R1   Morgan; 66
R2   Morgan; 135
R3   Morgan; 212
Lowest Scores
R2   Grady; 66
R3   Faldo, Scott Simpson (64), Sindelar; 68
R4   Montgomerie; Tyner; 70

16–19 July						**1992**

BRITISH OPEN

Honourable Company, Muirfield, Angus, Scotland
6970 yards PAR 71 (284)

Nick Faldo won his 3rd Open to match the feat of Jones, Cotton, Player, Nicklaus and Ballesteros this century. He still ties 11th on the all-time list of Open winners however, only halving Vardon's haul of titles. At the same venue in 1987, Paul Azinger was the American ground down by Faldo. This time, after wasting a 4 shot lead overnight, he stood on the 15th tee 2 behind John Cook, with the tide going the way of this American. Faldo's reserves of grit are famously deep, however, and *the* outstanding winner of Majors in recent years proved why when he birdied 15 and 17, forcing Cook to crack on 18, and win by one.

1	**NICK FALDO**	66	64	69	73	272
	(£95000)					
2	John Cook	66	67	70	70	273
3	Jose-Maria Olazabal	70	67	69	68	274
4	Steve Pate	64	70	69	73	276
5=	Gordon Brand, Jr	65	68	72	74	279
	Ernie Els	66	69	70	74	279
	Donnie Hammond	70	65	70	74	279
	Robert Karlsson	70	68	70	71	279
	Malcolm Mackenzie	71	67	70	71	279
	Andrew Magee	67	72	70	70	279
	Ian Woosnam	65	73	70	71	279
12=	Chip Beck	71	68	67	74	280
	Ray Floyd	64	71	73	72	280
	Sandy Lyle	68	70	70	72	280
	Mark O'Meara	71	68	72	69	280
	Larry Rinker	69	68	70	73	280
	Jamie Spence	71	68	70	71	280
18	Greg Norman	71	72	70	68	281
19=	Ian Baker-Finch	71	71	72	68	282
	Hale Irwin	70	73	67	72	282
	Tom Kite	70	69	71	72	282
22=	Paul Lawrie	70	72	68	73	283
	Peter Mitchell	69	71	72	71	283
	Tom Purtzer	68	69	75	71	283
25=	Billy Andrade	69	71	70	74	284
	Peter Senior	70	69	70	75	284
	Duffy Waldorf	69	70	73	72	284
28=	Mark Calcavecchia	69	71	73	72	285
	Russ Cochran	71	68	72	74	285
	Mats Lanner	72	68	71	74	285
	Mark McNulty	71	70	70	74	285
	Jodie Mudd	71	69	74	71	285
	Craig Parry	67	71	76	71	285

Round Leader(s)

R1 Floyd, Pate; 64
R2 Faldo; 130
R3 Faldo; 199

Lowest Scores

R2 Faldo; 64
R3 Beck, Irwin; 67
R4 Baker-Finch, Norman, Olazabal; 68

13–16 August						**1992**

US PGA

Bellerive CC, St Louis, Missouri
7024 yards PAR 71 (284)

John Cook was to be unlucky again at Bellerive, but this time he could take some comfort knowing that Nick Price was also a two-time second placer (British Opens in 1982 and 1988) before landing his 1st Major. Zimbabwean Nick Price, with an English father and Welsh mother, spent much of his early career on the European circuit before settling in the US. He was now establishing himself as one of the world's best players. Faldo's charge to become the 1st European to win the PGA did not fluster the calm African who, after the leader throughout, Gene Sauers, blew up, held on for a comfortable win.

1	**NICK PRICE**	70	70	68	70	278
	($280000)					
2=	John Cook	71	72	67	71	281
	Nick Faldo	68	70	76	67	281
	Jim Gallagher, Jr	72	66	72	71	281
	Gene Sauers	67	69	70	75	281
6	Jeff Maggert	71	72	65	74	282
7=	Russ Cochran	69	69	76	69	283
	Dan Forsman	70	73	70	70	283
9=	Brian Claar	68	73	73	70	284
	Anders Forsbrand	73	71	70	70	284
	Duffy Waldorf	74	73	68	69	284
12=	Billy Andrade	72	71	70	72	285
	Corey Pavin	71	73	70	71	285
	Jeff Sluman	73	71	72	69	285
15=	Mark Brooks	71	72	68	75	286
	Brad Faxon	72	69	75	70	286
	Greg Norman	71	74	71	70	286
18=	Steve Elkington	74	70	71	72	287
	Rick Fehr	74	73	71	69	287
	John Huston	73	75	71	68	287
21=	Bill Britton	70	77	70	71	288
	Fred Couples	69	73	73	73	288
	Lee Janzen	74	71	72	71	288
	Tom Kite	73	73	69	73	288
	Gil Morgan	71	69	73	75	288
	Tommy Nakajima	71	75	69	73	288
	Tom Purtzer	72	72	74	70	288
28=	Mike Hulbert	74	74	70	71	289
	Peter Jacobsen	73	71	72	73	289
	Larry Nelson	72	68	75	74	289
	Joe Ozaki	76	72	74	67	289
	Tom Wargo	72	72	73	72	289

Round Leader(s)

R1 Sauers, Craig Stadler (48); 67
R2 Sauers; 136
R3 Sauers; 206

Lowest Scores

R2 Gallagher, Steven Richardson (48); 66
R3 Maggert; 65
R4 Faldo, Ozaki; 67

1993
THE MASTERS
8–11 April

Augusta National GC, Augusta, Georgia
6925 yards _PAR 72 (288)_

1993
US OPEN
17–20 June

Baltusrol, Springfield, New Jersey
7152 yards _PAR 70 (280)_

8 years after winning his 1st Masters, Bernhard Langer proved he was still a force in world golf with a repeat victory at Augusta. It was also 10 years after Seve Ballesteros' 2nd win, which paved the way for Lyle, Faldo (twice) and Woosnam, along with Langer, to dominate the event for Europe. Jose-Maria Olazabal apart, the German was the only European to finish in this year's Top 10 – a signal, perhaps, along with form from the other Majors later in the year, that the US were to retain the Ryder Cup this year. Winner's prize money topped $300000 for the 1st time.

Failing to make the cut in 3 former attempts, it was deemed a little early in his career for 28 year-old Lee Janzen to win a Major. However, leading from R2, he headed a strong field thereafter and held on to be a worthy winner from 1991 Champion Payne Stewart. Joey Sindelar tied for the R1 lead with a 66. He then shot a 79 to miss the cut. John Daly, the 1991 PGA Champion and prodigious hitter, playing the 630 yard 17th - the longest hole in Majors history - drove, then 1-ironed the green in 2.

1	**BERNHARD LANGER**	68	70	69	70	277
	($306000)					
2	Chip Beck	72	67	72	70	281
3=	John Daly	70	71	73	69	283
	Steve Elkington	71	70	71	71	283
	Tom Lehman	67	75	73	68	283
	Lanny Wadkins	69	72	71	71	283
7=	Dan Forsman	69	69	73	73	284
	Jose-Maria Olazabal	70	72	74	68	284
9=	Brad Faxon	74	70	72	69	285
	Payne Stewart	74	70	72	69	285
11=	Seve Ballesteros	74	70	71	71	286
	Ray Floyd	68	71	74	73	286
	Anders Forsbrand	71	74	75	66	286
	Corey Pavin	67	75	73	71	286
	Scott Simpson	72	71	71	72	286
	Fuzzy Zoeller	75	67	71	73	286
17=	Mark Calcavecchia	71	70	74	72	287
	Jeff Sluman	71	72	71	73	287
	Howard Twitty	70	71	73	73	287
	Ian Woosnam	71	74	73	69	287
21=	Russ Cochran	70	69	73	76	288
	Fred Couples	72	70	74	72	288
	Sandy Lyle	73	71	71	73	288
	Jeff Maggert	70	67	75	76	288
	Larry Mize	67	74	74	73	288
	Mark O'Meara	75	69	73	71	288
27=	Nolan Henke	76	69	71	73	289
	Hale Irwin	74	69	74	72	289
	Jack Nicklaus	67	75	76	71	289
	Joey Sindelar	72	69	76	72	289

Round Leader(s)
R1 Lehman, Mize, Nicklaus, Pavin; 67
R2 Maggert; 137
R3 Langer; 207
Lowest Scores
R2 Beck, Maggert, Zoeller; 67
R3 Langer, 69
R4 Forsbrand; 66

1	**LEE JANZEN**	67	67	69	69	272
	($290000)					
2	Payne Stewart	70	66	68	70	274
3=	Paul Azinger	71	68	69	69	277
	Craig Parry	66	74	69	68	277
5=	Scott Hoch	66	72	72	68	278
	Tom Watson	70	66	73	69	278
7=	Ernie Els	71	73	68	67	279
	Ray Floyd	68	73	70	68	279
	Fred Funk	70	72	67	70	279
	Nolan Henke	72	71	67	69	279
11=	John Adams	70	70	69	71	280
	David Edwards	70	72	66	72	280
	Nick Price	71	66	70	73	280
	Loren Roberts	70	70	71	69	280
	Jeff Sluman	71	71	69	69	280
16=	Fred Couples	68	71	71	71	281
	Barry Lane	74	68	70	69	281
	Mike Standly	70	69	70	72	281
19=	Ian Baker-Finch	70	70	70	72	282
	Dan Forsman	73	71	70	68	282
	Tom Lehman	71	70	71	70	282
	Blaine McCallister	68	73	73	68	282
	Steve Pate	70	71	71	70	282
	Corey Pavin	68	69	75	70	282
25=	Chip Beck	72	68	72	71	283
	Mark Calcavecchia	70	70	71	72	283
	John Cook	75	66	70	72	283
	Wayne Levi	71	69	69	74	283
	Rocco Mediate	68	72	73	70	283
	Joe Ozaki	70	70	74	69	283
	Kenny Perry	74	70	68	71	283
	Curtis Strange	73	68	75	67	283

Round Leader(s)
R1 Hoch, Parry, Joey Sindelar (Cut); 66
R2 Janzen; 134
R3 Janzen; 203
Lowest Scores
R2 Cook, Price, Stewart, Watson; 66
R3 Edwards; 66
R4 Steve Lowery (33); 66

15–18 July	**1993**

BRITISH OPEN
Royal St George's, Sandwich, Kent, England
6860 yards **PAR 70 (280)**

12–15 August	**1993**

US PGA
Inverness Club, Toledo, Ohio
7024 yards **PAR 71 (284)**

Greg Norman set the lowest score in Majors history when his 64 in the last round gave him a 2-shot lead over reigning Champion, Nick Faldo. Norman's 13-under par 267 was one lower than Tom Watson's at Turnberry in 1977. In repeating his win he scotched further accusations of his fragility in Major Championships, but he was not to get rid of them completely. Ernie Els shot 4 sub-70 rounds, but only finished 6th - the lowest position for such an achievement. Nick Faldo and Payne Stewart each tied with the all-time low of 63. The winning prize money reached 6 figures in £s Sterling for the 1st time.

Paul Azinger, twice a runner-up in Majors (British Open 1987 and the PGA itself a year later) and close finisher in this year's US Open, eventually collected an overdue Major Championship. Greg Norman's propensity to fail in Majors showdowns continued, as he succumbed once again to events at Inverness. Here, in 1986, it was Bob Tway's greenside bunker blow: this time it was down to Greg himself. He rimmed the hole from 4 feet to bogey the 2nd extra hole in a play-off. Vijay Singh, from Fiji, easily the greatest golfer to come from the South Seas, shot a record-equalling 63 in R2.

1	**GREG NORMAN**	66	68	69	64	267
	(£100000)					
2	Nick Faldo	69	63	70	67	269
3	Bernhard Langer	67	66	70	67	270
4=	Corey Pavin	68	66	68	70	272
	Peter Senior	66	69	70	67	272
6=	Ernie Els	68	69	69	68	274
	Paul Lawrie	72	68	69	65	274
	Nick Price	68	70	67	69	274
9=	Fred Couples	68	66	72	69	275
	Wayne Grady	74	68	64	69	275
	Scott Simpson	68	70	71	66	275
12	Payne Stewart	71	72	70	63	276
13	Barry Lane	70	68	71	68	277
14=	Mark Calcavecchia	66	73	71	68	278
	John Daly	71	66	70	71	278
	Tom Kite	72	70	68	68	278
	Mark McNulty	67	71	71	69	278
	Gil Morgan	70	68	70	70	278
	Jose Rivero	68	73	67	70	278
	Fuzzy Zoeller	66	70	71	71	278
21=	Peter Baker	70	67	74	68	279
	Howard Clark	67	72	70	70	279
	Jesper Parnevik	68	74	68	69	279
24=	Rodger Davis	68	71	71	70	280
	David Frost	69	73	70	68	280
	Mark Roe	70	71	73	66	280
27=	Seve Ballesteros	68	73	69	71	281
	Mark James	70	70	70	71	281
	Malcolm Mackenzie	72	71	71	67	281
	Larry Mize	67	69	74	71	281
	Yoshinori Mizumaki	69	69	73	70	281
	Iain Pyman (a)	68	72	70	71	281
	Des Smyth	67	74	70	70	281

1	**PAUL AZINGER***	69	66	69	68	272
	($300000)					
2	Greg Norman	68	68	67	69	272
3	Nick Faldo	68	68	69	68	273
4	Vijay Singh	68	63	73	70	274
5	Tom Watson	69	65	70	72	276
6=	John Cook	72	66	68	71	277
	Bob Estes	69	66	69	73	277
	Dudley Hart	66	68	71	72	277
	Nolan Henke	72	70	67	68	277
	Scott Hoch	74	68	68	67	277
	Hale Irwin	68	69	67	73	277
	Phil Mickelson	67	71	69	70	277
	Scott Simpson	64	70	71	72	277
14=	Steve Elkington	67	66	74	71	278
	Brad Faxon	70	70	65	73	278
	Bruce Fleisher	69	74	67	68	278
	Gary Hallberg	70	69	68	71	278
	Lanny Wadkins	65	68	71	74	278
	Richard Zokol	66	71	71	70	278
20=	Jay Haas	69	68	70	72	279
	Eduardo Romero	67	67	74	71	279
22=	Lee Janzen	70	68	71	72	281
	Jim McGovern	71	67	69	74	281
	Frank Nobilo	69	66	74	72	281
	Gene Sauers	68	74	70	69	281
	Greg Twiggs	70	69	70	72	281
	Ian Woosnam	70	71	68	72	281
28=	Peter Jacobsen	71	67	74	70	282
	Billy Mayfair	68	73	70	71	282
	Loren Roberts	67	67	76	72	282

*Paul Azinger beat Greg Norman at 2nd extra hole in Sudden Death Play-off

Round Leader(s)
R1 Simpson; 64
R2 Singh; 131
R3 Norman; 203

Lowest Scores
R2 Singh; 63
R3 Faxon; 65
R4 Hoch; 67

Round Leader(s)
R1 Calcavecchia, Norman, Senior, Zoeller; 66
R2 Faldo; 132
R3 Faldo, Pavin; 202

Lowest Scores
R2 Faldo; 63
R3 Grady; 64
R4 Stewart; 63

1994
THE MASTERS
7–10 April

Augusta National GC, Augusta, Georgia
6925 yards _PAR 72 (288)_

The rich promise of Jose-Maria Olazabal matured at Augusta, as Seve's prodigy and countryman won a Major for the 1st time. 6 off the lead after R1, Olazabal powered his way up the leaderboard, going around the final 54 holes in 11 under par, to overtake R3 leader, Tom Lehman. This win made it 9 wins for Europeans since Ballesteros himself in 1980, and the 3rd for Spain.

1	**J-MARIA OLAZABAL**	74	67	69	69	279
	($360000)					
2	Tom Lehman	70	70	69	72	281
3	Larry Mize	68	71	72	71	282
4	Tom Kite	69	72	71	71	283
5=	Jay Haas	72	72	72	69	285
	Jim McGovern	72	70	71	72	285
	Loren Roberts	75	68	72	70	285
8=	Ernie Els	74	67	74	71	286
	Corey Pavin	71	72	73	70	286
10=	Ian Baker-Finch	71	71	71	74	287
	Ray Floyd	71	74	71	72	287
	John Huston	72	72	74	69	287
13	Tom Watson	70	71	73	74	288
14	Dan Forsman	74	66	76	73	289
15=	Chip Beck	71	71	75	74	291
	Brad Faxon	71	73	73	74	291
	Mark O'Meara	75	70	76	70	291
18=	Seve Ballesteros	70	76	75	71	292
	Ben Crenshaw	74	73	73	72	292
	David Edwards	73	72	73	74	292
	Bill Glasson	72	73	75	72	292
	Hale Irwin	73	68	79	72	292
	Greg Norman	70	70	75	77	292
	Lanny Wadkins	73	74	73	72	292
25=	Bernhard Langer	74	74	72	73	293
	Jeff Sluman	74	75	71	73	293
27=	Scott Simpson	74	74	73	73	294
	Vijay Singh	70	75	74	75	294
	Curtis Strange	74	70	75	75	294
30=	Lee Janzen	75	71	76	73	295
	Craig Parry	75	74	73	73	295

Round Leader(s)
R1 Mize; 68
R2 Mize; 139
R3 Lehman; 209
Lowest Scores
R2 Forsman; 66
R3 Lehman, Olazabal; 69
R4 Haas, Huston, Olazabal; 69

1994
US OPEN
16–20 June

Oakmont CC, Oakmont, Pennsylvania
6946 yards _PAR 71 (284)_

There was a 3-way play-off in the Open for the 1st time since Brookline in 1963. Arnold Palmer, along with Jack Cupit, missed out to Julius Boros that year – now Arnold, aged 64, started the Open for the last time: Ernie Els, 40 years his junior, became the 1st South African since Gary Player to win the Open, and only the 3rd after Bobby Locke and Player to win any Major Championship. After 18 holes, Colin Montgomerie was eliminated, leaving Els to fight it out, sudden death, with Loren Roberts. It took 2 holes before Roberts' bogey let in Ernie. The R1 leaderboard looked nostalgic – Tom Watson led Jack Nicklaus by one.

1	**ERNIE ELS**	69	71	66	73	279
	($320000)					
2=	Colin Montgomerie	71	65	73	70	279
	Loren Roberts	76	69	74	70	279
4	Curtis Strange	70	70	70	70	280
5	John Cook	73	65	73	71	282
6=	Tom Watson	68	73	68	74	283
	Clark Dennis	71	71	70	71	283
	Greg Norman	71	71	69	72	283
9=	Jeff Maggert	71	68	75	70	284
	Frank Nobilo	69	71	68	76	284
	Jeff Sluman	72	69	72	71	284
	Duffy Waldorf	74	68	73	69	284
13=	David Edwards	73	65	75	72	285
	Scott Hoch	72	72	70	71	285
	Jim McGovern	73	69	74	69	285
16=	Fred Couples	72	71	69	74	286
	Steve Lowery	71	71	68	76	286
18=	Seve Ballesteros	72	72	70	73	287
	Hale Irwin	69	69	71	78	287
	Scott Verplank	70	72	75	70	287
21=	Steve Pate	74	66	71	77	288
	Sam Torrance	72	71	76	69	288
23=	Bernhard Langer	72	72	73	72	289
	Kirk Triplett	70	71	71	77	289
25=	Chip Beck	73	73	70	74	290
	Craig Parry	78	68	71	73	290
	Mike Springer	74	72	73	71	290
28=	Lennie Clements	73	71	73	75	292
	Jim Furyk	74	69	74	75	292
	Davis Love III	74	72	74	72	292
	Jack Nicklaus	69	70	77	76	292
	Jumbo Ozaki	70	73	69	80	292

* Ernie Els (74) beat Colin Montgomerie (78) and tied with Loren Roberts (74) in the 18-Hole Play-off, before winning at the second extra hole.

Round Leader(s)   **Lowest Scores**
R1 Watson; 68   R2 Cook, Edwards, Montgomerie; 65
R2 Montgomerie; 136   R3 Roberts; 64
R3 Els; 206   R4 McGovern, Torrance, Waldorf; 69

14–17 July				**1994**

BRITISH OPEN

Turnberry GC, Ayrshire, Scotland
6957 yards PAR 70 (280)

Nick Price was to end 1994 atop the Sony World Rankings – the only player, along with Ballesteros (1988), Woosnam (1991) and Faldo (1992 & 1993) to oust Greg Norman from that spot since the computerized tables were 1st produced in 1986. Greg was to regain the No1 position for the 3rd time in 1995. Price's 2nd Major occurred in a display of blistering scoring over the Turnberry Links. His battle-royal throughout R4 with Jesper Parnevik, culminated with the Swede, going to the last 2 ahead, dropping a shot, while Price was holing a 17-yard putt for eagle at the 17th.

1	**NICK PRICE**	69	66	67	66	268
	(£110000)					
2	Jesper Parnevik	68	66	68	67	269
3	Fuzzy Zoeller	71	66	64	70	271
4=	David Feherty	68	69	66	70	273
	Anders Forsbrand	72	71	66	64	273
	Mark James	72	67	66	68	273
7	Brad Faxon	69	65	67	73	274
8=	Nick Faldo	75	66	70	64	275
	Tom Kite	71	69	66	69	275
	Colin Montgomerie	72	69	65	69	275
11=	Mark Calcavecchia	71	70	67	68	276
	Russell Claydon	72	71	68	65	276
	Jonathan Lomas	66	70	72	68	276
	Mark McNulty	71	70	68	67	276
	Larry Mize	73	69	64	70	276
	Frank Nobilo	69	67	72	68	276
	Greg Norman	71	67	69	69	276
	Ronan Rafferty	71	66	65	74	276
	Tom Watson	68	65	69	74	276
20=	Mark Brooks	74	64	71	68	277
	Peter Senior	68	71	67	71	277
	Vijay Singh	70	68	69	70	277
	Greg Turner	65	71	70	71	277
24=	Andrew Coltart	71	69	66	72	278
	Ernie Els	69	69	69	71	278
	Bob Estes	72	68	72	66	278
	Peter Jacobsen	69	70	67	72	278
	Paul Lawrie	71	69	70	68	278
	Tom Lehman	70	69	70	69	278
	Jeff Maggert	69	74	67	68	278
	Terry Price	74	65	71	68	278
	Loren Roberts	68	69	69	72	278
	Mike Springer	72	67	68	71	278
	Craig Stadler	71	69	66	72	278

Round Leader(s)

R1 Turner; 65
R2 Watson; 133
R3 Faxon, Zoeller; 201

Lowest Scores

R2 Brooks; 64
R3 Mize, Zoeller; 64
R4 Faldo, Forsbrand; 64

11–14 August				**1994**

US PGA

Southern Hills CC, Tulsa, Oklahoma
6824 yards PAR 70 (280)

Nick Price's 11-under par 269 was a new low for the PGA Championship and formed part of a remarkable 23-under par back-to-back Majors double for the World No1. He became the 1st golfer since Faldo in 1990 to win more than 1 Major in the same season – and only the 2nd person to achieve the British Open-PGA double in the same year since Walter Hagen's achievement 70 years before. His win by 6 strokes over an outstanding field emphasised Price's superiority in 1994.

1	**NICK PRICE**	67	65	70	67	269
	($310000)					
2	Corey Pavin	70	67	69	69	275
3	Phil Mickelson	68	71	67	70	276
4=	John Cook	71	67	69	70	277
	Nick Faldo	73	67	71	66	277
	Greg Norman	71	69	67	70	277
7=	Steve Elkington	73	70	66	69	278
	Jose Maria Olazabal	72	66	70	70	278
9=	Ben Crenshaw	70	67	70	72	279
	Tom Kite	72	68	69	70	279
	Loren Roberts	69	72	67	71	279
	Tom Watson	69	72	67	71	279
	Ian Woosnam	68	72	73	66	279
14	Jay Haas	71	66	68	75	280
15=	Glen Day	70	69	70	72	281
	Mark McNulty	72	68	70	71	281
	Larry Mize	72	72	67	70	281
	Kirk Triplett	71	69	71	70	281
19=	Bill Glasson	71	73	68	70	282
	Mark McCumber	73	70	71	68	282
	Craig Parry	70	69	70	73	282
	Craig Stadler	70	70	74	68	282
	Curtis Strange	73	71	68	70	282
	Fuzzy Zoeller	69	71	72	70	282
25=	Ernie Els	68	71	69	75	283
	David Frost	70	71	69	73	283
	Barry Lane	70	73	68	72	283
	Bernhard Langer	73	71	67	72	283
	Jeff Sluman	70	72	66	75	283
30=	Bob Boyd	72	71	70	71	284
	Lennie Clements	74	70	69	71	284
	Brad Faxon	72	73	73	66	284
	Wayne Grady	75	68	71	70	284
	Sam Torrance	69	75	69	71	284
	Richard Zokol	77	67	67	73	284

Round Leader(s)

R1 Colin Montgomerie (36),
   Price; 67
R2 Price; 132
R3 Price; 202

Lowest Scores

R2 Blaine McCallister (36); 64
R3 Elkington, Sluman; 66
R4 Faldo, Faxon,
   Woosnam; 66

1995

6–9 April

THE MASTERS

Augusta National GC, Augusta, Georgia
6925 yards PAR 72 (288)

Ben Crenshaw's 2nd Masters – and 2nd Major – was an emotional occasion. 'Gentle' Ben had been one of the game's most popular players for over 2 decades, and when he won his 2nd Green Jacket, 11 years after the 1st, and just a few days after the death of his friend and mentor, Harvey Penick, no-one complained. Davis Love III, whose grandfather and father had featured in various Majors over the years, was beginning to assume the mantle that Crenshaw once had – and Kite had discarded in 1992.

1	**BEN CRENSHAW**	70	67	69	68	274
	($396000)					
2	Davis Love III	69	69	71	66	275
3=	Jay Haas	71	64	72	70	277
	Greg Norman	73	68	68	68	277
5=	Steve Elkington	73	67	67	72	279
	David Frost	66	71	71	71	279
7=	Scott Hoch	69	67	71	73	280
	Phil Mickelson	66	71	70	73	280
9	Curtis Strange	72	71	65	73	281
10=	Fred Couples	71	69	67	75	282
	Brian Henninger	70	68	68	76	282
12=	Lee Janzen	69	69	74	71	283
	Kenny Perry	73	70	71	69	283
14=	Hale Irwin	69	72	71	72	284
	Jose-Maria Olazabal	66	74	72	72	284
	Tom Watson	73	70	69	72	284
17=	Paul Azinger	70	72	73	70	285
	Brad Faxon	76	69	69	71	285
	Ray Floyd	71	70	70	74	285
	John Huston	70	66	72	77	285
	Colin Montgomerie	71	69	76	69	285
	Corey Pavin	67	71	72	75	285
	Ian Woosnam	69	72	71	73	285
24=	David Edwards	69	73	73	71	286
	Nick Faldo	70	70	71	75	286
	David Gilford	67	73	75	71	286
	Loren Roberts	72	69	72	73	286
	Duffy Waldorf	74	69	67	76	286
29=	Bob Estes	73	70	76	68	287
	Jumbo Ozaki	70	74	70	73	287

Round Leader(s)
R1   Frost, Mickelson, Olazabal; 66
R2   Haas; 135
R3   Crenshaw, Henninger; 206

Lowest Scores
R2   Haas; 64
R3   Strange; 65
R4   Love; 66

1995

15–18 June

US OPEN

Shinnecock Hills GC, Southampton, New York
6912 yards PAR 70 (280)

Davis Love was inheriting the label 'the best player never to have won a Major', championship by championship, and this was reinforced when the Open celebrated its centennial at Shinnecock. Corey Pavin had also been linked with the tag, but his 1st win eliminated him from the maiden stakes to leave Love, with another creditable performance, looking over his shoulder for new competition in Mickelson and Montgomerie. Greg Norman finished 2nd for the 7th time in a Major.

1	**COREY PAVIN**	72	69	71	68	280
	($350000)					
2	Greg Norman	68	67	74	73	282
3	Tom Lehman	70	72	67	74	283
4=	Bill Glasson	69	70	76	69	284
	Jay Haas	70	73	72	69	284
	Neal Lancaster	70	72	77	65	284
	Davis Love III	72	68	73	71	284
	Jeff Maggert	69	72	77	66	284
	Phil Mickelson	68	70	72	74	284
10=	Frank Nobilo	72	72	70	71	285
	Vijay Singh	70	71	72	72	285
	Bob Tway	69	69	72	75	285
13=	Brad Bryant	71	75	70	70	286
	Lee Janzen	70	72	72	72	286
	Mark McCumber	70	71	77	68	286
	Nick Price	66	73	73	74	286
	Mark Roe	71	69	74	72	286
	Jeff Sluman	72	69	74	71	286
	Steve Stricker	71	70	71	74	286
	Duffy Waldorf	72	70	75	69	286
21=	Billy Andrade	72	69	74	72	287
	Pete Jordan	74	71	71	71	287
	Brett Ogle	71	75	72	69	287
	Payne Stewart	74	71	73	69	287
	Scott Verplank	72	69	71	75	287
	Ian Woosnam	72	71	69	75	287
	Fuzzy Zoeller	69	74	76	68	287
28=	David Duval	70	73	73	72	288
	Gary Hallberg	70	76	69	73	288
	Mike Hulbert	74	72	72	70	288
	Miguel Jimenez	72	72	75	69	288
	Colin Montgomerie	71	74	75	68	288
	Jose-Maria Olazabal	73	70	72	73	288
	Jumbo Ozaki	69	68	80	71	288
	Scott Simpson	67	75	74	72	288

Round Leader(s)
R1   Price; 66
R2   Norman; 135
R3   Lehman, Norman; 209

Lowest Scores
R2   Norman; 67
R3   Lehman; 67
R4   Lancaster; 65

20–23 July	1995

BRITISH OPEN

Royal & Ancient GC, St Andrews, Fife, Scotland
6933 yards PAR 72 (288)

10–13 August	1995

US PGA

Riviera CC, Pacific Palisades, California
6956 yards PAR 71 (284)

John Daly, flirting with alcoholics' rehabilitation centres since his 1991 PGA triumph, held his nerve to outplay an emotionally-drained Constantino Rocca in the 4-hole play-off. After completing R4, Daly was in the Clubhouse watching the Italian approach Tom Morris' green. He needed to chip and putt for 2 to tie. With not much green to work with, Rocca fluffed his shot, and saw his ball roll back into the Valley of Sin and stop 20 yards or so from the pin. Daly, with TV cameras watching his every gesture, kept calm, but must have thought the Claret Jug was his. His expression hardly changed when Constantino holed his next shot - but the Italian collapsed in a mixture of relief and exhaustion. Despite seeing the Jug dashed away from his lips at the last, it was Daly, in overtime, who stayed calmer to win his 2nd Major.

Quiz question: Which golfer ties the record low score in Major Championships, but has never won any? Answer: Colin Montgomerie. His 267 took him level with Steve Elkington, whose 25-foot birdie putt sealed the play-off. Their 72-hole record was one better than that of Nick Price the previous year, and tied Greg Norman's Majors record at Sandwich in 1993. If the Europeans had taken a shine to the Masters, then the PGA was starting to become the preserve of golfers from the Southern Hemisphere. Between 1916 and 1962 only Australia's Jim Ferrier and South Africa's Gary Player had taken the trophy ahead of native or naturalized Americans. Following Player's 2nd win in 1972, David Graham, Wayne Grady, Price (twice), Ernie Els and now Elkington had won the Championship – the last 5 in 6 years.

1	**JOHN DALY*** (£125000)	67	71	73	71	282
2	Constantino Rocca	69	70	70	73	282
3=	Steven Bottomley	70	72	72	69	283
	Mark Brooks	70	69	73	71	283
	Michael Campbell	71	71	65	76	283
6=	Steve Elkington	72	69	69	74	284
	Vijay Singh	68	72	73	71	284
8=	Bob Estes	72	70	71	72	285
	Mark James	72	75	68	70	285
	Corey Pavin	69	70	72	74	285
11=	Ernie Els	71	68	72	75	286
	Brett Ogle	73	69	71	73	286
	Payne Stewart	72	68	75	71	286
	Sam Torrance	71	70	71	74	286
15=	Robert Allenby	71	74	71	71	287
	Ben Crenshaw	67	72	76	72	287
	Brad Faxon	71	67	75	74	287
	Per-Ulrik Johansson	69	78	68	72	287
	Greg Norman	71	74	72	70	287
20=	Andrew Coltart	70	74	71	73	288
	David Duval	71	75	70	72	288
	Barry Lane	72	73	68	75	288
	Peter Mitchell	73	74	71	70	288
24=	Mark Calcavecchia	71	72	72	74	289
	Bill Glasson	68	74	72	75	289
	Lee Janzen	73	73	71	72	289
	Bernhard Langer	72	71	73	73	289
	Jesper Parnevik	75	71	70	73	289
	Katsuyoshi Tomori	70	68	73	78	289
	Steven Webster (a)	70	72	74	73	289

1	**STEVE ELKINGTON*** ($360000)	68	67	68	64	267
2	Colin Montgomerie	68	67	67	65	267
3=	Ernie Els	66	65	66	72	269
	Jeff Maggert	66	69	65	69	269
5	Brad Faxon	70	67	71	63	271
6=	Bob Estes	69	68	68	68	273
	Mark O'Meara	64	67	69	73	273
8=	Jay Haas	69	71	64	70	274
	Justin Leonard	68	66	70	70	274
	Steve Lowery	69	68	68	69	274
	Jeff Sluman	69	67	68	70	274
	Craig Stadler	71	66	66	71	274
13=	Jim Furyk	68	70	69	68	275
	Miguel Jimenez	69	69	67	70	275
	Payne Stewart	69	70	69	67	275
	Kirk Triplett	71	69	68	67	275
17=	Michael Campbell	71	65	71	69	276
	Constantino Rocca	70	69	68	69	276
	Curtis Strange	72	68	68	68	276
20=	Greg Norman	66	69	70	72	277
	Jesper Parnevik	69	69	70	69	277
	Duffy Waldorf	69	69	67	72	277
23=	Woody Austin	70	70	70	68	278
	Nolan Henke	68	73	67	70	278
	Peter Jacobsen	69	67	71	71	278
	Lee Janzen	66	70	72	70	278
	Bruce Lietzke	73	68	67	70	278
	Billy Mayfair	68	68	72	70	278
	Steve Stricker	75	64	69	70	278
	Sam Torrance	69	69	69	71	278

* John Daly beat Constantino Rocca in the 4-Hole Play-off

*Steve Elkington beat Colin Montgomerie at 1st extra hole in Sudden Death Play-off

Round Leader(s)
R1 Crenshaw, Daly; 67
R2 Daly, Faxon; 138
R3 Campbell; 207

Lowest Scores
R2 Faxon; 67
R3 Campbell; 65
R4 Bottomley; 69

Round Leader(s)
R1 Michael Bradley (54); 63
R2 Els, O'Meara; 131
R3 Els; 197

Lowest Scores
R2 Stricker; 64
R3 Haas; 64
R4 Faxon; 63

1996
11–14 April
THE MASTERS
Augusta National GC, Augusta, Georgia
6925 yards PAR 72 (288)

1996
12–16 June
US OPEN
Oakland Hills CC, Birmingham, Michigan
6996 yards PAR 70 (280)

Perhaps this was the most astounding final round in Majors history. World No1, Greg Norman, twice winner of the British Open, became a Majors runner-up for the 8th time when he surrendered a 6-shot overnight lead to Nick Faldo, to lose by 5. That Norman has a Majors weakness in a game he has otherwise dominated for much of the last decade, cannot now be questioned. His 8 runners-up places puts him tied with Sam Snead in 3rd place of all time. But Sam won 7 Majors as well, and proportionately the best players have a similar number of winning and 2nd place positions. Above Snead and Norman are Nicklaus with 19 2nds and 18 wins, followed by Palmer (9 and 7, respectively). Against Faldo, Norman's capitulation included a 7 shot swing in as many holes, and 10 over the last 12. Faldo, to his credit, still shot a best-of-the-day 67 for his 6th Major - joint-11th all-time with Lee Trevino – and remains one of the best head-to-head scrappers in the history of the Majors.

Steve Jones had to pre-qualify for the Open – being the 1st winner to do so since 1976, when Steve Pate had to endure the same ordeal. Jones had faded from the golf scene a few years previously due to an horrendous motorcycle accident, but it was he who had the right stuff as holes were running out. Jones, Davis Love and Tom Lehman were battling for supremacy. Love should have been in the Clubhouse with a 67, but missing a putt on the 18th reminiscent of that required to win the British Open in 1970 by Doug Sanders, and after bogeying 17, he could only sit and wait. Driving off the 18th tee Lehman found a fairway bunker to nullify any hope he had of making the green in regulation. Jones steadied and drove truly down the middle to set up the par that was to win it.

1	**NICK FALDO**	69	67	73	67	276
	($435000)					
2	Greg Norman	63	69	71	78	281
3	Phil Mickelson	65	73	72	72	282
4	Frank Nobilo	71	71	72	69	283
5=	Scott Hoch	67	73	73	71	284
	Duffy Waldorf	72	71	69	72	284
7=	Davis Love III	72	71	74	68	285
	Jeff Maggert	71	73	72	69	285
	Corey Pavin	75	66	73	71	285
10=	David Frost	70	68	74	74	286
	Scott McCarron	70	70	72	74	286
12=	Ernie Els	71	71	72	73	287
	Lee Janzen	68	71	75	73	287
	Bob Tway	67	72	76	72	287
15=	Mark Calcavecchia	71	73	71	73	288
	Fred Couples	78	68	71	71	288
17	John Huston	71	71	71	76	289
18=	Paul Azinger	70	74	76	70	290
	David Duval	73	72	69	76	290
	Tom Lehman	75	70	72	73	290
	Mark O'Meara	72	71	75	72	290
	Nick Price	71	75	70	74	290
23=	Larry Mize	75	71	77	68	291
	Loren Roberts	71	73	72	75	291
25=	Brad Faxon	69	77	72	74	292
	Ray Floyd	70	74	77	71	292
27=	Bob Estes	71	71	79	72	293
	Justin Leonard	72	74	75	72	293
29=	John Daly	71	74	71	78	294
	Jim Furyk	75	70	78	71	294
	Jim Gallagher, Jr	70	76	77	71	294
	Hale Irwin	74	71	77	72	294
	Scott Simpson	69	76	76	73	294
	Craig Stadler	73	72	71	78	294
	Ian Woosnam	72	69	73	80	294

Round Leader(s)

R1	Norman; 63	**Lowest Scores**	
R2	Norman; 132	R2	Pavin; 66
R3	Norman; 203	R3	Duval, Waldorf; 69
		R4	Faldo; 67

1	**STEVE JONES**	74	66	69	69	278
	($405000)					
2=	Tom Lehman	71	72	65	71	279
	Davis Love III	71	69	70	69	279
4	John Morse	68	74	68	70	280
5=	Ernie Els	72	67	72	70	281
	Jim Furyk	72	69	70	70	281
7=	Ken Green	73	67	72	70	282
	Scott Hoch	73	71	71	67	282
	Vijay Singh	71	72	70	69	282
10=	Lee Janzen	68	75	71	69	283
	Colin Montgomerie	70	72	69	72	283
	Greg Norman	73	66	74	70	283
13=	Dan Forsman	72	71	70	71	284
	Frank Nobilo	69	71	70	74	284
	Tom Watson	70	71	71	72	284
16=	David Berganio	69	72	72	72	285
	Mark Brooks	76	68	69	72	285
	Stewart Cink	69	73	70	73	285
	John Cook	70	71	71	73	285
	Nick Faldo	72	71	72	70	285
	Mark O'Meara	72	73	68	72	285
	Sam Torrance	71	69	71	74	285
23=	Billy Andrade	72	69	72	73	286
	Woody Austin	67	72	72	75	286
	Brad Bryant	73	71	74	68	286
	Peter Jacobsen	71	74	70	71	286
27=	John Daly	72	69	73	73	287
	Pete Jordan	71	74	72	70	287
	Jack Nicklaus	72	74	69	72	287
	Payne Stewart	67	71	76	73	287
	Curtis Strange	74	73	71	69	287

Round Leader(s)

R1	Austin, Stewart; 67	**Lowest Scores**	
R2	Stewart; 138	R2	Jones, Norman; 66
R3	Lehman; 208	R3	Lehman; 65
		R4	Hoch; 67

18–21 July					**1996**

BRITISH OPEN

Royal Lytham and St Anne's GC, Lancashire, England
6892 yards PAR 71 (284)

With the 1st prize doubling within 4 years, the 125th Open, although mostly dominated by the top Americans, was still not supported by too many of them. Demands imposed upon them by the ever-more competitive PGA Tour forced many to stay at home – especially those not exempt and who would have to have invested extra time in qualifying. Nick Faldo kept home hopes alive with 3 successive 68s, but was too far away from Tom Lehman's 54-hole record score of 198 to make an impression. 1994 US Open Champion, Ernie Els, and 45 year-old Mark McCumber, kept up the pressure, and Mark Brooks was in the hunt as he was the previous year, but Lehman's cushion was too comfortable. His 2-over par 73 still gave him a 2-stroke advantage at the end. After several good finishes in recent years, his 1st Major was well-deserved.

1	**TOM LEHMAN**	67	67	64	73	271
	(£200000)					
2=	Ernie Els	68	67	71	67	273
	Mark McCumber	67	69	71	66	273
4	Nick Faldo	68	68	68	70	274
5=	Mark Brooks	67	70	68	71	276
	Jeff Maggert	69	70	72	65	276
7=	Fred Couples	67	70	69	71	277
	Peter Hedblom	70	65	75	67	277
	Greg Norman	71	68	71	67	277
	Greg Turner	72	69	68	68	277
11=	Alexander Cejka	73	67	71	67	278
	Darren Clarke	70	68	69	71	278
	Vijay Singh	69	67	69	73	278
14=	David Duval	76	67	66	70	279
	Paul McGinley	69	65	74	71	279
	Mark McNulty	69	71	70	69	279
	Shigeki Maruyama	68	70	69	72	279
18=	Padraig Harrington	68	68	73	71	280
	Rocco Mediate	69	70	69	72	280
	Loren Roberts	67	69	72	72	280
	Michael Welch	71	68	73	68	280
22=	Jay Haas	70	72	71	68	281
	Mark James	70	68	75	68	281
	Carl Mason	68	70	70	73	281
	Steve Stricker	71	70	66	74	281
	Tiger Woods (a)	75	66	70	70	281
27=	Paul Broadhurst	65	72	64	71	282
	Ben Crenshaw	73	68	71	70	282
	Tom Kite	77	66	69	70	282
	Peter Mitchell	71	68	71	72	282
	Frank Nobilo	70	72	68	72	282
	Corey Pavin	70	66	74	72	282

Round Leader(s)   **Lowest Scores**

R1	Broadhurst; 65	R2	Hedblom, McGinley; 65
R2	Lehman, McGinley; 134	R3	Lehman; 64
R3	Lehman; 198	R4	Maggert; 65

8–11 August					**1996**

US PGA

Valhalla GC, Louisville, Kentucky
7144 yards PAR 72 (288)

Carrying on his good form from Royal Lytham, Mark Brooks from Texas was involved in the finish once again. This time his immediate competition came from Kenny Perry, who was 2 strokes clear of the field going to the last hole. R3 leader Russ Cochran had blown up and challenges from Vijay Singh and Steve Elkington were dissipating. With Perry's lead then reduced to one after a waywide drive, Brooks birdied the last to force extra holes. He repeated the dose at the same hole in the play-off. The 2 shot swing was a stern lesson to Perry, actively playing to the crowd going to the 18th tee. He should have remembered Jesper Parnevik's horror 2 years before at Turnberry, when he set off up the 18th 2 ahead of Nick Price – and failed to make the play-off.

1	**MARK BROOKS***	68	70	69	70	277
	($430000)					
2	Kenny Perry	66	72	71	68	277
3=	Steve Elkington	67	74	67	70	278
	Tommy Tolles	69	71	71	67	278
5=	Justin Leonard	71	66	72	70	279
	Jesper Parnevik	73	67	69	70	279
	Vijay Singh	69	69	69	72	279
8=	Lee Janzen	68	71	71	70	280
	Per-Ulrik Johansson	73	72	66	69	280
	Phil Mickelson	67	67	74	72	280
	Larry Mize	71	70	69	70	280
	Frank Nobilo	69	72	71	68	280
	Nick Price	68	71	69	72	280
14=	Mike Brisky	71	69	69	72	281
	Tom Lehman	71	71	69	70	281
	Joey Sindelar	73	72	69	67	281
17=	Russ Cochran	68	72	65	77	282
	David Edwards	69	71	72	70	282
	Brad Faxon	72	68	73	69	282
	Jim Furyk	70	70	73	69	282
	Greg Norman	68	72	69	73	282
	Tom Watson	69	71	73	69	282
	DA Weibring	71	73	71	67	282
24=	Emlyn Aubrey	69	74	72	68	283
	Miguel Jimenez	71	71	71	70	283
26=	Fred Funk	73	69	73	69	284
	Mark O'Meara	71	70	74	69	284
	Corey Pavin	71	74	70	69	284
	Curtis Strange	73	70	68	73	284
	Steve Stricker	73	72	72	67	284

*Mark Brooks beat Kenny Perry in the Sudden-death Play-off at the 1st extra hole

Round Leader(s)   **Lowest Scores**

R1	Perry; 66	R2	Leonard; 66
R2	Mickelson; 134	R3	Cochran; 65
R3	Cochran; 205	R4	Sindelar, Stricker, Tolles, Weibring; 67

Part 3

The Championships
Results 1997
Previews 1998

THE CHAMPIONSHIPS: RESULTS 1997

THE YEAR OF THE TIGER?

Just months after turning professional, and with three victories already on the US tour, Eldrick 'Tiger' Woods became the youngest player to win the Masters Tournament. In doing so he set up a stack of records over an Augusta course ideally suited to his long hitting and delicate approach work. He became the first person to win a Major in his rookie season since Jerry Pate picked up the 1976 US Open. He set new Masters records for the last 54 holes (200); his margin of victory (12 - thereby being the widest margin in any Major this century and second overall behind Tom Morris Sr and tied with Tom Morris Jr); low total (270); and the youngest winner (21 years 3 months 15 days). He is the also the fifth youngest winner of any Major this century (if you exclude the fact that both John McDermott and Gene Sarazen won two Majors while younger). Only McDermott (19 in the 1911 US Open and 20 the following year), Francis Ouimet (20 in the 1913 US Open), Sarazen (20 in the 1922 US Open and PGA) and Tom Creavy (also 20 in the 1931 PGA) were younger. He is the seventh youngest of all-time following the above-mentioned 'Young' Tom (17, 18 and 19 in 1868, 1869 and 1870) and Willie Auchterlonie (just 21 in 1892) in British Opens.

If there was one record closest to the heart of Woods, however, it would be that after 137 years of Major Championships - and 101 since John Shippen was begrudgingly allowed to play at Shinnecock Hills - he was the first black player to scale the golfing heights. Coming into the Tournament, Tiger had made some high-profile comments about the degree of racial prejudice still in some of America's most conservative golf clubs. After he was presented with his Green Jacket by outgoing Champion, Nick Faldo, Woods alluded to none of this but

AUGUSTA NATIONAL – Yardages and Pars						
	HOLE	YARDS	PAR	HOLE	YARDS	PAR
1	Tea Olive	400	4	10 Camellia	485	4
2	Pink Dogwood	555	5	11 White Dogwood	455	4
3	Flowering Peach	360	4	12 Golden Bell	155	3
4	Flowering Crab Apple	205	3	13 Azalea	485	5
5	Magnolia	435	4	14 Chinese Fir	405	4
6	Juniper	180	3	15 Firethorn	500	5
7	Pampas	360	4	16 Redbud	170	3
8	Yellow Jasmine	535	5	17 Nandina	400	4
9	Carolina Cherry	435	4	18 Holly	405	4
	OUT	3465	36	IN	3660	36
				TOTAL	6925	72

concentrated, in a speech of some dignity and no little maturity, on what positive effects his win would have on young people everywhere.

This historic win can been seen as a multi-faceted event, then. From a golfing viewpoint, before the Tournament, no less an observer than Jack Nicklaus was stating how Woods' prodigious power was adding a different dimension to the modern game (in much the same way as Bobby Jones acknowledged the arrival of Nicklaus himself nearly 40 years before!), and had even predicted that Tiger would go on and win as many Masters as he and Arnold Palmer put together. Throughout the four days, as Woods took a firmer and firmer hold on the Tournament, the eulogies from illustrious competitors and commentators came thick and fast. Eight-time Major Champion, Tom Watson, when asked to comment about Woods' performance for his age said, 'He's making the men look like boys.' Afterwards, the legendary Byron Nelson was to say, 'Tiger Woods is the best player of his age I have ever seen.' It was Gary Player, however, who took the theme further than golf itself when considering the world-wide implications of Woods' win. The South African winner of nine Majors suggested, 'Tiger has the opportunity to do something for the human race that no other golfer before him has'.

Some burden on the shoulders of one so young – but such was the impact of Woods' win at Augusta. Coming as it did on a wave of hype and publicity (some of it admittedly down to his father, Earl), the inevitability of the victory seemed never in doubt after the first day and the feeling was that here was the perfect sportsman who would not only go on to win this, his first Major as a professional, but the Grand Slam this year too – thus exuding a god-like aura of invincibility which in turn would raise the hopes and aspirations in the merely-mortal, much like a mediaeval warrior-saint may have done.

This was so much Tiger Woods' Masters, that it is scarcely recorded that the dogwoods, azaleas and the like had come and gone in the early spring, leaving Augusta without its usual splash of colour. Many people may have forgotten that those in centre-scene 12 months earlier – winner, Nick Faldo and the traumatized Greg Norman – both missed the cut in a welter of protest from many professionals who felt the pin positions must have been set by the Marquis de Sade. This was Faldo's first missed cut at Augusta since 1979, and only the second time in a run of 37 Majors. How many will remember the old hero, Arnold Palmer, shooting 32-over par for 36 holes in his 43rd consecutive Masters? How many will be aware that Woods' first Masters win would be the last time Ben Hogan would grace Augusta National when he ceremonially teed-off on Thursday with Gene Sarazen and Byron Nelson?

Sometimes a performance from one person in sport can negate those of a hundred others around him. That phenomenon happened at Augusta last April.

1997 MASTERS COMPLETED SCORES

6925 yards **PAR 72 (288)**

1	**TIGER WOODS** ($486000)	70	66	65	69	270
2	Tom Kite	77	69	66	70	282
3	Tommy Tolles	72	72	72	67	283
4	Tom Watson	75	68	69	72	284
5=	Constantino Rocca	71	69	70	75	285
	Paul Stankowski	68	74	79	74	285
7=	Fred Couples	72	69	73	72	286
	Bernhard Langer	72	72	74	68	286
	Justin Leonard	76	69	71	70	286
	Davis Love III	72	71	72	71	286
	Jeff Sluman	74	67	72	73	286
12=	Steve Elkington	76	72	72	67	287
	Per-Ulrik Johansson	72	73	73	69	287
	Tom Lehman	73	76	69	69	287
	Jose-Maria Olazabal	71	70	74	72	287
	Willie Wood	72	76	71	68	287
17=	Mark Calcavecchia	74	73	72	69	288
	Ernie Els	73	70	71	74	288
	Fred Funk	74	73	69	72	288
	Vijay Singh	75	74	69	70	288
21=	Stuart Appleby	72	76	70	71	289
	John Huston	67	77	75	70	289
	Jesper Parnevik	73	72	71	73	289
24=	Nick Price	71	71	75	74	291
	Lee Westwood	77	71	73	70	291
26=	Lee Janzen	72	73	74	73	292
	Craig Stadler	77	72	71	72	292
28=	Paul Azinger	69	73	77	74	293
	Jim Furyk	74	75	72	72	293
30=	Scott McCarron	77	71	72	74	294
	Larry Mize	79	69	74	72	294
	Colin Montgomerie	72	67	74	81	294
	Mark O'Meara	75	74	70	75	294
34=	Sandy Lyle	73	73	74	75	295
	Fuzzy Zoeller	75	73	69	78	295
36	Duffy Waldorf	74	75	72	75	296
37	David Frost	74	71	73	79	297
38	Scott Hoch	79	68	73	78	298
39=	Jack Nicklaus	77	70	74	78	299
	Sam Torrance	75	73	73	78	299
	Ian Woosnam	77	68	75	79	299
42	Jumbo Ozaki	74	74	74	78	300
43=	Corey Pavin	75	74	78	74	301
	Clarence Rose	73	75	79	74	301
44	Ben Crenshaw	75	73	74	80	302
45	Frank Nobilo	76	74	72	81	303

Those who missed the 36-hole cut included:

150	John Cook, Phil Mickelson
151	Brad Faxon, Greg Norman, Gary Player, Bob Tway
153	Mark McNulty, Jeff Maggert
154	Ray Floyd
155	Seve Ballesteros
155	Nick Faldo
159	Mark Brooks
160	Billy Casper, Steve Jones
162	Loren Roberts
176	Arnold Palmer

Leaders (Round-by-round)

R1	67	J Huston
	68	P Stankowski
	69	P Azinger
R2	136	T Woods; 70,66
	139	C Montgomerie; 72,67
	140	C Rocca; 71,69
R3	201	T Woods; 70,66,65
	210	C Rocca; 71,69,70
	211	P Stankowski; 68,74,69

Low Scores

R2	66	T Woods
	67	C Montgomerie, J Sluman
	68	S Hoch, T Watson, I Woosnam
R3	65	T Woods
	66	T Kite
	69	F Funk, T Lehman, V Singh, P Stankowski, T Watson, F Zoeller
R4	67	S Elkington, T Tolles
	68	B Langer, W Wood
	69	M Calcavecchia, P-U Johansson, T Lehman, T Woods

THE 97th US OPEN CHAMPIONSHIP

CONGRESSIONAL GOLF CLUB

Bethesda, Maryland
12–15 June 1997

MONTGOMERIE UNABLE TO OVERCOME ELS BOGEY

When Ernie Els won the US Open for the first time in 1994 at the demanding Oakmont course, Colin Montgomerie tied for the runners-up spot with Loren Roberts. That was after a play-off - a fate that was to revisit the Scot the following year in the PGA Championship. Montgomerie also lost to the South African in the final of the 1994 World Matchplay, so if Els was not in the field it is conceivable that Montgomerie may now be the winner of at least one Major Championship – instead of holding that overworked press title, 'The Best Player in the World Not to Have Won a Major Championship'. That logic may be somewhat simplistic, but with Ernie winning again at the Congressional Club – just outside Washington, DC – Montgomerie's recent failures to convert strong positions into winning ones may just have something to do with Els, and the Scotsman will surely be looking for the South African the next time he's in the running.

The 27 year-old from Johannesburg shadowed the field throughout the four days. Apart for a brief moment in the third round when he shared the lead with Montgomerie, Jeff Maggert and Tom Lehman, he only took the outright lead in the final round after drama at the 17th. Tying now with just Montgomerie, he played a perfect approach to within 15 feet of the flag. Colin, put under pressure to match it, left his putt for par a tantalizing 5 feet above the hole. If there was one criticism of the

Congressional course it was the juxtaposition of the 17th and 18th greens. While considering his putt, Montgomerie was distracted by the galleries on the 18th and decided to wait the several minutes it took for the pair playing to and on that green to hole out, before addressing his ball. He duly missed, took a bogey 5, and Ernie prevailed once again.

Since Tommy Armour in 1927, only four non-American born golfers had won the US Open – Gary Player of South Africa, Tony Jacklin of England, David Graham of Australia, and Els himself in 1994. By taking the title again he became the overseas player (not American-born or naturalized, that is) with the most wins in history.

However, for a while it looked like in-form Tom Lehman might emulate the likes of Tony Jacklin and Tom Watson in recent years, by adding the US Open to the British Open he already held, but both he and Jeff Maggert

CONGRESSIONAL – Yardages and Pars					
HOLE	YARDS	PAR	HOLE	YARDS	PAR
1	446	4	10	190	3
2	411	4	11	396	4
3	216	3	12	540	5
4	460	4	13	212	3
5	515	5	14	430	4
6	324	4	15	423	4
7	161	3	16	457	4
8	442	4	17	449	4
9	467	4	18	448	4
OUT	3442	35	IN	3545	35
			TOTAL	6987	70

1997 US OPEN COMPLETED SCORES

7213 yards PAR 70 (280)

1	**ERNIE ELS** ($465000)	71	67 69 69	276
2	Colin Montgomerie	65	76 67 69	277
3	Tom Lehman	67	70 68 73	278
4	Jeff Maggert	73	66 68 74	281
5=	Olin Browne	71	71 69 71	282
	Jim Furyk	74	68 69 71	282
	Jay Haas	73	69 68 72	282
	Tommy Tolles	74	67 69 72	282
	Bob Tway	71	71 70 70	282
10=	Scott Hoch	71	68 72 72	283
	Scott McCarron	73	71 69 70	283
	David Ogrin	70	69 71 73	283
13=	Billy Andrade	75	67 69 73	284
	Stewart Cink	71	67 74 72	284
	Loren Roberts	72	69 72 71	284
16=	Bradley Hughes	75	70 71 69	285
	Davis Love III	75	70 69 71	285
	Jose-Maria Olazabal	71	71 72 71	285
19=	Nick Price	71	74 71 70	286
	Paul Stankowski	75	70 68 73	286
	Hal Sutton	66	73 73 74	286
	Lee Westwood	71	71 73 71	286
	Tiger Woods	74	67 73 72	286
24=	Scott Dunlap	75	66 75 71	287
	Steve Elkington	75	68 72 72	287
	Edward Fryatt	72	73 73 69	287
	Len Mattiace	71	75 73 68	287
28=	Paul Azinger	72	72 74 70	288
	Kelly Gibson	72	69 72 75	288
	Paul Goydos	73	72 74 69	288
	Hideki Kase	68	73 73 74	288
	Mark McNulty	67	73 75 73	288
	Jeff Sluman	69	72 72 75	288
	Payne Stewart	71	73 73 71	288
	Fuzzy Zoeller	72	73 69 74	288
36=	Stuart Appleby	71	75 70 73	289
	John Cook	72	71 71 75	289
	Justin Leonard	69	72 78 70	289
	Frank Nobilo	71	74 70 74	289
	Mark O'Meara	73	73 71 72	289
	Steve Stricker	66	76 75 72	289
	Grant Waite	72	74 72 71	289
43=	Darren Clarke	73	74 73 70	290
	Fred Funk	73	70 72 75	290
	Phil Mickelson	75	68 73 74	290
	Craig Parry	70	74 69 77	290
	Chris Perry	70	73 71 76	290
48=	David Duval	74	73 70 74	291
	Nick Faldo	72	74 69 76	291
	Jesper Parnevik	72	75 73 71	291
51	David White	70	72 73 77	292
52=	Paul Broadhurst	77	69 72 75	293
	Fred Couples	75	72 72 74	293
	Hale Irwin	70	73 76 74	293
	Lee Janzen	72	73 75 73	293
	Jack Nicklaus	73	71 75 74	293

COMPLETED SCORES continued

	Peter Teravainen	71	73 74 75	293
58=	Larry Mize	70	74 76 74	294
	Clarence Rose	72	71 73 78	294
60=	Rodney Butcher	73	74 70 78	295
	Steve Jones	72	75 69 79	295
	Chris Smith	77	69 74 75	295
	Duffy Waldorf	73	73 73 76	295
64	Tom Watson	72	74 72 78	296
65=	Ben Crenshaw	73	74 76 74	297
	Brad Faxon	72	74 76 75	297
	Dave Schreyer	68	73 82 74	297
68=	Stephen Ames	73	73 75 77	298
	Thomas Bjorn	71	75 73 79	298
	Mike Hulbert	73	73 77 75	298
	Tom Kite	75	69 82 72	298
	Greg Kraft	77	69 76 76	298
	John Morse	71	74 76 77	298
74	Jimmy Green	75	72 79 73	299
75=	Andrew Coltart	74	71 76 79	300
	Randy Wylie	71	76 77 76	300
77=	Donnie Hammond	75	71 76 79	301
	Dick Mast	73	69 83 76	301
	Perry Parker	75	71 77 78	301
	Vijay Singh	71	76 77 77	301
	Greg Towne	71	73 83 74	301
82	Jack Ferenz	72	75 80 76	303
83	Marco Dawson	75	71 80 78	304
84	Slade Adams	71	74 78 83	306

Those who missed the 36-hole cut included:

148 Bernhard Langer, Corey Pavin
149 Mark Brooks, Mark Calcavecchia
150 Curtis Strange, Ian Woosnam
154 Greg Norman
Withdrawn   John Daly, 77

faded over the back nine. Over the four rounds, Congressional's narrow fairways and unrelenting rough rewarded long hitters only if they were straight. After the euphoria of Augusta, Tiger Woods had proved he was human with one or two indifferent performances, but still came to the Open the bookie's favourite to add the second leg of the Grand Slam to the Masters. His golf during the week, apart from a clutch of birdies in Round Two, was too erratic to meet the demands of Congressional. Other mighty hitters – double Majors winner, John Daly, and 1991 Masters Champion, Ian Woosnam – didn't have the required control

225

Leaders (Round-by-round)		
R1	65	C Montgomerie
	66	S Stricker, H Sutton
	67	T Lehman, M McNulty
R2	137	T Lehman; 67,70
	138	E Els; 71,67
	139	J Maggert; 73,66
		D Ogrin; 70,69
		H Sutton; 66,73
R3	205	T Lehman; 67,70,68
	207	E Els; 71,67,69
		J Maggert; 73,66,68
	208	C Montgomerie; 65,76,67

Low Scores		
R2	66	S Dunlap, J Maggert
	67	B Andrade, S Cink, E Els, T Tolles, T Woods
	68	S Elkington, J Furyk, S Hoch, P Mickelson
R3	67	C Montgomerie
	68	J Haas, T Lehman, J Maggert, P Stankowski
	69	B Andrade, O Browne, E Els, N Faldo, J Furyk, S Jones, D Love III, S McCarron, C Parry, T Tolles, F Zoeller
R4	68	L Mattiace
	69	E Els, E Fryatt, P Goydos, B Hughes, C Montgomerie
	70	P Azinger, D Clarke, J Leonard, S McCarron, N Price, B Tway

to succeed. Daly, just weeks after leaving the Betty Ford Clinic walked off the course after 9 holes of Round Two - 10 over par for the Championship – and left playing partners, Ernie Els and Payne Stewart, unaware of his actions. Woosnam missed the cut, simply saying, 'The course was too tough for me'. The Tournament threw up some interesting characters not expected to feature too strongly in Majors these days. 1983 PGA Champion, Hal Sutton came in just behind Colin Montgomerie in the first round, with a superb 66, while Bob Tway had only his second Top 10 finish in a Major since his PGA-winning year of 1986. Defending Champion, Steve Jones, despite a third round 69, never really mounted a serious challenge, and finished tied for 60th place.

THE 126th BRITISH OPEN CHAMPIONSHIP   ROYAL TROON GOLF CLUB

Ayrshire, Scotland
17–20 July 1997

LEONARD WINS THE MOST OPEN OPEN

Agony for Parnevik once more

25 year-old Texan, Justin Leonard, won his first Major Championship when he finished two strokes clear of Sweden's Jesper Parnevik and Northern Irishman, Darren Clarke, to take the 1997 Open Championship at Royal Troon. His win was the third victory for a Twentysomething after the feats of 21 year-old Tiger Woods and 27 year-old Ernie Els earlier in the season, and it may just be starting a new era in the history of golf.

Since the 1960s the game has just not seen the groups of two or perhaps three players which had dominated golf at certain times in the past. Lee Trevino flirted with Nicklaus and Watson in the 1970s as arguably the three greatest golfers for a while, but this was not such a strong three-pronged rivalry as say, 'The Big Three' – Nicklaus, Player and Palmer – a decade earlier. The original 'Great Triumvirate' of Vardon, Braid and Taylor had echoes in Hagen, Jones and, to a lesser extent, Sarazen in the 20s; there was Hogan, Nelson and Snead before and after the Second World War. Golf since 'The Big Three', however, has not been carved up so definitively. During the 1980s we find that wins in Major Championships have been shared out much more evenly, and in recent years only Nick Faldo has picked up titles with any regularity. The irridescence that was Ballesteros now seems to have burned out, and the two Major titles and eight

	HOLE	YARDS	PAR		HOLE	YARDS	PAR
	ROYAL TROON *—Yardages and Pars*						
1	Seal	364	4	10	Sandhills	438	4
2	Black Rock	391	4	11	The Railway	465	4
3	Gyaws	379	4	12	The Fox	431	4
4	Dunure	557	5	13	Burmah	465	4
5	Greenan	210	3	14	Alton	179	3
6	Turnberry	577	5	15	Crosbie	457	4
7	Tel-el-Kebir	402	4	16	Well	542	5
8	Postage Stamp	126	3	17	Rabbit	223	3
9	The Monk	423	4	18	Craigend	452	4
	OUT	3429	35		IN	3652	36
					TOTAL	**7081**	**71**

1997 BRITISH OPEN – COMPLETED SCORES

7079 yards PAR 71 (284)

1	JUSTIN LEONARD (£250000)	69	66	72	65	272
2=	Darren Clarke	67	66	71	71	275
	Jesper Parnevik	70	66	66	73	275
4	Jim Furyk	67	72	70	70	279
5=	Stephen Ames	74	69	66	71	280
	Padraig Harrington	75	69	69	67	280
7=	Fred Couples	69	68	70	74	281
	Peter O'Malley	73	70	70	68	281
	Eduardo Romero	74	68	67	72	281
10=	Robert Allenby	76	68	66	72	282
	Mark Calacavecchia	74	67	72	69	282
	Ernie Els	75	69	69	69	282
	Retief Goosen	75	69	70	68	282
	Tom Kite	72	67	74	69	282
	Davis Love III	70	71	74	67	282
	Shigeki Maruyama	74	69	70	69	282
	Frank Nobilo	74	72	68	68	282
	Tom Watson	71	70	70	71	282
	Lee Westwood	73	70	67	72	282
20=	Stuart Appleby	72	72	68	71	283
	Brad Faxon	77	67	72	67	283
	Mark James	76	67	70	70	283
	Jose-Maria Olazabal	75	68	73	67	283
24=	Jay Haas	71	70	73	70	284
	Tom Lehman	74	72	72	66	284
	Peter Lonard	72	70	69	73	284
	Phil Mickelson	76	68	69	71	284
	Colin Montgomerie	76	69	69	70	284
	David A Russell	75	72	68	69	284
	Tiger Woods	72	74	64	74	284
	Ian Woosnam	71	73	69	71	284
32	Mark McNulty	78	67	72	68	285
33=	Rodger Davis	73	73	70	70	286
	David Duval	73	69	73	71	286
	Jonathan Lomas	72	71	69	74	286
36=	Andrew Magee	70	75	72	70	287
	Greg Norman	69	73	70	75	287
38=	Michael Bradley	72	73	73	70	288
	John Kernohan	76	70	74	68	288
	Bernhard Langer	72	74	69	73	288
	Mark O'Meara	73	73	74	68	288
	Raymond Russell	72	72	74	70	288
	Vijay Singh	77	69	70	72	288
44=	Jose Coceres	76	70	71	72	289
	Jerry Kelly	76	68	72	73	289
	Curtis Strange	71	71	70	77	289
	David Tapping	71	66	78	74	289
48=	Richard Boxall	75	71	72	72	290
	Jim Payne	74	71	74	71	290
	Steve Jones	76	71	68	75	290
51=	Angel Cabrera	70	70	76	75	291
	Nick Faldo	71	73	75	72	291
	Jeff Maggert	76	69	71	75	291
	Peter Mitchell	75	69	76	71	291
	Corey Pavin	78	69	76	68	291
	Wayne Riley	74	71	75	71	291

COMPLETED SCORES – continued

	Peter Senior	76	70	73	72	291
	Greg Turner	76	71	72	72	291
59	Payne Stewart	73	74	71	74	292
60=	Barclay Howard (a)	70	74	76	73	293
	Jack Nicklaus	73	74	71	75	293
62=	Tom Purtzer	72	71	73	78	294
	Jamie Spence	78	69	72	75	294
	Steve Stricker	72	73	74	75	294
	Peter Teravainen	74	72	73	75	294
66=	Gary Clark	74	72	72	77	295
	Per-Ulrik Johansson	72	75	73	75	295
	Paul McGinley	76	71	77	71	295
69	Tommy Tolles	77	68	75	76	296
70	Billy Andrade	72	72	78	76	298

Those who missed the 36-hole cut included:

148 Steve Elkington
149 Lee Janzen, Gary Player, Craig Stadler
150 Mark Brooks, Nick Price
151 John Cook
153 Sandy Lyle
157 Paul Azinger

runner-up places graphically blot the Greg Norman copybook.

With the spread of global talent, top golfers find it less easy now to dominate the Majors – reasons why players of the calibre of Stewart, Azinger, Couples, Woosnam and Pavin have in the last decade only won token Majors, when much more could have been expected of them. Now with the arrival over the last two or three years of Els, Lehman, Woods – and at Troon, Leonard – as Majors winners, there are signs that the old order may be breaking up.

Certainly, the 126th Open was very 'open', and without denigrating Justin Leonard's achievement, when only the winner from the leading group of almost 20 players broke par in Round Four, the Championship perhaps cried out for a 'charge' from one of the greats of old to put pressure on the young Texan. Fred Couples, for example, was in a good position to challenge on the

Leaders (Round-by-round)		
R1	67	D Clarke, J Furyk
	69	F Couples, J Leonard, G Norman
	70	A Cabrera, B Howard, D Love III, A Magee, J Parnevik
R2	133	D Clarke; 67,66
	135	J Leonard; 69,66
	136	J Parnevik; 70,66
R3	202	J Parnevik; 70,66,66
	204	D Clarke; 67,66,71
	207	F Couples; 69,68,70
		J Leonard; 69,66,72

Low Scores		
R2	66	D Clarke, J Leonard, J Parnevik, D Tapping
	67	M Calcavecchia, B Faxon, M James, T Kite
	68	R Allenby, F Couples, J Kelly, P Mickelson, J-M Olazabal, E Romero, T Tolles
R3	64	T Woods
	66	R Allenby, S Ames, J Parnevik
	67	E Romero, L Westwood
R4	65	J Leonard
	66	T Lehman
	67	B Faxon, P Harrington, D Love III, J-M Olazabal

Scrappy play over the outward nine was balanced by a couple of birdies, to see Parnevik edge away from the Irishman. Up ahead, however, Leonard was burning up the course. He had played the easier front nine in 31, with six birdies, so that by the 11th Parnevik's lead (despite picking up a birdie himself) had been cut to two. The eccentric Swede then bogeyed 13 and 16 while the man from Dallas held his nerve over the testing homeward stretch. Once more the 17th proved fatal for Jesper when a wild drive resulted in a dropped shot after Justin had holed a 35-footer for birdie. A broken man, Parnevik finally capitulated with a bogey at 18.

The conditions on Day One, with the wind whipping in from the Firth of Clyde, spelt disaster for many players. 1991 Champion Ian Baker-Finch, continuing a prolonged fight against appalling form, must have been totally devastated when he shot a 92 and withdrew. The above –mentioned Nick Price, 78, Paul Azinger, 79, and 1996 PGA Champion, Mark Brooks, 80, all suffered and eventually missed the cut. Tiger Woods, despite a Championship low of 64 in Round Three, still had much to learn about links golf. With the wind helping on the front nine his driving was at times breathtaking. He drove 400 yards or so more than once on the par-5 4th, and once plopped his tee-shot into the green-side bunker at the 402-yard 7th. However, just like Jack Nicklaus 35 years earlier – in his first Open Championship – he discovered that Troon doesn't lie down for long drivers. Whereas Jack (who, incidentally, was continuing his unbroken run of appearances in 1997) took that famous 10 at the 11th, Tiger's challenge ended with a 7 at the same hole on Day One; also an 8 at the 10th in Round Two; and to finish off, a 6 at the 126-yard Postage Stamp.

last day in a leading group comprising relatively untried campaigners, but after birdying the first, Fred couldn't bring his experience to bear, and faded away badly.

The lead after 54 holes was held by Parnevik by two from halfway leader Clarke, and five from Leonard. The Swede, who was having a successful year on the PGA Tour in America, had overhauled Clarke with two 66s, and at least went into the last round in a position he had found himself before – in 1994, just down the road at Turnberry. Then his nemesis was in the form of Nick Price, who eagled the 17th while Jesper bogeyed the last to convert a two-shot lead into a one-stroke horror story. Surely it couldn't happen twice?

One oddity: three Swedes – Pierre Fulke (Round One) and Dennis Edlund and Daniel Olsson (Round Two) – all shot holes-in-one; and all missed the cut.

THE 79th US PGA CHAMPIONSHIP

WINGED FOOT GOLF CLUB

Mamaroneck, New York
14–17 April 1997

LOVE CONQUERS ALL

The previous year Davis Love was leading the US Open at Oakland Hills when he stood on the 71st tee. A bogey followed, and a miss with little more than a tap-in at 18 saw his lead overhauled by a grateful Steve Jones. More fuel was being added to the fire. A second place at the Masters in 1995 and four further Top 10 places between 1995 and 1997 put Love – a bit like Colin Montgomerie – in that monstrous media stranglehold which heaped pressure on him every time he entered a Major and then didn't win.

However, with Winged Foot at its most wicked, Love buried British Open Champion Justin Leonard over the final round - and that media tag forever. In doing so he stopped the march of the Twentysomethings (he is 33), but did strengthen the argument that it is becoming increasingly difficult for any one player, or group of players, to dominate the Majors. Davis Love III was the 13th consecutive different winner of a Major Championship, and one of 16 one-time winners in the 90s. His father, Davis Love, Jr, a respected putting teacher, achieved 6th place in the British Open of 1969, but was tragically killed in a plane-crash in 1988, and thus did not witness his son's finest hour.

Love's 4th Round 66 was a masterful display of long straight driving and sound approach play and putting. Tying for the lead overnight with Leonard – seven ahead of the pack and seven under par – it was going to take a

miraculous round from someone to impose on this duel at the top. The murderous rough either side of the narrow fairways ensured that would not happen, and, indeed, it was the rough that put paid to Leonard's hopes of back-to-back Majors victories. He conceded four shots to Love between holes 2 and 5 as Davis birdied two, and he strayed either side of the fairway to drop two. Although the lead thereafter fluctuated in the number of shots, Love was still three to the good at 16. The rain, which had caused some interruption to play during the weekend was driving in again. Love, according to Leonard, hit 'two shots...[which] were just incredible', to secure his par. He extended his winning margin to five when, with some style, he birdied the 448-yard last.

WINGED FOOT – Yardages and Pars					
HOLE	YARDS	PAR	HOLE	YARDS	PAR
1	402	4	10	466	4
2	235	3	11	415	4
3	455	4	12	187	3
4	434	4	13	461	4
5	407	4	14	439	4
6	475	4	15	583	5
7	174	3	16	441	4
8	362	4	17	480	4
9	607	5	18	190	3
OUT	3551	35	IN	3662	35
			TOTAL	7213	70

1997 PGA COMPLETED SCORES

6987 yards PAR 70 (280)

1	**DAVIS LOVE III** ($470000)	66 71 66 66	269
2	Justin Leonard	68 70 65 71	274
3	Jeff Maggert	69 69 73 65	276
4	Lee Janzen	69 67 74 69	279
5	Tom Kite	68 71 71 70	280
6=	Phil Blackmar	70 68 74 69	281
	Jim Furyk	69 72 72 68	281
	Scott Hoch	71 72 68 70	281
9	Tom Byrum	69 73 70 70	282
10=	Tom Lehman	69 72 72 70	283
	Scott McCarron	74 71 67 71	283
	Joey Sindelar	72 71 71 69	283
13=	David Duval	70 70 71 73	284
	Tim Herron	72 73 68 71	284
	Colin Montgomerie	74 71 67 72	284
	Greg Norman	68 71 74 71	284
	Mark O'Meara	69 73 75 67	284
	Nick Price	72 70 72 70	284
	Vijay Singh	73 66 76 69	284
	Tommy Tolles	75 70 73 66	284
	Kirk Triplett	73 70 71 70	284
	Bob Tway	68 75 72 69	284
23=	Mark Calcavecchia	71 74 73 76	285
	John Cook	71 71 74 69	285
	Bernhard Langer	73 71 72 69	285
	Doug Martin	69 75 74 67	285
	Shigeki Maruyama	68 70 74 73	285
	Kenny Perry	73 68 73 71	285
29=	Ronnie Black	76 69 71 70	286
	Fred Couples	71 67 73 75	286
	John Daly	66 73 77 70	286
	Paul Goydos	70 72 71 73	286
	Hale Irwin	73 70 71 72	286
	Phil Mickelson	69 69 73 75	286
	Frank Nobilo	72 73 67 74	286
	Don Pooley	72 74 70 70	286
	Payne Stewart	70 70 72 74	286
	Lee Westwood	74 68 71 73	286
	Tiger Woods	70 70 71 75	286
40=	Ignacio Garrido	70 71 75 71	287
	Steve Jones	69 73 75 70	287
	David Ogrin	74 72 71 70	287
	Eduardo Romero	71 72 72 72	287
44=	Paul Azinger	68 73 71 76	288
	Thomas Bjorn	72 68 77 71	288
	Steve Elkington	72 72 70 74	288
	Jesper Parnevik	76 70 71 71	288
	Sam Torrance	74 72 70 72	288
49=	Robert Allenby	67 77 74 71	289
	Brian Henninger	74 68 75 72	289
	Chris Perry	68 71 73 77	289
	Loren Roberts	76 70 74 69	289

COMPLETED SCORES – continued

53=	Olin Browne	70 73 74 73	290
	Ernie Els	70 76 74 70	290
	Billy Mayfair	75 68 75 72	290
	Taylor Smith	71 71 74 74	290
	Craig Stadler	72 72 74 72	290
58=	Steve Lowery	72 69 79 71	291
	Larry Mize	71 73 73 74	291
	Lanny Wadkins	72 72 77 70	291
61=	Stuart Appleby	75 70 69 78	292
	Russ Cochran	72 73 72 75	292
	Fred Funk	71 74 77 70	292
	Retief Goosen	72 70 74 76	292
	Jay Haas	71 69 73 79	292
	Lee Rinker	70 71 75 76	292
67=	Peter Jacobsen	74 72 75 72	293
	Per-Ulrik Johannson	73 69 73 78	293
	Paul Stankowski	68 71 77 77	293
70	Carlos Franco	69 74 76 75	294
71=	Michael Bradley	73 69 80 73	295
	Yoshinori Kaneko	72 73 76 74	295
	Larry Nelson	76 70 76 73	295
	Constantino Rocca	69 69 79 78	295
75	Andrew Magee	71 70 80 75	296
76=	Pete Jordan	76 70 75 76	297
	Kevin Sutherland	73 73 73 78	297

Those who missed the 36-hole cut included:

147 Billy Andrade
148 Fuzzy Zoeller
149 Mark Brooks, Ian Woosnam
150 Jack Nicklaus, Tom Watson
151 Brad Faxon, Jeff Sluman
152 Jose-Maria Olazabal
153 Darren Clarke, Nick Faldo, Curtis Strange
156 Hal Sutton
157 Ben Crenshaw
158 Wayne Grady

The up-and-down nature of double-Major Champion John Daly's life continued. After walking out mid-round at the US Open earlier in the year, he shot an opening 66 to share the lead with Davis Love. He then proceeded to toss an errant driver over a fence at the 12th in Round Two, before confronting a PGA official with some choice words when he was denied relief from a bad lie on Sunday. He finished on 286 – eight over par, tying for 29th place. The US continued to dominate this Major, filling the Top 10 places and ties. Only consistent overseas performers like Price, Norman, Singh, Nobilo and Montgomerie featured in

Leaders (Round-by round)		
R1	66	J Daly, D Love III
	67	R Allenby
	68	P Azinger, T Kite, J Leonard, S Maruyama, G Norman, C Perry, P Stankowski, B Tway
R2	136	L Janzen; 69,67
	137	D Love III; 66,71
	138	P Blackmar; 70,68 F Couples; 71,67 J Leonard; 68,70 J Maggert; 69,69 S Maruyama; 68,70 P Mickelson; 69,69 C Rocca; 69,69
R3	203	J Leonard; 68,70,65 D Love; 66,71,66
	210	L Janzen; 69,67,74 T Kite; 68,71,71
	211	F Couples; 71,67,73 D Duval; 70,70,71 S Hoch; 71,72,68 J Maggert; 69,69,73 P Mickelson; 69,69,73 T Woods; 70,70,71

Low Scores		
R2	66	V Singh
	67	F Couples, L Janzen
	68	T Bjorn, P Blackmar, B Henninger, B Mayfair, L Westwood
R3	65	J Leonard
	66	D Love III
	67	S McCarron, C Montgomerie, F Nobilo
R4	65	J Maggert
	66	D Love III, T Tolles
	67	M Calcavecchia, D Martin, M O'Meara

the Top 30 – with the notable exception of 24 year-old Lee Westwood, who achieved this in every 1997 Major. Spare a thought for Italian, Constantino Rocca. Swinging wonderfully for a man with a shoulder problem, he shot a half-way score of 138, and was in joint third place! He then shot 79-78 to finish 15 over par and tie for 71st.

THE 1998 MAJOR CHAMPIONSHIPS

1998 sees the return of two favourite Major Championship sites – the Olympic Country Club and Royal Birkdale, for the US and British Opens, respectively. It also welcomes a new venue to the roster – Sahalee Country Club – where the PGA Championship will be held in August.

THE MASTERS

The 62nd Masters, of course, will be held as usual at Augusta National, the dates in 1998 being 9–12 April. The talk this time around must be whether Tiger Woods can repeat his historic 1997 victory. There seems little doubt that in Woods there is a multiple Masters winner – and probable multi-Majors winner too – but how chastened was he by his 1997 experiences? It seemed that sheer hype would win him the Masters after starting his rookie season in almost unbeatable fashion. His record-breaking win at Augusta could not be sustained however, and his inconsistency, however long he might have been off the tee, proved his downfall at all the other Majors. At Congressional and Winged Foot the lush, unforgiving rough bordering the narrow fairways proved his undoing: at Troon he had nightmares with gorse bushes.

Unless his early season form dips, Woods will start favourite for the Masters, and if he performs like 1997, it will all be about second place. This book goes to press before the Ryder Cup starts at Valderrama, but the cross-season axis of this competition and the Masters in April will really tell whether the European resurgence is continuing – led by Colin Montgomerie, some gifted Scandinavians and Spaniards, and, perhaps, Lee Westwood – or running out of steam. Time may be running out for Faldo, Langer and Woosnam to win again the Major they have been most comfortable with, but a good Ryder Cup and a strong showing at Augusta may point to a few more good years yet.

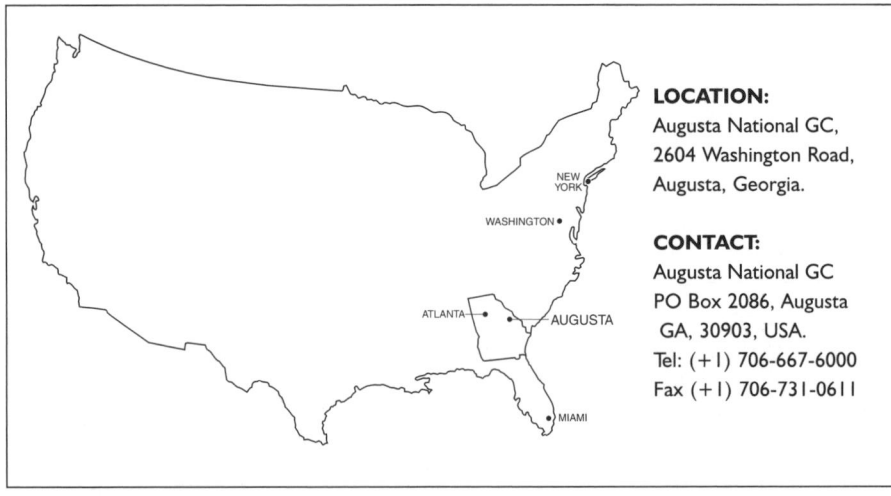

LOCATION:
Augusta National GC,
2604 Washington Road,
Augusta, Georgia.

CONTACT:
Augusta National GC
PO Box 2086, Augusta
GA, 30903, USA.
Tel: (+1) 706-667-6000
Fax (+1) 706-731-0611

Of the Americans, Justin Leonard could push Tiger, and at last the quality of Davis Love has won through. Lehman, Maggert, Furyk, Faxon and Tolles had their moments in 1997, and will do so again in 1998, but if they can repeat their early season form then relative newcomers Paul Stankowski and Australia's Stuart Appleby could spring a surprise or two. Will Greg Norman's 1996 experience ever be expunged – or has his marvellous career, too, seen its best days? Will Ernie Els take over the Norman mantle as best resident overseas player on the PGA Tour?

One last hope for the Masters – I do hope spring doesn't arrive too early again. Another year without the azaleas and dogwoods would be too much to bear!

THE US OPEN

Between 18–21 June the 98th US Open returns to Olympic Country Club (Lake Course), San Francisco, California. The Golf course has played host to three previous Opens – in 1955, 1966 and 1987 – as well as the US Amateur in 1958 and 1981 (when Nathaniel Crosby, son of Bing, won a poignant victory just four years after his father's death).

The course was sculpted from the Pacific shoreline sand-dunes by English emigré Wilfred Reid as long ago as 1917, but has had several revisions since – the last major one occurring in 1952, by the influential Robert Trent Jones. Characterized by its 35000 trees – a mix of Pacific conifers and broad-leafed deciduous – it is strikingly lacking in fairway sand for a course so naturally blessed with it. Being situated in the Bay area, just several hundred yards from the Ocean, Olympic often experiences one of San Francisco's trade marks – sea fog. This can affect play over the course of a day as it rolls out and in, and can cause an unexpected lushness in the fairway grass which prevents bounce and run-on.

LOCATION:
Olympic Country Club at
Lakeside
San Francisco, California.

CONTACT:
US Golf Association,
Golf House,
PO Box 708 Far Hills,
NJ 07931-0708, USA
Tel (+1) 908-234-2300
Fax (+1) 908-234-0319

In 1955, the trees were aided and abetted by longer rough than normal, and although Ben Hogan posted an unspectacular 287, most people thought that that was that. It was still going to be too good for any of the fancied players out on the course. But, like some rank outsider plodding just behind the thoroughbreds in a classic horse race, the going was to the liking of unknown Jack Fleck, and he came through the field as the more fancied entries were increasingly hampered by the cloying conditions. He tied Hogan's total to force a play-off, and golf's purest bloodstock of the time – aiming for a record fifth win – was also reined in.

Another play-off settled the 1966 Open at Olympic, with Billy Casper denying Arnold Palmer his second Open and eighth Major in all. It was a disaster for Arnie – and a totally inconceivable one with nine holes to play. Palmer led Casper by seven at the turn – the largest lead in any Major at such a stage not to go on to win – but that was totally negated by the 17th (including a 7-shot swing in six holes). Palmer then lost his third play-off in the US Open when, in a virtual replay of the previous day he dropped five strokes over six holes on the back nine.

Scott Simpson's win in 1987 couldn't match the previous two at Olympic for drama, but it did throw up an outsider as Champion. Tom Watson lost his Third Round lead with some early bogeys and Simpson played the marginally more solid golf thereon in to deny Tom his second Open, and elusive 9th Major. Tommy Nakajima's tragedies in Majors were more blackly comic here when he lost his ball in a tree and couldn't find it.

The spongy turf of the fairways will again favour the longer, straighter hitters off the tee, if they can obtain distance on the full, and not rely on the ball bouncing on. Once more, defending Champion Ernie Els will have the game to win at Olympic, but any of the 1997 Major Champions have the capability, along with Colin Montgomerie, Nick Price and Tom Lehman. Jim Furyk (he of the eccentric swing, which David Feherty has likened to an octopus falling out of a tree!) fits the bill if his 1997 driving stats can hold up in a Major – and this event may just provide the breakthrough he has been inching towards over the last year or two. Jeff Maggert, too, could come close again – but is it the last chance for Faldo or Norman?

THE BRITISH OPEN

The 127th Open Championship, between 16–19 July, will be the eighth to have been hosted over the classic links of Royal Birkdale. The course, designed by George Low (with amendments from others, including the legendary JH Taylor) is sited at the seaside resort of Southport, close to the city of Liverpool on the Lancashire (now Merseyside) coast.

Established in 1889, the Birkdale Club staged the Ladies' British Open as long ago as 1909, but was not added to the Opens roster until 1954 (the 1940 Championship was due to be held there but was called off by Hitler). It was accorded its 'Royal' status in 1951. As well as hosting eight Open Championships it was the venue for the Ryder Cup in 1965 and, famous for Jack Nicklaus' sporting concession to Tony Jacklin, in 1969. It has also held Walker and Curtis Cup matches as well as the British PGA Championship.

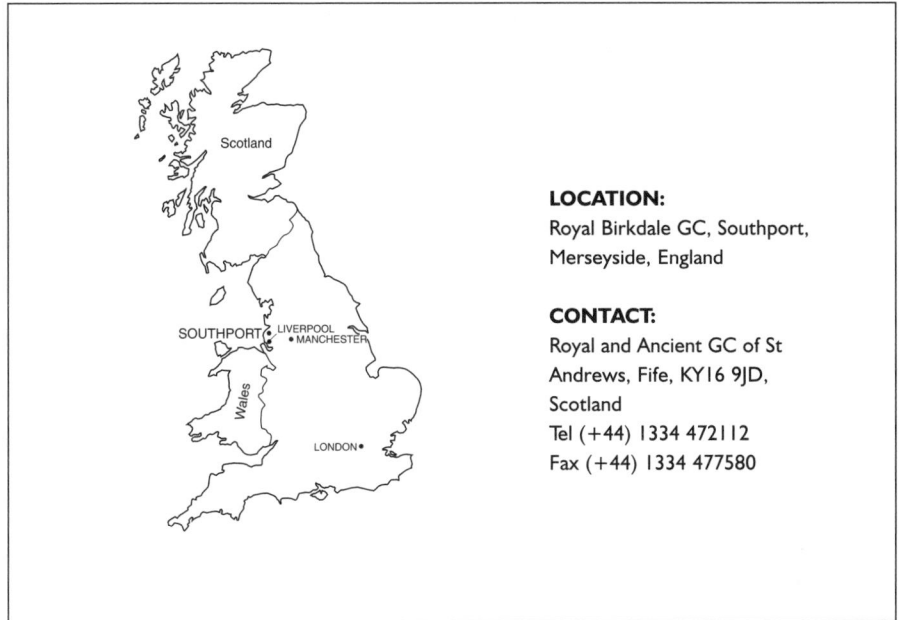

LOCATION:
Royal Birkdale GC, Southport,
Merseyside, England

CONTACT:
Royal and Ancient GC of St
Andrews, Fife, KY16 9JD,
Scotland
Tel (+44) 1334 472112
Fax (+44) 1334 477580

That first Championship saw Peter Thomson win his first Open – and it was also to witness his fifth and last in 1965, by which time the links had been extended to over 7000 yards.

In 1961, the great Arnold Palmer won his first Open Championship and reversed a 30 year trend by making the Open fashionable with American golfers again. He is commemorated by a plaque off the 16th fairway (then the 15th) when, some 140 yards from the green, his drive burrowed beneath a bush. Palmer, typically, scorned convention and, as Peter Unsworth, the Chairman of Birkdale's Championship Committee puts it, 'his 5 iron moved ball, bush and turf to get his par 4'. The 1961 Open will also be remembered for the atrocious weather when winds blew down marquees and the Friday was washed out.

Lee Trevino was starting to hex Tony Jacklin when the Open returned to Birkdale in 1971. The 1969 Champion was to suffer at the hands of the Texan more than once in the early 70s, which, many people believe, was the cause of Jacklin's rapid decline over the next few years. The 1971 event was made more popular with TV viewers by the sight of Taiwanese 'Mr' (Liang-Huan) Lu doffing his hat to the galleries as he strode up the fairways. He finally had to concede to Trevino, too, after Lee's last-round putting prowess (he single-putted seven of the first eight greens).

The 1976 Championship at Royal Birkdale was dominated by Johnny Miller who finished six better than Jack Nicklaus and the 19-year old Spanish tyro, Seve Ballesteros. His final-round 66 was exceptional, matched only by Mark James, (it formed part of a cautious last 36 holes when he used his 1 iron no fewer than 21 times off the tee), and was eight shots lower than the scrambling Seve.

Tom Watson won his only Open Championship (out of five) outside of Scotland at Birkdale in 1983. Hale Irwin lost by one – after completely missing a tap-in at the 14th in the Third Round – but Watson won in style, striking a majestic 213-yard 2 iron to within 20 feet on the last hole.

In better days for him, Ian Baker-Finch won the 1991 title – having finished in the Top Ten twice previously. Shooting a record 29 on the outward half, he had enough left to coast home ahead of fellow-Australian Mike Harwood, Freddie Couples, who shot a 64, and Mark O'Meara.

The Royal Birkdale Committee, aware of problems, have completely re-laid and, in some cases re-designed all the greens since the 1991 Championship. Fine-tuning the golf-course over the past 15 years or so had reduced the Championship yardage to 6940 by 1991. The 7th and 17th tees have since been re-sited, increasing the lengths respectively by 25 yards (to 177) and 47 yards (to 544), making the 1998 Championship course a demanding 7012 yards for its par 70.

Will 1998 see the first-ever British winner at Birkdale? The odds are not in favour, but Darren Clarke's effort in 1997 suggests he has the temperament to win. The Spaniards and Swedes who do well on the European tour find links golf as strange to them as most Americans, but Constantino Rocca of Italy nearly won at St Andrews in 1995 and Jesper Parnevik has come close twice to prove it is possible for a continental European to do well. Justin Leonard will be out to prove his Troon win was no fluke and Tom Lehman will again be a threat. So too – as at every event – will be Els, and perhaps Vijay Singh's time might come. Some of the more experienced campaigners may have something to say about it though – Couples, Langer, Norman, Faldo and Woosnam were all in the Top 20 the last time the Open came to Royal Birkdale.

THE US PGA

Unlike all the other Major Championships, the 80th US PGA Championship is breaking virgin ground in 1998 by playing the Sahalee Country Club (pronounced, so I'm advised by the PGA of America, 'Suh-HOLLY' – which may come out sounding a little different in Scotland than in Florida!). Translated from the Chinook Indian, Sahalee means 'high heavenly grounds', and in fact the golf course is perched 500 feet above the inlet of the Puget Sound on the Sammamish Plateau – rolling countryside west of the Cascade Mountains.

Spreading the PGA gospel (the Championship has visited half of the United States since its inauguration in 1916) – the site is approximately 30 minutes drive east of Seattle – it is only the second occasion for a PGA (or any other Major) Championship to have visited Washington State, and only the third time ever to play the beautiful Pacific North West. In 1944 the Championship was hosted by the Manito G&CC at Spokane, when Bob Hamilton beat Byron Nelson in the matchplay final. Two years later, Ben Hogan won the first of his nine Majors when he also won the PGA title, this time at neighbouring Portland, Oregon, demolishing Ed 'Porky' Oliver 6&4.

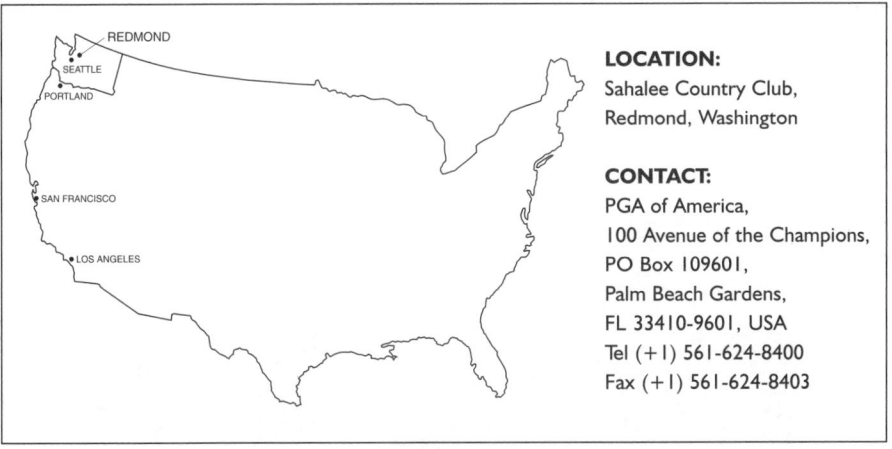

LOCATION:
Sahalee Country Club,
Redmond, Washington

CONTACT:
PGA of America,
100 Avenue of the Champions,
PO Box 109601,
Palm Beach Gardens,
FL 33410-9601, USA
Tel (+1) 561-624-8400
Fax (+1) 561-624-8403

Designed by Ted Robinson, Sahalee is a 27-hole complex and is listed in 1997 as one of *Golf Digest*'s Top 100 courses in America – set as it is among the cedar, hemlock and fir trees of a dense, natural forest. Although it has not played host to a Major Championship before, it can claim four regional qualifying events for the US Open and two for the US Amateur Championship. It also hosted the 1986 North West Classic.

With approximately 7000 tree-lined yards and a par of 70 it will be a worthy test for the world's best, who now play the PGA Championship regularly – making it a fitting climax to the Majors season. For the 80th PGA Championship, two of the existing par 5s will be reduced to 470 yards to provide excruciating par 4s. The Championship's front nine will be taken from Sahalee's South Course and the back nine from the North Course. The nine holes of the East Course will be dominated by the tented village – media headquarters and hospitality chalets – and the other paraphernalia which now forms such a huge part of any Major Championship.

Defending Champion, Davis Love, should have a new-found confidence following his overdue first Majors win, but this Championship is renowned for its difficulty to defend. No-one has done so since the event went strokeplay in 1958. Nick Price was the last double winner in 1994, and he has the game, if he still has the will, to win it again. Of the non-winners, Tommy Tolles could be a good outside bet and, not for the first time expect Jeff Maggert to feature. The more temperate climate of the North West United States may help Colin Montgomerie, who dislikes the draining heat of a Mid-West August more than most. The tradition that no European has ever won the PGA may be the psychological barrier in front of Colin this time though. If Ernie Els hasn't collected a Major before the PGA comes around, many people's money will go on him. The same might be said of Tiger Woods, but Augusta will always suit his game more than US Open/PGA-style courses. If he gets his power-play aiming in the right direction though, there is no Major title beyond his immense ability.

THE OLD COURSE, ST ANDREWS – The 17th, the 'Road Hole', with the R&A Clubhouse in the background. *Allsport/Hulton Deutsch*

ROYAL TROON – The Open Championship's shortest hole – the 8th – the 126-yard 'Postage Stamp'. *Allsport*

ROYAL LYTHAM & ST ANNE'S – The 18th hole and Clubhouse. *Allsport*

MUIRFIELD – Home of the Honourable Company of Edinburgh Golfers since 1892, having moved from Musselburgh. *Allsport*

AUGUSTA NATIONAL – The 12th – 'Golden Bell' and Hogan's Bridge. *Allsport*

OAKLAND HILLS – Host to 8 Major Championship since 1924. *Allsport*

OAKMONT – In 1994 it hosted its 7th US Open – a record – and has 3 PGA championships to its credit as well. *Allsport*

PEBBLE BEACH – Spectacular Pacific shoreline course – but not strictly a links. *Allsport*

Part 4

The Players
1860–1997

INTRODUCTION

This section of the book provides the only known record anywhere of the top players' Major Championship records. Adopting the Part 2 premise of Top 30 finishers (Round of the Last 32 in the PGA before 1958) some 2000 records, each a player's *Curriculum Vitae* of successful sorties into the Majors, are listed alphabetically. Within the individual lists, the records appear chronologically, but only the years where Top 30 appearances occur are recorded. Therefore, if a record omits the year 1937, for instance, then that player has no Top 30 Major Championship finishes in that year.

The symbol [a] after a player's name denotes that he was amateur for the whole period of his Majors Top 30 career: 'a' following a finishing position denotes the player was an amateur for that event only.

AARON, Tommy (US)

	MAS	USO	BOP	PGA
1960	25			
1964				21
1965	11			8
1966	13	30		22
1967	8			20
1968	7			26
1969	8			
1970	5			
1971	22			
1972				2
1973	W			
1975		29		
1979	28			

ABBOTT, Patrick (US)

	MAS	USO	BOP	PGA
1952		28		

ADAM, Robert [a] (SCO)

	MAS	USO	BOP	PGA
1890			25	

ADAMS, GC (US)

	MAS	USO	BOP	PGA
1916				Last 32

ADAMS, Jimmy (SCO)

	MAS	USO	BOP	PGA
1934			26	
1936			2	
1937			17	
1938			2	
1939			13	
1947			12	
1949			8	
1950			12	
1951			4	
1954			5	
1956			25	
1959			29	

ADAMS, John (US)

	MAS	USO	BOP	PGA
1993		11		

ADAMS, Sam (US)

	MAS	USO	BOP	PGA
1977		23		

ADWICK, James (ENG)

	MAS	USO	BOP	PGA
1925			27	

ADWICK, KWC (ENG)

	MAS	USO	BOP	PGA
1956			28	

ALBUS, Jim (US)

	MAS	USO	BOP	PGA
1984		30		

ALCROFT, Albert (US)

	MAS	USO	BOP	PGA
1927				Last 32
1928				Last 32
1929				Last 32

ALERIDGE, Clayton (US)

	MAS	USO	BOP	PGA
1944				Last 32

ALEXANDER, Andrew (SCO)

	MAS	USO	BOP	PGA
1882			13	

ALEXANDER, Skip (US)

	MAS	USO	BOP	PGA
1948		11		Last 16
1949	30	27		Last 32
1950	14	18		Last 32
1952	27			
1953	29			

ALLAN, Jamie (SCO)

	MAS	USO	BOP	PGA
1878			8	
1879			2	
1885			29	
1888			18	

ALLAN, John (SCO)

	MAS	USO	BOP	PGA
1866			8	
1868			5	
1870			8	
1878			9	
1890			15	
1893			23	

ALLAN, Matthew (SCO)

	MAS	USO	BOP	PGA
1875			13	
1884			11	

ALLEN, Brian (ENG)

	MAS	USO	BOP	PGA
1963			14	

ALLEN, Trevor (ENG)

	MAS	USO	BOP	PGA
1950			24	

ALLENBY, Robert (AUS)

	MAS	USO	BOP	PGA
1995			15	
1997			10	

ALLIN, Brian (Buddy) (US)

	MAS	USO	BOP	PGA
1974	15	10		
1975	20	25		10
1976	19			

ALLISS, Percy (ENG)

	MAS	USO	BOP	PGA
1922			10	
1925			5	
1927			9	
1928			4	
1929			4	
1930			17	
1931			3	
1932			4	
1934			9	
1935			15	
1936			5	
1937			15	
1939			9	
1946			17	

ALLISS, Peter (ENG)

MAS	USO	BOP	PGA
1953		9	
1954		8	
1957		12	
1958		11	
1959		16	
1961		8	
1962		8	
1963		18	
1966		20	
1968		13	
1969		8	

ALLOTT, Fred (ENG)

MAS	USO	BOP	PGA
1950		29	
1952		21	

ALVES, Grange (US)

MAS	USO	BOP	PGA
1911	20		

AMBO, Walter (US)

MAS	USO	BOP	PGA
1947			Last 32

AMES, Stephen (TRI)

MAS	USO	BOP	PGA
1997		5	

ANDERSON, Bill (SCO)

MAS	USO	BOP	PGA
1939		17	
1946		14	

ANDERSON, Brad (US)

MAS	USO	BOP	PGA
1971			22

ANDERSON, Carl (US)

MAS	USO	BOP	PGA
1919			Last 32
1923			Last 32

ANDERSON, D [a] (SCO)

MAS	USO	BOP	PGA
1890		17	

ANDERSON Jr, David (SCO)

MAS	USO	BOP	PGA
1888		2	
1890		14	
1891		22	
1892		16	
1893		22	
1895		6	
1896		24	
1900		14	

ANDERSON Sr, David (SCO)

MAS	USO	BOP	PGA
1876		14	
1879		7	
1882		21	
1885		21	

ANDERSON, Iain (SCO)

MAS	USO	BOP	PGA
1955		15	

ANDERSON, Jamie (SCO)

MAS	USO	BOP	PGA
1869		6	
1870		7	
1873		2	
1874		5	
1876		12	
1877		W	
1878		W	
1879		W	
1881		2	
1882		3	
1884		15	

ANDERSON, John G (US)

MAS	USO	BOP	PGA
1912	16		

ANDERSON, LS [a] (SCO)

MAS	USO	BOP	PGA
1893		19	

ANDERSON, PC [a] (SCO)

MAS	USO	BOP	PGA
1893		19	

ANDERSON, R (US)

MAS	USO	BOP	PGA
1896	27		

ANDERSON, Stuart [a] (SCO)

MAS	USO	BOP	PGA
1894		25	

ANDERSON Jr, Tom (US)

MAS	USO	BOP	PGA
1909	7		
1910	8		
1912	10		

ANDERSON Jr, Willie (SCO/US)

MAS	USO	BOP	PGA
1897	2		
1898	3		
1899	5		
1900	11		
1901	W		
1902	5		
1903	W		
1904	W		
1905	W		
1906	5		
1907	15		
1908	4		
1909	4		
1910	11		

ANDERSON Sr, Willie (SCO)

MAS	USO	BOP	PGA
1885		24	
1888		27	

ANDRADE, Billy (US)

MAS	USO	BOP	PGA
1990			14
1992		25	12
1995	21		
1996	23		
1997	13		

ANDREW, R [a] (SCO)

MAS	USO	BOP	PGA
1908		27	

249

ANDREW, Robert
(SCO)

	MAS	USO	BOP	PGA
1860			4	
1861			5	
1863			6	
1864			3	
1865			7	
1866			3	
1867			7	
1868			2	

ANDREWS, Robert [a]
(US)

	MAS	USO	BOP	PGA
1913		21		

ANGELINI, Alfonso
(IT)

	MAS	USO	BOP	PGA
1954			12	

ANNON, Fred
(US)

	MAS	USO	BOP	PGA
1944				Last 16

AOKI, Isao
(JAP)

	MAS	USO	BOP	PGA
1977	28			
1978			7	
1979			7	
1980		2	12	
1981		11	11	4
1982		30	20	
1983	19			
1984	25	16		
1985	16			
1987		14		
1988	25		7	
1989				17

APPLEBY, Stuart
(AUS)

	MAS	USO	BOP	PGA
1997	21		20	

ARCHER, George
(US)

	MAS	USO	BOP	PGA
1966		17		
1967	16			
1968	22	16		4
1969	W	10		
1970		30		
1971		5		
1972	12			
1977	19	27		19
1980				17
1981	11			
1982	30			
1983	12			
1984	25			

ARMITAGE, R [a]
(SCO)

	MAS	USO	BOP	PGA
1873			12	
1879			29	

ARMOUR, Tommy
(SCO/US)

	MAS	USO	BOP	PGA
1924		13		
1925				QF
1926		9	12	
1927		W		QF
1928		16		Last 32
1929		5	10	
1930				W
1931			W	QF
1932		21	17	
1933		4		
1934				Last 16
1935				RU
1936	20	22		
1937	8			
1938		23		
1939	10	22		
1940		12		
1942	28			

ARMOUR III, Tommy
(US)

	MAS	USO	BOP	PGA
1988			28	
1989				24

ARMSTRONG, Wally
(US)

	MAS	USO	BOP	PGA
1977		16		
1978	5	20		19
1979			13	

ARUNDEL, Thomas
(SCO)

	MAS	USO	BOP	PGA
1879			15	
1880			10	
1882			27	
1883			21	

AUBREY, Emlyn
(ENG)

	MAS	USO	BOP	PGA
1989		29		
1996				24

AUCHTERLONIE,
Laurie (SCO)

	MAS	USO	BOP	PGA
1888			14	
1891			18	
1895			13	
1899		9		
1900		4		
1901		5		
1902		W		
1903		7		
1904		4		
1905		24		
1906		3		
1907		11		
1908		21		
1909		23		

AUCHTERLONIE, Willie (SCO)

	MAS	USO	BOP	PGA
1888			18	
1891			8	
1893			W	
1894			23	
1896			12	
1897			18	
1900			5	
1901			29	
1910			28	

AULBACH, George (US)

	MAS	USO	BOP	PGA
1924				Last 32
1926				Last 32

AUSTIN, Woody (US)

	MAS	USO	BOP	PGA
1995				23
1996		23		

AVESTON, Willie (WAL)

	MAS	USO	BOP	PGA
1895			27	
1899			15	
1908			28	

AYCOCK, Tommy (US)

	MAS	USO	BOP	PGA
1974				11

AYTON, David (SCO)

	MAS	USO	BOP	PGA
1873			18	
1879			15	
1882			7	
1885			3	
1887			12	
1888			9	
1890			17	
1891			22	

AYTON Jr, Laurie (SCO)

	MAS	USO	BOP	PGA
1956			25	
1957			30	
1960			28	

AYTON Sr, Laurie (SCO/US)

	MAS	USO	BOP	PGA
1910			4	
1911			9	
1912			5	
1913			30	
1920		17		Last 16
1921		18		Last 16
1922		11		
1924		25		
1925		9		Last 32
1926		16		Last 32
1930				Last 16
1931		23		
1933			21	
1935			9	
1939			30	

AZINGER, Paul (US)

	MAS	USO	BOP	PGA
1987	17		2	
1988		6		2
1989	14	9	8	
1990		24		
1993				W
1995	17			
1996	18			
1997	28	28		

BAIOCCHI, Hugh (SA)

	MAS	USO	BOP	PGA
1973			18	
1974	22			
1975			23	
1980			29	
1984			9	

BAIRD, Butch (US)

	MAS	USO	BOP	PGA
1966				28
1976		4		

BAKER, Peter (ENG)

	MAS	USO	BOP	PGA
1993			21	

BAKER-FINCH, Ian (AUS)

	MAS	USO	BOP	PGA
1984			9	
1985			20	
1989			30	
1990			6	
1991	7		W	
1992	6		19	
1993		19		
1994	10			

BALDIE, D [a] (SCO)

	MAS	USO	BOP	PGA
1883			30	

BALDING, Al (CAN)

	MAS	USO	BOP	PGA
1956	29		17	
1957	16			
1958	26			
1961	27			
1962	24			
1967		12	8	
1968			9	
1970		18		

BALFOUR, Leslie [a] (SCO)

	MAS	USO	BOP	PGA
1885			16	
1888			5	
1892			28	

BALL, Donald (US)

	MAS	USO	BOP	PGA
1908		12		

BALL, Errie (US)

	MAS	USO	BOP	PGA
1934				Last 32
1936			23	Last 32
1948				Last 32
1956		22		

BALL, Frank
(US)

	MAS	USO	BOP	PGA
1921			19	
1923			16	
1924			3	
1925			23	
1928		22		
1935			26	

BALL Jr, John [a]
(ENG)

	MAS	USO	BOP	PGA
1878			4	
1890			W	
1891			11	
1892			2	
1893			8	
1894			13	
1895			18	
1897			17	
1899			25	
1902			15	
1904			17	
1907			15	
1908			13	
1910			19	

BALL, Tom
(ENG)

	MAS	USO	BOP	PGA
1906			24	
1907			10	
1908			2	
1909			2	
1910			12	
1911			15	
1912			26	
1913			30	

BALLESTEROS, Severiano
(Seve) (SP)

	MAS	USO	BOP	PGA
1976			2	
1977			15	
1978	18	16	17	
1979	12		W	
1980	W		19	
1982	3		13	13
1983	W	4	6	27
1984		30	W	5
1985	2	5		
1986	4	24	6	
1987	2	3		10
1988	11		W	
1989	5			12
1990	7			
1991	22		9	23
1992		23		
1993	11	18		
1994	18			

BALLINGALL, JH
(ENG)

	MAS	USO	BOP	PGA
1938			15	

BAMFORD, Brian
(ENG)

	MAS	USO	BOP	PGA
1962			24	
1965			21	

BANNERMAN, Harry
(SCO)

	MAS	USO	BOP	PGA
1971			11	
1972			19	

BANNISTER, Eric
(ENG)

	MAS	USO	BOP	PGA
1920			14	

BARBARO, Louis
(US)

	MAS	USO	BOP	PGA
1953		30		

BARBER, JM
(ENG)

	MAS	USO	BOP	PGA
1924			9	

BARBER, Jerry
(US)

	MAS	USO	BOP	PGA
1953	21	30		
1954	6			QF
1956	6			Last 32
1957	26	9		
1958		19		
1959				2
1960		9		
1961				W
1962	5			

BARBER, Miller
(US)

	MAS	USO	BOP	PGA
1962		22		
1966		26		
1967		18		
1968	12	24		8
1969	7	6	10	5
1970	21	6		
1971				4
1972		29		16
1973		25		24
1974	15			
1975	26	24		
1977				25
1978	24			
1979	12			28

BARBER, Tom
(ENG)

	MAS	USO	BOP	PGA
1923			16	
1926			5	
1930			9	

BARBIERI, Romualdo
(ARG)

	MAS	USO	BOP	PGA
1955			10	

BARKER, HH
(ENG/US)

	MAS	USO	BOP	PGA
1907			30a	
1908		17		
1909		7		
1910		8		
1911		7		
1915		24		

BARNES, Brian
(SCO)

	MAS	USO	BOP	PGA
1967			25	
1968			6	
1972			5	
1973			10	
1975			23	
1976			14	
1981			14	

BARNES, Jim (ENG/US)

	MAS	USO	BOP	PGA
1912		18		
1913		4		
1914		13		
1915		4		
1916		3	W	
1919		11	W	
1920		6	6	Last 16
1921		W	6	RU
1922		24	2	Last 32
1923		12		QF
1924				RU
1925		29	W	
1926			17	Last 32
1927		24	16	
1928			6	Last 16
1929			7	
1930			6	

BARNETT, Robert (US)

	MAS	USO	BOP	PGA
1921				Last 32
1923				Last 32

BARNUM, John (US)

	MAS	USO	BOP	PGA
1958				16

BARONI, Fred (US)

	MAS	USO	BOP	PGA
1922				Last 32
1924				Last 32
1927		15		Last 32

BARR, Dave (CAN)

	MAS	USO	BOP	PGA
1985		2		
1986	16			
1988		25		

BARRETT, Percy (ENG/CAN)

	MAS	USO	BOP	PGA
1904		6		
1905		3		
1908		8		
1912		15		

BARRON, Herman (US)

	MAS	USO	BOP	PGA
1929				Last 16
1930		28		
1931		15		
1933		13		QF
1934		23		Last 32
1935		14		
1936		11		
1939				Last 32
1941		5		
1945				Last 16
1946	25	4		Last 16
1947	17	27		Last 32
1948	25	7		
1949	13	27		Last 16

BASS, Vic (US)

	MAS	USO	BOP	PGA
1942				Last 32

BASSLER, Charles (US)

	MAS	USO	BOP	PGA
1951		21		SF
1953				Last 32
1954				Last 16
1957				Last 32
1961				29

BASSLER, Harry (US)

	MAS	USO	BOP	PGA
1938				Last 16
1941				Last 32
1944				Last 16
1946				Last 16
1947				Last 32

BASSLER, Newton (US)

	MAS	USO	BOP	PGA
1946				Last 32

BATLEY, Jas (ENG)

	MAS	USO	BOP	PGA
1912			27	
1914			21	

BATTELL, Bert (US)

	MAS	USO	BOP	PGA
1916		24		

BAXTER, Alex (SCO/US)

	MAS	USO	BOP	PGA
1906		17		

BAYER, George (US)

	MAS	USO	BOP	PGA
1957		22		
1958	29			
1960	29	12		
1961				22
1962				3
1963	28			
1964		11		
1965	15			

BEACH, Ralph (US)

	MAS	USO	BOP	PGA
1927				Last 16

BEAN, Andy (US)

	MAS	USO	BOP	PGA
1977	19	23		
1978	24	6		7
1979	28	25		12
1980	12		6	2
1982	10			
1983			2	30
1984	18	11	14	16
1985	25	15		3
1986		24	14	
1988		12	16	
1989				2

BEARD, Frank (US)

	MAS	USO	BOP	PGA
1965	8	3		
1966	22	17		11
1967	26			7
1968	5			6
1969	19			10
1970	9			
1971	9			13
1972			19	
1973	24	25		
1974	22	12		11
1975		3		

BECK, Alf (ENG)

	MAS	USO	BOP	PGA
1932			25	
1934			21	
1935			26	

BECK, Chip (US)

	MAS	USO	BOP	PGA
1982		12		
1983		10		23
1984		21		25
1986		2		16
1987	12			
1988	21	21	28	
1989	8	2	26	
1990		29		5
1991			17	23
1992			12	
1993	2	25		
1994	15	25		

BELFORE, Joe (US)

	MAS	USO	BOP	PGA
1938		27		

BELL, Art (US)

	MAS	USO	BOP	PGA
1935				Last 32
1944				QF
1946				Last 16
1947				SF
1948	23	25		
1955		28		

BELL, David (US)

	MAS	USO	BOP	PGA
1900		2		

BELL, RK [a] (ENG)

	MAS	USO	BOP	PGA
1946			23	

BELLWOOD, Frank (US)

	MAS	USO	BOP	PGA
1913		30		

BELLWORTHY, AE (ENG)

	MAS	USO	BOP	PGA
1904			29	
1909			26	

BEMAN, Deane (US)

	MAS	USO	BOP	PGA
1960	29a			
1961		12a		
1962		14a		
1964	25a			
1965		11a		
1966		30a		
1967		6		13
1969	19	2		
1970	23			

BEMBRIDGE, Maurice (ENG)

	MAS	USO	BOP	PGA
1968			5	
1970			13	
1972			19	
1974	9			
1975	26		16	

BEMISH, Walter (US)

	MAS	USO	BOP	PGA
1931				Last 32

BENEPE, Jim (US)

	MAS	USO	BOP	PGA
1988			28	
1990		14		

BENNETT, Stephen (ENG)

	MAS	USO	BOP	PGA
1989			26	

BERGANIO, David (US)

	MAS	USO	BOP	PGA
1996		16		

BERGIN, Bill (US)

	MAS	USO	BOP	PGA
1984			14	

BERNARDI, Sam (US)

	MAS	USO	BOP	PGA
1937				Last 32
1949		27		
1952				Last 32

BERNARDINI, Roberto (IT)

	MAS	USO	BOP	PGA
1969	29			
1970			17	
1972			13	

BERTOLINO, Enrique (ARG)

	MAS	USO	BOP	PGA
1939			13	
1956			6	

BESSELINK, Al (US)

	MAS	USO	BOP	PGA
1950		12		
1951	20	6		
1952	3			
1953	9			
1954	9			

BEVERIDGE, James (SCO)

	MAS	USO	BOP	PGA
1880			23	

BIAGETTI, Leo (US)

	MAS	USO	BOP	PGA
1957		30		

	MAS	USO	BOP	PGA

BIES, Don (US)

Year	MAS	USO	BOP	PGA
1967				7
1968		5		26
1969				11
1973		29		30
1974				9
1982		30		

BINNIE, William (SCO)

Year	MAS	USO	BOP	PGA
1910			24	

BISDORF, Bill (US)

Year	MAS	USO	BOP	PGA
1964				28
1967				30

BISHOP, Simon (ENG)

Year	MAS	USO	BOP	PGA
1985			16	

BLACK, David (SCO/US)

Year	MAS	USO	BOP	PGA
1912		30		

BLACK, Jimmy (ENG)

Year	MAS	USO	BOP	PGA
1938			20	

BLACK, John (US)

Year	MAS	USO	BOP	PGA
1922		2		
1923		26		

BLACK, Ronnie (US)

Year	MAS	USO	BOP	PGA
1984	6			
1986				21
1987				28
1988				25
1997				29

BLACKMAR, Phil (US)

Year	MAS	USO	BOP	PGA
1997				6

BLACKWELL, Edward BH (Ted) [a] (SCO)

Year	MAS	USO	BOP	PGA
1892			13	
1900			30	
1904			26	
1911			21	

BLACKWELL, Ernley RH [a] (SCO)

Year	MAS	USO	BOP	PGA
1891			22	
1892			27	

BLAIR, David [a] (SCO)

Year	MAS	USO	BOP	PGA
1950			30	
1960			9	

BLAKE, Jay Don (US)

Year	MAS	USO	BOP	PGA
1987		24		
1988				25
1989			18	
1991	27			13
1992		6		

BLAKESLEE, Jack (US)

Year	MAS	USO	BOP	PGA
1925				Last 32

BLANCAS, Homero (US)

Year	MAS	USO	BOP	PGA
1971		19		
1972	5	4		

BLAND, John (SA)

Year	MAS	USO	BOP	PGA
1980			16	

BLANTON, Julian (US)

Year	MAS	USO	BOP	PGA
1928				Last 16

BLISS Jr, Rodney [a] (US)

Year	MAS	USO	BOP	PGA
1934		28		

BLUM, Arnold (US)

Year	MAS	USO	BOP	PGA
1952	24			
1958	29			

BLYTH, AD [a] (ENG)

Year	MAS	USO	BOP	PGA
1894			10	

BOLETSA, George (US)

Year	MAS	USO	BOP	PGA
1951				Last 16

BOLSTAD, Lester [a] (US)

Year	MAS	USO	BOP	PGA
1933		19		

BOLT, Tommy (US)

Year	MAS	USO	BOP	PGA
1951		29		
1952	3	7		
1953	5			Last 32
1954	12	6		SF
1955	22	3		SF
1956	8	22		
1957				Last 16
1958		W		5
1959	30			17
1960	20			
1961	4	22		
1962				30
1965	8			
1966	17			
1967	26			
1971				3

BONALLACK, Michael [a] (ENG)

Year	MAS	USO	BOP	PGA
1959			11	
1966			27	
1968			21	
1971			22	

BONNAR, Tom (US)

Year	MAS	USO	BOP	PGA
1910		14		

BONTEMPO, Henry (US)

Year	MAS	USO	BOP	PGA
1935				Last 32

BOOBYER, Fred (ENG)

Year	MAS	USO	BOP	PGA
1960			28	
1965			25	
1966			30	
1967			29	
1969			25	

255

BOOMER, Aubrey (ENG)

Year	MAS	USO	BOP	PGA
1921			26	
1922			17	
1924			6	
1925			25	
1927			2	
1928			6	
1929			15	
1931			20	
1933			18	
1935			11	
1936			15	

BOON, Neil (SCO)

Year	MAS	USO	BOP	PGA
1875			11	
1878			19	

BOOTHBY, Fitz [a] (SCO)

Year	MAS	USO	BOP	PGA
1882			3	

BOOTHBY, RT [a] (SCO)

Year	MAS	USO	BOP	PGA
1892			16	

BOREK, Gene (US)

Year	MAS	USO	BOP	PGA
1971				30

BOROS, Julius (US)

Year	MAS	USO	BOP	PGA
1950		9		
1951	17	4		
1952	7	W		
1953	10	17		
1954	16	23		
1955	4	5		
1956	24	2		
1957		4		
1958		3		5
1959	8	28		
1960	5	3		24
1962	11			11
1963	3	W		13
1964				21
1965		4		17
1966	28	17	15	5
1967	5			5
1968	16	16		W
1969		13		25
1970	23	12		26
1972		29		
1973		7		
1974	26			

BOTTOMLEY, Steven (ENG)

Year	MAS	USO	BOP	PGA
1995			3	

BOURNE, Walter (US)

Year	MAS	USO	BOP	PGA
1921			26	
1924		17		

BOUSE, GJ (US)

Year	MAS	USO	BOP	PGA
1907		20		

BOUSFIELD, Ken (ENG)

Year	MAS	USO	BOP	PGA
1947			27	
1948			21	
1949			11	
1952			21	
1955			5	
1956			22	
1959			11	
1960			21	
1961			8	
1963			30	

BOWDEN, George (US)

Year	MAS	USO	BOP	PGA
1919		8		
1920		30		Last 32

BOYD, Bob (US)

Year	MAS	USO	BOP	PGA
1983				30
1990				19
1994				30

BOYD, James (SCO)

Year	MAS	USO	BOP	PGA
1875			14	
1887			20	

BOYD, Tom (US)

Year	MAS	USO	BOP	PGA
1919				Last 32
1920				Last 32
1921		26		Last 16
1922				Last 32
1925		20		
1929		30		

BOYD, W (SCO)

Year	MAS	USO	BOP	PGA
1870			15	

BOYER, Auguste (FRA)

Year	MAS	USO	BOP	PGA
1930			9	
1931		29		
1933			14	
1934			29	
1935			10	

BOYLE, Hugh (IRE)

Year	MAS	USO	BOP	PGA
1962			27	
1965			12	
1967			8	
1973			18	

BOYNTON, Frank (US)

Year	MAS	USO	BOP	PGA
1962		27		
1966				22
1968				8

BRADBEER, Bob (ENG)

Year	MAS	USO	BOP	PGA
1928			23	

BRADBEER, James (ENG)

Year	MAS	USO	BOP	PGA
1907			19	
1913			7	
1914			14	

BRADLEY, Jackson (US)

	MAS	USO	BOP	PGA
1948				Last 32
1950				Last 16
1951				Last 16
1953				Last 16
1960		19		

BRADSHAW, Harry (IRE)

	MAS	USO	BOP	PGA
1946			11	
1949			2	
1950			16	
1951			15	
1952			9	
1954			12	
1956			23	
1957			19	
1958			24	
1959			16	
1961			20	
1962			30	

BRADY, Mike (US)

	MAS	USO	BOP	PGA
1907		16		
1908		17		
1909		12		
1911		2		
1912		3		
1913		14		
1914		5		
1915		6		
1916		9		Last 16
1919		2		Last 16
1920		14		
1921		14		
1922		8		Last 32
1923		20		
1924		9		Last 32
1925		7		Last 16
1926		16		Last 16

BRAID, George (SCO/US)

	MAS	USO	BOP	PGA
1902		26		
1904		15		

BRAID, James (SCO)

	MAS	USO	BOP	PGA
1894			10	
1896			6	
1897			2	
1898			10	
1899			5	
1900			3	
1901			W	
1902			2	
1903			5	
1904			2	
1905			W	
1906			W	
1907			5	
1908			W	
1909			2	
1910			W	
1911			5	
1912			3	
1913			18	
1914			10	
1920			21	
1921			16	
1924			18	
1926			26	
1927			29	

BRAID, Robert (SCO/US)

	MAS	USO	BOP	PGA
1899		27		

BRANCH, William J (Bill) (ENG)

	MAS	USO	BOP	PGA
1935			8	
1937			13	
1949			14	
1950			24	
1955			23	

BRAND, D (SCO)

	MAS	USO	BOP	PGA
1873			22	

BRAND, Fred (US)

	MAS	USO	BOP	PGA
1906		18		
1907		11		
1914		28		
1922				Last 32

BRAND, Gordon J (ENG)

	MAS	USO	BOP	PGA
1981			19	
1985			25	
1986			2	

BRAND Jr, Gordon (SCO)

	MAS	USO	BOP	PGA
1987			26	
1988			20	
1992			5	

BRANNAN, Mike (US)

	MAS	USO	BOP	PGA
1982		22		

BRANTLY, Edward [a] (US)

	MAS	USO	BOP	PGA
1961		29		

BREDEMUS, John (US)

	MAS	USO	BOP	PGA
1919				Last 32

BREWER, Gay
(US)

	MAS	USO	BOP	PGA
1962	11	5		
1964	25	5		8
1965		16		28
1966	2			27
1967	**W**			28
1968		9	6	20
1969			15	25
1970		7		
1971		9		
1972		25		7
1973	10		10	
1974				17
1976	23			
1977		26		
1978	29			
1981	15			

BREWS, Sid
(ENG/SA)

	MAS	USO	BOP	PGA
1923			22	
1929			18	
1934			2	
1935		21	30	
1938			13	

BRIGGS, Eldon
(US)

	MAS	USO	BOP	PGA
1955				Last 32
1957				Last 32

BRION, Stan
(US)

	MAS	USO	BOP	PGA
1974				22

BRISKY, Mike
(US)

	MAS	USO	BOP	PGA
1996				14

BRITTON, Bill
(US)

	MAS	USO	BOP	PGA
1990	7			4
1992				21

BRITZ, Tienie
(SA)

	MAS	USO	BOP	PGA
1978			29	
1983			19	

BROADHURST, Paul
(ENG)

	MAS	USO	BOP	PGA
1990			12	
1991			17	
1996			27	

BROKAW, George T [a]
(US)

	MAS	USO	BOP	PGA
1903		26		

BROOKS, Mark
(US)

	MAS	USO	BOP	PGA
1990		5		26
1991		19		
1992				15
1994			20	
1995			3	
1996		16	5	**W**

BROSCH, Al
(US)

	MAS	USO	BOP	PGA
1936		28		
1937		6		
1939				Last 32
1940				Last 16
1948				Last 32
1949		13		Last 16
1950				Last 32
1951		10		QF
1952		15		

BROWN, A
(SCO)

	MAS	USO	BOP	PGA
1874			29	
1880			16	

BROWN, Billy Ray
(US)

	MAS	USO	BOP	PGA
1990		3		
1991		19		
1992	19			

BROWN, David
(SCO/US)

	MAS	USO	BOP	PGA
1880			4	
1883			24	
1886			**W**	
1887			9	
1889			4	
1890			10	
1891			7	
1892			24	
1894			13	
1895			6	
1896			7	
1897			7	
1901		7		
1902		12		
1903		2		
1907		8		
1908		27		

BROWN, Eric
(SCO)

	MAS	USO	BOP	PGA
1950			23	
1952			9	
1953			9	
1955			12	
1957			3	
1958			3	
1960			9	
1961			5	
1965			17	
1966			23	
1968			18	
1969			16	

BROWN, George
(SCO)

	MAS	USO	BOP	PGA
1860			5	
1861			9	
1863			5	

BROWN, Hugh
(SCO)

	MAS	USO	BOP	PGA
1872			7	

BROWN, J
(SCO)

MAS	USO	BOP	PGA
1870		11	

BROWN, Ken
(SCO)

MAS	USO	BOP	PGA
1979		19	
1980		6	
1982		19	
1984		14	
1987		17	24

BROWN, Stuart
(ENG)

MAS	USO	BOP	PGA
1970		28	

BROWN, T
(SCO)

MAS	USO	BOP	PGA
1874		17	
1880		10	

BROWN, W
(US)

MAS	USO	BOP	PGA
1916			Last 16

BROWN, Willie
(SCO)

MAS	USO	BOP	PGA
1874		24	
1877		5	
1880		8	
1883		3	
1885		23	
1889		7	

BROWNE, Olin
(US)

MAS	USO	BOP	PGA
1997	5		

BROWNING, Jim
(US)

MAS	USO	BOP	PGA
1953			Last 16
1954			Last 16
1955			Last 32

BRUE, Bob
(US)

MAS	USO	BOP	PGA
1961	22		
1973			12

BRUEN, Jimmy [a]
(IRE)

MAS	USO	BOP	PGA
1939		13	

BRYANT, Brad
(US)

MAS	USO	BOP	PGA
1992	23		
1995	13		
1996	23		

BUCKLE, GR
(ENG)

MAS	USO	BOP	PGA
1913		30	
1920		9	
1927		16	

BULLA, Johnny
(US)

MAS	USO	BOP	PGA
1939		6	2
1940	21		
1941		3	
1946	16	22	2
1947	13		6	Last 32
1948	13	8	7	QF
1949	2	14	27	Last 32
1950		12	14	
1951	8			QF
1952		4		
1956		24		

BULLOCK, Fred
(ENG)

MAS	USO	BOP	PGA
1938		8	
1947		15	
1950		7	
1952		8	
1959		2	

BUNN, Oscar
(US)

MAS	USO	BOP	PGA
1896	21		

BURGESS, Jack
(US)

MAS	USO	BOP	PGA
1922			Last 16

BURGESS, Michael [a]
(ENG)

MAS	USO	BOP	PGA
1965		29	

BURKE, Billy
(US)

MAS	USO	BOP	PGA
1928		18		Last 32
1929		15		
1930		28		Last 32
1931		W		SF
1932		7		
1934	3	6		
1936	28	18		Last 16
1937	29	16		Last 32
1938	13			Last 16
1939	3			Last 16
1940				Last 32
1942	22			
1947		27		
1950	29			

BURKE, Eddie
(US)

MAS	USO	BOP	PGA
1934			Last 32
1942			Last 32
1948			Last 32
1949			Last 32
1950			Last 16

BURKE Jr, Jack
(US)

MAS	USO	BOP	PGA
1949		27		
1951	11			QF
1952	2			Last 32
1953	8	14		
1954	6	15		
1955	13	10		QF
1956	W			W
1957	7			
1958				4
1959				17
1960	11			29
1961	7			
1962				17
1963		21		
1965				8
1969	24			

BURKE Sr, Jack (US)

	MAS	USO	BOP	PGA
1909		30		
1910		27		
1911		18		
1914		28		
1920		2		
1922		28		
1925				Last 16
1928				Last 32
1929		26		

BURKEMO, Walter (US)

	MAS	USO	BOP	PGA
1951				RU
1952				Last 16
1953				W
1954	22			RU
1955	15			
1956	17	29		Last 16
1957		4		SF
1958		5		16
1959	22			17
1960	6			22
1961	11			14
1963		8		
1964				17
1966		22		

BURNS, George (US)

	MAS	USO	BOP	PGA
1975	30		10	
1976			10	
1977			5	19
1978				19
1979				28
1980		28		
1981		2		
1982		30		

BURNS, Jack (SCO)

	MAS	USO	BOP	PGA
1882			23	
1885			7	
1888			W	
1889			14	

BURNS, Stewart (SCO)

	MAS	USO	BOP	PGA
1928			16	
1930			24	

BURROWS, Gaylord (US)

	MAS	USO	BOP	PGA
1977			26	

BURTON, Dick (ENG)

	MAS	USO	BOP	PGA
1936			12	
1938			4	
1939			W	
1946			12	
1947			5	
1948			18	
1949			14	
1951			12	

BURTON, John (ENG)

	MAS	USO	BOP	PGA
1934			12	
1937			29	

BUSSON, JH (Harry) (ENG)

	MAS	USO	BOP	PGA
1939			25	
1947			25	

BUSSON, JJ (Jack) (ENG)

	MAS	USO	BOP	PGA
1935			11	
1937			23	
1938			4	

BUTCHART, Arthur (SCO)

	MAS	USO	BOP	PGA
1909			26	
1921			26	
1924			23	

BUTEL, Fred (ENG)

	MAS	USO	BOP	PGA
1898			29	

BUTLER, Peter (ENG)

	MAS	USO	BOP	PGA
1957			30	
1961			20	
1964	13		30	
1966	13		16	
1967	24			
1971			25	
1972			15	
1973			6	
1976			10	
1977			15	

BUTLER, Tony (US)

	MAS	USO	BOP	PGA
1931				Last 32

BYMAN, Bob (US)

	MAS	USO	BOP	PGA
1978			17	
1979			7	21

BYRD, Sam (US)

	MAS	USO	BOP	PGA
1939		16		
1940	14			
1941	3	26		
1942	4			Last 32
1944				Last 16
1945				RU
1947		23		

BYRUM, Curt (US)

	MAS	USO	BOP	PGA
1987				14

BYRUM, Tom (US)

	MAS	USO	BOP	PGA
1997				9

CADLE, George (US)

	MAS	USO	BOP	PGA
1977				15
1978				26

CAHILL, Michael (AUS)

	MAS	USO	BOP	PGA
1978			11	
1985			25	

CAIRNCROSS, Douglas (SCO)

	MAS	USO	BOP	PGA
1937			25	

CALCAVECCHIA, Mark (US)

	MAS	USO	BOP	PGA
1986		14		
1987	17	17	11	
1988	2			17
1989			W	
1990	20			
1991	12			
1992			28	
1993	17	25	14	
1994			11	
1995			24	
1996	15			
1997	17		10	23

CALDWELL, Rex (US)

	MAS	USO	BOP	PGA
1978				3
1980				20
1984		11		25

CAMPBELL, Albert [a] (CAN)

	MAS	USO	BOP	PGA
1936	26			

CAMPBELL, Alec (US)

	MAS	USO	BOP	PGA
1923				Last 16

CAMPBELL, Alex (SCO/US)

	MAS	USO	BOP	PGA
1899		12		
1900		11		
1901		8		
1902		20		
1903		15		
1904		13		
1905		6		
1906		18		
1907		3		
1908		12		
1909		13		
1910		16		
1911		12		
1912		5		
1913		13		
1915		10		
1916		28		

CAMPBELL, Andrew (US)

	MAS	USO	BOP	PGA
1909		7		

CAMPBELL, Ben (SCO)

	MAS	USO	BOP	PGA
1883			10	
1885			22	
1886			3	
1887			10	
1890			15	
1892			16	

CAMPBELL, Jack (SCO/US)

	MAS	USO	BOP	PGA
1902		14		
1903		6		
1904		20		
1907		19		
1909		22		
1910		18		
1912		23		

CAMPBELL, James (SCO/US)

	MAS	USO	BOP	PGA
1902		26		
1903		26		
1907		22		

CAMPBELL, Joe (US)

	MAS	USO	BOP	PGA
1957		22a		
1958	29a			
1959		25		
1962		28		27
1969		25		

CAMPBELL, John (SCO)

	MAS	USO	BOP	PGA
1875			10	

CAMPBELL, Matt (US)

	MAS	USO	BOP	PGA
1913		15		

CAMPBELL, Michael (NZ)

	MAS	USO	BOP	PGA
1995			3	17

CAMPBELL, WW (SCO/US)

	MAS	USO	BOP	PGA
1896		25		

CAMPBELL, William [a] (US)

	MAS	USO	BOP	PGA
1954		23		

CAMPBELL, Willie (SCO/US)

	MAS	USO	BOP	PGA
1880			10	
1881			5	
1883			5	
1884			4	
1885			9	
1886			2	
1887			3	
1888			4	
1889			7	
1891			22	
1895		6		
1896		14		
1898		26		

CANAUSA, Fred (US)

	MAS	USO	BOP	PGA
1921				Last 32

CANIZARES, Jose-Maria (SP)

	MAS	USO	BOP	PGA
1982			22	
1985			11	
1986			11	

CARMICHAEL, Sam (US)

	MAS	USO	BOP	PGA
1967				14

CARMICHAEL, T [a] (SCO)

	MAS	USO	BOP	PGA
1893			23	

CARPENTER, Mel (US)

	MAS	USO	BOP	PGA
1952				Last 32

CARR, Joe [a] (IRE)

	MAS	USO	BOP	PGA
1951			24	
1960			8	

CARRICK, John [a] (SCO)

	MAS	USO	BOP	PGA
1887			25	

CARTER, G (ENG)

	MAS	USO	BOP	PGA
1907			19	

CASPER, Billy (US)

	MAS	USO	BOP	PGA
1956		14		
1957	16			
1958	20	13		2
1959		W		17
1960	4	12		24
1961	7	17		15
1962	15			
1963	11			
1964	5	4		9
1965		17		2
1966	10	W		3
1967	24	4		19
1968	16	9	4	6
1969	2		25	
1970	W	8	17	18
1971	13		7	2
1972	17	11		4
1973	17			
1975	6			5
1976	8			
1977	14			
1978		30		

CASTANON, Aurelio (ARG)

	MAS	USO	BOP	PGA
1939			29	

CATLIN, Arthur (ENG)

	MAS	USO	BOP	PGA
1913			27	

CAWKWELL, George (ENG)

	MAS	USO	BOP	PGA
1904			26	

CAWSEY, George (ENG)

	MAS	USO	BOP	PGA
1903			9	
1904			18	
1906			15	
1909			16	

CAWSEY, Harry (ENG)

	MAS	USO	BOP	PGA
1907			30	

CAYGILL, Alex (ENG)

	MAS	USO	BOP	PGA
1964			17	
1966			16	
1968			24	
1969			25	

CEJKA, Alexander (GER)

	MAS	USO	BOP	PGA
1996			11	

CERDA, Antonio (ARG)

	MAS	USO	BOP	PGA
1951			2	
1952			5	
1953			2	
1954			5	
1955			5	
1956			8	
1957			9	
1958			26	
1959			16	
1961	24			

CERRUDO, Ron (US)

	MAS	USO	BOP	PGA
1969				21
1974		30		

CHAMBERS, Peter [a] (SCO)

	MAS	USO	BOP	PGA
1863			11	

CHAMBERS Jr, Robert [a] (SCO)

	MAS	USO	BOP	PGA
1861			10	

CHAMP, Frank (US)

	MAS	USO	BOP	PGA
1939				Last 32
1952				QF

CHAPMAN, Dick [a] (US)

	MAS	USO	BOP	PGA
1941	19			
1947	14			
1951	20			
1954	11	21		

CHAPMAN, Roger (ENG)

	MAS	USO	BOP	PGA
1989			13	
1991			12	

CHARLES, Bob (NZ)

	MAS	USO	BOP	PGA
1962	25		5	
1963	15	19	W	13
1964		3	17	19
1968	19	7	2	2
1969	29		2	
1970	17	3	13	26
1971		13	18	13
1972	22		15	
1973	29	11	7	
1975			12	
1979			10	
1986			19	
1988			20	

CHARTER, Brien (US)

	MAS	USO	BOP	PGA
1955				Last 16
1957				Last 32

CHEN, Ching-Po (TAI)

Year	MAS	USO	BOP	PGA
1963	15			
1966	22			

CHEN, Tze-Chung (TAI)

Year	MAS	USO	BOP	PGA
1985		2		23
1986	23			
1987	12			
1988	19			

CHEN, Tze-Ming (TAI)

Year	MAS	USO	BOP	PGA
1985				3

CHERRY, Don [a] (US)

Year	MAS	USO	BOP	PGA
1955	30			
1959	25			
1960		9		

CHIAPETTA, Louis (US)

Year	MAS	USO	BOP	PGA
1929		16		

CHIN, Chick (JAP)

Year	MAS	USO	BOP	PGA
1936	20			

CHISHOLM, John (SCO)

Year	MAS	USO	BOP	PGA
1873			20	

CHRIST, George (US)

Year	MAS	USO	BOP	PGA
1926				QF
1928				Last 16
1934				Last 32

CHRISTIAN, Neil (US)

Year	MAS	USO	BOP	PGA
1924				Last 32
1928		18		
1929				Last 16
1944				Last 32

CHURIO, Marcos (ARG)

Year	MAS	USO	BOP	PGA
1931			7	

CINK, Stewart (US)

Year	MAS	USO	BOP	PGA
1996		16		
1997		13		

CIRCELLI, Pat (US)

Year	MAS	USO	BOP	PGA
1931				Last 32
1935				Last 16

CIUCI, Al (US)

Year	MAS	USO	BOP	PGA
1922				Last 16

CIUCI, Henry (US)

Year	MAS	USO	BOP	PGA
1924				QF
1928		6		
1929		7		Last 16
1930				Last 32
1931		29		Last 32
1932		14		
1933		15		
1934	25	17		

CLAAR, Brian (US)

Year	MAS	USO	BOP	PGA
1989		5		
1990		29		
1992				9

CLAMPETT, Bobby (US)

Year	MAS	USO	BOP	PGA
1978		30a		
1979	23			
1981				27
1982		3	10	
1987				28

CLARK, Arthur (US)

Year	MAS	USO	BOP	PGA
1940				Last 16
1948			30	

CLARK, Barney (US)

Year	MAS	USO	BOP	PGA
1945				Last 32

CLARK, Clarence (US)

Year	MAS	USO	BOP	PGA
1929				Last 32
1932		11		
1933		9		Last 16
1935	19			
1936		3		
1937	13	7		

CLARK, Clive (ENG)

Year	MAS	USO	BOP	PGA
1967			3	
1970			17	
1972			11	

CLARK, Howard (ENG)

Year	MAS	USO	BOP	PGA
1977			13	
1981			8	
1983			26	
1988			28	
1989			13	
1993			21	

CLARK, Jimmy (US)

Year	MAS	USO	BOP	PGA
1953				QF

CLARK, Walter (US)

Year	MAS	USO	BOP	PGA
1901		22		
1905		18		
1907		22		

CLARKE, Charles (US)

Year	MAS	USO	BOP	PGA
1921				Last 16

CLARKE, Darren (IRE)

Year	MAS	USO	BOP	PGA
1996			11	
1997			2	

CLARKSON, F (US)

Year	MAS	USO	BOP	PGA
1916				Last 32

CLAYDON, Russell (ENG)

Year	MAS	USO	BOP	PGA
1994			11	

CLAYTON, D (SCO)

Year	MAS	USO	BOP	PGA
1874			28	

CLEMENTS, Lennie (US)

Year	MAS	USO	BOP	PGA
1983		13		
1984		16		
1986		24		
1987		9		
1994		28		30

COBURN, George (SCO)

	MAS	USO	BOP	PGA
1900			26	
1903			29	
1904			16	
1908			24	

COCHRAN, Russ (US)

	MAS	USO	BOP	PGA
1984				10
1987				28
1992			28	7
1993	21			
1996				17

COE, Charles R [a] (US)

	MAS	USO	BOP	PGA
1949	16			
1951	12			
1953	16			
1954	20			
1958	23	13		
1959	6			
1961	2			
1962	9			
1970	23			

COLBERT, Jim (US)

	MAS	USO	BOP	PGA
1971		3		
1973		10		12
1974	4	5		28
1976	12			
1977	14			
1980	14			30
1981	25	26		
1982				16
1984				25

COLE, Bobby (SA)

	MAS	USO	BOP	PGA
1966			30a	
1968			13	
1969				21
1970		12	28	
1971		13		
1974			7	3
1975	15		3	
1977			15	
1978	28			

COLEMAN, Fay (US)

	MAS	USO	BOP	PGA
1934				Last 16
1936				Last 32
1941				Last 32
1946				Last 32

COLES, Neil (ENG)

	MAS	USO	BOP	PGA
1959			21	
1961			3	
1963			20	
1965			12	
1968			6	
1969			11	
1970			6	
1971			22	
1973			2	
1974			13	
1975			7	
1976			28	
1980			29	

COLLINGE, Tom (ENG)

	MAS	USO	BOP	PGA
1937			24	

COLLINS, Al (US)

	MAS	USO	BOP	PGA
1932				QF

COLLINS, Bill (US)

	MAS	USO	BOP	PGA
1960				12
1961	7			
1962	29			
1964		7		

COLLINS, Fred (ENG)

	MAS	USO	BOP	PGA
1901			15	
1904			18	
1905			22	
1907			15	
1908			13	
1909			21	
1911			12	
1912			7	
1913			11	
1923			16	

COLLINS, JB (US)

	MAS	USO	BOP	PGA
1935				Last 32

COLLINS, Jock (US)

	MAS	USO	BOP	PGA
1925				Last 32
1930				Last 16
1931				Last 32

COLLINS, WS (ENG)

	MAS	USO	BOP	PGA
1939			26	

COLTART, Andrew (SCO)

	MAS	USO	BOP	PGA
1994			24	
1995			20	

COLTART, Bruce (US)

	MAS	USO	BOP	PGA
1939				Last 16
1940		29		
1941				Last 16
1942				Last 32
1944				Last 32

COLTART, Frank (US)

	MAS	USO	BOP	PGA
1923				Last 32

COMPSTON, Archie (ENG)

	MAS	USO	BOP	PGA
1920			9	
1922			26	
1924			21	
1925			2	
1927		7	22	
1928		22	3	
1929			12	
1930			6	
1931			28	
1932			10	
1933			12	
1946			18	

CONGDON, Chuck (US)

	MAS	USO	BOP	PGA
1944				SF
1946				QF
1948		12		

CONNER, Frank (US)

	MAS	USO	BOP	PGA
1979				23
1981		6		

CONRAD, Joe [a] (US)

	MAS	USO	BOP	PGA
1955			18	23

COODY, Charles (US)

	MAS	USO	BOP	PGA
1967		28		
1968	30	16		8
1969	5	13		7
1970	12			
1971	W		5	
1972	12			15
1973	29	29		
1974	29			
1976	5			8
1977				4
1978		30		

COOK, John (US)

	MAS	USO	BOP	PGA
1980				19
1981	21	4		
1983				20
1987	24			28
1991		19		
1992		13	2	2
1993		25		6
1994		5		4
1996		16		
1997				23

COOP, AB (ENG)

	MAS	USO	BOP	PGA
1958			20	
1961			13	
1962			22	
1964			24	

COOPER, Derrick (ENG)

	MAS	USO	BOP	PGA
1986			21	
1989			19	

COOPER, Harry (ENG/US)

	MAS	USO	BOP	PGA
1923				Last 32
1925				SF
1926				Last 32
1927		2		Last 16
1930		4		Last 16
1931		15		
1932		7		
1933		29		Last 16
1934		3		Last 16
1935	25	28		
1936	2	2		Last 16
1937	4	4		QF
1938	2	3		
1939		12		
1940	4			
1941	14			
1942	18			QF

COOPER, Pete (US)

	MAS	USO	BOP	PGA
1948		25		Last 32
1949	21	8		
1950	29	29		
1953		4		Last 16
1954	22			
1955	24			
1956	12	14		
1958				25
1959				17
1960				15
1962				30

CORLETT, Charles (ENG)

	MAS	USO	BOP	PGA
1926			28	

CORSTORPHINE, D (SCO)

	MAS	USO	BOP	PGA
1879			23	
1880			16	
1883			26	

COSGROVE, Ned (SCO)

	MAS	USO	BOP	PGA
1880			3	
1881			3	

COSGROVE, R (SCO)

	MAS	USO	BOP	PGA
1874			21	

COSGROVE, William (SCO)

	MAS	USO	BOP	PGA
1874			20	
1877			3	
1878			6	
1883			16	
1884			16	
1885			29	
1886			20	

COTTON, Henry (ENG)

	MAS	USO	BOP	PGA
1927			8	
1928			18	
1930			8	
1931			9	
1932			10	
1933			7	
1934			W	
1935			7	
1936			3	
1937			W	
1938			3	
1939			13	
1946			4	
1947			6	
1948	25		W	
1952			4	
1956			6	
1957	13		9	
1958			8	

COTTON, LT (ENG)

	MAS	USO	BOP	PGA
1934			29	

COUPLES, Fred (US)

	MAS	USO	BOP	PGA
1982				3
1983				23
1984	10	9	4	20
1985	10			6
1988	5	10	4	
1989	11	21	6	
1990	5		25	2
1991		3	3	27
1992	W	17		21
1993	21	16	9	
1994		16		
1995	10			
1996	15		7	
1997	7		7	29

COURTNEY, Chuck (US)

	MAS	USO	BOP	PGA
1971				22

COWAN, Gary [a] (CAN)

	MAS	USO	BOP	PGA
1964	25			

COWAN, John (US)

	MAS	USO	BOP	PGA
1919		7		
1923				Last 32

COX, Bill (ENG)

	MAS	USO	BOP	PGA
1935			11	
1936			12	
1937			21	
1938			8	

COX, Reg (ENG)

	MAS	USO	BOP	PGA
1935			22	

COX, Wiffy (US)

	MAS	USO	BOP	PGA
1924		29		
1928				Last 32
1929		11		Last 32
1930				Last 32
1931		4		
1932		5		
1934		3		
1936	13	5		
1937	12			
1938	25			

COXON, Barry (AUS)

	MAS	USO	BOP	PGA
1967			18	

CRAMPTON, Bruce (AUS)

	MAS	USO	BOP	PGA
1956			13	
1957	21			
1958	26	19		
1960	16			
1961		22		
1962	29			17
1963	11	5		3
1964	21	14		
1965	11			20
1966	17			
1967				26
1968				23
1969	13	6		15
1970		30		6
1971	18			
1972	2	2		24
1973			18	2
1974	11	23		
1975				2
1976	27			

CRAPPER, H (ENG)

	MAS	USO	BOP	PGA
1930			21	

CRAWFORD, Charlie (SCO)

	MAS	USO	BOP	PGA
1886			29	
1892			30	

CRAWFORD, Dick (US)

	MAS	USO	BOP	PGA
1960	29			
1967				20
1968				26
1969		25		
1970		22		

CRAWLEY, LG [a] (ENG)

	MAS	USO	BOP	PGA
1939			23	

CREAVY, Tom (US)

	MAS	USO	BOP	PGA
1931				W
1932				SF
1933				QF
1934	25	8		

CREAVY, William (US)

	MAS	USO	BOP	PGA
1923		26		
1925				Last 32

CREMIN, Eric (AUS)

	MAS	USO	BOP	PGA
1951			16	

CRENSHAW, Ben (US)

	MAS	USO	BOP	PGA
1971		27a		
1972	19a			
1973	24a			
1974	22		28	
1975	30	3		10
1976	2	8		8
1977	8		5	
1978			2	16
1979		11	2	2
1980	6		3	
1981	8	11	8	
1982	24	19	15	
1983	2			9
1984	W		22	
1986	16	6	21	11
1987	4	4	4	7
1988	4	12	16	17
1989	3			17
1990	14			
1991	3			
1994	18			9
1995	W		15	
1996			27	

CRICHTON, Marshall (US)

	MAS	USO	BOP	PGA
1926				Last 16

CROKE, Jack (US)

	MAS	USO	BOP	PGA
1912		21		
1913		21		

CROWDER, Waldo (US)

	MAS	USO	BOP	PGA
1928		6		

CROWLEY, Bob (US)

	MAS	USO	BOP	PGA
1930				Last 16
1931				Last 16
1933		26		
1934				QF

CRUICKSHANK, Bobby (SCO/US)

	MAS	USO	BOP	PGA
1921		26		Last 16
1922		28		SF
1923		2		SF
1924		4		Last 16
1925				Last 16
1926				Last 32
1927		11		Last 32
1929			6	
1932		2		QF
1933				Last 16
1934	28	3		
1935	9	14		
1936	4			Last 16
1937	17	3		
1938	18			
1939		25		
1942	15			

CRUICKSHANK, JI [a] (SCO/ARG)

	MAS	USO	BOP	PGA
1925			16	

CULLEN, Gary (ENG)

	MAS	USO	BOP	PGA
1980			23	

CUMMINGS, George (US)

	MAS	USO	BOP	PGA
1903		22		
1904		28		
1905		9		
1906		18		
1910		14		
1911		20		
1912		23		

CUNNINGHAM, Alex (SCO/US)

	MAS	USO	BOP	PGA
1916		29		
1919		21		
1920				Last 16

CUNNINGHAM, James (SCO)

	MAS	USO	BOP	PGA
1890			27	

CUPIT, Buster (US)

	MAS	USO	BOP	PGA
1958				8
1959				17
1962				30

CUPIT, Jacky (US)

	MAS	USO	BOP	PGA
1961		9		
1962	20	17		
1963		2		
1964		28		17
1965				8
1966				6
1967	15			

CURL, Rod (US)

	MAS	USO	BOP	PGA
1975	15			
1978		30		26
1980				20

CURLEY, Jack (US)

	MAS	USO	BOP	PGA
1927				Last 32
1933				Last 32

CURTIS, Donald (ENG)

	MAS	USO	BOP	PGA
1927		19		

CURTIS, JF (US)

	MAS	USO	BOP	PGA
1898		16		

CUTHBERT, John (SCO)

	MAS	USO	BOP	PGA
1897			30	

DAILEY, Allan (SCO)

	MAS	USO	BOP	PGA
1933			27	
1934			16	
1938			4	

DALLEMAGNE, Marcel (FRA)

	MAS	USO	BOP	PGA
1931			16	
1934			4	
1936			3	
1937			26	
1938			23	

DALY, Fred (IRE)

	MAS	USO	BOP	PGA
1946			8	
1947			W	
1948			2	
1950			3	
1951			4	
1952			3	
1953			11	
1955			12	
1958			20	

DALY, John (US)

	MAS	USO	BOP	PGA
1991				W
1992	19			
1993	3		14	
1995			W	
1996	29	27		
1997				29

DALZIEL, C [a] (SCO)

	MAS	USO	BOP	PGA
1901			24	

D'ANGELO, Jimmy (US)

	MAS	USO	BOP	PGA
1944				Last 32

DARCY, Eamonn (IRE)

	MAS	USO	BOP	PGA
1976			15	
1981			14	
1983			26	
1985			11	
1987			17	
1990			22	
1991			5	

DAVENPORT, Robin (ENG)

	MAS	USO	BOP	PGA
1967			25	

DAVIES, Bill (ENG)

	MAS	USO	BOP	PGA
1925			5	
1928			10	
1929			18	
1930			24	
1931		29	7	
1932			7	
1934			13	
1936			14	
1939			20	

DAVIS, Mark (ENG)

	MAS	USO	BOP	PGA
1989			30	

DAVIS, Rodger (AUS)

	MAS	USO	BOP	PGA
1979			5	
1983			26	
1987			2	
1988	29		20	
1991			12	
1993			24	

DAVIS, WF (Willie) (SCO/US)

	MAS	USO	BOP	PGA
1895		5		
1896		13		
1897		15		
1898		18		
1901		27		

DAWSON, George [a] (US)

	MAS	USO	BOP	PGA
1933		17		

DAWSON, John [a] (US)

	MAS	USO	BOP	PGA
1934	23			
1935	17			
1936	9			
1949	16			

DAWSON, Peter (ENG)

	MAS	USO	BOP	PGA
1974			18	
1977			22	

DAY, Arthur (ENG)

	MAS	USO	BOP	PGA
1920			29	

DAY, Glen (US)

	MAS	USO	BOP	PGA
1994				15

DEBOYS, Alec [a] (SCO)

	MAS	USO	BOP	PGA
1960			21	

DeFOY, Craig (WAL)

	MAS	USO	BOP	PGA
1971			4	
1972			23	

de la TORRE, Angel (SP)

	MAS	USO	BOP	PGA
1920			16	
1923			19	

de la TORRE, Manuel (SP)

	MAS	USO	BOP	PGA
1963				17

de LUCA, Fidel (ARG)

	MAS	USO	BOP	PGA
1960			16	

del VECCHIO, Perry (US)

	MAS	USO	BOP	PGA
1927		15		
1928				QF

de MANE, Arthur (US)

	MAS	USO	BOP	PGA
1926		23		

DEMARET, Jimmy (US)

	MAS	USO	BOP	PGA
1937		16		
1938				Last 16
1939		22		
1940	W			Last 32
1941	12			
1942	6			SF
1946	4	6		SF
1947	W			
1948	18	2		SF
1949	8			QF
1950	W	20		SF
1951	30	14		
1952		15		
1953		4		
1954	29	29	10	
1957	3	3		
1958	14			
1962	5			

DEMASSEY, Mike (US)

	MAS	USO	BOP	PGA
1944				Last 32
1949				Last 32

DENNIS, Clark (US)

	MAS	USO	BOP	PGA
1994		6		

DENNY, CS (ENG)

	MAS	USO	BOP	PGA
1931			15	

DERR, Ray (US)

	MAS	USO	BOP	PGA
1923				Last 16
1924				SF
1925				Last 16

de VICENZO, Roberto (ARG)

	MAS	USO	BOP	PGA
1948			3	
1949			3	
1950	12		2	
1951	20	29		
1952				Last 16
1953			6	
1954				QF
1956	17	27		
1957		8		
1960			3	
1961	22			
1964			3	
1965			4	
1966	22		20	
1967	10		W	
1968	2	24	10	
1969			3	
1970			17	
1971	9		11	
1972	22			
1973			28	
1975			28	

DEVLIN, Bruce (AUS)

	MAS	USO	BOP	PGA
1964	4		5	
1965	15	6	8	6
1966	28	26	4	28
1967	10	23	8	
1968	4	9	10	
1969	19	10	16	
1970		8	25	18
1971	13	27		13
1972	5		26	
1973	8		18	24
1974				22
1975	15			
1976	19			
1980				30
1981		26		
1982		10		

de WIT, Gerard (HOL)

	MAS	USO	BOP	PGA
1956			22	
1958			24	

DICK, CE [a] (ENG)

	MAS	USO	BOP	PGA
1894			20	

DICKINSON, Gardner (US)

	MAS	USO	BOP	PGA
1953		21		
1959		17		
1961		9		
1962	15	23		
1963		21		8
1964				23
1965		21		5
1966	28			18
1967		6		28
1968	22			30
1969	29			
1972	22			
1973	10			

DICKSON, Bob (US)

	MAS	USO	BOP	PGA
1969				25
1973	17			

DIEGEL, Leo
(US)

	MAS	USO	BOP	PGA
1920		2		Last 32
1921		26		
1922		7		
1923		8	25	
1924		25		Last 32
1925		8		QF
1926		3		RU
1927		11		
1928		18		**W**
1929		8	3	**W**
1930		11	2	Last 16
1931		3		Last 32
1932		4		
1933		17	3	Last 32
1934	16	17		Last 32
1935	19			
1938				Last 32
1939				Last 32

DIEHL, Terry
(US)

	MAS	USO	BOP	PGA
1977		7		
1980				10

DIETZ, Mike
(US)

	MAS	USO	BOP	PGA
1956		29		

DILL, Terry
(US)

	MAS	USO	BOP	PGA
1964		14		
1965	24			
1966	17			
1970				26
1971				30
1975		18		

DILLARD, Andy
(US)

	MAS	USO	BOP	PGA
1992		17		

DINGWALL, John
(SCO/US)

	MAS	USO	BOP	PGA
1901		28		
1909		27		
1912		18		

DODSON, Leonard
(US)

	MAS	USO	BOP	PGA
1937		10		
1952				Last 32

DOERING, Arthur
(US)

	MAS	USO	BOP	PGA
1954				Last 32

DOLEMAN, A [a]
(SCO)

	MAS	USO	BOP	PGA
1870			9	

DOLEMAN, F
(SCO)

	MAS	USO	BOP	PGA
1870			14	

DOLEMAN, William [a]
(SCO)

	MAS	USO	BOP	PGA
1865			6	
1866			6	
1867			6	
1868			8	
1869			7	
1870			5	
1872			3	
1874			20	
1875			8	
1879			18	
1884			16	

DONALD, Mike
(US)

	MAS	USO	BOP	PGA
1990		2		

DONALDSON, James
(SCO/US)

	MAS	USO	BOP	PGA
1910		28		
1911		15		
1913		30		
1914		5		
1915		19		
1916		21		Last 32
1923				Last 32

DONOVAN, William
(US)

	MAS	USO	BOP	PGA
1899			30	

DORRESTEIN, Jan
(HOL)

	MAS	USO	BOP	PGA
1972			15	

DOSER, Clarence
(US)

	MAS	USO	BOP	PGA
1929				Last 32
1935				Last 32
1936				Last 32
1939				Last 16
1945				SF
1947				Last 32
1950				Last 32
1952		13		QF
1953		17		

DOUGHERTY, Ed
(US)

	MAS	USO	BOP	PGA
1975				22

DOUGLAS, Dave
(US)

	MAS	USO	BOP	PGA
1949		6		Last 16
1950				QF
1951	5	6		
1952	30			Last 32
1953				QF
1955				Last 32
1961		14		
1962		28		

DOUGLAS, Edward
(ENG)

	MAS	USO	BOP	PGA
1926			22	

DOUGLAS, Findlay [a]
(SCO/US)

	MAS	USO	BOP	PGA
1897		19		
1903		8		
1909		23		

DOUGLAS, George (SCO/US)

	MAS	USO	BOP	PGA
1892			25	
1896		4		

DOUGLASS, Dale (US)

	MAS	USO	BOP	PGA
1969	19	13		
1971	27			
1974		18		
1975		24		27
1978		24		

DOW, George (US)

	MAS	USO	BOP	PGA
1924				Last 32

DOW, J (SCO)

	MAS	USO	BOP	PGA
1874			23	

DOW, Robert (SCO)

	MAS	USO	BOP	PGA
1879			23	

DOW, William (SCO)

	MAS	USO	BOP	PGA
1861			3	
1862			4	
1864			5	
1865			3	
1867			8	
1868			7	
1870			17	

DOWIE, A [a] (SCO)

	MAS	USO	BOP	PGA
1946			27	

DOWLING, Jack (US)

	MAS	USO	BOP	PGA
1912		7		
1913		26		
1915		22		
1916		12		QF

DOYLE, Pat (US)

	MAS	USO	BOP	PGA
1913		10		
1919		18		Last 32
1920				Last 32
1926				QF
1928				Last 16

DREW, Norman (ENG)

	MAS	USO	BOP	PGA
1954			20	
1957			15	
1958			20	

DRUMMOND, R (SCO)

	MAS	USO	BOP	PGA
1880			21	

DUDAS, Stan (US)

	MAS	USO	BOP	PGA
1958		27		

DUDLEY, Ed (US)

	MAS	USO	BOP	PGA
1925				Last 16
1927				Last 16
1928			6	QF
1929		18		
1930		17		
1931		15		Last 32
1932		14		SF
1933			7	QF
1934	5			
1935	19	21		QF
1936	6			Last 16
1937	3	5	6	Last 16
1938	6			Last 32
1939	10	12		
1940	4	10		Last 16
1941	5	10		Last 32
1942				QF
1944				QF
1945				Last 32
1947				Last 32
1948	18			

DUFFY, Matt (US)

	MAS	USO	BOP	PGA
1922				Last 32

DUNCAN, George (SCO)

	MAS	USO	BOP	PGA
1906			8	
1907			7	
1908			18	
1909			21	
1910			3	
1911			8	
1912			4	
1914			10	
1920			W	
1921		8	5	
1922		6	2	
1923			6	
1924			6	
1925			27	
1926			20	
1928			18	
1929			22	

DUNLAP, Scott (US)

	MAS	USO	BOP	PGA
1997		24		

DUNN, Jamie (SCO)

	MAS	USO	BOP	PGA
1861			11	

DUNN, John (SCO/US)

	MAS	USO	BOP	PGA
1898		25		

DUNN, Tom (SCO)

	MAS	USO	BOP	PGA
1878			9	
1879			8	
1882			18	
1883			17	
1884			7	
1886			16	

DUNN Jr, Willie
(SCO/US)

	MAS	USO	BOP	PGA
1883			9	
1884			11	
1886			27	
1895		2		
1896		12		
1897		3		
1898		7		

DUNN Sr, Willie
(SCO)

	MAS	USO	BOP	PGA
1861			7	
1866			10	
1867			10	
1868			10	
1874			21	

DUPREE, Charles
(US)

	MAS	USO	BOP	PGA
1956				Last 32

DURNIAN, Denis
(ENG)

	MAS	USO	BOP	PGA
1983			8	

DUTRA, Mortie
(US)

	MAS	USO	BOP	PGA
1924				Last 16
1925				SF
1927				QF
1928				Last 32
1929				Last 32
1930		17		
1931		7		
1932		23		
1933		6		Last 32
1934	11	28		
1935		14		Last 32
1936				Last 32

DUTRA, Olin
(US)

	MAS	USO	BOP	PGA
1928				Last 32
1930		25		
1931		21		
1932		7		W
1933		7	6	Last 16
1934		W		
1935	3	12		
1937				Last 32
1938		16		
1939		16		

DUVAL, David
(US)

	MAS	USO	BOP	PGA
1995		28	20	
1996	18		14	
1997				13

EASTERBROOK, Syd
(ENG)

	MAS	USO	BOP	PGA
1932			13	
1933			3	
1935			7	

EASTWOOD, Bob
(US)

	MAS	USO	BOP	PGA
1980				30
1987		14		
1988		21		

EATON, Zell
(US)

	MAS	USO	BOP	PGA
1934		28a		
1936		28		
1948				Last 32
1952		28		Last 32

EDGAR, JD (Douglas)
(ENG/US)

	MAS	USO	BOP	PGA
1909			26	
1912			20	
1914			14	
1919		21		QF
1920		20		RU
1921			26	

EDMUNDSON, James
(IRE)

	MAS	USO	BOP	PGA
1908			11	

EDWARDS, Danny
(US)

	MAS	USO	BOP	PGA
1974			5	
1975			23	
1976		19		
1977	19			
1982	24	12		22
1983				20
1984	18			
1986	28		21	
1987		24	29	

EDWARDS, David
(US)

	MAS	USO	BOP	PGA
1980		28		30
1981				16
1984	3			
1987				14
1988				25
1993		11		
1994	18	13		
1995	24			
1996				17

EDWARDS, Kenneth
(US)

	MAS	USO	BOP	PGA
1904		26		

EDWARDS, Thurman
(US)

	MAS	USO	BOP	PGA
1944				Last 32

EGAN, H Chandler [a]
(US)

	MAS	USO	BOP	PGA
1904		20		
1906		8		
1911		23		

EHRESMAN, Clarence
(US)

	MAS	USO	BOP	PGA
1932				Last 32

EICHELBERGER, Dave
(US)

	MAS	USO	BOP	PGA
1971	20	19		
1972		29		
1976		21		
1986		24		

ELDER, Lee (US)

	MAS	USO	BOP	PGA
1972		29		24
1973				24
1974				11
1976				15
1977	19			
1978		30		
1979	17	11		
1980				26

ELDRED, Vincent (US)

	MAS	USO	BOP	PGA
1931				Last 32
1932		12		Last 16
1933				Last 32
1935		12		

ELKINGTON, Steve (AUS)

	MAS	USO	BOP	PGA
1989		21		
1990		21		
1991	22			
1992				18
1993	3			14
1994				7
1995	5		6	W
1996				3
1997	12	24		

ELLIS Jr, Wes (US)

	MAS	USO	BOP	PGA
1956		9		
1960				6
1961				5
1962				30
1963	24			17
1965	15	24		13
1966		8		
1967	16	12		25

ELPHICK, Jack (US)

	MAS	USO	BOP	PGA
1923				Last 32

ELS, Ernie (SA)

	MAS	USO	BOP	PGA
1992			5	
1993		7	6	
1994	8	W	24	25
1995			11	3
1996	12	5	2	
1997	17	W	10	

ELSWORTHY, Sherman (US)

	MAS	USO	BOP	PGA
1948				Last 32

EMERY, Clare (US)

	MAS	USO	BOP	PGA
1959				28

EMMETT, Devereux (US)

	MAS	USO	BOP	PGA
1897		28		

ENDERBY, Kep [a] (AUS)

	MAS	USO	BOP	PGA
1951			17	

ERICKSON, Bob (US)

	MAS	USO	BOP	PGA
1968		24		

ESPINOSA, Abe (US)

	MAS	USO	BOP	PGA
1924		7		
1925				Last 32
1926				QF
1931				QF
1932				Last 16
1933		24		
1939				Last 32

ESPINOSA, Al (US)

	MAS	USO	BOP	PGA
1924				QF
1925		9		Last 16
1926		13		Last 32
1927		18		SF
1928		14		RU
1929		2		QF
1930				QF
1931		10		Last 32
1933				Last 16
1934	7	21		
1935	17	28		
1936	15			
1937	29			Last 32

ESTES, Bob (US)

	MAS	USO	BOP	PGA
1993				6
1994		24		
1995	29			6
1996	27			

EVANS Jr, Charles (Chick) [a] (US)

	MAS	USO	BOP	PGA
1914		2		
1915		18		
1916		W		
1919		10		
1920		6		
1921		4		
1922		16		
1923		14		
1924		10		
1926		13		

EVANS, Max (US)

	MAS	USO	BOP	PGA
1954		23		Last 32
1955	27	28		

EVERARD, HSC [a] (SCO)

	MAS	USO	BOP	PGA
1885			18	
1888			11	
1891			28	

FABEL, Brad (US)

	MAS	USO	BOP	PGA
1987				28

FAIRBAIRN, THT (ENG)

	MAS	USO	BOP	PGA
1953			14	

FAIRFIELD, Don (US)

	MAS	USO	BOP	PGA
1955				QF
1957		17		
1958		27		
1961				22
1964		28		

FAIRLIE, FA [a]
(SCO)

	MAS	USO	BOP	PGA
1892			19	
1893			28	

FAIRLIE, JO [a]
(SCO)

	MAS	USO	BOP	PGA
1861			8	

FALDO, Nick
(ENG)

	MAS	USO	BOP	PGA
1976			28	
1978			7	
1979			19	
1980			12	
1981			11	
1982			4	14
1983	20		10	
1984	15		6	20
1985	25			
1986			5	
1987			W	28
1988	30	2	3	4
1989	W	18	11	9
1990	W	3	W	19
1991	12	16	17	16
1992	13	4	W	5
1993			2	3
1994			8	4
1995	24			
1996	W		4	

FALLON, Johnny
(SCO)

	MAS	USO	BOP	PGA
1936			23	
1938			26	
1939			3	
1948			21	
1949			8	
1955			2	
1957			19	

FARINA, Armand
(US)

	MAS	USO	BOP	PGA
1948				Last 32

FARLOW, Charles
(US)

	MAS	USO	BOP	PGA
1949		27		
1957				Last 32

FARQUHAR, John [a]
(US)

	MAS	USO	BOP	PGA
1964		28		

FARRELL, Billy
(US)

	MAS	USO	BOP	PGA
1962				17
1966				22
1967		23		11

FARRELL, Jack
(US)

	MAS	USO	BOP	PGA
1927				Last 32

FARRELL, Johnny
(US)

	MAS	USO	BOP	PGA
1919				Last 32
1921				Last 32
1922		11		Last 16
1923		5	19	Last 16
1924		19		QF
1925		3		QF
1926		3		SF
1927		7		Last 32
1928		W		
1929		2		RU
1930		8		QF
1931		10	5	Last 32
1933		9		SF
1934				Last 32
1936	29	22		
1937				Last 16
1939				Last 32
1940	14	28		

FAULKNER, Gus
(ENG)

	MAS	USO	BOP	PGA
1922			27	
1931			12	

FAULKNER, Max
(ENG)

	MAS	USO	BOP	PGA
1936			21	
1939			23	
1948			15	
1949			6	
1950			5	
1951			W	
1952			17	
1953			12	
1954			20	
1957			9	
1958			16	
1963			20	
1965			10	
1969			30	

FAXON, Brad
(US)

	MAS	USO	BOP	PGA
1988		11		
1992				15
1993	9			14
1994	15		7	30
1995	17		15	5
1996	25			17
1997		20		

FAZIO, George
(US)

	MAS	USO	BOP	PGA
1941				Last 32
1946				Last 32
1948	30	25		QF
1949				Last 32
1950	21	3		Last 32
1951	18			
1952	14	5		
1953		4		
1954		27		
1958				25

FEHERTY, David (IRE)

	MAS	USO	BOP	PGA
1987			26	
1989			6	
1991				7
1994			4	

FEHR, Rick (US)

	MAS	USO	BOP	PGA
1984		25		
1985		9		
1991		26		27
1992				18

FEMINELLI, Al (US)

	MAS	USO	BOP	PGA
1960		23		

FENN, AH (US)

	MAS	USO	BOP	PGA
1901		17		
1903		30		

FENTON, Jas (SCO)

	MAS	USO	BOP	PGA
1873			12	
1874			23	

FERGUS, Keith (US)

	MAS	USO	BOP	PGA
1979		9		
1980	26	3		
1981				4
1983	16			14
1984				29

FERGUSON, Bob (SCO)

	MAS	USO	BOP	PGA
1874			8	
1875			4	
1877			3	
1879			6	
1880			W	
1881			W	
1882			W	
1883			2	
1886			4	

FERGUSON, Jacky (SCO)

	MAS	USO	BOP	PGA
1886			24	

FERGUSON, James (SCO/US)

	MAS	USO	BOP	PGA
1916		29		32

FERGUSON, R (SCO)

	MAS	USO	BOP	PGA
1953			29	

FERGUSSON, J (SCO)

	MAS	USO	BOP	PGA
1874			10	

FERNANDEZ, Vicente (ARG)

	MAS	USO	BOP	PGA
1971			25	
1976			10	
1986			21	

FERNIE, George (SCO)

	MAS	USO	BOP	PGA
1884			7	
1885			18	
1887			17	
1890			21	

FERNIE, Peter (SCO)

	MAS	USO	BOP	PGA
1882			21	
1884			9	
1886			22	
1887			24	

FERNIE, Tom (SCO)

	MAS	USO	BOP	PGA
1911			29	
1923			5	
1925			13	

FERNIE, Willie (SCO)

	MAS	USO	BOP	PGA
1873			10	
1879			12	
1881			8	
1882			2	
1883			W	
1884			2	
1885			4	
1886			8	
1887			7	
1888			14	
1889			6	
1890			2	
1891			2	
1892			8	
1893			23	
1894			5	
1895			6	
1896			3	
1897			22	
1898			7	
1899			5	
1902			12	
1903			24	

FERREE, Jim (US)

	MAS	USO	BOP	PGA
1957		17		
1958		19		
1964				28

FERREE, Purvis (US)

	MAS	USO	BOP	PGA
1944				Last 32

FERRIER, Jim (AUS/US)

	MAS	USO	BOP	PGA
1940	26a	29a		
1941	29	30		
1942	15			
1946	4			Last 16
1947	6	6		W
1948	4			Last 32
1949	16	23		SF
1950	2			Last 32
1951	7			Last 16
1952	3			Last 32
1953	16			
1960				2
1961		22		
1963				7
1964	5			

FETCHICK, Mike (US)

	MAS	USO	BOP	PGA
1956				Last 32
1957	16	13		
1958		27		
1963		14		
1964				23
1967		28		

FEZLER, Forrest (US)

	MAS	USO	BOP	PGA
1974		2		
1975	30	24		

FIELD, Stewart (ENG)

	MAS	USO	BOP	PGA
1950			24	

FINDLAY, AH (Alex) (SCO/US)

	MAS	USO	BOP	PGA
1898		13		
1899		11		
1902		30		

FINSTERWALD, Dow (US)

	MAS	USO	BOP	PGA
1955		28		
1956	24			
1957	7	13		RU
1958	17			W
1959	18	11		4
1960	3	3		15
1961		6		
1962	3			11
1963	5	12		3
1964	9	8		
1965	21			
1966				12

FIORI, Ed (US)

	MAS	USO	BOP	PGA
1980	6			

FISCHER, Johnny [a] (US)

	MAS	USO	BOP	PGA
1932		27		

FITZJOHN, Ed (US)

	MAS	USO	BOP	PGA
1901		28		

FITZJOHN, Val (US)

	MAS	USO	BOP	PGA
1899		2		
1900		10		
1901		12		

FITZSIMONS, Pat (US)

	MAS	USO	BOP	PGA
1975	22	9		

FLECK, Jack (US)

	MAS	USO	BOP	PGA
1955		W		Last 16
1956				Last 32
1957	26	26		
1959	18	19		
1960		3		
1961		27		19
1962	11			7
1965				20

FLECKMAN, Marty (US)

	MAS	USO	BOP	PGA
1967		18a		
1968				4

FLEISHER, Bruce (US)

	MAS	USO	BOP	PGA
1992	25			
1993				14

FLOYD, Raymond (US)

	MAS	USO	BOP	PGA
1964		14		
1965		6		17
1966	8			18
1967				20
1968	7			W
1969		13		
1970		22		8
1971	13	8		
1972				4
1973		16		
1974	22	15		11
1975	30	12	23	10
1976	W	13	4	2
1977	8		8	
1978	16	12	2	
1979	17			
1980	17			17
1981	8		3	19
1982	7		15	W
1983	4	13	14	20
1984	15			13
1985	2	23		
1986		W	16	
1987			17	14
1988	11	17		9
1989		26		
1990	2			
1991	17	8		7
1992	2		12	
1993	11	7		
1994	10			
1995	17			
1996	25			

FOORD, Ernest (ENG)

	MAS	USO	BOP	PGA
1905			24	
1906			30	
1909			21	
1910			28	
1914			19	

FORD, Bob (US)

	MAS	USO	BOP	PGA
1983		26		

276

FORD, Doug (US)

	MAS	USO	BOP	PGA
1952	21	19		
1953	21	21		
1955		7		W
1956	6	9		Last 32
1957	W	17		Last 16
1958	2			11
1959	25	5		11
1960	25			7
1961		6		5
1962		8		5
1963	11			27
1964			24	
1965				20
1966	17			

FOREMAN, J (SCO)

	MAS	USO	BOP	PGA
1880			10	

FOREMAN, Roger (ENG)

	MAS	USO	BOP	PGA
1962			16	

FORRESTER, George (SCO)

	MAS	USO	BOP	PGA
1882			23	

FORRESTER, Jack (US)

	MAS	USO	BOP	PGA
1921				Last 32
1923		4		Last 32
1924				Last 32
1925		20		
1926		13		
1928		17		
1929		23		
1930		28		

FORSBRAND, Anders (SWE)

	MAS	USO	BOP	PGA
1985			8	
1986			16	
1987			29	
1992				9
1993	11			
1994			4	

FORSMAN, Dan (US)

	MAS	USO	BOP	PGA
1992				7
1993	7	19		
1994	14			
1996		13		

FORTINO, Tony (US)

	MAS	USO	BOP	PGA
1956				Last 32

FOSTER, Martin (ENG)

	MAS	USO	BOP	PGA
1975			23	
1977			26	

FOTHERINGHAM, Arthur (US)

	MAS	USO	BOP	PGA
1916		24		

FOTHERINGHAM, George (US)

	MAS	USO	BOP	PGA
1912			13	
1916				Last 32
1919		29		Last 16

FOUGHT, John (US)

	MAS	USO	BOP	PGA
1983				5

FOULIS, David (SCO/US)

	MAS	USO	BOP	PGA
1897		8		
1899		18		

FOULIS, James (SCO/US)

	MAS	USO	BOP	PGA
1895		3		
1896		W		
1897		3		
1899		20		
1900		14		
1901		11		
1902		20		
1904		9		
1906		22		

FOULIS, Jim (US)

	MAS	USO	BOP	PGA
1928				Last 32
1931				Last 16
1934	28			Last 32
1937				Last 16
1938		19		QF
1939		25		
1940	29	16		Last 16
1941	29			Last 32
1942	26			
1946	11			

FOULIS, Robert (SCO/US)

	MAS	USO	BOP	PGA
1897		15		
1900		29		

FOULIS, TJ (SCO/US)

	MAS	USO	BOP	PGA
1911		29		

FOURIE, John (SA)

	MAS	USO	BOP	PGA
1976			15	
1977			22	

FOVARGUE, Walter (US)

	MAS	USO	BOP	PGA
1906		14		
1909		18		
1911		28		
1914		24		
1916		13		Last 32

FOWLER, WH [a] (SCO)

	MAS	USO	BOP	PGA
1900			26	

FOWNES Jr, WC [a] (US)

	MAS	USO	BOP	PGA
1913		11		

FRANCIS, Francis [a] (ENG)

	MAS	USO	BOP	PGA
1936			23	
1937	28			

FRANCIS, Red (US)

	MAS	USO	BOP	PGA
1940				Last 32

FRANCIS, William (US)

	MAS	USO	BOP	PGA
1939				Last 32

FRANK, Joe (US)

MAS	USO	BOP	PGA
1930			Last 32

FRANKLIN, Barry (SA)

MAS	USO	BOP	PGA
1967		25	

FRASER, Leo (US)

MAS	USO	BOP	PGA
1934			Last 32

FRENCH, Emmett (US)

MAS	USO	BOP	PGA
1915	10		
1916			Last 16
1919			QF
1921	5	26	SF
1922	19		RU
1923	22		
1924	22		QF
1925	20		Last 32
1926	27	8	
1927	4		

FROST, David (SA)

MAS	USO	BOP	PGA
1985		23	25	
1986		15		21
1987		17	6	10
1988	8		7	
1989	18	18		27
1993			24	
1994				25
1995	5			
1996	10			

FROSTICK, FH (ENG)

MAS	USO	BOP	PGA
1912			24	

FRY, Earl (US)

MAS	USO	BOP	PGA
1930			Last 32

FRY, Mark (US)

MAS	USO	BOP	PGA
1930			Last 32
1934		16		
1941			Last 16
1944			Last 16

FRY, SH [a] (ENG)

MAS	USO	BOP	PGA
1902			14	

FRYATT, Edward (ENG)

MAS	USO	BOP	PGA
1997		24		

FUNK, Fred (US)

MAS	USO	BOP	PGA
1985		23		
1993		7		
1996				26
1997	17			

FUNSETH, Rod (US)

MAS	USO	BOP	PGA
1965				8
1966		13		
1968		16		
1971				30
1972		25		
1973		20		
1976		11		
1977	14	10		
1978	2			
1979				23

FURGOL, Ed (US)

MAS	USO	BOP	PGA
1946		12		
1947		13		
1948	6			
1951	15			
1953				Last 16
1954		W		Last 32
1955	24		20	Last 16
1956	24	4		SF
1957	6			
1963	5			
1964		14		13

FURGOL, Marty (US)

MAS	USO	BOP	PGA
1948		28		
1949				Last 16
1950		20		
1951		23		Last 32
1952				Last 32
1953		9		Last 32
1954	22	18		
1955		25		Last 16
1957	11			
1958		13		

FURYK, Jim (US)

MAS	USO	BOP	PGA
1994		28		
1995				13
1996	29	5		17
1997	28	5	4	6

GADD, Bert (ENG)

MAS	USO	BOP	PGA
1933			22	
1934			21	
1935			4	
1936			21	
1938			10	

GADD, Chas (ENG)

MAS	USO	BOP	PGA
1927			27	

GADD, George (ENG)

MAS	USO	BOP	PGA
1922			12	
1923			29	
1924			9	
1926			22	
1928			23	

GADDIE, Clay (US)

MAS	USO	BOP	PGA
1949				Last 32

GAFFORD, Ray (US)

Year	MAS	USO	BOP	PGA
1950				QF
1951		19		Last 32
1952		28		

GAIRDNER, JR [a] (ENG)

Year	MAS	USO	BOP	PGA
1898			21	

GAJDA, Bob (US)

Year	MAS	USO	BOP	PGA
1952				Last 32
1957				Last 32
1958				25

GALE, Terry (AUS)

Year	MAS	USO	BOP	PGA
1979			13	
1983			29	
1984			28	

GALLACHER, Bernard (SCO)

Year	MAS	USO	BOP	PGA
1973			18	
1974			24	
1975			19	
1978			22	
1982			25	
1983			19	

GALLAGHER Jr, Jim (US)

Year	MAS	USO	BOP	PGA
1989				12
1991	17	11		3
1992	25			2
1993	29			

GALLARDO, Angel (SP)

Year	MAS	USO	BOP	PGA
1974			24	
1977			26	

GALLETT, Francis (US)

Year	MAS	USO	BOP	PGA
1922				Last 16
1923		5		
1924				Last 16
1925		20		
1926				Last 32
1927				QF
1930		25		

GAMEZ, Robert (US)

Year	MAS	USO	BOP	PGA
1990			12	

GARAIALDE, Jean (FRA)

Year	MAS	USO	BOP	PGA
1958			14	
1959			21	
1961			26	
1962			12	
1963			9	
1964			13	
1969			30	

GARDNER, Buddy (US)

Year	MAS	USO	BOP	PGA
1985	6			
1989	17			

GARDNER, Robert (US)

Year	MAS	USO	BOP	PGA
1911		23		

GARDNER, Robert W (US)

Year	MAS	USO	BOP	PGA
1961	11			

GARDNER, Stewart (US)

Year	MAS	USO	BOP	PGA
1900		9		
1901		4		
1902		2		
1903		3		
1904		6		
1905		5		
1906		7		
1907		21		

GARNER, John (ENG)

Year	MAS	USO	BOP	PGA
1972			28	
1974			11	

GARRIDO, Antonio (SP)

Year	MAS	USO	BOP	PGA
1978			24	

GASSIAT, Jean (FRA)

Year	MAS	USO	BOP	PGA
1912			7	
1913			22	
1914			14	
1920			29	
1922			7	
1926			28	
1927			19	
1928			23	

GAUDIN, A (ENG)

Year	MAS	USO	BOP	PGA
1920			16	

GAUDIN, EP (ENG)

Year	MAS	USO	BOP	PGA
1909			14	
1910			8	

GAUDIN, HA (Herbert) (ENG)

Year	MAS	USO	BOP	PGA
1925			12	
1926			10	

GAUDIN, JW (ENG)

Year	MAS	USO	BOP	PGA
1921			15	
1923			29	
1924			16	
1925			5	

GAUDIN, PJ (Philip) (ENG/US)

Year	MAS	USO	BOP	PGA
1900			22	
1901			9	
1904			23	
1906			19	
1907			11	
1908			9	
1910			12	
1912			23	
1914			8	
1922				Last 32

GAUDIN, WC (ENG/US)

Year	MAS	USO	BOP	PGA
1907		30		

GAUNTT, Jimmy (US)

Year	MAS	USO	BOP	PGA
1942				Last 32

GEIBERGER, Al (US)

	MAS	USO	BOP	PGA
1961		12		
1963				5
1964	13	14		19
1965	24	4		19
1966		30		W
1967		28		5
1968	30	9		8
1969	13	2		
1970				16
1971	24			30
1972	12	21		
1973		13		18
1974		18	13	8
1976	15	2		
1977		10		6
1979		19		

GENTA, Tomas (ARG)

	MAS	USO	BOP	PGA
1931			11	

GERLAK, Alex (US)

	MAS	USO	BOP	PGA
1933				Last 32
1940				Last 32

GETCHELL, George (US)

	MAS	USO	BOP	PGA
1948				Last 32

GHEZZI, Vic (US)

	MAS	USO	BOP	PGA
1932				Last 32
1933				Last 32
1934	25			Last 16
1935	8	20		Last 32
1936	15	18		Last 16
1937	8	20		Last 16
1938	10	11		
1939	12	29		Last 32
1940		15		Last 32
1941	6	19		W
1942				Last 32
1945				QF
1946	13	2		Last 32
1947	21	6	18	SF
1948	18	14		
1950	14			
1951				Last 16
1952	30			Last 16
1954	29			
1955				Last 32
1956	29			

GIANFERANTE, Jerry (US)

	MAS	USO	BOP	PGA
1936		22		
1941		30		

GIBSON, Andrew (US)

	MAS	USO	BOP	PGA
1940		20		

GIBSON, Charles (ENG)

	MAS	USO	BOP	PGA
1894			28	
1897			30	

GIBSON, John (US)

	MAS	USO	BOP	PGA
1940				Last 32
1945				Last 32

GIBSON, Kelly (US)

	MAS	USO	BOP	PGA
1997		28		

GIBSON, Leland (US)

	MAS	USO	BOP	PGA
1942				Last 16
1946		26		
1947		6		QF
1948		14		Last 16
1949	13			
1950	14			
1952		22		
1953	13			
1954		18		
1955		25		

GILBERT, Gibby (US)

	MAS	USO	BOP	PGA
1971				6
1973				18
1975				17
1979				5
1980	2			
1981	28			

GILDER, Bob (US)

	MAS	USO	BOP	PGA
1978				19
1979		16		16
1981	15			4
1982	14			8
1985				18
1988		8		6
1991				5
1992		6		

GILES III, Marvin [a] (US)

	MAS	USO	BOP	PGA
1968	22			
1973		17		

GILFORD, David (ENG)

	MAS	USO	BOP	PGA
1995	24			

GILLAN, DH[a] (SCO)

	MAS	USO	BOP	PGA
1890			30	

GINN, Stewart (AUS)

	MAS	USO	BOP	PGA
1976			21	

GLASSON, Bill (US)

	MAS	USO	BOP	PGA
1984		25		
1986	25			
1989		21		
1994	19			19
1995		4	24	

GLENZ, David (US)

	MAS	USO	BOP	PGA
1974		30		

GLOVER, Randy (US)

	MAS	USO	BOP	PGA
1976		19		

GOALBY, Bob
(US)

	MAS	USO	BOP	PGA
1959				5
1960		19		
1961		2		15
1962	25	14		2
1963				17
1966		22		
1967		6		7
1968	W			8
1971		19		
1972	17			
1973	6			18
1974	22			

GODFREY, Walter
(NZ)

	MAS	USO	BOP	PGA
1970			22	

GOETZ, Bob
(US)

	MAS	USO	BOP	PGA
1958		16		
1963		30		

GOFF, Bruce [a]
(SCO)

	MAS	USO	BOP	PGA
1885			29	

GOFF, WH [a]
(SCO)

	MAS	USO	BOP	PGA
1885			26	

GOGGIN, Willie
(US)

	MAS	USO	BOP	PGA
1933		9		RU
1934				Last 32
1936		18	23	Last 16
1937				Last 32
1940	4			
1941	9			
1942	14			Last 16
1944				QF
1952			9	

GOLDEN, John
(US)

	MAS	USO	BOP	PGA
1920		17		
1921		22		QF
1922		8		SF
1923				Last 16
1924		25		
1925		18		Last 16
1926				SF
1927		7		SF
1928				Last 32
1929			13	Last 32
1930		5		Last 32
1931		27		Last 16
1932				Last 16
1933		21		QF
1934	21	17		

GOLDSTRAND, Joel
(US)

	MAS	USO	BOP	PGA
1970		12		

GONZALES, Mario
(BRA)

	MAS	USO	BOP	PGA
1948			11	

GONZALEZ, Jaime
(BRA)

	MAS	USO	BOP	PGA
1984			28	
1985			20	

GOOD, DJ
(ENG)

	MAS	USO	BOP	PGA
1973			18	

GOOD, Gordon
(ENG)

	MAS	USO	BOP	PGA
1936			19	

GOODLOE Jr, William [a]
(US)

	MAS	USO	BOP	PGA
1955	28			

GOODMAN, Johnny [a]
(US)

	MAS	USO	BOP	PGA
1930		11		
1932		14		
1933		W		
1936		22		
1937		8		

GOOSEN, Retief
(SA)

	MAS	USO	BOP	PGA
1997			10	

GOOSIE, JC
(US)

	MAS	USO	BOP	PGA
1963				27

GOSS, Dan
(US)

	MAS	USO	BOP	PGA
1922				Last 32

GOSSETT, Thomas
(SCO)

	MAS	USO	BOP	PGA
1886			4	

GORDON, George
(US)

	MAS	USO	BOP	PGA
1919				Last 16

GORDON, Jack
(US)

	MAS	USO	BOP	PGA
1920				Last 32
1921				Last 16

GOULD, Harold
(WAL)

	MAS	USO	BOP	PGA
1948			30	

GOURLAY, Tom
(SCO/US)

	MAS	USO	BOP	PGA
1896		19		

GOURLAY, Walter
(SCO)

	MAS	USO	BOP	PGA
1873			6	
1876			8	
1879			8	

GOYDOS, Paul
(US)

	MAS	USO	BOP	PGA
1997		28		29

GRADY, Wayne
(AUS)

	MAS	USO	BOP	PGA
1986				21
1987			17	
1989			2	
1990	27			W
1991			26	
1992	13	17		
1993			9	
1994				30

GRAHAM, David (AUS)

	MAS	USO	BOP	PGA
1973	29			
1974		18	11	
1975		29	28	10
1976			21	4
1977	6			
1978	9			
1979		7		W
1980	5		29	26
1981	7	W	14	
1982	19	6	27	
1983		8	14	14
1984	6	21		
1985	10	23	3	
1986	28	15	11	7
1987	27			
1988				17
1990			8	

GRAHAM, Jack [a] (ENG)

	MAS	USO	BOP	PGA
1897			18	
1901			9	
1904			7	
1906			4	
1907			13	
1908			18	
1913			11	

GRAHAM, Lou (US)

	MAS	USO	BOP	PGA
1965		23		
1967		28		
1968				8
1970				22
1972		19		
1973	17			30
1974		3		
1975		W		
1976	12	28		22
1977	6	2		6
1979	23	25		10
1980	26			

GRANT, D [a] (ENG)

	MAS	USO	BOP	PGA
1920			29	

GRANT, David (SCO)

	MAS	USO	BOP	PGA
1879			23	
1880			8	
1883			24	
1884			20	
1886			8	
1887			7	
1888			6	
1889			7	
1890			7	
1891			14	
1893			17	
1894			20	

GRANT, James A [a] (US)

	MAS	USO	BOP	PGA
1966	28			

GRAPPASONI, Ugo (IT)

	MAS	USO	BOP	PGA
1949			28	
1951			19	
1953			27	
1954			17	

GRAVATT, Morrie (US)

	MAS	USO	BOP	PGA
1944				Last 32

GRAY, Claude (ENG)

	MAS	USO	BOP	PGA
1913			18	

GRAY, Ernest (ENG)

	MAS	USO	BOP	PGA
1903			15	
1904			18	
1905			5	
1906			24	
1908			13	

GRAY, Reg (ENG)

	MAS	USO	BOP	PGA
1907			18	

GREEN, Hubert (US)

	MAS	USO	BOP	PGA
1972	22			16
1973	14			
1974	9	26	4	3
1975	8	18		
1976	19	6	5	30
1977	8	W	3	
1978	2		29	26
1979	10	24		16
1980	4	6		
1981	11		23	27
1983		19		
1984		30		14
1985				W
1988	19			
1989		9		

GREEN, Ken (US)

	MAS	USO	BOP	PGA
1983		26		
1986				26
1987			29	
1989	11			
1991				16
1996		7		

GREEN, Tom (ENG)

	MAS	USO	BOP	PGA
1930			29	
1934			26	
1936			5	

GREEN, WH (ENG)

	MAS	USO	BOP	PGA
1939			19	

GREENE, Bert (US)

	MAS	USO	BOP	PGA
1969				3
1970	12			
1971	12			

GREENE, Christy (IRE)

	MAS	USO	BOP	PGA
1958			20	
1964			13	
1965			21	
1966			30	

GREENWALDT, Phil (US)

	MAS	USO	BOP	PGA
1941				Last 32

GREGSON, Malcom (ENG)

	MAS	USO	BOP	PGA
1964			19	
1968			27	
1971			25	

GREIG, William [a] (SCO)

	MAS	USO	BOP	PGA
1885			16	
1888			23	
1891			28	
1900			16	

GREINER, Otto (US)

	MAS	USO	BOP	PGA
1948		14		
1963		27		

GRIFFIN, George (US)

	MAS	USO	BOP	PGA
1925				Last 32

GRIFFITHS, AS (US)

	MAS	USO	BOP	PGA
1902		16		

GROH, Gary (US)

	MAS	USO	BOP	PGA
1975		18		

GROSSART, T (SCO)

	MAS	USO	BOP	PGA
1883			14	

GROUT, Dick (US)

	MAS	USO	BOP	PGA
1926				Last 16

GROUT, Jack (US)

	MAS	USO	BOP	PGA
1941				Last 16
1945				Last 16
1953				Last 32

GUEST, Charles (US)

	MAS	USO	BOP	PGA
1927				Last 16
1929				Last 16
1930		17		Last 32
1931		19		

GUILFORD, Jesse [a] (US)

	MAS	USO	BOP	PGA
1919		24		
1921		26		
1922		19		
1924		29		

GULDAHL, Ralph (US)

	MAS	USO	BOP	PGA
1933		2		
1934		8		
1936		8		
1937	2	W	11	Last 32
1938	2	W		Last 32
1939	W	7		Last 32
1940	14	5		SF
1941	14	21		Last 16
1942	21			
1949		22		

GULLANE, Henry (SCO/US)

	MAS	USO	BOP	PGA
1899		8		
1900		25		

GULLICKSON, Lloyd (US)

	MAS	USO	BOP	PGA
1920				Last 32
1922		28		

GUSA, Arthur (US)

	MAS	USO	BOP	PGA
1931				Last 32

GUSTIN, John (US)

	MAS	USO	BOP	PGA
1964				9

GUTHRIE, James (SCO)

	MAS	USO	BOP	PGA
1875			12	

HAAS, Fred (US)

	MAS	USO	BOP	PGA
1946	15			
1947	17			
1948	18			
1949	29	19		
1950	10	18		
1951		29		
1952				QF
1953	26	12		Last 32
1954		6		Last 32
1955				Last 32
1956	29	14		Last 32
1962				23
1963				27

HAAS, Jay (US)

	MAS	USO	BOP	PGA
1975		18a		
1977		5		
1979				7
1980	17			
1981				19
1982		6	27	5
1983	27		19	9
1984	21	11		
1985	5	15		
1986	6			
1987	7			28
1988		25		
1992		23		
1993				20
1994	5			14
1995	3	4		8
1997		5	24	

HACKBARTH, Alfred (US)

Year	MAS	USO	BOP	PGA
1921		11		

HACKBARTH, Otto (US)

Year	MAS	USO	BOP	PGA
1906		22		
1910		23		
1911		29		
1912		7		
1914		27		
1915		29		
1916		19		
1919		26	Last 16	
1920			Last 32	
1921		22		

HACKNEY, Clarence (US)

Year	MAS	USO	BOP	PGA
1919		13		Last 32
1920		12		QF
1921		8	23	Last 32
1923				Last 16
1924		13		
1925		17		
1926		22		
1930				Last 32
1935				Last 32

HACKNEY, Dave (US)

Year	MAS	USO	BOP	PGA
1929				Last 32
1931				Last 32
1933				Last 32

HACKNEY, George (US)

Year	MAS	USO	BOP	PGA
1922		17		

HAGAWA, Yakata (JAP)

Year	MAS	USO	BOP	PGA
1982	15			

HAGEN, Walter (US)

Year	MAS	USO	BOP	PGA
1913		4		
1914		W		
1915		10		
1916		7		SF
1919		W		
1920		11		
1921		2	6	W
1922		5	W	
1923		18	2	RU
1924		4	W	W
1925		5		W
1926		7	3	W
1927		6		W
1928		4	W	QF
1929		19	W	SF
1930		17		
1931		7	22	Last 32
1932		10		Last 32
1933		4		
1934	13			Last 32
1935	15	3		
1936	11			
1937			26	
1940				Last 16

HAGER, Joe (US)

Year	MAS	USO	BOP	PGA
1980		12		
1982		22		
1984		25		

HALIBURTON, Tom (SCO)

Year	MAS	USO	BOP	PGA
1946			30	
1948			23	
1953			29	
1959			29	
1963			30	

HALL, Charles (US)

Year	MAS	USO	BOP	PGA
1920		30		

HALLBERG, Gary (US)

Year	MAS	USO	BOP	PGA
1980		22a		
1984				6
1985	6			
1993				14
1995		28		

HALLDORSAN, Dan (US)

Year	MAS	USO	BOP	PGA
1982				16

HALLETT, Jim (US)

Year	MAS	USO	BOP	PGA
1987				21
1991				27

HALSALL, Bobby (ENG)

Year	MAS	USO	BOP	PGA
1954			15	
1955			23	

HAM, Arthur (US)

Year	MAS	USO	BOP	PGA
1924				Last 32

HAMBLETON, Walter (ENG)

Year	MAS	USO	BOP	PGA
1914			25	

HAMBRICK, Archie (US)

Year	MAS	USO	BOP	PGA
1933		21		

HAMBRO, CE [a] (ENG)

Year	MAS	USO	BOP	PGA
1894			25	
1899			21	

HAMILL, Harry (IRE)

Year	MAS	USO	BOP	PGA
1906			19	

HAMILTON, Bob (US)

Year	MAS	USO	BOP	PGA
1944				W
1945				Last 32
1946	3			Last 32
1947		29		
1948	18			
1949	23			Last 32
1951				Last 32
1952				SF
1953	4			

HAMMOND, Donnie (US)

	MAS	USO	BOP	PGA
1984				16
1986	11			11
1987	27			
1990	24		8	
1992		23	5	

HAMPTON, Harry (US)

	MAS	USO	BOP	PGA
1919		11		Last 16
1920		22		SF
1921		22		Last 32
1922		19		Last 16
1924				Last 32
1925		20		
1926		27		QF
1927		7		
1928		25		

HANCOCK, Phil (US)

	MAS	USO	BOP	PGA
1978		20		16

HANCOCK, Roland (US)

	MAS	USO	BOP	PGA
1927				Last 32
1928		3		

HARBERT, Chick (US)

	MAS	USO	BOP	PGA
1939	18			
1942	10			
1946	7	8		
1947		12		RU
1948	3	28		QF
1949		23		
1950	24			Last 16
1951				Last 32
1952		24		RU
1953	5			
1954	12			W
1955				Last 32
1957		8		
1958	17			
1959	14	26		28
1961		29		
1962				11

HARCKE, Byron (US)

	MAS	USO	BOP	PGA
1945				Last 32

HARDEN, Jack (US)

	MAS	USO	BOP	PGA
1949				Last 32
1951				Last 16

HARGREAVES, Jack (ENG)

	MAS	USO	BOP	PGA
1948			3	
1951			19	
1952			27	
1954			20	
1956			17	

HARLAND, John (US)

	MAS	USO	BOP	PGA
1895		7		
1898		17		
1901		28		
1902		20		

HARMON, Claude (US)

	MAS	USO	BOP	PGA
1945				SF
1946	18	15		
1947	26	19		Last 16
1948	W		27	SF
1949	11	8		Last 32
1950				Last 16
1952	14			
1953				SF
1954		15		Last 32
1955	28			Last 16
1956				Last 32
1957				QF
1958	9			
1959		3		
1960	16	27		

HARMON Jr, Tom (US)

	MAS	USO	BOP	PGA
1924				Last 32
1926		27		Last 16
1927		29		Last 16

HARNEY, Paul (US)

	MAS	USO	BOP	PGA
1959	25			14
1960		12		18
1961	6			11
1962	15	28		7
1963		4		23
1964	5			
1965	11			
1966	8			15
1967	6	18		
1970		18		
1972	22			
1973	24			

HARPER, Chandler (US)

	MAS	USO	BOP	PGA
1942	13			
1946	19	15		Last 16
1947	8			Last 32
1948				Last 32
1950				W
1952				Last 32
1953	10			
1959	14			

HARPER Jr, Charles (US)

	MAS	USO	BOP	PGA
1956				Last 16
1957				Last 32

HARRIMAN, HM [a] (US)

	MAS	USO	BOP	PGA
1899		13		

HARRINGTON, Padraig (IRE)

	MAS	USO	BOP	PGA
1996			18	
1997			5	

HARRIS, Bob (US)

	MAS	USO	BOP	PGA
1955		21		
1960		15		

HARRIS Jr, Labron (US)	MAS	USO	BOP	PGA
1964		28		
1965		24		
1967		28		

HARRIS Sr, Labron (US)	MAS	USO	BOP	PGA
1952				Last 32
1953				Last 16
1958		27		

HARRIS, Robert [a] (SCO)	MAS	USO	BOP	PGA
1911			27	
1925			10	

HARRISON, Dutch (US)	MAS	USO	BOP	PGA
1939		25		SF
1941		7		
1942	7			Last 32
1945				Last 32
1946		10		Last 16
1947	29	13		
1948	13			
1949	23			
1950		4		
1951	15			
1953		14		Last 32
1954	4			Last 16
1956		17		
1958		23		
1960		3		
1961		17		
1965		28		
1967		16		

HARRISON, John (US)	MAS	USO	BOP	PGA
1896		24		
1897		24		

HARRISON, Robert (US)	MAS	USO	BOP	PGA
1961		29		

HART, Dick (US)	MAS	USO	BOP	PGA
1962				30
1963				17
1964				28

HART, Dudley (US)	MAS	USO	BOP	PGA
1992		23		
1993				6

HART, PO (US)	MAS	USO	BOP	PGA
1921		30		
1923		24		
1926		23		
1927		24		
1929		13		Last 32

HARTER, Charles (US)	MAS	USO	BOP	PGA
1952				Last 32

HARTLEY, Lister [a] (ENG)	MAS	USO	BOP	PGA
1926			13	
1932			25	

HARWOOD, Mike (AUS)	MAS	USO	BOP	PGA
1991			2	

HASSANEIN, H (EGY)	MAS	USO	BOP	PGA
1950			30	
1953			17	
1955			28	

HASTINGS, Willie (SCO)	MAS	USO	BOP	PGA
1938			23	

HATALSKY, Morris (US)	MAS	USO	BOP	PGA
1982	24			
1990				14
1991	29			

HAVERS, Arthur (ENG)	MAS	USO	BOP	PGA
1920			7	
1921			4	
1922			12	
1923			W	
1924			29	
1925			19	
1926			26	
1927		15	7	
1929			11	
1931			9	
1932			3	
1933			14	
1937			17	
1947			27	

HAWKES, Jeff (SA)	MAS	USO	BOP	PGA
1989			30	

HAWKINS, Fred (US)	MAS	USO	BOP	PGA
1951		6		
1952	7			
1953	10			
1955		19		QF
1956	29			QF
1957	16	6		
1958	2			14
1959	7	11		28
1960	16			10
1961	24			22

HAYES, Dale (SA)	MAS	USO	BOP	PGA
1971			17	
1978			11	
1976	19			

HAYES, Mark (US)	MAS	USO	BOP	PGA
1975				22
1976		14		15
1977			9	19
1978			14	
1979			30	
1980		6		
1981		14		
1982	10			
1983	20	26		

HAYES, Otway (SA)

	MAS	USO	BOP	PGA
1948			28	

HAYES Jr, Ted (US)

	MAS	USO	BOP	PGA
1970		22		

HEAFNER, Clayton (US)

	MAS	USO	BOP	PGA
1939		16		
1941	12	21		
1946	7	12		
1947	29			Last 32
1949	8	2		QF
1950	7			
1951	20	2		
1952	24			
1953		26		

HEAFNER, Vance (US)

	MAS	USO	BOP	PGA
1981				11

HEARD, Jerry (US)

	MAS	USO	BOP	PGA
1971		13		9
1972	5	29	28	7
1973		7		
1974	11			
1975	26	29		25
1976				22

HEBERT, Jay (US)

	MAS	USO	BOP	PGA
1953		9		
1954	16	17		
1955	15			Last 32
1956		17		
1957	10			QF
1958	9	7		5
1959	8	17		25
1960				W
1961	30			13
1962		17		10
1963	27			
1964	30			
1966	10			12
1967	21			
1968	28			

HEBERT, Lionel (US)

	MAS	USO	BOP	PGA
1955				Last 32
1956				Last 16
1957				W
1958				16
1959		28		
1960	9	27		18
1961	30			
1962	20	23		
1963		14		
1964		21		
1967	8			14
1968	7			30
1969	8			

HEDBLOM, Peter (SWE)

	MAS	USO	BOP	PGA
1996			7	

HEINLEIN, William (US)

	MAS	USO	BOP	PGA
1941				Last 32
1946				Last 32

HEINTZELMAN, Webb (US)

	MAS	USO	BOP	PGA
1990		24		

HELD, Eddie [a] (US)

	MAS	USO	BOP	PGA
1923		26		

HENDERSON, Willie John (SCO)

	MAS	USO	BOP	PGA
1951			19	
1955			15	

HENDRY, Jock (SCO/US)

	MAS	USO	BOP	PGA
1926				Last 32
1929				Last 32

HENDRY, TS [a] (SCO)

	MAS	USO	BOP	PGA
1885			27	

HENKE, Nolan (US)

	MAS	USO	BOP	PGA
1989		21		
1991		7		
1992	6			
1993	27	7		6
1995				23

HENNING, Alan (SA)

	MAS	USO	BOP	PGA
1966			30	

HENNING, Harold (SA)

	MAS	USO	BOP	PGA
1957			29	
1958			13	
1959			23	
1960			3	
1961			10	
1962	11		30	
1963			20	
1964			8	
1966	22		13	
1967			6	
1968	22			
1969	13		16	
1970			3	
1973			10	
1983			6	

HENNINGER, Brian (US)

	MAS	USO	BOP	PGA
1995	10			

HENRY, Bunky (US)

	MAS	USO	BOP	PGA
1969		9	11	
1970		30		

HEPBURN, James (SCO)

	MAS	USO	BOP	PGA
1903			24	
1904			29	
1905			24	
1906			30	
1908			24	
1909			8	
1910			19	
1911			10	

HERD, David (SCO)

Year	MAS	USO	BOP	PGA
1894			20	
1895			20	
1896			27	
1898			21	
1899			28	
1901			25	
1902			28	

HERD, Alex (Sandy) (SCO)

Year	MAS	USO	BOP	PGA
1888			8	
1891			13	
1892			2	
1893			3	
1894			8	
1895			2	
1896			5	
1897			5	
1898			17	
1899			16	
1900			10	
1901			5	
1902			W	
1903			4	
1904			9	
1905			15	
1906			19	
1907			12	
1908			4	
1909			8	
1910			2	
1911			3	
1912			5	
1913			11	
1914			29	
1920			2	
1921			6	
1923			22	
1924			13	
1925			13	
1926			20	
1927			9	

HERD, Fred (SCO/US)

Year	MAS	USO	BOP	PGA
1898		W		
1899		25		
1900		16		
1902		24		

HERON, Al [a] (US)

Year	MAS	USO	BOP	PGA
1930		11		

HERON, George (US)

Year	MAS	USO	BOP	PGA
1925		29		

HERRESHOFF, Fred [a] (US)

Year	MAS	USO	BOP	PGA
1910		20		
1913		16		

HERRON, Tim (US)

Year	MAS	USO	BOP	PGA
1997				13

HESLER, Phil (US)

Year	MAS	USO	BOP	PGA
1920				Last 32

HEZLET, Charles [a] (IRE)

Year	MAS	USO	BOP	PGA
1928			17	

HIGGINS, Doug (US)

Year	MAS	USO	BOP	PGA
1956		27		

HILGENDORF, Charles (US)

Year	MAS	USO	BOP	PGA
1922				Last 32
1928		18		
1929		13		
1930		28		

HILL, Dave (US)

Year	MAS	USO	BOP	PGA
1963				17
1966		22		
1967		18		11
1968		16		17
1969	24	13		15
1970	5	2		
1971	27			6
1972		29		
1973			18	
1974	11			3
1975	7			7
1976	15			22

HILL, Mike (US)

Year	MAS	USO	BOP	PGA
1970				16
1973				24
1974				11
1975				17
1976				15

HILL, Ray (US)

Year	MAS	USO	BOP	PGA
1940				Last 32
1949				QF
1955				Last 32

HILLS, Percy (ENG)

Year	MAS	USO	BOP	PGA
1904			29	
1905			22	

HILTON, Harold [a] (ENG)

Year	MAS	USO	BOP	PGA
1892			W	
1893			8	
1896			23	
1897			W	
1898			3	
1899			12	
1900			16	
1901			4	
1902			6	
1903			24	

HILTON, Horace [a] (ENG)

Year	MAS	USO	BOP	PGA
1911			3	

HINCKLE, Lon
(US)

	MAS	USO	BOP	PGA
1975			19	
1980		3		3
1981	28	6		
1982				9

HINES, Jimmy
(US)

	MAS	USO	BOP	PGA
1932				Last 32
1933				SF
1934	7	8		
1935	9			Last 32
1936				QF
1937	10	20		QF
1938	10	11		SF
1939	22	20		
1940	27	20		Last 16
1941	19	24		QF
1942				Last 32
1944				Last 16
1948				Last 32
1950				Last 32
1952			21	

HINSON, Larry
(US)

	MAS	USO	BOP	PGA
1970				4
1971	30	9		13
1973				12
1974		23		26
1975				28

HIRIGOYEN, Pierre
(FRA)

	MAS	USO	BOP	PGA
1930			21	
1932			29	

HISKIE, Babe
(US)

	MAS	USO	BOP	PGA
1973				17

HITCHCOCK, Jimmy
(ENG)

	MAS	USO	BOP	PGA
1954			29	
1957			23	
1959			11	
1962			30	
1963			26	
1966			16	

HOARE, WT
(US)

	MAS	USO	BOP	PGA
1896		15		
1897		5		

HOARE, WV
(US)

	MAS	USO	BOP	PGA
1898		6		
1900		27		

HOBDAY, Simon
(ZIM)

	MAS	USO	BOP	PGA
1975			28	
1976			21	
1979			30	
1983			19	

HOBENS, Jack
(US)

	MAS	USO	BOP	PGA
1902		14		
1903		9		
1904		11		
1905		7		
1906		10		
1907		4		
1908		6		
1909		4		
1910		7		
1916				Last 16
1919				Last 32

HOCH, Scott
(US)

	MAS	USO	BOP	PGA
1983	27			
1985				12
1987				3
1988		21		25
1989	2	13		7
1990	14	8		
1991		6		
1993		5		6
1994		13		
1995	7			
1996	5	7		
1997		10		6

HODSON, Bert
(WAL)

	MAS	USO	BOP	PGA
1927			7	
1930			12	
1931			25	
1932			17	
1934			7	

HOFFNER, Charles
(US)

	MAS	USO	BOP	PGA
1914		13		
1915		24		
1919		13		
1920				Last 32
1922		19		Last 32
1924				Last 32
1925				Last 32

HOGAN, Ben (US)

	MAS	USO	BOP	PGA
1938	25			
1939	9			Last 16
1940	10	5		QF
1941	4	3		QF
1942	2			QF
1946	2	4		W
1947	4	6		
1948	6	W		W
1950	4	W		
1951	W	W		
1952	7	3		
1953	W	W	W	
1954	2	6		
1955	2	2		
1956	8	2		
1958	14	10		
1959	30	8		
1960	6	9		
1961		14		
1964	9			9
1965	21			15
1966	13	12		
1967	10			

HOLGUIN, Tony (US)

	MAS	USO	BOP	PGA
1949	19			
1955				Last 32
1957				Last 32

HOLLAND, Len (ENG)

	MAS	USO	BOP	PGA
1920			5	
1921			16	
1922			12	
1923			25	
1924			6	
1927			22	
1931			22	
1935			26	

HOLLAND, Mike (US)

	MAS	USO	BOP	PGA
1982				29

HOLSCHER, Bud (US)

	MAS	USO	BOP	PGA
1955		7		

HONEYMAN, David (US)

	MAS	USO	BOP	PGA
1910		28		
1912		30		

HONEYMAN, W (SCO)

	MAS	USO	BOP	PGA
1882			16	

HONSBERGER, Ray (US)

	MAS	USO	BOP	PGA
1952				Last 16

HOOD, Tom [a] (SCO)

	MAS	USO	BOP	PGA
1865			10	
1866			11	
1874			14	

HOOPER, Herb (US)

	MAS	USO	BOP	PGA
1971				18

HOPE, WL [a] (ENG)

	MAS	USO	BOP	PGA
1928			23	
1932			15	

HORNE, Reg (ENG)

	MAS	USO	BOP	PGA
1947			2	
1948			28	
1949			20	
1950			17	
1953			20	
1955			23	
1957			24	

HORNE, Stanley (CAN)

	MAS	USO	BOP	PGA
1938	15			

HORNE, William (ENG)

	MAS	USO	BOP	PGA
1907			23	
1909			7	
1912			20	
1920			9	

HORTON, Tommy (ENG)

	MAS	USO	BOP	PGA
1965			17	
1967			8	
1968			13	
1969			11	
1970			9	
1975			19	
1976			5	
1977			9	

HORVATH, Rudy (CAN)

	MAS	USO	BOP	PGA
1954		13		

HOUGHTON, Al (US)

	MAS	USO	BOP	PGA
1933				Last 32
1934				QF

HOWARD, George (US)

	MAS	USO	BOP	PGA
1925				Last 32

HOWELL, Ron (US)

	MAS	USO	BOP	PGA
1966				28

HOYLE, M (ENG)

	MAS	USO	BOP	PGA
1967			13	

HSU, Chi-San (TAI)

	MAS	USO	BOP	PGA
1976			21	

HUCKABY, Charles (US)

	MAS	USO	BOP	PGA
1965		17		

HUGE, Ted (US)

	MAS	USO	BOP	PGA
1945				Last 32

HUGGETT, Brian (WAL)	MAS	USO	BOP	PGA
1961			26	
1962			3	
1963			14	
1965			2	
1967			25	
1968			13	
1969			16	
1970			28	
1971			25	
1972			26	

HUGHES, Bradley (AUS)	MAS	USO	BOP	PGA
1997		16		

HUGHES, Cyril (ENG/US)	MAS	USO	BOP	PGA
1913			22	
1914			19	
1920			25	
1922		24		
1923		11		

HUISH, David (SCO)	MAS	USO	BOP	PGA
1976			21	

HULBERT, Mike (US)	MAS	USO	BOP	PGA
1986				7
1989				27
1990		29		
1991				23
1992	19	6		28
1995		28		

HUME, Jimmy (ENG)	MAS	USO	BOP	PGA
1967			29	

HUNT, Bernard (ENG)	MAS	USO	BOP	PGA
1955			5	
1957			24	
1958			30	
1959			11	
1960			3	
1962			16	
1963			11	
1964			4	
1965	26		5	
1969			23	
1971			20	

HUNT, Geoff (ENG)	MAS	USO	BOP	PGA
1960			28	
1964			30	

HUNT, Guy (ENG)	MAS	USO	BOP	PGA
1972			7	
1975			28	
1977			15	
1978			17	

HUNTER, Charlie (SCO)	MAS	USO	BOP	PGA
1860			6	
1861			12	
1862			3	
1863			7	
1868			9	
1870			9	
1872			6	
1874			26	

HUNTER, David (SCO/US)	MAS	USO	BOP	PGA
1899		30		
1901		25		
1902		30		
1907		16		
1908		16		
1909		30		

HUNTER, J (SCO)	MAS	USO	BOP	PGA
1870			15	

HUNTER, James [a] (SCO)	MAS	USO	BOP	PGA
1882			29	
1884			18	

HUNTER, John (SCO)	MAS	USO	BOP	PGA
1893			15	
1896			18	
1898			8	
1903			21	

HUNTER, Mac (US)	MAS	USO	BOP	PGA
1959		19		

HUNTER, P [a] (SCO)	MAS	USO	BOP	PGA
1921			19	

HUNTER, Robert [a] (SCO/US)	MAS	USO	BOP	PGA
1904		23		

HUNTER, T [a] (SCO)	MAS	USO	BOP	PGA
1867			8	
1870			13	
1874			16	

HUNTER, William [a] (SCO)	MAS	USO	BOP	PGA
1872			8	
1878			20	

HUNTER Jr, William I (SCO/US)	MAS	USO	BOP	PGA
1920			26a	
1922		24a	22a	
1923				Last 32
1925		13		
1926		8		
1928		28		
1929		26		
1930		17		
1931			16	
1934		14		
1935		28		
1938		15		

HUNTER Sr, Willie (SCO/US)

	MAS	USO	BOP	PGA
1901		28		
1902		20		
1903			13	
1905			24	
1906			12	
1914			17	

HUSKE, Al (US)

	MAS	USO	BOP	PGA
1938		24		
1940		29		

HUSTON, John (US)

	MAS	USO	BOP	PGA
1990	3	14		
1991	29			7
1992	25			18
1994	10			
1995	17			
1996	17			
1997	21			

HUTCHINGS, Charles [a] (ENG)

	MAS	USO	BOP	PGA
1891			18	
1893			13	
1894			25	

HUTCHINSON, Denis (SA)

	MAS	USO	BOP	PGA
1961			18	
1962			16	
1965			21	
1966			27	
1967			22	

HUTCHINSON, Horace [a] (ENG)

	MAS	USO	BOP	PGA
1885			11	
1886			16	
1887			10	
1890			6	
1891			22	
1892			10	

HUTCHINSON, James (SCO)

	MAS	USO	BOP	PGA
1898			21	
1901			25	

HUTCHINSON Tom (SCO/US)

	MAS	USO	BOP	PGA
1899			22	
1900		7		

HUTCHISON, CK [a] (SCO)

	MAS	USO	BOP	PGA
1909			19	
1910			24	
1914			29	

HUTCHISON, James (SCO)

	MAS	USO	BOP	PGA
1866			12	

HUTCHISON, Jock (SCO/US)

	MAS	USO	BOP	PGA
1908		8		
1909		23		
1910		8		
1911		5		
1912		23		
1913		16		
1915		8		
1916		2		RU
1919		3		QF
1920		2		W
1921		18	W	Last 16
1922		8	4	QF
1923		3		
1924				Last 32
1925		27		
1927		23		
1928				QF

HUTCHISON Jr, Jock (US)

	MAS	USO	BOP	PGA
1940		23		

HUTCHISON, Ralph (US)

	MAS	USO	BOP	PGA
1945				QF

HUTCHISON, W (SCO)

	MAS	USO	BOP	PGA
1874			25	

HYNDMAN III, William [a] (US)

	MAS	USO	BOP	PGA
1957		13		
1958	26			
1959	18			

INGHAM, Mike (ENG)

	MAS	USO	BOP	PGA
1969			30	

INGRAM, David (SCO)

	MAS	USO	BOP	PGA
1977			26	

INMAN Jr, Joe (US)

	MAS	USO	BOP	PGA
1975		14		
1976		23		22
1977		16		11
1978	9	12		11
1979	23			
1980		16		17
1981				19

INMAN, John (US)

	MAS	USO	BOP	PGA
1990		14		

INMAN Jr, Walker (US)

	MAS	USO	BOP	PGA
1955		14		
1956	29			

IRWIN, Hale (US)

	MAS	USO	BOP	PGA
1971	13	19		22
1972				11
1973				9
1974	4	W	24	
1975	4	3	9	5
1976	5	26		
1977	5			
1978	8	4	24	12
1979	23	W	6	
1980	25	8		30
1981				16
1983	6		2	14
1984	21	6	14	25
1985		14		
1986				26
1988		17		
1990		W		12
1991	10	11		
1992			19	
1993	27			6
1994	18	18		
1995	14			
1996	29			
1997				29

ISAACS, Jack (US)

	MAS	USO	BOP	PGA
1949		23		Last 32
1952				Last 16
1953				SF
1954				Last 32

ISHII, Tomoo (JAP)

	MAS	USO	BOP	PGA
1964	26			

IVERSON, Don (US)

	MAS	USO	BOP	PGA
1973				6
1974	29			

JACK, Reid [a] (SCO)

	MAS	USO	BOP	PGA
1959			5	
1960			16	

JACKLIN, Tony (ENG)

	MAS	USO	BOP	PGA
1963			30	
1965			25	
1966			30	
1967	16		5	
1968	22		18	
1969		25	W	25
1970	12	W	5	
1971			3	
1972	27		3	
1973			14	
1974			18	
1979			24	
1981			23	

JACKSON, D [a] (IRE)

	MAS	USO	BOP	PGA
1896			24	

JACKSON, F (ENG)

	MAS	USO	BOP	PGA
1902			23	

JACKSON, Gardner (US)

	MAS	USO	BOP	PGA
1961				19

JACKSON, Hugh (IRE)

	MAS	USO	BOP	PGA
1970			8	
1971			22	

JACKSON, James [a] (US)

	MAS	USO	BOP	PGA
1959		19		

JACOBS, JA (ENG)

	MAS	USO	BOP	PGA
1935			15	
1946			23	
1948			25	
1952			25	

JACOBS, John (ENG)

	MAS	USO	BOP	PGA
1952			27	
1953			14	
1954			20	
1955			12	
1956			16	
1961			20	

JACOBS, Tommy (US)

	MAS	USO	BOP	PGA
1958		10		
1959				14
1962		6		23
1963	28			8
1964		2		
1965	15	28		
1966	2			

JACOBSEN, Gary (US)

	MAS	USO	BOP	PGA
1977		5		

JACOBSEN, Peter (US)

	MAS	USO	BOP	PGA
1979				23
1980		22		10
1981	11			27
1982	20			
1983	20		12	3
1984	25	7	22	18
1985			11	10
1986	25			3
1987		24		20
1988		21		
1989		8	30	27
1990	30		16	26
1991	17			
1992				28
1993				28
1994			24	
1995				23
1996		23		

JAECKEL, Barry (US)

	MAS	USO	BOP	PGA
1976		28		

JAGGER, David (ENG)

	MAS	USO	BOP	PGA
1974			28	

JAMES, Mark (ENG)

	MAS	USO	BOP	PGA
1976			5	
1979			4	
1981			3	
1983			29	
1985			20	
1989			13	
1991			26	
1993			27	
1994			4	
1995			8	
1996			22	
1997			20	

JAMIESON, Jim (US)

	MAS	USO	BOP	PGA
1971				6
1972	5			2
1973	3			18
1974		26		

JANUARY, Don (US)

	MAS	USO	BOP	PGA
1958		7		
1959		19		
1960	20			5
1961	4			2
1962	20			27
1963	9	11		
1964	18	11		
1966	6	17		12
1967	16	3		W
1968	14	24		
1969	5			15
1970	12			12
1971	4	27		
1972		11		
1973	10			
1975		29		10
1976		14		2
1977	8			6
1978	11			19
1979				7
1981				19

JANZEN, Lee (US)

	MAS	USO	BOP	PGA
1992	·			21
1993		W		22
1994	30			
1995	12	13	24	23
1996	12	10		8
1997	26			4

JARMAN, Edward (ENG)

	MAS	USO	BOP	PGA
1934			13	

JENKINS, JLC [a] (SCO)

	MAS	USO	BOP	PGA
1914			8	

JENKINS, Tom (US)

	MAS	USO	BOP	PGA
1974				17
1976		26		

JEWELL, FC (ENG)

	MAS	USO	BOP	PGA
1922			12	
1923			25	

JIMENEZ, Miguel (SP)

	MAS	USO	BOP	PGA
1995		28		13
1996				24

JOB, Nick (ENG)

	MAS	USO	BOP	PGA
1978			22	
1981			14	

JOHANSSON, Per-Ulrik (SWE)

	MAS	USO	BOP	PGA
1995			15	
1996				8
1997	12			

JOHNS, Charlie (ENG)

	MAS	USO	BOP	PGA
1909			4	
1920			16	
1922			11	
1924			16	
1927			16	

JOHNSON, Gunnar (US)

	MAS	USO	BOP	PGA
1930				Last 32
1933				Last 32

JOHNSON, Howie (US)

	MAS	USO	BOP	PGA
1967		23		
1969		13		19
1970	18			
1971			20	

JOHNSON, Jimmy (US)

	MAS	USO	BOP	PGA
1949				Last 32

JOHNSON, Norman (ENG)

	MAS	USO	BOP	PGA
1961			14	

JOHNSON, Terl (US)

	MAS	USO	BOP	PGA
1938				Last 32
1945				Last 16
1956				QF

JOHNSTON, Bill (US)

	MAS	USO	BOP	PGA
1956				SF
1957	28			
1960			26	
1963				8

JOHNSTON, Harrison [a] (US)

	MAS	USO	BOP	PGA
1926		23		
1927		18		
1928		22		

JOHNSTON, JF [a] (SCO)

	MAS	USO	BOP	PGA
1862			6	
1863			11	

JOHNSTON, Ralph (US)

	MAS	USO	BOP	PGA
1971		27		
1973		13		
1974	15			
1975	20			

JOHNSTON, RH [a] (SCO)	MAS	USO	BOP	PGA
1891			28	

JOHNSTONE, JC (SCO)	MAS	USO	BOP	PGA
1905			18	
1911			29	

JOLLY, Herbert (ENG)	MAS	USO	BOP	PGA
1923			8	
1926			21	
1929			15	

JOLLY, Jack (US)	MAS	USO	BOP	PGA
1905		26		
1906		14		
1907		25		

JONES, Brian (AUS)	MAS	USO	BOP	PGA
1981			8	

JONES, DC (WAL)	MAS	USO	BOP	PGA
1933			22	

JONES, Ernest (ENG)	MAS	USO	BOP	PGA
1911			24	
1913			18	
1914			21	

JONES, Gordon (US)	MAS	USO	BOP	PGA
1965				20

JONES, Grier (US)	MAS	USO	BOP	PGA
1975		18		
1976		28		30
1977				25
1978				16

JONES, JW [a] (ENG)	MAS	USO	BOP	PGA
1952			27	

JONES, Jack (US)	MAS	USO	BOP	PGA
1952				Last 32

JONES, John (US)	MAS	USO	BOP	PGA
1898		8		
1901		12		
1908		5		

JONES, RT (Bobby) [a] (US)	MAS	USO	BOP	PGA
1920		8		
1921		5		
1922		2		
1923		W		
1924		2		
1925		2		
1926		W	W	
1927		11	W	
1928		2		
1929		W		
1930		W	W	
1934	13			
1935	25			
1937	29			
1938	16			
1942	28			

JONES, Rowland (ENG)	MAS	USO	BOP	PGA
1894			29	
1901			11	
1902			12	
1903			24	
1904			26	
1905			2	
1906			5	
1908			24	
1909			26	
1911			16	
1912			27	
1924			23	

JONES, Steve (US)	MAS	USO	BOP	PGA
1988	30			9
1990	20	8	16	
1996		W		

JORDAN, Pete (US)	MAS	USO	BOP	PGA
1995		21		
1996		27		

JOSEPH, Eddie (US)	MAS	USO	BOP	PGA
1947				Last 16

JOWLE, Frank (ENG)	MAS	USO	BOP	PGA
1946			18	
1948			18	
1955			3	

JURADO, Jose (ARG)	MAS	USO	BOP	PGA
1926			8	
1928			6	
1929			25	
1931			2	
1932		6		

KAISER, Bill (US)	MAS	USO	BOP	PGA
1935		21		

KANE, C (IRE)	MAS	USO	BOP	PGA
1954			17	

KANE, Jim (US)	MAS	USO	BOP	PGA
1992		23		

KARLSSON, Robert (SWE)	MAS	USO	BOP	PGA
1992			5	

KASE, Hideki (JAP)	MAS	USO	BOP	PGA
1997		28		

KAY, James
(SCO)

	MAS	USO	BOP	PGA
1887			12	
1890			11	
1891			14	
1892			5	
1893			6	
1895			25	
1896			14	
1897			25	
1898			12	
1900			22	
1905			30	
1906			30	

KAY, Robert
(US)

	MAS	USO	BOP	PGA
1956		24		Last 16

KEDDIE, James
(SCO)

	MAS	USO	BOP	PGA
1886			29	

KEISER, Herman
(US)

	MAS	USO	BOP	PGA
1940				Last 32
1941		26		
1942	22			
1946	W			
1947	24			
1948	10	14		
1949	11			
1950	14			
1957				Last 32

KELLER, Bob
(US)

	MAS	USO	BOP	PGA
1961				29

KELLY, Paul
(US)

	MAS	USO	BOP	PGA
1965				28

KENNEDY, Les
(US)

	MAS	USO	BOP	PGA
1949		19		

KENNETT, Tom
(US)

	MAS	USO	BOP	PGA
1920				Last 16

KENNETT, William
(US)

	MAS	USO	BOP	PGA
1927			29	

KENNEY, Dan
(US)

	MAS	USO	BOP	PGA
1914		20		
1922				Last 32

KENNY, Donald
(SCO)

	MAS	USO	BOP	PGA
1906			24	

KENNY, Joseph
(US)

	MAS	USO	BOP	PGA
1930				Last 32

KENYON, Ernest WH
(ENG)

	MAS	USO	BOP	PGA
1931			28	
1932			22	
1935			11	
1938			28	
1939			9	
1949			29	

KEPLER, Bob
(US)

	MAS	USO	BOP	PGA
1945				Last 16

KERRIGAN, Tom
(US)

	MAS	USO	BOP	PGA
1914		20		
1915		10		
1916		29		QF
1919		26		Last 16
1920		23		
1921			3	Last 32
1922				QF
1924		19		
1925		18		QF
1936		11		

KERTES, Stanley
(US)

	MAS	USO	BOP	PGA
1938		27		

KESSELRING, Gerald
(CAN)

	MAS	USO	BOP	PGA
1957		26		

KETTLEY, AF
(ENG)

	MAS	USO	BOP	PGA
1911			29	

KIDD, Harry
(SCO)

	MAS	USO	BOP	PGA
1907			23	

KIDD, Tom
(SCO)

	MAS	USO	BOP	PGA
1873			W	
1874			8	
1879			5	
1882			11	

KIDD, Willie
(SCO/US)

	MAS	USO	BOP	PGA
1919				Last 32
1920		30		
1927				Last 32
1928				Last 32

KIMBALL, Richard
(US)

	MAS	USO	BOP	PGA
1908		10		

KINCH, Henry
(US)

	MAS	USO	BOP	PGA
1921		23		
1927		22		

KINDER, Joe
(US)

	MAS	USO	BOP	PGA
1932				Last 16

KINDER, John
(US)

	MAS	USO	BOP	PGA
1931		21		
1940				Last 32

KING, Alex
(ENG)

	MAS	USO	BOP	PGA
1963			11	

296

KING, Sam
(ENG)

	MAS	USO	BOP	PGA
1935			22	
1936			28	
1937			29	
1938			23	
1939			3	
1947			6	
1948			7	
1949			4	
1950			9	
1952			5	
1953			7	
1954			8	
1957			24	
1958			30	
1959			5	

KING Jr, Tom
(ENG)

	MAS	USO	BOP	PGA
1927			27	

KING Sr, Tom
(ENG)

	MAS	USO	BOP	PGA
1922			22	

KINGSLEY, EC [a]
(US)

	MAS	USO	BOP	PGA
1948			11	

KINNELL, David
(SCO)

	MAS	USO	BOP	PGA
1898			6	
1903			18	
1906			11	
1908			5	

KINNELL, James
(SCO)

	MAS	USO	BOP	PGA
1895			23	
1897			20	
1898			15	
1899			7	
1901			7	
1902			6	
1903			15	
1905			4	
1906			28	
1907			28	
1910			8	

KINSMAN, George
(US)

	MAS	USO	BOP	PGA
1951		29		

KINSMAN, Robert
(SCO)

	MAS	USO	BOP	PGA
1876			11	
1879			18	
1882			29	
1885			27	

KIRK, Bob
(SCO)

	MAS	USO	BOP	PGA
1865			4	
1866			5	
1867			5	
1868			4	
1869			4	
1870			2	
1873			3	
1876			8	
1878			2	

KIRK, Eddie
(US)

	MAS	USO	BOP	PGA
1940		23		QF

KIRK, James
(SCO)

	MAS	USO	BOP	PGA
1882			28	

KIRK, Walter
(ENG)

	MAS	USO	BOP	PGA
1896			24	

KIRKALDY, Andrew
(SCO)

	MAS	USO	BOP	PGA
1879			2	
1880			7	
1888			6	
1889			2	
1890			4	
1891			2	
1892			13	
1893			4	
1894			3	
1895			3	
1896			14	
1897			10	
1898			21	
1899			3	
1900			10	
1901			18	
1902			10	
1903			11	
1904			7	
1905			24	

KIRKALDY, Hugh
(SCO)

	MAS	USO	BOP	PGA
1887			19	
1888			11	
1889			10	
1890			7	
1891			W	
1892			2	
1893			4	
1894			13	
1895			15	

KIRKALDY, John
(SCO)

	MAS	USO	BOP	PGA
1879			12	
1882			3	
1884			9	
1885			11	
1887			12	
1888			18	
1891			14	
1900			19	

KIRKWOOD Jr, Joe (US)

	MAS	USO	BOP	PGA
1948		21		
1949	7			
1950	14	5		
1951	20	21		
1952	19			
1957				Last 32

KIRKWOOD Sr, Joe (AUS/US)

	MAS	USO	BOP	PGA
1921			6	
1922		13	19	
1923		12	4	QF
1924		22		
1925			13	
1926			22	
1927			4	
1929		19		Last 32
1930				SF
1931			25	Last 32
1932		23		Last 32
1933		9	14	
1934		12	4	
1936	29			
1942				Last 16
1946		8		
1947		23		
1948		28		

KITE, Tom (US)

	MAS	USO	BOP	PGA
1972	27	19a		
1974		8		
1975	10			
1976	5		5	13
1977	13			13
1978	18	20	2	
1979	5		30	
1980	6		27	20
1981	5	20		4
1982	5	29		9
1983	2	20	29	
1984	6		22	
1985		13	8	12
1986	2			26
1987	24			10
1988			20	4
1989	18	9	19	
1990	14			
1992		W	19	21
1993			14	
1994	4		8	9
1996			27	
1997	2		10	5

KLEIN, Willie (US)

	MAS	USO	BOP	PGA
1923				Last 32
1926		9		
1927				Last 16
1928				Last 32
1931		23		
1933				Last 32
1936				Last 32

KNIGHT, Dick (US)

	MAS	USO	BOP	PGA
1959		10		

KNIGHT, G (ENG)

	MAS	USO	BOP	PGA
1946			21	

KNIGHT, James [a] (SCO)

	MAS	USO	BOP	PGA
1862			5	
1863			8	

KNIGHT, Reg (ENG)

	MAS	USO	BOP	PGA
1953			24	
1957			30	
1959			23	
1961			14	

KNIPE, J (ENG)

	MAS	USO	BOP	PGA
1949			14	

KNOX, Kenny (US)

	MAS	USO	BOP	PGA
1987		17		
1988				9
1991				4

KNUDSON, George (CAN)

	MAS	USO	BOP	PGA
1964				28
1965	10	17		20
1966	6			
1968	28			
1969	2			25

KOCH, Gary (US)

	MAS	USO	BOP	PGA
1979				10
1982		6		
1983		24	14	
1985	16		11	
1986	16	15	6	
1987	22			
1988	25		4	
1989			30	

KOCSIS, Charles [a] (US)

	MAS	USO	BOP	PGA
1936		14		
1937		10		
1938	22			
1951		16		
1952	14			
1959	22			

KOCSIS, Emerick (US)

	MAS	USO	BOP	PGA
1929		30		
1939				QF

KONO, Takaaki (JAP)

	MAS	USO	BOP	PGA
1969	13			
1970	12			
1972	19			

KOONTZ, Charles (US)

	MAS	USO	BOP	PGA
1927				Last 32

KOVACH, Steve (US)

	MAS	USO	BOP	PGA
1946		15		

KOWAL, Matt
(US)

	MAS	USO	BOP	PGA
1939		25		

KOZAK, Walter
(US)

	MAS	USO	BOP	PGA
1930		28		

KRAK, Mike
(US)

	MAS	USO	BOP	PGA
1956				Last 32
1957				Last 32

KRATZERT, Bill
(US)

	MAS	USO	BOP	PGA
1977	24	19		25
1978	5	6		12
1979	17			
1980	19			
1985	14			

KRINGLE, Frank
(US)

	MAS	USO	BOP	PGA
1945				Last 32

KROLL, Ed
(US)

	MAS	USO	BOP	PGA
1964				23

KROLL, Ted
(US)

	MAS	USO	BOP	PGA
1950		25		Last 16
1951	25			
1952	14	7		SF
1953	7	7		
1954		27		Last 16
1955				Last 32
1956		4		RU
1957				Last 16
1958	23			20
1959	14	11		25
1960	13	3		12
1961	24	27		4
1962	25			30
1964				23
1965		24		

KRUEGER, Alvin
(US)

	MAS	USO	BOP	PGA
1934		14		
1935		6		Last 16
1936				Last 32
1937				Last 32
1938		27		Last 32

KUNES, Gene
(US)

	MAS	USO	BOP	PGA
1932				Last 16
1934				SF
1935	28	21		
1940		16		
1941	19	20		Last 32
1942	10			
1944				Last 32
1946	29	19		
1947		19		
1951				Last 16

KURAMOTO, Masahiro
(JAP)

	MAS	USO	BOP	PGA
1982			4	
1986			30	

KYLE, Alex [a]
(SCO)

	MAS	USO	BOP	PGA
1939			20	

KYLE, DH [a]
(SCO)

	MAS	USO	BOP	PGA
1921			26	

LACEY, Arthur
(ENG)

	MAS	USO	BOP	PGA
1930			24	
1931			8	
1932			7	
1935			22	
1936			8	
1937			7	
1938			17	
1949			20	

LACEY, Charles
(US)

	MAS	USO	BOP	PGA
1930		7		SF
1932		23		Last 32
1938		22		

LAFFOON, Ky
(US)

	MAS	USO	BOP	PGA
1933		26		
1934	18	23		Last 16
1935	28	28		Last 16
1936	6	5		Last 32
1937	5	20		SF
1938	27			Last 32
1939	22	9		Last 32
1940				Last 32
1942				Last 16
1945				QF
1946	4			
1947				QF
1948				Last 16

LAFITTE, L
(FRA)

	MAS	USO	BOP	PGA
1920			13	

LAGERBLADE, Herbert
(US)

	MAS	USO	BOP	PGA
1916		15		
1919		26		

LAIDLAY, Johnny [a]
(SCO)

	MAS	USO	BOP	PGA
1885			13	
1886			8	
1887			4	
1888			10	
1889			4	
1890			11	
1891			18	
1893			2	
1895			17	
1896			18	
1897			29	
1900			26	
1901			7	

LAIDLAW, W
(SCO)

	MAS	USO	BOP	PGA
1935			17	
1937			7	

LAMB, David [a]
(ENG)

	MAS	USO	BOP	PGA
1876			12	

LAMB, Henry [a]
(ENG)

	MAS	USO	BOP	PGA
1873			9	
1876			7	
1879			15	
1882			11	

LAMBERGER, Larry
(US)

	MAS	USO	BOP	PGA
1946				Last 32

LAMBERT, John
(SCO)

	MAS	USO	BOP	PGA
1886			12	

LANCASTER, Neal
(US)

	MAS	USO	BOP	PGA
1995		4		

LANDRUM, Ralph
(US)

	MAS	USO	BOP	PGA
1983		8		

LANE, Barry
(ENG)

	MAS	USO	BOP	PGA
1991			17	
1993		16	13	
1994				25
1995			20	

LANGER, Bernhard
(GER)

	MAS	USO	BOP	PGA
1981			2	
1982			13	
1984			2	
1985	W		3	
1986	16	8	3	
1987	7	4	17	21
1988	9			
1989	26			
1990	7			
1991			9	
1992		23		
1993	W		3	
1994	25	23		25
1997	7			23

LANNER, Mats
(SWE)

	MAS	USO	BOP	PGA
1992			28	

L'ANSON, John
(ENG/US)

	MAS	USO	BOP	PGA
1896		22		

LARGE, Bill
(ENG)

	MAS	USO	BOP	PGA
1971			25	

LARGE, Harry
(ENG)

	MAS	USO	BOP	PGA
1930			21	

LARGE, William
(ENG)

	MAS	USO	BOP	PGA
1930				
			17	

LASSEN, EA (Bertie) [a]
(ENG)

	MAS	USO	BOP	PGA
1909			10	
1913			14	
1914			17	

LAWRIE, Paul
(SCO)

	MAS	USO	BOP	PGA
1992			22	
1993			6	
1994			24	

LEACH, Bill
(US)

	MAS	USO	BOP	PGA
1921				Last 32
1925				Last 32
1926				Last 16
1928		6		

LEACH, Fred
(ENG)

	MAS	USO	BOP	PGA
1911			27	
1912			17	
1914			21	
1920			29	
1921			6	
1924			23	

LEAVER, William
(ENG)

	MAS	USO	BOP	PGA
1903			8	
1906			12	
1908			13	

LEE, Robert
(ENG)

	MAS	USO	BOP	PGA
1985			25	
1986			21	

LEEDER, Malcolm
(ENG)

	MAS	USO	BOP	PGA
1963			20	

LEEDS, HC [a]
(US)

	MAS	USO	BOP	PGA
1898		8		

LEES, Arthur
(ENG)

	MAS	USO	BOP	PGA
1946			18	
1947			6	
1948			11	
1949			6	
1950			7	
1952			9	
1953			13	

LEES, Walter
(ENG)

	MAS	USO	BOP	PGA
1949			17	

LeGRANGE, Cobie
(SA)

	MAS	USO	BOP	PGA
1965			17	
1969			11	

LEHMAN, Tom
(US)

	MAS	USO	BOP	PGA
1993	3	19		
1994	2		24	
1995		3		
1996	18	2	W	14
1997	12	3	24	10

LEITCH, D [a]
(SCO)

	MAS	USO	BOP	PGA
1883			20	
1888			26	
1890			13	

LEITCH, Dan
(US)

	MAS	USO	BOP	PGA
1899		22		

LEMA, Tony
(US)

	MAS	USO	BOP	PGA
1963	2	5		13
1964	9	20	W	9
1965	21	8	5	
1966	22	4	30	

300

LEONARD, Justin (US)

	MAS	USO	BOP	PGA
1995				8
1996	27			5
1997	7		W	2

LEONARD, P (IRE)

	MAS	USO	BOP	PGA
1975			12	

LEONARD, Stan (CAN)

	MAS	USO	BOP	PGA
1955	8			
1956	24			
1957	11			
1958	4			
1959	4			
1960	9			
1961	15			
1962		25		
1963	21			

LEPRE, Charles (US)

	MAS	USO	BOP	PGA
1956				Last 32

LESLIE, R (US)

	MAS	USO	BOP	PGA
1897		21		

LESTER, Eric (ENG)

	MAS	USO	BOP	PGA
1953			17	
1954			20	
1956			22	
1957			15	
1958			8	
1961			26	

LEVI, Wayne (US)

	MAS	USO	BOP	PGA
1976		28		
1979		25		
1981	25			
1982	24			
1983	12			
1984	11			
1985	18			18
1986				30
1991				16
1993		25		

LEWIS, Alf (ENG)

	MAS	USO	BOP	PGA
1901			18	

LEWIS, Hugh (ENG)

	MAS	USO	BOP	PGA
1963			14	

LICHARDUS, Milton (Babe) (US)

	MAS	USO	BOP	PGA
1956				Last 32
1959				17

LIETZKE, Bruce (US)

	MAS	USO	BOP	PGA
1977	28	19		15
1978		20		
1979	6			16
1980			19	30
1981	11	17	6	4
1982	20			16
1983				6
1985	6			18
1986				5
1987				28
1991				2
1992	13			
1995				23

LINNARS, Dick (US)

	MAS	USO	BOP	PGA
1926				Last 16

LISTER, John (US)

	MAS	USO	BOP	PGA
1898		14		

LISTER, John (NZ)

	MAS	USO	BOP	PGA
1971			25	
1977		27		

LITTLE, Lawson (US)

	MAS	USO	BOP	PGA
1934		25a		
1935	6a		4a	
1936	20			
1937	19			
1938	10			
1939	3			
1940	19	W		
1941	8	17		
1942	7			
1946	21	10	10	Last 32
1947	14			
1949	23			
1950	9			
1951	6			Last 32
1956	28			

LITTLER, Gene (US)

Year	MAS	USO	BOP	PGA
1954	22	2		
1955	22	15		
1956	12			
1958		4		
1959	8	11		10
1960				18
1961	15	W		5
1962	4	8		23
1963	24	21		
1964	13	11		
1965	6	8		28
1966				3
1967	26			7
1968				30
1969	8			
1970	2	12		4
1971	4			
1973	17			
1974			18	28
1975	22			7
1976	12			22
1977	8			2
1978	24			
1979	10			16
1982		22		

LIVIE, David (US)

Year	MAS	USO	BOP	PGA
1912		30		

LLOYD, Joe (ENG/US)

Year	MAS	USO	BOP	PGA
1893			17	
1894			17	
1896		3		
1897		W	20	
1898		4		
1901		20		
1903		24		
1905		16		

LOCKE, AD (Bobby) (SA)

Year	MAS	USO	BOP	PGA
1936			8a	
1937			17a	
1938			10	
1939			9	
1946			2	
1947	14	3		
1948	10	4		
1949	13	4	W	
1950			W	
1951		3	6	
1952	21		W	
1953		14	8	
1954		5	2	
1955			4	
1957			W	
1958			16	
1959			29	

LOCKHART, Gordon (SCO)

Year	MAS	USO	BOP	PGA
1923			12	

LOCKWOOD, AG [a] (US)

Year	MAS	USO	BOP	PGA
1901		17		
1905		11		

LOEFFLER, Emil (HOL/US)

Year	MAS	USO	BOP	PGA
1921		10		Last 32
1922				QF

LOMAS, Jonathan (ENG)

Year	MAS	USO	BOP	PGA
1994			11	

LONARD, Peter (AUS)

Year	MAS	USO	BOP	PGA
1997			24	

LONG, Harold (US)

Year	MAS	USO	BOP	PGA
1927				Last 32

LONGMUIR, Bill (SCO)

Year	MAS	USO	BOP	PGA
1979			30	

LONGWORTH, Ted (US)

Year	MAS	USO	BOP	PGA
1929		23		
1932				Last 32
1944				Last 32

LONIE, JC (SCO)

Year	MAS	USO	BOP	PGA
1914			29	

LoPRESTI, Tom (US)

Year	MAS	USO	BOP	PGA
1936				Last 32

LOOS, Eddie (US)

Year	MAS	USO	BOP	PGA
1919				Last 32
1920		17		Last 32
1921		12		
1922		15		
1924		10		
1927		11		
1934		25		Last 32
1935				Last 32

LOTT, Lyn (US)

Year	MAS	USO	BOP	PGA
1976		8		
1977		7		25
1982		12		

LOTZ, Dick (US)

Year	MAS	USO	BOP	PGA
1970	18			8
1971	24	24		

LOVE III, Davis (US)

Year	MAS	USO	BOP	PGA
1989			23	17
1991		11		
1992	25			
1994		28		
1995	2	4		
1996	7	2		
1997	7	16	10	W

LOVE Jr, Davis (US)

Year	MAS	USO	BOP	PGA
1963		14		
1969			6	

LOVEKIN, WR (US)

Year	MAS	USO	BOP	PGA
1906		22		

LOVING, Ben (US)

	MAS	USO	BOP	PGA
1942				Last 32

LOVING, Elmer (US)

	MAS	USO	BOP	PGA
1913		11		

LOW Jr, George (SCO/US)

	MAS	USO	BOP	PGA
1899		2		
1900		6		
1901		9		
1902		12		
1904		23		
1905		15		
1906		11		
1907		5		
1908		12		
1909		27		
1910		12		
1911		15		
1915		7		

LOW Sr, George (SCO)

	MAS	USO	BOP	PGA
1878			18	
1882			13	

LOW, GW (George) (SCO)

	MAS	USO	BOP	PGA
1962			29	

LOWERY, Steve (US)

	MAS	USO	BOP	PGA
1994		16		
1995				8

LU, CS (TAI)

	MAS	USO	BOP	PGA
1983			29	

LU, Liang-Huan (TAI)

	MAS	USO	BOP	PGA
1964			24	
1971			2	
1974			5	

LUCAS, PB (Laddie) [a] (ENG)

	MAS	USO	BOP	PGA
1935			22	

LUMSDEN, A (ENG)

	MAS	USO	BOP	PGA
1894			30	

LUNN, Bob (US)

	MAS	USO	BOP	PGA
1968		24		30
1969				21
1970	10	3		
1971		27		9

LUTHER, Ted (US)

	MAS	USO	BOP	PGA
1934		12		
1935		26		

LYE, Mark (US)

	MAS	USO	BOP	PGA
1980		26		
1984	6			
1989		13		

LYLE, Sandy (SCO)

	MAS	USO	BOP	PGA
1979			19	
1980			12	
1981	28		14	
1982			8	
1984			14	
1985	25		W	
1986	11		30	
1987	17		17	
1988	W	25	7	
1990			16	
1991		16		16
1992			12	
1993	21			

LYNCH, Levi (US)

	MAS	USO	BOP	PGA
1935				Last 16

LYONS, Denny (US)

	MAS	USO	BOP	PGA
1973		20		12

LYONS, Toby (US)

	MAS	USO	BOP	PGA
1953		30		
1954				Last 32
1956				Last 16

McANDREWS, RG (SCO/US)

	MAS	USO	BOP	PGA
1897		21		
1898		8		
1900		23		

McBEE, Rives (US)

	MAS	USO	BOP	PGA
1966		13		

M'CACHNIE, G (SCO)

	MAS	USO	BOP	PGA
1874			10	

McCALLISTER, Blaine (US)

	MAS	USO	BOP	PGA
1988				25
1989				17
1990				19
1993		19		

McCALLISTER, Bob (US)

	MAS	USO	BOP	PGA
1962				11
1963		21		
1965				8

McCARRON, Scott (US)

	MAS	USO	BOP	PGA
1996	10			
1997	30	10		10

McCOLL, Bill (SCO)

	MAS	USO	BOP	PGA
1980			23	

McCULLOCH, Duncan (SCO)

	MAS	USO	BOP	PGA
1925			19	
1927			26	
1928			18	
1930			30	
1931			28	

McCULLOUGH, Mike (US)

	MAS	USO	BOP	PGA
1977		10		
1978		12		
1983			29	

McCUMBER, Mark (US)

Year	MAS	USO	BOP	PGA
1979				28
1984		16	8	
1985	18			
1986	11	8		
1987	12			5
1988	24			
1989		2		
1991	17			
1992		13		
1994				19
1995		13		
1996			2	

McDEEVER, Tom (SCO/US)

Year	MAS	USO	BOP	PGA
1904		29		

McDERMOTT, Fred (US)

Year	MAS	USO	BOP	PGA
1928				Last 32

McDERMOTT, John (US)

Year	MAS	USO	BOP	PGA
1910		2		
1911		W		
1912		W		
1913		8	5	
1914		9		

MacDONALD, Bob (US)

Year	MAS	USO	BOP	PGA
1913		28		
1915		3		
1916		8		Last 16
1919		29		SF
1920		10		QF
1922		13		
1925		15		
1926		27		
1927		29		
1928				Last 16
1932		27		

MacDONALD, Charles Blair [a] (SCO/US)

Year	MAS	USO	BOP	PGA
1897		11		
1900		30		

MacDONALD, Ian (ENG)

Year	MAS	USO	BOP	PGA
1963			14	

MacDONALD, John (ENG)

Year	MAS	USO	BOP	PGA
1960			21	
1963			20	
1964			19	

MacDONALD, Keith (ENG)

Year	MAS	USO	BOP	PGA
1962			27	
1966			26	
1968			24	

McDONALD, Robert (US)

Year	MAS	USO	BOP	PGA
1911		29		

MacDOWALL, James (SCO)

Year	MAS	USO	BOP	PGA
1926			28	
1934			16	

McELLIGOTT, Ed (US)

Year	MAS	USO	BOP	PGA
1928				Last 32

McEVOY, Peter [a] (ENG)

Year	MAS	USO	BOP	PGA
1979			17	

McEWAN, David (SCO)

Year	MAS	USO	BOP	PGA
1887			27	
1895			25	
1896			18	
1901			29	
1906			19	
1907			23	

McEWAN, Douglas (SCO)

Year	MAS	USO	BOP	PGA
1892			25	
1895			27	

McEWAN Jr, Peter (SCO)

Year	MAS	USO	BOP	PGA
1896			11	
1897			14	
1898			17	
1900			21	

McEWAN Sr, Peter (SCO)

Year	MAS	USO	BOP	PGA
1862			6	

McEWAN, William (SCO)

Year	MAS	USO	BOP	PGA
1890			9	
1892			19	
1893			28	
1899			24	
1902			25	
1907			30	

MacFARLANE, Willie (SCO/US)

Year	MAS	USO	BOP	PGA
1912		18		
1916				SF
1920		8		Last 32
1923				QF
1924				Last 16
1925		W		
1926		20		
1927		18		
1928		14		Last 16
1929		26		
1931				Last 16
1934	6			
1937		19		Last 32

MacFIE, Allan [a] (SCO)

Year	MAS	USO	BOP	PGA
1887			22	
1888			18	

McGEE, Jerry (US)

Year	MAS	USO	BOP	PGA
1971		13		22
1972	5			29
1974		30		
1976	15			8
1977	28	19		6
1978	11	27		
1979				12

McGINLEY, Paul (IRE)

Year	MAS	USO	BOP	PGA
1996			14	

McGOVERN, Jim (US)

Year	MAS	USO	BOP	PGA
1993				22
1994	5	13		

McGOWAN, Pat (US)

Year	MAS	USO	BOP	PGA
1978		27		
1980		16		
1983		13		4

McHALE Jr, James [a] (US)

Year	MAS	USO	BOP	PGA
1947		23		
1949		27		
1950			17	
1953		26		

McINTOSH, D (SCO/US)

Year	MAS	USO	BOP	PGA
1906		22		

McINTOSH, Gregor (SCO)

Year	MAS	USO	BOP	PGA
1949			20	

McINTYRE, Neal (US)

Year	MAS	USO	BOP	PGA
1926				Last 16
1929				Last 32
1932				Last 32

McKAY, James (SCO)

Year	MAS	USO	BOP	PGA
1890			29	

McKENNA, Charles (US)

Year	MAS	USO	BOP	PGA
1927				Last 32

McKENNA, John (IRE)

Year	MAS	USO	BOP	PGA
1951			28	

MacKENZIE, Fred (SCO/US)

Year	MAS	USO	BOP	PGA
1904		3		
1905		16		
1910			16	

MacKENZIE, JH (SCO)

Year	MAS	USO	BOP	PGA
1923			8	

MacKENZIE, Malcolm (ENG)

Year	MAS	USO	BOP	PGA
1992			5	
1993			27	

MacKENZIE, W Willis [a] (SCO)

Year	MAS	USO	BOP	PGA
1929			25	

MACKEY Jr, Lee (US)

Year	MAS	USO	BOP	PGA
1950		25		

MACKIE, Isaac (US)

Year	MAS	USO	BOP	PGA
1901		16		
1903		13		
1905		29		
1907		22		
1908		23		
1909		4		
1919		13		
1920				Last 32

MACKIE, John (US)

Year	MAS	USO	BOP	PGA
1902		29		

McCLELLAND, Doug (ENG)

Year	MAS	USO	BOP	PGA
1972			23	
1973			14	
1974			28	

MACKRELL, JN (US)

Year	MAS	USO	BOP	PGA
1896		16		

M'LEAN, Jack [a] (SCO)

Year	MAS	USO	BOP	PGA
1933			18	
1934			16	
1937			26	
1938			22	

McLEAN, George (SCO/US)

Year	MAS	USO	BOP	PGA
1916		19		Last 16
1919		5		SF
1920		30		SF
1921			26	QF
1923				SF
1926		16		

McLENDON, Mac (US)

Year	MAS	USO	BOP	PGA
1968		22		
1975				25
1978	29			

McLEOD, Fred (SCO/US)

Year	MAS	USO	BOP	PGA
1903		26		
1904		29		
1905		19		
1907		5		
1908		W		
1909		13		
1910		4		
1911		4		
1912		13		
1914		3		
1915		8		
1916		24		
1919		8		RU
1920		13		
1921		2		QF
1923				QF
1924				Last 32
1926			7	Last 32

McMINN, William (SCO)

Year	MAS	USO	BOP	PGA
1931			28	
1949			20	

MACNAMARA, TL (IRE)

Year	MAS	USO	BOP	PGA
1913			25	

McNAMARA, Frank (US)

Year	MAS	USO	BOP	PGA
1920		14		

McNAMARA, Tom
(US)

	MAS	USO	BOP	PGA
1905		20		
1907		14		
1908		10		
1909		2		
1910		5		
1911		29		
1912		2		
1913		16		
1914		13		
1915		2		
1916		15	Last 32	
1919		3	Last 16	

McNEILL, Hughie
(IRE)

	MAS	USO	BOP	PGA
1912			15	
1913			18	

McNICKLE, Artie
(US)

	MAS	USO	BOP	PGA
1978		16		
1979	17			28
1980				30

McNULTY, Mark
(ZIM)

	MAS	USO	BOP	PGA
1980			23	
1981			23	
1987			11	
1988	16	17	28	17
1989			11	
1990			2	8
1991				27
1992			28	
1993			14	
1994			11	15
1996			14	
1997		28		

McNULTY, Robert
(US)

	MAS	USO	BOP	PGA
1916				Last 32

McSPADEN, Harold
(US)

	MAS	USO	BOP	PGA
1934	7			
1935	19			
1936	15	18		QF
1937		20		RU
1938	16	16		Last 32
1939	12	9		
1940	17	12		SF
1941	9	7		Last 16
1942	18			Last 16
1944				QF
1945				Last 32
1946	29			SF
1947	4			
1948		12		

McWATT, Thomas
(SCO)

	MAS	USO	BOP	PGA
1886			12	

MADISON, Les
(US)

	MAS	USO	BOP	PGA
1936				Last 32

MAGEE, Andrew
(US)

	MAS	USO	BOP	PGA
1991	7			13
1992	19	17	5	

MAGEE, Jerry
(US)

	MAS	USO	BOP	PGA
1958		19		

MAGGERT, Jeff
(US)

	MAS	USO	BOP	PGA
1992				6
1993	21			
1994		9	24	
1995		4		3
1996	7		5	
1997		4		3

MAGUIRE, Willie
(US)

	MAS	USO	BOP	PGA
1926				Last 32

MAHAFFEY, John
(US)

	MAS	USO	BOP	PGA
1973		29		30
1974		12		9
1975		2	10	28
1976		4		
1978				W
1980		28		15
1981	8			
1982		22		
1984		30		20
1985	14			23
1986			30	
1987		24		
1988				15

MAHON, PJ
(IRE)

	MAS	USO	BOP	PGA
1938			20	

MAIR, James [a]
(SCO)

	MAS	USO	BOP	PGA
1890			26	

MAIDEN, James
(US)

	MAS	USO	BOP	PGA
1905		26		
1906		3		
1909		27		

MAKALENA, Ted
(US)

	MAS	USO	BOP	PGA
1963		27		
1964		23		

MALLORY, Leo
(US)

	MAS	USO	BOP	PGA
1937		28		

MALTBIE, Roger
(US)

	MAS	USO	BOP	PGA
1976	9			
1977		26		
1983				14
1985				28
1986	23			
1987	4			28

MANERO, Tony
(US)

	MAS	USO	BOP	PGA
1927				Last 16
1928				Last 32
1929				QF
1931		19		
1933		29		
1935				Last 16
1936	W			QF
1937	13			SF
1938	27			Last 32
1939	26			Last 32
1940	29			
1944				Last 16

MANGRUM, Lloyd
(US)

	MAS	USO	BOP	PGA
1940	2	5		
1941	9	10		SF
1942				Last 16
1946	16	W		
1947	8	23		QF
1948	4	21		Last 32
1949	2	14		SF
1950	6	2		QF
1951	3	4		Last 16
1952	6	10		Last 32
1953	2	3	24	
1954	4	3		
1955	7			
1956	4			
1957	28			
1960		23		

MANGRUM, Ray
(US)

	MAS	USO	BOP	PGA
1935	13	4		Last 32
1936	6	11		Last 32
1937	24	14		
1938		27		Last 16
1939				Last 32
1940		27		Last 32
1941	28			

MANSFIELD, James [a]
(SCO)

	MAS	USO	BOP	PGA
1882			7	

MANTON, HR
(ENG)

	MAS	USO	BOP	PGA
1936			28	

MANZIE, R
(SCO)

	MAS	USO	BOP	PGA
1873			16	

MARCHBANK, Brian
(SCO)

	MAS	USO	BOP	PGA
1986			8	
1989			30	

MARR, Dave
(US)

	MAS	USO	BOP	PGA
1959		15		
1960		17		10
1961				22
1962	2			
1963		21		
1965				W
1966		4	8	18
1967	16	9		
1968	20			
1969		10		
1970		30		
1972			11	

MARSH, Graham
(AUS)

	MAS	USO	BOP	PGA
1970			25	
1975	22		6	
1976	9		17	
1977			15	
1978				7
1979	28	16	7	16
1981			19	
1982			25	
1983			4	
1984			9	
1985			20	
1987			11	

MARSHALL, William
(US)

	MAS	USO	BOP	PGA
1897		11		
1906		22		

MARSTON, Max [a]
(US)

	MAS	USO	BOP	PGA
1915		19		

MARTI, Elroy
(US)

	MAS	USO	BOP	PGA
1954				Last 16

MARTI, Fred
(US)

	MAS	USO	BOP	PGA
1969				25
1971				9

MARTIN, Bob
(SCO)

	MAS	USO	BOP	PGA
1873			10	
1874			4	
1875			2	
1876			W	
1878			4	
1879			21	
1881			4	
1882			3	
1885			W	
1887			2	
1888			16	

MARTIN, Doug
(US)

	MAS	USO	BOP	PGA
1997				23

MARTIN, Earl
(US)

	MAS	USO	BOP	PGA
1947				Last 32

MARTIN, Hutt
(US)

	MAS	USO	BOP	PGA
1923		29		

MARTIN, Iverson (US)	MAS	USO	BOP	PGA
1953	1953			Last 32

MARTIN, Jimmy (IRE)	MAS	USO	BOP	PGA
1960	1960		28	
1962	1962		16	
1964	1964		24	

MARTIN, Miguel (SP)	MAS	USO	BOP	PGA
1989	1989		30	

MARTINDALE, Bill (US)	MAS	USO	BOP	PGA
1966	1966			15

MARTUCCI, Louis (US)	MAS	USO	BOP	PGA
1919	1919			Last 32

MARUSIC, Milon (US)	MAS	USO	BOP	PGA
1951	1951			Last 32
1952	1952	15		Last 16
1957	1957			Last 16
1961	1961	29		

MARUYAMA, Shigeki (JAP)	MAS	USO	BOP	PGA
1996	1996		14	
1997	1997		10	23

MASON, Carl (ENG)	MAS	USO	BOP	PGA
1978	1978		24	
1980	1980		4	
1996	1996		22	

MASON, George (SCO)	MAS	USO	BOP	PGA
1891	1891		22	

MASSENGALE, Don (US)	MAS	USO	BOP	PGA
1966	1966			28
1967	1967			2
1972	1972	15		
1974	1974			24
1976	1976			22

MASSENGALE, Rik (US)	MAS	USO	BOP	PGA
1974	1974	30		
1975	1975	14		
1976	1976	23		30
1977	1977	3		26
1981	1981	26		

MASSY, Arnaud (FRA)	MAS	USO	BOP	PGA
1902	1902		10	
1905	1905		5	
1906	1906		6	
1907	1907		W	
1908	1908		9	
1910	1910		22	
1911	1911		2	
1912	1912		10	
1913	1913		7	
1914	1914		10	
1920	1920		29	
1921	1921		6	

MATTHEWS, Alf (ENG)	MAS	USO	BOP	PGA
1904	1904		23	
1906	1906		28	
1907	1907		17	

MATTIACE, Len (US)	MAS	USO	BOP	PGA
1997	1997	24		

MAXWELL, Billy (US)	MAS	USO	BOP	PGA
1955	1955	18	27	
1956	1956		12	
1957	1957		8	
1958	1958	9	27	25
1959	1959	8	26	11
1960	1960	25		24
1961	1961		22	27
1962	1962	5	8	
1963	1963	15	5	5
1964	1964	18		13
1965	1965	26	14	
1970	1970			10

MAXWELL, Robert [a] (SCO)	MAS	USO	BOP	PGA
1900	1900		7	
1902	1902		4	
1903	1903		13	
1904	1904		10	
1906	1906		7	
1909	1909		13	

MAY, Dick (ENG)	MAS	USO	BOP	PGA
1925	1925		23	

MAYER, Dick (US)	MAS	USO	BOP	PGA
1950	1950		12	
1951	1951	25		
1952	1952		28	
1953	1953	16		
1954	1954	29	3	
1955	1955	10		
1957	1957		W	QF
1958	1958		23	14
1959	1959	4		
1961	1961	19		
1963	1963	15		

MAYFAIR, Billy (US)	MAS	USO	BOP	PGA
1988	1988		25a	
1990	1990			5
1991	1991	12		
1992	1992		23	
1993	1993			28
1995	1995			23

MAYFIELD, Shelley (US)	MAS	USO	BOP	PGA
1954	1954		6	QF
1955	1955		12	SF
1956	1956	8	29	Last 32
1961	1961			22
1962	1962			30

MAYO, Charles (ENG/US)

	MAS	USO	BOP	PGA
1907			17	
1908			30	
1911			16	
1912			11	
1913			27	
1920				Last 16
1925		26		

MEARNS, Bob (SCO)

	MAS	USO	BOP	PGA
1890			23	
1891			14	
1893			23	

MEDIATE, Rocco (US)

	MAS	USO	BOP	PGA
1991	22			16
1993	25			
1996	18			

MEEHAN, James (US)

	MAS	USO	BOP	PGA
1923				Last 32

MEHLHORN, Bill (US)

	MAS	USO	BOP	PGA
1919				Last 32
1920		27		Last 16
1922		4	16	
1923		8		
1924		3		Last 32
1925		15		RU
1926		3	8	
1927		5		Last 32
1928			9	Last 32
1929				Last 16
1930		9		Last 32
1931		4		Last 16
1934				Last 32
1936				SF

MEISTER Jr, Edward [a] (US)

	MAS	USO	BOP	PGA
1962		25		

MELNYK, Steve (US)

	MAS	USO	BOP	PGA
1971	24			
1973	12			
1975		29		17
1977		16		

MENGERT, Al (US)

	MAS	USO	BOP	PGA
1953	23	21		
1954		13		
1955		16		
1956	24			
1957	21			
1958	9			
1961				29
1966		26		
1968				20
1970				18

MERCER, JH (US)

	MAS	USO	BOP	PGA
1898		23		

METZ, Dick (US)

	MAS	USO	BOP	PGA
1933				Last 32
1934				QF
1935		10		Last 32
1936	27	28		Last 32
1938	8	2		Last 16
1939		7		SF
1940	21	9		Last 16
1941	19	10		
1942				Last 32
1946		8		Last 32
1947	8	13		Last 16
1948	10			
1949	30			
1950		20		Last 32
1952		6		
1953	23	7		
1954		29		
1958		7		

MICKELSON, Phil (US)

	MAS	USO	BOP	PGA
1990		29a		
1993				6
1994				3
1995	7	4		
1996	3			
1997			24	29

MIDDLECOFF, Cary (US)

	MAS	USO	BOP	PGA
1946	12a			
1947	29			
1948	2	21		
1949	23	W		
1950	7	10		
1951	12	24		
1952	11	24		QF
1953	27			Last 32
1954	9	11		SF
1955	W	21		RU
1956	3	W		
1957		2	14	
1958	6	27		20
1959	2	19		8
1960				29
1961				11
1962	29			15

MIGUEL, Angel (SP)

	MAS	USO	BOP	PGA
1956			13	
1957			4	
1958			29	
1959	25			
1960			16	
1961			14	
1964		8		

MIGUEL, Sebastian (SP)

	MAS	USO	BOP	PGA
1957			15	
1958			26	
1960			26	
1961			14	
1962			12	
1963			9	
1965			8	
1966			8	
1967			6	
1968			21	

MILLAR, J (SCO)

	MAS	USO	BOP	PGA
1870			12	

MILLER, Allen (US)

	MAS	USO	BOP	PGA
1975	15			

MILLER, David (ENG)

	MAS	USO	BOP	PGA
1961			30	

MILLER, G [a] (SCO)

	MAS	USO	BOP	PGA
1883			19	

MILLER, James [a] (SCO)

	MAS	USO	BOP	PGA
1863			9	

MILLER, Johnny (US)

	MAS	USO	BOP	PGA
1966		8a		
1970		18		12
1971	2	5		20
1972		7	15	20
1973	6	W	2	18
1974	15		10	
1975	2		3	
1976	23	10	W	
1977		27	9	11
1978		6		
1981	2	23		
1982			22	
1983	12			30
1984		4		
1985	25	8		
1986	28			

MILLER, Lindy [a] (US)

	MAS	USO	BOP	PGA
1978	16			

MILLER, Massie (US)

	MAS	USO	BOP	PGA
1929		21		

MILLER, William (SCO)

	MAS	USO	BOP	PGA
1865			9	

MILLS, Peter (ENG)

	MAS	USO	BOP	PGA
1959			23	
1960			20	
1967			22	

MILNE, John (SCO)

	MAS	USO	BOP	PGA
1903			24	

MINER, RS (US)

	MAS	USO	BOP	PGA
1922				Last 16
1923				Last 32

MITCHELL, Abe (ENG)

	MAS	USO	BOP	PGA
1914			4	
1920			4	
1921			13	
1922		17	18	
1923			8	
1925			4	
1926			5	
1928			21	
1929			4	
1930			13	
1931			11	
1932			10	
1933			7	

MITCHELL, Bobby (US)

	MAS	USO	BOP	PGA
1969		25		
1970		12		
1971	22	27		
1972	2	21		
1974		23		

MITCHELL-INNES, G [a] (SCO)

	MAS	USO	BOP	PGA
1869			8	

MITCHELL, Joe (US)

	MAS	USO	BOP	PGA
1900		23		
1914		13		
1915		26		
1916		21		Last 16

MITCHELL, Peter (ENG)

	MAS	USO	BOP	PGA
1992			22	
1995			20	
1996			27	

MITCHELL, William [a] (SCO)

	MAS	USO	BOP	PGA
1862			6	
1863			13	

MIZE, Larry (US)

	MAS	USO	BOP	PGA
1984	11			6
1985				23
1986	16	24		
1987	W	4	26	
1988		12		
1989	26		19	17
1990	14	14		12
1991	17			
1992	6			
1993	21		27	
1994	3		11	15
1996	23			
1997	30			

MIZUMAKI, Yoshinori (JAP)

	MAS	USO	BOP	PGA
1993			27	

MOE, Donald [a] (US)

	MAS	USO	BOP	PGA
1930			15	

MOE, Kristen (US)

	MAS	USO	BOP	PGA
1985			25	

	MAS	USO	BOP	PGA

MOFFAT, William [a]
(SCO)

	MAS	USO	BOP	PGA
1863			14	

MOFFITT, Ralph
(ENG)

	MAS	USO	BOP	PGA
1960			21	
1961			26	
1962			11	
1964			13	

MONAGHAN, A
(SCO)

	MAS	USO	BOP	PGA
1887			17	

MONK, Arthur
(ENG)

	MAS	USO	BOP	PGA
1922			27	

MONTGOMERIE, Colin
(SCO)

	MAS	USO	BOP	PGA
1991			26	
1992		3		
1994		2	8	
1995	17	28		2
1996		10		
1997	30	2	24	13

MONTI, Eric
(US)

	MAS	USO	BOP	PGA
1949		11		
1950	30			
1955		28		
1958				20
1961		6	`	
1965		21		

MOODY, Orville
(US)

	MAS	USO	BOP	PGA
1969		W	16	8
1970	18			
1971	20	27		
1972		15		
1973				30
1978			11	
1979			19	

MOORE, Eric
(SA)

	MAS	USO	BOP	PGA
1950			5	
1956			25	
1958			16	

MOORE, Frank
(US)

	MAS	USO	BOP	PGA
1936		14		
1938		7		Last 32
1939	22			
1946				QF
1948		28		Last 32
1949				Last 32

MOORE, James
(SCO)

	MAS	USO	BOP	PGA
1878			21	

MORAN, Michael
(IRE)

	MAS	USO	BOP	PGA
1909			21	
1910			14	
1911			21	
1912			15	
1913			3	
1914			25	

MORE, WD
(ENG)

	MAS	USO	BOP	PGA
1891			5	
1892			21	

MORELAND, Gus [a]
(US)

	MAS	USO	BOP	PGA
1933		7		

MORGAN, Gil
(US)

	MAS	USO	BOP	PGA
1975				17
1976				8
1977				15
1978	18			4
1979				28
1980	19	16	10	3
1981	21			19
1982		22		22
1983	8	3		
1984	3	21	22	
1985		23		28
1987				21
1990				3
1991				16
1992		13		21
1993			14	

MORGAN, John
(ENG)

	MAS	USO	BOP	PGA
1974			13	
1978			29	

MORLEY, Mike
(US)

	MAS	USO	BOP	PGA
1976		14		15
1977		27		
1980		8		

MORRIS, JOF
(SCO)

	MAS	USO	BOP	PGA
1873			12	
1874			10	
1878			3	
1879			8	
1884			13	
1885			9	
1886			11	
1888			23	

MORRIS, Jack
(SCO)

	MAS	USO	BOP	PGA
1873			17	
1878			16	
1887			25	

MORRIS, Johnny
(US)

	MAS	USO	BOP	PGA
1941		26		

MORRIS Jr, Tom
(SCO)

	MAS	USO	BOP	PGA
1866			4	
1867			4	
1868			W	
1869			W	
1870			W	
1872			W	
1873			3	
1874			2	

311

MORRIS Sr, Tom (SCO)

	MAS	USO	BOP	PGA
1860			2	
1861			**W**	
1862			**W**	
1863			2	
1864			**W**	
1865			5	
1866			4	
1867			**W**	
1868			6	
1869			2	
1870			4	
1872			4	
1873			7	
1874			18	
1876			4	
1878			11	
1879			18	
1881			5	
1883			10	
1884			13	
1885			29	
1886			27	
1888			27	

MORRISON, Fred (US)

	MAS	USO	BOP	PGA
1929				Last 16
1932		14		

MORRISON, Hugh (SCO)

	MAS	USO	BOP	PGA
1875			8	

MORSE, John (US)

	MAS	USO	BOP	PGA
1996		4		

MOSEL, Stan [a] (US)

	MAS	USO	BOP	PGA
1952		28		

MOSES, JR (ENG)

	MAS	USO	BOP	PGA
1959			23	

MOTHERSOLE, Charles (US)

	MAS	USO	BOP	PGA
1921		22		Last 16
1923		16		

MOULAND, Mark (WAL)

	MAS	USO	BOP	PGA
1991			17	

MOWRY, Larry (US)

	MAS	USO	BOP	PGA
1969				11

MOZEL, Joe (US)

	MAS	USO	BOP	PGA
1944				Last 32

MUDD, Jodie (US)

	MAS	USO	BOP	PGA
1982	20a			
1986		15		
1987	4	17		
1989	7		5	
1990	30		4	
1991	7	26	5	
1992			28	

MUNDAY, Rod (US)

	MAS	USO	BOP	PGA
1939				QF
1942				Last 32
1950				Last 32
1951				Last 32

MUNGER, Jack [a] (US)

	MAS	USO	BOP	PGA
1936		28		

MUNN, LO [a] (ENG)

	MAS	USO	BOP	PGA
1932			29	

MUNRO, Jack (US)

	MAS	USO	BOP	PGA
1914		25		

MURE FERGUSSON, R [a] (SCO)

	MAS	USO	BOP	PGA
1891			4	

MURE FERGUSSON, S [a] (SCO)

	MAS	USO	BOP	PGA
1869			3	
1873			15	
1885			24	
1892			15	
1893			15	
1894			18	
1897			12	
1901			15	

MURPHY, Bob (US)

	MAS	USO	BOP	PGA
1966		15a		
1967		23a		
1969		5		
1970	23			2
1971	13			
1973		20		
1975		3		25
1976	28			
1977				25
1979		25		
1980	20			
1981	18			

MURPHY, Eddie (US)

	MAS	USO	BOP	PGA
1926		27		
1927				Last 32

MURRAY, A (SA)

	MAS	USO	BOP	PGA
1964			19	

MURRAY, AH (US)

	MAS	USO	BOP	PGA
1912		26		

MURRAY, Charles (SCO/CAN)

	MAS	USO	BOP	PGA
1904		11		
1905		29		
1909		30		
1912		9		
1913		21		
1921		21		

MURRAY, D (IRE)

Year	MAS	USO	BOP	PGA
1927			29	

MURRAY, Walter (US)

Year	MAS	USO	BOP	PGA
1931				Last 16

MUSCROFT, Hedley (ENG)

Year	MAS	USO	BOP	PGA
1967			18	
1969			28	

MYLES, Reggie (US)

Year	MAS	USO	BOP	PGA
1932				Last 16
1933				Last 32
1947				Last 16
1951				QF

NABHOLTZ, Larry (US)

Year	MAS	USO	BOP	PGA
1924				SF
1926				Last 32
1927		24		
1929				Last 16

NAGLE, Kel (AUS)

Year	MAS	USO	BOP	PGA
1951			19	
1955			20	
1960			W	
1961		17	5	
1962			2	
1963			4	
1964	21			
1965	15	2	5	20
1966			4	
1967		9	22	
1968	30		13	
1969			9	
1970		30		
1971			11	

NAKAJIMA, Tommy (JAP)

Year	MAS	USO	BOP	PGA
1978			17	
1983	16	26		
1984				10
1986	8		8	
1987		9		
1988				3
1991	10			
1992				21

NAKAMURA, Tohru (JAP)

Year	MAS	USO	BOP	PGA
1979			24	
1982			20	
1983			29	

NARY, Bill (US)

Year	MAS	USO	BOP	PGA
1947		13		
1950		8		
1951	25			
1953		17		QF
1954				Last 32
1955				Last 32

NEAVES, Charles (SCO)

Year	MAS	USO	BOP	PGA
1901			22	

NELSON, Al (US)

Year	MAS	USO	BOP	PGA
1946				Last 32

NELSON, Byron (US)

Year	MAS	USO	BOP	PGA
1932				Last 32
1935	9			
1936	13			
1937	W	20	5	QF
1938	5	5		QF
1939	7	W		RU
1940	3	5		W
1941	2	17		RU
1942	W			SF
1944				RU
1945				W
1946	7	2		QF
1947	2			
1948	8			
1949	8			
1950	4			
1951	8			
1952	24			
1953	29			
1954	12			
1955	10	28		
1957	16			
1958	20			
1965	15			

NELSON, CP (US)

Year	MAS	USO	BOP	PGA
1911		14		
1914		28		

NELSON, Gunnar (US)

Year	MAS	USO	BOP	PGA
1926				Last 32
1932				Last 32

NELSON, Larry (US)

Year	MAS	USO	BOP	PGA
1976		21		
1978				12
1979		4		28
1980	6		12	
1981		20		W
1982	7	19		
1983		W		
1984	5			
1985				23
1987				W
1988			13	
1989		13		
1990		14		
1991		3		
1992				28

NELSON, Wallie (US)

Year	MAS	USO	BOP	PGA
1920				Last 32

NETTLEBLADT, Harry (US)

	MAS	USO	BOP	PGA
1938				Last 32
1940				Last 32
1942				Last 32
1944				Last 32
1945				Last 32

NEWTON, Jack (AUS)

	MAS	USO	BOP	PGA
1975			2	
1976			17	
1978			24	
1979	12			
1980	2		10	20

NICHOLLS, Bernard (ENG/US)

	MAS	USO	BOP	PGA
1897		6		
1898		8		
1899		17		
1901		5		
1902		28		
1903		19		
1904		4		
1905		20		
1906		10		
1907		8		
1909			10	

NICHOLLS, Gilbert (US)

	MAS	USO	BOP	PGA
1898		23		
1899		20		
1901		14		
1902		18		
1903		15		
1904		2		
1905		7		
1906		8		
1907		2		
1909		17		
1910		5		
1911		5		
1915		10		
1916		4		
1919		16		
1920		23		
1924			13	

NICHOLS, Bobby (US)

	MAS	USO	BOP	PGA
1962		3		6
1963	24	14		23
1964	25	14		W
1966	22	7		
1967	2	23		14
1968	30	4		
1969	29			
1970				26
1971		9		
1972		11		
1973	24	20		
1974	7			
1975	4			
1978				19
1979		25		

NICKLAUS, Jack (US)

	MAS	USO	BOP	PGA
1960	13a	2a		
1961	7a	4a		
1962	15	W		3
1963	W		3	W
1964	2	23	2	2
1965	W		12	2
1966	W	3	W	22
1967		W	2	3
1968	5	2	2	
1969	24	25	6	11
1970	8		W	6
1971	2	2	5	W
1972	W	W	2	13
1973	3	4	4	W
1974	4	10	3	2
1975	W	7	3	W
1976	3	11	2	4
1977	2	10	2	3
1978	7	6	W	
1979	4	9	2	
1980		W	4	W
1981	2	6	23	4
1982	15	2	10	16
1983			29	2
1984	18	21		25
1985	6			
1986	W	8		16
1987	7			24
1988	21		25	
1989	18		30	27
1990	6			
1991				23
1993	27			
1994		28		
1996		27		

NICOLETTE, Mike (US)

	MAS	USO	BOP	PGA
1983		13		

NIELSON, Lonnie (US)

	MAS	USO	BOP	PGA
1986				11

314

NIEPORTE, Tom (US)

	MAS	USO	BOP	PGA
1958		17		
1960				18
1962				30
1964	5			26

NOBILO, Frank (NZ)

	MAS	USO	BOP	PGA
1990			16	
1993				22
1994		9	11	
1995		10		
1996	4	13	27	
1997			10	29

NOKE, Eddie (ENG)

	MAS	USO	BOP	PGA
1952			21	

NOLAN, William (IRE)

	MAS	USO	BOP	PGA
1929			23	
1934			21	

NORDONE, Augie (US)

	MAS	USO	BOP	PGA
1941				Last 32
1945				Last 32

NORMAN, Greg (AUS)

	MAS	USO	BOP	PGA
1978			29	
1979			10	
1981	4			4
1982			27	5
1983	30		19	
1984	25	2	6	
1985		15	16	2
1986	2	12	W	
1987	2			
1988	5			9
1989	3		2	12
1990		5	6	19
1991			9	
1992	6		18	15
1993			W	2
1994	18	6	11	4
1995	3	2	15	20
1996	2	10	7	
1997				13

NORTH, Andy (US)

	MAS	USO	BOP	PGA
1975		12		4
1976		14		
1977	24			
1978		W		
1979	12	11		
1980	24	8		15
1981				11
1982		22		
1983	30	10		
1985		W		
1990	27			

NORTON, Willie (ENG/US)

	MAS	USO	BOP	PGA
1896		26		
1900		19		
1902		11		
1903		20		

OAKLEY, Bud (US)

	MAS	USO	BOP	PGA
1941				Last 32

OBENDORF, Herbert (US)

	MAS	USO	BOP	PGA
1923				Last 32

O'BRIEN, JJ (US)

	MAS	USO	BOP	PGA
1914		13		
1916		9		QF
1920		23		

OCKENDEN, James (ENG)

	MAS	USO	BOP	PGA
1911			29	
1914			7	
1923			25	
1925			19	
1928			23	

O'CONNOR Jr, Christy (IRE)

	MAS	USO	BOP	PGA
1983			8	
1985			3	
1986			11	
1990			25	

O'CONNOR Sr, Christy (IRE)

	MAS	USO	BOP	PGA
1953			24	
1954			20	
1955			10	
1956			10	
1957			19	
1958			3	
1959			5	
1961			3	
1962			16	
1963			6	
1964			6	
1965			2	
1966			13	
1967			21	
1969			5	
1970			17	
1972			23	
1973			7	
1974			24	
1976			5	

O'CONNOR, Tom (US)

	MAS	USO	BOP	PGA
1939				Last 16

O'DONNELL, John (US)

	MAS	USO	BOP	PGA
1954				Last 32

OGDEN, Bill (US)

	MAS	USO	BOP	PGA
1953		12		
1956		17		
1963		30		
1965		21		

OGG, Willie (US)

	MAS	USO	BOP	PGA
1922		19	Last 32	
1923		18	Last 16	
1924		15	Last 32	
1925			Last 32	
1928			Last 32	

OGILVIE, David (SCO/US)

	MAS	USO	BOP	PGA
1903		20		
1907		26		
1908		27		
1909		18		
1912		16		
1915		29		

OGILVIE, W (SCO/US)

	MAS	USO	BOP	PGA
1907		30		

OGLE, Brett (AUS)

	MAS	USO	BOP	PGA
1995		21	11	

O'GRADY, Mac (US)

	MAS	USO	BOP	PGA
1987		9		
1988	30			

OGRIN, David (US)

	MAS	USO	BOP	PGA
1983		13		
1997		10		

O'HARA, Pat (US)

	MAS	USO	BOP	PGA
1920				Last 32
1921		30		Last 32

O'HARA, Peter (US)

	MAS	USO	BOP	PGA
1920		27		QF
1921		18		Last 32
1924		7		
1929		8		
1930		11		
1931				Last 16

OKE, JH (ENG)

	MAS	USO	BOP	PGA
1901			15	
1903			29	
1907			28	

OKE, William (ENG)

	MAS	USO	BOP	PGA
1931			16	

OLAZABAL, Jose-Maria (SP)

	MAS	USO	BOP	PGA
1985			25a	
1986			16	
1987			11	
1989	8	9	23	
1990	13	8	16	14
1991	2	8		
1992			3	
1993	7			
1994	W			7
1995	14	28		
1997	12	16	20	

O'LEARY, John (IRE)

	MAS	USO	BOP	PGA
1977			26	
1979			13	

OLIVER, Ed (US)

	MAS	USO	BOP	PGA
1939		29		
1940	19			
1946		6		RU
1947	8	3		Last 16
1948				Last 16
1951		24		Last 32
1952	30	2		
1953	2			
1954	22			Last 16
1957		22		
1958				8
1959	14			11
1960	20			

O'LOUGHLIN, Martin (IRE/US)

	MAS	USO	BOP	PGA
1907		16		
1910		23		

O'MALLEY, Peter (AUS)

	MAS	USO	BOP	PGA
1997			7	

O'MEARA, Mark (US)

	MAS	USO	BOP	PGA
1984		7		25
1985	24	15	3	28
1987	24			
1988		3	27	9
1989	11			
1990				19
1991	27		3	
1992	4		12	
1993	21			
1994	15			
1995				6
1996	18	16		
1997	30			13

O'NEILL, George (US)

	MAS	USO	BOP	PGA
1906		29		

OOSTERHUIS, Peter (ENG)

	MAS	USO	BOP	PGA
1970			6	
1971			18	
1972			28	
1973	3		18	
1974			2	
1975		7	7	
1976	23			
1977		10		
1978	14	27	6	26
1980			23	
1982	24	30	2	22
1983	20			
1984		25		

OOSTHUIZEN, Andries (SA)

	MAS	USO	BOP	PGA
1975			12	

OPPERMAN, Steve (US)

	MAS	USO	BOP	PGA
1965		15		

OSBORNE, HE (ENG)

	MAS	USO	BOP	PGA
1949			26	

OSBORNE, HJ (Herbert) (ENG)

	MAS	USO	BOP	PGA
1922			19	

OTT, Leonard (US)

	MAS	USO	BOP	PGA
1941				Last 16

OUIMET, Francis [a] (US)

	MAS	USO	BOP	PGA
1913	W			
1914	5			
1919	18			
1923	29			
1925	3			

OVERTON, Jay (US)

	MAS	USO	BOP	PGA
1988				17

OWEN, Simon (NZ)

	MAS	USO	BOP	PGA
1978			2	
1979			13	
1981			23	

OZAKI, M (Jumbo) (JAP)

	MAS	USO	BOP	PGA
1973	8			
1978			14	
1979			10	
1987		17	11	
1989	18	6	30	
1990	23	24		
1992		23		
1994		28		
1995	29	28		

OZAKI, N (Joe) (JAP)

	MAS	USO	BOP	PGA
1992				28
1993		25		

PADGETT, Don (ENG)

	MAS	USO	BOP	PGA
1977		27		

PADGHAM, Alf (ENG)

	MAS	USO	BOP	PGA
1932			4	
1933			7	
1934			3	
1935			2	
1936			W	
1937			7	
1938			4	
1946			30	
1947			13	
1948			7	
1950			20	

PALETTI, Joe (US)

	MAS	USO	BOP	PGA
1934				Last 32

PALMER, Arnold (US)

	MAS	USO	BOP	PGA
1955	10	21		
1956	21	7		
1957	7			
1958	W	23		
1959	3	5		14
1960	W	W	2	7
1961	2	14	W	5
1962	W	2	W	17
1963	9	3	26	
1964	W	5		2
1965	2		16	
1966	4	2	8	6
1967	4	2		14
1968			10	2
1969	27	6		2
1970			12	
1971	18	24		18
1972		3	7	16
1973	24	4	14	
1974	11	5		28
1975	13	9	16	
1976				15
1977		19	7	19
1980	24			
1981			23	
1982			27	

PALMER, Johnny (US)

	MAS	USO	BOP	PGA
1941		21		
1942	26			
1947	17	6		
1948	28			Last 32
1949	4	8		RU
1950	24	10		QF
1951	30	24		
1952	12			
1953	13			
1955	18			Last 16
1956	11			
1957	24			

PANTON, John (SCO)

	MAS	USO	BOP	PGA
1950			20	
1951			11	
1952			15	
1953			27	
1956			5	
1957			15	
1959			5	
1962			16	
1965			10	
1970			9	

PARK, David (SCO)

	MAS	USO	BOP	PGA
1861			4	
1863			3	
1866			2	
1872			4	
1874			6	

317

PARK, Jack
(SCO/US)

	MAS	USO	BOP	PGA
1899		6		
1901		9		
1902		25		
1915		10		

PARK, Mungo
(SCO)

	MAS	USO	BOP	PGA
1874			W	
1875			3	
1876			4	
1877			7	
1878			17	
1880			20	
1883			27	

PARK Jr, Willie
(SCO)

	MAS	USO	BOP	PGA
1880			15	
1881			5	
1882			18	
1883			8	
1884			4	
1885			4	
1886			4	
1887			W	
1888			11	
1889			W	
1890			4	
1891			6	
1892			7	
1893			19	
1894			12?	
1896			14	
1897			22	
1898			2	
1899			14	
1900			6	
1901			18	
1902			23	
1903			15	
1904			12	
1905			13	

PARK Sr, Willie
(SCO)

	MAS	USO	BOP	PGA
1860			W	
1861			2	
1862			2	
1863			W	
1864			4	
1865			2	
1866			W	
1867			2	
1868			3	
1870			6	
1874			13	
1875			W	
1876			3	
1878			6	
1880			14	
1882			7	
1883			22	

PARKIN, Philip
(WAL)

	MAS	USO	BOP	PGA
1985			25	
1986			21	

PARKS Jr, Sam
(US)

	MAS	USO	BOP	PGA
1935	15	W		Last 16
1936	20			
1937		16		Last 32
1938	24			
1940		29		
1941	19			
1942				Last 32

PARNEVIK, Jesper
(SWE)

	MAS	USO	BOP	PGA
1993			21	
1994			2	
1995			24	20
1997	21		2	

PARRY, Craig
(AUS)

	MAS	USO	BOP	PGA
1990			22	
1991		11	8	
1992	13		28	
1993		3		
1994	30	25		19

PATE, Jerry
(US)

	MAS	USO	BOP	PGA
1975		18a		
1976		W		4
1977	14		15	5
1978	18	16		2
1979		2	26	5
1980	6		16	10
1981	5	26	19	11
1982	3			9
1983				23

PATE, Steve
(US)

	MAS	USO	BOP	PGA
1987		24		
1988		3		
1989	26		13	
1990			8	
1991	3			7
1992	6		4	
1993		19		
1994		21		

PATRICK, Alexander
(SCO)

	MAS	USO	BOP	PGA
1878			15	

PATRICK, AH
(SCO/US)

	MAS	USO	BOP	PGA
1896		16		
1899		13		

PATRICK, John
(SCO/US)

	MAS	USO	BOP	PGA
1895		7		
1896		19		

PATRICK, N
(SCO)

	MAS	USO	BOP	PGA
1874			27	

PATRICK, RS
(SCO/US)

	MAS	USO	BOP	PGA
1899		27		
1901		25		
1902		30		

PATRONI, Jack
(US)

	MAS	USO	BOP	PGA
1932		23		
1936				Last 32
1949				Last 16

PATTON, Billy Joe [a]
(US)

	MAS	USO	BOP	PGA
1954	3	6		
1956	12	13		
1957		8		
1958	8			
1959	8			
1960	13			

PATTON, Mike
(US)

	MAS	USO	BOP	PGA
1925				Last 32
1926				Last 32

PAULSEN, Guy
(US)

	MAS	USO	BOP	PGA
1929				Last 32
1931		13		

PAUTKE, Ben
(US)

	MAS	USO	BOP	PGA
1933				Last 32

PAVELLA, Mike
(US)

	MAS	USO	BOP	PGA
1951				Last 32
1955				Last 32

PAVIN, Corey
(US)

	MAS	USO	BOP	PGA
1984			22	20
1985	25	9		6
1986	11			21
1987	27			
1988				17
1990		24	8	14
1991	22	8		
1992	3			12
1993	11	19	4	
1994	8			2
1995	17	W	8	
1996	7		27	

PAXTON, Edwin
(SCO)

	MAS	USO	BOP	PGA
1878			13	
1879			23	

PAXTON, George
(SCO)

	MAS	USO	BOP	PGA
1874			3	
1876			8	
1879			4	
1880			4	
1883			5	

PAXTON, James
(SCO)

	MAS	USO	BOP	PGA
1863			10	

PAXTON, Peter
(SCO)

	MAS	USO	BOP	PGA
1880			2	
1883			10	
1885			8	
1886			23	
1896			30	
1898			21	
1900			19	

PAYTON, George
(US)

	MAS	USO	BOP	PGA
1947		19		

PEACH, Stanley
(AUS)

	MAS	USO	BOP	PGA
1967			13	

PEARCE, Eddie
(US)

	MAS	USO	BOP	PGA
1975		14		
1976				28

PEARSON, George
(US)

	MAS	USO	BOP	PGA
1897		21		

PEEBLES, Frank
(SCO/US)

	MAS	USO	BOP	PGA
1912		10		

PEEBLES, Robert
(SCO/US)

	MAS	USO	BOP	PGA
1905		28		
1908		12		
1914		13		
1916		15		

PEEBLES, Tom
(SCO/US)

	MAS	USO	BOP	PGA
1909		7		

PEETE, Calvin
(US)

	MAS	USO	BOP	PGA
1976		23		
1979		11		
1980	19	28		
1981	21	14		
1982	30	10		3
1983		4		
1984	15			4
1985				18
1986	11	24		30

PEMBERTON, RH (Bob)
(ENG)

	MAS	USO	BOP	PGA
1938			28	

PENECALE, Sam
(US)

	MAS	USO	BOP	PGA
1957		26		

PENNA, Toney
(US)

	MAS	USO	BOP	PGA
1937		28		
1938		3		
1939	10			
1940	10			
1941	19			Last 32
1942	22			Last 16
1944				Last 16
1945				Last 16
1946	21	15		Last 32
1947	8			Last 32
1948		8		
1949	23			
1959	21			
1951				Last 32

PERELLI, Johnny
(US)

	MAS	USO	BOP	PGA
1927				Last 32
1932				Last 16

PERKINS, Phil
(ENG/US)

	MAS	USO	BOP	PGA
1927			9a	
1928			14a	
1929			23a	
1931		7a		
1932		2		
1934		21		
1935	28			

PERNICE, Tom
(US)

	MAS	USO	BOP	PGA
1989		13		

PERRY, Alf
(ENG)

	MAS	USO	BOP	PGA
1930			30	
1932			17	
1933			26	
1934			26	
1935			W	
1938			15	
1939			3	
1946			25	
1947			18	
1948			23	

PERRY, Chris
(US)

	MAS	USO	BOP	PGA
1987				28
1989				17
1990				26

PERRY, Kenny
(US)

	MAS	USO	BOP	PGA
1993		25		
1995	12			
1996			2	
1997				23

PERSONS, Peter
(US)

	MAS	USO	BOP	PGA
1991		19		

PFEIL, Mark
(US)

	MAS	USO	BOP	PGA
1982				22
1983				30

PHELPS, Mason
(US)

	MAS	USO	BOP	PGA
1911		20		

PHILLIPS, Frank
(AUS)

	MAS	USO	BOP	PGA
1963			18	
1964			12	

PICARD, Henry
(US)

	MAS	USO	BOP	PGA
1932				Last 16
1933				Last 16
1934	23			
1935	4	6	6	
1936	9	5		Last 16
1937		10	15	QF
1938	W	7		SF
1939	8	12		W
1940	7	12		Last 16
1941		26		
1942	15			
1946	25	12		
1947	6			
1948	25			
1949	21			
1950	14	12		SF
1951		24		Last 32

PINERO, Manuel
(SP)

	MAS	USO	BOP	PGA
1981			6	
1985			25	
1986			19	

PIPER, J
(ENG)

	MAS	USO	BOP	PGA
1911			13	

PIRIE, Jack
(US)

	MAS	USO	BOP	PGA
1921				Last 32

PITTMAN, Jerry
(US)

	MAS	USO	BOP	PGA
1958		17		
1967		16		
1968	7	7		

PLATTS, Lionel
(ENG)

	MAS	USO	BOP	PGA
1961			20	
1962			24	
1967			13	

PLAYER, Gary (SA)

	MAS	USO	BOP	PGA
1956			4	
1957	24		24	
1958		2	7	
1959	8	15	W	
1960	6	19	7	
1961	W	9		29
1962	2	6		W
1963	5	8	7	8
1964	5	23	8	13
1965	2	W		
1966	28	15	4	3
1967	6	12	3	
1968	7	16	W	
1969			23	2
1970	3			12
1971	6	27	7	4
1972	10	15	6	W
1973		12	14	
1974	W	8	W	7
1975	30			
1976	28	23	28	13
1977	19	10	22	
1978	W	6		26
1979	17	2	19	23
1980	6			26
1981	15	26		
1982	15			
1983		20		
1984	21			2
1990	24			

PLAYFAIR, N [a] (SCO)

	MAS	USO	BOP	PGA
1888			25	

PLEMMONS, Broyles (US)

	MAS	USO	BOP	PGA
1953				Last 32

POHL, Dan (US)

	MAS	USO	BOP	PGA
1981				3
1982	2	3		
1983	8			8
1985				12
1986				26
1987		9		14
1988	16	12		8
1989		29		24

POLLAND, Eddie (IRE)

	MAS	USO	BOP	PGA
1973			18	

POLLOCK, R [a] (SCO)

	MAS	USO	BOP	PGA
1862			6	

POMEROY, Ewing (US)

	MAS	USO	BOP	PGA
1957				Last 32

POOLEY, Don (US)

	MAS	USO	BOP	PGA
1981	19			19
1983				23
1985		15		
1986		24		16
1987		24		5
1988	5		16	
1989	14	26	19	
1990				8
1997				29

POPE, Charles (ENG)

	MAS	USO	BOP	PGA
1912			27	

PORTER, Joe (US)

	MAS	USO	BOP	PGA
1976				29

POSE, Martin (ARG)

	MAS	USO	BOP	PGA
1939			8	
1941	29			

POTT, Johnny (US)

	MAS	USO	BOP	PGA
1959		19		
1960		15		15
1961	19			5
1962	20			27
1963	21			
1964	13	9		
1965				28
1969				
		28		19

POULTON, Alan (Tiger) (ENG)

	MAS	USO	BOP	PGA
1951			28	
1952			25	
1953			29	

POWERS, Greg (US)

	MAS	USO	BOP	PGA
1978				26
1982		30		

PRICE, Nick (ZIM)

	MAS	USO	BOP	PGA
1980			27	
1981			23	
1982			2	
1985				5
1986	5			
1987	22	17	8	10
1988	14		2	17
1990			25	
1991		19		
1992	6	4		W
1993		11	6	
1994			W	W
1995		13		
1996	18			
1997	24	19		13

	MAS	USO	BOP	PGA

PRICE, Terry
(AUS)

1994			24	

PRINGLE, Bob
(SCO)

1873			21	
1874			14	
1875			7	
1877			2	
1878			22	
1880			4	
1882			23	
1883			4	
1886			16	

PROWSE, H
(ENG)

1932			13	

PRUITT, Dillard
(US)

1992	13			

PULFORD, George
(ENG)

1895			4	
1897			3	
1898			13	
1902			22	
1903			18	
1906			30	
1907			3	
1908			18	
1909			10	

PURSE, W
(US)

1932			29	

PURSEY, W
(ENG)

1921			13	
1922			22	

PURTZER, Tom
(US)

1977		4		
1978		24		
1979		8		
1981				19
1982			4	16
1984	25	16	.	
1989	24			
1992			22	21

PYMAN, Iain [a]
(ENG)

1993			27	

QUICK, Smiley
(US)

1946		26a		
1948		8		
1951		10		
1952	27			
1955		16		

QUIGLEY, N
(ENG)

1947			27	

RACHELS, Sammy
(US)

1981		6		

RAFFERTY, Ronan
(IRE)

1984			9	
1986			21	
1990	14			
1994			11	

RAGAN, Dave
(US)

1960	25			22
1962	25			7
1963		12		2

RAINFORD, Peter
(ENG)

1899			16	
1902			28	
1909			14	

RAJOPPI, TJ
(US)

1921				Last 32

RANDOLPH, Sam [a]
(US)

1985	18			

RANSOM, Henry
(US)

1940		29		
1941		13		
1946		22		Last 32
1947		29		Last 32
1948				Last 16
1949				Last 32
1950		5		
1951	25	16		
1953				QF
1954				Last 32
1956				QF
1957	21			Last 16
1959		28		

RASSETT, Joey
(US)

1983		26		

RAUTENBUSCH, WM [a]
(US)

1914		11		

RAWLINS, Harry
(ENG/US)

1900		19		
1908		21		

RAWLINS, Horace
(ENG/US)

1895		**W**		
1896		2		
1897		8		
1898		19		
1899		13		
1901		17		
1902		16		
1903		12		
1904		14		
1907		26		

RAY, Ted (ENG)

	MAS	USO	BOP	PGA
1899			16	
1900			13	
1901			12	
1902			9	
1903			23	
1904			12	
1905			11	
1906			8	
1907			5	
1908			3	
1909			6	
1910			5	
1911			5	
1912			W	
1913		3	2	
1914			10	
1920		W	3	
1921			19	
1923			12	
1925			2	
1926			28	
1927		27	29	
1930			24	

REASOR, Mike (US)

	MAS	USO	BOP	PGA
1974		15		

REED, Elmer (US)

	MAS	USO	BOP	PGA
1950				Last 16

REEKIE, WM [a] (US)

	MAS	USO	BOP	PGA
1923		5		

REES, Dai (WAL)

	MAS	USO	BOP	PGA
1935			30	
1936			11	
1937			21	
1938			13	
1939			12	
1946			4	
1947			21	
1948			15	
1950			3	
1951			12	
1952			27	
1953			2	
1954			2	
1955			28	
1956			13	
1957			30	
1958			14	
1959			9	
1960			9	
1961			2	

REFRAM, Dean (US)

	MAS	USO	BOP	PGA
1962		28		
1963		14		
1964	30			
1965		28		
1969		13		

REGALADO, Victor (MEX)

	MAS	USO	BOP	PGA
1974				28
1975	30			
1978		24		
1984				10

REID, John (US)

	MAS	USO	BOP	PGA
1895		10		
1896		16		
1903		24		

REID, Mike (US)

	MAS	USO	BOP	PGA
1979		25		
1980		6		
1981		20		
1983				9
1984				14
1985		23		
1986		24		
1988				2
1989	6			
1991		26	26	

REID, Steve (US)

	MAS	USO	BOP	PGA
1968				26

REID, Wilfred (ENG/US)

	MAS	USO	BOP	PGA
1909			21	
1910			24	
1911			16	
1912			20	
1913		16	26	
1915		10		
1916		4		Last 32
1919		21		Last 16
1923				Last 32
1925		27		

REINHART, FO (US)

	MAS	USO	BOP	PGA
1903		13		

RENNER, Jack (US)

	MAS	USO	BOP	PGA
1979				12
1980	14			
1981		17		
1982	20	30		
1983	16			
1984	11			
1985		9		

RENNIE, James (SCO)

	MAS	USO	BOP	PGA
1875			5	
1879			12	
1881			7	
1885			18	

RENOUF, TG (ENG)

	MAS	USO	BOP	PGA
1897			14	
1898			9	
1899			12	
1901			12	
1902			20	
1904			22	
1905			16	
1906			8	
1907			17	
1908			28	
1909			5	
1910			8	
1911			13	
1912			19	
1913			5	

REVOLTA, Johnny (US)

	MAS	USO	BOP	PGA
1933		15		Last 16
1934	18	8		Last 16
1935	13			W
1936	25	14		Last 32
1937	13	28		Last 32
1938	18	16		Last 32
1939		22		Last 16
1940	27	16		
1945				Last 16
1951		19		
1952	13			
1954		29		Last 16
1957		30		

RHYAN, Dick (US)

	MAS	USO	BOP	PGA
1964				23
1968				20

RICHARDSON, JC (SCO)

	MAS	USO	BOP	PGA
1970			13	

RICHARDSON, Steven (ENG)

	MAS	USO	BOP	PGA
1991				5

RICKETTS, Alfred (ENG/US)

	MAS	USO	BOP	PGA
1896		10		
1897		6		
1899		16		

RIEGEL, Skee (US)

	MAS	USO	BOP	PGA
1948	13a			
1949	30a	14a		
1950	21	12		
1951	2	10		
1952	14			
1953	29			
1955	13			
1956				Last 32
1957				Last 32

RINKER, Larry (US)

	MAS	USO	BOP	PGA
1982		15		
1986		24		
1992			12	

RISDON, PWL [a] (ENG)

	MAS	USO	BOP	PGA
1935			26	

RISEBOROUGH, Ernest (ENG)

	MAS	USO	BOP	PGA
1906			24	

RISEBOROUGH, Herbert (ENG)

	MAS	USO	BOP	PGA
1910			28	

RITCHIE, William (SCO)

	MAS	USO	BOP	PGA
1910			16	
1920			29	

RIVERO, Jose (SP)

	MAS	USO	BOP	PGA
1985			3	
1988			16	
1990			25	
1993			14	

ROBB, J (SCO)

	MAS	USO	BOP	PGA
1895			13	

ROBBINS Jr, Hillman [a] (US)

	MAS	USO	BOP	PGA
1955	24			
1956	17			

ROBERTS, Charles (ENG)

	MAS	USO	BOP	PGA
1907			23	
1910			24	
1912			27	
1913			14	

ROBERTS, Hugh (WAL)

	MAS	USO	BOP	PGA
1921			26	

ROBERTS, Loren (US)

	MAS	USO	BOP	PGA
1990				5
1991				27
1993		11		28
1994	5	2	24	9
1995	25			
1996	23		18	
1997		13		

ROBERTSON, AM (SCO)

	MAS	USO	BOP	PGA
1946			27	

ROBERTSON, Argyll, [a] (SCO)

	MAS	USO	BOP	PGA
1879			28	

ROBERTSON, DD [a]
(SCO)

	MAS	USO	BOP	PGA
1890			23	

ROBERTSON, Dave
(US)

	MAS	USO	BOP	PGA
1904		19		
1906		29		
1907		13		
1908		20		
1912		28		
1922			Last 32	
1924		10		

ROBERTSON, Fred
(SCO)

	MAS	USO	BOP	PGA
1933			22	
1937			17	

ROBERTSON, Jock
(SCO/US)

	MAS	USO	BOP	PGA
1924			Last 32	

ROBERTSON, Peter
(US)

	MAS	USO	BOP	PGA
1904		29		
1905		3		
1906		14		
1907		5		
1908		6		
1909		20		
1911		9		
1912		28		
1913		21		

ROBERTSON, William
(SCO)

	MAS	USO	BOP	PGA
1924			23	

ROBINSON, WD
(US)

	MAS	USO	BOP	PGA
1907		26		
1910		26		

ROBSON, Fred
(ENG)

	MAS	USO	BOP	PGA
1908			18	
1910			5	
1911			10	
1923			29	
1924			23	
1925			10	
1926			17	
1927			2	
1928			4	
1930			4	
1931			20	
1932			9	

ROCCA, Constantino
(IT)

	MAS	USO	BOP	PGA
1995			2	17
1997	5			

RODGERS, Phil
(US)

	MAS	USO	BOP	PGA
1958	22			
1962		3	3	
1963			2	
1964	25		19	
1966	17	6	4	
1967				28
1969		13		
1972				7
1973	23			
1974	7			

RODGERS, Phillip H
(ENG)

	MAS	USO	BOP	PGA
1927			9	
1930			15	
1931			28	
1932			25	
1935			17	

RODRIGUEZ, Chi Chi
(PR)

	MAS	USO	BOP	PGA
1964	21			
1967	26			
1969				15
1970	10	27		
1971	30	13		
1972		9		24
1973	10	29	28	24
1974	20	26		
1975				22
1981		6		

ROE, Mark
(ENG)

	MAS	USO	BOP	PGA
1987			17	
1990			16	
1993			24	
1995		13		

ROGERS, Bill
(US)

	MAS	USO	BOP	PGA
1978	29			
1979		4		
1980	16		19	8
1981		2	W	27
1982		3	22	29
1983			8	

ROGERS, Jock
(SCO/US)

	MAS	USO	BOP	PGA
1924		19		
1926		20		
1929		11		

ROGERS, Johnny
(US)

	MAS	USO	BOP	PGA
1938		24		
1939		20		

ROLLAND, Douglas
(SCO)

	MAS	USO	BOP	PGA
1882			13a	
1883			10	
1884			2	
1894			2	

325

ROMANS, Walter (US)

MAS	USO	BOP	PGA
1949			Last 16

ROMERO, Eduardo (ARG)

MAS	USO	BOP	PGA
1988		13	
1989		8	
1991		26	
1993			20
1997		7	

ROONEY, Michael (US)

MAS	USO	BOP	PGA
1956			Last 32

ROSBURG, Bob (US)

MAS	USO	BOP	PGA
1953	21		
1954	6	29	
1955	4	5	
1956	16		
1958		5	11
1959	30	2	W
1960	20	23	
1961	15	21	19
1962		13	
1964		9	
1966	10		
1967	21		
1968	30		
1969		2	
1971		3	9

ROSE, DG [a] (SCO)

MAS	USO	BOP	PGA
1888		27	

ROSE, James (US)

MAS	USO	BOP	PGA
1919			Last 32

ROSMAN, Joe (US)

MAS	USO	BOP	PGA
1919			Last 32
1920			Last 32

ROSS, AM [a] (SCO)

MAS	USO	BOP	PGA
1889		13	
1895		27	

ROSS, Alex (SCO/US)

MAS	USO	BOP	PGA
1902	10		
1903	9		
1904	15		
1905	13		
1906	6		
1907	W		
1908	23		
1910	22		
1911	9		
1914	22		
1919	16		
1920	27		

ROSS, Donald (SCO/US)

MAS	USO	BOP	PGA
1901	21		
1902	9		
1903	5		
1904	10		
1905	25		
1907	10		
1910		8	

ROSS, Jack (SCO)

MAS	USO	BOP	PGA
1895		24	
1896		18	
1901		25	

ROSS, Jack B (SCO)

MAS	USO	BOP	PGA
1913		30	

ROSSI, Ricardo (ARG)

MAS	USO	BOP	PGA
1956		17	

ROTAR, Charles (US)

MAS	USO	BOP	PGA
1955	28		

ROWE, Charles (US)

MAS	USO	BOP	PGA
1909	20		
1912	27		
1920	14		
1922			QF

ROWE, John (ENG)

MAS	USO	BOP	PGA
1894		23	
1897		28	
1902		15	
1904		16	
1905		11	
1907		21	
1910		22	

ROYER Jr, Hugh (US)

MAS	USO	BOP	PGA
1968	22		

RUDOLPH, Mason (US)

MAS	USO	BOP	PGA
1960			22
1961	28		
1962		28	
1963	15	27	23
1964	18		4
1965	4	11	20
1966		8	22
1967	10		28
1968	14		17
1969	11		
1970		27	10
1973	14		3

RUIZ, Leopoldo (ARG)

MAS	USO	BOP	PGA
1958		5	
1959		9	

RUMMELLS, Dave (US)

MAS	USO	BOP	PGA
1988			6
1989			5

RUNYAN, Paul (US)

	MAS	USO	BOP	PGA
1931				Last 16
1932		12		Last 32
1933				QF
1934	3	28		W
1935	7	10		QF
1936	4	8		
1937	19	14		Last 16
1938	4	7		W
1939	16	9		QF
1940	12			QF
1941		5		
1942	3			
1946		21		
1947		6		
1950		25		
1951		6		
1952		22		
1961			18	

RUSSELL, David A (ENG)

	MAS	USO	BOP	PGA
1997			24	

RUSSELL, David J (ENG)

	MAS	USO	BOP	PGA
1988			11	

RUTHERFORD, W [a] (US)

	MAS	USO	BOP	PGA
1898		28		

RYAN, Jack (US)

	MAS	USO	BOP	PGA
1939				Last 32
1940		29		
1941	17			Last 32

SAAVEDRA, Armando (ARG)

	MAS	USO	BOP	PGA
1979			30	

SALERNO, Gus (US)

	MAS	USO	BOP	PGA
1955				Last 32

SAMPSON, Harold (US)

	MAS	USO	BOP	PGA
1930				QF
1935				Last 32

SANDERS, Doug (US)

	MAS	USO	BOP	PGA
1958				2
1960	29			3
1961	11	2		3
1962		11		15
1963	28	21		17
1964			11	28
1965	11	11		20
1966	4	8	2	6
1967	16		18	28
1968	12			8
1970			2	
1971			9	
1972			4	7
1973			28	
1976			28	

SANDERSON, AJ (US)

	MAS	USO	BOP	PGA
1915		21		

SANDERSON, J (US)

	MAS	USO	BOP	PGA
1919		24		

SANUDO, Cesar (US)

	MAS	USO	BOP	PGA
1972		9		

SARAZEN, Gene (US)

	MAS	USO	BOP	PGA
1920		30		
1921		17		QF
1922		W		W
1923		16		W
1924		17		Last 16
1925		5		Last 32
1926		3		Last 16
1927		3		QF
1928		6	2	SF
1929		3	8	QF
1930		28		RU
1931		4	3	SF
1932		W	W	
1933		26	3	W
1934		2	21	Last 16
1935	W	6		Last 32
1936	3	28	5	
1937	19	10		Last 32
1938	13	10		QF
1939	5			
1940	21	2		QF
1941	19	7		SF
1942	28			
1945				Last 32
1947	26			Last 16
1948	23			Last 16
1950	10			
1951	12			Last 32
1952			17	
1954			17	
1955				Last 32
1956				Last 16
1958			16	

SARGENT, Alfred (US)

	MAS	USO	BOP	PGA
1931				Last 32

SARGENT, George (ENG/US)

	MAS	USO	BOP	PGA
1909		W		
1910		16		
1911		7		
1912		6		
1913		21		
1914		3		
1915		10		
1916		4		
1919		29		
1923		29		

SAUBABER, Jean (FRA)

	MAS	USO	BOP	PGA
1936			28	

SAUERS, Gene (US)

	MAS	USO	BOP	PGA
1986				30
1987				24
1992				2
1993				22

SAVEL, Steve (US)

	MAS	USO	BOP	PGA
1944				Last 32

SAWYER, DE [a] (US)

	MAS	USO	BOP	PGA
1911		18		

SAWYER, Pat (US)

	MAS	USO	BOP	PGA
1937		16		

SAYERS, Ben (SCO)

	MAS	USO	BOP	PGA
1878			12	
1879			22	
1880			19	
1882			18	
1883			7	
1884			6	
1885			15	
1886			16	
1887			5	
1888			2	
1889			3	
1890			19	
1891			9	
1892			5	
1893			12	
1894			5	
1895			9	
1896			7	
1897			12	
1898			19	
1899			11	
1900			9	
1902			19	
1903			21	
1905			10	
1908			30	
1909			17	
1915		29		

SAYERS, George (ENG/US)

	MAS	USO	BOP	PGA
1915		28		

SAYNER, Cedric (ENG)

	MAS	USO	BOP	PGA
1925			27	
1929			25	
1932			29	

SCHEIDER, F (US)

	MAS	USO	BOP	PGA
1935				Last 32

SCHLEE, John (US)

	MAS	USO	BOP	PGA
1973		2		
1974	26			17
1975				10
1976				4
1977	8			

SCHLOTMAN, JB (US)

	MAS	USO	BOP	PGA
1900		22		

SCHMUTTE, Leonard (US)

	MAS	USO	BOP	PGA
1928		25		
1929		26		
1950				Last 32
1952				Last 32

SCHNEIDER, Charles (US)

	MAS	USO	BOP	PGA
1930				Last 32
1933				Last 32
1935				Last 32
1937				Last 32

SCHNEITER, George (US)

	MAS	USO	BOP	PGA
1934		28		
1941				Last 32
1944				SF
1945				Last 32
1946	13			Last 16
1947	26			Last 32
1948		14		
1949				Last 32
1955		19		

SCHROEDER, John (US)

	MAS	USO	BOP	PGA
1971		27		22
1977			9	19
1978			7	12
1979				21
1981		4		
1982	24			

SCHULTZ, Eddie (US)

	MAS	USO	BOP	PGA
1929				Last 16
1931				Last 32
1932				Last 32
1935				QF

SCHULZ, Ted (US)

	MAS	USO	BOP	PGA
1992	6			

SCHWAB, Pat (US)

	MAS	USO	BOP	PGA
1968		24		

SCHWARTZ, Bill (US)

	MAS	USO	BOP	PGA
1933		29		
1934		28		

SCOTT, Andrew (SCO)

	MAS	USO	BOP	PGA
1896			7	
1897			16	
1898			29	
1899			25	
1900			22	
1901			18	
1903			6	

SCOTT, Michael [a] (ENG)

	MAS	USO	BOP	PGA
1922			19	

SCOTT Jr, R [a] (SCO)

	MAS	USO	BOP	PGA
1923			22	

328

SCOTT, Syd (ENG)

	MAS	USO	BOP	PGA
1952			9	
1953			22	
1954			2	
1955			20	
1956			28	
1959			4	
1960			9	
1961			10	
1962			10	
1964			19	

SCHWARTZ, WJ (US)

	MAS	USO	BOP	PGA
1934	18			

SEAVALL, Eric (US)

	MAS	USO	BOP	PGA
1930				Last 32

SECKEL, Albert [a] (US)

	MAS	USO	BOP	PGA
1911		11		

SELLMAN, Jack (US)

	MAS	USO	BOP	PGA
1963				13

SENIOR, Peter (AUS)

	MAS	USO	BOP	PGA
1991			17	
1992			25	
1993			4	
1994			20	

SERAFIN, Felix (US)

	MAS	USO	BOP	PGA
1928		28		
1936		22		
1937	19			
1938	6			Last 16
1939	16	29		
1940		20		
1941	19			
1942	18			
1945				Last 32
1946	21			

SERRA, Enrique (URU)

	MAS	USO	BOP	PGA
1939			17	

SERVAS, LC (US)

	MAS	USO	BOP	PGA
1901		28		

SEWELL, Doug (ENG)

	MAS	USO	BOP	PGA
1963			26	
1965			25	
1966			20	
1971			25	

SEWGOLUM, Sewsunker (SA)

	MAS	USO	BOP	PGA
1963			13	

SEYMOUR, Mark (ENG)

	MAS	USO	BOP	PGA
1924			29	
1929			18	
1931			22	
1932			22	
1935			17	

SHADE, Ronnie (SCO)

	MAS	USO	BOP	PGA
1966			16a	
1970			25	
1974			22	

SHAFER, George (US)

	MAS	USO	BOP	PGA
1950				Last 32

SHANKLAND, Bill (ENG)

	MAS	USO	BOP	PGA
1938			18	
1939			3	
1946			13	
1947			4	
1949			11	
1951			6	

SHANKS, PJ (ENG)

	MAS	USO	BOP	PGA
1959			29	

SHAVE Jr, Bob (US)

	MAS	USO	BOP	PGA
1960		27		
1966		26		

SHAVE Sr, Bob (US)

	MAS	USO	BOP	PGA
1925		20		
1927				Last 32
1929				Last 32
1930		17		Last 16
1938				Last 32

SHAW, Bob (US)

	MAS	USO	BOP	PGA
1968			27	
1972				20

SHAW, QA [a] (US)

	MAS	USO	BOP	PGA
1898		21		

SHAW, Tom (US)

	MAS	USO	BOP	PGA
1969				21
1970			28	
1973		25		

SHEA, Leo (US)

	MAS	USO	BOP	PGA
1926				Last 32

SHEARER, Bob (US)

	MAS	USO	BOP	PGA
1976			21	
1977			15	
1978		16	7	26

SHELTON, Ben (ENG)

	MAS	USO	BOP	PGA
1954			29	

SHEPARD, B (ENG)

	MAS	USO	BOP	PGA
1947			27	

SHEPPARD, Charles (US)

	MAS	USO	BOP	PGA
1938		26		
1940				Last 32
1941				Last 32
1957				QF

SHERBORNE, Andrew (ENG)

	MAS	USO	BOP	PGA
1991			17	

SHERLOCK, James
(ENG)

	MAS	USO	BOP	PGA
1897			27	
1902			17	
1904			6	
1905			8	
1910			28	
1911			16	
1913			7	
1920			16	
1924			9	

SHERMAN, Mike
(US)

	MAS	USO	BOP	PGA
1916				Last 32

SHIPPEN, John
(US)

	MAS	USO	BOP	PGA
1896		6		
1899		25		
1900		27		
1902		5		

SHOEMAKER, Dick
(US)

	MAS	USO	BOP	PGA
1946				Last 16
1951				Last 16
1958				29

SHUTE, Denny
(US)

	MAS	USO	BOP	PGA
1928		6		
1929		3		Last 32
1930		25		Last 16
1931		25		RU
1932		14		Last 32
1933		21	W	
1934	13		20	SF
1935	5	4		Last 16
1936	11	10		W
1937	13	10	14	W
1938		11		Last 16
1939	15	3		Last 16
1941	18	2		QF
1942				Last 32
1945				QF
1946	25			
1947	20			
1950				Last 16
1951				Last 32

SIECKMANN, Tom
(US)

	MAS	USO	BOP	PGA
1985		23		
1990		8		
1991		19		

SIFFORD, Charles
(US)

	MAS	USO	BOP	PGA
1964		27		
1972		21		

SIGEL, Jay [a]
(US)

	MAS	USO	BOP	PGA
1980	26			

SIKES, Dan
(US)

	MAS	USO	BOP	PGA
1963	15	10		
1964	13			
1965	5			
1966				28
1967				3
1968		15		8
1969	12			25
1970		27		18
1972				13
1973				6
1974	15			17

SIKES, RH
(US)

	MAS	USO	BOP	PGA
1965				13
1966			12	28
1967				14

SILLS, Tony
(US)

	MAS	USO	BOP	PGA
1985		15		
1986				16

SIMONS, Jim
(US)

	MAS	USO	BOP	PGA
1971		5a		
1972		15a		
1977				25
1979	23	16		
1980	19	22		
1981	15			
1982	15			5
1983				30

SIMPSON, Archie
(SCO)

	MAS	USO	BOP	PGA
1885			2	
1886			4	
1887			5	
1888			16	
1889			12	
1890			2	
1891			11	
1892			9	
1893			14	
1894			13	
1895			5	
1896			12	
1897			7	
1898			16	
1899			16	
1900			7	
1902			30	
1903			29	

SIMPSON, Bob
(SCO)

	MAS	USO	BOP	PGA
1885			4	
1886			15	
1887			16	
1888			30	
1893			6	
1898			29	

SIMPSON, David
(SCO)

MAS	USO	BOP	PGA
1882		23	
1886		26	
1891		18	

SIMPSON, George
(SCO/US)

MAS	USO	BOP	PGA
1911	2		
1912	13		
1914	13		
1916	24		Last 16

SIMPSON, Harry
(ENG)

MAS	USO	BOP	PGA
1914		3	

SIMPSON, Jack
(SCO)

MAS	USO	BOP	PGA
1883		17	
1884		W	
1885		13	
1886		12	
1887		12	
1892		28	

SIMPSON, James
(SCO/US)

MAS	USO	BOP	PGA
1914	11		

SIMPSON, JB
(SCO/US)

MAS	USO	BOP	PGA
1911	23		
1916	15		

SIMPSON, RL
(SCO/US)

MAS	USO	BOP	PGA
1911	17		

SIMPSON, Robert
(SCO/US)

MAS	USO	BOP	PGA
1900	14		
1901	14		
1904	6		

SIMPSON, Scott
(US)

MAS	USO	BOP	PGA
1980			30
1981	23		
1982	15		
1983	11	13		9
1984		25		6
1985		15		12
1986	25		
1987	27	W	
1988		6	
1989		6	26
1990	7	14	
1991	22	2	
1992	13		
1993	11		9	6
1994	27		
1995		28	
1996	29		

SIMPSON, Tim
(US)

MAS	USO	BOP	PGA
1984		11		25
1985	18		
1987		14	
1989				27
1990		5	12	8

SIMPSON, Tom
(ENG)

MAS	USO	BOP	PGA
1900		14	
1905		9	
1906		15	
1908		7	
1913		27	

SINDELAR, Joey
(US)

MAS	USO	BOP	PGA
1985		15		28
1986		15	
1988		17	
1992		6	
1993	27		
1997				10

SINGH, Vijay
(FIJ)

MAS	USO	BOP	PGA
1989		23	
1990		12	
1991		12	
1993				4
1994	27		
1995		10	6	
1996		7	11	
1997	17			13

SKERRITT, Paddy
(IRE)

MAS	USO	BOP	PGA
1968			18	

SLINGERLAND, G
(US)

MAS	USO	BOP	PGA
1935				Last 32

SLUMAN, Jeff
(US)

MAS	USO	BOP	PGA
1986				30
1987				14
1988				W
1989	8			24
1990	27	14	25	
1991	29		
1992	4	2		12
1993	17	11	
1994	25	9		25
1995		13		8
1997	7	28	

SMALLDON, DF
(WAL)

MAS	USO	BOP	PGA
1955			17	
1956			28	

SMITH (Cambridge)
(ENG)

MAS	USO	BOP	PGA
1879			23	

SMITH, AW [a]
(SCO/US)

MAS	USO	BOP	PGA
1879			11	
1895		3	
1896		4	

SMITH, Al (US)

	MAS	USO	BOP	PGA
1948	16			Last 16
1952				Last 16
1953				Last 16
1957				Last 32

SMITH, Alexander (SCO)

	MAS	USO	BOP	PGA
1860			7 or 8	

SMITH, Alex (SCO/US)

	MAS	USO	BOP	PGA
1898		2		
1899		7		
1900		13		
1901		2		
1902		18		
1903		4		
1904		18		
1905		2	16	
1906		W		
1907			23	
1908		3		
1909		3		
1910		W		
1911		23		
1912		3		
1913		16		
1915		22		
1916				Last 16
1921		5		

SMITH, Alfred (US)

	MAS	USO	BOP	PGA
1947		19		
1948		21		

SMITH, Arthur (SCO/US)

	MAS	USO	BOP	PGA
1900		16		
1903		26		
1905		10		
1908		29		
1914		9		

SMITH, Bob E (US)

	MAS	USO	BOP	PGA
1971		24		20
1972				24
1976		28		
1979		25		

SMITH, C Ralph (SCO)

	MAS	USO	BOP	PGA
1897			30	
1898			27	
1900			30	
1902			27	
1914			21	
1920			28	

SMITH, G (SCO)

	MAS	USO	BOP	PGA
1884			20	

SMITH, GG (Garden) [a] (SCO)

	MAS	USO	BOP	PGA
1892			21	

SMITH, George (SCO/US)

	MAS	USO	BOP	PGA
1906		18		
1910		21		

SMITH, George B (US)

	MAS	USO	BOP	PGA
1925				Last 32
1929		16		
1932		21		Last 32
1934				Last 32

SMITH, George M (US)

	MAS	USO	BOP	PGA
1930		11		

SMITH, Horton (US)

	MAS	USO	BOP	PGA
1928		28		SF
1929		10	25	Last 32
1930		3	4	QF
1931		27	11	QF
1932				Last 32
1933		24	14	Last 32
1934	W	17		
1935	19	6		QF
1936	W	22		QF
1937	19		10	Last 16
1938	22	19		QF
1939	26	15		QF
1940		3		
1941	19	13		Last 16
1942	5			
1946		21		
1947		22		
1949	23	23		Last 32
1950	12			
1952	30	15		
1954				Last 16

SMITH, Ian (ENG)

	MAS	USO	BOP	PGA
1960			16	

SMITH, Jack (US)

	MAS	USO	BOP	PGA
1925			16	
1927			22	
1928			13	
1947				Last 32

SMITH, Macdonald (SCO/US)

	MAS	USO	BOP	PGA
1910		2		
1913		4		
1923		20	3	
1924		4		
1925		11		
1926		9		
1927		18		
1928		6		
1929		23	15	
1930		2	2	
1931		10	5	
1932		14	2	
1933		19		
1934	7	6	4	
1935		14	17	
1936		4		

SMITH, Mel (US)

	MAS	USO	BOP	PGA
1927				Last 32

SMITH, Norman (US)

	MAS	USO	BOP	PGA
1930				Last 32

SMITH, WB [a] (US)

	MAS	USO	BOP	PGA
1897		29		

SMITH, WD (Dick) [a] (SCO)

	MAS	USO	BOP	PGA
1957			5	

SMITH, Warren (US)

	MAS	USO	BOP	PGA
1957				Last 16

SMITH, William B (ENG)

	MAS	USO	BOP	PGA
1920			21	
1922			22	

SMITH, Willie (SCO/US)

	MAS	USO	BOP	PGA
1898		5		
1899		W		
1900		4		
1901		3		
1902		4		
1903		9		
1905		13		
1906		2		
1907		2		
1908		2		
1910			5	

SMITHERS, Wally (ENG)

	MAS	USO	BOP	PGA
1936			15	
1949			8	
1950			12	
1951			28	
1952			17	

SMYTH, Des (IRE)

	MAS	USO	BOP	PGA
1982			4	
1993			27	

SNEAD, JC (US)

	MAS	USO	BOP	PGA
1972	30			20
1973	2			3
1974	26	21		24
1975	10			28
1976			14	15
1977			27	19
1978			2	
1979	22			
1980	14	22		
1981				15
1982			15	
1983	12			

SNEAD, Sam (US)

	MAS	USO	BOP	PGA
1937	18	2	11	Last 16
1938				RU
1939	2	5		
1940	7	16		RU
1941	6	13		QF
1942	7			W
1946	7	19	W	Last 32
1947	22	2		Last 32
1948	16	5		QF
1949	W	2		W
1950	3	12		Last 32
1951	8	10		W
1952	W	10		
1953	16	2		Last 32
1954	W	11		QF
1955	3	3		Last 32
1956	4	24		QF
1957	2	8		Last 16
1958	13			3
1959	22	8		8
1960	11	19		3
1961	15	17		27
1962	15		6	17
1963	3			27
1965		24		6
1966				6
1967	10			
1968		9		
1970	23			12
1972	27			4
1973	29	29		9
1974	20			3

SNEED, Ed (US)

	MAS	USO	BOP	PGA
1975		29		
1978	18			
1979	2	11	26	28
1980		8		

SNELL, David (ENG)

	MAS	USO	BOP	PGA
1958			30	

SOMERS, Vaughan (AUS)

	MAS	USO	BOP	PGA
1986			21	

SOMERVILLE, Ross [a] (CAN)

	MAS	USO	BOP	PGA
1933			28	

SOTA, Ramon (SP)

	MAS	USO	BOP	PGA
1960			15	
1961			12	
1963			7	
1964			30	
1965	6		25	
1971			11	

SOTO, Arturo (ARG)

	MAS	USO	BOP	PGA
1955			17	

SOUCHAK, Frank [a] (US)

	MAS	USO	BOP	PGA
1953		9		

SOUCHAK, Mike (US)

	MAS	USO	BOP	PGA
1955	4	10		
1956	17	29	8	
1957				Last 16
1958	14			8
1959	25	3		5
1960	16	3		12
1961	28	4		
1962	5	14		
1963	11			23
1964	9			12
1965				15
1967				20
1972				29

SOUTHERDEN, EA (ENG)

	MAS	USO	BOP	PGA
1949			20	

SPARK, W (SCO)

	MAS	USO	BOP	PGA
1933			28	

SPEARS, Herschel (US)

	MAS	USO	BOP	PGA
1948		14		
1949		11		
1950	27			

SPENCE, Jamie (ENG)

	MAS	USO	BOP	PGA
1990			22	
1992			12	

SPENCE, TW (Bill) (ENG)

	MAS	USO	BOP	PGA
1954			12	

SPENCER, Glen (US)

	MAS	USO	BOP	PGA
1928				Last 16

SPRAY, Steve (US)

	MAS	USO	BOP	PGA
1968		5		

SPRINGER, Mike (US)

	MAS	USO	BOP	PGA
1994		25	24	

SPROGELL, Frank (US)

	MAS	USO	BOP	PGA
1922				Last 16

STACKHOUSE, WA (US)

	MAS	USO	BOP	PGA
1944				Last 32

STADLER, Craig (US)

	MAS	USO	BOP	PGA
1978				6
1979	7			
1980	26	16	6	
1981		26		
1982	W	22		16
1983	6	10	12	
1984			28	18
1985	6			18
1986		15		30
1987	17	24	8	28
1988	3	25		15
1989			13	7
1990	14	8		
1991	12	19		7
1992	25			
1994			24	19
1995				8
1996	29			
1997	26			

STAHL, Marvin (US)

	MAS	USO	BOP	PGA
1938				Last 16

STAIT, Jack (US)

	MAS	USO	BOP	PGA
1923				Last 16
1924		25		

STANDLY, Mike (US)

	MAS	USO	BOP	PGA
1993		16		

STANKOWSKI, Paul (US)

	MAS	USO	BOP	PGA
1997	5	19		

STANLEY, Ian (AUS)

	MAS	USO	BOP	PGA
1986			30	

STANTON, Bob (US)

	MAS	USO	BOP	PGA
1966			27	
1969		22		
1970				22

STARK, George (US)

	MAS	USO	BOP	PGA
1922				Last 32

STARKS, Nate (US)

	MAS	USO	BOP	PGA
1975		29		

STEEL, William (SCO)

	MAS	USO	BOP	PGA
1860			7 or 8	

STEELSMITH, Jerry (US)

	MAS	USO	BOP	PGA
1961		29		

STEPHENSON, David (SCO)

	MAS	USO	BOP	PGA
1905			28	

STEVENS, LB [a] (ENG)

	MAS	USO	BOP	PGA
1911			24	

STEVENS, Tom (US)

	MAS	USO	BOP	PGA
1926		23		
1927			19	

STEWART, Earl (US)

Year	MAS	USO	BOP	PGA
1951		24		
1952		10		
1953	16			
1954	22			
1958		23		
1962		17		
1963				27
1967				26

STEWART, Payne (US)

Year	MAS	USO	BOP	PGA
1984	21			
1985	25	5	2	12
1986	8	6		5
1987			4	24
1988	25	10	7	9
1989	24	13	8	W
1990			2	8
1991		W		13
1993	9	2	12	
1995		21	11	13
1996		27		
1997		28		29

STEWART, WG [a] (US)

Year	MAS	USO	BOP	PGA
1897		20		

STICKLEY, Arnold (ENG)

Year	MAS	USO	BOP	PGA
1959			11	

STILL, Ken (US)

Year	MAS	USO	BOP	PGA
1963		19		
1970		5		
1971	6	19		

STINCHCOMB, Verl (US)

Year	MAS	USO	BOP	PGA
1945				Last 32

STOCKTON, Dave (US)

Year	MAS	USO	BOP	PGA
1968		9		17
1969	18	25		
1970	5			W
1971	9		11	
1972	10			
1973	14			12
1974	2			26
1975	26			
1976				W
1978		2		19
1980	26			

STODDART, WE (US)

Year	MAS	USO	BOP	PGA
1898		29		

STONEHOUSE, Ralph (US)

Year	MAS	USO	BOP	PGA
1932				QF
1934	16			
1941				Last 32

STOREY, Eustace [a] (ENG)

Year	MAS	USO	BOP	PGA
1938			26	

STRAFACI, Frank [a] (US)

Year	MAS	USO	BOP	PGA
1937		9		

STRANAHAN, Frank (US)

Year	MAS	USO	BOP	PGA
1946	20a			
1947	2a	13a	2a	
1948			23a	
1949	19a		13a	
1950	14a		9a	
1951			12a	
1952	19a			
1953	14a	21a	2a	
1954			29a	
1955	15	12		
1956	22		12	
1957		13	19	
1958		10		
1962				17

STRANAHAN, Richard (US)

Year	MAS	USO	BOP	PGA
1960		27		

STRANGE, Curtis (US)

Year	MAS	USO	BOP	PGA
1976	15a			
1980		16		5
1981	19	17		27
1982	7		15	14
1983		26	29	
1984		3		
1985	2			
1986	21		14	
1987	12	4		9
1988	21	W	13	
1989	18	W		2
1990	7	21		
1992		23		
1993		25		
1994	27	4		
1995	9			17
1996		27		

STRATH, Andrew (SCO)

Year	MAS	USO	BOP	PGA
1860			3	
1863			4	
1864			2	
1865			W	
1866				6
1924			5	
1925			5	
1926			10	

STRATH, Davie (SCO)

Year	MAS	USO	BOP	PGA
1869			5	
1870			2	
1872			2	
1873			5	
1874			18	
1875			6	
1876			2	
1877			5	

335

	MAS	USO	BOP	PGA

STRATH, George
(SCO/US)

	MAS	USO	BOP	PGA
1878			14	
1879			29	
1880			16	
1883			29	
1886			24	
1896		22		

STRATH, William
(SCO)

	MAS	USO	BOP	PGA
1864			6	
1865			8	

STRECK, Ron
(US)

	MAS	USO	BOP	PGA
1977	23			
1979				4
1982				22

STRICKER, Steve
(US)

	MAS	USO	BOP	PGA
1995		13		23
1996			22	

STRINGER, Irving
(US)

	MAS	USO	BOP	PGA
1910		28		

STRONG, Herbert
(US)

	MAS	USO	BOP	PGA
1908		29		
1913		9		
1915		26		

STUART, A [a]
(SCO)

	MAS	USO	BOP	PGA
1887			22	

STUPPLE, Bob
(US)

	MAS	USO	BOP	PGA
1937		20		

SULLIVAN, Mike
(US)

	MAS	USO	BOP	PGA
1980				30
1983			14	
1984	25			
1989				12

SULLIVAN, Vince
(US)

	MAS	USO	BOP	PGA
1966		30		

SUNESSON, Magnus
(SWE)

	MAS	USO	BOP	PGA
1991			12	

SUTTON, Hal
(US)

	MAS	USO	BOP	PGA
1982		19	29	
1983	27	6	29	W
1984		16		6
1985		23		
1986		4		21
1987			11	28
1989		29		
1991				7
1997		19		

SUTTON, Norman
(ENG)

	MAS	USO	BOP	PGA
1930			24	
1936			23	
1947			17	
1949			19	
1951			6	
1952			20	
1953			29	
1954			27	
1955			28	
1957			30	

SUZUKI, Norio
(JAP)

	MAS	USO	BOP	PGA
1976			10	
1977			26	
1980			19	

SWAELENS, Don
(BEL)

	MAS	USO	BOP	PGA
1958			11	
1962			23	
1969			30	
1974			7	

SWEETSER, Jess [a]
(US)

	MAS	USO	BOP	PGA
1921		14		
1939	29			

SWEENY, HR [a]
(US)

	MAS	USO	BOP	PGA
1898		27		

SYLVESTER, Joe
(US)

	MAS	USO	BOP	PGA
1919				Last 32
1920				Last 16
1921				Last 32
1923		24		

SZWEDKO, Andrew
[a] (US)

	MAS	USO	BOP	PGA
1940		29		

TAGGART, Fred
(SCO)

	MAS	USO	BOP	PGA
1928			11	
1939			26	

TAILER, Tommy
(US)

	MAS	USO	BOP	PGA
1938	18			
1939	21			

TAIT, Bob
(SCO)

	MAS	USO	BOP	PGA
1883			28	
1886			20	
1888			18	

TAIT, Freddie [a]
(SCO)

	MAS	USO	BOP	PGA
1891			28	
1892			21	
1894			9	
1895			15	
1896			3	
1897			3	
1898			5	
1899			7	

THE PLAYERS

TAPIE, Alan (US)

	MAS	USO	BOP	PGA
1974			13	
1975			16	
1976			21	
1979				23
1980				20

TAYLOR, Alex (US)

	MAS	USO	BOP	PGA
1901		22		
1904		23		

TAYLOR Jr, Frank [a] (US)

	MAS	USO	BOP	PGA
1956		29		
1957	13			
1960	20			

TAYLOR, Gerard (AUS)

	MAS	USO	BOP	PGA
1987			25	

TAYLOR, HE [a] (ENG)

	MAS	USO	BOP	PGA
1911			16	

TAYLOR, JH (ENG)

	MAS	USO	BOP	PGA
1893			10	
1894			W	
1895			W	
1896			2	
1897			10	
1898			4	
1899			4	
1900		2	W	
1901			3	
1902			6	
1903			9	
1904			2	
1905			2	
1906			2	
1907			2	
1908			7	
1909			W	
1910			14	
1911			5	
1912			11	
1913		30	W	
1914			2	
1920			12	
1921			26	
1922			6	
1924			5	
1925	5			
1926			10	

TAYLOR, Josh (ENG)

	MAS	USO	BOP	PGA
1911			24	
1913			14	
1914			25	

TAYLOR, JW (ENG)

	MAS	USO	BOP	PGA
1896			29	
1897			30	
1898			27	
1899			25	
1900			18	

TAYLOR, Philip (ENG)

	MAS	USO	BOP	PGA
1912			24	
1913			17	
1920			16	

TAYLOR, Scott (US)

	MAS	USO	BOP	PGA
1989		29		

TELLIER, Louis (FRA/US)

	MAS	USO	BOP	PGA
1913		4	22	
1914		8		
1915		4		
1916		13		Last 32
1919		5		Last 32
1921		14		

TENNYSON, Brian (US)

	MAS	USO	BOP	PGA
1989				27
1990				26

TERRY, Orrin (US)

	MAS	USO	BOP	PGA
1908		17		
1909		15		

TEWELL, Doug (US)

	MAS	USO	BOP	PGA
1980				30
1982				22
1983				9
1984				25
1985				12
1986				10
1988	14			

THOM, Charles (US)

	MAS	USO	BOP	PGA
1902		7		
1910		12		
1913		26		
1921				Last 32

THOMAS, Dave (WAL)

	MAS	USO	BOP	PGA
1956			17	
1957			5	
1958			2	
1959	30			
1962			8	
1963			26	
1964			13	
1966			2	
1968			27	

THOMAS, Emery (US)

	MAS	USO	BOP	PGA
1950				Last 32

THOMPSON, Alec (SCO)

	MAS	USO	BOP	PGA
1904			25	

THOMPSON, Alvie (CAN)

	MAS	USO	BOP	PGA
1963	28			

THOMPSON, George (US)

	MAS	USO	BOP	PGA
1920				Last 16

THOMPSON, John (SCO)

	MAS	USO	BOP	PGA
1876			14	

THOMPSON, Leonard (US)

	MAS	USO	BOP	PGA
1974		21		17
1975				10
1976				22
1977				15
1978	24			
1979	7			
1980				26
1981				22

THOMPSON, RM (US)

	MAS	USO	BOP	PGA
1914		25		

THOMPSON, Rocky (US)

	MAS	USO	BOP	PGA
1973		18		

THOMPSON, W (US)

	MAS	USO	BOP	PGA
1899		24		

THOMSON, Cyril (ENG)

	MAS	USO	BOP	PGA
1935			30	

THOMSON, George (US)

	MAS	USO	BOP	PGA
1904		15		

THOMSON, Hector (SCO)

	MAS	USO	BOP	PGA
1936			15a	
1950			14	
1953			22	

THOMSON, James (SCO/US)

	MAS	USO	BOP	PGA
1910		18		
1916				Last 32

THOMSON, Jimmy (SCO/US)

	MAS	USO	BOP	PGA
1926		16		
1929			13	
1935		2		Last 32
1936	15	14		RU
1937	6	28		Last 16
1938	8			Last 32
1939	18			
1942	12			Last 32
1946	25			Last 32
1949				Last 32

THOMSON, Peter (AUS)

	MAS	USO	BOP	PGA
1951			6	
1952			2	
1953		26	2	
1954	16		W	
1955	18		W	
1956		4	W	
1957	5	22	2	
1958	23		W	
1959			23	
1960			9	
1961	19		7	
1962			6	
1963			5	
1964			24	
1965			W	
1966			8	
1967			8	
1968			24	
1969			3	
1970			9	
1971			9	
1977			13	
1978			24	
1979			26	

THOMSON, R (SCO)

	MAS	USO	BOP	PGA
1873			18	

THOMSON, Robert (SCO)

	MAS	USO	BOP	PGA
1903			6	
1904			12	
1905			7	
1906			30	
1909			17	
1911			29	
1912			13	

THOMSON, William (SCO)

	MAS	USO	BOP	PGA
1874			6	
1876			4	
1880			21	
1882			16	
1883			23	
1889			10	

THOREN, John (US)

	MAS	USO	BOP	PGA
1938				Last 32
1957				Last 32

THORPE, Jim (US)

	MAS	USO	BOP	PGA
1981		11		
1982		30		
1983		13		14
1984		4		
1985	18			
1986				7
1987		9		

TILLINGHAST, AW [a] (US)

	MAS	USO	BOP	PGA
1910		25		

TIMBERMAN, Wayne (US)

Year	MAS	USO	BOP	PGA
1945				Last 32

TINGEY Jr, Albert (ENG)

Year	MAS	USO	BOP	PGA
1924			18	

TINGEY Sr, Albert (ENG)

Year	MAS	USO	BOP	PGA
1895			21	
1896			28	
1897			30	
1899			9	
1908			30	

TINSLEY, Dave (US)

Year	MAS	USO	BOP	PGA
1946			'	Last 32

TODA, Torchy (JAP)

Year	MAS	USO	BOP	PGA
1936	29			

TODD, Harry (US)

Year	MAS	USO	BOP	PGA
1941		13a		
1946		22		
1947	29	13		
1948	8			
1949		14		
1952		13		

TOLIFSON, AC (US)

Year	MAS	USO	BOP	PGA
1897		30		
1900		25		

TOLLES, Tommy (US)

Year	MAS	USO	BOP	PGA
1996				3
1997	3	5		13

TOLLEY, Cyril [a] (ENG)

Year	MAS	USO	BOP	PGA
1924			18	
1925			27	
1929			25	
1933			18	
1938			28	

TOMORI, Katsuyoshi (JAP)

Year	MAS	USO	BOP	PGA
1995			24	

TOOGOOD, AH (ENG)

Year	MAS	USO	BOP	PGA
1894			4	
1895			9	
1896			17	
1897			22	
1899			23	
1903			18	
1904			12	
1907			22	
1908			18	

TOOGOOD, Peter [a] (AUS)

Year	MAS	USO	BOP	PGA
1954			15	

TOOGOOD, Walter (ENG)

Year	MAS	USO	BOP	PGA
1895			27	
1896			22	
1897			26	
1898			19	
1899			20	
1901			28	
1902			20	
1905			28	
1906			15	
1907			13	
1908			18	

TOPPING, Lambert (ENG)

Year	MAS	USO	BOP	PGA
1954			20	

TORPEY, Bunny (US)

Year	MAS	USO	BOP	PGA
1933				Last 32
1937				Last 32

TORRANCE, Sam (SCO)

Year	MAS	USO	BOP	PGA
1975			19	
1981			5	
1982			12	
1984			9	
1985			16	
1986			21	
1994		21		30
1995			11	23
1996		16		

TORRANCE, TA [a] (SCO)

Year	MAS	USO	BOP	PGA
1932			22	

TORRANCE, WB [a] (SCO)

Year	MAS	USO	BOP	PGA
1927			9	

TORZA, Felice (IT)

Year	MAS	USO	BOP	PGA
1952		24		
1953	29			RU

TOSKI, Bob (US)

Year	MAS	USO	BOP	PGA
1950		20		Last 16
1951	18			
1953				Last 32
1954	22	18		Last 32
1956		17		Last 32
1958				20

TOWNS, Eddie (US)

Year	MAS	USO	BOP	PGA
1916				Last 32
1921				Last 32
1922				Last 16
1924				Last 16

TOWNSEND, Peter (ENG)

Year	MAS	USO	BOP	PGA
1966			23a	
1969			16	
1972			13	
1974			13	
1981			19	

339

TRAVERS, Jerome [a]
(US)

	MAS	USO	BOP	PGA
1907		26		
1913		28		
1915		W		

TRAVIANI, P
(IT)

	MAS	USO	BOP	PGA
1951			24	

TRAVIS, Walter [a]
(AUS/US)

	MAS	USO	BOP	PGA
1902		2		
1903		15		
1905		11		
1908		23		
1909		7		
1912		10		

TREVINO, Lee
(US)

	MAS	USO	BOP	PGA
1967		5		
1968		W		23
1969	19			
1970		8	3	26
1971		W	W	13
1972		4	W	11
1973		4	10	18
1974				W
1975	10	29		
1976	28			
1977		27	4	13
1978	14	12	29	7
1979	12	19	17	
1980	26	12	2	7
1981			11	
1982			12	
1983	20		5	14
1984		9	14	W
1985	10		20	2
1986		4		11
1987			17	
1989	18			
1990	24		25	
1991			17	

TRIPLETT, Kirk
(US)

	MAS	USO	BOP	PGA
1994		23		15
1995				13
1997				13

TRISH, John
(US)

	MAS	USO	BOP	PGA
1952				Last 32

TROMBLEY, Bill
(US)

	MAS	USO	BOP	PGA
1952		19		
1954				Last 32

TUCKER, Ken
(US)

	MAS	USO	BOP	PGA
1939				Last 32

TUCKER, Samuel
(US)

	MAS	USO	BOP	PGA
1895		9		
1897		25		

TUCKER, Willie
(ENG/US)

	MAS	USO	BOP	PGA
1896		8		
1897		15		
1898		14		
1899		27		

TUPLING, Peter [a]
(ENG)

	MAS	USO	BOP	PGA
1969			28	

TURNBULL, George
(US)

	MAS	USO	BOP	PGA
1905		20		
1916		21		

TURNER, Greg
(NZ)

	MAS	USO	BOP	PGA
1994			20	
1996			7	

TURNER, Ted
(US)

	MAS	USO	BOP	PGA
1934				Last 16
1935		14		
1936			15	

TURNESA, Jim
(US)

	MAS	USO	BOP	PGA
1942				RU
1945				Last 16
1946				QF
1947				Last 16
1948		3		
1949	4	4		Last 16
1951				Last 32
1952				W
1953	27	17		Last 32
1954			5	
1956	22			Last 16

TURNESA, Joe
(US)

	MAS	USO	BOP	PGA
1923		14		
1924		15		
1925		11		
1926		2		Last 32
1927		27		RU
1928		6		
1929			25	
1930		17		
1932				Last 32
1935	9			

TURNESA, Mike
(US)

	MAS	USO	BOP	PGA
1934	28			
1935	25			
1939				Last 32
1941				Last 16
1942				Last 32
1945				Last 16
1946		26		
1947				Last 16
1948				RU
1953				Last 32

TURNESA, Willie [a]
(US)

	MAS	USO	BOP	PGA
1939	26			

340

TURPIE, Harry (SCO/US)

	MAS	USO	BOP	PGA
1897		14		
1898		12		
1899		18		
1900		8		
1901		22		
1902		8		
1903		23		
1904		20		
1906		13		
1911		12		

TUTEN, Billy (US)

	MAS	USO	BOP	PGA
1990		24		

TWAY, Bob (US)

	MAS	USO	BOP	PGA
1986	8	8		W
1988		25	20	
1991		26	5	
1995		10		
1996	12			
1997		5		13

TWEDDELL, W [a] (ENG)

	MAS	USO	BOP	PGA
1927			29	

TWIGGS, Greg (US)

	MAS	USO	BOP	PGA
1993				22

TWINE, William (ENG)

	MAS	USO	BOP	PGA
1927			29	
1928			14	
1931			25	
1932			25	
1934			11	

TWITTY, Howard (US)

	MAS	USO	BOP	PGA
1979				7
1980				5
1989				27
1991				16
1993	17			

TYNER, Tray (US)

	MAS	USO	BOP	PGA
1992		17		

TYNG, JA [a] (US)

	MAS	USO	BOP	PGA
1897		15		
1898		19		

ULRICH, Wally (US)

	MAS	USO	BOP	PGA
1953				Last 16
1954				Last 32
1955				Last 16

UPTON Jr, FR [a] (US)

	MAS	USO	BOP	PGA
1909		15		

URZETTA, Sam (US)

	MAS	USO	BOP	PGA
1951	25a	29a		
1956	12			

VALENTINE, Tommy (US)

	MAS	USO	BOP	PGA
1981		26		11

van DONCK, Flory (BEL)

	MAS	USO	BOP	PGA
1946			27	
1947			21	
1948			7	
1950			9	
1951			24	
1952			7	
1953			20	
1954			10	
1955			5	
1956			2	
1957			5	
1958			5	
1959			2	

VARDON, Harry (ENG)

	MAS	USO	BOP	PGA
1893			23	
1894			5	
1895			9	
1896			W	
1897			6	
1898			W	
1899			W	
1900		W	2	
1901			2	
1902			2	
1903			W	
1904			5	
1905			9	
1906			3	
1907			7	
1908			5	
1909			26	
1910			16	
1911			W	
1912			2	
1913		2	3	
1914			W	
1920		2	14	
1921			23	
1922			8	

VARDON, Tom (ENG)

	MAS	USO	BOP	PGA
1891			9	
1892			12	
1893			28	
1894			19	
1895			9	
1896			10	
1897			7	
1900			10	
1902			5	
1903			2	
1904			4	
1906			12	
1907			3	
1908			13	
1909		23	19	
1912		21		
1916		9		

VAUGHAN, David (WAL)

	MAS	USO	BOP	PGA
1972			7	

VENTURI, Ken (US)

	MAS	USO	BOP	PGA
1954	16a			
1956	2a	8a		
1957	13	6		
1958	4			20
1959				5
1960	2	23		9
1961	11			
1962	9			
1964		W		5
1966	16	17		15
1967	21	28		11

VERPLANK, Scott (US)

	MAS	USO	BOP	PGA
1986		15		
1994		18		
1995		21		

VERWEY, Bob (SA)

	MAS	USO	BOP	PGA
1965		17		
1966		22		
1967		18		
1979			30	

VICKERS, RD (ENG)

	MAS	USO	BOP	PGA
1927			9	

VINES, Ellsworth (US)

	MAS	USO	BOP	PGA
1946		26		
1947	24			
1948	28	14		
1949		14		
1950				Last 32
1951				SF
1957				Last 32

VINES, Randall (AUS)

	MAS	USO	BOP	PGA
1971			25	

von ELM, George [a] (US)

	MAS	USO	BOP	PGA
1926			3	
1928		4		
1929		5		
1930		11		
1931		2		
1932		27		
1934		28		
1938		11		

von NIDA, Norman (AUS)

	MAS	USO	BOP	PGA
1946			4	
1947			6	
1948			3	
1950	27			
1952	27		9	

VOSSLER, Ernie (US)

	MAS	USO	BOP	PGA
1955		21		
1959		5		17
1960				24
1961				15
1966				18

WADE, Jim (ENG)

	MAS	USO	BOP	PGA
1949			25	

WADKINS, Bobby (US)

	MAS	USO	BOP	PGA
1980		12		
1983				27
1986		15		
1987	21	4		7

WADKINS, Lanny (US)

	MAS	USO	BOP	PGA
1971		13a		
1972	19	25		16
1973	29	7	7	3
1974		26		
1975			22	
1977				W
1978	18			
1979	7	19		
1980				30
1981	21	14		
1982		6		2
1983	8	7	29	
1984		11	4	3
1985	18	5		10
1986		2		11
1987	12		29	2
1988	11	12		25
1989	26		26	
1990	3			
1991	3			
1993	3			14
1994				

WADKINS, Lloyd (US)

	MAS	USO	BOP	PGA
1947				Last 32

WAGNER, Leonard (US)

	MAS	USO	BOP	PGA
1955				Last 32

WAITES, Brian (ENG)

	MAS	USO	BOP	PGA
1983			19	

WALDORF, Duffy (US)

	MAS	USO	BOP	PGA
1992			25	9
1994		9		
1995	24	13		20
1996	5			

WALKER, Cyril (ENG/US)

	MAS	USO	BOP	PGA
1916				QF
1921		13		SF
1923		23		Last 16
1924		W		
1926			17	
1931				QF

	MAS	USO	BOP	PGA

WALKER, Harry (ENG)

	MAS	USO	BOP	PGA
1926			13	

WALKER, Peter (SCO/US)

	MAS	USO	BOP	PGA
1899		9		

WALL, Art (US)

	MAS	USO	BOP	PGA
1953		26		
1955		16		
1956				Last 32
1958	6			11
1959	W			25
1961				5
1962		11		23
1963	21			8
1967		9		
1968	22			
1971	27			
1972				24
1975	15			
1976	28			

WALPER, Leo (US)

	MAS	USO	BOP	PGA
1936				Last 16

WALSH, Frank (US)

	MAS	USO	BOP	PGA
1928		27		
1929				Last 32
1930		28		
1931		13		
1932				RU
1933		29		Last 16
1935		26		
1936				Last 32
1937		20		
1938	27			Last 32
1939	29			
1940	12	10		Last 32

WALSH, Peter (US)

	MAS	USO	BOP	PGA
1922				Last 32

WALTON, Philip (IRE)

	MAS	USO	BOP	PGA
1989			13	

WALTON, Thomas (ENG)

	MAS	USO	BOP	PGA
1922			8	
1923			19	

WALZEL, Bobby (US)

	MAS	USO	BOP	PGA
1979		19		
1980				8

WAMPLER, Fred (US)

	MAS	USO	BOP	PGA
1959		28		

WARD, Charlie (ENG)

	MAS	USO	BOP	PGA
1932			17	
1933			28	
1934			13	
1939			30	
1946			4	
1947			6	
1948			3	
1949			4	
1951			3	
1953			17	
1956			17	

WARD Jr, E Harvie [a] (US)

	MAS	USO	BOP	PGA
1952	21			
1953	14			
1954	20			
1955	8	7		
1957	4	26		

WARD, Marvin (Bud) (US)

	MAS	USO	BOP	PGA
1939		4a		
1940	21a			
1941		30a		
1942	14a			
1946		26a		
1947		5a		
1948	30a			
1955	30			
1957		17		

WARGO, Tom (US)

	MAS	USO	BOP	PGA
1992				28

WARRENDER, T (US)

	MAS	USO	BOP	PGA
1896		28		

WATERS, Alan (ENG)

	MAS	USO	BOP	PGA
1947			23	
1948			11	
1949			18	
1951			17	

WATERS, L (SCO/SA)

	MAS	USO	BOP	PGA
1895			18	
1901			22	

343

WATROUS, Al (US)

Year	MAS	USO	BOP	PGA
1922				Last 32
1923		8		
1924				Last 16
1925		13		Last 32
1926			2	Last 32
1927		18		
1928			8	Last 16
1929				SF
1930		17		Last 16
1931		15		
1932				Last 32
1933		13		
1934	11			QF
1935		14		SF
1936	29			
1937	7			Last 32
1938	27			
1939	25			Last 16
1940	21			Last 32
1950				Last 32

WATSON, Denis (ZIM)

Year	MAS	USO	BOP	PGA
1982			15	
1985		2		
1986		12		
1987	27			

WATSON, James (SCO/US)

Year	MAS	USO	BOP	PGA
1904		29		
1906		27		

WATSON, RC (US)

Year	MAS	USO	BOP	PGA
1911		23		

WATSON, Tom (US)

Year	MAS	USO	BOP	PGA
1972		29		
1973				12
1974		5		11
1975	8	9	W	9
1976		7		15
1977	W	7	W	6
1978	2	6	14	2
1979	2		26	12
1980	12	3	W	10
1981	W	23	23	
1982	5	W	W	9
1983	4	2	W	
1984	2	11	2	
1985	10			6
1986	6	24		16
1987	7	2	7	14
1988	9		28	
1989	14		4	9
1990	7			19
1991	3	16	26	
1993		5		5
1994	13	6	11	9
1995	14			
1996		13		
1997	4		10	

WATT, David (SCO)

Year	MAS	USO	BOP	PGA
1914			25	

WATT, Tom (SCO)

Year	MAS	USO	BOP	PGA
1905			18	
1908			11	

WATT, William (SCO)

Year	MAS	USO	BOP	PGA
1911			21	
1921			19	
1922			27	
1923			8	

WAY, Ernest (US)

Year	MAS	USO	BOP	PGA
1899		23		
1900		21		
1906		27		

WAY, Paul (ENG)

Year	MAS	USO	BOP	PGA
1984			22	

WAY, WH (US)

Year	MAS	USO	BOP	PGA
1896		11		
1897		25		
1899		2		
1900		16		
1903		15		
1904		26		
1905		20		
1908		29		

WEASTALL, BS (ENG)

Year	MAS	USO	BOP	PGA
1924			21	

WEAVER, Bert (US)

Year	MAS	USO	BOP	PGA
1963				27

WEAVER, Dewitt (US)

Year	MAS	USO	BOP	PGA
1974		18		

WEBB, Gene (US)

Year	MAS	USO	BOP	PGA
1949		19		

WEBSTER, DL (SCO)

Year	MAS	USO	BOP	PGA
1968			21	

WEBSTER, Steven [a] (ENG)

Year	MAS	USO	BOP	PGA
1995			24	

WEETMAN, Harry (ENG)

Year	MAS	USO	BOP	PGA
1951			6	
1952			15	
1953			14	
1955			5	
1956			10	
1957			12	
1958			8	
1959			16	
1960			9	
1962			12	
1964			6	
1965			29	

WEHRLE, Wilfred [a] (US)

	MAS	USO	BOP	PGA
1939		16		
1940		23		

WEIBRING, DA (US)

	MAS	USO	BOP	PGA
1979		19		
1983		20		
1985			8	
1986			30	4
1987	7			3
1988		3		
1989		21		
1991		11		
1992	25			

WEISKOPF, Tom (US)

	MAS	USO	BOP	PGA
1967		15		
1968	16	24		
1969	2	22		
1970	23	30	22	
1971	6			22
1972	2	8	7	
1973		3	W	6
1974	2	15	7	3
1975	2	29	15	
1976	9	2	17	8
1977	14	3	22	
1978	11	4	17	4
1979		4		
1980			16	10
1981				27
1982	10			
1983	20	24		30

WEITZEL, Johnny (US)

	MAS	USO	BOP	PGA
1954		21		

WELCH, Michael (ENG)

	MAS	USO	BOP	PGA
1996			18	

WEST, James (US)

	MAS	USO	BOP	PGA
1916				Last 32
1919		18		QF
1920		20		
1921				Last 26
1923				Last 32
1924		22		

WESTON, Percy (ENG)

	MAS	USO	BOP	PGA
1924			9	
1932			29	
1934			21	

WESTWOOD, Lee (ENG)

	MAS	USO	BOP	PGA
1997	24	19	10	29

WETHERED, Roger [a] (ENG)

	MAS	USO	BOP	PGA
1921			2	

WHEILDON, Dick (ENG)

	MAS	USO	BOP	PGA
1920			21	
1922			17	

WHIGHAM, Charles [a] (SCO)

	MAS	USO	BOP	PGA
1890			27	

WHIGHAM, HJ [a] (SCO/US)

	MAS	USO	BOP	PGA
1896		6		
1897		8		

WHITCOMBE, Charles (ENG)

	MAS	USO	BOP	PGA
1922			5	
1923			6	
1926			22	
1927			6	
1930			9	
1931			28	
1932			4	
1934			7	
1935			3	
1936			19	
1937			4	
1938			10	

WHITCOMBE, Ernest E (ENG)

	MAS	USO	BOP	PGA
1937			29	
1946			21	
1947			18	
1948			15	
1950			17	
1951			24	
1959			29	

WHITCOMBE, Ernest R (ENG)

	MAS	USO	BOP	PGA
1914			29	
1922			12	
1924			2	
1925			25	
1927			4	
1930			17	
1931			22	
1933			12	
1934			9	
1935			17	
1938			19	

WHITCOMBE, Reg (ENG)

	MAS	USO	BOP	PGA
1925			19	
1926			13	
1928			23	
1930			13	
1931			16	
1932			17	
1933			7	
1934			16	
1936			8	
1937			2	
1938			W	
1939			3	
1946			14	
1947			13	
1948			18	

WHITE, Buck (US)

	MAS	USO	BOP	PGA
1949		6		
1951		16		Last 32
1953				Last 32
1957				Last 32

WHITE, DK (US)

	MAS	USO	BOP	PGA
1920		23		
1923				Last 32

WHITE, GM (Bill) (ENG)

	MAS	USO	BOP	PGA
1949			30	
1950			24	

WHITE, Jack (SCO)

	MAS	USO	BOP	PGA
1893			10	
1895			21	
1898			13	
1899			2	
1900			4	
1901			6	
1902			18	
1903			3	
1904			W	
1905			18	

WHITE, Orville (US)

	MAS	USO	BOP	PGA
1934				Last 32
1935		25		Last 32
1936	15			

WHITE, R (US)

	MAS	USO	BOP	PGA
1897		27		

WHITE, Ronnie [a] (ENG)

	MAS	USO	BOP	PGA
1946			30	

WHITECROSS, Robert [a] (SCO)

	MAS	USO	BOP	PGA
1906			15	

WHITEHEAD, George (US)

	MAS	USO	BOP	PGA
1938				Last 32

WHITEHEAD, Ross (ENG)

	MAS	USO	BOP	PGA
1962			12	

WHITING, Albert (ENG)

	MAS	USO	BOP	PGA
1928			11	

WHITT, Don (US)

	MAS	USO	BOP	PGA
1957				SF
1958				29
1960		17		
1961				15
1962		17		30

WHITTEN, Buddy (US)

	MAS	USO	BOP	PGA
1983				27

WIEBE, Mark (US)

	MAS	USO	BOP	PGA
1988		25		
1989				12
1990				19

WIECHERS, Jim (US)

	MAS	USO	BOP	PGA
1972		25		29
1975		14		

WILCOCK, Peter (ENG)

	MAS	USO	BOP	PGA
1973			18	

WILCOX, Leland (US)

	MAS	USO	BOP	PGA
1940		23		

WILCOX, Pat (US)

	MAS	USO	BOP	PGA
1937				Last 32

WILCOX, Terry (US)

	MAS	USO	BOP	PGA
1965		28		
1969				7
1970	21			

WILKES, Brian (SA)

	MAS	USO	BOP	PGA
1963			20	

WILKES, Trevor (SA)

	MAS	USO	BOP	PGA
1957			24	
1958			26	

WILL, George (SCO)

	MAS	USO	BOP	PGA
1961			30	
1964			29	
1965			21	
1966			23	

WILLIAMS, Dan (US)

	MAS	USO	BOP	PGA
1924				Last 16
1925				Last 16
1926		9		

WILLIAMS, David (ENG)

	MAS	USO	BOP	PGA
1991			12	

WILLIAMS, Eddie (US)

	MAS	USO	BOP	PGA
1931		25		

WILLIAMS, Harold (US)

	MAS	USO	BOP	PGA
1950		20		Last 32

WILLIAMS Jr, Henry (US)

	MAS	USO	BOP	PGA
1944				Last 32
1948				Last 32
1949				QF
1950		29		RU
1952				Last 16
1953				Last 16
1954				Last 32

WILLIAMSON, EB (ENG)

	MAS	USO	BOP	PGA
1954			27	

WILLIAMSON, JM (SCO)

	MAS	USO	BOP	PGA
1900			29	

WILLIAMSON, Tom (ENG)

	MAS	USO	BOP	PGA
1898			21	
1899			9	
1902			30	
1903			11	
1905			13	
1906			19	
1907			7	
1910			19	
1912			17	
1913			7	
1914			4	
1920			26	
1921			6	
1922			27	
1923			12	
1924			13	
1926			13	
1927			9	
1928			21	
1929			25	
1931			11	

WILSON, Dave (US)

	MAS	USO	BOP	PGA
1919				Last 32

WILSON, JC [a] (SCO)

	MAS	USO	BOP	PGA
1946			25	

WILSON, P [a] (SCO)

	MAS	USO	BOP	PGA
1887			20	

WILSON, Robert (ENG)

	MAS	USO	BOP	PGA
1890			22	
1896		9		
1897		11		

WILSON, Reg (ENG)

	MAS	USO	BOP	PGA
1912			7	
1914			6	
1920			21	
1923			29	
1928			23	

WILSON, Sandy (SCO)

	MAS	USO	BOP	PGA
1968			27	

WINGATE, Sydney (ENG)

	MAS	USO	BOP	PGA
1920			7	
1923			12	
1924			23	
1925			5	
1928			23	

WINNINGER, Bo (US)

	MAS	USO	BOP	PGA
1951		29a		
1952		24		
1953	29			
1957		21		
1958	17	27		16
1959	18	19		
1960				29
1962		17		
1963	8			27
1964	21			7
1965	26			4

WISE, Larry (US)

	MAS	USO	BOP	PGA
1972				20

WOLFF, Randy (US)

	MAS	USO	BOP	PGA
1970		18		

WOLSTENHOLME, Guy (ENG/AUS)

	MAS	USO	BOP	PGA
1959			16a	
1960			6	
1962			24	
1965			17	
1967			13	
1969			11	
1970			22	
1976			17	

WOOD, Craig (US)

	MAS	USO	BOP	PGA
1929		16		QF
1930		9		
1932		14		Last 32
1933		3	2	
1934	2			RU
1935	2	21		
1936	20			SF
1937	26			Last 32
1939	6	2		
1940	7	4		Last 32
1941	**W**	**W**		Last 32
1942	22			QF
1944				Last 16
1949		27		

WOOD, Larry (US)

	MAS	USO	BOP	PGA
1971				22

WOOD, Warren [a] (US)

	MAS	USO	BOP	PGA
1914		22		

WOOD, Willie (US)

	MAS	USO	BOP	PGA
1985				23
1992		17		
1997	12			

WOODS, Tiger (US)

	MAS	USO	BOP	PGA
1996			22a	
1997	**W**	19	24	29

WOODWARD, Jim (US)

	MAS	USO	BOP	PGA
1987		17		

WOOSNAM, Ian (WAL)

Year	MAS	USO	BOP	PGA
1985			16	
1986			3	30
1987			8	
1988			25	
1989	14	2		6
1990	30	21	4	
1991	W		17	
1992	19	6	5	
1993	17			22
1994				9
1995	17	21		
1996	29			
1997			24	

WORSHAM, Lew (US)

Year	MAS	USO	BOP	PGA
1946		22		Last 32
1947		W		QF
1948	30	6		Last 16
1949	6	27		Last 16
1950				Last 32
1951	3	14		Last 32
1952	7	7		Last 32
1954	12	23		
1955				QF
1956				Last 16
1961	22			
1962	29			

WORTHINGTON, JS [a] (ENG)

Year	MAS	USO	BOP	PGA
1904			21	

WRENN, Robert (US)

Year	MAS	USO	BOP	PGA
1988	25			
1989		26		

WRIGHT, A (SCO)

Year	MAS	USO	BOP	PGA
1890			20	

WRIGHT Jr, Fred [a] (US)

Year	MAS	USO	BOP	PGA
1922		24		

WRIGHT, Jimmy (US)

Year	MAS	USO	BOP	PGA
1969				4
1970	29			

WYNN, Bob (US)

Year	MAS	USO	BOP	PGA
1975				28
1977	24			

WYNNE, Philip (SCO)

Year	MAS	USO	BOP	PGA
1898			10	

WYSONG, Dudley (US)

Year	MAS	USO	BOP	PGA
1964		23		
1965		8		
1966				2

YANCEY, Bert (US)

Year	MAS	USO	BOP	PGA
1966				23
1967	3			
1968	3	3		
1969	13	22	16	
1970	4	22	13	22
1971		9	11	22
1972	12	11	19	29
1973		25	5	24
1974		3		
1975	30			

YATES, Charlie [a] (US)

Year	MAS	USO	BOP	PGA
1934	21			
1935	19			
1937	26			
1939	18			
1940	17			
1942	28			

YEOMAN, Tom (ENG)

Year	MAS	USO	BOP	PGA
1901			12	
1902			25	

YOUDS, Jack (ENG/US)

Year	MAS	USO	BOP	PGA
1898		21		

YOUNG, Arthur (ENG)

Year	MAS	USO	BOP	PGA
1930			17	

YUNG-YO, Hsieh (TAI)

Year	MAS	USO	BOP	PGA
1970	29			

ZARHARDT, Joe (US)

Year	MAS	USO	BOP	PGA
1939				Last 32
1941		25		
1944				Last 32

ZARLEY, Kermit (US)

Year	MAS	USO	BOP	PGA
1968	20			8
1969		13		
1970				22
1969		13		
1971		27		
1972		6		
1973	17			9
1975		24		
1978				19

ZENDER, Bob (US)

Year	MAS	USO	BOP	PGA
1976				30
1978				26

ZIEGLER, Larry (US)

Year	MAS	USO	BOP	PGA
1968		24		
1969				5
1970		8		
1971	30			
1973		13		
1974		12		
1975	13			
1976	3			

ZIMMERMAN, Al
(US)

	MAS	USO	BOP	PGA
1932		27		
1935				SF
1936				Last 32
1938		19		
1946	29			

ZIMMERMAN, Emery
(US)

	MAS	USO	BOP	PGA
1938		5		

ZOELLER, Fuzzy
(US)

	MAS	USO	BOP	PGA
1978				10
1979	W			
1980	19			
1981				2
1982	10	15	8	
1983	20		14	6
1984		W	14	
1985		9	11	
1986	21	15	8	
1987	27		29	
1988	16	8		
1989	26			
1990	20	8		14
1991	12	5		
1992	19			
1993	11		14	
1994			3	19
1995		21		
1997		28		

ZOKOL, Richard
(US)

	MAS	USO	BOP	PGA
1988				17
1993				14

Part 5

The Records 1860–1997

INTRODUCTION

These records both complement, and/or are a result of, all the previous sections of this book. The most important historical records only are included, in an attempt not to trivialize the statistics, but the author would be happy to consider readers' comments on this for future editions.

The last section of Part 5 is devoted to Performance Charts which show the Majors results of all the greatest players throughout history, both in lists comparing them with their contemporaries, and in an 'All-Time Greats' Hall of Fame.

MOST WINS IN MAJOR CHAMPIONSHIPS

Jack Nicklaus	18
Walter Hagen	11
Ben Hogan	9
Gary Player	9
Tom Watson	8
Bobby Jones	7
Arnold Palmer	7
Gene Sarazen	7
Sam Snead	7
Harry Vardon	7
Nick Faldo	6
Lee Trevino	6
Seve Ballesteros	5
James Braid	5
Byron Nelson	5
JH Taylor	5
Peter Thomson	5
Willie Anderson Jr	4
Jim Barnes	4
Ray Floyd	4
Bobby Locke	4
Tom Morris Jr	4
Tom Morris Sr	4
Willie Park Sr	4
Jamie Anderson	3
Tommy Armour	3
Julius Boros	3
Billy Casper	3
Henry Cotton	3
Jimmy Demaret	3
Bob Ferguson	3
Ralph Guldahl	3
Hale Irwin	3
Cary Middlecoff	3
Larry Nelson	3
Nick Price	3
Denny Shute	3

MOST WINS IN INDIVIDUAL MAJORS

British Open

Harry Vardon	6
James Braid	5
JH Taylor	5
Peter Thomson	5
Tom Watson	5
Walter Hagen	4
Tom Morris Jr	4
Tom Morris Sr	4
Willie Park Sr	4

US Open

Willie Anderson Jr	4
Ben Hogan	4
Bobby Jones	4
Jack Nicklaus	4
Hale Irwin	3
Julius Boros	2
Billy Casper	2
Ernie Els	2
Ralph Guldahl	2
Walter Hagen	2
John McDermott	2
Cary Middlecoff	2
Andy North	2
Gene Sarazen	2
Alex Smith	2
Curtis Strange	2
Lee Trevino	2

PGA

Walter Hagen	5
(All Matchplay – MP)	
Jack Nicklaus	5
(All Strokeplay – SP)	
Gene Sarazen (All MP)	3
Sam Snead (All MP)	3
Jim Barnes (All MP)	2
Leo Diegel (All MP)	2
Ray Floyd (All SP)	2
Ben Hogan (All MP)	2
Byron Nelson (All MP)	2
Larry Nelson (All SP)	2
Gary Player (All SP)	2
Nick Price (All SP)	2
Paul Runyan (All MP)	2
Denny Shute (All MP)	2
Dave Stockton (All SP)	2
Lee Trevino (All SP)	2

The Masters

Jack Nicklaus	6
Arnold Palmer	4
Jimmy Demaret	3
Nick Faldo	3
Gary Player	3
Sam Snead	3
Seve Ballesteros	2
Ben Crenshaw	2
Ben Hogan	2
Bernhard Langer	2
Byron Nelson	2
Horton Smith	2
Tom Watson	2

MULTIPLE WINS IN THE SAME YEAR

Jack Nicklaus (5)	1963	**MAS, PGA**
	1966	**MAS, BOP**
	1972	**MAS, USOP**
	1975	**MAS, PGA**
	1980	**USOP, PGA**
Ben Hogan (3) *	1953	MAS, USOP, BOP
	1948	USOP, PGA
	1951	MAS, USOP
Bobby Jones (2)	1926	USOP, BOP
	1930	USOP, BOP
Arnold Palmer (2)	1960	MAS, USOP
	1962	MAS, BOP
Gene Sarazen (2)	1922	USOP, PGA
	1932	USOP, BOP
Tom Watson (2)	1977	MAS, BOP
	1982	USOP, BOP
Jack Burke Jr (1)	1956	MAS, PGA
Nick Faldo (1)	1990	MAS, BOP
Walter Hagen (1)	1924	BOP, PGA
Gary Player (1)	1974	MAS, BOP
Nick Price (1)	1994	BOP, PGA
Sam Snead (1)	1949	MAS, PGA
Lee Trevino (1)	1971	USOP, BOP
Craig Wood (1)	1941	MAS, USOP

The only occasion where three Majors were won

YOUNGEST WINNERS

Tom Morris Jr (BOP, 1868)
17 years 5 months 8 days

Tom Morris Jr (BOP, 1969)
  18 years 5 months 1 day
Tom Morris Jr (BOP, 1870)
  19 years 5 months
John McDermott (USOP, 1911)
  19 years 10 months 12 days
Francis Ouimet (USOP, 1913)
  20 years 4 months 11 days
Gene Sarazen (USOP, 1922)
  20 years 4 months 16 days
Gene Sarazen (PGA, 1922)
  20 years 5 months 20 days
Tom Creavy (PGA, 1931)
  20 years 7 months 17 days
John McDermott (USOP, 1912)
  20 years 11 momths 21 days
Willie Auchterlonie (BOP, 1893)
  21 years 24 days
Tiger Woods (MAS, 1997)
  21 years 3 months 15 days

OLDEST WINNERS

Julius Boros (PGA, 1968)
48 years 4 months 18 days

Tom Morris, Sr (BOP, 1867)
  46 years 3 months 9 days
Jack Nicklaus (MAS, 1986)
  46 years 2 months 23 days
Jerry Barber (PGA, 1961)
  45 years 3 months 6 days
Hale Irwin (USOP, 1990)
  45 years 15 days
Lee Trevino (PGA, 1984)
  44 years 8 months 18 days
Roberto de Vicenzo (BOP, 1967)
  44 years 3 months 3 days
Ray Floyd (USOP, 1986)
  43 years 9 months 11 days
Ted Ray (USOP, 1920)
  43 years 4 months 16 days
Julius Boros (USOP, 1963)
  43 years 3 months 20 days
Ben Crenshaw (MAS, 1995)
  43 years 2 months 29 days

LARGEST WINNING MARGINS

13 Tom Morris Sr	BOP, 1862	
12 Tom Morris Jr	BOP, 1870	
Tiger Woods	MAS, 1997	
11 Willie Smith	USOP, 1899	
9 Jim Barnes	USOP, 1921	
Jack Nicklaus	MAS, 1965	
8 James Braid	BOP, 1908	
Ray Floyd	MAS, 1976	
JH Taylor	BOP, 1900	
JH Taylor	BOP, 1913	
7 Fred Herd	USOP, 1898	
Tony Jacklin	USOP, 1970	
Cary Middlecoff	MAS, 1955	
Jack Nicklaus	PGA, 1980	

LONGEST GAPS BETWEEN WINS

11 years	**Julius Boros** **(USOP 1952 to USOP 1963)** **Henry Cotton** **(BOP 1937 to BOP 1948)** **Ben Crenshaw** **(MAS 1984 to MAS 1995)** **Hale Irwin** **(USOP 1979 to USOP 1990)**
10 years	Lee Trevino (PGA 1974 to PGA 1984)

Coincidentally these time spans bridge between the same Major Championship. The longest span between victories in two different Majors is 9 years for Gene Sarazen (PGA 1923 to BOP 1932). The longest gap between two wins in the same Major (although they achieved success elsewhere between-times) was 13 years for Gary Player (MAS 1961 to 1974) and Ray Floyd (PGA 1969 to PGA 1982).

MOST RUNNERS-UP

Jack Nicklaus	(BOP 7; USOP 4; PGA 4; MAS 4)	19
Arnold Palmer	(BOP 1; USOP 4; PGA 3; MAS 2)	10
Greg Norman	(BOP 1; USOP 2; PGA 2; MAS 3)	8
Sam Snead	(USOP 4; PGA 2; MAS 2)	8
JH Taylor	(BOP 6; USOP 1)	7
Tom Watson	(BOP 1; USOP 2; PGA 1; MAS 3)	7
Ben Hogan	(USOP 2; MAS 4)	6
Byron Nelson	(USOP 1; PGA 3; MAS 2)	6
Gary Player	(USOP 2; PGA 2; MAS 2)	6
Harry Vardon	(BOP 4; USOP 2)	6
Ben Crenshaw	(BOP 2; PGA 1; MAS 2)	5
Ray Floyd	(BOP 1; PGA 1; MAS 3)	5
Tom Weiskopf	(USOP 1; MAS 4)	5
Craig Wood	(BOP 1; USOP 1; PGA 1; MAS 2)	5

It is also worth noting that the following players have recorded the most Runner-Up positions without ever winning a Major title:

Harry Cooper	(USOP 2; MAS 2)	4
Bruce Crampton	(USOP 1; PGA 2; MAS 1)	4
Doug Sanders	(BOP 2; USOP 1; PGA 1)	4
Macdonald Smith	(BOP 2; USOP 2)	4
Andy Bean	(BOP 1; PGA 2)	3
Chip Beck	(USOP 2; MAS 1)	3
Johnny Bulla	(BOP 2; MAS 1)	3
Andrew Kirkaldy	(BOP 3)	3
Tom McNamara	(USOP 3)	3
Colin Montgomerie	(USOP 2; PGA 1)	3
Ed Oliver	(USOP 1; PGA 1; MAS 1)	3
Dai Rees	(BOP 3)	3
Frank Stranahan	(BOP 2; MAS 1)	3
Davie Strath	(BOP 3)	3

Colin Montgomerie is the only current player in this invidious position. On every occasion he was runner-up, Bruce Crampton was beaten by Jack Nicklaus!

MOST TOP 5 FINISHES
(3rd to 5th and aggregated)

	3–5	Agg
JACK NICKLAUS	**19**	**56**
Arnold Palmer	10	26
Sam Snead	11	26
Gene Sarazen	13	24
Tom Watson	9	24
Walter Hagen	8	22
Ben Hogan	7	22
Gary Player	8	19
Nick Faldo	10	18
Byron Nelson	7	18
Greg Norman	8	18
JH Taylor	6	18
Harry Vardon	5	18

The players with most Top 5 finishes who have never recorded a win are:

Harry Cooper	7	11
Macdonald Smith	6	10
Bobby Cruickshank	6	8
Andrew Kirkaldy	4	4
Doug Sanders	4	8

The players with most Top 5 finishes who have never recorded a win or a second place are:

Jay Haas	7
Ed Dudley	6
Bruce Devlin	5

MOST TOP 10 FINISHES
(6th to 10th and aggregated)

	6–10	Agg
JACK NICKLAUS	**16**	**71**
Sam Snead	20	46
Tom Watson	20	44
Gary Player	21	40
Ben Hogan	17	39
Arnold Palmer	12	38
Gene Sarazen	11	35
Ray Floyd	15	28
Walter Hagen	6	28
Byron Nelson	10	28

The players with most Top 10 finishes who have never recorded a win are:

Ed Dudley	13	19
Bruce Devlin	11	16
Macdonald Smith	5	15

MOST TOP 20 FINISHES
(11th to 20th and aggregated)

	11–20	Agg
JACK NICKLAUS	**10**	**81**
Sam Snead	19	65
Tom Watson	16	60
Ray Floyd	31	59
Gary Player	16	56
Palmer	17	55
Ben Hogan	6	45
Billy Casper	20	44
Gene Sarazen	9	44
Lee Trevino	21	43

The players with most Top 20 finishes who have never recorded a win are:

Ed Dudley	12	31
Bruce Devlin	9	25
Doug Sanders	11	24

MOST TOP 30 FINISHES
(21st to 30th and aggregated)

	21–30	Agg
JACK NICKLAUS	**19**	**100**
Sam Snead	16	81
Gary Player	19	75
Tom Watson	7	67
Ray Floyd	7	66
Arnold Palmer	9	64
Gene Sarazen	10	54
Lee Trevino	9	52
Tom Kite	9	51
Ben Crenshaw	9	50

The players with most Top 30 finishes who have never recorded a win are:

Ed Dudley	5	36
Bruce Devlin	11	34
Bruce Crampton	11	33

LOWEST SCORES

Totals

267	Steve Elkington	Riviera CC	PGA 1995
	Colin Montgomerie*	Riviera CC	PGA 1995
	Greg Norman	Royal St George's	BOP 1993
268	Nick Price	Turnberry	BOP 1994
	Tom Watson	Turnberry	BOP 1977
269	Ernie Els*	Riviera CC	PGA 1995
	Nick Faldo*	Royal St George's	BOP 1993
	Davis Love III	Winged Foot	PGA 1997
	Jeff Maggert*	Riviera CC	PGA 1995
	Jack Nicklaus*	Turnberry	BOP 1977
	Jesper Parnevik*	Turnberry	BOP 1994
	Nick Price	Southern Hills	PGA 1994
270	Nick Faldo	St Andrews	BOP 1990
	Bernhard Langer*	Royal St George's	BOP 1993
	Tiger Woods	Augusta National	MAS 1997
271	Brad Faxon*	Riviera CC	PGA 1995
	Ray Floyd	Augusta National	MAS 1976
	Tom Lehman	Royal Lytham	BOP 1996
	Bobby Nichols	Columbus CC	PGA 1964
	Jack Nicklaus	Augusta National	MAS 1965
	Tom Watson	Muirfield	BOP 1980
	Fuzzy Zoeller*	Turnberry	BOP 1994
272	Paul Azinger	Inverness	PGA 1993
	Ian Baker-Finch	Royal Birkdale	BOP 1991
	Ben Crenshaw*	Oakland Hills	PGA 1979
	Nick Faldo	Muirfield	BOP 1992
	Ray Floyd	Southern Hills	PGA 1982
	David Graham	Oakland Hills	PGA 1979
	Lee Janzen	Baltusrol	USOP 1993
	Jack Nicklaus	Baltusrol	USOP 1980
	Greg Norman*	Inverness	PGA 1993
	Corey Pavin*	Royal St George's	BOP 1993
	Peter Senior*	Royal St George's	BOP 1993
	Jeff Sluman	Oak Tree GC	PGA 1988

* Not winning totals

18 Holes

63	Michael Bradley	Riviera CC	PGA 1995
	Ray Floyd	Southern Hills	PGA 1982
	Jack Nicklaus	Baltusrol	USOP 1980
	Greg Norman	Augusta National	MAS 1996
	Tom Weiskopf	Baltusrol	USOP 1980
64	Rodger Davis	Muirfield	BOP 1987
	Mike Donald	Augusta National	MAS 1990
	Ray Floyd	Muirfield	BOP 1992
	Jim Gallagher Jr	Riviera CC	PGA 1995
	Lee Mackey Jr	Merion	USOP 1950

Lloyd Mangrum	Augusta National	MAS 1940
Bobby Nichols	Columbus CC	PGA 1964
Christy O'Connor Jr	Royal St George's	BOP 1985
Mark O'Meara	Riviera CC	PGA 1995
Steve Pate	Muirfield	BOP 1982
Scott Simpson	Inverness	PGA 1993
Craig Stadler	Royal Birkdale	BOP 1983
Doug Tewell	Cherry Hills	PGA 1985

36 Holes

130	Nick Faldo (66,64)	Muirfield	BOP 1992
131	Ernie Els (66,65)	Riviera CC	PGA 1995
	Ray Floyd (65,66)	Augusta National	MAS 1976
	Mark O'Meara (64,67)	Riviera CC	PGA 1995
	Vijay Singh (68,63)	Inverness	PGA 1993
	Hal Sutton (65,66)	Riviera CC	PGA 1983
132	Nick Faldo (67,65)	St Andrews	BOP 1990
	Nick Faldo (69,63)	Royal St George's	BOP 1993
	Ray Floyd (63,69)	Southern Hills	PGA 1982
	Nick Price (67,65)	Southern Hills	PGA 1994

Best US Open Scores

134	Tze-Chung Chen (65,69)	Oakland Hills	1985
	Lee Janzen (67,67)	Baltusrol	1993
	Jack Nicklaus (63,71)	Baltusrol	1980

54 Holes

197	Ernie Els (66,65,66)	Riviera CC	PGA 1995
198	Tom Lehman (67,67,64)	Royal Lytham	BOP 1996
199	Nick Faldo (67,65,67)	St Andrews	BOP 1990
200	Ray Floyd (63,69,68)	Southern Hills	PGA 1982
	Jeff Maggert (66,69,65)	Riviera CC	PGA 1995
	Mark O'Meara (64,67,69)	Riviera CC	PGA 1995
201	Ray Floyd (65,66,70)	Augusta National	MAS 1976
	Tiger Woods (70, 66,65)	Augusta National	MAS 1997

Best US Open Scores

203	George Burns (69,66,68)	Merion	1981
	Tze-Chung Chen (65,69,69)	Oakland Hills	1985
	Lee Janzen (67,67,69)	Baltusrol	1993

LOW ROUNDS

2nd Round

63	Bruce Crampton	Firestone CC	PGA 1975
	Nick Faldo	Royal St George's	BOP 1993
	Mark Hayes	Turnberry	BOP 1977
	Greg Norman	Turnberry	BOP 1993
	Gary Player	Shoal Creek	PGA 1984
	Vijay Singh	Inverness	PGA 1993

64	Miller Barber	Augusta National	MAS 1979
	Don Bies	NCR CC	PGA 1969
	Mark Brooks	Turnberry	BOP 1994
	Horacio Carbonetti	Muirfield	BOP 1980
	Nick Faldo	Muirfield	BOP 1992
	Jay Haas	Augusta National	MAS 1995
	Tommy Jacobs	Congressional	USOP 1964
	Rives McBee	Olympic Club	USOP 1966
	Blaine McCallister	Southern Hills	PGA 1994
	Gary Player	Augusta National	MAS 1974
	Dave Rummells	Oak Tree GC	PGA 1988
	Craig Stadler	Kemper Lakes	PGA 1989
	Curtis Strange	Oak Hill	USOP 1989
	Steve Stricker	Riviera CC	PGA 1995

3rd Round

63	Isao Aoki	Muirfield	BOP 1980
	Paul Broadhurst	St Andrews	BOP 1990
	Nick Price	Augusta National	MAS 1986

64	Ian Baker-Finch	St Andrews	BOP 1990
	Ian Baker- Finch	Royal Birkdale	BOP 1991
	Miller Barber	NCR CC	PGA 1969
	Keith Clearwater	Olympic Club	USOP 1987
	Ben Crenshaw	Merion	USOP 1981
	Wayne Grady	Royal St George's	BOP 1993
	Hubert Green	Muirfield	BOP 1980
	Jay Haas	Riviera CC	PGA 1995
	Larry Mize	Turnberry	BOP 1994
	Jack Nicklaus	Augusta National	MAS 1965
	Loren Roberts	Oakmont	OSOP 1994
	Hal Sutton	Shoal Creek	PGA 1984
	Bob Tway	Inverness	PGA 1986
	Tom Watson	Muirfield	BOP 1980
	Fuzzy Zoeller	Turnberry	BOP 1994

4th Round

63	Brad Faxon	Riviera CC	PGA 1995
	Johnny Miller	Oakmont	USOP 1973
	Jodie Mudd	Royal Birkdale	BOP 1991
	Payne Stewart	Royal St George's	BOP 1993
64	Seve Ballesteros	Turnberry	BOP 1986
	Maurice Bembridge	Augusta National	MAS 1974
	Fred Couples	Royal Birkdale	BOP 1991
	Steve Elkington	Riviera CC	PGA 1995
	Nick Faldo	Turnberry	BOP 1994
	Anders Forsbrand	Turnberry	BOP 1994
	Hale Irwin	Augusta National	MAS 1975
	Peter Jacobsen	Brookline	USOP 1988
	Graham Marsh	Royal Birkdale	BOP 1983
	Jack Nicklaus	Columbus CC	PGA 1964
	Greg Norman	Augusta National	MAS 1988
	Greg Norman	Royal Troon	BOP 1989
	Greg Norman	Royal St George's	BOP 1993
	Gary Player	Augusta National	MAS 1978

PERFORMANCE CHARTS

INTRODUCTION

The following pages take the statistics of Parts 2, 3 and 4 in an effort to quantify the performances (by way of allocating points for positions attained) of the leading golfers in Major Championships. It is divided into three main areas, and using the premise that was adopted in Part 2, the Top 30 players in each era using this system are listed in charts.

i Leading Players of Different Generations

This section identifies five naturally-defined eras in the history of golf covering the first century of Major Championships, 1860–1960 – and the ensuing completed decades (1961–70; 1971–80; 1981–90), making eight charts in all.

The first chart covers the period 1860–1894, when there was only the British Open to play for (and the points allocation here is adjusted to accommodate that); then 1895–1916 – the years of the 'Great Triumvirate' and the rapid progress of golf in America; the third – 1919-30 – the days of Hagen, Jones and Sarazen; fourth, 1931-1942, from the beginnings of the Masters to the start of World War II; and 1944–60 – Nelson, Hogan and Snead and the polarization of the British Open. The remaining three look at succeeding decades in more detail.

ii Last 5 and 10 Years

Here the most recent history is analyzed with rolling charts which will be updated every year, depicting the most current trends and performances. The first chart takes the last 10 years (including 1997), while the second considers the last five. These charts show the positions of players over the same period up to the previous year, in much the same way as a music, film or book chart does, so that comparative performances this year against last can be identified.

iii The Top 100 All-Time List

Taking the statistics from all three charts above (and from Parts 2 and 4 for certain individuals who did not achieve a Top 30 place in any of the defined eras), this section collates all the points accruing for each golfer and calculates from their totals which golfers make up the Top 100 of all time – a kind of statistical Hall of Fame. Like the 5- and 10-year charts, these will be updated annually, so that there will be positional movement, and – from time to time – the loss of some older 'great' to accommodate a younger one. C'est la vie.

It is appreciated that with quantity, the very best should also have quality, and that the Bobby Jones's and Ben Hogan's of this world should be higher in such a listing than their points accumulation over a relatively short, or interrupted career, can permit. However, the points tallies are remarkably close to what most people would surmise - and how else is one ever going to settle the 19th-hole argument as to who actually was, or is, the best player never to win a Major?

LEADING PLAYERS OF DIFFERENT GENERATIONS

The following tables take the performances of the leading players of different eras and apply points to the positions they achieved in Major Championships during that time. With the exception of the period 1860-1894 (see below for details), which pertains to the period when only the British Open was contested and fields were often limited in size and standard, uniform points-to-positions values apply throughout. They are: 20 points for 1st place; 8 for 2nd; 5 for 3rd to 5th (SF in PGA when matchplay); 3 for 6th to 10th (QF); 2 for 11th to 20th (Last 16); and 1 for 21st to 30th (Last 32).

					1860-1894		
Pos.	**Player**	**Win** (12pts)	**R/UP** (5pts)	**3-5** (3pts)	**6-10** (2pts)	**11-20** (1pts)	**Total Points**
1	Tom Morris, Sr	4 (48)	3 (15)	6 (18)	3 (6)	4 (4)	91
2	Willie Park, Sr	4 (48)	4 (20)	3 (9)	3 (6)	2 (2)	85
3	Tom Morris, Jr	4 (48)	1 (5)	3 (9)			62
4	Jamie Anderson	3 (36)	2 (10)	2 (6)	2 (4)	2 (2)	58
5	Bob Ferguson	3 (36)	1 (5)	3 (9)	2 (4)		54
6	Willie Fernie	1 (12)	4 (20)	2 (6)	6 (12)	2 (2)	52
7	Willie Park, Jr	2 (24)		5 (15)	3 (6)	5 (5)	50
8	Bob Martin	2 (24)	2 (10)	4 (12)	1 (2)	1 (1)	49
9=	Bob Kirk		2 (10)	6 (18)	1 (2)		30
	Ben Sayers		1 (5)	4 (12)	3 (6)	7 (7)	30
11	Andrew Kirkaldy		3 (15)	3 (9)	2 (4)	1(1)	29
12	Andrew Strath	1 (12)	1 (5)	3 (9)	1 (2)		28
13=	Hugh Kirkaldy	1 (12)	1 (5)	1(3)	2 (4)	3 (3)	27
	Davie Strath		3 (15)	3 (9)	1 (2)	1 (1)	27
15	Willie Campbell		1 (5)	5 (15)	3 (6)		26
16	David Brown	1 (12)		2 (6)	3 (6)	1 (1)	25
17	John Ball, Jr (a)	1 (12)	1 (5)	1 (3)	1 (2)	2 (2)	24
18=	Robert Andrew		1 (5)	4 (12)	3 (6)		23
	Mungo Park	1(12)		2 (6)	1 (2)	3 (3)	23
	Archie Simpson		2 (10)	2 (6)	1 (2)	5 (5)	23
21	William Doleman (a)			2 (6)	6 (12)	3 (3)	21
22=	Tom Kidd	1 (12)		1 (3)	1 (2)	1 (1)	18
	Johnny Laidlay (a)		1 (5)	2 (6)	2 (4)	3 (3)	18
24	William Dow			4 (12)	2 (4)	1 (1)	17
25=	David Grant				6 (12)	4 (4)	16
	David Park		1 (5)	3 (9)	1 (2)		16
	Jack Simpson	1 (12)				4 (4)	16
28=	Willie Auchterlonie	1 (12)			1 (2)	1 (1)	15
	Jack Burns	1 (12)			1 (2)	1 (1)	15
	Bob Pringle		1 (5)	2 (6)	1 (2)	2 (2)	15

The 1892 Open Champion, amateur Horace Hilton, was 31st - tied with the emerging genius, JH Taylor. Sandy Herd, only just beginning his 54-year span of Opens, was 33rd.

1895 –1916

Pos.	Player	Win (20pts)	R/UP (8pts)	3-5 (5pts)	6-10 (3pts)	11-20 (2pts)	21-30 (1pt)	Total Points
1	Harry Vardon	7 (140)	5 (40)	4 (20)	4 (12)	1 (2)	1 (1)	215
2=	James Braid	5 (100)	4 (32)	6 (30)	3 (9)	1 (2)		173
	JH Taylor	4 (80)	7 (56)	4 (20)	4 (12)	2 (4)	1 (1)	173
4	Willie Anderson, Jr	4 (80)	1 (8)	6 (18)		3 (6)		112
5	Alex Smith	2 (40)	3 (24)	4 (20)	1 (3)	5 (10)	3 (3)	100
6	Sandy Herd	1 (20)	2 (16)	7 (35)	3 (9)	6 (12)	1 (1)	93
7	Ted Ray	1 (20)	1 (8)	5 (25)	4 (12)	5 (10)	1 (1)	76
8	Willie Smith	1 (20)	3 (24)	5 (25)	1 (3)	1 (2)		74
9	John McDermott	2 (40)	1 (8)	1 (5)	2 (6)			59
10	Gilbert Nicholls		2 (16)	3 (15)	3 (12)	5 (10)	1 (1)	54
11=	Fred McLeod	1 (20)	2 (20)		1 (3)	3 (6)	3 (3)	52
	Arnaud Massy	1 (20)	1 (8)	1 (5)	6 (18)		1 (1)	52
13	Laurie Auchterlonie	1 (20)		4 (20)	2 (6)	1 (2)	3 (3)	51
14	Jack White	1 (20)	1 (8)	2 (10)	1 (3)	3 (6)	1 (1)	48
15	Tom Vardon		1 (8)	3 (15)	5 (15)	3 (6)	2 (2)	46
16	Horace Rawlins	1 (20)	1 (8)		1 (3)	6 (12)	1 (1)	44
17	Tom McNamara		3 (24)	1 (5)	1 (3)	5 (10)	1 (1)	43
18=	Alex Campbell			2 (10)	3 (9)	11 (22)	1 (1)	42
	James Foulis	1 (20)		2 (10)	1 (3)	4 (8)	1 (1)	
	George Sargent	1 (20)		2 (10)	3 (9)	1 (2)	1 (1)	42
21=	Jim Barnes	1 (20)		3 (15)		2 (4)		39
	Harold Hilton (a)	1 (20)		2 (10)	1 (3)	2 (4)	2 (2)	39
	Alex Ross	1 (20)			4 (12)	2 (4)	3 (3)	39
24=	Joe Lloyd	1 (20)		2 (10)		3 (6)	1 (1)	37
	TG Renouf			2 (10)	3 (9)	8 (16)	2 (2)	37
26=	Walter Hagen	1 (20)		2 (10)	2 (6)			36
	George Low, Jr		1 (8)	1 (5)	3 (9)	6 (12)	2 (2)	36
28	Jock Hutchison		2 (16)	1 (5)	3 (9)	1 (2)	2 (2)	34
29	Stewart Gardner		1 (8)	3 (15)	3 (9)		1 (1)	33
30=	Charles Evans, Jr (a)	1 (20)	1 (8)			1 (2)		30
	Andrew Kirkaldy			2 (10)	4 (12)	3 (6)	2 (2)	30

Mike Brady tied for 33rd, while the 1913 US Open conquerer of Vardon and Ray, Francis Ouimet – who struck a blow for the amateur and the native-born American golfer - tied 36th.

	1919–1930						
Pos.	**Player**	**Win** (20pts)	**R/UP** (8pts)	**3-5** (5pts)	**6-10** (3pts)	**11-20** (2pts)	**21-30 Total** (1pt) **Points**
1	Walter Hagen	10 (200)	3 (24)	6 (30)	4 (12)	4 (8)		274
2	Bobby Jones (a)	7 (140)	4 (32)		1 (3)	1 (2)		177
3	Gene Sarazen	3 (60)	2 (16)	5 (25)	5 (15)	5 (10)	3 (3)	129
4	Jim Barnes	3 (60)	3 (24)		7 (21)	5 (10)	5 (5)	120
5	Leo Diegel	2 (40)	3 (24)	2 (10)	5 (15)	4 (8)	5 (5)	102
6=	Johnny Farrell	1 (20)	2 (16)	4 (20)	5 (15)	4 (8)	3 (3)	82
	Jock Hutchison	2 (40)	1 (8)	3 (15)	4 (12)	2 (4)	3 (3)	82
8	Tommy Armour	2 (40)		1 (5)	4 (12)	3 (6)	1 (1)	64
9	Bill Mehlhorn		1 (8)	4 (20)	4 (12)	4 (8)	6 (6)	54
10	George Duncan	1 (20)	1 (8)	1 (5)	4 (12)	2 (4)	2 (2)	51
11	John Golden			4 (20)	3 (9)	5 (10)	5 (5)	44
12	Al Espinosa		2 (16)	1 (5)	4 (12)	4 (8)	1 (1)	42
13=	Emmett French		1 (8)	3 (15)	3 (9)	2 (4)	5 (5)	41
	Arthur Havers	1 (20)		1 (5)	2 (6)	4 (8)	2 (2)	41
	Ted Ray	1 (20)	1 (8)	1 (5)		2 (4)	4 (4)	41
	Macdonald Smith		2 (16)	2 (10)	2 (6)	4 (8)	1 (1)	41
17=	Bobby Cruickshank		1 (8)	3 (15)	1 (3)	4 (8)	4 (4)	38
	Willie MacFarlane	1 (20)			2 (6)	5 (10)	2 (2)	38
19=	Joe Kirkwood, Sr			3 (15)	2 (6)	5 (10)	3 (3)	34
	Al Watrous		1 (8)	1 (5)	2 (6)	6 (12)	3 (3)	34
21	Mike Brady		1 (8)		3 (9)	7 (14)	2 (2)	33
22=	Fred McLeod		2 (16)		4 (12)	1 (2)	2 (2)	32
	Abe Mitchell			4 (20)	1 (3)	4 (8)	1 (1)	32
	Cyril Walker	1 (20)		1 (5)		3 (6)	1 (1)	32
25	Joe Turnesa		2 (16)		1 (3)	4 (8)	3 (3)	30
26	Archie Compston		1 (8)	1 (5)	3 (9)	1 (2)	4 (4)	28
27	Harry Hampton			1 (5)	2 (6)	5 (10)	6 (6)	27
28	Fred Robson		1 (8)	2 (10)	1 (3)	1 (2)	2 (2)	25
29=	Harry Cooper		1 (8)	2 (10)		2 (4)	2 (2)	24
	George MacLean			4 (20)		1 (2)	2 (2)	24
	Horton Smith			3 (15)		2 (6)	3 (3)	24

American dominance, and the opportunity to play in more Majors (the PGA started in 1916), paints a totally different picture to the previous era, so much the preserve of the 'Great Triumvirate'. It was the end of Majors success for JH Taylor (38th) and Sandy Herd (33rd) – both of whom had featured in the 1860–1894 and 1894–1916 league tables. Percy Alliss was 32nd and 1916 US Open winner, the amateur Chick Evans, was tied for 34th.

Pos.	Player	Win (20pts)	R/UP (8pts)	3-5 (5pts)	6-10 (3pts)	11-20 (2pts)	21-30 (1pt)	Total Points
								1931–1942
1	Gene Sarazen	4 (80)	2 (16)	8 (40)	6 (18)	4 (8)	7 (7)	169
2	Byron Nelson	4 (80)	3 (24)	6 (30)	4 (12)	3 (6)		152
3	Denny Shute	3 (60)	2 (16)	4 (20)	3 (9)	11 (22)	4 (4)	131
4	Craig Wood	2 (40)	5 (40)	3 (15)	4 (12)	2 (4)	7 (7)	118
5	Ralph Guldahl	3 (60)	3 (24)	2 (10)	3 (9)	4 (8)	5 (5)	116
6	Paul Runyan	2 (40)		5 (25)	9 (27)	7 (14)	2 (2)	108
7	Horton Smith	2 (40)		2 (10)	7 (21)	11 (22)	7 (7)	100
8	Henry Picard	2 (40)		3 (15)	8 (24)	8 (16)	2 (2)	97
9	Sam Snead	1 (20)	4 (32)	1 (5)	4 (12)	5 (10)		79
10	Ed Dudley				6 (30)	10 (30)	7 (14)	77
11	Harry Cooper		3 (24)	5 (25)	2 (6)	7 (14)	3 (3)	72
12=	Henry Cotton	2 (40)		2 (10)	4 (12)	1 (2)		64
	Olin Dutra	2 (40)		1 (5)	3 (9)	4 (8)	2 (2)	64
14	Vic Ghezzi	1 (20)			4 (12)	11 (22)	8 (8)	62
15	Billy Burke	1 (20)		3 (15)	2 (6)	6 (12)	5 (5)	58
16	Tommy Armour	1 (20)	1 (8)	1 (5)	3 (9)	4 (8)	5 (5)	55
17	Harold McSpaden		1 (8)	1 (5)	5 (15)	12 (24)	1 (1)	53
18=	Jimmy Hines		8 (24)	2 (10)		6 (12)	6 (6)	52
	Johnny Revolta	1 (20)			1 (3)	11 (22)	7 (7)	52
20	Lawson Little	1 (20)		2 (10)	4 (12)	4 (8)	1 (1)	51
21	Alf Padgham	1 (20)	1 (8)	3 (15)	2 (6)			49
22	Reg Whitcombe	1 (20)	1 (8)	1 (5)	2 (6)	3 (6)		45
23	Dick Metz		1 (8)	1 (5)	6 (18)	3 (6)	7 (7)	44
24	Bobby Cruickshank		1 (8)	3 (15)	2 (6)	6 (12)	2 (2)	43
25=	Ky Laffoon			3 (15)	2 (6)	5 (10)	11 (11)	42
	Tony Manero	1 (20)		1 (5)	1 (3)	4 (8)	6 (6)	42
27	Ben Hogan		1 (8)	3 (15)	5 (15)	1 (2)	1 (1)	41
28	Macdonald Smith		1 (8)	3 (15)	3 (9)	4 (8)		40
29=	Jimmy Demaret	1 (20)		1 (5)	1 (3)	3 (6)	2 (2)	36
	Jimmy Thomson		2 (16)		2 (6)	5 (10)	4 (4)	36

The post Jones-Hagen era brought a more even spread of victories, and with the advent of the Masters in 1934, an even greater imbalance between the US and Britain. Some Brits, such as Cotton, Padgham and Reg Whitcombe, may have featured even more strongly in this table if they had competed in the American Majors and had performed as well as they had done in the British Open. Other British Open winners included Alf Perry (32nd) and Dick Burton (37th): the last amateur winner of the US Open, Johnny Goodman, tied 38th, and 1931 PGA Champion, Tom Creavy, was 31st.

		1944–1960						
Pos.	Player	Win (20pts)	R/UP (8pts)	3-5 (5pts)	6-10 (3pts)	11-20 (2pts)	21-30 (1pt)	Total Points
1	Ben Hogan	9 (180)	5 (40)	4 (20)	9 (27)	1 (2)	1 (1)	270
2	Sam Snead	6 (120)	4 (32)	7 (35)	10 (30)	9 (18)	8 (8)	243
3	Bobby Locke	4 (80)	2 (16)	6 (30)	3 (9)	4 (8)	2 (2)	145
4	Cary Middlecoff	3 (60)	4 (32)	2 (10)	6 (18)	7 (14)	10 (10)	144
5	Peter Thomson	4 (80)	3 (24)	2 (10)	2 (6)	2 (4)	4 (4)	128
6	Lloyd Mangrum	1 (20)	3 (24)	8 (40)	6 (18)	3 (6)	6 (6)	114
7	Jimmy Demaret	2 (40)	1 (8)	7 (35)	4 (12)	5 (10)	2 (3)	108
8	Arnold Palmer	3 (60)	1 (8)	2 (10)	4 (12)	1 (2)	3 (3)	95
9	Julius Boros	1 (20)	1 (8)	8 (40)	3 (9)	3 (6)	4 (4)	87
10	Doug Ford	2 (40)	1 (8)	1 (5)	4 (12)	5 (10)	6 (6)	81
11	Jack Burke, Jr	2 (40)	1 (8)	1 (5)	5 (15)	5 (10)	2 (2)	80
12	Jim Ferrier	1 (20)	2 (16)	4 (20)	3 (9)	4 (8)	4 (4)	77
13=	Claude Harmon	1 (20)		4 (20)	3 (9)	10 (20)	7 (7)	76
	Byron Nelson	1 (20)	3 (24)	1 (5)	6 (18)	3 (6)	3 (3)	76
15	Walter Burkemo	1 (20)	2 (16)	3 (15)	1 (3)	6 (12)	4 (4)	70
16	Tommy Bolt	1 (20)		6 (30)	2 (6)	4 (8)	5 (5)	69
17	Chick Harbert	1 (20)	1 (8)	2 (10)	4 (12)	5 (10)	8 (8)	68
18	Frank Stranahan		3 (24)		2 (6)	13 (26)	4 (4)	60
19	Lew Worsham	1 (20)		1 (5)	6 (18)	5 (10)	6 (6)	59
20	Jim Turnesa	1 (20)		4 (20)	1 (3)	5 (10)	4 (4)	57
21=	Johnny Bulla		2 (16)	1 (5)	6 (18)	6 (12)	5 (5)	56
	Ted Kroll		1 (8)	3 (15)	3 (9)	9 (18)	6 (6)	56
	Bob Rosburg	1 (20)	1 (8)	3 (15)	1 (3)	3 (6)	4 (4)	56
24	Ed Oliver		3 (24)	1 (5)	3 (9)	6 (12)	5 (5)	55
25	Jay Hebert	1 (20)		1 (5)	5 (15)	5 (10)	2 (2)	52
26=	Ed Furgol	1 (20)		2 (10)	2 (6)	6 (12)	3 (3)	51
	Gary Player	1 (20)	1 (8)	1 (5)	4 (12)	2 (4)	2 (2)	51
28	Fred Daly	1 (20)	1 (8)	3 (15)	1 (3)		3 (3)	49
29	Flory van Donck		2 (16)	3 (15)	4 (12)	1 (2)	3 (3)	48
30=	Billy Casper	1 (20)	1 (8)	1 (5)		6 (12)	1 (1)	46
	Dick Mayer	1 (20)		2 (10)	2 (6)	3 (6)	4 (4)	46

The British Open became increasingly marginalized as the Americans stayed away in droves. The Ryder Cup, which had been in existence since 1927 had, up to 1955, gone 9-2 in favour of the Americans over the British - a clear indication of the gulf in standards. The momentum swung back momentarily in 1957 with a famous victory for the home team at Lindrick in Yorkshire. Its captain, Dai Rees, was 32nd in this table. Henry Cotton was 31st, Bob Hamilton, winner of the 1944 PGA was 33rd, Ken Venturi 34th, tied with Roberto de Vicenzo, and 1951 British Open Champion, Max Faulkner, 36th.

Pos.	Player	Win (20pts)	R/UP (8pts)	3-5 (5pts)	6-10 (3pts)	11-20 (2pts)	21-30 (1pt)	Total Points
				1961–1970				
1	Jack Nicklaus	8 (160)	7 (56)	6 (30)	4 (12)	3 (6)	4 (4)	268
2	Arnold Palmer	4 (80)	8 (64)	5 (25)	5 (15)	5 (10)	2 (2)	196
3	Gary Player	4 (80)	3 (24)	6 (30)	8 (24)	5 (10)	4 (4)	172
4	Billy Casper	2 (40)	2 (16)	5 (25)	6 (18)	9 (18)	2 (2)	119
5	Julius Boros	2 (40)		5 (25)		10 (20)	5 (5)	90
6	Bob Charles	1 (20)	3 (24)	3 (15)	1 (3)	8 (16)	3 (3)	81
7	Gene Littler	1 (20)	1 (8)	4 (20)	5 (15)	4 (8)	6 (6)	77
8	Don January	1 (20)	1 (8)	3 (15)	2 (6)	11 (22)	2 (2)	73
9	Doug Sanders		3 (24)	2 (10)	3 (9)	11 (22)	4 (4)	69
10	Al Geiberger	1 (20)	1 (8)	3 (15)	2 (6)	7 (14)	4 (4)	67
11	Gay Brewer	1 (20)	1 (8)	2 (10)	4 (12)	4 (8)	5 (5)	63
12	Tony Jacklin	2 (40)		2 (10)		3 (6)	5 (5)	61
13	Bruce Devlin			4 (20)	9 (27)	4 (8)	5 (5)	60
14	Tony Lema	1 (20)	1 (8)	3 (15)	3 (9)	2 (4)	3 (3)	59
15	Roberto de Vicenzo	1 (20)	1 (8)	3 (15)	2 (6)	2 (4)	3 (3)	56
16	Bobby Nichols	1 (20)	1 (8)	2 (10)	1 (3)	3 (6)	8 (8)	55
17	Bob Goalby	1 (20)	2 (16)		3 (9)	3 (6)	2 (2)	53
18	Kel Nagle		2 (16)	4 (20)	2 (6)	3 (6)	4 (4)	52
19	Dave Marr	1 (20)	1 (8)	1 (5)	3 (9)	3 (6)	3 (3)	51
20	Peter Thomson	1 (20)		2 (10)	5 (15)	1 (2)	2 (2)	49
21=	Ray Floyd	1 (20)			4 (12)	5 (10)	1 (1)	43
	Mason Rudolph			2 (10)	3 (12)	7 (14)	7 (7)	43
23	Ken Venturi	1 (20)		1 (5)	1 (3)	5 (10)	2 (2)	40
24	Bruce Crampton			2 (10)	2 (6)	8 (16)	6 (6)	38
25	Lee Trevino	1 (20)		2 (10)	1 (3)	1 (2)	2 (2)	37
26=	George Archer	1 (20)		1 (5)	1 (3)	3 (6)	2 (2)	36
	Paul Harney			2 (10)	4 (12)	6 (12)	2 (2)	36
28=	Phil Rodgers		1 (8)	3 (15)	1 (3)	3 (6)	2 (2)	34
	Sam Snead			1 (5)	5 (15)	5 (10)	4 (4)	34
30=	Frank Beard			2 (10)	5 (15)	3 (6)	2 (2)	33
	Dave Stockton	1 (20)		1 (5)	1 (3)	2 (4)	1 (1)	33

Thanks to Jack Nicklaus, Gary Player and – most significantly – Arnold Palmer, the British Open regained its former perceived status among the Major Championships. More transatlantic journeys were made from west to east, and from this decade, the tables can be said to be representative of the world's best players competing in the world's best tournaments. Failing to make this Top 30 were Christy O'Connor, Sr, Dow Finsterwald and Bob Rosburg (all tied 32nd).

		1971–1980						
Pos.	**Player**	**Win** (20pts)	**R/UP** (8pts)	**3-5** (5pts)	**6-10** (3pts)	**11-20** (2pts)	**21-30** (1pt)	**Total Points**
1	Jack Nicklaus	9 (180)	8 (64)	12 (60)	6 (18)	2 (4)		326
2	Tom Watson	4 (80)	3 (24)	2 (10)	8 (24)	6 (12)	2 (2)	152
3	Gary Player	4 (80)	1 (8)	1 (5)	9 (27)	7 (14)	9 (9)	143
4	Lee Trevino	4 (80)	1 (8)	3 (15)	4 (12)	10 (20)	5 (5)	140
5	Tom Weiskopf	1 (20)	4 (32)	6 (30)	8 (24)	7 (14)	3 (3)	123
6	Hale Irwin	2 (40)		7 (35)	5 (15)	4 (8)	7 (7)	105
7	Johnny Miller	2 (40)	3 (24)	2 (10)	5 (15)	6 (12)	2 (2)	103
8	Hubert Green	1 (20)	1 (8)	5 (25)	6 (18)	5 (10)	6 (6)	87
9	Ray Floyd	1 (20)	2 (16)	2 (10)	4 (12)	10 (20)	3 (3)	81
10	Jerry Pate	1 (20)	2 (16)	3 (15)	2 (6)	6 (12)	1 (1)	70
11	Ben Crenshaw		4 (32)	2 (10)	5 (15)	3 (6)	5 (5)	68
12	Seve Ballesteros	2 (40)	1 (8)			6 (12)		60
13	Lou Graham	1 (20)	1 (8)	1 (5)	3 (9)	3 (6)	6 (6)	54
14	Dave Stockton	1 (20)	2 (16)		2 (6)	4 (8)	3 (3)	53
15	David Graham	1 (20)		2 (10)	4 (12)	2 (4)	6 (6)	52
16	Arnold Palmer			3 (15)	2 (12)	10 (20)	4 (4)	51
17=	Tom Kite		1 (8)	3 (15)	3 (9)	7 (14)	3 (3)	49
	Lanny Wadkins	1 (20)		1 (5)	3 (9)	5 (10)	5 (5)	49
19	Charles Coody	1 (20)		1 (15)	1 (3)	2 (4)	4 (4)	46
20	John Mahaffey	1 (20)	1 (8)	1 (5)	1 (3)	2 (4)	4 (4)	44
21	Bruce Crampton		4 (32)			3 (6)	3 (3)	41
22	Andy North	1 (20)		1 (5)	1 (3)	5 (10)	2 (2)	40
23	JC Snead		2 (16)	1 (5)	1 (3)	4 (8)	7 (7)	39
24=	Billy Casper		1 (8)	2 (10)	3 (9)	5 (10)	1 (1)	38
	Don January		1 (8)	1 (5)	5 (15)	4 (8)	2 (2)	38
26	Peter Oosterhuis		1 (8)	1 (5)	4 (12)	3 (6)	5 (5)	36
27	Gene Littler		1 (8)	1 (5)	3 (9)	4 (8)	4 (4)	34
28	Al Geiberger		1 (8)		3 (9)	6 (12)	3 (3)	32
29	Tommy Aaron	1 (20)	1 (8)				3 (3)	31
30=	Jim Colbert			3 (15)	1 (3)	4 (8)	1 (1)	27
	Gil Morgan			2 (10)	2 (6)	5 (10)	1 (1)	

A second decade of Nicklaus domination, with Jack's two Majors in 1980 suggesting he was finishing as strongly as he started it. Bert Yancey, Jerry Magee and the unfortunate Jack Newton shared 31st place, while 1979 Masters Champion, Fuzzy Zoeller, was just emerging on the scene and claimed 33rd spot.

1981–1990

Pos.	Player	Win (20pts)	R/UP (8pts)	3-5 (5pts)	6-10 (3pts)	11-20 (2pts)	21-30 (1pt)	Total Points
1	Tom Watson	4 (80)	4 (32)	3 (15)	9 (27)	5 (10)	4 (4)	168
2	Nick Faldo	4 (80)	1 (8)	5 (25)	3 (9)	8 (16)	3 (3)	141
3	Seve Ballesteros	3 (60)	2 (16)	7 (35)	4 (12)	4 (8)	3 (3)	134
4	Greg Norman	1 (20)	4 (32)	6 (30)	3 (9)	6 (12)	3 (3)	106
5	Ray Floyd	2 (40)	2 (16)	2 (10)	3 (9)	12 (24)	2 (2)	101
6	Curtis Strange	2 (40)	2 (16)	2 (10)	3 (9)	8 (16)	6 (6)	97
7	Ben Crenshaw	1 (20)	1 (8)	5 (25)	5 (15)	10 (20)	3 (3)	91
8	Jack Nicklaus	1 (20)	3 (24)	1 (5)	6 (18)	5 (10)	9 (9)	86
9	Payne Stewart	1 (20)	2 (16)	3 (15)	7 (21)	2 (4)	5 (5)	81
10	Larry Nelson	3 (60)		1 (5)	1 (3)	5 (10)	1 (1)	79
11	Lanny Wadkins		3 (24)	4 (20)	4 (12)	7 (14)	6 (6)	76
12=	Tom Kite		2 (16)	4 (20)	5 (15)	8 (16)	4 (4)	71
	Bernhard Langer	1 (20)	2 (16)	3 (15)	4 (12)	3 (6)	2 (2)	71
14	Fuzzy Zoeller	1 (20)	1 (8)		7 (21)	8 (16)	4 (4)	69
15	Craig Stadler	1 (20)		1 (5)	6 (18)	9 (18)	7 (7)	68
16	David Graham	1 (20)		1 (5)	7 (21)	7 (14)	5 (5)	65
17	Lee Trevino	1 (20)	1 (8)	2 (10)	2 (6)	9 (18)	2 (2)	64
18	Sandy Lyle	2 (40)			2 (6)	6 (12)	4 (4)	62
19	Fred Couples		1 (8)	5 (25)	6 (18)	2 (4)	3 (3)	58
20	Scott Simpson	1 (20)			5 (15)	6 (12)	5 (5)	52
21	Hale Irwin	1 (20)	1 (8)		2 (6)	6 (12)	3 (3)	49
22	Larry Mize	1 (20)		1 (5)	1 (3)	8 (16)	4 (4)	48
23	Peter Jacobsen			2 (10)	3 (9)	8 (16)	10 (10)	45
24	Hal Sutton	1 (20)		1 (5)	2 (6)	3 (6)	7 (7)	44
25	Andy Bean		2 (16)	1 (5)	1 (3)	8 (16)	3 (3)	43
26=	Chip Beck		2 (16)	1 (5)	2 (6)	3 (6)	8 (8)	41
	Nick Price		2 (16)	2 (10)	2 (6)	3 (6)	3 (3)	41
28	Mark Calcavecchia	1 (20)	1 (8)			6 (12)		40
29	Bill Rogers	1 (20)	1 (8)	1 (5)	1 (3)		3 (3)	39
30	Jay Haas			2 (10)	4 (12)	4 (8)	5 (5)	35

The 80s proved to be much more open, with Tom Watson the only obvious successor to the 'Big Three'. It also saw the re-emergence of Europe as a power in golf, with Ballesteros and Faldo in the vanguard. PGA Champions Andy North (for the second time in 1985), Bob Tway (1986), Jeff Sluman (1988) and Wayne Grady (1990) were out of the Top 30 at, respectively, 37th (tied with Gil Morgan), 36th, 34th (tied with Paul Azinger) and 31st (tied with Ian Woosnam).

LAST 10 YEARS

Pos. 1997	1996	Player	Win (20pts)	R/UP (8pts)	3-5 (5pts)	6-10 (3pts)	11-20 (2pts)	21-30 (1pt)	Total Points
1	1	Nick Faldo	5 (100)	2 (16)	8 (40)	2 (6)	8 (16)	2 (2)	180
2	2	Greg Norman	1 (20)	4 (32)	5 (25)	7 (21)	9 (18)		116
3	3	Nick Price	3 (60)	1 (8)	1 (5)	2 (10)	8 (16)	2 (2)	101
4=	5	Fred Couples	1 (20)	1 (8)	5 (25)	7 (21)	5 (10)	6 (6)	90
	4	Payne Stewart	2 (40)	2 (16)		6 (18)	5 (10)	6 (6)	90
6	13	Ernie Els	2 (40)	1 (8)	3 (15)	4 (12)	3 (6)	2 (2)	83
7	6	Curtis Strange	2 (40)	1 (16)	1 (5)	2 (6)	3 (6)	6 (6)	79
8	15	Tom Kite	1 (20)	1 (8)	3 (15)	4 (12)	6 (12)	2 (2)	69
9	7	Corey Pavin	1 (20)	1 (8)	2 (10)	5 (15)	6 (12)	3 (3)	68
10	11	Jose-Maria Olazabal	1 (20)	1 (8)	1 (5)	6 (18)	7 (14)	2 (2)	67
11	9	Ian Woosnam	1 (20)	1 (8)	2 (10)	3 (9)	5 (10)	7 (7)	64
12	15	Tom Lehman	1 (20)	2 (16)	3 (15)	1 (3)	3 (6)	2 (2)	64
13	13	Jeff Sluman	1 (20)	1 (8)	1 (5)	4 (12)	5 (10)	7 (7)	62
14	–	Davis Love III	1 (20)	2 (16)	1 (5)	3 (9)	3 (6)	4 (4)	60
15	8	Tom Watson			5 (25)	6 (18)	7 (14)	2 (2)	59
16	22	John Daly	2 (40)		1 (5)		2 (4)	3 (3)	52
17	23	Steve Elkington	1 (20)		3 (15)	2 (6)	3 (6)	4 (4)	51
18	19	Scott Hoch		1 (8)	2 (10)	8 (24)	3 (6)	2 (2)	50
19	23	Mark Calcavecchia	1 (20)	1 (8)		1 (3)	7 (14)	4 (4)	49
20	12	Paul Azinger	1 (20)	1 (8)		3 (9)	3 (6)	3 (3)	46
21	20	Ray Floyd		2 (16)		5 (15)	6 (12)	2 (2)	45
22	25	Mark Brooks	1 (20)		3 (15)	4 (8)	1 (1)		44
23=	21	Bernhard Langer	1 (20)		1 (5)	4 (12)		6 (6)	43
	–	Colin Montgomerie		3 (24)	1 (5)	2 (6)	2 (4)	4 (4)	43
25	–	Lee Janzen	1 (20)		1 (5)	2 (6)	2 (4)	6 (6)	41
26	–	Justin Leonard	1 (20)	1 (8)	1 (5)	2 (6)		1 (1)	40
27	29	Mark O'Meara			3 (15)	2 (6)	7 (14)	3 (3)	38
28	28	John Cook		2 (16)	2 (10)	1 (3)	3 (6)	2 (2)	37
29	–	Jeff Maggert			5 (25)	3 (9)		2 (2)	36
30	25	Chip Beck		2 (16)	1 (5)		3 (6)	8 (8)	35

Nick Faldo, with five wins in the rolling decade 1988–1997, has been the collector of Major Championships in a period where few players have dominated for any meaningful period of time. This chart is a dynamic one and positions will change annually. Already Ernie Els is pressurizing the 'old guard' and Davis Love is the highest new entry.

LAST 5 YEARS

Pos. 1997	1996	Player	Win (20pts)	R/UP (8pts)	3-5 (5pts)	6-10 (3pts)	11-20 (2pts)	21-30 (1pt)	Total Points
1	4	Ernie Els	2 (40)	1 (8)	2 (10)	4 (12)	3 (6)	2 (2)	78
2	2	Greg Norman	1 (20)	3 (24)	2 (10)	3 (9)	6 (12)		75
3	5	Tom Lehman	1 (20)	2 (16)	3 (15)	2 (6)	4 (8)	2 (2)	67
4	2	Nick Price	2 (40)			2 (6)	5 (10)	1 (1)	57
5	21	Davis Love III	1 (20)	2 (16)	1 (5)	3 (9)	1 (2)	1 (1)	53
6	1	Nick Faldo	1 (20)	1 (8)	3 (15)	1 (3)	1 (2)	1 (1)	49
7	6	Corey Pavin	1 (20)	1 (8)	1 (5)	3 (9)	2 (4)	2 (2)	48
8	7	Steve Elkington	1 (20)		3 (15)	2 (6)	2 (4)	2 (2)	47
9	9	Lee Janzen	1 (20)		1 (5)	2 (6)	3 (6)	5 (5)	42
10	–	Justin Leonard	1 (20)	1 (8)	1 (5)	2 (6)		1 (1)	40
11=	15	Colin Montgomerie		3 (24)		2 (6)	2 (4)	3 (3)	37
	11	Jose-Maria Olazabal	1 (20)			2 (6)	5 (10)	1 (1)	37
13	21	Jeff Maggert			5 (25)	3 (9)		1 (1)	35
14=	12	Mark Brooks	1 (20)		2 (10)		1 (2)	1 (1)	33
	15	Bernhard Langer	1 (20)		1 (5)	1 (3)		5 (5)	33
16	17	Paul Azinger	1 (20)		1 (5)		2 (4)	2 (2)	31
17=	14	John Daly	1 (20)		1 (5)		1 (2)	3 (3)	30
	9	Tom Kite		1 (8)	2 (10)	3 (9)	1 (2)	1 (1)	30
	26	Tom Watson			3 (15)	3 (9)	3 (6)		30
20=	24	Jay Haas			4 (20)	1 (3)	2 (4)	2 (2)	29
	20	Phil Mickelson		1 (8)	2 (10)	3 (9)		2 (2)	29
22	19	Ben Crenshaw	1 (20)			1 (3)	2 (4)	1 (1)	28
23	27	Scott Hoch			2 (10)	5 (15)	1 (2)		27
24	24	Loren Roberts		1 (8)	1 (5)	1 (3)	3 (6)	4 (4)	26
25=	23	Brad Faxon			1 (5)	2 (6)	6 (12)	2 (2)	25
	–	Jim Furyk			3 (15)	1 (3)	2 (4)	3 (3)	25
	27	Vijay Singh			2 (10)	3 (9)	2 (4)	2 (2)	25
	–	Tiger Woods	1 (20)				1 (2)	3 (3)	25
29	30	Frank Nobilo			1 (5)	4 (12)	2 (4)	3 (3)	24
30	8	Fred Couples				5 (15)	3 (6)	2 (2)	23

This chart pin-points current form and trends. Covering the period 1993–1997 it is the most volatile and highlights the shooting stars of today. This is typified by Davis Love's upward bound of 16 places, and the first – high – appearance by Justin Leonard. It also shows the downward trend of players. The Top 30 lost Ian Woosnam and Faldo's poor year sees him deposed from the top. Not too much should be read into Fred Couples' plunge, however. 1997 was a reasonable year for Fred, but not as good as the year that fell out the other end –1992 – when he won the Masters.

HALL OF FAME – THE TOP 100							
POS	Player	Win	R/UP	3-5	6-10	11-20	21-30	Total Points
1	Jack Nicklaus	18	19	19	16	10	19	694
2	Gary Player	9	6	8	21	16	19	382
3	Sam Snead	7	8	11	20	19	16	373
4	Tom Watson	8	7	9	20	16	7	360
5	Arnold Palmer	7	9	10	12	17	9	344
6	Walter Hagen	11	3	8	6	8	5	339
7	Ben Hogan	9	6	7	17	6	3	329
8	Gene Sarazen	7	4	13	11	9	10	314
9	Ray Floyd	4	5	4	15	31	7	254
10	Lee Trevino	6	2	7	7	21	9	243
11	Nick Faldo	6	2	10	5	15	5	236
12	Harry Vardon	7	6	5	5	1	1	232
13	Byron Nelson	5	6	7	10	6	3	230
14=	Seve Ballesteros	5	3	7	5	13	6	206
	JH Taylor	5	7	6	7	3	2	206
16	Billy Casper	3	4	8	9	20	4	203
17	Greg Norman	2	8	8	9	13	4	193
18	Ben Crenshaw	2	5	8	11	15	9	192
19	Julius Boros	3	1	13	4	13	11	185
20	Peter Thomson	5	3	4	8	4	8	184
21	James Braid	5	4	6	4	3	4	182
22	Bobby Jones	7	4		1	1		177
23	Tom Kite	1	4	9	11	17	9	173
24	Hale Irwin	2	1	7	9	15	13	143
25	Jim Barnes	4	3	3	7	7	5	159
26	Denny Shute	3	2	5	5	14	8	152
27=	Jimmy Demaret	3	1	9	5	8	5	149
	Cary Middlecoff	3	4	2	6	9	11	149
29	Tom Weiskopf	1	5	6	9	10	11	148
29	Bobby Locke	4	2	6	3	4	2	145
31	Lloyd Mangrum	1	4	10	8	4	6	140
32=	Gene Littler	1	3	6	10	11	13	139
	Lanny Wadkins	1	3	7	7	14	11	139
34	Horton Smith	2		5	9	14	13	136
35	Johnny Miller	2	4	3	7	9	7	133
36	Leo Diegel	2	3	5	5	8	10	130
37	Sandy Herd**	1	4	8	5	10	2	127
38=	Nick Price	3	2	3	4	9	5	126
	Craig Wood	2	5	3	5	4	8	126
40	Don January	1	2	5	8	18	4	125
41	Payne Stewart	2	3	3	8	6	9	124
42	Curtis Strange	2	2	4	4	11	10	122
43	Hubert Green	2	1	5	7	9	9	121
44=	Tommy Armour	3	1	2	7	7	6	119
	Paul Runyan	2		5	11	8	5	119
46=	Henry Cotton	2		4	10	3	1	117
	David Graham	2		3	11	9	11	117
	Ralph Guldahl	3	3	2	3	4	6	117
	Ted Ray	2	2	6	4	7	5	117
50=	Jock Hutchison	2	3	4	7	3	5	116

POS	Player	Win	R/UP	3-5	6-10	11-20	21-30	Total Points
							HALL OF FAME – THE TOP 100 – continued	

POS	Player	Win	R/UP	3-5	6-10	11-20	21-30	Total Points
	Fuzzy Zoeller	1	1	2	8	14	6	116
52=	Fred Couples	1	1	7	11	6	6	114
	Henry Picard	2		4	9	11	5	114
54	Willie Anderson Jr	4	1	6		3		112
55	Johnny Farrell	1	2	6	7	6	9	108
56	Bernhard Langer	2	2	4	6	3	7	107
57	Roberto de Vicenzo	1	2	6	6	7	8	106
58	Bob Charles	1	3	3	3	16	5	105
59=	Doug Ford	2	1	1	8	8	8	101
	Vic Ghezzi	1	1	1	6	18	14	101
61	Alex Smith	2	3	4	1	5	3	100
62	Al Geiberger	1	2	3	5	13	7	99
63=	Ed Dudley			6	13	12	5	98
	Doug Sanders		4	4	5	11	7	98
65	Larry Nelson	3		3	2	7	4	97
66=	Harry Cooper		4	7	2	9	5	96
	Craig Stadler	1	3	1	11	13	12	96
68	Macdonald Smith		4	6	5	8	1	94
69	Jim Ferrier	1	2	5	4	5	9	92
70=	Jack Burke Jr	2	1	1	7	6	5	91
	Tom Morris Sr*	4	3	6	3	4		91
72=	Dow Finsterwald	1	1	6	4	8	3	89
	Jerry Pate	1	2	5	3	8	3	89
74	Tommy Bolt	1		8	3	5	9	88
75=	Bruce Crampton		4	2	2	14	11	87
	Bruce Devlin			5	11	9	11	87
	Bob Rosburg	1	2	4	4	6	7	87
78	Dave Stockton	2	2	1	3	6	4	86
79	Willie Park Sr*	4	4	3	3	2		85
80	Fred McLeod	1	2	4	5	4	5	84
81=	Gay Brewer	1	1	2	8	6	9	83
	Ernie Els	2	1	3	4	3	2	83
83=	Cory Pavin	1	1	2	7	8	7	82
	Ken Venturi	1	2	3	4	8	3	82
85	Bobby Cruickshank		2	6	3	10	6	81
86	Walter Burkemo	1	2	3	2	9	5	80
87	Kel Nagle	1	2	4	2	6	4	78
88	Tony Jacklin	2		4		5	8	77
89=	George Duncan	1	1	3	8	3	3	76
	Jay Haas			7	5	6	7	76
	Chick Harbert	1	1	2	5	7	9	76
	Claude Harmon			4	3	10	7	76
93=	Jose Maria Olazabal	1	1	1	6	9	3	75
	Willie Park Jr**	2	1	5	4	11	2	75
	Ian Woosnam	1	1	3	4	6	8	75
96=	Bobby Nichols	1	1	3	3	6	10	74
	Willie Smith	1	3	5	4	5	1	74
98=	Johnny Bulla		3	2	7	6	6	73
	Sandy Lyle	2			2	11	5	73
	Dick Metz	1	1		12	6	12	73

* Points as per 1860–1894 scoring system
** Points using both scoring systems

LIST OF ABBREVIATIONS

a	Amateur
ARG	Argentina
AUS	Australia
BEL	Belgium
BOP	British Open
BRA	Brazil
CAN	Canada
EGY	Egypt
ENG	England
FIJ	Fiji
FRA	France
GER	Germany (including former West Germany)
HOL	Holland
IRE	Ireland (including Northern Ireland and the former Irish Free State)
IT	Italy
JAP	Japan
MAS	US Masters
MEX	Mexico
NZ	New Zealand
PGA	US PGA Championship, or Professional Golfers' Association
PR	Puerto Rico
R&A	Royal and Ancient Club of St Andrews
SA	South Africa
SCO	Scotland
SP	Spain
SWE	Sweden
TAI	Taiwan (including former Formosa)
TRI	Trinidad and Tobago
URU	Uruguay
US	United States
USGA	US Golf Association
USO(P)	US Open
WAL	Wales
ZIM	Zimbabwe (including former Southern Rhodesia and Rhodesia)

BIBLIOGRAPHY

The Open Championship Annuals, 1894–1994/6 (R&A)
History of the Open Golf Championship, (The Guardian)
The British Professional Golfers, 1887–1930 – A Register, Alan F Jackson
USGA Record Books, 1895–1959; 1960–1980; 1981–90, (USGA)
The Official US Open Almanac, Salvatore Johnson
Official Guide of the PGA Championships (PGA's media guide, effectively)
Records of the Masters Tournament, 1934–81, (Augusta National GC)
The Who's Who of Golf, Peter Alliss
Golf and All its Glory, Bruce Critchley with Bob Ferrier
Encyclopedia of Golf, Webster Evans